Ordinary Heroes

The extraordinary tale of
106 Army Troops Company
Royal Engineers

'Most people live worthy, dutiful

lives which are not recorded –

Their deeds are remembered by

family, friends and workmates –

So they live on in memory.

But history chose to take a group

of us away from home and put us

in crucial places at critical times,

out of sight of those who knew us.

I want to record the deeds of these

ordinary men.'

Bill Harvey
April 2002

Bill encouraged me to make
this record. I have tried to let
the words of those who were
there, tell their tale.

Ordinary Heroes

The extraordinary tale of 106 Army Troops Company Royal Engineers

Charles Jones

WritersPrintshop

First published in Great Britain 2004 by WritersPrintshop

ISBN 1902623085

Designed by gavin ward design associates

Maps by Frances Colling

Cover Photographs

The Sapper Cap Badge
In 1782 Sapper officers wore the King's cypher on their sword belt with the crown over it. Later this was surrounded by the royal garter and the Corps of Royal Engineers was inscribed. This was later abbreviated to Royal Engineers. A similar badge was worn by the Royal Sappers and Miners from 1823. The laurel wreaths were probably added in recognition of the work done by the Corps during the Napoleonic Wars.

The company photo, Christmas 1939, Rennes. The 'Sitzkrieg', as the German's termed it, was 3 months old. It would be another 4 months before the 'Blitzkrieg' was launched. The company continued to make their way home after the fall of France in June 1940.

Bill Harvey and Alan Jones met up in June 1998 more than 56 years to the day after their capture at Tobruk.

Dhoby day in the desert
Sunday was dhoby day when the washing was done. The flimsy cans used to supply petrol were converted to washing bowls.

Dropping the NCOs tent
The Mechanists section pose just after they have dropped the NCOs tent which had been strategically situated in one of the many folds in the rocky desert.

The book is dedicated to the memory of

all those who served in 106 Company

Acknowledgements

My thanks go to the library staff at the Imperial War Museum who do an outstanding job conserving source material. I wish to record how much it meant that that they took me seriously when I started to question the official record. The days spent working in their cupola provided the structure of the book.

I am also immensely grateful to the Public Records Office at Kew for the outstanding service they provide. The people who staff the help desks are the knowledgeable and patient servants of scholarship. I cannot thank them, and their predecessors who have bequeathed us the Public Record, enough. Specifically, I am grateful to the Public Records Office for permission to use the air photographs of the POW camp and the chart of Tobruk plus several quotes from war diaries that are listed in the reference section.

My thanks are also due to the families of Bill Harvey and Bob Borthwick for their permission to us their father's diaries. I am grateful to Ken Venables and my own dad for the information they have provided.

I am grateful to my sisters, Sue and Fan, who have made the completion of the project very much a family affair by providing support rather than pressure at just the right moments.

Finally to my partner Kate who has given a home to this project for too many years.

Thank you all, very much.

Chas Jones
June 2004

Maps, Illustrations & Photographs

Contents

Foreword

This is the book about a group of men who soldiered for their country from September 1939 until liberated in May and June 1945. They are real people who recorded their stories in narratives and interviews. I hope they can stand as representatives of all the men from Doncaster and surrounding district who formed 106 Army Troops Company Royal Engineers.

Bill Harvey sparked the project with his original diary. He told me about Bob Borthwick's diary. Bob promised to complete his story and I spent many hours questioning Bill about details uncovered in the Public Records Office. The simple task of editing the diaries together soon became a fascinating detective story. Months later I found myself holding a scrap of paper packed with poignancy which tried to alert the HQ in Rennes that sappers were scattered through north east France as the final evacuation was ordered.

There were many memorable moments in the preparation of this book. The first was the remarkable set of coincidences that put Bill Harvey's story in my hands. The company clerk, Mr Simmons, recalled seeing a picture of Alan Jones in the local Salisbury paper where both lived. A search of the phone directory yielded a phone number and an address. About a week later I found myself reading what my dad had done in the war for the first time.

Still later there were documents with Winston Churchill's handwritten footnotes reluctantly agreeing to bury the investigations about the events of June 1940. The release of German records held by the former Soviet Union allowed the situation surrounding the last days of the BEF to be plotted. A year later I was reading high-level complaints about the maverick activities of the company's neighbours at Kabrit in Egypt while I investigated why the skilled engineers who had built such steam locomotives as 'The Flying Scotsman' were undertaking commando training. The maverick was Capt David Stirling who was preparing his warriors to found the SAS. Their RAF host complained that accommodation had been prepared but Stirling insisted on sleeping in the desert.

When I read the diaries it was obvious that the writers were not told, and had not discovered, the wider drama in which they were players. I have tried my best to verify the many stories that were hinted at in the diaries. The historical issues opened by these diaries were substantial:

✧ Could they really have been the first unit to go to France in 1939?

✧ Were some still in France after the Armistice in June 1940?

✧ Could this small unit have played a significant role in the battle of El Alamein even though they were struggling to survive as POWs by the time the battle took place?

✧ Were they present at the birth of the legend that has become the Special Air Service?

The answer to all these questions is, I believe, 'Yes'.

✧ Did British soldiers take over and run a death camp when the war ended as they waited for liberation? Certainly, as Alan Jones returned with photos to prove it.

The modest rail workers and miners who formed this Territorial Army Unit made none of these claims. They just did the jobs that were asked of them. Afterwards, they went back to their families and their work. They left for France a week after war was declared and some did not return until a month after the end of the war.

I am no historian and this was not designed as a book of reference. It was intended as the book about 3 men, balanced with the narrative of their tormenter, Erwin Rommel. I must take full responsibility for any inaccuracies in the historic narrative. Because the story raises some significant issues, and seeks to revise parts of the accepted narrative, a list of source material has been compiled which I hope will assist any historians who wanted to pursue the threads unravelled in this book.

As Bill returned to Doncaster in June 1945 he offered his fare to the conductress on the tram taking him home. She refused it. 'You have already paid enough.' The debt remains unpaid and will soon be cancelled as these ordinary heroes pass away. I hope these words have done them some justice.

Chas Jones
York, June 2004

Chapter One

First In, Last Out

September 1939

Map of expanding Germany

The expansion of Nazi-governed Germany steadily destroyed the balance crafted by France at the Treaty of Versailles in 1919. First, the demilitarised Rhur was occupied and later the Sudetenland. Plebiscites, conducted by the League of Nations, were used to justify German claims to bring ethnic German in adjacent territories into German 'protection'. Later the democratic façade was dropped as Czechoslovakia and Poland were invaded.

Facing the facts

Alan

Friday, the first day of September 1939 dawned as a fine, Yorkshire day. Everybody was tense.

In London Prime Minister Chamberlain's Cabinet was assembling for its regular meeting. At 4.45 that morning the German army had stormed the Polish border.

As ministers set out for Downing Street most had heard the reports relayed by the United States ambassador in London. But it would be two days before the Cabinet declared war on Germany.

For Staff Sergeant Alan Jones, the war had already begun. The previous morning the order to mobilise the specialist non-commissioned officers had been received by telegram from York. Alan had been ordered to report to the Commanding Officer of the Royal Engineers at Catterick Garrison in the North Riding of Yorkshire.

The CRE removed a set of four brown envelopes from his safe and handed one to each of the four sapper staff sergeants who shuffled into his office and now stood at the other side of his desk. The envelopes were received in silence.

They knew they were off to war. They had been sure of that for months although it was rarely a topic of conversation. There were plenty of old soldiers around to compensate for this reticence. They were anxious to tell tales of trench life. Alan Jones expected to join a unit who would spend their abbreviated lives in the trenches. He guessed they would be fighting in France again.

The Government had promised to send an army to France and experienced soldiers such as Alan would fill posts in reserve units of the Territorial Army. They would redeem the pledge Chamberlain's Government had made to the French in order to achieve the Munich Agreement.

The quartet of young men opened their envelopes as if participating in a well-rehearsed parade drill. The index finger slit the envelope. Each then pulled the almost translucent piece of folded paper from its envelope. They focused immediately on the key information. Amid all of the neat rows of information one line stood out. Some weeks before, a busy clerk had taken these anonymous sheets and given them a name.

Each page of duplicated instructions had been roughly aligned in the typewriter. Names and places had been keyed into the blank spaces using a crisp new typewriter ribbon. It took a few moments to absorb all the information. Some squinted. Others turned the paper to catch the light pouring through the window.

The instructions that determined each man's fate were brief. They named the unit they were to join, where the unit was located and their war role. There was no allowance for leave. They were to go immediately. Alan would not have to travel far. He had been posted to join 106 Army Troops Company Royal Engineers based in Doncaster.

For Alan Jones the timing of the looming war could have been worse. The international tension of the previous months had been an exciting professional time for him. The postponement bought at Munich permitted him the satisfaction of seeing his first major engineering job commissioned and working.

With 5 Division at Catterick, with his colleague Don Burton, Alan had worked alongside an experienced staff of civilians. He had obtained his Electrical & Mechanical Certificate just one year before. This provided invaluable experience for his posting to Doncaster where he would again be supervising staff with diverse engineering experience.

Now in his twenty-fifth year he had seen light, power and heating come to the new infantry battalion barracks at Bourlon Lines. This provided hot water and central heating for the first time to soldiers in their barracks. He felt confident for the tasks he knew lay ahead. He was even a little excited. He digested the rest of his instructions.

In training organisations and military bases all over Britain, soldiers were opening their orders as the mobilisation plan was activated. That same Thursday morning the German High Command was issuing its own instructions to unit commanders to invade Poland. The holiday month of August was over.

There was a short pause before the CRE dismissed them. The instructions were replaced in their envelopes and handed back. He wished them luck; they replaced their berets, saluted and left the room. The orders had been marked SECRET so it would be inappropriate to talk about their destinations. But as usual the barrack room rumour mill had revealed almost all before they made it back to their rooms. The Garrison clerks had prepared posting orders and travel warrants, and could tell them exactly who was going where and always implied that they knew a great deal more.

Leaving the job at Catterick would not be a professional wrench. He had only been in Catterick for five months, hardly long enough to become attached to the place, but just enough time to see his project completed. He had been brought up in Nottinghamshire but both parents were dead, and one married sister on the South Coast was all the close family he had.

However, he had recently met a wonderful girl at a dance. Visits to her parents in Ashton-under-Lyne had followed. But the Army now allowed him no time to make romantic arrangements. There was little time to wonder if that relationship had a future and he was in no mood to think about it. Unbeknown to him, the object of his affections, Kathleen, would not let time, distance, or the stressful uncertainty of the next five and a half years alter what she knew was inevitable.

Kathleen

Kathleen was prepared. Her father had put down his cabinet making tools in December 1914 and picked up his rifle as a member of the Territorial Force. He spent the next three years with the Gordon Highlanders in the Yprés Salient. In 1919 he came home. Kathleen's mother had warned her what war would mean for lovers. Her own engagement and the wood-bound pocket sized copy of Burns' love poems she had presented her betrothed had survived the Great War. She could tell Kathleen what it meant to be left at home.

Her mother confided in her how much a lover's constancy had meant to her father. Among the family treasures was the photo of his sweetheart, chaperoned even in the photo by her mother, which had been tucked inside the copy of Burns' poems that the reluctant warrior kept in his tunic for the four years he was away.

There had been plenty of time to talk about the coming war. Kathleen was certain there would be another along soon. A year before with fellow students she had played with a Ouija board and it had spelled out the month of the coming war. Kathleen would soon volunteer for war service and abandon her studies at Glasgow School of Art.

Bill

Bill Harvey had started on his road to war earlier in the year. The world news had been bad and was getting worse. Early 1939 he knew a clash with Germany was inevitable. He had been unimpressed by the failure of world governments to intervene following Italy's invasion of Ethiopia or the re-arming of Germany in breach of the Treaty of Versailles.

'Their massive build-up of military, air, and naval forces,' he recalled 'was answered by the pathetic performance of our government under Chamberlain.'

As long ago as March 1935, the Nazi Party had introduced compulsory military service. German shipyards were busy with orders for an expanding Navy. Diplomats were regularly invited to watch German tanks exercising. For Bill the conclusion was clear even before the newsreels showed German tanks rolling into the Saarland or goose-stepping to reoccupy the Rhineland. Finally there was the disgrace of Czechoslovakia. That was a simple matter of deserting your friends, according to Bill.

Bill was in turmoil. If there was a war, he guessed that all men between the ages of eighteen and twenty-six would be mobilised. He would prefer to serve in a unit of tradesmen. Many of his colleagues at the Railway Plant in Doncaster had reached the same conclusion.

Bill, along with thousands of others, had faced the facts and decided that another war was probable, so he volunteered for the Territorial Army. Bill admits that he had mixed motives 'At this time we were living in Balby and our next door neighbour, Frank Bone, was already serving in a Supplementary Reserve Unit. He received a bounty of £12 per year which was a goodly sum in those days when wages averaged £4 a week.'

If the threat of war went away he would just be left to do a fortnight's camp and a number of drill nights. It seemed like a reasonable deal at the time.

'Things went reasonably quiet again after I joined in May 1939. I did a fortnight's camp at Leeds and some local training. As the days went by everyone was buoyed up by the lack of action from Germany. We even began to think that the threat of war would disappear.'

Training consisted of little more than learning to look like a soldier. There was some weapon training but there was not enough ammunition for any live firing. Nevertheless, Bill was now a sapper in the Royal Engineers. He felt more secure about the future. Perhaps there would be peace in his time.

'About this time our first child, Janet, was about three years old and we decided the time was right for a second baby.'

As the situation in Europe deteriorated, Britain began a cautious programme of rearmament constrained by public opinion that inflicted by-election defeats on any party advocating more military spending. The expansion of the Army would have to be done on the cheap. In April 1939, the size of the Territorial Army was doubled from thirteen to twenty-six divisions and some limited, compulsory military service was introduced.

106 Army Troops Company (Royal Engineers), was formed in April 1939 and designated a Supplementary Reserve Company. Two words in their title were important. They helped account for the diverse tasks assigned to the company over the next three active years. They were *Army Troops*, not to be assigned to any divisional commander to be moved around a battlefield. They worked for the man at the top, the army commander.

The title 'Army Troops' emerged during the debate accompanying the Royal Commission in 1904. The title was an embodiment of the military maxim that armchair generals talk about tactics while professionals sort out their logistics. It was recognised that the man in charge needed some engineering resources at his disposal.

Army Troops were defined as 'battalions of infantry and other units not required to complete the division' The working title was the unflattering 'General Utility Troops.' Knowing the military inclination to abbreviate, there was immediate recognition of the anatomical possibilities. 106 GUT Company Royal Engineers was not to be.

The other word in the title with which they were christened was 'Supplementary.' The railway men and miners now preparing to go to war had little interest or understanding of the heated discussions that had surrounded the selection of their unit's title. No dictionary would explain the significance of these five syllables. The definition lay in the long history of defending the British shores.

As the nineteenth century drew to a close it was feared that the revolutions in Europe might be exported. Such fears were not without foundation. Europe was being politically reorganised. The French Emperor, Napoleon III, was threatening invasion while the Prussian Chancellor, Count von Bismarck, was employing the Prussian army in an effective campaign to unify the German peoples and establish a dominant place for Germany in the world order. The popular response in Britain was to form volunteer units to defend the country.

The Navy was jealous of its role as defender of the nation. A serious debate had already raged for a generation about whether there was any need for a home-based army. The Navy claimed it would prevent any invader from reaching British shores. But the Duke of Wellington opposed the 'Blue Water School.' With a force of twenty-five thousand men, 'I defy all the fleets of England to save it without the assistance of an army in the field,' he wrote to Peel.

The need to protect the Empire was easier for the Navy to accept. The small local garrisons around the globe could call on the Navy to deliver an Expeditionary Army to suppress any rebellion or repel an invasion. However, the dispatch of a sizable Expeditionary Force would deprive the country of its defensive garrison. The Volunteers were the political compromise. The Admirals, even with their royal patronage, found it hard to resist the diversion of modest funds to the Generals.

The force was only partly funded by the Exchequer. Much of the administrative expense for the Volunteers fell on their commanding officers. In times of peace they could be the plaything of the gentry. These local defence corps had already been formalised into the Volunteer Force in 1859. The answer to the Continental crisis was to incorporate the Volunteers into the Army.

So in March 1908 the Territorials joined the Army with an establishment of three hundred and fourteen thousand and the task of defending the coast and country if the Regular Army troops had to be sent overseas. These Volunteers were restyled the Territorial Force. They would hold the line in Flanders after half the Regular Army was destroyed in 1914 until Kitchener's Army arrived a year later.

But there was yet another 'army' whose origins would impact the fate of the Doncaster company. The Militias, the most ancient defenders of the coastline, were also 'abolished' under the 1908 reforms. They refused to be assigned to serve within the army which they saw as a junior service. However, they were eventually placated with a bit of flattery and became the 'Special Reserve.' Their sole task was to bring Regular Army units up to war establishment in time of need.

After the Great War the Special Reserve was itself abolished and the role of providing skilled personnel was taken over by the Territorial Army. The Militia ceased to exist as an independent force in 1920. The rules said the Volunteers would not be sent overseas unless they were part of the Special Service Section of the TA. The TA could be sent overseas, but only after a special Act of Parliament.

Students of the military reorganisations will not be surprised that political forces continued to manoeuvre and four years later, in 1924, the SR was reintroduced. This time the 'SR' stood for Supplementary Reserve. Once again Territorials could be sent abroad as a part of an expeditionary force.

Among the Supplementary Reserve were six Army Troops Companies and eleven other Specialist Companies formed by the Royal Engineers. The establishment was six officers and two hundred and forty-two men. Their wartime role was to undertake construction work for any British Expeditionary Force.

As well as establishing the principle that Territorials should be equipped and provided with facilities by the Exchequer, the Royal Commission of 1904 also set down another key role for the Volunteers. 'The Volunteer Force has had a great effect in educating the people of Great Britain to think of the Army as a national institution…' The Commission continued, 'We deprecate any changes which would modify the spirit which this force has cherished', noting that sympathy between the Army and the nation had been defective before the rise of the Volunteer Force. They were to be ordinary folk in uniform.

Doncaster

The company was to be based in Scarborough Barracks, Doncaster, sharing the building with the 5th Battalion of the King's Own Yorkshire Light Infantry. The officers and men were all Doncaster-based. They came from the surrounding pit villages and the railway workshops which was known in that depressed area as 'The Plant.' As so many of the company were recruited from the Doncaster Railway Works, they were known as the 'plant men'.

The Thirties had been a decade of remarkable technological advance. Electricity had reached most large towns. Everybody had seen an aeroplane and the ancient road network was now filling with vehicles. 106 Army Troops Company was filled with tradesmen who possessed the skill required to install and maintain this modern equipment. It was recognised that these craftsmen, drawn from industry, were normally better qualified than their Regular Army counterpart.

In 1939, the world was still recovering from the great depression but skilled tradesmen could still be found. By the time the unit returned from France seven months later, the true value of craftsmen would be appreciated as the industrial war effort accelerated. The company would later lose several of the older men whose contribution to the war effort would be from the work-bench.

As a Supplementary Reserve Unit, 106 Army Troops Company was to travel to France with a British Expeditionary Force (BEF). It was allocated to work with the Lines of Communication and 104 Army Troops Company. Their job would be to prepare the way for the arrival of the army.

Mobilisation

August was normally a quiet month when families took their holidays, but these were tumultuous times. In August 1939 Hitler continued to raise tension in Europe. He denounced the terms of the non-aggression pact a previous German government had signed with Poland. At the same time he abrogated the Naval Pact signed with Great Britain. The likely course of events was unfolding for those willing to face the unpleasant fact that Hitler would have to be confronted sooner or later.

But it was still possible to be optimistic. Germany was bordered by powerful, hostile nations, France in the west and Soviet Russia in the East. There was a hope that Germany's expansion could be checked. Hitler's actions were always cloaked with some legal niceties. Maybe respect for the rule of law would eventually triumph. Once the borders of Germany had been rearranged to undo the mistakes of Versailles, tranquillity might return, they speculated.

There were other distractions. The Poles, who were soon to become Germany's next victim, were forcing the weakened Czech state to cede territory to them under the terms set out in the Munich Agreement. Hungary also demanded, and received, a strip of erstwhile Czechoslovakian land. Jan Masaryk, whose father was known as the founder of Czechoslovakia, noted that 'My little country has paid almost the supreme price to preserve European democracy. …If it is for peace…I am glad. If it isn't, may God have mercy on our souls.'

Alan returned to his billet to complete the packing he had started some days before. It did not take long. His three sets of tunic, shirts and trousers were always correctly folded and stowed. These, plus the spare pair of boots, almost filled the issued kitbag. There was just room for his washing roll with his shaving equipment and a small repair kit that was universally know as a 'housewife.' Plate, mug and cutlery went in last so they could be accessed quickly if a meal was in prospect.

Everything else was packed in a suitcase and left for dispatch by rail to his sister's safekeeping. With both parents dead, this was his only close relative. Alan's father had died just days before he was born and his mother soon after he entered the army as a boy soldier. Soldiers going on active service had no need of civilian clothes. Opportunities for 'marching out' would be limited. The army of the 1918 had learned to keep its soldiers busy with parades and cleaning when out of the line. Civilian clothes were considered a passport to desertion. In uniform, the army was visible at work or relaxing. Alan's private life was packed and dispatched to Worthing.

He arrived with his kit bag in Doncaster late on Thursday. He was already at Scarborough Barracks when full mobilisation was ordered. The Regular Army provided two 'Military Mechanists (Electrical & Mechanical).' The other regular was WOII Ernest Fox. However, men of his rank and experience were in short supply and he was soon posted to a larger unit, leaving Alan Jones as the only military mechanist.

The life of a young soldier involved much hanging about and inspections.

1.1

Kit is set out in the regulation fashion for inspection at Blackdown in 1933.

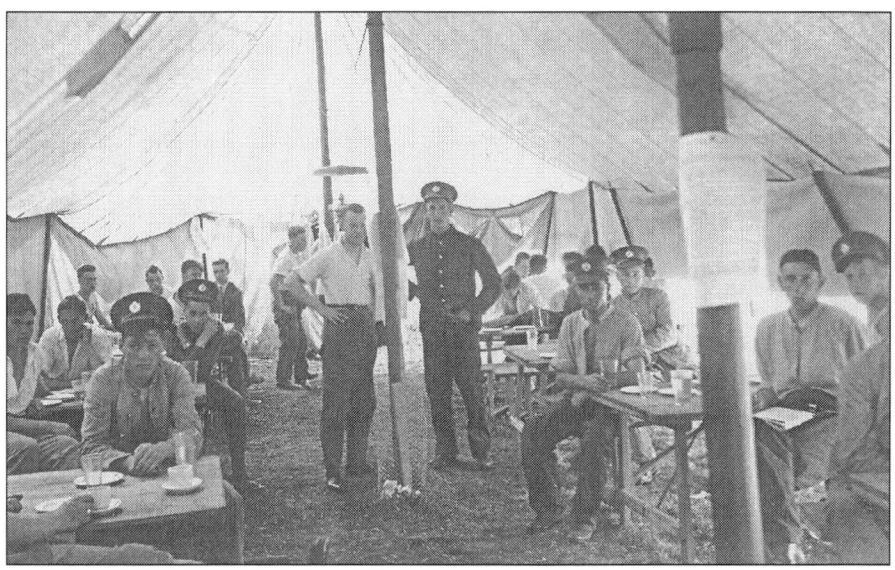

1.2
Inside the mess tent.

1.3
Corporals Alan Jones and Jock
Hazeldine showing their new stripes.

1.4
The 19 year old corporals, posted to
Malta in 1936, prepare to go to town.
To avoid getting stranded so far from
home, they applied for a long course
to get back to England.

The first entry in the 106 ATC war diary records that the 'Mobilise' telegram arrived from York at 20.55 on 1 September 1939. At 1800 the following day the diary records that TA Reservists were already assembled in the drill hall.

The pace of activity gave little time to reflect on the events that were unfolding. Bill recalled:

'By the middle of August things were moving quickly. The critical factor became Hitler's intention to invade Poland. This was the benchmark of British policy. In late August things happened quickly and dramatically, culminating in a radio broadcast for Reservists and Territorials to report to their barracks.'

Bill heard about the broadcast. His unit had been mobilised but at first he found it impossible to believe, so he went to work as usual. There he found many of the workbenches deserted. Clearly, others had been able to comprehend and obey this unwelcome call to arms. Several hours passed and the benches remained empty. Bill tried hard to concentrate on the work on his bench. There were frequent visitors asking if he had heard the announcement. It was obviously not a mistake or some simple misunderstanding.

Bill tidied away his work and returned home. He exchanged few words with Edith as they gathered his few items of kit. She hunted for a piece of soap he could take. Then he put on his uniform, laced his boots and reported to the barracks just before lunch on Friday. There were no long good-byes, no tears. The situation was a nuisance, a disruption, probably just a precaution.

It would take a few days to gather the whole unit. Some were working away or taking a late summer holiday. However, on Tuesday evening the unit log could note that the mobilisation personnel were complete except for one driver who was known to be in Canada.

One week before, on 24 August, the Western world was stunned when Hitler's foreign minister, Count von Ribbentrop, announced that a non-aggression pact had been signed with Russia. The pact had been signed late the night before. It came into effect immediately.

Nobody had predicted such an alliance. The two signatories had made no secret of their ideological enmity. German communists were in exile or filling Hitler's new concentration camps. Most of the Soviet High Command had been liquidated in the purges. Chief among their crimes was that they had trained with German staff officers in the Russian staff college during the decades when a German equivalent was banned. Stalin's army was not yet fit for war. They had just twenty-two months to prepare.

The pact with the Soviets had a short gestation. It was perhaps conceived in May when Molotov replaced Litvinov as Foreign Commissar and the Soviet policy of collective security came under review. While Britain and France negotiated their own security treaties with the Soviet Union during the summer, the German government waited. Germany had another plan to neutralise the Soviet Army. It was hoping that Poland could still be persuaded to cede Danzig and the Polish Corridor that left this fragment of ancient Prussia isolated and ostracised. In exchange for the corridor, Germany would support the Polish claim to the Ukraine, now part of the Soviet Union. If Poland could contain the Soviet Army, Germany military planners would be well content. Confrontation with their natural enemy could be postponed.

The secret negotiations between Germany and the Soviets did not start well. They produced little more than an increasing list of demands from Stalin. However, the two countries did manage to conclude a trade agreement that gave Germany a supply of energy and raw materials in exchange for industrial technology needed by the Soviet weapons industry. The German machine tools involved in this technology transfer would move east when the Germans attacked in 1942 to continue the production of the weapons that would defeat their invasion.

The German-Soviet non-aggression pact flowed from this straightforward trade deal. For the benefit of the astonished world the pact was justified by both parties as a way to contain the Imperialist powers of Britain, France, Belgium and Holland.

Chamberlain's government now reacted with uncharacteristic speed. The Anglo-Polish Defence Alliance was agreed on the 25 August. If the intention had been to outface Hitler, it failed. The bluff was called at dawn on the 1 September. Nine spearhead German divisions supported by forty-seven in reserve launched their attack on Western Poland to be followed by the Soviet army seventeen days later from the East.

Erwin Rommel

As the ink was drying on the Anglo-Polish treaty, General Erwin Rommel reported to Hitler's field HQ. His role was to organise the military around the headquarters and he would regularly accompany the Chancellor

The young Erwin was a child of the freshly united German Empire, born in 1891.The Germany of his youth, and later military career, were to be dominated by Prussian politicians. Rommel's family, however, came from the opposite side of the country, from the rather unfashionable state of Wüerttemberg.

Rommel admired the man he often referred to as 'the boss' in his diary. Hitler was, like himself, an outsider. They shared an admiration for the role that will-power and determination played in the life of any nation. The military aristocracy felt they could control both of these mavericks.

Young Erwin had harboured ambitions to be an engineer. With school friends he had experimented with flying machines. He always sought to understand how things worked and would later horrify his young bride by insisting on stripping their new motorbike to its nuts and bolts before they could use it for their honeymoon.

After graduation he planned to apply for a job at the Zeppelin factory in Friedrichshafen. But he also wanted to be financially independent of his parents. When his father advised him to follow a safer career path he become a soldier. He joined the army as an officer cadet member of the 7th Württhemberger Infantry Regiment.

After a short time in the ranks, he departed for Danzig where he would learn the Prussian officer's code. He graduated just before the outbreak of war in 1914. He was very familiar with the territory of Eastern Prussia that would be isolated under the terms of the Versailles Treaty. Twenty-five years later he would find himself fighting to re-join Prussia to the body of Greater Germany.

But throughout his life, Rommel never let his identity as a German smother his identity as a Swabian. So he returned to serve with his local regiment. He had survived the Great War with three serious wounds after distinguished service on the Western and Italian fronts. His daring tactics had gained him rapid promotion as one of the youngest Colonels in the German Army. Now at Hitler's HQ, he was still an outsider, not one of the aristocratic General Staff. However, he enjoyed the respect of the Commander in Chief and the General Staff as a brave, decisive soldier.

His appointment would provide a channel of communication for the military as they edged towards war. In a unique stream of letters home, Rommel confided to his wife that he hoped the Poles would accept the logic, backed by military might, of allowing Eastern Prussia, home to many of the General Staff, to be territorially reunited with Germany.

He witnessed the failure of diplomacy. It was his task to explain to Hitler the military imperatives that forced the staff to demand a decision. An army could not be kept on standby indefinitely, nor could its plans be concealed from the enemy for long. If the latter were given time to reinforce the frontier, the battle would be harder and they would risk loosing Poland to the Russians, whose forces would be ready to attack in a few weeks. An immediate attack made sense to Rommel's military mind.

Late on 25 August, Rommel moved with his escort battalion to Bad Polzin. His move brought with it a backdated promotion to major-general. They waited another ten days for Hitler to arrive aboard the special train that would serve as the Führer's mobile HQ during the invasion of Poland.

War

The inevitability of war could no longer be denied. Britain would have to support her new Polish ally. But Chamberlain was still not convinced that it was impossible to find a peace formula. The French Government frustrated the attempt to send an early communiqué demanding an end to hostilities. France had been mobilised but their Parliament had not approved the war budget. The communiqué had to wait. The French Foreign Minister, George Bonnet, was unhappy with the text. He was unwilling to specify any time limit for compliance.

When Chamberlain addressed a sceptical House of Commons that fateful Friday evening, he was left in no doubts about the House's determination to assist Poland. Chamberlain remained cautious. He insisted that he must first follow the arcane diplomatic practice of indicating a country's intention of declaring war. He was therefore able to assure a packed House that the British Ambassador would ask for the restoration of his passport in order to return home if a satisfactory reply was not received to the British communiqué.

In Berlin that evening, the British and French ambassadors therefore presented identical messages to the German Foreign Minister, Count von Ribbentrop.

Saturday morning brought the first detailed reports of the Blitzkrieg that had been unleashed upon Poland. Hopes that the impressive Polish army could block the Germans began to crumble. Chamberlain was now pressed by the French to allow them forty-eight hours to complete their mobilisation before declaring war.

To add to Chamberlain's dilemma, the Italian Foreign Minister Count Ciano offered to use his good offices to help resolve the matter. Ciano had interceded at Munich and was respected by Chamberlain and later by Churchill. When Chamberlain returned to the Commons on Saturday evening he confounded his Cabinet colleagues by advocating the path of negotiation once again. When he left the Chamber he was informed by his foreign minister, Lord Halifax, that the members of his cabinet would not tolerate any further delay. The Prime Minister faced the inevitable and agreed that the ultimatum, resolved by the Cabinet the previous day, should be delivered.

The Cabinet meeting broke up in the early hours of Sunday morning. It had been agreed that Sir Neville Henderson would see the German Foreign Minister at nine o'clock that morning. The Ambassador would say that a state of war would exist between Britain and Germany unless a favourable reply was received by eleven o'clock to the communiqué delivered on Friday.

Time had already been reserved in the BBC schedule for the Prime Minister to address the nation. Few doubted there would be no response to the ultimatum. In his famous broadcast of Sunday 3 September, Prime Minister Chamberlain explained the sequence of events.

'Our ambassador in Berlin handed a note to the Germans stating that a state of war would exist between Britain and Germany unless a favourable reply was received by eleven o'clock. I must tell you now that no such undertaking has been received and consequently we are at war with Germany.'

Bill Harvey recalled the events. 'Everything was in a terrible state of confusion. The only certainty was that we were to be confined to barracks. Confusion lasted through the Saturday but on Sunday morning we were assembled and informed that the government had issued an ultimatum to Germany. It had been ignored and as a consequence we were now at war with Germany.' They would be in France before the shock and feeling of unreality lifted.

For Staff Sergeant Alan Jones there was no confusion. He had his instructions. He had arranged for his party of soldiers to be able to listen to the declaration of war as they worked. 'All of our 1098 (mobilisation) equipment had started to arrive. We had to unpack, check and then issue it. There was no time to stand around and speculate.'

In 1939 most families in Doncaster had a radio. However, most homes lacked electricity so the radios relied on a dry battery or a rechargeable accumulator. The radios had been on continuously as the fateful events unfolded. Now it was the weekend and many sets faded and then fell silent as no spare batteries could be bought. But Bill Harvey's family heard the broadcast.

For the married men their predicament slowly dawned. 'It was then that I began to realise what a terrible thing I had done to my wife, heavily pregnant at that time, to leave her unprotected at a time when she would need me most.' Bill remembers 'My only consolation was that Edith's mother would look after her. I was conscious of a deep sense of guilt involving Edith in such hardship. This feeling was uppermost in my mind throughout the war years. We did not know how long it would last or even the eventual outcome.'

'I am sure the majority shared the same worries and fears for the families they left behind. One poor man was so beset with the worry of it all, that he got out one night, went home and gassed himself and all his family. I knew him quite well because he was a coach painter in the Plant.'

Activity was the military antidote to worry. 'Mobilised on the Friday and on a war footing on the Sunday. Things happened too quickly to get upset. A new daily routine took over our lives. If you paused for a moment it just seemed unbelievable.'

Their first brush with war occurred on Sunday night. The air raid siren sounded and there was a general rush outside to see one little plane caught in the search-lights and very high up. It was interesting rather than threatening. However the intervention of some officious person spoiled the occasion by ordering that gas masks had to be worn.

In London, a pilot had become the first casualty of the war. As Chamberlain's broadcast ended the London air-raid sirens sounded, as two fighters climbed to intercept a French aircraft that had strayed into British airspace. The RAF fighters collided over the Thames. After a quarter of an hour the 'all clear' was sounded.

At noon, Chamberlain repeated his message to the House of Commons, meeting for the first time on Sunday in a hundred and twenty years. He did not stay to listen to the criticism of his policy of appeasement. Chamberlain left the House after delivering his pathetic admission of failure. 'Everything I have worked for, everything that I have worked for in my public life, has crashed in ruins.' His faith that freeing Germany from the burdens imposed at Versailles in 1919 would bring peace had failed. France, in particular, was unwilling to recognise another great power.

Britain would stand alone until five o'clock that evening when the French ultimatum expired by which time the War time Cabinet was assembling for the first time, still with Chamberlain as Prime Minister.

'Get ready'

It was a busy week. Kit was issued and the necessary vaccinations administered. Three times a day they were marched down to the Lyceum Cafe in the High Street of Doncaster for meals. The weather was warm so they marched without tunics, their brand new white braces announcing that they had just been issued with new kit. During the daytime the senior NCOs gradually knocked them into some sort of military shape.

But the level of activity at the barracks simply raised the level of anxiety among relatives. France, the ally that Britain was committed to supporting, seemed a long way from Yorkshire in the days when a week's holiday at Scarborough or Skegness made you a cosmopolitan.

The anxiety among the local community was heightened when on Wednesday they received instructions to dig trenches around the drill hall for use as a refuge in the event of air raids. Along with the fear of a gas attack, much had been made in the press of the ability of modern bombers to destroy whole cities and their inhabitants. This fear would permit a breed of petty tyrant, the Air Raid Precautions warden to flourish for the next six years.

After a few days sleeping on the drill hall floor with just an army blanket for bedding they were allocated civilian billets. Bill was dumped with a couple of old souls in Chequer Road, near the Park entrance in Doncaster. 'I may have stopped there the first night but after that I used to call in to let them know where I was going, then went home to see my wife. I'm sure everyone else did the same.'

Each day of the first week of the war there was the heartbreaking spectacle of wives and family arriving at the barrack gates in a quest for news. Were they going to move? There was no hard news and in its place rumours abounded. The men could only assure their relatives that they had been given no orders to move. Frequently, before the relatives or girlfriends had arrived home after a lengthy journey by train and bus, another rumour informed them that 106 was due to leave the next day. This would necessitate a return journey to the barracks.

The level of activity certainly indicated that the unit was preparing to go to war.

'Looking back I know we all had our troubles and worries but it must have been an organisational nightmare for the administration. Staff Sergeant Jack Hurren was responsible for transport and Sergeant Cliff Barron for men and equipment.'

'We were also told at this time that the pay for a sapper was three shillings and three pennies a day and we would be expected to make some provision for our wives or families.'

'I was pleased to make a contribution of two shillings and six pence a day out of my army pay. What a terrible shock. As a Grade 1 electrician in the Plant my average wage was £4 10 shillings a week. Our financial situation was worse than I had anticipated.' Bill's pay packet shrank to under a quarter of its peacetime size. Not only was he deserting his family but he was impoverishing them. There would be no luxuries from his new pay. Even the annual bounty would be withheld now they had been mobilised. Bill never received his 'bounty'.

The company had six sections, one HQ admin section, one electrical and mechanical section plus four normal working sections. All electrical and mechanical trades were represented. They would be required to create or convert buildings for accommodation, stores, personnel and hospitals in advance of the BEF. Altogether there were two hundred and sixty officers and men.

The Officer Commanding was Captain Wentworth-Smith with Lieutenant Peter Yates as his second in command. Bill was assigned to No 2 section, a general section under Lieutenant Bell, a volunteer like himself, whose family ran a local jewellery firm. Bill Abel as the section sergeant. The section was filled with men from the Plant or surrounding pit villages.

Staff Jones was the only regular soldier at that stage. He was kept busy sorting out their mobilisation equipment which arrived efficiently according to plan from depots around the country. Clothing, weapons as well as an impressive range of engineering tools, equipment and instruments arrived each day. The kit Alan Jones had checked was now repacked and already on its way in whatever transport could be requisitioned. So far the plan had worked well. Some of their equipment would be transferred to their new lorries waiting near the ports. The lorries requisitioned from local removal firms had been given a coat of green paint and joined the army sailing to France to meet them.

'Go'

With the equipment packed and dispatched there was little left to do except worry. They did not have much time to worry. There were many heavy hearts marching down the main street of Doncaster to the station on Monday morning as 106 headed for France. It was an early start. They marched out promptly at seven o'clock. They had received notice two days before that they would be moving on Monday 10 September. It had taken just ten days from the time they were called up.

The need for transport was acute. The army had abandoned horses and was turning itself into the world's first 'transportised' army. The programme to motorise the army was far from complete. There was no time for 106 to wait for an allocation of transport to arrive. Doncaster removal and transport firms had to surrender a few vehicles from their fleet. The army was choosy and took the most modern vehicles in exchange for modest compensation.

For Bill, the actual moment of parting arrived with little warning. 'Edith was fortunate. With my father's help she managed to be on the platform for a last heartbreaking farewell. To see the agony on her poor, dear face as the train pulled away was unbearable. Not a moment to be savoured! So we were on our way but far too miserable to care where we would end up.'

'One laughable thing was that they issued each of us with a ration of one tin of bully and one hard biscuit for the journey. The biscuit was about five inches square and three-quarters of an inch thick. It was most likely a left over from the First World War.' Most of the rations went out of the window.

At 2.30 that afternoon they arrived in Southampton, matching the speed of the modern train service. This time the troops disembarked within the confines of the dockyard without an audience. For three days the ships had been assembling to transport the BEF to France. Key liaison personnel had been taken across by air or by Navy destroyer during the first three days of war.

It was now 'Day 7' of the mobilisation plan. The advanced parties had reached France, heavy equipment was underway and the dock workers essential for the build- up were in place. And now it was time for the first units to head for France. 106 ATC was among them. A system had now been established at the docks to process the volume of soldiers expected. There were pay books to be checked and amended, injections to be administered and rations to be issued. It took the rest of the warm afternoon to reach their ship but by 6.15 p.m. they were embarked and ready to go.

'Once in Southampton we embarked on a ship called the Monals Queen, a former ferry boat on the Liverpool to Isle of Man service. By this time most of us were nursing sore arms due to the vaccination and immunisation jabs which didn't improve our general misery.'

The boat pulled out to sea and anchored, waiting for darkness to fall before crossing the Channel. The Navy checked that their channel was clear of mines and hunted the planned route for U-boats. When the route had been thoroughly checked the troop-ships were told to make best speed to their destination.

The ferryboats were not renowned for comfort. There were a few benches and the limited saloon space was taken over by the officers. So it was a case of securing a small space either on deck or in a gangway and sleeping the time away with a greatcoat for protection from the autumn breeze and their pack for a pillow.

There had been plenty of talk of mines and U-boats as they prepared for their crossing. The Navy looked reassuringly busy. Some men talked knowledgeably of mine sweepers and destroyers and how nothing would be able to sneak past the Royal Navy. But Bill stayed on the deck. That way he was nearer the lifeboats.

'If anyone was waiting to sink us there was not much we could do about it so why worry? We woke up the next morning to disembark at Cherbourg where another train was waiting for us and away we went again.' This was the day that Bill Harvey and his comrades received their real introduction to army life. 'Every time we expected to settle down the call came, "Fall in lads, we're moving again".' 'Hurry up and wait' had frustrated generations of soldiers before them. The sappers of 106 Company would not be spared.

At 6.45 am they started to disembark at Cherbourg. Bill, half expected a cheering crowd or some reception committee from the French they had come to defend. But instead, the only activity on the quay, or in the town, was the dockers and military movements personnel. The town was surprisingly tranquil.

There was little time to notice much about this piece of foreign field they had come to defend as they marched to the waiting train. Shortly after noon the train began a leisurely journey. The first stop would be Le Mans. This excited some of the mechanics who recognised this as the home of the famous 24-hour car race. This was the first of three 'Haltes-Repas', French food stops, arranged along the way.

In truth it was more 'haltes' than 'repas' as they had to wait for one of the limited slots that the French authorities had allocated to the train before they could join the mainline heading west for Brittany and their final destination, Brest.

The company has the distinction of being the first unit to arrive in France after mobilisation. The transport sergeant, Jack Hurren, received a medal for his effort to move the company and its equipment to France.

Poland

On 26 September, Rommel returned to Berlin to prepare for Hitler's return after the defeat of Poland. Rommel had witnessed the rapid evolution of Blitzkrieg. Having smashed through the crust of a still-mobilising Polish defence, the Germans employed Schrecklichkeit (frightfulness) to awe their enemies. The other key words were 'Surprise, Speed.'

Polish generals could not comprehend a tactic that bypassed strong points. But Rommel observed how the bypassed Poles had to withdraw as the panzers pressed on East. In the euphoria that followed victory, Rommel felt able to hint that he would like to lead an operational unit. As an infantry officer, this was an unlikely move but on 6 February, Rommel was ordered to proceed to take command of 7th Panzer Division.

On 27 February the Polish Government capitulated. The one and a half million-strong German army had taken forty thousand casualties.

Chapter Two

France

September 1939

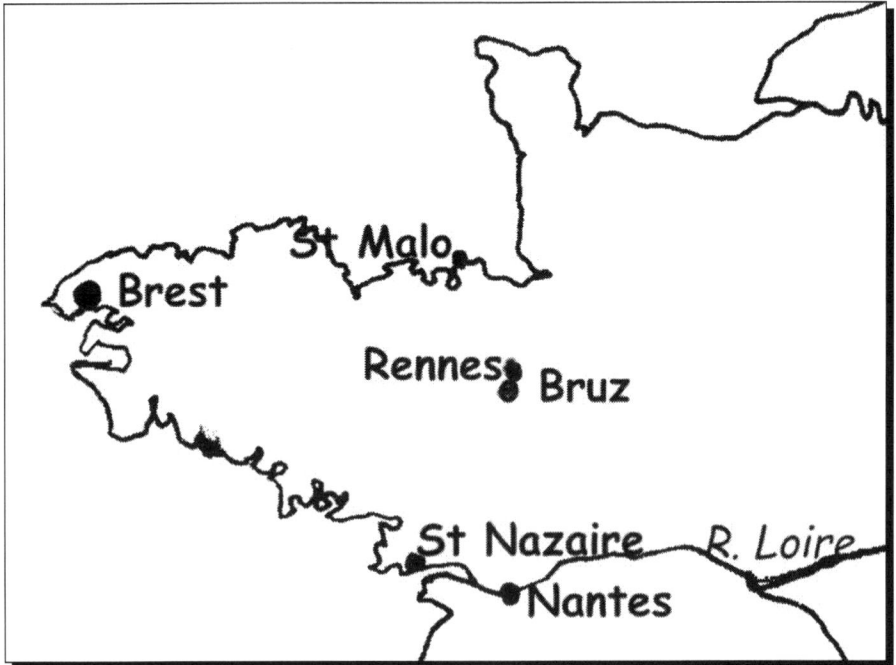

Map of North-west France

Brittany was chosen as the supply base for the BEF in 1939 with its easy access to
the Empire trade routes and reinforcements. The 'Lines of Communication' would
feed troops and supplies forward. It was further from the anticipated interference
expected from German naval and air forces. In practice, the short Channel to was
able to operate successfully as the tide and sandbanks made it difficult for U-boats.
The Lines of Communications were therefore not as exercised as intended as the
forces built up during the first six months of the war.

For the military planners this war would be just like the previous war. A steady flow of men and matériel would be landed and fed to the front for as long as it took to wear down the Germans. The company's role was to work in the Lines Of Communication. The Plant Men would form an LOC unit.

The intervening two decades had done little to change the military philosophy of the victors. The downsized German Army had meanwhile, changed the rules of war. The Poles were learning what the mobile, armoured force, illegally rebuilt under the Nazi leadership, could achieve.

The company would prepare the way for others to reinforce the French left flank. Constrained by Belgian neutrality there could be no move forward. The BEF would be forced to stay in the featureless flatlands along the border. The British Divisions would have to wait along the French/Belgian border, among the well-tended cemeteries of the Great War.

It was anticipated that as much as a year would be needed to build up the BEF. Once in position, fresh troops and supplies would flow from the secure ports along the west coast of France to the front along the established Line of Communication.

The threat from the air and from U-boats had prompted the planners to move their base away from Calais to the Brittany on the west coast. Brittany was also chosen as the base area for this war because it provided access to the Atlantic, over which men and supplies were expected to flow from the British and French Empires in due course. Apart from this, it would be war as usual.

The French were, however, determined that the battles should be fought beyond its borders this time. The French reluctance to engage in an active war was a natural consequence of the losses they had suffered in the Great War. A quarter of their young men had been killed. Plans for a strong border defence were born after the Great War ended. France had suffered major attacks across its frontier in 1870 and 1914 from the newly emerging nation that was Germany. A fortified line was politically and militarily attractive.

'Maginot Mentality'

The Germans had demonstrated how difficult it was to breach a well-sited and fortified defensive line during the bloody campaigns of 1916 and 1917. Constructed behind their front line during 1915 after the advances of 1914, the Germans withdrew to the Hindenburg Line, which forced the Allies to spent millions of men capturing each fort and elaborate defence. So the military lesson appeared clear.

Perhaps the German offensive in early 1918 should have warned French Generals that a fixed defence would not work. The successful Allied counter-offensive, supported by the new British tanks, should have reinforced to post-war military strategists the need for mobility.

The Germans had matched the construction of the Maginot line with a modest one of their own. The Siegfried line, behind the Western Wall, was not on the scale or sophistication of its French counterpart. However, it betrays the defensive thinking that had pervaded the mentality of all the combatants who had survived the horrors of the Great War.

The Czechs, Poles, Russians and Belgians also invested in frontier defence during the thirties. All these defences were sited to deter a resurgent German nation from aggression. The Belgian position was singularly inconsistent. Their defence apparently relied on neutrality. This prevented the British army taking up defensible positions during the early months of the war. However, the Belgian defence was reinforced with a set of impressive, concrete forts at strategic points along their frontier with Germany. Neither forts nor neutrality would ultimately prove effective.

The French Maginot Line was a set of fortifications which ran from the Swiss frontier to Luxemburg. It covered all the likely invasion routes and protected the industrial regions of the North East. It was never envisaged as a continuous defensive line, although this myth was propagated to the public.

Ending the line near the Belgium frontier was not a naïve or incompetent oversight. The terrain of the Lowlands would be protected by demolishing bridges over the numerous waterways that crossed Belgium and northern France. Flooding was seen as the best weapon to use against any invasion. But once the British army had raced forward to defend Belgium, any flooding risked stranding the BEF. Ultimately, flooding would be used effectively to protect the evacuation beaches in May and June 1940.

There was another sound reason not to build the Maginot line along its common border with Belgium. France enjoyed good relations with this constitutionally-neutral land where half the population spoke French. Extending the line could be misinterpreted as a political statement of abandonment or an invitation to Germany to violate Belgian neutrality in the future. Gestures and politics were at the core of French military strategy.

When the BEF was dispatched, the Secretary of State for War, Hore-Belisha, ignored French sensibilities and sent X Force of Royal Engineers to complete the line along the French-Belgian frontier. The water-table would render the engineering task of excavations and fortifications difficult and expensive. They managed to construct over four hundred pillboxes and associated defences in the few months available.

For Bill the Maginot line made sense. It made him feel secure. Even if the defence did not deter a German attack, there was a good chance it could hold them up and keep them a very long way from Rennes. What upset Bill was the prospect that the stalemate might go on for years. The 'Maginot Mentality' that encouraged the military to believe that they could sit behind fixed defences would soon be discredited.

The First and Second British Corps were immediately ordered to France. They were not part of any attempt to assist Poland. No plan existed to attack Germany or try to divert the forces attacking our new ally to another front. Realistically, there was little the Allies could do to provide direct or indirect support to the Poles at the Eastern edge of Europe.

It was unrealistic to expect much from the Army in the short term. The only roles set for the British Army were the defence of the homeland and protection of its overseas territories. No plan existed to reinforce any Continental ally or to fight a technically advanced army. The early arrival of an engineering company from Doncaster did nothing to upset the military balance.

The Polish military planners quickly understood their own predicament. They could not expect to defeat the German army. However, the Poles and their new Allies expected to fight the invaders to a standstill. This was the first of many miscalculations to afflict the Allied cause.

The fate of Poles was effectively sealed when the Soviet army joined the attack on Poland from the East in late September. Further resistance was futile. Polish forces were told to make their way to France. An astonishing number of Polish army and air-force units left Poland. Nearly a quarter of a million men eventually made their way to Allied territory. Most passed through Romania where they were interned before being taken out by boats chartered by the British and French governments. In eight months they would be waiting at ports around Bordeaux for ships once again, this time to bring them to Britain.

The Allies might have attacked Germany in the south. However, the French did not want to fight on their homeland but had no plans to leave their territory. This contradiction was resolved with a series of probing attacks towards Germany's Western Wall in the area of Saarbruecken during September.

This was an early test of the notion of 'armed deterrence.' The French wanted to demonstrate their willingness to fight in the hope it might replace an actual trial of strength. The fallback position was to wait for the German army to blunt itself against their elaborate defences before any counter-attack would be considered.

Apart from dispatching the BEF, British aggression was confined to dropping leaflets and attacking shipping. Bombing munitions factories was ruled out by Sir Kingsley Wood, the Secretary of State for Air, as they were private property. Even Churchill's plan as First Sea Lord to float mines down the Rhine was vetoed by the French for fear that such an aggressive act would provoke German reprisals. Safe behind their fortification, the hope persisted that hostilities could be avoided. A war of gestures and occasional demonstrations might be necessary before peace could be concluded.

Bill was not privy to such strategic thinking. In common with the other soldiers rushing to France, he thought the speedy collapse of Polish resistance was ominous. The discomfort, lack of leadership and loneliness did nothing to improve his morale. He was glad of the Maginot Line, which made a lot of sense to an engineer.

Army Plan W

The plan that had sent the company to France after the declaration of war was the result of a political decision made under pressure from the French. It was a key concession offered to the French by the British Prime Minister, Chamberlain, when he pressured French Premier Daladier to concede the demilitarisation of the Czech Sudetenland in September 1938. Plan W was completed just in time for this new crisis.

The Munich Agreement shattered the military balance of Continental Europe. In contrast to the British Prime Minister who received a hero's welcome at Hendon Airdrome, his French counterpart expected a hostile reception from his countrymen. When the French pilot returning from Munich observed the crowds at the airfield he suggested diverting.

French diplomacy had constructed a set of alliances to provide a check to the growing military might of National Socialist Germany. The loss of thirty-five Czech Divisions and a sophisticated armaments industry upset the French calculations. This was a diplomatic coup for the Nazis and a disaster for France. The French saw themselves being isolated to face the might of the German army once again.

The pressure on Britain to abandon its isolation and rejoin Europe was recognised but so were the political dangers. A credible gesture of support for the French was required from the British Government. In late February 1939, after much dissent within the Cabinet, it was agreed to commit up to ten Divisions to reinforce France in the event of war.

The French had over a hundred divisions. During the autumn of 1939 they faced twenty-three weak German Divisions that had been left out of the order of battle for the invasion of Poland. The ten British Divisions would help defend the forty-five mile section of the French/Belgian frontier to the Channel coast. As a very junior partner they would be under French command as in the First War.

When Brigadier L A Hawes set his staff to check the existing plans for the move of the British Army to France, he discovered the plans were seriously out of date. A major defect was the plan's reliance on horse-drawn transport. The army had been mechanised so the provision of fodder and grooms had to be replaced with fuel and mechanics.

The Army plan, W4, was prepared between June and September 1939. These six months of thorough staff work produced a plan to move the army through the ports of Nantes, St Nazaire, Cherbourg and Brest. The western ports were chosen for disembarkation as they were the furthest from the anticipated German air and submarine threats. A southern base between St Nazaire and Nantes would be the main logistic port, providing easy access to transatlantic shipping.

Two main land bases were to be used. The northern base was at the important railhead of Rennes which would be linked to the port of Brest. Whichever engineer unit was given the serial number 1583 would construct and maintain a transit base. Weeks later, 106 ATC RE was on the way to Rennes.

The plan, whose formal title was 'First Maintenance Project', allowed just enough time for all the necessary preparations before being activated. The haste with which these plans were prepared is well illustrated by the inclusion of local tourist maps to indicate key locations. Nevertheless, it all worked surprisingly well.

The plan listed 9099 entries in the mobilisation plans. The first phase was to run from Mobilisation day plus three to Mobilisation day plus ten. The early serials list hundreds of advance parties and thousands of individual liaison officers. The first units would start to cross a week after mobilisation, Mobilisation plus seven, M+7.

In position 2637, 106 (West Riding) Army Troop Company (SR) is listed with the first contingent of troops. The company would lead the way on M+7 to arrive with some other specialist units and the first infantry companies. These would be the first units of the BEF to arrive in France.

Phase Two would deliver the First British Corps and Second echelon troops. By M+19 the Second Corps would set off and be in place by M+26. Thereafter the rest of the Lines of Communication troops would arrive to be followed by the fighting troops. These included Military Police to run a three hundred place jail on M+30 and vets to look after staff officers' horses on M+60.

A deception plan was put in place to persuade German intelligence that the short channel crossing would be used for the deployment of the BEF as in the First World War. The bluff might have worked as the Navy enjoyed early success against U-boats waiting to ambush the first convoys. Ironically, the Navy soon chose to adopt this shorter Dover-Calais route when it became vital to economise on shipping and escorts.

Consequently, the supply organisation would be underused as the short Channel crossing was used until the western Blitzkrieg was launched in May 1940. The company and other Lines of Communications troops would not be as busy as planned.

Settling in

Going to war was an anticlimax for Bill. 'We had slipped in by a side door without fuss or ceremony.' There were none of the cheering crowds they had often seen on newsreels as the locals welcomed their protectors. The train journey was long and dull. It was late afternoon when they arrived at Brest.

They did not know what they were here for. The favourite rumour had it that they were to establish a transit camp for following troops, thought to be Canadians.

They climbed off the train and formed up again to march up to a castle where they were to be billeted. To their surprise and some open amusement an officer appeared, mounted on a horse. 'We discovered he was to be our adjutant. I thought we had slipped back to the 1914/18 war. He might have made a gesture of being an officer in a modern army.'

'As we marched along everyone was weary and hungry. After a while, being new to army discipline, there were shouts of 'How about a rest?' which caused the officer to ride up and down the column to inform us if he heard anymore he would give us a route march. Needless to say discretion prevailed and we eventually arrived. We found the fort surrounded by a dry moat and were told we would sleep there until the tents arrived.'

2.1

Alan Jones beside the moat of the castle at Brest where the company spent their first weeks in France preparing a transit camp. Most would escape to Rennes before the onset of the harsh winter of 1939. Below is the commercial port where Alan would escape in June 1940.

2.2

The Central Café, Lesnervanes fed the soldiers who were converting the abandoned monastery into a special hospital during the early months of the war.

As the first to arrive, accommodation was indeed basic. The next days were occupied in making their 'home' habitable. There were neither running water nor latrines. But thirty-six hours later the services had been laid on.

The days were occupied with odd jobs which seemed to Bill designed to keep them busy. It continued the practice established over the centuries of keeping servicemen active. Sailors scrubbed decks while soldiers swept and polished. It could have been worse. Soldiers of the Great War were paraded up to five times a day when they were not in the trenches. It all served to provide a constant reminder that they were subject to military discipline. As civilians just ten days before, they recognised this charade but they fell in and got on with the imposed tedium.

Real work was hard to find. The stores and vehicles had yet to arrive. The tasks had not been agreed with the French. But as the days passed the lucky ones were taken to do a variety of odd jobs along the intended reinforcement route and escaped Brest and the clutches of its comical Adjutant. The trucks and tools began to arrive.

On 25 September a group of thirty-three sappers under Staff Sergeant Alan Jones was detached to Lesnevans. The Abbey at Lesnevans had been gutted by fire in 1938 but the solid stone walls had survived. Their task was set up a 'special' hospital inside the hollow monastery.

The north and east wings housed the accommodation while a chapel occupied a third side. The monastic architects had not closed the quadrangle on the south side, thereby trapping the autumn sun's light and heat. Work on the two floors progressed slowly. The restored building and the improved facilities would never be used by the military, but survive to this day as a monument to the detailed, if mysterious, work of military planners.

The task was technically simple. The sappers however had to master the use of local materials as they worked alongside the local craftsmen. The main difficulty was driving holes through the granite walls but the coal-miners among them were used to cutting through rock. Work was slow but gradually the path for the central heating pipes and other services was opened around the two residential wings of the cloister.

In the evenings Alan Jones headed for the Café Central, a few minutes' walk from the Abbey, overlooking the central square. Here he impressed the proprietors with his schoolboy French. After a few days Madame introduced her niece, Marie-Claire. In a country still short of marriageable men, here perhaps was a suitable husband for her sister's most beautiful daughter.

She had come here from Paris as war threatened. Marie-Claire would be allowed to wait on the tables used by the English soldiers although Madame was never far away. As the evenings darkened and autumn surrendered to the wet winter westerlies, they abandoned the tables in the square and took refuge inside for their nightly drink. A platonic friendship flourished between two young people far from home.

Armies overseas are less noted for the meeting of minds as for carnal contact. The high command recognised VD as a serious problem. However, they were not willing to countenance the advice issued by Brigadier Montgomery to his soldiers. He told them to ask a Military Policeman where they could find a licensed brothel instead of using the unregulated prostitution that developed around the Channel Ports. He received a reprimand for this honesty.

The 'special' hospital at Lesnevans was designed to deal with the casualties from this conflict. The doctor from 8th Field Hospital informed Alan this establishment was to be for the treatment of Venereal Diseases. The hospital was to be the centre for the treatment of soldiers who were expected to succumb during the campaign.

The work took many weeks to complete. It was a good start to the war for Alan who kept up his regular flow of letters home to Kathleen. Letters flowed both ways. She had written to say that she had abandoned her art school to train for war work. There seemed little point in painting while all she loved was in peril. The unexpected bonus was that she found herself supervising an overbearing bully of a tutor from her old college who was a few years later assigned to do war work.

This pattern continued through the winter months as working parties were dispatched from Brest to build or adapt facilities. The lucky ones were given Army French Form 706 to allow them to purchase food from local cafes. For the adventurous this was fun. For those used to a plain Yorkshire diet it was an unwelcome adventure.

Alan enjoined the experience of foreign food. These were new tastes. They reminded him of the tastes he had enjoyed in his early years back home. He recalled his weekly trip to meet the train from Lincoln where he would receive a basket of freshly baked pork pies and potted meats. In the little village of Tuxford the customers would queue at his mother's guest house, ready to purchase these luxuries.

Bill was willing to try foreign food but was happy when the café was persuaded to produce some plain fare for the Yorkshiremen. Instead of spending their evenings at the café, Bill and the other soldiers were happy to collect their rations and return to their billets in the Abbey. There was time to talk, read and write. The war seemed a long way away. Bill had come to do his duty but really wanted to be at home.

On 28 September Number Two Section under Lieutenant Bell left the moat at Brest. They headed for their permanent base in Rennes. Sapper Bill recalls, 'We occupied the house, with officers and senior NCOs on the ground floor and other ranks on the upper floors. I finished up in an attic with several others. We acquired a dartboard which became a treasured possession. We spent most of our nights in darts competitions, between the inevitable guard duties.'

Good administrative order was gradually imposed on the HQ at Rennes. On 9 October they were instructed to start keeping a log of the company's activities on the army form known as a War Diary. In true British fashion, the early entries are all about the weather. October was wet in Rennes. So was November. There was little else to report.

A workshop was taken over and instructed to supply four thousand beds for the transit camp at Brest. But the order for the construction of beds had to be adjusted a week later as the production of 'duck boards' to provide a dry floor in the tented camps became the priority. More wood was then found and the beds completed.

Local businesses flourished at first. The locally produced huts, known as 'Tomines' were built at the rate of one a day in November. These would provide more comfortable accommodation for troops moving back and forth along the Lines Of Communication. Production slowed in December when the shortage of timber required to produce floors for the tents caused the design to be modified to save wood.

None of the plans seemed to have taken account of the shortage of resources that would emerge as world trade was disrupted. The conscription of two million Frenchmen into the armed forces further reduced the flow of constructional timber. Corrugated metal Nissen huts were now proposed as the alternative when the supply of timber effectively ran out at the end of the year and were starting to arrive from factories in Britain.

During October other sections escaped the confinement of Brest and joined the company in the Chateau Des Loges in Rennes with its extensive grounds. Their new home was at the edge of town on the main road to Lorient. On the pavement outside their base ran a light gauge railway, used by the farmers to haul their produce to the railhead or quay where trains and barges would distribute it to the markets of France.

At the end of October Number One Section and the Electrical & Mechanical specialists were moved out of Brest to join the company when their work on the hospital was complete. As each section arrived from Brest, huts filled the grounds at the back of the house that had become their home and working base.

The planners had located the engineers' base well. The site had excellent road, rail and canal connections. For the soldiers it had the great benefit of being on the opposite side of Rennes, away from all the other barracks and Headquarters, offering the prospect of a life relatively free from military manners.

The location had been particularly well chosen for Alan Jones. The city's football stadium was just 200 yards up the road. Regular competitive matches would be a feature of his life. The army produced a team to play other French, professional club team. Alan was a regular member of that British Army team which toured northern France in the autumn of 1939.

Alan could even lay claim to have represented his country as he was able to hold his place in the team even though a member of the England team, now conscripted, was competing for his place.

The other recreation was walking into town just a mile away. As building resources became scarce and the plans were incomplete, the workload was not excessive. On their way to the centre they would have to be alert to the clanging bell on the train that ran right along the pavement. They learned to respect this iron monster. Its brakes were suspect and they learned to listen carefully before attempting to drive a truck across the line or even step on it.

On the way to town, they passed a solid stone stall on which, during the hours of daylight, sat a sombre, uniformed tax collector with the title 'Octroi' carved on a scroll above the arch. This was an ancient tax levied on goods going in and out of the city of Rennes. Alan recalled that similar tax points were strategically situated around some English market towns of his youth. The visiting army was naturally exempt from this levy as, it appeared, were many others who bustled past the post or who contrived to associate themselves with British soldiers as they carried their bundles past the check-point.

As they approached the town they were regularly greeted by the sight of the local washer-women slapping and scrubbing their clothes on the flat stones by the river. For the men from Yorkshire this was something their mothers talked of. It was now a rare sight as most Yorkshire homes boasted a boiler and dolly which had replaced the trip to the local pump or river on washing day.

Drudgery was still the fate of many of the craftsmen from Doncaster. The general shortage of sappers would force Number Four Section to remain in Brest during the harsh winter that was to follow. This was in spite of constant complaint from their OC who wanted his men for similar tasks that needed strong backs at Rennes. The troops were much needed but not for their engineering expertise.

What the army wanted in Rennes were more porters to unload the supplies that were starting to flow from factories and depots in Britain. The logistics continued to arrive into the base area while the troops who could have carried out the task of shifting ammunition and equipment were going direct to the front.

However the last section did eventually escape from the freezing moat to the more favourable accommodation at Caserne Potangern. They moved just in time to miss the spectacular explosion and fire that engulfed MV Pacific Coast on 9 November, which showered debris on the vacated tented camp around the port.

The vessel was laden with the flimsy, two gallon petrol cans used by the army. A spark from the motor in a crane used to remove the hatch covers was blamed for the explosion, which killed many dock workers and their supervising officers. Only much later, after the recognition of the benefits of the 'jerry cans' captured from the Germans in the desert war, was this robust and enduring design adopted and manufactured for British forces.

Operations staff at the Rennes Area HQ noted that loaded wagons were attractive targets. It was not so much the Luftwaffe that bothered them as pilferers. A lot of material seemed to be falling off the back of these rail trucks. The staff requested police and more military pioneers. They suggested a corps of veterans and retired policeman might be formed to fulfil the role of guardian of military supplies.

Plan W had proposed the use an infantry battalion for this unloading. While they waited for their vehicles and stores to arrive from the southern port, the soldiers would provide a strong set of backs to shift the equipment, fuel and ammunition now flowing into France. But now the infantry were bypassing Rennes on their move forward as the Navy opted for the shorter crossing.

Life in the rear area was never allowed to settle into a regular pattern. There were constant, mostly pointless, changes to the routine. Early November saw the introduction of daily training with gas masks. The original plan was to undertake a half hour route march with gas mask and wearing a gas cape to acclimatise the wearers to the discomfort. But faced with the amount of work and shortage of workers, the order was amended. It was agree that gas masks would be worn each day from ten o'clock each day for half an hour. After a few weeks with sappers keeping out of sight during gas mask drill, the order was forgotten.

November also witnessed some arrivals and departures. The unit was instructed to return Sapper K Venables to Doncaster as it had now been proved that he was under the nineteen year minimum age set for members of the BEF. Ken's mother was alarmed to discover that her son had put himself in harm's way and took her case to her Member of Parliament.

Sapper Ken Venables was taken out of the line, only to be returned to the front as the Germans launched their second 'blitzkrieg' in the Spring, forcing Ken back across the Channel. It was impossible to cheat his fate. Unknown to Ken or his comrades, they would all eventually be captured on the same day, in the same battle and spend the rest of the war as captives. Ken would learn to mine coal in Poland.

The 'phoney war' brought very little military activity to Rennes. Just a single air raid warning early on 16 November was as near as the war had come so far and that had been a false alarm. The same day, Sergeant Sillick of the Norfolk Regiment and Corporal Drew of the Wiltshires arrived to run an infantry cadre for the company NCOs. For a few weeks, rifle inspections become part of the routine but attempts to turn the busy engineers into infantry soldiers were abandoned and the trainers soon vanished from the ration roll.

The company had all volunteered to play their part but they all expected their role would be as engineers. This view was unpopular with commanders at all levels who made several attempts over the years to turn technical tradesmen into warriors. These attempts all failed. Each time the fighting did close around the company it was not rifle drill or any field craft skills that would help them.

Once again, it was Number Four Section back near Brest that had to endure the worst of the serious military training while those in Rennes, out of sight of higher command, bent the rules and soldiered on with these diversionary tasks. The Rennes routine was regularly disrupted by the demand for working parties to unload the supply trains that were now arriving. Complaints about skilled men working as porters, working parties turning up late or short-staffed, and the continuing problem of pilferage kept the officers at all levels busy. The call went back to Britain again for more pioneers.

Divine inspiration?

A second regular soldier joined the company during the winter. Staff Sergeant Bob Borthwick joined the company at Rennes. His journey through France to join the company had taken him via Pont de l'Arche on the Seine. He had come to appreciate the diverse skills that made up military engineering.

'One problem we had was a lack of water. A sapper major arrived, accompanied by a French civilian, both armed with forked twigs ready for water divining. I must admit that I was sceptical but because it was official I went along with it.'

His scepticism seemed to be confirmed when they marked a spot half way up the slope of the Seine valley well away from the river.

'A few days later a lorry load of equipment and sappers arrived. After boring two holes they installed two 'nodding donkey' pumps to lift the water from 300 feet below.' Bob recalled that he had seen men from the English Drilling Equipment Company being allocated ranks and turned into a specialist RE company prior to his own dispatch to France. Now he had seen them in action.

Water diviners would be in action at their new base at the Hermitage just west of Rennes in late November. This time a geological expert, Professor Milon, would locate the spring to supply their new transit camps with water.

Before heading to France, Bob was employed forming up two other Army Troops Companies in Liverpool earlier in the year but had to confess to the Company Sergeant Major, Bill Somerville, that he was ignorant of the multiple military roles required of 'Army Troops Companies.' Bob had joined the army as a draughtsman and had completed only six months of the two-year, military mechanists course early in 1939 as the war loomed and his training was interrupted.

They agreed that Alan Jones, the other Regular, would take responsibility for planning the engineering work and would oversee electrical work while Bob would concentrate on mechanical engineering. Bob would have Lance Sergeant Bill Richardson, a foreman fitter from Doncaster Main Colliery, as his assistant. Lance Sergeant Harold Crowecroft, a plumber by trade, would be Alan's number two in the electrical and mechanical section.

The unit Bob was joining had been a community before they became soldiers. Away from their workplace they had grown even closer. Bob was one of the first 'foreigners' to join the company. 'The unit seemed like a happy family' recalled Bob.

The patriarch of this family was Sergeant Sam Shaw. He was a ruddy faced, ginger- haired giant of a man. He exuded good cheer. As a foreman fitter at The Plant, all of the officers and many of the men had been supervised by him when they were apprentices. The value of such unity had long been recognised among Territorial Army units well before Kitchener's 'Pals' Battalions.

The Officer Commanding was Captain Yates. Before the war, Peter Yates had been a manager in the railway work-shops in Doncaster with a reputation as a stickler for detail which made him a good 'Officer Commanding.' He had a difficult job as the unit was normally scattered. Nevertheless he managed to keep a proprietorial eye on his workers and tried to make sure they lacked for nothing. His real role was to insulate the company from the many bright ideas for military training or unloading trains that arrived almost every day.

As the desperate winter of 1939 descended the company continued its diverse tasks preparing the many facilities that would be required to support the troops at the front. New skills were learnt. There was no time for formal teaching and there was much learning on the job. By good luck rather than any planning they found they had the range of skills required.

Plouret and St Thégonieux received working parties to install lighting and water systems. But all too frequently the jobs were left incomplete awaiting material and spare parts. When replacement parts were not forthcoming, the art of improvisation began to emerge. Instead of the textbook solution that would satisfy inspectors, the sappers sought solutions that worked. They fabricated pipes, manufactured machine parts and brazed broken shafts to get things working whenever there was a problem.

Bill, an expert electrician, became proficient at overhead power lines in a few hours. One of the first jobs was to provide electric supply and lighting in hutted accommodation built in Rennes.

'Overhead line work was new to me' says Bill. 'Fortunately Fred Robinson had a good knowledge of it, and taught me about dressing poles, strain supports and running the wires. These skills were to prove invaluable much later.'

A new unit arrived and moved into the camp that Bill had just illuminated. They were eagerly awaited. A freshly enlisted Pioneer Corps battalion was provided to unload the trains that now arrived daily to relieve the sappers of this chore. The Stores Depot at the railhead was under pressure to unload the wagons as soon as possible to supply the fuel, ammunition and rations to support the growing army.

Bill was not impressed when he saw the Pioneers arrive. 'We turned out of our billet to watch them go by to their new accommodation. I've never seen a scruffier bunch of soldiers in my life. They looked more like a bunch of newly captured POW's than representatives of the British Army.'

One of their sergeants also told Bill that as he had approached the signing-on table, the recruiting officers looked at him and said he could immediately be enrolled as a sergeant. This did not endear the Pioneers to Bill. 'Here I was looking for ways and means to achieve my first stripe in order to increase Edith's pay allocation. He had been handed three promotional steps, to a sergeant, without any effort. I don't mean to be unkind but he didn't look the part of a senior NCO.' Bill felt he was a long way from understanding the military mind.

2.3a
The Company assembles for its Christmas photo in the grounds of its Headquarters
to the west of Rennes. It was rare for the company to be assembled in one place
as their projects were spread along the Lines of Communications.

As 1939 drew to a close, life was settling into a comfortable routine for the company. The chore of unloading railway wagons was completely relieved following the arrival of three companies of Italian labourers. And the weather in December had so far been kind.

Buildings were being pressed into diverse, sometimes incomprehensible, uses. The casino at St. Malo was rewired but continued as a casino. Chateaux were requisitioned as head quarters or hospitals. The situation was deemed sufficiently stable to permit a royal visit. The King crossed the channel on 4 December and spent a week visiting troops and commanders along the Franco-Belgian border. Although British papers were not allowed to report the visit until the royal party was back home, the foreign press were not restrained.

Perhaps responding to the royal visit, the Germans launched their first attack on the western front with a raid in the Saar sector where French troops had advanced a short distance into German territory. The skirmish achieved nothing of military significance except that some British troops attached to the French saw action on 11 December. It gave the papers some news for Christmas.

2.3b

The OC and senior non-commissioned officers of the company. The officers spent much of their time on reconnaissance missions or attending senior officers at the several headquarters to which they were beholden, leaving it to the senior ranks to run the projects that were scattered round Brittany.

Glad tidings

'In early December I received news of the arrival of our second child, a boy. Edith had already decided to call him William George. I suppose she reasoned that if I didn't survive at least she would have another Billy. I felt that being tagged William George made him an early war casualty.'

There were still no plans to attack Germany. With many of the men and some matériel for the BEF taking the shortest route to the front, the pace of activity slowed. As Christmas approached they were told that some home leave would be allowed. Applications on compassionate grounds would be considered first.

'Naturally I applied on the grounds of Billy's birth and was accepted. I had saved a little money and there was a store in Rennes called 'Prisunic' so I was able to buy a few small presents. They included a wooden plaque with a peasant girl's head carved on it, a doll for my daughter Janet and a little woollen outfit for the new baby.'

'The sea crossing on the small ferryboat was considerably rougher than my first crossing. I remembered an old man's advice - if you feel you may be seasick get laid down - so using the wooden blocks they called a life jacket, I flopped down in a gangway and slept the trip away. I was very much looking forward to seeing Edith and the children.' The field postal system was efficient so news of his expected arrival had reached Doncaster. ' I remember arriving home at 10.30 p.m., in full army kit. Edith's mother had kept William George junior up so I could get my first look at the new baby.'

'Much to my dismay I found that Edith was very poorly with a breast abscess and was due at Doncaster Infirmary the next morning for an operation to remove it. I was also informed that my father was in the same hospital with blood clot trouble arising from a leg wound he received serving in the Scots Guards during the Boer War.'

'He was delirious and the khaki uniform agitated him. He didn't know me so I only stayed with him for a few minutes. I didn't know at the time it would be the last time I would ever see him.'

'When I got back to Edith's mother I found Edith was already in the operating theatre and we had to sweat it out. When the operation was completed Edith looked terrible and was in an ague condition. It was an hour before they said we could take her home. We decided to get a taxi home. The operation took some clearing and the nurses confined her to bed all the time I was on leave. I did apply for a compassionate extension but the doctor wouldn't support it.'

As a home leave it was a disaster. Bill's only comfort was that he had been with Edith for the operation. When the time came for him to cross the water again the sea was rougher than ever. The sea matched his mood.

He returned to duty feeling more miserable than before. Within the week news arrived that his father had died. 1940 was off to an ominous start. Over half of the company managed to obtain a valued leave pass for two weeks back home before Christmas. Being the first to arrive in France did earn that one, dubious privilege.

In early January, Bill was detailed to accompany Lieutenant Richmond to St Thegonnic, to a chateau which had been converted into an officer training centre. The scenery was beautiful. Lieutenant Richardson explained that the area along this coast near Morlaix was known as 'Little Switzerland.' Any thoughts of a war were far from everyone's mind as they motored through the picturesque scene.

After this sortie they proceeded to Brest where they joined some of the company were shivering under canvas within the castle moat again. They would have to spend a night there before heading back to Rennes.

'It was terribly cold and made me wonder how they managed to survive. They had a canteen of sorts and a small marquee with a stove in it, but you couldn't warm the bell tents we slept in. For the first time in my life I was pleased to wear long john underwear.' Bill recalled.

Bill had come to accept that he was not lucky. Instead of a speedy return to the relative comfort of his own billet in Rennes, 'I was detailed to join a party of electricians working in a building in the town. We were to install lighting. I was working from a ladder, when the foot of the ladder slipped on the ice and dropped me about twelve feet. I managed to keep going that day but the next morning I had to report sick. I was diagnosed as having strained or torn my shoulder muscles.'

After a few days they all returned to Rennes. Although under pressure to complete the many building and conversion tasks, most of the company had received home passes before the end of January. Bill had been fortunate to go on leave before Christmas. In January leave trains would be delayed by the weather and various scares. On 10 January Major Helmut Reinberger, a junior German staff officer, accidentally gifted details of the attack planned for 17 January to the Belgians when his plan crashed. On 14 January all leave was cancelled until 17 January when the immediate threat was deemed to have passed.

The weather changed abruptly in mid-January. It started with a number of hard frosts. On 16 January snow began to fall. The pattern of frost and snow settled on the battlefield for the next three months. Travelling became hazardous and uncomfortable. Outside work was often impossible. The slow pace of life was frozen.

With time on their hands there were opportunities to read the limited news and magazines brought back by those returning from leave. They read how Poland had succumbed to the combined might of the German and Russian armies after a stubborn but unequal fight. There was time to talk but very little happening to feed rumours. They knew so little of what was happening elsewhere that speculation was a pointless activity as well as one that was strongly discouraged.

Everyone accepted that their build-up was nearing completion and that the Germans would attack the border in the spring. This eventuality was neither looked forward to nor feared. The BEF had been able to set up the supply system to support the defensive battle to come. They were ready.

The weather did not improve as February turned to March. Bill was left wondering what kind of a war this was. 'At our end of France the war seemed rather remote and I remember the section being turned out to build a POW compound on the outskirts of Rennes. Our command evidently had visions of a counter attack before we could all bed down to trench warfare, like in 1914/18' Bill conjectured.

Alan Jones was one of the few to miss out on a leave trip home. Without a wife or elderly parents to visit he did not bother to apply for a pass. He had other duties to attend to. He had a football team to lead. Under their coach, the company would produce a formidable team during the winter.

Regular football matches had become a feature of the routine. In the early months they had played against the local team. Now, with new units arriving each week to pass along the Lines of Communication, there was plenty of competition. The team made use of the requisitioned furniture van that had brought much of their personal equipment to France as their team bus when they played fixtures away from the convenient local stadium.

Inside the spacious box body the team could travel in relative warmth and luxury. Unlike all soft-topped military vehicles, the van was not draughty with its enclosed, plywood body and it doubled as a changing room when they reached the ground. When the time came to start the match they could drop the loading ramp and run, ready and warm, on to the pitch.

However, the snow curtailed even that activity. The winter of 1939/40 was exceptional. The cobblestone roads covered with a layer of ice were almost impassable. Many vehicles had thoughtfully been fitted with wide tyres suitable for soft ground. These were ideal for mud or sand but could not cut into the ice. Each week, as a dozen or more members of the company were given home leave, they faced a treacherous road journey to the coast followed by a rough passage. But there was no shortage of volunteers.

Getting the vehicles going could be just as much a problem as keeping them moving along the road. The issue of antifreeze for the radiators was restricted to armoured vehicles. Trucks had to be drained each night or started up every hour. However, minute traces of wax in petrol would freeze in the carburettors. Even diesel fuel was not immune to the cold. The fuel turned to jelly and resisted attempts to spray it into the cylinders. Warming the radiator, sump and fuel tank provided a daily challenge. The company drivers happily avoided the ignominious roll call of those who set fire to their vehicles as they tried to warm their engines to get them started.

In spite of the cold, the company was commissioned to start building an enormous stores depot. The civilian skills of Lance-Sergeant Bill Hartland, proved invaluable. As a steel erector he soon turned an unskilled team into a proficient construction unit. As craftsmen, they enjoyed acquiring a new skill. Soon they had erected a steel framed shed with galvanised sheet cladding, about forty feet wide, a hundred feet long and about twenty-five to thirty feet to the apex, which remains in use by the French Army.

Before the roof cladding was complete, Alan Jones collected Bill for another electrical job at Thorigné-Fouillard, a village on the outskirts of Rennes where a locally constructed 'Tomine' hutted camp had been built. They would be away from the main unit for some time.

'It was then that I received news that Edith's mother had died. I knew that she would be very much on her own. This only added to my daily worries.' He was glad he was going to be kept busy by Alan. They were going to live in a little village, lodging with local families, which was comforting.

Relations with the locals remained cordial. The arrival of foreign troops was a boost to the local economy. There were no French army units in the area so there was none of the problem encountered wherever two 'friendly' armies met. British soldiers were also paid three times as much as their French counterparts. To reduce this source of friction the British limited the amount of money that could be drawn. Soldiers were allowed to draw roughly the same amount of pay as that of a French Army private, 'poilu', whose allowance was 50 centimes or 'sous' per day.

German propagandists exploited this differential in pay. In the leaflet war of the winter of 1939 one picture showed a pretty French lady in bed beside a man dressed only in a monocle

However, not all cross-border propaganda was so successful. One board on the German side read 'Soldiers of the Northern Provinces, beware of the English. They are destroying your properties, eating your food, sleeping with your wives, raping your daughters.' The French erected their own sign with the words 'On s'en fout, on est du Midi' (We don't give a damn, we're from the south).

For a non-drinker such as Bill, the local cafés had few attractions. One night, curiosity led him to explore the nightlife he had heard so much about. He set off with two Doncaster mates but the expedition did not last long. The three of them were surrounded by girls as soon as they sat down. Bill was between his two friends and was able to make his escape. Shortly after the gang was reunited without any mishap for the walk home along the quay. 'I think we gave up the high, or low, life after that.'

The infrastructure for the army at the front was now more or less ready as planned. The BEF was in position protecting the left flank of the French. The lines of communication for the flow of matériel of war from supply depots to the front were complete. Repair workshops were in place. Transit camps had washing facilities. The hospitals were now staffed and equipped to cope with the battle that was anticipated.

In spite of all these preparations which had kept them busy for 6 months, the workload on 106 Army Troops Company did not seem to diminish. Alan recalls a steady flow of requests for work. The medics asked him to set up a water pump and filtration system. The undiminished workload provoked yet more complaints from the new OC, Captain Yates, every time troops were taken away from their engineering task.

The 7th Panzer Division also had a new commander. General Erwin Rommel had used his short time as commander of Hitler's close protection battalion to secure a field command for himself. His tales of the exploits that had promoted this outsider to the rank of general and would soon make Rommel his Fürher's 'favourite general' The Commander-in-Chief empathised with another boy from the country who had made it to the top. This respect was mutual.

This posting, which removed Rommel from the supreme headquarters, served the German High Command's plans. This brilliant young general was not from the aristocratic clique that still hoped to guide and control their country's destiny. It made sense to send him to a front-line unit to ensure he could not exercise too much influence over their Commander-in-Chief, Hitler.

The harsh surrender terms insisted on by France had included the disbanding of the institution of the German military staff. The new generation of German generals would not fight in the way advocated by the staff colleges of the other European nations. The Germans could not be relied upon to launch massive attacks against prepared defences in a repeat of the trench war or the pitched battled of the previous centuries. Rommel had observed the success of the new theories when they were put to the test in Poland.

Rommel welcomed his exile from the charmed circle he had so effectively protected during the opening act of the war. During his short stay he had learned many political lessons. These would be vital for his future survival as a commander, as he ignored and transgressed orders. He would become an astute if ultimately unsuccessful practitioner of the system of influence.

In March it was finally accepted that the company's skills were in short supply so a demand was made for two labour companies to be assigned to each section. Had it actually happened, the company would have had eight companies attached to them to do the moving and holding for the craftsmen.

Meanwhile, military routine continued. Early April saw the unit being lined up to receive a booster for the anti-tetanus injection. The resulting sore arms reduced the effectiveness of the workforce for some days.

There was another touch of ominous normality. Among the arrivals at Rennes had been nine mobile cinemas. Five of these had been allocated to serve the Lines of Communication units. The records of Expeditionary Forces Institute, EFI, show that nearly a quarter of a million men watched film shows at one of the mobile cinemas, which were capable of accommodating ten showings per night.

Nothing likely to inflame the passions or depress the spirits was screened. Along with patriotic feature films, Pathé News projected images of the devastation the German army had brought to Poland. It was the latter that provoked conversation as they returned to their frosty reality.

2.4
The marshalling yard at Bruz, south of Rennes, leaves the main line. Alan Jones was completing the construction of the main rail base for the BEF when it was overrun in June 1940. Many of the sheds constructed by the company are still in use by the French Army.

Chapter Three

Last Out

May – June 1940

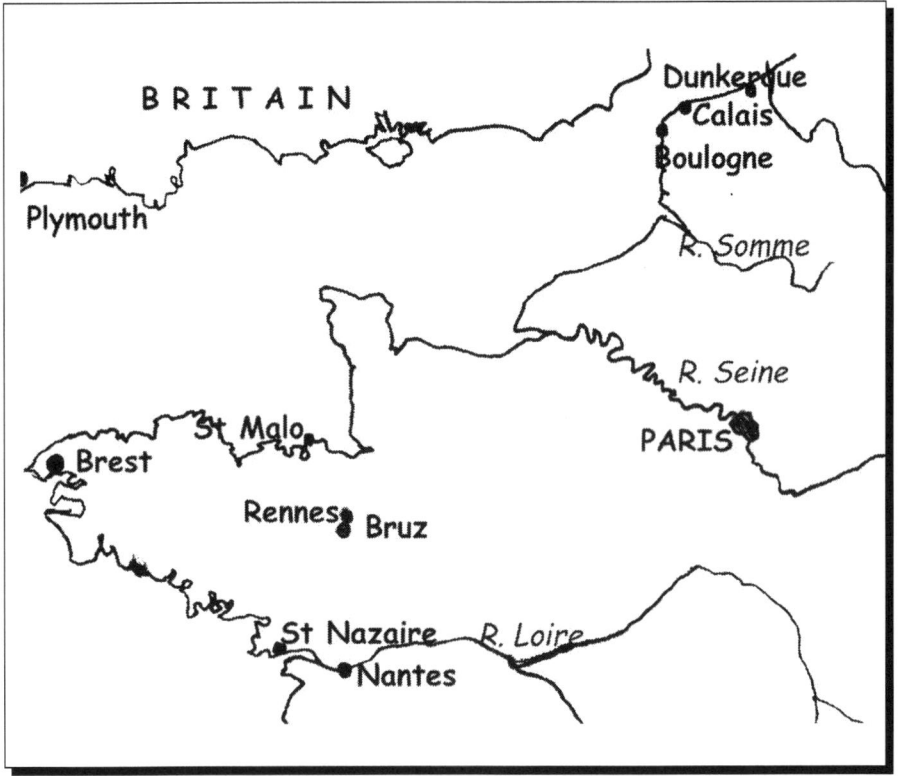

Map of English and French coastlines

The Dunkirk evacuation ended in early June. Two weeks later the operation was repeated using large vessels to extract the rest of the army from France.

At 0325 on10 May 1940, the first flight of Ju52 of II/KGr.zbV.172 aircraft took off from Butzweilerhof and Ostheim followed at thirty second intervals by forty more, each towing a DFS 230 heavy assault glider. Operation Granite was launched. A line of flashing beacons had been set up on the ground to guide them to the German border near Aachen.

Their task was to secure key crossing points for von Bock's Army Group B before they could be destroyed by their defenders. Without these bridges, the German invasion force would be struggling to cross the many tributaries of the Rhein. Four years and four months later, the Allies would carry out an airborne operation with similar objectives to secure the crossing to invade Germany.

Just after 0400 Belgian and Dutch air defences opened fire against tug planes as they turned home without ever crossing the German border. A force of eleven gliders was tasked to capture the Belgian fort at Eben Emael which commanded the Albert Canal just south of Maastricht. Three other groups would capture bridges at Vroenhoven, Veldwezelt and Kanne.

The commander of Operation Granite ended up in field after his tow plane took evasive action to avoid a collision with another in the formation. Undeterred, he unpacked his collapsible bike to reach a road where he hitched a lift back to base and then waited for a replacement plane. At 0730 Lieutenant Witzig arrived on Eban Emael and slid to a halt near bunker 19 where his troops had neutralised the fort with their innovative hollow charge explosives.

The silent surprise from the sky quickly destroyed the surface defences and most of the ability to observe the advancing German army. The defenders clung on to their foothold on the top of the fort and twenty-four hours later were relieved by German sappers who used flame weapons to subdue remaining resistance.

It took 36 hours to subdue the ineffectual fort. Meanwhile the German Sixth Army continued its advance to cover the right flank of the armoured divisions preparing to bypass the Maginot Line. The fort and around one thousand defenders surrendered at midday.

The long-expected news of the invasion reached the company quickly. For Bob Borthwick the Blitzkrieg was an unwelcome birthday present. Along with Alan Jones he was the only other soldier used to firing their personal weapon. They were now ordered to draw some ammunition and carry out some target practice with their rifles. But there were two major obstacles to carrying out this order. First, the majority of the men had never fired a weapon. But the second problem was the shortage of ammunition. They were surrounded by munitions of all sorts but none had been allocated for them.

Bob carried two rounds for his revolver while Alan had been issued with five rounds for his personal weapon. The sappers had carried their 303 rifles all the way from Doncaster. They were certainly experts at carrying and cleaning their weapons. The attempt to acquire the necessary competence to use their rifles was frustrated by this acute shortage of ammunition. In spite of the intermittent attempts to make them into fighting soldiers, no one had anticipated that they would need any ammunition at this distance from the front.

The BEF now rushed forward to defend Belgium. This well-rehearsed manoeuvre was efficiently executed and they prepared to face Army Group B as it made its way south and west. This was the cue for German Army Group A to reveal itself. In a rehearsal for the Battle of the Bulge three and a half years later, the elite Panzer Divisions broke cover and set out across the plains of Northern France.

Rommel, an infantryman by training, had trained the units of his command hard in the few months available. He quickly adapted the shock tactics that exploited each success to keep the enemy in turmoil. In spite of his hard routine, those under his command already understood and respected the drive of their commander.

Rommel had kept them calm during the anxious wait for action. During the night there had been numerous postponements. At ten p.m., less than eight hours before they were due to cross the border, the code word 'Danzig' was received. Fighting was bitter but Rommel's 7th Panzer Division began to earn its title 'The Ghost Division.'

The Division appeared where it was not expected. For the Allies, these unscheduled appearances were most unwelcome. For the High Command and flanking German generals, this smacked of indiscipline and provoked anger and envy in equal measure.

By the 15 May, Rommel had assaulted and crossed half a dozen water obstacles. To the military mind, this was deemed to be impenetrable territory for armour. Rommel, with his engineering mind, rose to the challenge and rolled on, never allowing his troops to loose their momentum.

The advancing Allies of the BEF had already reached their defence line along the river Dyle deep inside Belgium. But they now risked being cut off from their supply lines by the rapid German breakthrough much further south, with Rommel's 7th Panzer now at the spearhead. The BEF could do nothing except turn round and retreat in front of the advancing and outflanking German Divisions. The Belgians were fighting fiercely but being driven back. The military position of the Allies was untenable.

The flooding that should have turned Holland into a fortress had also been defeated in another series of brilliant moves by German airborne troops. Bridge demolitions that should have slowed the progress of the invaders were regularly captured intact by the Germans for their advancing army. Where there were no bridges, the tanks used canal lock gates or other improvised crossing to allow the invasion to gain a succession of footholds. Holland's defences were by-passed before the plans to evacuate the people and livestock prior to flooding the polders could be put into effect.

The lines of communication, so carefully constructed over the previous seven months, could no longer provide the logistics required by the isolated BEF. The supply lines had been cut by the German tanks pouring from the Eiffel Mountains. The BEF had been beaten without, at that stage, the main British units contacting their enemy.

The first Panzer Division reached the Channel coast at Abbeville near Calais on 19 May. Now, ironically, it was the German spearhead that was threatened. Both flanks had been left dangerously exposed by the speed of their own advance, with the French to the south and the BEF retreating through Belgium. The British launched a counter-attacks at Arras on 21 May which exploited this vulnerability. A co-ordinated response from the Allies might have isolated and destroyed the German tanks.

Rommel, as always, commanded from the front. He watched as the new British Matilda tanks advanced, and destroyed, his German Panzers. He saw that the German anti-tank guns could not pierce the tough armour of the Matildas, which threatened his exposed position. He looked around for a gun with a heavier calibre and ordered his heavy anti-aircraft guns to come forward and hold the line. At last, with the 88mm rounds, he had a weapon to stop the advance.

In this one encounter, he lost four times as many tanks as he had suffered since the breakthrough began. He also witnessed the death of his young ADC, Joachim Most, who had been at his side throughout the brief campaign but was killed as he directed the improvised defence ordered by Rommel.

The hasty counter attack petered out for lack of support from the south. But the shock bought the Allies a vital break. The German High Command now paused to sort out the tasks for the converging Germany Army Groups A and B. Having rushed through Belgium and France it was important that the two German armies did not smash into each other. The Fürher's order went out at 12.31 on the 24 May ordering the advance to the coast to halt.

Consequently, the German encirclement of the evacuation beaches was not completed until Monday 27 May. This pause broke the momentum so vital to any military operation. It gave the defenders time to organise an effective perimeter defence and flood the open approaches. The halt-order was lifted after forty-eight hours. It would take over a week to close the evacuation beaches, just fifteen kilometres beyond the halt-line.

The Belgian army had been ordered to cease fire at 0400 on 28 May after eighteen days of hard fighting. With the French 1st Army facing defeat, their troops in the north joined those waiting their turn to be evacuated. The evacuation begun in late May was able to continue until 4 June by which time 338,226 Allied troops had been returned to Britain from the beaches around Dunkirk.

Aware that an evacuation was underway the German High Command wisely decided not to commit their panzer divisions to taking the beachhead. The countryside ahead was crossed with canals and dikes. This was not tank terrain and German infantry was rushing to catch up. In this fractured terrain, tanks could easily become the filling in a water sandwich where the infantry could stalk and kill armoured vehicles.

The German High Command were already concentrating on the coming battle to the south with the French Army. The job of securing the beaches was left to the following infantry and artillery with support from the Luftwaffe, who were supposed to prevent the BEF from escaping until the army was ready.

Fortunately for the company, the Germans' next objective lay with the million French soldiers still waiting in and behind the Maginot Line. The hundred thousand British troop along the Lines of Communication inherited the mantle and tasks of the BEF. There were no thoughts of withdrawal among the troops or commanders. There was a new 'front line'.

The first battle had been lost but the plan was clear. Troops from Dunkirk would be reorganised and returned to France to join the flow that continued to disembark at Cherbourg during June. French troops returning from Britain would be allowed a month's home leave to prepare them for the expected battles. Allied commanders had still failed to grasp the pace of modern warfare.

The HQ at Rennes prepared to do its job. It would feed units and supplies up to the new front. But in early June the front was much nearer than it had been a month before.

Administrative matters continued to occupy the OC, Captain Peter Yates. On the day that the German army reached the Channel coast, Peter Yates was writing to the War Office, answering a charge that his establishment had increased by seven soldiers. He set out his case in detail. Three months earlier, someone had complained about the cost of feeding troops at local cafés. He explained that detachments were working throughout Brittany. So extra cooks were allocated to feed them and save the cost of café meals. Now the system was complaining about the cost of the cooks and wanted them back.

Stores are for storing

Time was also found to prepare a considered report on the defects of Plan W. Key among the recommendations was the shortage of engineers. Another point noted was the dubious logic of sending clerks and cooks via Cherbourg while their office equipment and field kitchens took the longer route to St

Nazaire. The result was that many units were stranded at the coast until catering and clerical transport made its way across Brittany to the Normandy coast to meet them.

Military policemen were also noted as another key deficiency. Thefts of equipment and stores had accumulated since the BEF landed in September. The precise nature of these thefts could not be identified. Guards and barbed wired had proved ineffective. When they counted what was on the shelves or issued out and tried to match it with the quantity sent from Britain, the numbers did not balance. For any quartermaster, this was a nightmare.

For the staff in their chateaux, balancing the books was important. They asked for an infantry battalion to guard the stores and arrest this haemorrhage of supplies. When the request was turned down they called for a company of military police. This suggestion was also rejected. In desperation the staff officers proposed the formation of a special corps of investigators formed by retired Metropolitan Police Officers to protect and investigate the losses.

Had this plan had matured, a short interview with Alan Jones or Bob Borthwick might have gone a long way towards resolving the missing stores problem. Both could certainly have 'helped the police with their enquiries.' They could have provided an alternative, perfectly innocent, solution to this 'crime.' They would have admitted that they kept their team busy by obtaining equipment wherever and in whatever way they could.

The engineering stores had initially been dumped on open ground opposite the Rennes football stadium. This was designated as the stores depot but the material was simply ground dumped and left unguarded. The company quickly moved many lorry loads of vital equipment to a controlled store in the centre of Rennes.

A trip back to the base store or railhead to pick up some lighting equipment might lead them to fill their small trucks with many other items for use in the future. If a job was being held up, they would send a fixer back along the supply line to obtain, by whatever means, the equipment required. Paperwork was not their priority. In the early days no one bothered about paperwork although nobody would admit this at the headquarters.

Arriving first in France had this one small reward. They knew the system. They had helped set it up. It also helped that the company were so often called on to supply the manpower to offload the supply trains. The transport that delivered them and returned them to their base seldom left without some items to add to their informal inventory.

It made sense to these recent civilian converts and saved a lot of paperwork and transport. The company had their cache stashed in a store down a small alley a short distance from the main station in Rennes. Hidden away in the centre of town the storeroom was well away from prying eyes of inspecting officers and other visitors. It must have been a wonderful windfall for the first local who ventured into their store after the company departed in late June.

The initial impact of the Blitzkrieg on the lives of those in Rennes was limited. The 139th Infantry Brigade that had been based at Rennes was moved forward, to be followed a few days later by all the transport attached to units along the Lines of Communication. Construction would regularly be delayed by the shortage of labour and late delivery of materials caused by the lack of necessary transport.

The first military impact on the troops in Rennes occurred the day after the forward units of the BEF were cut off. The enormity of what had occurred was not even hinted at in Operating Instruction Number 1 issued by the HQ in Rennes on 20 May. This ordered that each unit was to prepare to form a mobile column at one hour's notice. This fighting unit was to consist of an officer, five NCOs and twenty-one men. Each would carry fifty rounds with five hundred rounds for the Light Machine Gun plus fifty special rounds for the anti-tank rifle that had been issued.

Without the need or indeed the ability to supply the isolated BEF, ammunition now became available. In addition to their ammunition they were to carry one day's dry rations to allow these menacing columns to operate away from their unit for twenty-four hours. These instructions were duly noted in company orders. With the officers away preparing for future tasks and the Regular NCOs deployed carrying out work, no action was taken, so it is fortunate that the company was never asked to hold back the German advance on Rennes.

On 24 May, with the Germans at the Channel coast, air raid precautions were imposed. Vehicles or troops were to stop under cover, black-out was to be strictly enforced and fire pickets to be stood by to deal with any fires started. They were suddenly in the firing line.

Withdrawal

The German armoured divisions had outrun the ability of the follow-on units, which still relied substantially on horse-drawn transport, to keep up. After a short pause, while the German army pressed every available civilian truck into service to bring the fresh units and supplies forward, the advance was resumed on 6 June.

While troops were being taken off the beaches around Dunkirk, ships were already delivering reinforcements to hold the line of the River Seine. The Somme had been lost but in the minds of the Allied Commanders the Seine provided another formidable obstacle. The Germans were held for just one day by the river when they assaulted the next defensive position, the Weygand line. This held for a few days. The steady progress of the Germans through France then resumed.

On 11 June, the 51st Division raised in the Scottish Lowlands began to disembark at Brest and move forward. But on the same day the first plans were being discussed for the evacuation of Rennes and the withdrawal of the entire BEF from France.

Attempts were made to sabotage bridges in order to slow German progress. Royal Engineer firing parties were told to wait for any stragglers before blowing their bridge. The demolitions were seldom guarded and the firing party would take the approach of a German reconnaissance party as their cue to blow the bridge and 'bug out' in their fifteen hundredweight truck.

The destruction of bridges initially slowed the progress of the German army to the west. But Rommel ordered his pontoon bridges to move forward along with the tanks and mobile infantry. They had come well prepared to fight their way through the lowlands where rivers, canals and dikes dissected the landscape. The German sappers were equipped and trained to cross water obstacles quickly.

The Germans had already discovered enough bridges intact and had crossed the rivers in the French sector and pushed on. As the fast moving panzers outflanked the British, successive, defensive positions were abandoned. Although the Germans' main effort was directed at isolating the million-strong French force in and behind the Maginot line, there was little respite for the troops on the Lines of Communication. French units continued to withdraw from contact to the south to keep in touch with their main force behind the Maginot line much further east. A wedge had now been driven between the retreating British and French allies.

The Germans could now swing north and concentrate their fighting resources on the smaller BEF. The plains of northern France were much better tank country than the hilly interior and the Germans took advantage of this terrain.

Without air superiority or forward observers for the artillery, nothing would stop the rapid German progress towards Brittany. But small as they were, these accumulated delays might provide the crucial hours needed to take the rest of the forces out of France. The timetable would be very tight.

After the exertion and substantial losses the Navy and commercial shipping had suffered evacuating a third of a million soldiers from Dunkirk, they prepared to mount their second evacuation. After Dynamo, Operation Cycle was prepared to lift the troops of the 51st Division from the coast around Le Havre. Elements of First Armoured Division along with the 51st Division had attempted to hold the northern sector of the Weygand line but had been trapped north of the Seine.

Bad weather and lack of communications prevented the planned evacuation taking place on the night of the 11/12 June. The German 7th Panzer Division, commanded by General Rommel had closed in by the morning leading to the largest surrender of British troops as the 51st Division became prisoners.

In a scene that would be re-enacted almost two years later, Rommel sent some tanks forward to prevent an orderly evacuation. A few of his panzers were able to reach high ground overlooking the harbour making it suicidal for the Navy to attempt an evacuation. He would repeat this tactic in Tobruk and demonstrate how effective a few tanks could be against ships. Next time he would capture most of the company.

The remnants of the 1st Armoured Division were more fortunate. Their armour was able to prevent Rommel's Panzers dominating the evacuation beach and over 2 thousand were lifted from Veules-les-Roses the next small port along the coast.

The loss of a Division brought home the need to risk no further delays. The Navy activated Operation Aerial. There would be no time wasted while orderly convoys were assembled. Ships were dispatched as soon as they were available. The 'Arandora Star', 'Strathaird' and 'Otranto' were dispatched to St Malo to take out the troops and equipment from the Rennes HQ.

With the fighting element of the BEF again outflanked and evacuated, the only course open was to fall back once again. The substantial infrastructure and all the supporting logistic units even with the recent reinforcements could now do little against Rommel's 7th Panzers. It was an unequal struggle. The diversion of Rommel into the Cherbourg peninsula bought the withdrawing British troops perhaps an extra day while the following German formation took up the race to the west and Brittany.

Less than a week after Rommel had surged across the Seine, no organised defensive force existed to protect the British foothold in France. 'Everyone was very apprehensive especially when Jerry turned his thrust towards Paris, which capitulated on 14 June. This brought him a stone's-throw from us, judging the speed at which they moved' recalled Bill Harvey.

The same day, Bob Borthwick mustered his men to help outload the recently completed Stores Depot for shipment back to Britain. Soon the welcome news that the unit had been ordered to withdraw to the port of St. Malo, about thirty miles north would follow. Bob would prefer to have been heading west or even south but guessed that the coast probably still offered the best chance of getting home. The news was received calmly.

General Alanbrooke had been sent to take command of the BEF but within days issued his order to evacuate the rest of the BEF anticipating that it would take at least 48 hours. The Navy was told that there were 123,600 troops and their equipment to remove. The time scale was optimistic. Alanbrooke would not himself get away until early on the 18 June.

Inspecting the original plan tells the tale of the speed of this operation. There was not enough time to have the evacuation plan typed up. Much is written in pencil including a list of all the units and the forty-nine ships that could be called on. Neither of the brave ships that brought Bob Borthwick or Bill Harvey home appear on these lists. Clearly there was a substantial amount of 'hot planning' as extra transport was pressed into service by the Navy.

Ships were to be stocked with five days water and rations and told to load military equipment only if this would not delay their departure from France. They were dispatched on the night of 15/16 June to all the main ports of the Brittany Peninsular. At the same time the convoys of troops were leaving their bases in Brittany and heading for the coast. The low cloud and calm seas that had shrouded the Dunkirk evacuation held.

In less than four days, the advanced force of 10th Panzer Division would be occupying Rennes. But plans were still being laid for the ammunition to be out-loaded. The three Italian labour companies were kept very busy until 17 June when they were paid off. They were given two day's pay in lieu of notice and assigned to the French military as work-parties. With Italy now in the war but now on the German side their future must have seemed uncertain.

Major General de Fonblanque, the British commander of the Lines of Communication visited Rennes at lunchtime on the 16th to confirm General Alanbrooke's order for evacuation. For senior officers this was a particularly fraught time. They were not willing or prepared to leave the passage of the crucial withdrawal plan to the increasingly unreliable telephone or radio or to delegate this vital task to subordinates. Their energy, recorded in their surviving log books, lists continuous trips and meetings which probably contributed significantly to the success of the evacuation.

One anonymous Royal Engineer officer was evidently distraught at his inability to take the news to all of his troops. In one of the final entries in the log of the Rennes HQ made at 2300 hours on the 16 June a scrap of paper is attached as an appendix *(Fig. 3.1)*. It looks as if it has been hastily torn from an exercise book. On it, the anguished author notes that one hundred and eleven members of 106 are in Lake camp at Plouneran. 'Ensure that they get orders and transport for move.' The proximity of Plouneran to Plouaret along the main supply route is noted by the author to help the harassed staff officers locate these troops. The 'action' column alongside this entry in the log is ominously blank.

At 9.30 the following morning, Brigadier Greenwood gives the order to 'clear everybody out.' By then, much of the company were already on the move.

There was remarkably little speculation among the troops about why they should be returning to Britain. There was a reluctance to ask too many questions. Something had obviously gone seriously wrong further east with the BEF. Many in Rennes thought that the Allied army had been driven south leaving them isolated.

Very little news filtered back. However, the lines of refugees told their own story. Bob Borthwick remembers, 'The sight of old ladies pushing prams or handcarts, overloaded farm wagons and even a fire-engine from Soissons with firemen and their families hanging on filled the roads. They were mixed with French soldiers who were desperately helping their families to a place of safety.' Good military order in the French army was evidently failing.

As the requirement for military work dried up, the company set up a table outside the mess to serve hot drinks including soup to the pathetic flow of humanity. The refugees provided little information. They learned not to ask or answer questions. Apart from the language barrier, refugees would have heard of the summary executions carried out by all the armies of those suspected to be spies or fifth columnists. In the absence of news, nothing but rumours passed through the army. Few of these rumour matched the reality.

'The main units at Rennes moved out at midday, 15 June. The doors of our NAAFI were opened. Vehicles, haversacks, pack and pockets of the lucky ones were filled with the little luxuries the NAAFI could supply. The night was spent, packing and re-packing personal equipment. Everything that could not be packed was given to their French neighbours.'

Blankets and other bedding, along with spare clothing, was thrown out of the windows into the arms of the waiting locals and the trickle of refugees. Even in retreat the habit, or perhaps the discipline, of leaving everything in

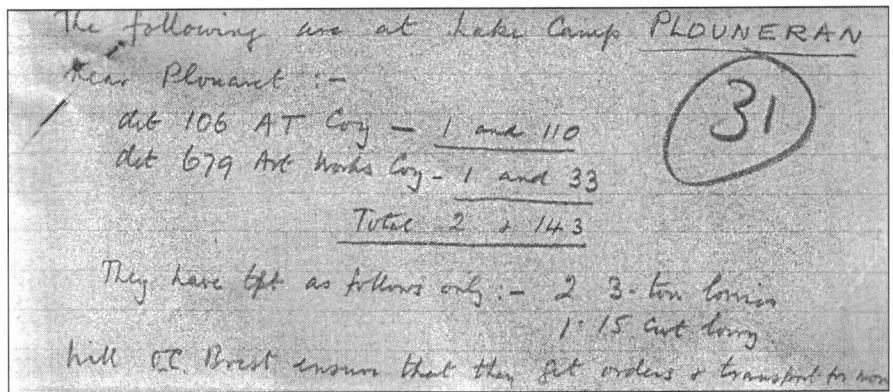

3.1 The last word:

This poignant note, written on a scrap of paper, was pinned as an official annex to the contemporary record made by the HQ in Rennes. It is easy to imagine the anguish of the unknown author who had been told to abandon those under his command and return to England. The company was not at the locations identified but they managed to make their own way home. *(Reproduced by the kind permission of the Public Records Office)*

good order survived. The irony of this final act amused Bill. 'Naturally everything was locked up and left neat and tidy, why I'll never know.' Unlike the open door policy at the NAFFI, the stores had been left tidy and securely locked.

Early on the morning of 16 June the company climbed into its available vehicles and set out for St Malo. But not everyone was on the move. In time-honoured tradition, the army would leave a group of soldiers to protect their rear. Bill Harvey was selected for the dubious privilege of holding up the German advance.

'I drew my usual short straw and was one of a detachment of six sappers and a sergeant detailed to stay as a rear guard.' A fifteen cwt truck was thoughtfully provided for their escape.

Others were also left behind. Staff Sergeant Alan Jones' party was still working away from the base and knew nothing of the move. The lack of supplies and visitors from the base at Rennes was making him uneasy. Occasional German and Allied aircraft crossed the horizon but there were no sounds of war. It would be another day before he decided to investigate.

Bill Harvey carried out a last inspection of their accommodation. 'I remember wandering through the billet and saw numerous small items, military manuals, issue watches etc. I would like to have purloined but there was the inherent streak of honesty which stopped me.' Military logic had prevented these items being handed over to the locals. Another instinct prevented them from destroying these items. They were locked up and safe awaiting the German troops.

A few store items would be taken. Engineering stores were a priority. Wire and bridging equipment was loaded and sent to the coast a few days before. Much of the hard work of the previous months had to be disposed of. The evening before they departed a decision was taken to hand the petrol and stores over to the French. The French promptly announced their intention to burn it or blow it up before the Germans arrived.

Bill and the rear party did not stay long. 'At four o'clock all hell broke loose. Fortunately for us, the Germans were bombing the French Barracks on the other side of the town. It was getting a bit hectic, so our Sergeant decided enough was enough and we pulled out. There was plenty of refugee activity on the roads but we managed to make reasonable time and eventually found the main unit at Chateauneuf a few miles outside of St. Malo.'

The following morning, as if to hurry the withdrawal, the Luftwaffe attacked the rail junction known as the Triage. The bombing from the 3 planes hit the troop train waiting its turn to head for the coast. The raid was small but accurate. The train was destroyed and there were many casualties. There were 30 officers and 1450 other ranks listed on the train. The train had been scheduled to depart at 9 o'clock, 40 minutes ahead of the raid. But the junction was congested as 2 ammunition trains were shunted to take their loads back to the coast and Britain.

Thirty vehicles were assembled to carry the injured as well as the survivors to St Malo. The number of casualties is not known. There were 50 slightly wounded and 80 stretcher cases. Nearly 500 of the Rennes personnel failed to pass through the checkpoints constructed by Bob Borthwick on the route to St Malo. This is unlikely to represent the true number of fatalities. In the confusion, many survivors might have bypassed the official route. No one from the company was listed on the train's manifest.

 Progress for the main body of the company had been slow. The thirty mile trip had taken all day. At Mangaval they were stopped by the Military Police, dressed in their familiar redcaps. The 'Redcaps' had collected several abandoned vehicles and wanted them to be formed into a roadblock.

Experiences gained in the retreat from Belgium towards Dunkirk less than a month before had demonstrated how effectively the Germans used fifth columnists to infiltrate refugee columns. The roadblocks would allow the MPs to carry out some sort of check on those passing through, both military and civilian. The aim was to ensure that enemy agents would not be able to reach the docks where, it was feared, they could pass information and carry out sabotage.

The vehicles were man-handled into the road leaving a gap through which a single vehicle could pass. Rolls and coffee in a local café was their reward. Once the task was done and refreshment taken, the company prepared to move again. But the Redcaps were not finished with them.

They now had to tow some vehicles to the next village so that a roadblock could be constructed there. It was late afternoon before the second roadblock was finished to the satisfaction of the Military Police. The Redcaps consulted their radio for instructions. The exchanges seemed to go on for hours and it was late afternoon before they were told they could proceed to St Malo. Over the radio came the news that Rennes had been bombed again. The enemy was reported to be approaching Rennes along the Route Nationale.

There was no time to waste. They passed through the other checkpoints quickly and soon found themselves approaching St Malo. They were forced to stop at the town of Chateauneuf. The town beyond was jammed and there were no ships to take those already waiting in the dock back to Britain. In retreat, good order was maintained and the company patiently waited their turn on the approach road to the town.

The only sort of luck that flowed Bill's way continued to be bad. 'In the evening I was again roped in to go with a party of senior ranks, on a 3 ton truck, to the NAAFI, somewhere near the docks. Apparently word had got round they were opening the doors and anyone could have what they liked. Some stuff was loaded on the truck but needless to say I was not included in the division of the spoils.'

There was little rest as they waited there turn to move. The next morning their orders came to move. It took two hours to creep into the town as units converged on the port. The Military Police passed along the convoy and ordered all vehicles to be abandoned and disabled. The expedient of removing the rotor arm from the distributor was all they were required to do. Some drivers chose to let the oil out of the engine and destroy the bearings by running the motor until it seized. The destruction of this abandoned fleet was completed when the vehicles were torched by the last troops to leave.

Bill was selected to provide the rear guard once again. The Germans were known to be not far behind. 'We slept at Chateauneuf and again next morning I was detached to accompany a Lance-Corporal and three other sappers to a point on the main road linking Rennes to St. Malo with instructions to look out for tanks. We were armed with a single anti-tank rifle, which nobody in the unit had ever fired. It would have been just as effective to throw our caps at a tank. We had a fright when we heard the roar of an aeroplane approaching but fortunately it turned out to be one of our Coastal Command planes. They waved to us and I thought you lucky blighters you'll be having breakfast in England.'

They were mightily relieved when their 15 cwt truck came back and took them to rejoin the company during the late morning and the unit made its way on foot onto the docks.

The Second Dunkirk

For the troops approaching the port everything seemed utter confusion. But the Navy had dispatched the ships and the Military Police seemed to know what was going on as they herded the army towards their getaway vehicle. There was no attempt to keep units together even though the experience from Dunkirk had shown that units with their command structure were easier to control and load.

Equipment of all sorts being destroyed. Redcaps were trying to maintain order but stragglers kept disappearing into the walled city apparently looking for a last drink. 'Some of them must have been left behind and they must have got a shock when they sobered up' reflected Bill Harvey.

As they approached the dock they were ordered to dump their precious pack and other luggage. They moved on carrying just their rifles and haversack. Walking along the quay beneath the old town they came in the failing light to what appeared to be a sailing ship that was just starting to load. By late afternoon on the 17 June they were lined up on the dock. Their lifeboat was the aptly named 'Alt' which Bill knew meant 'Old.'

'The boat was medium sized, possibly a Dutch cross channel ferry. Someone had the foresight to salvage a Bren gun and tripod and mount it on the upper deck. Who knows, it may even have had some ammunition as well' Bill recalls.

As they started to board, Bob watched another boat leaving. The 'Prince Bedouin' set sail at 14.45 taking with it most of the personnel from the Rennes Headquarters. He wondered if the rest of the company was on board. He hoped that no one had been left behind as the Redcaps told them this was the last boat to leave and a Naval unit was ready to demolish the harbour lock gates.

The loading went without incident and they finally got away in the early hours. Bob decided to stay on deck again. He was relieved to hear the ship's engine starting and fell asleep immediately. After an uneventful crossing, the dawn light woke Bob as they approached Poole Harbour. It was now the 18 June and Rennes was already being occupied by the advanced contingent of the German Army.

The evacuation from Brest was running concurrently. Attempts were made to take out some of the more valuable equipment. In particular, the modern artillery of the Canadian army was to be rescued. In the confusion order were issued to destroy vehicles which were required to tow the guns only to be countermanded hours later.

The French commander in Brittany, now isolated from the central authority, threatened to take action against any Allied troops who destroyed equipment. When vehicles were reported to be burning along the road leading to the port, the local British commander went to impose his authority and avoid the risk of conflict within the crumbling alliance.

Discipline on the harbour was difficult to maintain and some Canadians decided to give their vehicles a last run by racing them round the docks. The harbour master was not amused and threatened action if this demolition Derby was not stopped. It was nevertheless an imaginative way to reduce the value of their new vehicles to the approaching enemy.

Allied relationships in the Brest area were tense. Each night a chain was raised across the harbour to prevent any ships or U-boats entering the harbour. For the Royal Navy, this was a big problem. Loaded ships presented an obvious target for attacking aircraft which could only drop their load accurately in daylight. Closing the harbour at 10 each night prevented the ships being loaded at dusk and then slipping out of the harbour in the dark to get lost in the open sea before daybreak.

Instead, the loaded ships had to make their run for the protection of the open sea in daylight when the boom was opened at 7 o'clock.

Just over thirty two thousand troops were evacuated through Brest and the evacuation ended, officially, with the departure of the appropriately named, HMS Broke, late on the 19 June. However, the destroyer had left a dock party and some military police.

Unlike many other harbours, Brest was not to blocked or facilities destroyed. Perhaps the pointlessness of rendering the most westerly port unusable prevented its destruction. In fact, the French Navy was firmly in control of this Atlantic base and threatening violence to any who violated their harbour. They would not let the Royal Navy pen them in. For Alan Jones and his team of electricians, still working south of Rennes, the preservation of the military harbour and the civilian port would be a blessing.

Fortunately the Luftwaffe were engaged elsewhere in support of the German troops. Western France was at the limit of their range for aircraft whose bases remained inside Germany. The main enemy activity directed against the evacuation was aerial mine laying. Naval minesweepers cleared the areas before the troop-carrying ships set sail. This involved some tense delays, especially as it sometimes meant waiting in the estuary in broad daylight.

Some skippers who had survived Dunkirk were even prepared to run the risk of mines. On 15 June the SS Manxmaid with the 10th Hussars aboard followed a rusty cargo vessel whose skipper had taken bearing on the fall of the mines and then led the little convoy to the relative safety of the open sea. The harbour was not reopened until 4pm the following day. Faced with such delays, General Alanbrooke now ordered the evacuation to be completed that day. Everybody was to head for the coast.

A French armistice or even a complete surrender had been recognised as a possibility during Churchill's flying visit to France on 14 June. Shipping could easily be detained at Brest by simply refusing to remove the boom at dawn. Given the frosty relations with the local French commander further evacuation would be blocked if the anticipated armistice was signed.

The end was neigh. On 17 June, General Petain had broadcast to the French nation announcing an armistice. He ordered all French forces to cease fighting. The subtle distinction between an armistice and surrender preserved French military honour. The armistice agreement was actually signed in the Forest of Compiègne on June 22, 1940, at 6:50 p.m., German summer time. There was some scope for ambiguity.

Article XXIII of the armistice 'becomes effective as soon as the French Government also has reached an agreement with the Italian Government regarding cessation of hostilities. Hostilities will be stopped six hours after the moment at which the Italian Government has notified the German Government of the conclusion of its agreement. The German Government will notify the French Government of this time by wireless.' Technically the Armistice did not come into effect until 25 June 1940.

The order was not immediately obeyed by everyone. While some of the French military were happy to celebrate the 'peace' others fought on. The last forts on the Maginot Line did not surrender until 30 June. Plans to continue the fight from French territory advocated by both Allied Prime Ministers did not find favour among the military or the new French government established at Bordeaux.

By this time, most British troops had been withdrawn so a confrontation with the French was avoided. Happily, Brest remained active and a few stragglers would be grateful even though the French had been told the armistice was already effective.

On 19 June, Churchill was already asking why so much equipment had been left behind. Major General P de Fonblanque, the BEF commander of the Lines of Communication force, explained his decision for the apparent premature closure of Brest. 'Time of closing of ports and clearing of British shipping was based on the application by the French for an armistice, with the consequent risk of internment of personnel and shipping.' After an attempt to chase up a full explanation Churchill pencilled a note to his military secretary, General Ismay, that he should 'let it die.'

Back Home

Bob remembers the home coming. 'On Poole quay, buses were waiting to take us to a hotel in Bournemouth. We were treated like royalty. First a meal, then clean uniforms and the chance of a bath. But my first priority was to send off a field post card to Wynne with the message 'Arrived home safe.'

After the hotel they were taken to some schools in Bournemouth. They spent a few days in Bournemouth while medicals were carried out and details

3.2
The Lancastria was sunk of St Nazaire on 17 June 1940 with the loss of an estimated three thousand lives. News of this tragedy was not released at the time. *Photo Frank Clements taken from the destroyer HMS Highlander.*

of returnees taken. In the meantime they had the run of the town. Everything was free, even cups of tea in some of the cafes. But the novelty soon wore off and became impatient to get home to their families.

Bill had mixed feeling. 'It was good to be back in England and everyone was so kind with offers of washing, sewing repairs and meals. But it left a sour feeling when I thought of our ignominious retreat from France.'

Field Postcards were available and a pay office was set up at the harbours to cope with this new influx.

The unit seemed to have had a safe escape. 'We were lucky. Another boat left St Naizaire about the same time and they were sunk by a German aircraft' Bill recalls. The Lancastria had been hit by a bomb as it prepared to sail for England. The news of this disaster was suppressed on the instructions of Churchill. He felt there was too much bad news around at the time.

The news of the Lancastria was very bad. It is estimated that over 3000 people died but no accurate figure exists. The surface of the water became covered in oil from the stricken vessel. Among the casualties were many sappers who had been preparing airfields for the RAF. More soldiers are believed to have perished in this one disaster than on the beaches of Dunkirk. It remains the forgotten disaster of the evacuation.

Back in France

Meanwhile still in France, Staff Sergeant Alan Jones had grown increasingly uneasy as no news arrived from the company base in Rennes. Four days had passed since most of the company headed for the coast. The nearby base depot at Bruz was getting emptier each day. Everybody was heading home. German planes were frequent visitors. They had heard the sound of bombs at the rail junction and they saw the plumes of smoke from the French arsenal at Redon that they regularly passed on their way to the company base.

Along with a small team, Alan Jones had been providing an electrical supply to the substantial base complex of workshops, accommodation and stores. Their temporary billets were a mile south of the base. To keep them fed they had their own cook. They were well supplied with food and rations but had augmented these with trout taken from a fishpond beside their billet. The supply of fresh fish was quickly exhausted by the cook. It was a steady enough life but something was wrong.

It was impossible to escape the conclusion that everybody was being evacuated. Maybe they were being moved or redeployed. Nobody he talked to knew what was going on. The other units in Bruz had received instructions to carry this or that to the port. Would they be returning? Were the camps the other side of town still full of troops? There were no answers available. It was hard to sleep with these thoughts and the portentous silence from the depot was hard to ignore. He slept soundly until dawn.

A decision had to be made. Staff Sergeant Jones could take his truck and investigate. He would need to find someone in authority. This could take much of the day. If he was then told to withdraw, valuable time would be lost returning to pick up his team. He knew it would be an anxious wait for those he left behind, deprived of their leader and their transport.

Leaving his post felt like desertion but this was Alan's decision. He told them to have their breakfast then load up all their kit. It was a brave decision, taken quickly. So Alan with his driver Dave Roberts loaded their little truck with their personal weapons and equipment. Six sappers climbed in the back and took the road to the West. Into every space their vital tools were crammed for the journey. As they reached the depot at Bruz there was an oppressive silence. It was clear that all the other units had departed.

'It should have been a difficult decision. After all I was walking off the job which as a soldier one never did' recalled Alan. His heart felt like a deserter but his head told him it was time to depart.

Passing south of Rennes all was quiet. In truth it was too quiet. The message was clear. The garrison in Rennes had withdrawn. They did not bother to stop. They continued their way, squeezed in their PU truck, towards the main highway through Brittany.

The road remained clear and they made good progress. The jams and checkpoints associated with the evacuation of troops from Brest were gone. The withdrawal had been completed four days ago. They paused in Morlaix. Saturday was market day. There was an air of normality. For the French, peace had returned. The Germans had allegedly stopped their advance and seemed to have vanished.

Alan Jones spent his remaining French Francs. They had adequate provisions so the money went on presents for the art student, Kathleen, whom he had not seen since August. He found a jewellery shop under the giant viaduct that dominates the town. A deal was quickly done and Alan stuffed an ivory necklace and matching, chunky bracelet into his battle dress.

There was no news and everyone was too cautious to ask questions. Warnings about the fate of fifth columnists were whispered whenever friends encountered each other. A straggling truck could easily attract attention from the Gendarmerie. Fortunately, nobody wanted to delay them and they were soon on their way west again oblivious of events elsewhere.

Spirits remained high. They were after all, heading home. They had no knowledge of the debacle that had befallen the BEF. Nobody had told them about the armistice announced five days earlier. Their time in France had not been disagreeable. However, their mood sobered as they passed the lines of abandoned vehicles. Some had been burnt out.

3.3 & 3.4

Alan Jones in the market place at Morlaix where in June 1940 he paused to buy some jewellery for his fiancée, Kathleen confident that he would find some transport back to Britain although France was already out of the war.

HOME	16 · 1 · 39	11 · 9 · 39	2	239
B.E.F.	12 · 9 · 39	23 · 6 · 40	–	285
HOME	24 · 6 · 40	16 · 3 · 41	–	266
M. EAST.	17 · 3 · 41	19 · 6 · 42	1	95
GERMANY	20 · 6 · 42	24 · 5 · 45	2	339
HOME	25 · 5 · 45	5 · 58	1	263

3.5

An extract from Staff Sergeants Alan Jones' record of service show his return from France on 24 June 1940. The same record shows his return from captivity on 24 May 1945, over 2 weeks after the end of the war.

Their route to the harbour was lined by army vehicles abandoned over the previous days. They had reached the main roundabout almost a mile from the harbour. The area was quiet. There were no troops to be seen and few locals were out of doors. They drove to the harbour they remembered from their time in the castle moat in September. When the route became impassable, they unpacked the truck that had carried them the 100 miles from Rennes.

Loaded with their kitbags, knapsack and weapons Alan Jones slung one of the precious instruments around the neck of each man and set off for the quay. In spite of their burden, they lost no time in marching to the docks past the deserted transit camp that now stretched for half a mile along the walls leading to the naval harbour. At the western end of the quay, the castle whose moat had been their early home already cast a shadow in their direction as the late afternoon sun dipped to the horizon.

Unbeknown to Alan, a contingent of Germans was already installed in the castle. Brest had already surrendered to the Germans late on Wednesday. The signs of occupation were not obvious. The town was deceptively still with no police or troops in evidence. It was a very quiet Saturday evening in Brest.

The town had not recovered from the shock of France's defeat or the particular threats uttered to their city a few days before. On Wednesday, 19 June news had reached them that the German 11th Division had moved through the 7th and 10th Divisions and launched a three pronged advance along the Brittany Peninsular. To his surprise, they encountered some opposition. General Petain had declared an armistice two days earlier but not all Bretons accepted this situation.

The aerodrome at Lanvéoc-Polmic was well defended. Small parties of Germans were sent forward to demand the surrender. At 15.30 the mayor of Brest met the Germans to parley at Gouesnou but the invaders were in no mood to negotiate. At 17.00 the mayor was issued with an ultimatum. Five divisions and their artillery were now in position to destroy Brest and the surrounding territory. Forty-five minutes later, the City agreed to a cease-fire. Brest had officially surrendered. The burghers of Lorient were made of sterner stuff and negotiated until Friday. Ironically their city would also be one of the last in France surrendered by the Germans in 1944.

That evening, a small party of signallers was sent to accept the surrender at the town hall before heading for the relative security of the castle, which served as the harbour office. There was little they could to enforce their rule. They were surrounded by the French Navy and in the territory of the fiercely independent Brettons.

The exhausted German army, still many miles from Brest, paused after the second breathtaking phase of their blitzkrieg that had taken them from the Somme to the west coast in two weeks. It would be several days before the German army was ready to advance and occupy Brest in force.

The Germans had won a stunning victory and their lines of supply had been stretched beyond all previous limits. But somehow they had kept going. It is unlikely that the stragglers were even aware of the drama that had been played out in the city. The small party of Germans did nothing to interfere with their escape plans. The city fathers were no longer exercising control. The residents were preparing themselves for the unthinkable reality that was about to invest them.

The 'Redcaps' were still at their post controlling the embarkation of stragglers. They were taking no notice of any armistice or surrender. They were not about to allow any exceptions to their 'arms and knapsack only' rule even if there was space. The salvaged tools of their trade, especially the precious equipment used to test electrical installations before any power is switched on, were condemned.

They protested but to no avail. Their assembled tools and meters were thrown into the harbour. Once this sacrifice was complete they were then directed towards two boats where small groups from all three services were waiting to be taken home.

The navy had been exercising their diplomatic skills on the ships in the harbour trying to persuade French naval and maritime vessels to sail to England and continue the fight with limited success. Activity at the harbour continued as fishermen and coasters plied their trade. The large vessels loaded with troops had departed on Monday. But a few of the slower, smaller vessels sent by the navy continued to arrive in Brest.

The navy had been unsuccessful in their attempt to persuade two skippers, recently arrived from the Dunkirk evacuation, that they should load up and set sail immediately. They could not be ordered or cajoled into departing with some stragglers. After three almost sleepless weeks the boat crews refused to move. It was, after all, Saturday night and they were in France. The exhausted sailors headed for town for some recreation.

They were finally taken out of France on one of the shortest nights of the year on a small coastal trader SS the Lady of Mann, and had an uneventful crossing to Plymouth on Sunday night. For the men on the deck it was an anxious time. There was no sign of any naval escort. They were alone. Everybody was aware of the U-boat threat. U49 had surfaced in view of the harbour to demonstrate the reality of this threat.

The threat the seamen most feared came from the air. They had seen many ships sunk by bombs as they sat trapped within the confines of the sand channels off the Belgian coast. The soldiers had witnessed the effects of bombing in Rennes as they passed the Triage. They all longed for the open sea and the freedom to manoeuvre and evade the expected bombardment.

The full moon illuminated them through the channel while their wake glistened in the moonlight pointing any potential attacker towards them. Alan kept a tense watch as they steamed through the channel to the open sea. 'The sea was like a millpond. The ripples ran away to the distant shore reflecting the moonlight.' Soon sleep took over. As the light of early dawn arched over the receding Brittany coast they reached open water. The sunlight extinguished their wake. There was still plenty to worry about but they were all soundly asleep.

They slipped into the dock at Plymouth but had to wait aboard their escape vessel while another arrival was unloaded. This ship receiving priority treatment was carrying some of the last wounded survivors rescued from the Lancastria sunk by German bombers on 17 June. The sight brought home their good fortune. They were impatient to get ashore but willing to wait.

As they disembarked, Hitler was just beginning his only trip around a deserted Paris. He had been on hand the day before to witness the humiliation of the French in the Forest of Compiègne where the Armistice between the French and Germans was signed on the 22 June. It had been a narrow escape for Alan and his section.

Alan Jones and the other stragglers were sent on to Blandford where they were accommodated and given new uniforms. After a few days, he was given a rail warrant to stay with his sister in Worthing. He was told to wait there until he received orders to report back. It would not be a long wait.

The first overseas posting of 106 Army Troops Company had come to an end. It had been uneventful but not without some honour. Bill Harvey recalls: 'Apparently we not only had the honour to be the first unit to arrive in France but most certainly we were also among the last to leave it.'

The influx of over 1/3 million troops changed the domestic perspective of this phoney war. Legislators had also worked hard during the opening months to reintroduce the many wartime provisions that had evolved during the Great War. The restricted output from vehicle headlights and the blackout contributed to a record 4,133 deaths on the road during the first 4 months of war. They introduced a multiplicity of petty regulations and promoted a new class of officials empowered to arrest the discomfited citizenry for any of a growing list of infringements.

The threat of mass bombing and gas attacks had not yet materialised. It was nearly Christmas before the first civilian was killed during a bombing raid on Scapa Flow. The war would not be fought the other side of the Channel as everybody had hoped and believed. Now the possibility of German troops landing in Britain had to be contemplated. 106 Army Troops Company, Royal Engineers had returned to a country where there was no longer any room for illusions.

The War had come home.

Chapter Four

Back Home

June 1940 – March 1941

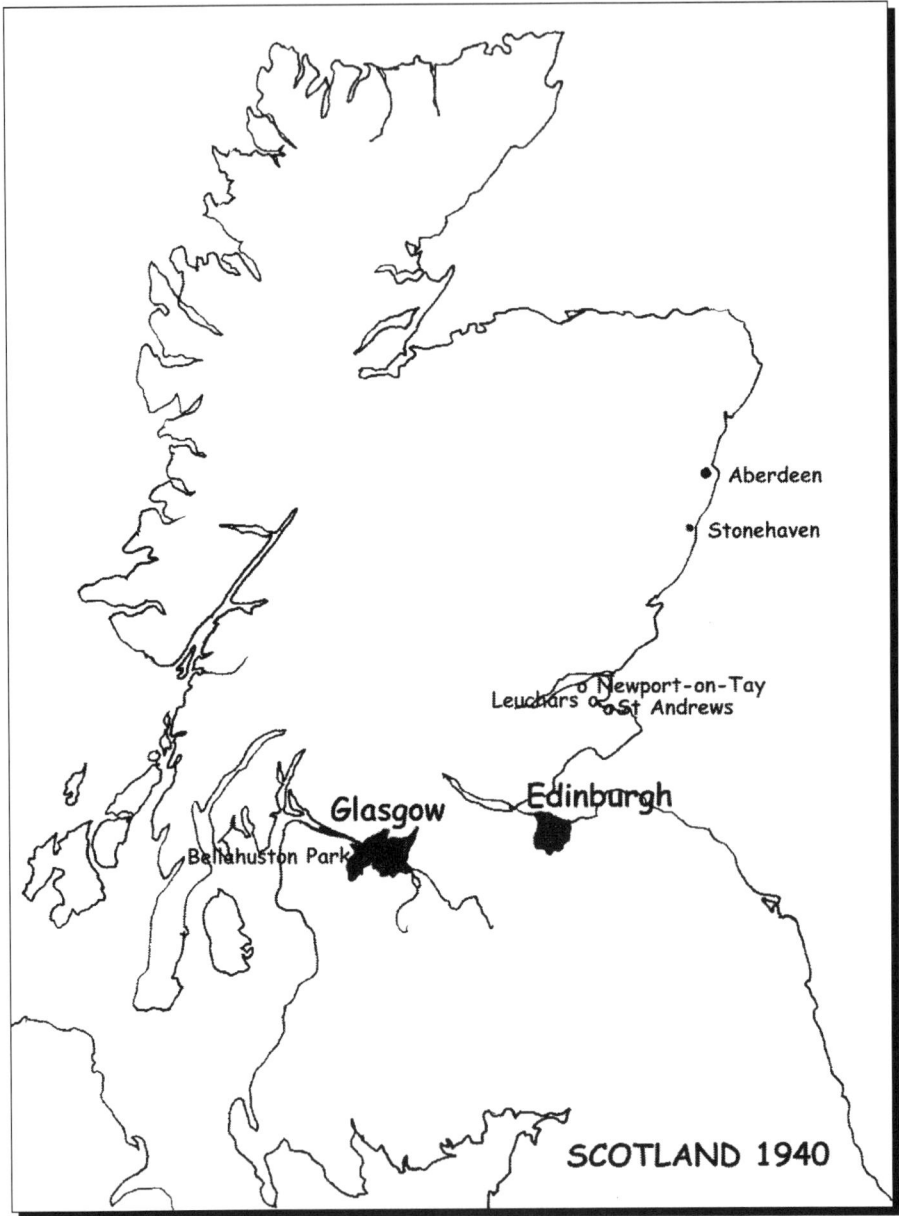

Map of Scotland

A minor miracle

The miracle that processed and dispersed a third of a million men from Dunkirk in May had to be repeated in June. The German army was not held at the Somme this time or on the far bank of the river Seine. The Weygand Line was outflanked and dissolved. The rest of the army would have to be brought home. The weary organisers moved along the south coast to welcome another quarter of a million soldiers and airmen of many nations.

The 'little ships' had staggered home. They were replaced by small cruise liners and refugee Dutch coasters unsuited to the conditions at the fringe of the Atlantic. There was neither the time nor the ships available to form convoys. These bigger, 'little ships' sailed alone. For two weeks over ten thousand soldiers disembarked each morning. The members of 106 Army Troops Company Royal Engineers were home after nine months in France.

A timely decision to abandon the position and then to leave much of their equipment in France ensured that most of the troops from the Lines of Communication had been brought home. But another minor miracle was required to bring some order from this chaos. Little attempt was made to put or to keep units together when they landed on the south coast. The military priority was to bring as many individuals back as the situation permitted. There would be plenty of time to reorganise later.

The Directorate of Quartering was given the task of managing this re-invasion. They were handed the brief to prepare for the return of all the forward elements of the BEF cut off from their supplies by the rapid advance of the German army to the coast. Their task would include finding homes for up to a third of a million returning troops. By the end of June, the directorate would have processed 522,752 men and women.

The first priority was to get the troops away from the ports. At the peak period, shortly after dawn each day, a train left Dover Marine station every eight minutes. Passenger trains had been sucked south to provide the first stage of this shuttle and remove the tide of humanity coming ashore.

There was an uncharacteristic neglect of normal military procedure. No attempts would be made to document returning troops at the port. Names would be noted so that next-of-kin could be informed. The initial plan was to let everyone send a telegram. However, a quick calculation proved that the system would be unable to cope. There were simply not enough telegraphers, lines, delivery people or motorbikes to cope. The soldiers might get home before their telegram. Instead free field service post cards would be issued upon arrival and collected at the feeding stops along the way. These were then posted in the normal way. The GPO worked round the clock.

Along the way, fourteen 'halte-repas' were set up, staffed by catering students and the Women's Royal Voluntary Service. A hot drink, a sandwich of meat or fish paste plus some cigarettes and matches were provided for the returnees. It was impossible to assemble enough cups. The call went out for the waxed paper cups used at fairs and garden parties designed for cold drinks. The hot brew melted the wax if the tea was too hot and the paper quickly disintegrated. So they were filled with warm tea and the cups lasted just long enough to quench the thirst.

A brew of tea was all that most could expect. The Horlicks Company donated its malted milk drink for the troops passing through Paddock Wood and Addison Road halts. Some were lucky enough to tag along with French and Belgian troops who were scheduled to receive wine to slake their thirst.

Once the soldiers had been taken away from the ports they were to be allocated somewhere to stay. The official term applied to their host was 'mother.' Every returnee would have an individual 'mother' in a unit stationed somewhere in the south of the country. Trains delivered their troops to their waiting mother units. As they left the train, a NAAFI ration bag with more sandwiches and cigarettes was given to each soldier.

The mother units would allocate one evacuee to each soldier. They would share beds, blankets, eating utensils, kitchens and rations. By personalising the problem, resourceful individuals invented a million unique solutions. Unused supplies of cutlery and crockery were discovered and surplus bedding was uncovered in countless cupboards and boxes. The system worked. Communal generosity and individual initiative solved every problem. By this means the returning army was housed and fed in the days following their evacuation. This was more then the 'feeding of the five thousand.' This miracle housed half a million.

Churchill recognised the achievement. It had been a victory of sorts. But he told the House of Commons that organising a massive retreat was not the sort of victory that defeated their enemy. The extraction of the BEF had undermined the appeasers in the War Cabinet and strengthened his own authority. There would be no more talk of negotiation in Churchill's Cabinet.

Morale was remarkably buoyant. They had just been driven from the Continent by an impressive army, yet Alan Jones recalls that there was no thought of defeat. 'It never crossed our minds that we would not defeat the Germans sooner rather than later.'

The spontaneous generosity of the population was infectious. Many cheered the exhausted troops as they left their evacuation trains. Most who saw the evacuees were moved to tears by their pitiful state. The popular intuition sensed these soldiers were victims of a disaster that was not of their making. They were victims who had done their best. They were doubly welcome. The soldiers provided the only insurance that Britain would not suffer the same fate as the continental countries that had fallen before the conquering German army.

This improvised armada had brought home something more than just the troops that had set out in the autumn and winter of 1939. People now understood the military power that opposed them. This comprehension was brought home with the army from France.

Home leave was ordered once arms and equipment had been accounted for. After that, troops were to report to a part of the country nominated to receive their unit.

For the French and Belgians the plan was to feed and return them to the continent. They were directed to Southampton, Bournemouth and Plymouth before being shipped home at the rate of 15,000 a day in boats destined to bring more allied troops home.

Other nationalities were concentrated around the country. The 24,000 Poles were directed towards Scotland while Lancashire was divided between the French in the South, the 5,000 Czechs towards the West with Latvians around Oldham.

Some French troops were less fortunate. Some 20,000 had opted not to join de Gaulle's Free French Forces after the armistice signed by the French Government. With accommodation in short supply, it was decreed that they were the ones who had to endure a winter under canvas until secure arrangements could be made to send them home in the spring of 1941.

The final task was to gather the troops to their original formation to reform a fighting force. It is to the credit of the Directorate of Quartering that they gave humane considerations precedence over normal military methods. Caring for the individuals helped to restore morale. The 'Phoney War' was over. There was a returnee in every community. Within a month units were reassembling.

For Alan Jones this meant a trip from his 'mother' unit at Blandford Camp along the south coast to his sister at Worthing. Bill Harvey had to face the longer journey from Bournemouth to Doncaster on one of the packed trains heading north.

4.1 Sunnyside follies:
Back from France Alan, centre, enjoyed the summer in Worthing with his sister before the company was reformed in Leeds. A group of friends prepare to head for a beach fancy-dress party in July 1940.

Bob Borthwick set off for the station as soon as he had his rail warrant, heading for Aldershot with a seven day leave pass in his hands. As the journey started he began to feel ill. It started with a sore mouth and throat but it did nothing to diminish the joy of meeting Wynn again. However, the next morning he reported to the Cambridge Hospital where he was made to feel most welcome. Hospitals throughout the south of England had been prepared for the anticipated mass of casualties returning from France. They had been mercifully underused but were pleased to play some part in the evacuation effort.

Although not a war wound, Bob had developed Vincennes disease, a common complaint in the First World War known to the soldiers as 'Trench Mouth.' It was believed to be a disease of malnutrition and brought on by a deficiency of vitamin B. Two patients had already been diagnosed with the disease. The staff seemed pleased to have a third case which helped confirm the diagnosis of this rare disease.

Two weeks of liver for breakfast, dinner and tea was the remedy. Once the symptoms vanished there was four weeks home convalescence with a ration card for extra liver. Modern medicine would have deprived Bob of both of these luxuries. The disease was later identified as a bacterial infection that thrives when dental hygiene breaks down. As August approached, Bob was told to head north to link up with 106 Coy in Leeds.

Reunion

The popular certainties of the first winter at war had been shattered in the spring offensive. The Expeditionary Force plus 150,000 refugees had arrived unannounced. Failure on such a massive scale helped to sweep away complacency. Solutions were needed and the sappers would soon be hard at work. With military camps already filled with units preparing to join the battle for France, there was nowhere to put over the half million men who had flooded back in June. The company, like so many around the country, was re-established in private houses.

Bill Harvey was one of the first to find a billet. 'I found myself with a family of steeplejacks by the name of Tomlinson who lived in Dib Lane, Leeds. They were very good to us. Military activity seemed to be standing guard at the Main GPO and examining staff passes as they went on duty. I found it slightly irritating as it was obvious that it was just a duty to keep us occupied.'

The BEF brought home tales of the fifth columnist who had joined the refugees fleeing the advancing Germans in the Low Countries. They had been blamed for everything from preventing bridge demolitions to marking targets for the Stukas that terrorised retreating armies and civilians. Soldiers told tales of summary executions of those suspected of spying. Liaison officers from all armies lived dangerously as they attempted to pass between the different nations. Back home in Britain, vigilance became an obsession.

Dib Lane was the company's home in the autumn of 1940. Their hut-building activity begun around Rennes was resumed when they built a camp in Roundhay Park, north of Leeds. All over the country contractors and Royal Engineers were converting civic parks to military camps. 106 Company would now work their way up the country building camps for others to occupy.

The experiences of France had taught everyone to live for the moment. Bill joined the exodus to Doncaster for weekend leave with their families and loved ones. 'Oh what a joy it was to see Edith, Janet and Billie, although every time it re-opens all the worries of the family welfare.' But it was worth it.

Bob was able to find accommodation for Wynn in Leeds while Alan Jones' landlady was able to find space for the weekend visits from Manchester of his new love, Kathleen.

Leuchars

However, it was too good to last and the next move was to Leuchars in Scotland near St Andrews. After three months billeted in the Dib Lane area the unit headed north to build their first base in Scotland.

The primitive set of huts they took over as accommodation was on the edge of woodland. Their first priority was to build latrines. These were constructed according to the military manual. A clump of trees sensibly screened the ablutions from the accommodation. While this site was logical it took no account of the habits and habitat of the local wildlife.

Bill painfully recalls the cost of this mistake. 'It is unnecessary to go into all the gruesome details but the lesson was quickly and very painfully learnt. Never to go to the toilets after tea. Jerry may have had his dive bombers but the midges at Leuchars were just as vicious.'

The standard of dental health in the conscript army was not good. The dangers of bad teeth, as Bob Borthwick's experience had shown, were recognised as a problem for the forces. Commanders did not want to have their effectiveness depleted by lack of dental fitness. Toothache among civilians was a common, debilitating condition of the working man. Some could not afford to pay for the attentions of a dentist. Others could not face the crude drills and pliers that dentists employed as remedies.

For some, the solution was to have all their teeth pulled out. A rich uncle might give a 'top set' of false teeth as a 21st birthday present. The natural teeth would be extracted in one traumatic session and replaced with a false set two weeks later after a diet of bread and milk. The shortcomings of false teeth had shown up when they were asked to chew the five inch square of army biscuit first issued when they left Doncaster station nine months earlier. 'False teeth were no match for such tough army fodder' Alan recalls.

Each night daily orders were posted for the next day's events. One night Bill Harvey noted that he was to proceed to St Andrews for dental inspection. 'I ran my tongue round my teeth and thought "I'm OK. It will just be a pleasant day out." Next morning I took my place in the lorry and off we went. We all sat in the waiting room until we were called. When my turn came I walked in expecting the all clear. When the dentist said "Umph not too good, I shall have to remove these three teeth and put a filling in another one." It was too late to dodge it and so I was parted with some of my teeth. When it was over, my mouth and jaw were frozen. I couldn't drink a cup of tea before we returned. Some pleasant day out!'

Along with their construction work, their military task was to defend a portion of the coastline which included the fairways and greens of the ancient golf course at St Andrews. While other sappers cut and embanked a modern-day Hadrian's Wall across the Scottish Lowlands, 106 ATC had to stop any invasion at the coast! The decision was made to erect obstacles to prevent the club's fairways being used as a bridgehead for an airborne assault.

But the Club at St Andrews had friends in high places. As a result they were able to negotiate the precise positioning of the poles, humps and trenches set up along the fairways. The location of these cross-hazards was designed to make it impossible for planes or gliders to land safely. The steep sides of the new trenches however, made it impossible for golf balls to be played out. A 'lift and drop' rule was introduced for those falling into one of these new traps which did not incur any penalty at first.

However, the 'Golfing' magazine at Christmas 1940 was already suggesting that these military modifications actually enhanced some courses, forcing players to place their shot rather than simply driving their ball down the fairway.

The daily routine for most sappers remained boring. In France, the unit had been overworked. After the burst of construction activity in Leeds they had nothing very useful to do. There was however a prevalent fear of invasion or coastal raids. Whether this was real or manufactured to keep them alert mattered little. Many doubted if the Germans would choose the rocky Scottish coast for any sort of attack. The fear of attack meant regular coastal guard duty. Keeping everybody busy in an expanding army was a problem so the ragged coastline provided lots of pointless patrolling. There was not yet enough fighting to occupy them all or equipment to employ them. But it would not be long before they were moved again.

This time their destination was a short distance north in Newport, a small town on the opposite bank of the river Tay facing Dundee. Their accommodation was a warehouse. Bill Harvey was a happy man. He had been able to secure lodgings for Edith and the children in the village. This was a lucky time for Bill Harvey.

Sapper Dave Barwell from Edlington, a miner by trade, was released from the army to return to work in the mines. Dave had been acting as the unit medical orderly. He had to persuade Bill to take the job as this was a precondition for the former's release back to civvy street. 'As soon as I agreed to take on the medical job he got away very quickly. The next morning when the sick reported I was surprised to see my first patient with some kind of a head covering. On examination it was evidently some kind of eczema and I put him on one side to see a doctor.'

The next person on sick parade was also a case for the doctor's attention. Bill's predecessor had been treating the victim with *Thermogene* on his chest. The result of the medication was some painful burns on his chest. For Bill this was a useful introduction to medicine. He learnt that his cures might be just as bad as the original problem.

'My first day as a medical orderly was not very encouraging. The usual need was to treat cuts, bruises and boils. On one occasion, I mentioned to the doctor that my experience was one year's training for a St John's certificate for first aid. He laughed and said all I needed was some aspirins, some *Number 9s*, the army's laxative, sodium sulphate for waxed ears and plenty of common sense.'

Bellahouston Park

In November, the company was on the move again this time to Bellahouston Park in Glasgow. The plan was to make it into a transit camp for overseas troops. The Canadians were mustering their forces to send them to Europe. The Americans were still keeping out of the war but had introduced the draft. Wise heads understood that the United States could not escape the effect of a war that was spreading round the world. When asked why he was so sure that America would be drawn into the war Churchill simply replied 'History.' In November 1940 nearly twenty thousand US men were called up for a year's military service although it would be another year before Churchill's prophecy would be fulfilled following the Japanese attack on Pearl Harbour.

Bellahouston Park was close to the river Clyde and had been chosen above Kelvingrove Park as the best site for the Empire Exhibition of 1938. The latter had housed the previous exhibitions of 1888, 1901 and 1911. These great exhibitions provided the city with an opportunity to advertise its industry to the world in the days before mass communication. Industrialists journeyed from around the world to inspect and buy the products of the northern factories.

But Bellahouston was preferred as it lay at the junction of two new, main roads which would allow visitors to arrive in automobiles along with the groups in charabancs. Visitors no longer had to rely on trains and trams.

Glasgow was struggling to recover after the Great Depression and this was intended to advertise the heavy engineering skills of the area. The exhibition attracted over twelve million visitors but still lost its backers three shillings and five pence for each pound invested; a loss of 17% of their stake.

Alan Jones already had an affinity for the park. Much of the electrical cable for his first major project as a clerk of works on Bourlon Lines in Catterick had come from Bellahouston Park when the exhibition and its equipment was dismantled and re-cycled.

Fifty Nissen huts had to be erected and connected to the services to provide the transit accommodation. This was the type of project where the expertise of the regular army staff sergeants was put to good effect.

There was a trick to lining up the pre-drilled sheets of corrugated iron on the Nissen huts. Done correctly, the curved sheets came together easily. However, an over tightened nut or a bent sheet could turn the exercise into a wrestling match with tempers fraying.

The Nissen hut was originally developed by a Canadian engineering officer during World War I. The roof and sides were made of corrugated metal. Two layers of metal were used on the lower sides and a single layer above on the roof. The whole structure was supported by eight foot radius, curved steel ribs.

The huts had been designed to be simple to assemble. A crew of six could erect one in a few hours. With practice erection could become even faster, although preparing the base and fitting electrical and plumbing took longer.

The curve of the side-walls resulted in a loss of effective width but careful positioning of beds and lockers ensured that the space was not wasted. The Americans however modified the design to produce the Quonset family of buildings. They introduced a side-wall to increase the headroom but reverted to the traditional, semi-circular rib to save shipping space and material.

For Bill Harvey there was professional satisfaction in this work. 'It went like clockwork. Separate gangs were allocated to perform various functions such as the footings and floors, assembly and erection. The bases were dug out and the floors concreted. Then the erection team moved in while the surveyors, excavators and concreters moved ahead putting in the next footings and floors. Finally there was the outfitting with doors and windows. We electricians moved in next. We could fit one hut a day. It was professionally most satisfying. The project went very smoothly as well as quickly.'

Glasgow was in festive mood in spite of the war in November 1940. They had been spared attacks by bombers so far. The war was getting closer. The local papers reported the arrival of survivors from sinkings of merchantmen bringing supplies from North America.

Everything seemed to be doubling. Prices and taxes were doubling. There was now double British summer time. Now Glasgow's 'War Weapons Week' would last a fortnight. Concerts and parades took place daily as the city sought to raise £10 million for the war effort. The warm welcome for the company afforded by War Weapons Week was a coincidence.

The Corporation of Glasgow, and especially its Parks' Department, were 'at war' with the military. The problem was over 'correct procedure.' In July the army had agreed to rent the sporting buildings and the Glasgow pavilion. These pavilions were the only permanent reminder of the exhibition of 1938. However, areas around them were being requisitioned leading to the formation of a special sub-committee of the corporation to resolve the problem of procedure. They met with military surveyors and were able to report on 18 September that the correct procedures would be followed in future by the military. The park remained requisitioned.

After the war the process of de-requisitioning the huts created even more friction. Once the transit camp had seen the last of the Canadians home, ten of the huts were occupied by squatters, among them many former soldiers. The corporation retaliated by cutting off their electricity. The Department of Health objected and it was restored. It would be April 1949 before all the administrative chaos was resolved and the land, with its huts, returned to the corporation. In time, the huts were removed and in 1993, the design of Glasgow's famous artist and architect, Charles Rennie Mackintosh, was realised. The 'house of an art lover' now occupies most of the site.

While working in the park, Joe Beckitt joined them as Company Sergeant Major. Bill Summersgill had been invalided out while in France due to ill-health. Bill Harvey's time as a medical orderly was also about to come to an end. 'I was surprised and somewhat apprehensive to be summoned to the presence of the new CSM one day. I was informed that his Orderly Corporal was also being recalled to civilian duties.' The incumbent had recommended Bill as his replacement. The rank of lance-corporal went with the job. Bill took the job. 'I found a desk job surprisingly enjoyable and rewarding.'

The work in Glasgow was completed in six weeks. Fifty huts erected in forty two days! Sadly no one was looking for record makers. If they had been, the company might have merited another footnote in the wartime history book for speed of this construction. Nor would they have the pleasure of occupying this excellent accommodation they had created.

Stonehaven

The company was to head north again and back to the east coast. They were being transferred even further north to Stonehaven, just down the coast from Aberdeen, for intensive training prior to another overseas posting. Embarkation leave would start immediately.

Bill Harvey was among the first to be given leave. Being company clerk had its perks. He set off direct from Glasgow heading for Doncaster to see Edith and the children. For Alan the move north would take him a long way from his love in Ashton-under-Lyne. Kathleen was now supervising the repair of aircraft radios and there was no embarkation leave for lovers engaged in war work. The move north would bring a parting that would last four and a half years. The country was settling in for a long war. Meanwhile, the architect of appeasement, Neville Chamberlain, had slipped quietly from the scene, dying on 9 November 1940.

'By the time my leave was over the unit had already moved and I returned to Stonehaven.' As the Company Sergeant Major's orderly corporal, Bill moved into a comfortable room in the large St Leonard's Hotel on the sea front. 'I found the CSM a good man to work for and I enjoyed the work and the responsibility.'

Everyone, including the clerks, had to undertake the military training, irrespective of their trade or duties. 'One aspect of the training was popular with the senior NCOs who organised it. We were placed in groups of six. The leader was appointed and given a map with a reference number denoting a particular landmark. We were to run to this landmark in a given amount of time. It was now the middle of winter with thick snow to run through. As soldiers, we didn't enjoy it at all, but apparently it had to be done to demonstrate our physical fitness.'

The war was also getting nearer. There were nightly air-raid warnings at Stonehaven. While the land war in Europe was quiet and the Battle of Britain had denied the Germans air supremacy. At sea, the war was intense. The coastal shipping lanes were the target for regular raids by the Luftwaffe. A tripod mounted Bren gun stood ready at the front of the hotel. 'Although we had occasional sightings of enemy aircraft I regret I cannot say we shot any down. It would have made a good story', recalls Bill.

Bill was kept busy with his book-keeping. 'As the CSM's Orderly Corporal one of my duties was to requisition rations in accordance with the number of men on the strength. Embarkation leave was still proceeding and what with some men going on leave and some returning it became an impossible task as far as accuracy was concerned. I can only say I muddled through. Thanks to my calculation the cooks were never short of food. As Orderly Corporal I kept clear of a lot of the humdrum side of training such as square bashing, rifle drill and incessant kit inspections.'

Stonehaven, was not far from the heartland of the quality malt whiskeys. It was certainly the right place to welcome the New Year. Bob Borthwick recalls that this led to the event that he later recalled as the most embarrassing of his life. 'At the Hogmanay ball in the Sergeant's Mess, Wynne and I were dancing the Dashing White Sergeant. I released my partner too soon only to see Wynne sliding over the dance floor with her kilt over her head.' Years of applying soap flakes to the wooden dance floor had the effect of making the transit smooth if no less embarrassing for both parties.

January 1941 was occupied with even more training while the easterly wind carried the chill of Siberia to the Scottish coast. There was little sight of the mild east coast weather of which the locals boasted. There was little coal and even the plentiful local firewood was effectively rationed. Life was slow and cold. But morale was maintained by the prospect or remembrance of a recent home leave.

Many men had taken advantage of their home leave to bring their wives back to Stonehaven. Because Bill Harvey had taken his last leave from Glasgow, he did not have a chance to assess the local possibilities for families. Edith became aware of the exodus of Doncaster wives and had taken charge of events. One evening Bill was summoned back to the orderly room to take a telephone call. He was apprehensive as he ran to take the call but he was instantly relieved. 'It was Edith announcing that she was in Edinburgh and would arrive in Stonehaven about midnight with the children. I quickly managed to fix up some accommodation and meet her. The news had evidently reached Doncaster that we should be on the move soon. So much for security!'

All the wives were desperate to spend the last few days together. War was a time for love and lovers. Everyone understood that once overseas the best they could hope for was a separation running into years. Bill Harvey knew how tough it was for those left behind. 'I salute the courage of all the wives in those troubled days and the hardships they endured.'

In late January the company was told to be ready to go overseas on or after 15 February. Among the items that featured in the news on the 22nd was the fall of Tobruk. A force of British, Australian and Free French burst through two lines of Italian defenders after several days of aerial bombardment. The news made little impact in the company whose fateful journey with Tobruk was about to begin. North Africa was a side show run by Field Marshal Wavell. Nevertheless it was good to have a victory.

The news that General Irwin Rommel had been dispatched three weeks later did not reach their ears either. Hitler had instructed his general to reverse the setbacks in Libya and stiffen the Italian resistance. They would in due course clash with the leader of the 9th Panzer formation that had chased the Lines of Communications units out of France about sixteen months later. The result would be the same for the company.

Partings now replaced parties. Many wives had contrived to follow their husbands every time the company was posted. There was a plentiful supply of rooms vacated by sons or fathers who were engaged in war service elsewhere. Landladies seemed to enjoy adopting these Yorkshire families into their homes. Bob recognised his good fortune. 'Most servicemen were already separated from their wives and families. We had enjoyed more than seven months together but it had to end.'

As January drew to a close, Bob put Wynne on the overnight sleeper for home. They recognised the uncertainty they now faced. They did not waste any time in speculation. Wynne knew that overseas posting meant years apart. Bob knew that Wynne was returning to the south where the Luftwaffe was still blitzing London.

Civilian casualties now outnumbered army losses. At sea the navy and merchant marine were also suffering significant losses as the Battle of the Atlantic built towards its bloody climax. Wynne knew that Bob would soon have to run the gauntlet patrolled by U-boats and bombers. There were no comfortable words to exchange just love and unquestioning optimism.

In February, with departure time drawing nearer, the company was to be 'knocked into shape.' This ritual began with the arrival of a regular army drill sergeant. Bill Harvey was to be one of his early victims. He takes up the story. 'This sergeant was a veritable ogre of a man, a born regular from the angle of his forage cap to the mirror-polished on his boots. He had a loud, gravely voice to match. When he gave orders it had a foghorn quality which made everyone in Stonehaven jump. After putting the complete unit through their paces for a few days he decided to give each NCO an individual test.

'A squad of twelve men was paraded on the esplanade running along the sea front. The terrifying drill sergeant with the NCO being tested at his side were stationed on the piece of flat waste ground which we used as a parade ground. The squad was at least two hundred yards from the NCO giving the orders.

'We not only had the distance to overcome but the sound of the sea at the back of the squad. For us it was a terrifying ordeal, due to the distance and background noise. You could shout an order. Then wait for what seemed like ten seconds before the squad moved. When my turn came I managed to get through without criticism. It seemed I had passed the test, to my great relief.'

Not everyone escaped without a tongue lashing. 'One poor lad, who did not possess a powerful voice got his squad all tangled up. Eventually the squad marching away out of earshot. Helpfully the instructor said, "For heavens sake say something, even if it's only goodbye".'

Bill was relieved to get back to the peace of the orderly room. His reward for having a loud voice was another stripe. He was now a full corporal in the 'Electrical and Mechanical' section. 'I thought just one more stripe and I should realise my immediate ambition to be a lance sergeant.'

Everyone had been warned that 'walls have ears' but it was recognised that soldiers would talk. To help provide a confusing flow of information to German intelligence the military were prepared to play a few tricks. A few days before embarkation 106 Army troops company were kitted out for the Far East or India. The company was paraded in the Wellington sun-helmets, favoured by the marines for ceremonial dress, for any enemy agents to observe. Their kit would not have looked out of place in Delhi or Singapore. This embarrassing spectacle also helped to confuse the company.

'I made the guess that we were off to the Far East but I was proved wrong' recalls Bob.

Eventually the departure date was fixed for 24 March. Sleeping-out passes were withdrawn the day before. It was another emotional time for Bill and Edith. 'I well remember our last hour together. We sat in a beach shelter on the seafront at Stonehaven trying hard to be brave but inevitably it became very tearful. I was very fearful about the mental ordeal she must face travelling back to Doncaster', recalls Bill.

The fateful day dawned and the company were formed up and marched to the station to board yet another train. This time the destination was Glasgow and the quays along the Clyde. They had lost several of their experienced tradesmen; their benefit to industry was now better appreciated and they had been classified as 'essential workers.' It had taken a year to harness industry to the war effort. The army now had to fight hard to keep its engineering tradesmen when they were also needed to produce and maintain the facilities providing military hardware.

In most cases only age, or certain medical or compassionate conditions resulted in a discharge. While 106 Company held on to most of its craftsmen, the engineering industry was just as effective at keeping hold of the workers it had. By 1941 any craftsman was likely to be classified as an essential worker and consequently not liable to call up. Expanding the unit had proved very difficult.

There were imperfections in the system. Bob lost two welders skilled in the art of oxyacetylene work. They were replaced by welders who knew nothing of the finer points of adjusting the gases to bond two pieces of metal. The skills of the recruits were in joining ships plates and spot welding using electric arc welders. Retraining would be necessary. Bill Richards set to the task immediately.

It was nine months to the day since the company had embarked for their hurried departure from St Malo. It had been a busy time but now they prepared for a mystery cruise going perhaps half way round the world. On 17 March they embarked on board HM Troopship G14 a few days ahead of their original schedule. G14 was better known as The Empress of Canada. The Empress of Canada was an Atlantic liner. 'She was a really beautiful sight. She looked magnificent' remembered Bill.

As they passed through the outskirts of Glasgow there were plenty of signs of the devastation caused by the recent air-raids. The docks, ship slipways and heavy industry had previously escaped damage but had now been targeted for a forty eight hour-long 'blitz.' The German bombers had pounded the city on the 13, 14 and 15 March with the benefit of a clear sky and full 'bombers' moon.

The fires were still burning. Because of several, fatal delayed explosions, other sappers were at work dealing with the many timed fuses dropped by the Luftwaffe eventually plotting the position of each bomb to give workers confidence to return to their workplace. Over 500 people died but remarkably limited damage was done to local industry much of which was continued operation.

This was a sanguine send off for the company.

4.2 Bob and Wynne:
It was common to have a photo before an overseas posting. The formality of the pose cannot disguise the tension of the impending parting.

Chapter Five

Out to Africa

March – May 1941

Map of Africa

They boarded the Empress quickly. No one knew if the bombers would return to blitz the docks for another night. The sappers were billeted in what had been the steward's card room. Hammocks were provided but there were no instructors to demonstrate the correct way to rig or use this aerial trampoline. Everyone tried but most failed to master their hammock. It provided some entertainment as bodies were deposited on the ground and loaded hammocks sagged to suffocate those below.

The company divided into the 'hammock' and the 'deck' dwellers. Bill Harvey abandoned his attempts at nest building sooner than most and took over one of the tables which would serve him as a bed for the voyage. The stowed hammock served him as a pillow. They were still sorting out their living space when the gentle vibration that would accompany them for the coming months began. They were moving.

As soon as they were aboard, the Empress of Canada moved down the Clyde where it stayed for two days. They could see more of the extensive devastation dealt by enemy bombers on the docks and dockyards of the Clyde as they moved out of the danger zone. Perhaps remembering the tragic loss of the Lancastria, they anchored in a sheltered location and waited for the rest of the convoy to form up.

The buzz had it that two German warships, Scharnhorst and Gneisenau, were suspected to be in Atlantic waters. There would be no move while these formidable hunters were prowling. But soon the rumour machine gave the all clear. It was reported they had withdrawn to French coast and the convoy was able to proceed. Rumours on board were more frequent and, it turned out, much more accurate than the idle barrack speculation they were used to ignoring. Within the community of a ship, walls certainly did have ears but there was nobody listening beyond the hull so their secret was safe at least until they went ashore.

The convoy moved towards the Atlantic. The Empress of Canada had been made the convoy flagship with Commander R Elliott on board as the Convoy Commodore. In command of the escorts was HMS Nelson although this magnificent battleship remained out of sight to the company for much of the voyage. The Convoy Commodore took up his position as the leading transport and the Empress of Canada headed into the Atlantic. When observed from deck level, their ship seemed very much alone.

HMS Nelson had spent the early months of the war following up reports of the formidable German surface fleet without making contact. Nelson's limited speed however, made it the ideal battleship to escort convoys. In March 1941 she had been replaced as the flagship of the home fleet by the modern HMS King George V.

Bill remembers his powerful feelings of loneliness and sadness as the green fields of home slipped astern. Their last view of the British Isles was the north of Ireland. Before they reached the emptiness of the ocean they were joined by twenty liners from other ports to form their considerable convoy. On the morning of 25 March 1941 the largest troop convoy of the war, designated WS7, formed up off the Isle of Oronsay. They were no longer alone on the high seas. The cruisers HMS Edinburgh and HMS Revenge now took up the lead position in the centre of the convoy with twelve destroyers providing flank protection from the U-boats.

This was a troop convoy destined to provide reinforcements for the defence of the Far East, India, North Africa and a special group to ensure the security of Crete. On 29 October 1940 Winston Churchill had written to his chiefs of staff that they should 'establish ourselves in Crete and that risks should be run for this valuable prize.' Five month on, the company were part of the response to this instruction.

With the Axis forces dominating continental Europe, the Mediterranean islands were seen as fortresses for the Allies to contain further expansion and a base from which to defend the sea routes. The threat to Crete was seen as a seaborne invasion. To meet this threat, naval guns were gathered and delivered to the island. In mid November Col V E G Guiness was begging for Engineers to be sent to build the gun emplacements and prepare other fortification.

At the time the company was hard at work in Glasgow. Their mix of skills made them the obvious choice for dispatch to Crete. Two weeks earlier convoy WS6 had sailed for the Middle East with a battalion of Marine Special Forces to hold the fort on Crete until the defences were in place. Neither convoy would arrive in time.

The promenade deck was reserved for officers, some nurses and senior NCOs. The small area at the back of the ship, normally occupied by the crew, was the area allocated to the other ranks. After each meal there was the ritual of cleaning that dominated their life aboard. 'We were herded to the stern deck while the sleeping or messing areas were cleaned again. We had little option but to study the ships following in the convoy' Bill recalls.

The ship following them was the MV Pasteur. It had been annexed from the French and had a single, large funnel, which to Bill Harvey, made her look unwieldy. 'Just try and imagine the situation. It was March and the waves appeared mountainous. Being at the back of the ship with the crew, one moment we were looking into the ocean, next as the stern lifted we could see the Pasteur and other ships of the convoy spread out across the ocean and finally we would be looking at the sky. A real roller coaster, guaranteed to induce sea-sickness.'

It was awe-inspiring to watch the two battleships. They did not ride the waves. They just smashed through with showers of water and spray running the full length of their decks. The heavy swell would lift the sterns of the smaller ships clear of the water. Alan Jones recalls the sight of the propellers racing as the vessel straddled the swell. It was an impressive demonstration of the power of the sea.

As the ships rose and fell, Alan could count 21 ships plus so many destroyers that bobbed about he found them hard to number. He was glad that they were aboard one of the larger vessels. The ship's crew took pleasure in assuring their precious cargo that the uncomfortable swell made it difficult for both U-boats and aircraft to spot them. This provided some consolation to the company as they hunted for their sea legs in basins, buckets and toilets.

Alan Jones sought out the ship's electrician. He knew from earlier troop-ships the tedious, time-wasting routine they could expect. He offered the services of his electricians which were gratefully accepted. The technical and craft skills of many of the company were put to good use on board, where each was assigned to one of the ship's engineers. This gave the members of 106 many privileges. They did not have to participate in the mindless drudgery of long voyages. Not for them the endless rota of cleaning or pointless PT.

They could vanish into the un-visited part of the Empress to carry out some vital maintenance. Away from the gaze of the ship's officers as well as the patrolling sergeant majors, they could also settle down for a quiet cigarette while the less fortunate soldiers carried out another boat drill or scrubbed and polished the spotless ship.

When the convoy was two days out, the jobs were handed out. Bill Harvey, Wilf Mossman, Joe Edwards and a young man called Clements, were seconded to assist the ship's electricians for the duration of the voyage. Others were assigned to work for the Second Officer whose responsibility was for deck machinery such as hoists. The remaining electricians did the everyday maintenance on the ship's complex electrical systems. Others such as Russ Starr were seconded to assist the plumbing staff.

5.1 Aboard the SS Empress of Canada: The electricians worked with the crew and enjoyed a more interesting time during the 10 week voyage. Many of the company were spared the chores and boredom of troopship life by working with the crew.

Bill Harvey was happy to be given the extra work. He enjoyed learning. 'I was delighted because it gave us all insight into different types of electrical installations. I also enjoyed this extra work because it took me away from the stern, watching the roller-coaster waves and the other ships in the convoy. The work also mitigated the apprehension, which I know I shared with many others, as to whether we should reach our unknown destination safely.'

'One of the jobs gave us the run of the ship.' Bill recalls. 'The propeller revolution counter on the ship's bridge was defective. It was especially important because of the presence of the commodore and we were the flagship. It became necessary to trace the cable through the ship from the engine room to the bridge and even up one of the dummy funnels.' This occupied much of the first leg of the voyage.

The main ballroom had been equipped with long tables and forms. This was their mess room. Rations at sea were meagre. Their portion of bread and jam was made less appetising when they discovered that the cooks had an endless supply of tomato jam. The food technologists in wartime Britain sought to provide the correct nutritional balance but took little account of sensibilities. At least aboard ship they were spared the undercooked or raw vegetables that officialdom encouraged them all to consume at home.

With the mist, fog and sea swell providing effective protection against all types of enemy raider; much of the destroyer screen was withdrawn after a week at sea and turned for home. The navy was still preoccupied with the possibility of the fast battleship, Bismarck, escaping into the Atlantic.

The convoy moved west at a steady sixteen knots to put it out of range of enemy aircraft that could direct U-boats or surface raiders. The approach of any aircraft provoked tension. If they could avoid having their position being reported, they were less likely to receive attention from the U-boats that patrolled the likely convoy routes. The only aerial activity was friendly but the passengers did not know this. The early days were tense.

The routine aboard was relaxed when they cleared the Bay of Biscay. The sea subsided and the weather became warmer as each day they drew three hundred miles nearer the equator. It was now a delight to stand in the glorious evening light and watch shoals of flying fish skim the water while porpoises played along the ship's bow wave.

Freetown

Their first port of call was Freetown which was reached on 4 April. No shore leave was allowed for soldiers who had now been aboard for twenty days although sailors were allowed their 'run ashore' during their three-day-stay.

The ship's engineers were particularly grateful that the company undertook the job of reversing the polarity of the ship's anti-mine protection.

Alan Jones describes the job as being as 'hot as hell.' 'We had to go down into the bowels of the ship where a cable carried a current to neutralise the fuses of magnetic mines.' These mines were laid along known shipping routes by U-boats and detonated when a ship disturbed the earth magnetic field as it passed overhead. 'By controlling the current and its direction they could counteract the magnetic effect of the ship. As we were going to cross the equator, we needed to be able to reverse the polarity of the coil.'

On 7 April the convoy headed south again towards the equator which was reached on 9 April. On the Empress of Canada the Court of King Neptune assembled to sentence those 'Crossing the Line' for the first time to a bath in a brine tub for some imagined transgression such as looking at the legs of one of the King's 'daughters.' The shells of halved coconuts, plus the coir from the husk transformed some shorter, squat sailors into unlikely maidens.

To refuse a kiss earned a dunking. To laugh might merit the smile being scrubbed away with a deck brush. Many of the company escaped this ritual humiliation as they were given 'very important tasks' by their maritime colleagues. But they heard all about it from those who had attended as courtiers for King Neptune.

Cape Town

As the convoy approached The Cape it divided. Half of the convoy was destined for the ill-fated defence of Singapore and moved on to Durban but the Empress of Canada docked at Cape Town. They approached the port as the new day was dawning. The site was unforgettable. 'The sun was rising above the Table Mountain with its cloth of clouds resting on it' recalls Bob. Bill too recalls the thrill he felt when he saw the frill of clouds lit by the rising sun on Table Mountain.

Docking a convoy seemed to take a very long time. They hung about the stern or sides as the flagship was slowly manoeuvred up to a berth. The procedures lasted until mid-afternoon.

To their surprise and pleasure, they were told that they would all be given shore leave. This was to be the start of a remarkable wartime friendship. Bob Borthwick and Cliff Barren wasted no time in preparing to test their land legs again. They showed their shore passes at the dock gate and stepped out for town but were approached by a gentleman who introduced himself as Mr Vye.

He invited them to be his guests for the duration of their stay. He explained that he ran an advertising agency which he was leaving his sons to run. The amazed soldiers readily accepted this generous and unexpected offer and climbed aboard his De Soto limousine.

South Africa was a country divided in many different ways. Both soldiers noted the signs listing facilities for *Whites Only* or *Blacks Only*. They had been warned about this aspect of the country and had been told to make no comment. They were also told to watch out for enemy agents.

The country was home to a large population of Germanic origin. The Boers made little secret of their sympathy to the Germans in their war against the British. This tension was resolved by interning many Boers and sometime whole families for the duration of the war.

Mindful of this espionage warning, the visitors were initially suspicious. However, the blatant way that they were approached and the number of other cars waiting outside the port, rather like a taxi rank, persuaded Bob and Cliff that they were not being seduced by a spy.

After a tour of the town they went to their host's home for lunch to meet the family. After three days of feasting and soft living at the Vye's home, they were driven back to the dock gates just in time for the 11 p.m. curfew. They went aboard loaded with fruit, magazines and memories of selfless hospitality. The generosity did not end with their departure. The Vye's said they would send food parcels to their wives regularly, a promise which they honoured.

Bill Harvey had a similar experience. 'I remember Russ Starr and I left the ship with the intention of a saunter round the town, just sightseeing and shop window gazing. There was no black-out in this part of the world and we could enjoy walking in the glorious street lighting and looking at the astounding array of goods in the shop windows. Suddenly a car drew up at the kerbside and a gentleman asked if we would like to go to his house for supper. This was an invitation we couldn't resist. After enjoying an excellent meal and talking with him and his charming wife, he returned us to the ship with a further invitation to join them the following day.'

'After so long on army food and only each others company this was luxury indeed. The man was of Danish extraction while his wife was a descendant of the original Dutch settlers. Fortunately for us one of the ships developed a fault so we had three days ashore. Our hosts took us further afield to see farms and the countryside. Before we left them on the last day, we told them we had been overwhelmed by their kindness and generosity, which greatly exceeded anything that we had received in our own country. They explained that it was part of a general campaign, instituted by the people of Cape Town, hoping that the recipients of their hospitality might be encouraged to emigrate to South Africa when the war was over. However, whatever their motives, we were very grateful.'

The shrunken convoy was joined by the aircraft carrier HMS Eagle whose role was to provide cover from U-boats which had claimed several victims around the Cape. They sailed on 20 April with their final destination still unknown. They spent the following days comparing stories of the wonders experienced at the foot of Table Mountain.

A few days later, the convoy split again with several troopships and freighters heading towards India. The rest of the convoy moved up the east coast of Africa. It was now safe to assume that the destination would be Egypt. During this leg of the voyage the alarming news of the loss of HMS Hood to a well-aimed salvo from the Bismarck was received. Bismarck had escaped to the open sea they had recently passed through and they were thankful to be half a world away. However, within three days the Bismarck itself was on the bottom. This news was greeted with delight and the surviving provisions gifted in Cape Town provided the ingredients for a few parties, made the merrier by the bottles smuggled aboard.

Port Tufik

The final destination was Port Tufik at the southern end of the Suez Canal which they reached on the evening of 5 May after forty nine days at sea. It was dark as the liner manoeuvred and tied up. At dawn the following day people were anxious to view their new home since they had been told nothing of their destination. They were amazed to be greeted by the sight of the two great passenger liners, the Queen Mary and Queen Elizabeth already docked.

These liners had arrived the day before loaded with reinforcements from Australia and New Zealand. Both 'Queens' were now troopships that employed their speed and unpredictable course to defeat pursuers.

The simultaneous arrival of so many personnel had overwhelmed the port facilities and so 106 had to wait two long, sticky days to disembark. The company set foot in Egypt on 8 May 1941. Leaving one section as a baggage party, the rest were moved by train to Cairo.

There were mixed emotions as they exchanged their floating home for the scorching barren landscape of the Suez Canal area. Before they left many of the sappers were given some duty free from the ship's issue cigarettes as a reward for the help they had given the ship's staff.

There was a sad footnote to this journey. After two more years working as a troopship, SS Empress of Canada was hit by a torpedo on the night of 13 March 1943 when travelling unescorted approaching the equator (01,12 S 09, 57 W). It was one of the rare occasions when an unescorted liner moving along its zigzag course at 18 _ knots was sunk by U-boats. The survivors had been adrift for twenty four hours before help arrived. All the boats and rafts were cleared and casualties were mercifully light although nine of the Italian prisoners died after rescue having survived thirty six hours in the water.

Chapter Six

Cairo and Alex

May – July 1941

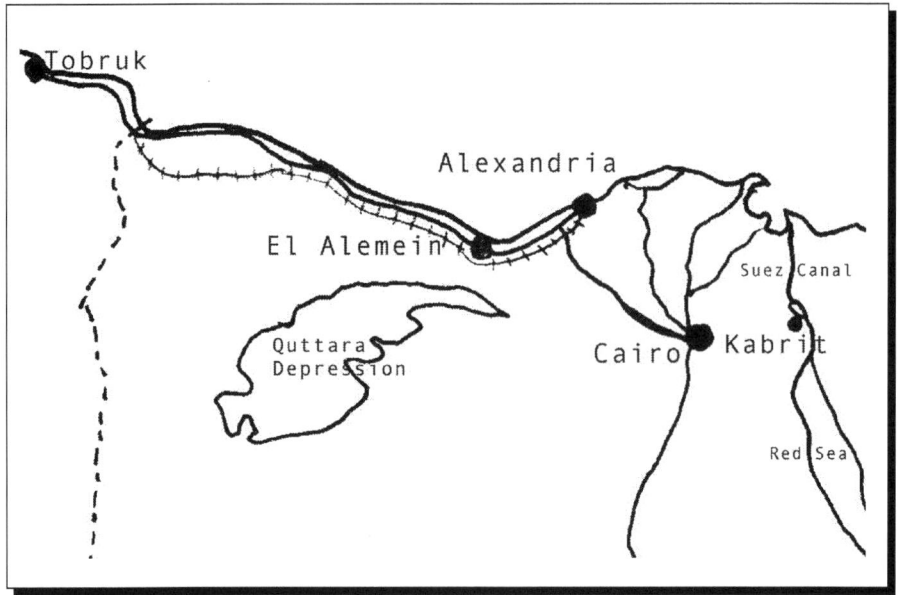

Map of North Africa

The company arrived too late for their planned task in Crete but were gainfully employed after a month acclimatising and sight-seeing. The war in the desert was going well but Rommel, who had chased the company out of France, was arriving to reinforce their Italian allies.

Bill Harvey was not impressed.

'So here we were in Egypt, apparently a land of great beauty. Its charm was not evident to us as we sat in the heat at the smelly dock waiting hours for a train that would take us somewhere else just as uncomfortable.' Nobody pretended that there was any sort of timetable. 'When we did get on the train it was like the "slow boat to China." Each time it stopped there was always a crowd of natives tapping at the window and seeking to sell us things.'

The most popular line was a quarter bottle of whisky. The hawkers were keen to show us that the seal was intact and it contained liquid. A few succumbed to greed or curiosity and naturally the native disappeared as soon as the transaction was completed. The victims discovered the bottle contained a liquid of very dubious quality. Bill had heard the tale many times and always told about the friend of a friend.

It was a hot and miserable journey. The novelty of the country compensated for some of the discomfort. As they lumbered away from the canal zone, the children took up the more honest trade of scrounging. They ran beside the train shouting their few words of English. The cry was for cigarettes. In exchange the children began to teach the soldiers the essential vocabulary of their country.

Baksheesh was their first word. The children held up coins and gestured the soldiers to throw coins to them. 'Fleuce' would soon be added to the vocabulary meaning 'loose change.' When the company became an employer of local labour the vocabulary increased. 'Naafi-egg-box' sufficed as the Arabic for thank you.

Alan Jones had made some progress with French when the company was in Brittany. He had regularly employed local labourers or craftsmen and he also had to seek out local materials. However, most sappers adopted familiar transliterations. 'Silver-plate' replaced *s'il vous plais* for the French expression for 'please.' Alan discovered that his smattering of French would serve him in this new land where many workmen had also picked up a few words of the language.

The company reached Cairo in the late afternoon and were transferred by lorry to the tented transit camp at Mena, situated west of the city with the pyramids in the background. The military system had re-learnt the lesson of past campaigns and recognised the need to provide soldiers with the time to get used to the heat and a meagre water ration. Two weeks were allowed for their bodies to adapt to their new environment.

Acclimatisation

The four mile march from the drop off point to their new home near Gaza was part of the acclimatisation. It was one of the few times they marched during the heat of the day as they learned to respect its intensity. The unaccustomed heat was not the only problem. The stomachs of 106 proved particularly susceptible to the native bugs. On 16 June the company diary records that one fifth was in hospital with stomach disorders. All recovered and soon developed a degree of immunity to the local bugs.

Mema was tented transit-accommodation situated in a wadi. The wadi was a dry river bed, like a miniature valley, with high sand dunes on all sides. It was not far from the famous Mema Hotel where affluent visitors to the pyramids and the Sphinx stayed. This was the story book desert of rich golden sand. This was the desert they recognised from the movies. Throughout their later travels they would not view such an idyllic piece of desert-scape. The reality would be rocky, rough and dusty.

Bill found himself back on medical duties for a time. 'Some of the worst cases I had to deal with were from individuals who went to Cairo on the local train. It was common to get an electric shock entering or leaving this ramshackle conveyance. I had several cases where men had hold of the handrail when leaving the train. As they touched the ground they got a proper electric shock which not only burnt their hand but caused an open wound further up the arm.' They quickly learnt to jump from the train, touching nothing on the way.

Once again the company was waiting. This was always frustrating. No one was allowed to know where they were going. One rumour had it that they had been destined for Crete. But by the time they were ready to move, Crete had fallen to the Germans so new plans had to be made. The German parachute army had temporarily put them out of a job. It was a lucky escape. Another hasty evacuation saved fourteen thousand but the same quantity of freshly arrived troops was captured.

Inactivity followed their acclimatisation. Early in June Major Yates took one of the two vehicles assigned to the company and paid a call on the HQ in Alexandria to request some work for his little, forgotten force of engineers. The Army HQ had more pressing concerns following the fall of the Balkans than the fate of a company of sappers assigned to them. It did allow some to wander from the wadi to do some sightseeing.

In the company of Stan Fox and Billie Cracknall, Bill Harvey went to explore the pyramids. Armed with a torch they were able to go inside to the burial chamber of one of the pyramids. They clambered over the Sphinx and had the whole episode recorded by a photographer who was on hand for those wanting a camel ride. Bill remembers it as a wonderful and awesome experience. 'On reflection, it was a one of the most wonderful experiences in our lives.'

The pyramids and the Sphinx provided the engineers with hours of amazed speculation. As experts in construction, none of them could come up with a satisfactory solution to how the massive stones could have been shaped and dropped into position.

6.1 & 6.2 & 6.3
While their skin adapted to the sun and their stomachs to local conditions there was time to explore the local sights while high command, focused on driving the Italians out of Africa, looked for suitable tasks for their craftsmen.

Bob Borthwick was put off trips into Cairo by the number of smartly dressed base personnel who seemed to fill the city. This made him feel uncomfortable.

One morning Alan Jones was detailed to gather some electricians for a job the staff in Cairo had found for them. Bill Harvey was among those nominated to go with the electricians. The company would now be split into three working parties. Two sections under SSgt Alan Jones were to go to Buselli where a new hospital was under construction.

The mechanical section led by Bob Borthwick was to take over a workshop in Alexandria and with it some proper accommodation. The HQ section moved on to Amiriya, another uncomfortable transit camp. There was little motor transport spare so they were ferried to the railhead for a move, with all their modest stores and equipment, to travel to their new places of work.

There were twelve electricians and representatives of most other construction trades in the sections headed by Alan Jones. From the railhead somewhere in the desert they were loaded into three ton lorries and set off for another unknown destination. The army was economical with information. Often the drivers were ignorant of their destination and had no maps. They just followed the vehicle in front.

This allowed ample scope among soldiers in the back to speculate. Would they turn west and head for the front or go east for the base area? It was oddly empowering to attempt to predict their destination even though they were powerless to influence it. 'We soon left the confines of Cairo, proceeding north and passing through agricultural areas not looking much like English farms.' Their destination could still be the desert war.

'The next major conurbation turned out to be Alexandria, which looked very clean and smart, compared to Cairo. We didn't stop but proceeded on our way and there was now distinct change in the scenery. No longer did we see the magical quality of sand dunes surrounding Cairo but a scrub landscape and a country road interspersed with small villages.'

They were now in Delta country. 'We established later that it was the coast road, which ran along the Mediterranean coast line to Musa Matri, Tobruk and beyond.' It looked as if they were off to war. Soon they came to the small, crowded village, of Buselli. This was their destination. About half a mile beyond the village, was an extensive arena that had been cleared of rocks which a bulldozer had built into neat walls. Here, a large hospital was in the course of construction.

Buselli

The existing six hundred bed hospital was nearing completion. There had been significant labour problems with the contractor which was stalling the plan to double the size of Buselli hospital. The source of the problem was friction between the local workforce and the soldiers overseeing them. In the four months that Alan's men were at work no labour problems were recorded among the construction teams.

Life at Buselli had just two drawbacks. The first was mosquitoes. 'We had a marquee to house the twenty of us and we fed with the medics. We had captured Italian cots to sleep on. Each cot had its own mosquito net and part of standard orders was that the net was to be properly tucked in by sundown. Also included in these orders, was the instruction that our shorts designed with a turn-up should be turned down as a further guard against mosquitoes' Bill recalls.

The second problem was discipline which was surprisingly strict among the medics. Bill had cause to remember. 'One of their officers was a proper pig who seemed to take an instinctive dislike to us engineers.

'One of his foibles was to inspect the tents each night to make sure the mosquito nets were properly fitted. One night he caught us with one of the nets up so the lads could play cards. Naturally he collared me as the NCO in charge and told me to report to the orderly room next morning.

'I reported next morning, and was waiting to be called, when our boss Staff Sergeant Alan Jones arrived and glanced at us. I didn't say anything because he seemed to be in a terrible rage and who could blame him. When the call came for me to march in he told me to stand fast and he went in himself.'

The orderly room was just a tent and with flaps up to allow ventilation so everyone could watch what transpired. 'He certainly had a field day. I was so proud of him. He told the officer that if he didn't drop this ridiculous charge, he would report to the Chief Medical Officer, remove all the engineering staff from the site and bring the whole matter to the attention of the Chief Engineer Officer in Cairo.' In the face of this threat the officer was quick to climb down and they had no further trouble during their stay at Buselli.

'The prevailing condition was extremely hot. Even natives were dying of heat-stroke' recalls Bill. The proximity of the sea did nothing to reduce the temperature. 'It was now mid June and although we had managed to get rid of the terrible pith helmets we'd carried all the way from England, they had been replaced by a lighter Indian pattern head-dress. The heat was still well nigh unbearable and to think that a few months previously we had been training in thick snow of Scotland.'

The tropical dress was a drill shirt and shorts, with the standard army boots and knee length stockings and short puttees which were wound round the top of the boot in regulation fashion. The medical staff and nurses were already established in tented accommodation with separate compounds for the nurses' accommodation and the operating theatres.

Alan Jones briefed them on the layout of the hospital. It was three parallel facilities. One was designated for Indian personnel, another for the colonial contingents and one hospital was for British troops. This roughly represented the contribution each was making to the desert war at the time.

The wards were being constructed by native labour under the supervision of a Greek overseer. Each ward was about 50 foot long, twenty foot wide and the sides approximately ten foot high with window apertures. The whole structure was topped with a semi-circular roof which gave a remarkable spacious and airy atmosphere inside. The huts were cool and constructed using local techniques and materials. Each panel was pre-fabricated by working a liquid plaster into a mat of reeds. They were cast in metal formers with reeds worked into the wet plaster by the hands and feet of the workforce. The result was strong, light and kept out the terrible heat.

When a panel was removed from its mould its colour was pinky-white, giving a very pleasing appearance, both inside and outside. A few of the wards were already complete when they arrived so the fitting out work could begin immediately.

The first task was to obtain a link from the local 11 kilovolt overhead power line that ran parallel to the road and railway line strategically alongside the hospital site but on the opposite side. This necessitated the establishment of an electrical sub-station in the centre of the hospital area from which low voltage lines could radiate to the various buildings. Life at Buselli was professionally very satisfying.

The team that broke records at Bellahouston Park were quickly into their stride. Split into two gangs they wired the existing huts, training the local labour to cleat the wires to the reed and plaster walls. Next they turned to the overhead line. One of the difficulties encountered was that the English climbing irons depended on spurs digging into the pole. This was all right in England, where the poles were heavily creosoted, which made the skin soft enough for the spur to penetrate. Egyptian poles, baked by a fierce sun, were hard as rock. They could not scale the poles with the climbing irons they had brought.

Fortunately, someone found a store of Italian climbing irons. These had a serrated semi-circular blade which went round the pole. For men who had never done any work up poles before, adopting a new design of climbing iron was taken in their stride. Stan Rogers was used to this work and quickly taught Bill what was required. 'If someone had told me a few years before that I would find myself climbing a 35 foot pole and working for an hour or two I would have laughed at them, but this was army life. We did lot of jobs we weren't used to.'

Bill had three or four locals in his team to lay out and pull the cables. 'One thing I can remember with affection was that all the native labourers knew me as 'Umbasha Bill.' Umbasha was the equivalent rank to a corporal in the Egyptian army.' It sounded good. The bad feeling, walk-outs and suspected sabotage of equipment ceased to be a feature of this construction site.

6.4 Working at Buselli:
The labour-force for the technicians was found locally. Before the company arrived, there were many reports of unrest and sabotage by local labour but relationships while working with the company were excellent. A supply of sweet, local tea was provided at regular intervals, served on a tray.

6.5
Part of the hospital at Buselli. *(Photo from press cutting – origin unknown)*

As the work was going well their Boss, Alan Jones let them take a three ton lorry into Alexandria to visit the NAAFI for a change of scenery and a meal on Sundays. But it was too far away to leave enough time to explore the city. It was not unusual to encounter a shower of stones as they passed through the small villages en route. So, some preferred to enjoy their limited time off to relax at Buselli.

Alan Jones knew how to put on a good show. When they were ready for the big 'switch-on' he chose dusk as the time to demonstrate their handiwork to the assembled medics and the local workforce. Alan led a few of the team round the camp, putting the fuses in as the tension among their audience mounted. As they left, each ward burst into light to the delight and appreciation of the residents.

The moment was not without some tension for Alan. He had ordered up the required length of heavy duty cable he required which had been cut with not an inch to spare. This was not itself a disaster but the ends had been left unprotected, damaging the cable's insulation. According to the book, the end should have been cut off and discarded but there was no leeway.

Much to Alan's relief, the cable took the load. To celebrate, Alan bought everybody a bottle of beer. 'Since I was not used to drinking, having drunk half the bottle it made my eyes shine like big lamps' Bill recalls.

6.6
The Electrical and Mechanical section pose for a photo after the successful commissioning of the lighting and electrical supply to the hospital at Buselli.

Meanwhile in Alexandria

Bob Borthwick arrived with his team in Alexandria. From the station in Alex, the mechanical section was delivered by lorry to a block of flats in Rue Prince Abdul Monheim in the north-west outskirts of the city.

The street consisted of Italian houses, shops and factories, now deserted as the owners had fled or been interned. Their new home was an ideal base for engineers. The ground floor was the workshop and office. The machine shop was reminiscent of an old Yorkshire mill shop driven by overhead belts. Above it were eight floors of luxurious flats. The only occupant was the original foreman, a friendly Maltese known as Joseph, who had been left to look after the machinery.

There is no law that says soldiers have to be uncomfortable. When such an opportunity presented itself they took full advantage. The first floor was given over to the Officers Mess for its sole resident, Lt Tony Lumkin with space for the other company officers visiting Alex. The next floor was divided between the three Sergeants plus enough space for a mess. The section had the run of the remaining floors. This was unaccustomed luxury.

The first soldierly priorities were to sort out the bed space and feeding. As they did not have much use for their three experts in concrete mixing and laying at the time they were appointed cooks. Their expertise as mixers extended well beyond concrete. There were no complaints with their appointment and the 'cooks' were happy with the routine and freedom offered.

Bob took charge of inspecting the beds. He had been in Singapore earlier in his military career and picked up some tips on how to detect and if necessary dispose of bed bugs. There was plenty of evidence of and infestation by bugs which would now be hungry for a meal. Joseph was able to produce a blowlamp from the workshop. The skilful incineration began.

When Sam returned with the rations he ordered all the section to carry out the 'debugging' on all the bedsteads. The smell of hot wood and metal mixed with the singed mattress masking the early attempts of the caterers.

Joseph, the caretaker, was added to the army payroll. He lived with his wife and children in a flat across the road. As well as a skilled machinist he could speak fluent Arabic, and good English. His advice would also prove invaluable in keeping the old, unfamiliar machines functioning.

His stream of colloquial invective was effective at keeping unwanted local visitors away. He franchised an Arab peddler with a cart, selling iced tea and lemonade to be stationed in the street outside the workshop. He also kept them supplied with safe, filtered water and ice for their refrigerators. Charging one piastre a glass, the peddler made a good profit from the workshop and surrounding area. Soon the franchise expanded to include water melon slices. The monopoly was maintained by imposing a ban on eating or drinking anything from the other carts. Consequently few suffered with the uncomfortable 'gippy tummy' that upset so many soldiers.

Things got even better when space was found for a couple of dhobi boys to wash and iron their clothes. Under the watchful eye of the cooks, the boys would wash starch and iron for two piastres per item. Their 'barrack' block was an enclave set in the Arab town that was otherwise 'out of bounds' to troops. The road was busy during the day with traffic of donkey and carts passing from the Arab quarter to trade in the town. Whole families, with father riding the donkey, mother and children following on foot, caused amusement at first. The rider perched precariously on the donkey's haunches looking liable to fall off at any moment.

There was plenty of call for the company's engineering skills. They would install machines for a planned expansion of the Wardian Ordnance workshop complex for tank and vehicle repair on the western outskirts of the town. Their other task was everything else that required their special skills.

The 7th Armoured Division, now renamed the 'Desert Rats', had returned to the Delta after pushing the Italians out of Egypt to regroup and take over their new tanks. They brought with them a mass of older tanks and vehicles recovered from the desert awaiting repair.

The new tanks needed desert proofing, particularly to excluded dust from the engine and improve cooling. The abrasive desert dust turned a tank's engine oil into a fine grinding compound. As a result any pistons and connecting rods bathed in this muddy oil were quickly ground down. These engine failures could render a tank's engine useless after a few weeks in the desert. The pistons could be fitted with new sealing rings but the connecting rods were a problem. The repair entailed boring out of the worn white metal, of the big-end bearing and recasting new metal in place. This was a factory job but the factory was a convoy journey away in England. In the meantime, the fighting vehicles would be out of action.

Corporal Stan Fox, a sheet metal worker by trade, was used to working with solder. His services were suggested as a possible solution. He soon became proficient pouring white metal and his failure rate for rebuilds soon dropped to zero. Assisted by Bill Cracknell, he set up a 'production line' at the far end of the workshop turning useless metal into usable connecting rods. The workshop at Wardian was soon refitting working motors in the tanks.

Other minor miracles were being performed with milling machines repairing gears. This team was Joe and Bill Richards. The latter would build up or replace broken teeth as he had seen welders do at Yorkshire Main Colliery in Doncaster. Joe would machine the gears to their original shape. This work would keep the antique milling machinery in their workshop busy all day and often into the night.

Bill Richards was another quick learner. His pit trade union forbade him to do any welding in his civilian job. Such job demarcations were not uncommon among industrial trades from which the company recruited. One sheet-plate welder who had joined them at Stonehaven claimed it would be a waste of time learning new skills: He was an oxyacetylene welder and his union would never agree to him also using an electric-welder. But the improvisation ethos took over and he soon mastered arc welding.

The reluctant learner came in to his own, when two Greek pilots appeared at the workshop with two burnt out exhaust manifolds. After the fall of Greece, many Greek Air Force pilots had escaped to Egypt and had been flying some older planes on reconnaissance missions. There were no spare parts for their old planes and their ground crew had not been able to patch the holes burned in the manifold, thus grounding the aircraft.

The plate welder agreed to have a go and with his expertise with thin plate and a delicate touch, he successfully patched the hole in one manifold by taking a patch from the other. The pilots were delighted and another stream of work was established keeping the vestigial Greek Air Force airborne.

While these 'stars' undertook these special repairs, the rest of the section was busy repairing the old and installing the new machinery at the Wardian Ordnance base.

The local Stores Officer also turned to them to ask when a stock of metal in an Egyptian store yard was up for sale. Bill Richards and Bob Borthwick went along armed with a portable electric grinding-wheel, files and a hacksaw. The odd lengths of rod and bar had been roughly sorted and inaccurately labelled.

The material was discreetly tested and tool steel, cast iron rod, phosphor bronze and duralumin were all identified. The British Army acquired a valuable stock of special metals all of which were in short supply. Bob was an expert at doing deals and the Stores Officer returned the favour and remained a valuable source of supply whatever they needed.

Bob was also a bit of an inventor. A number of broken 'Universal Type Sun Compasses' was offered for possible repair. These sun compasses were issued along with a complicated sheet of instructions to facilitate cross-desert navigation. Accurate use depended on latitude and longitude, date and time, and reference to tables and curves that, once understood, were an accurate means of direction finding in the desert.

With a few modifications Bob realised a simpler but marginally less accurate version of the compass could be made. This would require only minor corrections every few days plus an occasional check with a magnetic compass. In anticipation of a possible move into the desert Bob kept a number of the simplified sun compasses to mount on their own vehicles in due course. His foresight would be rewarded.

The mechanical section remained busy during the hot, summer months taking advantage of the cool hours after dawn for heavy work. The evenings were often spent in their antique workshop attempting some new repair. They were long days, fuelled by a plentiful supply of cold water, fresh fruit and excellent food from the 'mixers.'

There was time off which they were happy to spend in the cool luxury of their flats. On Saturday nights the Metro cinema or the YMCA provided attractions. On Sunday the Section would head for bingo. Four at a time would pile in to a horse drawn carriage meant for two and take the five piastres ride to the Union Jack Club.

The bingo was always well attended because girls were allowed in. There was a large contingent of expatriate Europeans in cosmopolitan Alex. Both clubs were run by volunteer ladies who, more or less, chaperoned the girls but the troops were well behaved. Nobody wanted to spoil this oblique contact with normal life by rowdy behaviour. Bob's 'sergeant-majorly' voice plus his smattering of French earned him the part time job of calling the numbers.

In the middle of June, the first mail since the sad partings in Stonehaven three months earlier reached them. Much had happened since March. A hush fell over the flats as letters were read and re-read. Good and bad news was shared. The meanings of words, phrases and what was left unsaid was discussed.

It was impossible to escape the subdued atmosphere as the remembrance of the months missed was quietly re-lived. For a week the evenings were quiet. The men looked for the right phrase to fit the limited space of an airgraph. With so many questions to ask and answer, and such limited news permitted by the censor, words had to be carefully weighed. It could take an evening or more to compose a letter as they struggled to express their thoughts and feelings in words that would not embarrass them when they thought of any intimate words being read by a censor.

At the end of the month Bob's first parcel from the Vyes in Cape Town arrived, containing cigarettes and chocolate. This was quickly followed by another parcel from Wynne with a belated birthday cake. The parcel from the Vyes became a fortnightly supply of quality cigarettes. He would in time learn that his wife too, was receiving regular food parcels from the Vyes in South Africa.

The war was never far away with frequent night-time air raids aimed at the ships in the harbour. Anti-aircraft fire was provided by Egyptian army guns. It did not seem to be very effective and it was necessary for the HQ Section at Amiriya to take cover from the falling shrapnel which arched over Alex and showered their fragile tented camps.

The heaviest raid occurred on Saturday 7 June 1941, when a land-mine fell on Rue de Soeur, the local red light area of Alexandria, a few hundred yards behind the flats. The flats shook in the blast and all the back windows were blown in. Everyone was up and dressed to offer help, not realising that it was 'Sister Street.' The devastation was equal to any Bob had seen in the London blitz but enough help was on hand so they returned to clear up their flats.

By the end of the month the air raids became so regular that a civilian exodus began. The trains left the station with carriages festooned with natives on the roof and hanging on wherever there was a tenuous hand or foot hold. The labour shortage became acute but this time these skilled tradesmen would not be employed as porters. But it was nearly time for the company to move on to another task.

The rest of the company had been less fortunate in their accommodation. The HQ and two sections had moved from the reception camp at Mena on 24 May to Amiriya, a large tented transit camp on the western outskirts of Alexandria. Their first job was to prepare the camp for the Australian and New Zealand troops evacuated after the fall of Crete.

The 'Plant Men' were being kept busy. As the bombing raids on the base area in Alex increased, the company were called in to repair or remove the damaged sheds. During June they applied their experience gained in constructing sheds in France and Scotland to de-construct the sheds damaged during the heavy raids of 5 June and re-cycle the materials to fix others.

The local command was so impressed with the effectiveness of the company's work that a demonstration was organised for local contractors and other military men on 17 June. The company did not employ explosives or cut the metal-work up. Instead they disconnected a few key components and then collapsed the structure with the aid of a few trucks and tow ropes. Their technique sometimes permitted the contents of the shed to be recovered.

The second of July brought an abrupt order to collect construction equipment, and move into the desert to make a start on some defensive construction work. For those in the crowded and uncomfortable tents for six weeks, news that they appeared to be heading towards the front was almost welcome.

6.7
The senior ranks pose for a photo at Kabrit where they are undertaking commando training at the HMS Saunders, the combined operation training centre. They were part of the original conception of what became the Special Air Service. Unlike their normal routine as engineers and craftsmen, which kept them busy all day, the company discovered that soldiering involved a lot of hanging about.

Chapter Seven

El Alamein

July – October 1941

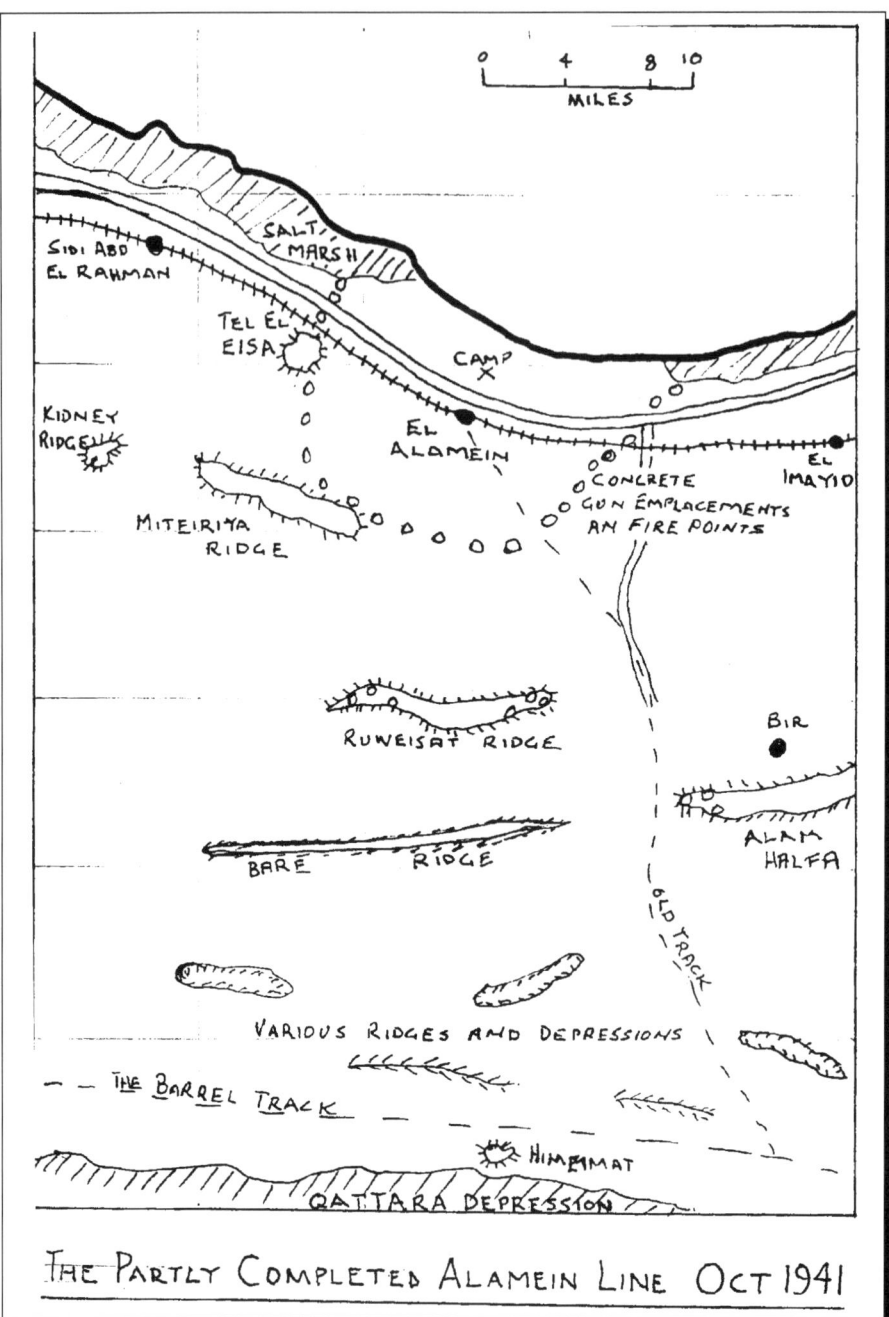

Map of the early defences around El Alamein
A sketch map produced by Bob Borthwick of the defences prepared at a convenient rail
halt north of the Quattara Depression but with handy access to the sea for a swim after a
hot day's work.

On 2 July the advanced party set out. The company's task was to prepare an army-sized defensive position. This, they were told, would involve quarrying road-making materials and preparing roads suitable for heavy traffic and armour, and constructing defensive positions.

El Alamein was the name of an insignificant railway halt some sixty miles out in the desert to which they set out in July 1941. The place would, in time, give its name to the battle which Churchill styled 'The end of the beginning.' But when the advance party arrived it was just another piece of dusty desert.

The Desert War had seen both sides make spectacular advances which were lost when supply lines and equipment became overstretched. El Alamein was eventually to become the 'line in the sand', the barrier that had to be held in order to keep the Allies in North Africa.

Bob saw the plans prepared by General Wavell's staff in September 1940 when he was fighting to save Greece, Iraq and North Africa for the Allies with his meagre force. A final line of defence was designed to protect his overstretched army if it was attacked while the troops were deployed in another theatre. It was a sensible precaution. A modest force should be able to hold a well-prepared defence until a counter force could be assembled and deployed.

General Wavell had observed the success of the blitzkrieg operations in Europe and in August 1940 noted that 'further instructions will be issued about defence based on KAFR, EL DAUWAR.' This was very much the final line of defence protecting the Nile Delta. The Delta was traditional defensive terrain crossed with numerous bridges and with land that could be flooded. But this was not the area to which the advance party set out in their search for a suitable place to unload their heavy equipment.

As the troops available had built up during 1941, so did the need to expand the area they could secure. A decision was made to move the line further west to provide space for the Eighth Army should it ever have to retreat from its position four hundred miles east, poised to sweep on through Libya to Tunisia. The line was just a sensible, military precaution on which these army troop engineers could be temporarily employed.

Bob recalls his first journey into the desert. They passed through fig plantations as they climbed out of the fertile delta. As they ascended the ridge, the view was of salt flats that stretched towards the sea on their right and sand dunes fringing the desert to the left. When they reached the ridge the road ran straight and parallel with the railway across a barren rock-strewn desert. The transition was dramatic.

Bob continued along the rail track with the recce officer. They passed several halts. They were attracted to Fuka, a significant halt to the west which was also well sited for defence. Time was pressing as the train loaded with the company and their first equipment could arrive soon and they would not be allowed to block the line for long to unload equipment. So they settled on the halt at El Alamein as their base. To the south rose an impressive escarpment which ran along many sections of the coast. Beyond the Miteiria Ridge and the larger Ruweisat Ridge was a basin of loose sand which would be a trap for vehicles. Quattara Depression was a vast area of shifting sand which made it impossible to use tracked and heavy trucks. Rommel made a habit of going in to the desert to bypass previous defensive lines. If the enemy wanted to win through to the Delta area it must pass through the El Alamein gap.

But it was currently Rommel's turn to retreat. He had spent his main effort attempting to dislodge the Australians besieged in Tobruk. He desperately wanted another port for his supplies. With an effective naval blockade around Bengahzi, his logistics overstretched, Rommel was on the defensive.

Just before they set out from Alex, the company learned the exciting news that the Germans had invaded their erstwhile ally, Russia. This engendered a hope that military support might be diverted from Rommel and the side-show in North Africa. If the 15 Panzer Division was starved of replacement after their failure to take Tobruk there was a real chance they could win through here. 'With this hope, coupled with a similar hope of a victory in the battle taking place up in the desert, we set to packing up for our move' Bob Borthwick later noted in his diary.

There was just one solid building and an assortment of small out buildings at El Alamein when they arrived. Certainly not enough space to house the company. The decision was made to establish their base on the seaward side of the railway line. It afforded access to the sea which was rare along the coast, he noted.

Bob mused on the purpose of this deserted station as he waited for the company to arrive. It appeared to have no reason to exist. He had not seen any signs of life for ten miles either way. The only residents were flies that plagued them whenever they stood still in the limited shade available.

It was July and the sun was at its hottest. Although new to the desert, conditions there caused few cases of sunburn or heat exhaustion. The long sea trip and the time at Amiriya had acclimatized them. Their heavy Wellington helmets had been withdrawn and everyone was issued with a pith helmet which was a lighter and more comfortable sun hat. Overalls were abandoned in favour of shorts and helmet as working dress. Even army boots were discarded in favour of sandals purchased in Alex. Bob bought himself a pair of sand-boots unofficially reserved for officers and perhaps for that reason known universally as 'brothel creepers.'

Visits to Alexandria or Cairo still demanded the restoration of proper, uniform dress as both destinations swarmed with those whose job was to enforce the dress rules. As the sun moved back south, the weather cooled, making work more pleasant. By September, everyone changed back into overalls, with their battledress beneath when the wind brought a chill and many small sandstorms.

Another way to defeat the heat was to dig the tents in. The sand was just two feet deep and the rock they reached provided a good base and revealed less canvas for the sun to beat on. This arrangement also kept the temperature stable in the cold desert nights and went down well with inspecting offers who noted that they were 'dug in.'

Between the rail line, the coast road and the sea were extensive salt marshes with small, saline lakes. An occasional causeway of sand led down to the shore. The camp was pitched on a prominent sand bar giving easy access to the beach for a refreshing swim after work. Every day there was a chance to cool off and wash in the sea before dinner. There was a pathway through the salt flats leading down to a passable beach. Bob laughed when he read that Lady Astor was complaining in the House of Commons that 'Our troops are lounging on the beaches of the Mediterranean.'

The flies waited for them whenever they took shelter from the sun in the tents. It was almost a relief to get to work in the heat as the flies did not follow. After dark, the sand flies took over and scorpions prowled the ground hunting their prey. These sandy coloured pests delivered a nasty, but not fatal, nip. Going barefoot was not an option.

The first working day was spent marking out where roads could be built to ring the strong points round El Alamein. Their long expected transport also began to arrive. Along with their small fleet of lorries came some Canadian built, Dodge utility trucks. Bob was particularly pleased with his two workshop lorries.

The larger was made by Dennis and came with a heavy DC generator for welding and many other purposes. It had a lathe, saw, drill and blacksmith's workshop. The smaller workshop vehicle was on an American Ford chassis and also had a generator that proved powerful enough to run the machines and the lights in the camp when air raids were not expected. This was the workshop for finer work with another lathe and drill. Both vehicles came packed with tools.

The problem with these power-packed workshops was that they allowed little room to work and under the desert sun they would soon become ovens. Bob set off in one of the new trucks back to Alexandria to acquire the bits everybody needed to customise their workshop. Bob was soon back with tubular scaffolding and canvas.

A shaded workshop was created between the two vehicles where all the equipment, except the lathes would be set up. With the extra carrying capacity, Bob was able to expand his special reserve of metals. He also managed to acquire another power saw and the wood for extra workbenches. They were now open for business.

Work had to be suspended next day when a train arrived unannounced with three road rollers, two stone crushers, three sizable concrete mixers, six dumper trucks and a truck full of picks, shovels, buckets and barrows.

The valuable cargo sat blocking the line. There was no means to off-load it. They anticipated that some means would be provided on the train to assist with the offloading. What they really needed was some road-making equipment to build a ramp.

The train commander was unsympathetic. His train was packed with other valuable cargos that were expected further up the line at Mersa Matruh. An improvised platform was rapidly assembled using their precious supply of wood and stone. But the unloading ramp was just the first of their problems. Nobody had ever driven a road roller before.

While the ramp was rising to meet the train, they found and digested the operating manuals. There was some experimenting with the steering mechanism. The steering handle had to be rotated many times to nudge the large front roller. There was limited scope for experiment before the moment of truth arrived and the first, mighty road roller was edged off the rail car and on to the ramp.

It was a tense moment as the roller rocked, compacting the improvised ramp. With Bob at the wheel, the first and second rollers were successfully landed. The third machine might have defeated a less experienced operator. Bob tried to put it into gear but this proved impossible. 'It felt all wrong. The clutch felt like the brake on the other rollers. So I reversed the operation of the two pedals and persuaded the roller onto our ramp.' A proper inspection confirmed Bob's suspicion that the cables had been reversed. This was an ominous sign but nobody thought to institute further investigations at that stage.

Three permanent drivers were nominated and, after a short study of the manual, the rollers set off with their apprentices at the wheel. By the time they reached their camp, a kilometre away, they would be masters of their machines. The third roller had another surprise for them. Halfway to camp it came to an abrupt, grinding halt. The noise of grinding, rushing, cracking metal led Bob straight to the focus of the problem. A tommy bar, used to extract nails or lever heavy items into position was firmly wedged in the five-foot gear wheel.

The damage was substantial. There seemed little doubt that it was the result of deliberate sabotage. There had been many such reports of damage being done to equipment left unattended. There were two more immediate problems. The first was to get the roller back to camp. The second was to get everything ready for some VIPs due later that day. The first problem was solved with a tow rope but there seemed no way to resolve the problem of the missing teeth from the giant gear wheel.

The OC reported the problem to their visitors who had come to discuss the plan for the defences. To Bob's embarrassment his expert welder Bill Richards had told the VIPs he could fix the broken teeth if he was given some *Sifbronze* welding rods. Bob had no idea how they could heat the massive wheel in their small blacksmith furnace. However, he immediately backed his man against his better judgement.

Bill Richards had a cunning plan to bury the wheel in the sand which would insulate the wheel while they heated and repaired the broken teeth. The next day a dispatch rider duly appeared with a supply of the rods and Bill went to work. Once he had rebuilt the teeth, Bill Cracknell set to work with a file to shape the missing teeth. It took him two days to match the gears and reassemble the drive.

There were a few tense moments as the engine started and the clutch slowly released. There were some ghastly grinding noises but the roller moved off. A bit more oil was diagnosed to eliminate the grinding noise and road-roller number three went back to work.

Bob inspected the plan prepared for the Alamein 'box.' In April the staff of 50 Division had set out a plan for the defensive line. To the north, the coastal marshes formed an impassable barrier for troops and armour. In the south, the ridges would provide good defensive and observation positions. Construction began either side of the coast road about three miles to the west of the station at the point where the ridge that had carried the road from Cairo petered out. On their new maps the place was called Tel el Lisa but they all knew it as the 'rocky knoll.'

Exactly twelve months later, on 10 July 1942, the General Auchinleck would go on the offensive and launch the first battle of El Alamein. The defences at Tel el Lisa would see many weeks of fierce fighting as the Axis advance was arrested and forced on the defensive.

In the desert war, attack could come from any direction so all-round defence was essential. To the south east of their defences was a low ridge of rock, the Miteiriya Ridge, which would form the southern limit of the semi-circular 'box' centred on the station and looping round to end at the marsh, about two miles further east

Each 'box' had a string of strong points. These consisted of a circular defensive position connected to its neighbour by a trench. Concrete observation points were planned plus anti-tank gun pits. Rocks would be levelled to give a clear view for the gunners. The barbed-wire, tank traps and mine fields were marked on the plan but would be added by others if required.

The staff at HQ had attempted to get a design for the defences agreed among the units who might one day have to occupy them. Each unit had their own view on how a gun pit or trench should be built. Exasperated, one anonymous brigadier had appended the note to the latest design for an anti tank gun pit.

'My experience is that no artillery commanders, except those with whom it was worked out, will accept any design.' The message was clear. The company got on with the task of making defensive positions that fitted the terrain.

The next 'box' would be on the western edge of the Ruweisat Ridge. The plan indicated that the Alamein line was to continue south to the Quattara Depression with boxes on the ridges to cover the sand depressions in between. Tobruk had proved during 1941 that a desert defensive-line could be held, provided it was not by-passed.

For the next four months the company at El Alamein would survey and make roads, prepare harbour areas and build defensive positions. The entire complex had to be accurately mapped for the staff in Cairo. The soon-to-be-famous 'boxes' were then neatly filed away for use in an emergency. That emergency was less than a year away.

Alan Jones' team stayed at Buselli as the capacity of the hospital was doubled again. The team upgrading the Wardian repair facility would follow when their installation task was complete. By the end of July the whole of the mechanical section swapped their luxury accommodation in Alex for a tent, half buried in the desert.

While south of the ridge, pegging out the next stage of the track to be consolidated, Bob decided to take a look at the Qattara Depression. It meant following a poorly defined track south for another eight miles until they met a track running east-west marked on the map as the 'Barrel Track'. This was a better defined track, well used by the Arabs, running all the way back to Cairo, one hundred and fifty miles to the east.

'The Depression was a few miles further on and when we reached the edge, the view was breathtaking. The cliffs were very rugged and broken, dropping away some three hundred feet or more to a flat expanse of alternate patches of white and yellow as it glistened in the heat. These were obviously areas of salt marsh and quicksand which stretched to the horizon. What a desolate place it looked. The whole area of the Depression, all of it below sea level, stretched for two hundred miles south west where it met the Great Sand Sea at the Siwa oasis'

From Bob's viewpoint on the encompassing cliff, the Depression widened to over one hundred miles across. 'It was possible to cross on a narrow path, weaving between salt flats and quick sands, but it was impassable to any large force in either direction. It formed therefore, a perfect barrier to the south from Alamein and I was most impressed having had the opportunity to see it.'

The compressor truck and pneumatic drills were dispatched with a section to start work on the strong points. A stone crusher was towed very slowly along the marked-out road by a road-roller during the day. The stone crusher would prepare material for making concrete. The rough rock removed from the gun pits was fed straight into the stone cruncher and then on to the mixer before being formed in to an observation point. It was a virtuous cycle leaving no waste.

While this construction team worked around the station, the other crusher was dispatched to the Ruweisat Ridge. The desert there was covered with boulders that had been eroded from the ridge and could be turned into hard core for the road producing a good field of fire at the same time. The rock-strewn landscape might provide good cover for attacking soldiers.

A metalled road running south from the station behind the planned defences was a priority task. An experimental road was built to test the surface. Quarried limestone had been delivered by rail. On this well rolled surface, tarmac was laid using the local salt-sand. The surface was satisfactory but the limestone base quickly collapsed under lorries loaded with material. A second road using the locally crushed rock however stood up to the load.

One hundred Arabs were recruited to feed the two stone crushers, collecting the rocks, loading them into the crusher and then loading the trucks with the hard core. A lance corporal supervised each group of local labourers. The gang of local workers and their supervisors camped out on the Ruweisat Ridge to save time, with Bob arriving each day with fuel for man and machines.

Paddy Kelly, a regular sapper who had joined the company after France, was a happy-go-lucky Irishman in charge of the stone crusher near the Ruweisat Ridge. One day the ration truck brought a message from Paddy that the diesel engine on his stone crusher would not start. The output of these machines dictated the pace of their work so Bob set off to see what was wrong.

Paddy had filled up with diesel as usual to start the day but all he could get was a sucking noise out of the engine as he turned it over. A quick look at the injectors pointed to the likely cause. They were coated in dark oil, lubricating oil. A quick inspection confirmed Bob's diagnosis. 'The fuel tank was full of lubricating oil. The fuel tank was high on the crusher frame and he admitted he picked up the jerrycan which he thought held the diesel, and, reaching overhead, had poured it in without being able to see the result. I told him it was not his fault. It taught me the lesson to have the jerrycans marked for identification in future.' After a clean and flush, the crusher was back in action.

'Jerrycans' was the name given to the excellent containers supplied to the Afrika Korps but acquired in quantity by the Allies during their advances of 1941. They had a capacity of twenty litres which could just about be comfortably handled when full. The jerrycan was made of pressed steel, had a spring cap on a well designed pouring spout. They were even internally galvanizing which made it handy for carrying water.

The company obtained a few at Amiriya. The Germans marked water cans with a white marking. Bob now decided to extend the company's captured cans with red for petrol, green for oil, and yellow for diesel fuel. Apart from their individual water bottles they had to improvise containers to carry additional water so necessary in the desert, and the jerrycan was ideal for this purpose.

Petrol continued to be issued in the flimsy British, four gallon tin cans but immediately transferred to a jerrycan which unlike its counterpart, would not leak if roughly handled. As the supply of captured cans proved insufficient, a factory was set up in the Delta to manufacture British jerrycans. Soon every vehicle had its complement of petrol and water jerrycans. The name has stuck ever since.

The empty petrol tins had their use. Tin plate was in demand by the workshop for repairs and miscellaneous fabrications. The water cart brought water every day from Amiriya for cooking. The official water ration was one gallon per day for all purposes. This went to the kitchen who would issue what was left after cooking and cups of tea. There was precious little water to spare for ablutions.

The company made water filters from empty petrol cans. Some small holes punched in the bottom were covered with a piece of cloth and the can then

7.1
Sunday was dhoby day when the washing was done. The flimsy cans used to supply petrol were converted to washing bowls. At this stage, water was not in short supply but later washing water would be repeatedly filtered for re-use.

filled with sand. Four soldiers would pool their weekly allowance of washing water. They would take it in turns each day to go first. After a wash and shave the basin was emptied into the filter. Moments later the water flowed back to the basin as clear as crystal. The process could be repeated for seven days before the smell of the filtered water became intolerable. The water was then relegated to a vehicle radiator and the whole filter, tin and all was thrown away.

The food remained good. Each day the cooks turned out the standard meal of 'meat and two veg' and most days the ration lorry returned from Alexandria with extra rations. In the evening there was normally some beer and soft drinks to satisfy the thirsts of the day. Everyone had learned to be careful with water. No drink was taken during the day, except for a brew at tea breaks.

'On one of my tours of inspection in the desert, I found the remains of a Norton motor cycle with its wheels and saddle missing plus the front forks bent. How it came to be out in the desert, miles from any road, is anyone's guess. Possibly it had been left by Arabs who might have found the wreck, stripped the useful parts and dumped the rest.

'On inspection the engine seemed in good order except for some sand. I put it on the truck and took it back to camp. The engine was in good order after cleaning; the forks were not so badly bent that they could not be straightened so all I needed was two wheels and a saddle.' The Signals dispatch riders at

7.2
It was possible to arrange a few luxuries
even in the desert. Showing tonight
is one of Charlie Chaplin's classics,
Modern Times, plus a beer obtained
on the regular supply run to Alexandria.

Amiriya were able to fix Bob up with a pair of wheels and a well worn saddle. After a struggle with the brakes, 'Bitsa' was born. Thereafter Bob could do his rounds mounted on Bitsa which served him well until its dispatch at Tobruk.

On one trip with Major Yates and Sergeant Spink, Bob was introduced to 'birs.' On the way, the OC explained that birs were water cisterns found along the North African coast hewn out of the rock beneath the desert sand whose builders were long forgotten. They were not marked on their maps and this one had only been discovered by a recent survey patrol and marked with a stake in the sand by the entrance hole.

It was to the east of the Ruweisat Ridge. The OC explained that the Staff wanted to open up the bir to form an underground headquarters. Armed with a rough sketch of the layout required, they would see if it was feasible. The proposal was to enlarge the entrance hole, cut some steps and to excavate additional chambers and dug-outs around the bir.

When the sand was cleared away, it revealed a hole in the rock about three feet in diameter. They stuck their heads through the entrance to make out a cavern some thirty or forty feet in diameter and about twenty feet deep. They were amazed to discover how cool it was. The defensive strength was obvious and it was easy to see how useful the bir would have been for water storage.

Around the entrance they could see grooves worn by the ropes attached to ancient buckets. They pondered how the cisterns were filled and concluded that caravans of camels carrying water skins, or perhaps troops might carrying water on the outward march to be recovered on the return journey.

'The last time I visited this bir, the work was progressing well but the company moved from Alamein before it was completed. Possibly this was the HQ used in the Battle of Alamein a year later.' Twenty five miles of the track east of Ruweisat Ridge was completed and linked to the rail halt at El Alamein.

Having completed the Alamein 'box', the company, began work on similar strong points on the Ruweisat Ridge, when they were moved in October. The company had been at El Alamein for over three months. The order to move came on 29 October. They were to leave all of their construction equipment in place.

The importance of the company's task was evidently not yet appreciated. At the end of January 1942 the CRE who signs himself 'Kisch' is reporting that the 'CinC has given final instruction as to an insurance line covering the frontier.' It was to run from Upper Salom: Musaid: Bir Wair: El Silciya: Pt 207: Abu Talaq: Halfaya. This was an ambitious position to defend previous gains when the Allies were in the ascendancy and well to the west of El Alamein.

Thoughts of higher command were focused on the build-up in the western desert designed to drive the Axis forces out of Africa. After the successes of the autumn, all attention was turning to offensive operations. Resources could be diverted from building doubtful defensive locations so far in the rear. The company could be better employed as part of the ambitious plans that would, it was hoped, end the desert war early in the New Year.

The whole company was to be gathered together from their diverse tasks and be prepared to undertake some more collective training.

'It was with some regret that we were warned to pack up in October with the work incomplete' Bob recalls. The company was to move down to a place called Kabrit on the Suez Canal. Bob had twice passed this remote signal station on the canal on his way to and from Singapore before the war. There was much speculation on the reason for this move well to the rear given that there was so much to be done at El Alamein.

Previous experience of 'military training' had not been enjoyable. It was marked by days of tedium followed by intense activity which seemed rather pointless. The skilled craftsmen had received few lessons in what to do if confronted by the enemy. They had still not yet fired their weapons but had come to accept that their contribution to the war effort would be primarily constructive.

7.3

The Mechanists section pose just after they have dropped the NCOs tent. The tent had been strategically situated in one of the many folds in the rocky desert. During the previous months hundreds of local workers had removed thousands of tones of material that might have sheltered enemy troops approaching El Alamein and crushed it to make roads and fortified positions.

Other sappers would keep some work going on the fortifications begun by the company over the next nine months. In late June and July 1942 these preparations would prove their worth in the first battle of El Alamein when the Afrika Korps was stopped on its charge across the desert. Rommel determined to break through the line but also decided to consolidate his position following an effective counter attack.

Auchinleck attacked again on 10 July at Tel el Eisa and took over a thousand prisoners. Rommel's counter against the defences achieved little. The battle then moved to Ruweisat Ridge where two battles on 14 and 21 July failed to drive the Germans back. A week later a two-pronged attack launched from the El Alamein defences again failed but valuable lessons were learned for the battle to come in October.

For a month, the defensive boxes built by the company held. The Eighth Army was exhausted and Auchinleck ordered an end to offensive operations. The defences would be used to launch a major counter-offensive. General Montgomery now took over and would make this position his own and give it a place in military history.

The fortifications of Ruweisat Ridge would play a critical role in preventing the Axis breakthrough to Alexandria. It would be another six months before General Montgomery could consolidate behind these defences and then launch his forces to begin the eviction of Axis troops from Africa.

Chapter Eight

Kabrit – Commando Training

November 1941 – January 1942

Just as Alan Jones prepared to commission the final part of the hospital and wrap up the work at Buselli he learned that the company had unexpectedly left nearby El Alamein and headed well to the rear. Soldiers are seldom kept informed of the plans of their leaders. They get used to guessing. Troops can usually anticipate events or discern some logic in what they are told to do. But the electricians were to rejoin the company at a place called Kasfaret in the south of Egypt near the Bitter Water Lakes, at least one hundred miles from the nearest action. Were they shipping out to the Far East?

Bob Borthwick was equally surprised by the move to the rear. Their work creating a last line of defence was going really well. But there was still so much to do. The orders were clear. But why the haste? In a matter of hours they were packed and ready to move. There was just time to wash off the desert dust of another hard day's work and grab a little sleep before the early morning move.

For the journey, the company was to move in two groups. All the transport headed east along the coast road on the 29 October. The other group would follow by rail the next day. Before that they would have to endure a night in the bitter desert cold without their bedding and limited home comforts; these had departed, loaded on the vehicles.

Their greatcoats provided some protection from the desert night chill with their pack providing a pillow. They were given tins of bully beef and hard biscuits to sustain them until they were reunited with their cooking pots. Bill was glad he had not joined the infantry as he imagined that this temporary hardship was their normality.

Bob travelled with his compressor truck now piled with the materials, equipment and personal gear they had accumulated to make life more comfortable including an iron bedstead. There was no rule that said a soldier had to be uncomfortable. His suspicions about the purpose of their unexpected posting were roused when they were not given a map or route card. A foreign posting would mean dumping all his hard won home comforts and starting again.

Their one instruction for the journey was to stay together whatever happened. Not knowing his destination, such an order was superfluous. Stating the obvious was normal for any chain of command. However, the instruction would have unforeseen consequences.

The convoy turned off at Amriya to by-pass Alexandria before following the desert road towards Cairo. There was time for a short pause for refreshment. When they set off again Bob took a turn at the wheel. His truck had a hand throttle in addition to the accelerator foot pedal, used when running the compressor. Officially it was not supposed to be used on the move but it was relaxing as the convoy trundled along at a nifty 40 mph keeping the regulation wide spacing designed to limit the effect of any attack from the air.

However, such gaps were tempting to other drivers. Half way along the desert road a small military truck came from a track on the right and tried to cut into the convoy. With the hand throttle engaged Bob was neither able nor willing to stop his heavy truck. Bob hit the passenger door of the van pushing it off the road into the desert and sailed on. The look of disbelief and horror on the face of the officer in the passenger seat of the truck provided a vivid memory. Bob smiled back.

'Red Caps' on motorcycles were ready to escort them through the chaotic Cairo and put them on the road to Kabrit. They were now briefed to close up and on no account were they to stop. Red traffic lights in Cairo would be ignored by the convoy.

This time it was a little, open Citroen 'deux chevaux', driven by an Egyptian sporting a red fez who challenged Bob. Having successfully cut into the convoy the little car stopped at a red traffic light until Bob's bumper nudged him gently forward. Amid much shouting on both sides, the Citroen driver exercised discretion and took off under his own power and out of the path of Bob's behemoth. But the convoy had already vanished round several corners.

Happily Bob knew his way from previous visits to the rear stores areas and closed up with the convoy outside Cairo, where the company paused for another short break decreed by standard operating procedures. After one hundred and eighty miles in five hours it was welcome. The Suez road ran out to the east of Cairo. The build-up of allied troops was obvious. The road was lined with tented camps full of troops preparing for the coming battle. Not for them the luxury of a transit camp beside the Great Pyramids to compensate for the flies, dust and heat.

Bob recognized the signals station at Kabrit that he has passed on his two transits through the Canal and knew this eventful journey was nearly over. They were beside the Suez Canal so this was journey's end. Kabrit is a small village on the edge of the Bitter Lake, one hundred miles south east of Cairo and well away from the fighting. It was home to the Commando Training School, HMS Saunders.

When the electricians with Alan Jones and Bill Harvey caught up with the company next day, it was already established in tented accommodation next to the naval camp. Their journey, by contrast, had been a pleasant drive through the historic heart of Egypt. They were even told where they were going and were given adequate time and information to complete the journey. There was an opportunity to pause and take in the spectacle of the Great Pyramids before passing the miles of tented camps that now lined the previously deserted roads from the canal ports towards the desert.

They found two other units in training at Kabrit. A New Zealand infantry battalion, and a small group of irregulars who were referred to as 'L detachment.' This bunch of veterans indulged in a training regime that seemed excessive to the others based at Kabrit. L detachment would go for hikes in the desert with a full load of 75 pounds on their backs. Watching them depart on their marches terrified the watching sappers who wondered if they were about to embark on some tough military training rather than on to a boat that would take them off to another war.

Bill had almost mastered the ability to suspend the rational part of his mind when contemplating the orders of his military masters. He wondered at the wisdom of turning craftsmen and artisans into storm troopers but resigned himself to whatever the military fates had in store for him.

On 31 October, the unit together for the first time since arriving in North Africa, were informed that they were at Kabrit for *combined operations training*. The briefing that followed made little sense to the troops used to exercising their technical craft, rather than their limited military skills. 'Combined Operations' interpreted from military speak means that the various arms and services of the military work together. In practical terms it meant they would be learning to use the navy's landing craft.

The camp at Kabrit was used to prepare troops for attacks behind the enemy line including various parachute, overland and seaborne missions that were being planned. The distances in the desert meant that any advance ran out of air cover. Plans were being hatched to seize airfields behind the enemy lines to improve the air support to forward troops during the next advance.

After settling in for a day there was another briefing from where the 'invasion training' was explained. They would work with the New Zealanders who were already installed across the canal road. They inspected some square shaped pontoons beached in the naval camp HMS Saunders. There was an assortment of barges and other queer looking craft designed, they were told, for landing behind enemy lines.

They were pleased to discover that they would be using some of the largest, most solid looking craft. These would transport them across the Great Bitter Lake and back as they practised boarding and landing. There was no indication when or where they were to 'invade.' They guessed that the company's task would be to form a beach workshop to provide their diverse range of engineering services to the others.

Two new skills were added to their repertoire. They learned to lay 'beach roads' made of rolls of wire netting. Laying the road was the easy part. But it took hours to wind it up in preparation for the next 'assault.' A company that had specialised in construction and repair were now required to master the use of explosives and demolition.

They were also introduced to the 'tommy cooker.' This was a rectangular tin filled with blocks of solid fuel, similar to fire lighters and was to be used for brewing tea or warming food. It packed away neatly inside their mess tins displacing the domestic keepsakes such as photos that often lived there. They had survived for over two years' active service without the need to prepare their own food. The novelty soon wore off as the difficulty of cleaning the soot off their mess tins and the poor quality of the weak tea produced was understood. The work of the company cooks was suddenly appreciated.

The cooks were also mastering new skills. They would not be left behind but had to learn to deal with tinned rations, including bully beef, tins of stew. The brew of tea for which they were renowned was now spoilt with the addition of condensed milk. The company had, until that time, enjoyed a healthy diet of fresh rations obtained from the local supply depot.

Attempts to enliven the tinned rations with spices and curry powder were not a success with the engineers from Doncaster who preferred their food plain and simple. However, with the aid of the tinsmiths and metalworkers they began to devise and construct numerous home comforts from the plentiful supply of catering tins that was a by-product of their dull rations.

In typical military fashion, several days were spent sorting out what was to be taken while they practised loading men and vehicles. These were, quite literally, dry runs. The sidewalls of a tent set up near the edge of the lake replaced the actual craft. They would assemble and then be 'loaded' into the space. Engineering vehicles come with potentially useful 'sticking out' pieces which would collect the canvas as they 'embarked'. The navy was not impressed. They could see these 'prickly' vehicles ripping one of their fragile craft open with disastrous results. Some modifications were required to please their boat men.

After a number of practice runs with the canvas they graduated to beached craft. But soon it was time to put to sea. 'We were required to crouch in the gunnels of the boat and when the Beach Master called us in, we had to wait until the vessel grounded and the front flap was dropped. We had to make a rapid but orderly exit dropping from the flap into the sea wading ashore using our imagination to anticipate a hail of bullets.' It all felt very real to Bill.

They were also required to wear battledress, rather than the hat, shorts and boots that was their normal working attire. To add to the discomfort of full military dress, for these exercises they would be in full marching order plus greatcoats and spare clothing in their packs. There would be no concession to the desert heat. Haversacks were crammed with towel, shaving kit, emergency rations of biscuits and concentrated chocolate and water bottles which the sergeant major decreed they were not allowed to drink.

Only one workshop lorry was to go. The heavier one was chosen for the work expected after a landing plus the compressor truck. Bob was relieved that the other vehicle was not removed. He drew some comfort from this. Evidently someone intended that they would be returning after their adventure.

After several days of dry runs the navy actually let them board the real landing craft. Military, beach landing craft were new and these were the first of this type of craft they had seen. The larger UDs might have motored out from England but the HICs were much smaller and barely seaworthy. Both had ramps for loading with an engine and crew house at the back. The first could accommodate a couple of lorries, the other twenty men and their equipment.

A Royal Engineer officer was to be 'beach master.' He was in charge of all their initial training. The landing drill was explained by the beach master. This involved deploying to what natural cover was available as soon as the ramp on the landing craft went down.

This intensive training in amphibious landings was designed to prepare them to go ashore on enemy occupied territory. Training consisted of loading the landing craft, then sailing across the Bitter Lake from the beach at Kabrit to land on the opposite shore, half an hour's bumpy ride away. After a great deal of messing about they would pack up, load up and assault the beach at Kabrit.

Getting on and off was soon mastered but they only ever managed one round trip per day for there were so many snags. Left to the navy, the vehicles sometimes arrived without their crew. The beach master would intervene and the vehicles would be ordered to disperse to the dunes where they hid so well that the crew were unable to find them.

After several round trips, people and their vehicles contrived to arrive together but it took little imagination to see how rough water, a rocky shore, enemy fire or darkness could disrupt proceedings. They could expect to meet at least three of the disruptive elements on any operation so the chaos was of itself, good training.

The sand on the opposite shore was soft. The small trucks could manage if driven steadily but the workshop lorry got stuck every time. They practised laying wire net roadway which came in long rolls and was not easy to handle. The coiled wire seemed to have a mind of its own, it had a preference for uncoiling like a spring or alternatively, snagging on itself and refusing to unwind. In daylight they could handle it but in the dark it would pose a problem, leaving the workshop truck stranded.

Experiments were carried out to lay a pathway of wire mesh laid on the sand as foundation for heavy vehicles. However, the training was intensive and Bill began to suspect they might be working to some deadline.

The beach master's task was to sort out the tactics and tasks once ashore. For the workshop team this involved getting ashore and setting up. For the rest there was lots of real soldiering involving digging in and defending the beach while Bob and his fitters developed the skill of camouflage, remaining inconspicuous and brewing tea. Practice paid off as they were always able to disembark and disperse quickly to their tents when they landed back at Kabrit.

They made the acquaintance of their neighbours who said they had moved in a couple of months before.

'They were a very fit and merry lot of men, many drawn from commando units and all volunteers. We got to know them very well, visiting their recreation tent while their sergeants came to our mess. Although they said little of their previous exploits, their security was very tight, we heard of trips to Italy, and during November, of an unsuccessful raid in the desert. Many were old desert campaigners and we learned a lot of desert lore from them' Bob recalls.

The neighbours

When 106 Company arrived the neighbours were busy with initial parachute training and were quickly persuaded to build a proper jump training facility to the design of the detachment commander, Capt David Sterling. The first structure was a tower for parachute jump and landing training. Later, ramps and slides were constructed to add variety and excitement to the training. Bob's ability to conjure up construction material and arrange for its delivery in the desert impressed these hard men.

Just two weeks after making their acquaintance many of the neighbours left. Sadly, many were not to return. The mission was thwarted by sand storms and half the men were lost. However, the SAS was born on this mission and the regiment have adopted the 17 November 1941 as their birthday. It had been conceived as the opening act of Operation Crusader designed to destroy the newly arrived Meschershmit 109 squadrons at Tmini and Mekili and then provide observation in the area behind Tobruk until the Army arrived.

Through November and into December they spent two days each week on these landings. The other neighbours, the New Zealanders practised landing on their off days. Bob felt very sorry for them as they marched past their camp on the way for a hot, dusty and boring day. Bob preferred his boredom to be served up by itself without the accompanying discomfort.

However CSM Sam Shaw was anxious to impose his special brand of military boredom. He seemed to be getting very irritable. There was much marching and rifle drill 'I think he was peeved because we had been away from the unit for such a long time. His favourite phrase was 'now for some serious soldiering.' Each morning we had a normal parade and then someone had the bright idea of doing a special inspection on a particular piece of equipment, such as cleanliness of our rifles. Next day it was our name and number tags or properly folded field dressings. I believed this was just to make a soldier's life unpleasant' Bill records.

To be fair, the CSM had another motive. He did not know their mission but he knew that his men had to be 'licked into shape' and quickly. The only way he knew how was the tried and tested military method of parade drilling and inspections. With nothing but loose shifting sand for a parade ground, the drill nearly always ended in a shambles. With dust everywhere and limited cleaning material or facilities, the turnout steadily deteriorated rather than improved much to the disgust of their sergeant major.

Apart from their messes, and occasional runs to Suez for stores, the only entertainment was Tommy's. This small blessing was a nearby open air cinema and snack bar, owned and operated by a Greek Cypriot known universally as Tommy Shafto. They sat on long wood forms surrounded by a curtain of tent that blocked out the dust and local reality staring at the cloth that served as a screen. 'I remember and enjoyed, in the dusk of a beautiful starlit evening, a film in which Grace Moore sang 'One Night of Love', or something similar, which awakened fresh thoughts of home. She certainly had a wonderful voice' Bill recalls.

The price for the cinema and drinks in his canteen was reasonable. The canteen operation was run by his wife assisted by half a dozen pretty local girls. This contributed to the popularity of the canteen. The sign outside announced 'Night Twicely.' As a projectionist, Tommy was not a success. He was frequently guilty of running films backwards, with reels in the wrong order and without sound. The audience of five hundred packed in the tent would quickly alert Tommy, and whole surrounding area, to his mistake and what he should do after he had rectified the situation.

Shortly before the company left Kabrit the canteen and projection room were burned to the ground. Many sappers rushed to the scene and did their best to rescue the canteen stock from the inferno.

8.1 Tommy Shafto's cinema at Kabrit:
The patchwork tent had elaborate, light proof ventilation shafts to maintain a comfortable temperature inside. Shortly before their departure, a fire started in the projection and destroyed this piece of private enterprise in spite of the strategically positioned fire appliance at the entrance.

They were issued with Benzadrine tablets as part of a medical experiment. It was only to be taken after hard work and if they were unable to complete the task. The OC. stressed that these were being issued for test and were only to be used when troops were exhausted. Bob's part in the landing exercises was not particularly exhausting so he had little need for the drug but decided to try them for the experience.

'I found the effect after taking a tablet was a feeling of being capable of dealing with any situation, carefree rather than careless.' This was followed by sudden feeling of tiredness when the effect wore off. Bob decided they would be unnecessary during for these exercises.

An advantage of a base location was regular, airmail letters, parcels and some airgraphs. The latter were letters written on an army form and photographed, sent by airmail as a miniature negative. These rolls of film were printed at H.Q. and delivered as normal post. Airgraph reached them in a week, or less, while the other mail took several weeks. In spite of the speed, a letter remained more personal. A letter felt as if it had not been exposed to the gaze of strangers, although they knew their outgoing mail was censored, and there was room for much more news in them.

December brought news of the Japanese attack on Pearl Harbour. It also brought Bob sad news in the form of a letter-card from his wife. These cards had replaced telegrams. The sender chose numbers from a printed card held in the Post Office with a curt sentence alongside. They were allowed three numbers to convey their message.

The first two sentences did not register but the third struck home. 'Dad has died.' I knew this meant my father because my wife's father was no longer alive. I was not sure of the term 'died.' My father was Chief Engineer on the cable ship HMTS Alert. In the First World War he served on her sister ship HMTS Monarch when it hit a mine, fortunately Dad and most of the crew were saved.

'My guess was that something similar had happened this time, I was very upset. Cliff Barron and Jack Hurren found me in my tent. Immediately sensing something was wrong I showed them the card and speculated on what could have happened. They did their best to cheer me up, eventually persuading me to go with them to the cinema and take my mind off the news. There was nothing much to be done but to accept their tact and I was thankful for their thoughtfulness.'

An explanatory letter followed. His wife had to be careful of her words because of censorship and Bob was not much the wiser. After the war Bob discovered that his father was killed in Falmouth by a jettisoned bomb. He had nipped ashore to post a letter to my mother. A few weeks later the 'Alert' hit a mine and was lost with all hands.

He also discovered that Wynne received a telegram stating 'Regret to inform you that your husband had been killed by enemy action.' It was delivered to Mrs Borthwick. Her anguish lasted until another telegram arrived from her mother in Dover. 'Come at once. Accident to Dad.' Wynne inspected the first message again. It was signed by Gates, Captain of the 'Alert', not Yates, Bob's OC. The bad news was for the other Mrs Borthwick.

They were also getting some world news. Alan Jones was in charge of fixing a radio they had acquired. By rigging the wire aerial he could sometimes pick up the BBC news if atmospheric conditions were favourable. This provided material for their main entertainment which was talking. No one ever complained of boredom. They enjoyed this spare time; what was not spent talking was devoted to sleeping.

Operation Bootjack

Late in 1941, the planners had identified the need for some forward air cover. The solution they produced was to land a brigade sized group on the coast. They would advance inland and seize the lightly defended airfields and hold them for up to four days when they would be relieved by the advancing forces. Long range Hurricanes from Malta (armed with cannons rather than the normal machines guns) would then operate from these airfields, thus extending the striking range of the air force for the advancing army.

The New Zealand brigade, already committed to the planned offensive, would provide the troops. 106 ATC would provide the engineering and all aspects of logistic support. The plan was to take the supplies and heavy equipment in two 'Glen' ships. Most of the infantry would be carried on the four escorting destroyers.

There was no plan for any re-supply or for the force to be withdrawn if the advance did not go to schedule. Once they were ashore, they were on their own. The planned airfields were at Agheila, Buerat and Misurata. Any of the airfields were able to accommodate the planned two squadrons of Hurricanes and were some distance from the nearest reinforcements. The hope was that any spare enemy troops would be directed to bolster their retreating front line rather than to retake the airfields.

The operation mounted by L detachment under Capt Stirling on 17 November 1941 did much to dent the enthusiasm of High Command for daring raids. The realities of war cruelly intervened, as it frequently does, to scatter the attackers. The raid nearly destroyed the future SAS. Their attack on the airfields was a disaster but proved that they were well defended.

However, it was the navy who killed off 'Bootjack.' They pointed out that the weather in January offered very few days suitable to land such a force on this inhospitable coast, the supply ships would be out of action at a vital time especially if the weather prevented the landing and the troops had to be taken all the way back to a suitable harbour. To reinforce their case, they questioned whether four destroyers could be spared during a major assault when the naval gunnery for air and shore bombardment would be vital.

So determined were the navy to kill off this operation that they questioned the military logic of sending such a large force to attack lightly defended airfields. This was the last entry in the file. Operation Bootjack was quietly shelved and the training regime relaxed.

Bill detected the change in plans. 'Towards the end of November, while we listened avidly to news of the attack by the newly named Eighth Army, our invasion plan was suddenly cancelled. Having noticed a decline in numbers of personnel next door, we guessed it was something to do with the push taking place to relieve Tobruk.'

'Later in December it was learned that one of several raids made for the attack, had been a reconnaissance party landed in the area of Derna. Unfortunately they had been captured and rumour spread that this was a reconnaissance for our invasion. Whether it was this fiasco or the relief of Tobruk that made it unnecessary, we may never know. The latest rumour was that the company would soon be on the move again now that there was not an 'Invasion' to stage.'

Instead of practising the beach landing, the sappers began experiments with fabricating landing stages and improvised quays. These were called 'crib' and 'drum' piers.

With the cancellation of their exercises, the company was allowed to go on leave. Cairo with its museums and monuments, plus the nightlife was the popular choice. Bob headed back to the cosmopolitan atmosphere Alexandria by train for a quiet stay at the Union Jack Club away from the crowd and smartly dressed base personnel.

Rumours were now flying about that we were to move again. These were reinforced when Number three section left for Tobruk, just before Christmas. However, the Quarter Master let slip that Christmas rations had been drawn and preparations were made for a military version of a Merry Christmas. Officers and sergeants always served the men their Christmas dinners.

There was turkey and Christmas pudding plus a bottle of Australian beer and lemonade. Afterwards each man was given fruit, nuts and a packet of cigarettes before the 'servants' retired to the mess for their own meal. Bob's inexperience as a beer drinker was noticed by his comrades who attempted to help by marching him outside and putting fingers down his throat. When this plan failed, Bob retired to bed. When he awoke late next day to discover that the plan hatched to shave off one half of Captain Bell's elegant moustache had failed. Evidently, the outnumbered officers had won the drinking battle. 'More practice', mused Bob as he discovered what a hangover felt like.

On 27 December 1941 the Chief Royal Engineer in Alexandia issues his fateful instruction.

'One section of 106 AT Coy RE is leaving for Tobruk today and will take some BRC fabric – Try this form of construction for the jetty repair. We do not wish this section of 106 AT Coy RE to be employed on work other than concrete drum construction as they are training for this type of work.'

The introduction to Tobruk that would lead to their capture had begun.

Two days later E & M section and Number Four section were told to pack up and be ready to move with their transport and equipment. Two sections and the company H.Q. would stay behind to conduct more experiments and trials. They would develop and test improvised pier and causeway constructions. January saw the company assembling crib and drum piers at first by day and then by night.

As transport was drawn into the offensive, the experiments were delayed several times as there was no way to move enough drinking water to the site to stop the men dehydrating as they worked. Once they had restored the piers at Tobruk, Number Four section returned to Kabrit leaving Alan Jones and the electricians restoring the facilities of Tobruk after its eight month siege.

8.2

Christmas morning was celebrated with a football match. Alan Jones' electricians took on the rest of the company and won 3–1. Alan modestly notes 'We were not the better team but used the wind to good effect.'

8.3

It is a long-established army tradition that the soldiers are served their Christmas lunch by the officers and senior ranks. The platter of food carried by Alan Jones is loaded with chicken and potatoes. The photo is inscribed 'one doing his stuff.'

With work at a standstill the monotonous routine of wasting time while looking busy took over. As January drew to a close some transport returned and work continued. The drum pier design was perfected along with the routines for assembling it speedily. Plans were drawn up for another improvised bridge, this time a scaffolding causeway.

Bill departs

Bill Harvey was fed up. 'We spent Christmas 1941 at this desolate spot with the usual formalities of officers serving the Christmas dinner to other ranks, not a very uplifting time.' But he was about to escape. In the New Year the CSM sent for me and told me to get ready for a trip to Gabel Maryan, a training school for NCOs. 'He also told me if I came back with a good pass I would be favourably considered for promotion to a lance sergeant. So away I went with full kit to join up with twenty others, from various units, on the same course.'

Bill enjoyed his ride in the train. The view was much improved compared with the back of a truck. 'The journey from Kabrit to Alexandria remains in my memory for its diversity of scenery for, to avoid Cairo, we were to drive across the Delta, via a place with the bizarre name of Zagazig. Being the passenger for this part of the journey, I was looking forward to enjoying the many aspects of the Delta. Each village, nestling under shady palm trees, produced a horde of yelling children "Shufti, tommy, cigarettes, choco-late" offering the hood of their burnoose to catch any offerings.'

The lush green of the Delta was a pleasure for the eyes with fields of rice, cotton and vegetables set in straight canals. The irrigation was now provided by pumps but there was still the occasional donkey-operated water wheel to be seen and even the ancient 'shadoof' where a manually operated bucket rhythmically raised water from the river.

'Each individual was required to give an instruction lecture, to last about thirty minutes, on a subject selected by the lecturer. The mystery of the military mind was again revealed when, as an electrician, I was detailed to speak on the subject of concreting, preparation, mixing to specific strengths and laying.' When his time came he presented his lesson lucidly for the allotted time. 'Whether anyone apart from me was much wiser when I finished is debatable.'

After three weeks at NCO school, Bill was sent to Moascar a re-deployment centre. 'I fully expected to be sent to another unit. If I had been drafted elsewhere who knows what might have happened. But I had no wish to be separated from the lads of the 106 for whom I had great affection and respect.'

The company had no wish to loose such a skilled technical to general field engineering. So a 15 hundred-weight runabout was dispatched with some credible paperwork to spirit Bill, back to the company before the system had a chance to assign him elsewhere.

At the end of January the company was told to pack up. On 4 February 1942 the road party was on the move. Bob recalls: 'At the briefing it was made clear that there would be no convoy, each vehicle would travel independently. The workshop lorries and the MT truck would be at the rear and I was to take the compressor truck again with a driver.'

The troops were ferried to the railhead at Port Tewfik for a dawn departure on the 5 February for the Western Desert. They were off 'Into the blue.' In the early hours of the following day they reached Mersa Metrun. They were greeted by an enemy bomber that dropped a single stick of small bombs half a mile away as a welcome to the war zone. The fateful year of 1942 began with a move to Mersa Matuh where the unit had to dig in with army HQ based at Bir Habata.

8.4
Alan Jones with the truck that ferried men and machinery across the desert for 15 months. Photo taken by his driver, Dave Roberts. Both had contracted malaria and missed the commando training.

Chapter Nine

Into the Blue

January – April 1942

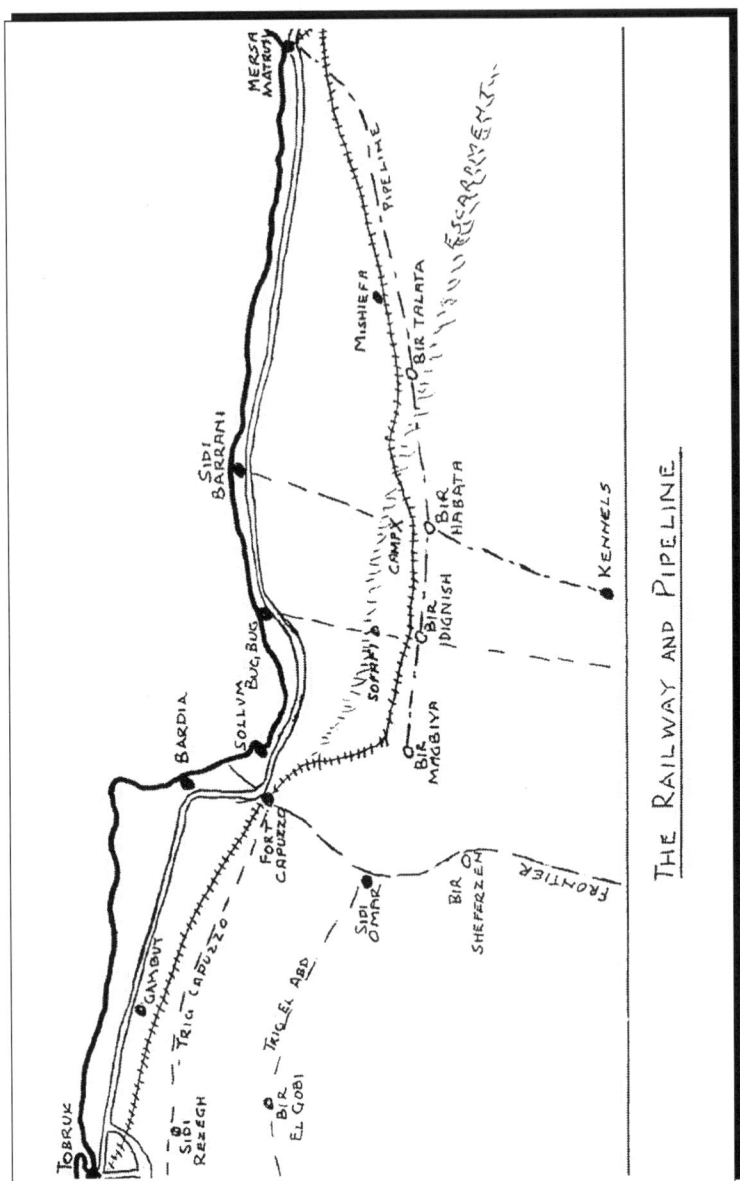

Plan showing pipeline and reservoirs

In November 1941 planning was all for the next big offensive so the defensive work
on El Alamein was suspended. The transport available could not move all the supplies.
By pumping water the logistic load could be much eased. The ancient storage cisterns
knows as 'birs' were excavated and used as reservoirs. This road and rail map prepared
by Staff Sergeant Bob Borthwick shows the pipeline and reservoirs set up by the company.

Winning wars is normally a numbers game. The trick is to have the larger numbers at the right place and the right time. Rommel had mastered this trick and used mobility to appear in force at the wrong place for the defenders. His Afrika Korps could achieve local superiority and force the allies to retreat. His manoeuvres were designed to isolate a superior Allied force that depended on a coastal corridor for supplies. While Wellington's army 'marched on its stomach', the Eighth Army depended on its flow of fuel and water to keep fighting. If these supplies were threatened, the forward troops would have to withdraw.

As 1942 began, the forces led by General Claude Auchinleck, appreciated the importance of the uninterruptible flow of materiel to the fighting formation. An ambitious logistic plan had been prepared to help win the numbers game and keep the Afrika Korps in retreat after the next offensive. So the final phase of the company's war began with a move 'into the blue.' They were heading into the desert but covered with a clear blue sky.

The staff had done their calculations and worked out that the only way to sustain an advance was to find some other way to get vital supplies forward. There were not enough trucks in the army to bring everything forward. If a pipeline could be laid to carry the water, it would be possible to maintain the army in its advance. Those assigned this task would have to lay 2.6 miles of pipe each day.

 The water points and all of the associated installations were not to be marked on any maps and all information about plans had a 'top secret' classification. The operational order send out to all commanders in February told them that activity was to focus on logistics to enable offensive operations to be resumed and sustained. The landings behind the enemy lines to seize airfields were once again being planned by senior staff.

The first staging post for the company on their way to the hot war was Mersa Matruh, some two hundred and fifty miles west, along the coast railway from Alexandria. They travelled in the chill of the night to avoid the attention of enemy aircraft. Early on the 7 February they left Mersa Matruh and by evening had reached the railhead just before the first contingents of the road party.

Along the line of the railway built by Royal Engineers from Britain, Australia and New Zealand ran a water pipeline. The starting point for the pipeline was the rail junction with the main line at Similla, eleven miles south-east of Mersa Matruh. It ran westward some ninety miles to Mashiefa, more usually called the railhead, but the pipe was now being extended to Fort Capuzzo on the Egyptian border as the army advanced.

The plan to move the water was based on the use of ancient birs as reservoirs. These caverns, hollowed out of the rock, were known in Roman times but their antiquity is uncertain. They had been constructed at regular intervals along the desert, a few miles inland from the coast road. Over the centuries, the desert had reclaimed them and they were now full of sand. The intention was to provide a facility to pump water 'from bir to bir.' This would provide a reserve along the way to allow for the inevitable interruptions caused by breakdown, supply problems or enemy action.

The company's task was to continue this pipeline towards the current front line where they would set up water supply points at Bir Habata and Bir Dignach to supply the fighting forces. A four inch pipe would be laid between Maghliya and the bir at Habata, a distance of twenty miles. A four inch and a three inch main would connect the bir at Dignach to Habata a further twelve and a half miles away.

Bob Borthwick was struck by the scale of the railhead. 'It was one huge store dump and the main railway depot for the army, with sidings and repair yards. The tented area was occupied by a RASC stores unit as well as the sapper railway people and had a large NAFFI compound.' It reminded him of the depot they had build at Bruz in 1939. This was a key link in the supply chain leading to the front. Here they would be kitted out for their new task in the desert.

Railhead

After two pleasant days in the transit camp at the railhead they were on the move again. Leaving some of Number Four section to load the piping and pumps on the train, the remainder set off from the railhead, travelling along the hardened track beside the railway perched on their trucks. Their first base was near Bir Habata forty-five miles westwards along the railway north of the railway on the plateau.

The desert was different from that so far experienced and certainly nothing like the sand dunes that piled up around the Nile Delta. Here there were no hills. The land was flat and rocky with only a few inches of sand on solid rock. The going could be good for vehicles provided you were careful. 'It was advisable to keep a good lookout' Bob recalls. 'Not only would there be loose rocks but there were places where a dip in the rock base had created a sand trap. A vehicle could get stuck up to its axles. In day-light these patches were easily seen as a stretch of smooth sand, devoid of rocks or stones, but not so easily anticipated at night.'

The temptation to travel fast left little time to avoid these traps. Getting stuck and the chore of digging out were more common than they need have been. Experience taught them to balance the benefit of speed against time and temper lost when getting stuck. The tyres and springs paid a price for bad driving with numerous punctures and occasional broken springs.

They were also learning the art of desert navigation. Maps were of limited use in a featureless landscape with few tracks and there were certainly no signs pointing to Bir Habata. You had to rely on the description of those who had been there before. The railway halts with names such as *Wahed* or *Etnin* had been replaced with unofficial army signboards christening each station with a familiar name such as 'Charing Cross' or 'Piccadilly.'

They passed the forty-five mile marker from the railhead and found a railway crossing point for vehicles. Following the advice given, they crossed the line and headed north towards a plateau in search of a suitable campsite. About a mile north and a bit to the west of the crossing there was an area of smooth sand. This dip in the rock base would give a couple of feet of sand to pitch tents. By dusk on the 10 January the remaining men of the section and equipment had been ferried to the new base.

With the constant threat of air raids or German raiders, a day was spent digging in to provide some protection. There was plenty of evidence they were now on land that had been fought over. Abandoned equipment and burnt lorries were much in evidence along their route and out in the desert. Digging was difficult in the rocky ground but, as engineers, they were well equipped. Suitable shelters were prepared for the rest of the company before the dark, cold, clear desert night began.

After their day settling and digging in, Tony Lumkin, Sam Shaw and Bob Borthwick set out to locate the first bir. It was somewhere 'south of the railway.' Fortunately a previous visitor had the foresight to erect a cairn of stones near the entrance. The work had been started by 566 Army Troops Company assisted by a Cypriot labour company. By means of a ladder they climbed down and inspected the interior. Bob describes what he saw.

'This bir was very similar to the one I had seen at El Alamein but smaller in diameter, about thirty feet and twenty feet in depth. It had been divided in half by a wall some ten feet high. Access to the dry side was by a ladder down to where the two pumps were positioned. The four inch delivery pipe rose alongside the ladder and the two exhaust pipes from the diesel engines that would power the pumps. These stood six feet up in the air waiting for the pumps.'

Bir Habata

It was easy to locate the incoming water supply pipe that had already been set up near the railway. This was their starting point. The company was to continue the line onward from Bir Habata via Bir Dignash and then on to Bir Magbiya before running the line south back along the rail route.

Bir Habata was near to Sofafi Fort, which had been the HQ for Eighth Army and was still occupied by the administrative echelon for the army so a major water point was to be set up there. Nothing of their work could be marked on any maps or mentioned in any messages.

Bob had a problem. 'Tony Lumkin and I spent a little time assessing how the pumps could be dismantled to pass down through the small entrance hole down into the bir. We were also worried about the seal where the suction pipe passed through of the dividing wall.' They were satisfied that they could take over the existing design with a few modifications and continued on their journey.

The following day the OC, Peter Yates, took a party to find the next bir at Dignash. But they were quickly able to locate it and mark it for the clearing parties. No work had begun here. Work on clearing it of the accumulated sand and rock started immediately. It went on in three eight hour shifts and in four days the bir was clear.

The rock walls of the bir were surprisingly clean and relatively clear of cracks, particularly lower down where water would be stored. Inside the bir, the walls and floor on the water side of the wall were cleaned and painted with waterproof cement. Simultaneously, the dividing wall was constructed.

The depth of the bir was slightly more than twenty feet. The buttressed, dividing wall was ten feet high. The design was for a maximum depth of eight feet of water so the bir could hold some eighteen thousand gallons. The rendering of the surface was delayed a day because, ironically, there was not enough water to make the mix.

During the following week, two Lister-Worthington three-throw ram pumps arrived for installation at Habata. Each pump was known and logged at headquarters. Among the staff papers at headquarters, each pump was given a name. Their 'health' was to be reported back along the chain of command. They kept the water flowing along the armies arteries and were very precious commodities. Orders had been given that in the even of any retreat, the pumps had to be salvaged. Each pump was stripped and passed in pieces into the bir where it was reassembled.

The work had to go on day and night as a convoy of water wagons was scheduled for the 28 February, just 21 days after the advance party had left Kabrit. To achieve their target, a slick and integrated operation was required.

For the pipe laying parties there were no tents. Laying pipes was a progressive job and they camped at the point where the days work finished. Each night, home was an individual pit to sleep in. Desert rats were friendly visitors but they had to be vigilant as scorpions would also tumble into their overnight home.

Unknown to the engineers, local labour was being employed to lay dummy pipelines near the real runs. This piece of deception relied on the infiltration of the native workforce by enemy agents. These pipelines used the supply of damaged and defective material which was left on the surface to attract the attention of pilots looking for the pipe.

Similar techniques were employed by the rail builders who created dummy railheads and track with scaffolding poles, paint and canvas. By constructing the real railheads in the shape of a very large circle, trucks could approach and depart from any direction making it hard for reconnaissance aircraft to predict where the material would be unloaded.

Only when the moon was full did the bombers have their way. There was no way to hide the silver trail of track to guide them to the precious and dangerous cargo. The only solution was to suspend night operation when there was a 'bomber's moon'. The Axis had discovered that a few cannon shells through the boiler of the steam engine closed the line. The response was to add some armour plate but the job of the defenders was made easier by the regularity of the air attacks. Given the timetable, it was possible for the rail men to hide their valuable load when an attack was anticipated.

The work on the first bir was completed on time. The pump and pipe were installed in time to take the water from the twenty truck water-tank train that arrived in the night. The fourteen tons of water was spilled into the bir in just three and a half hours. The forward troops now had another underground water storage facility. Attention could now turn to the pipe line to Dignach.

Their reputation had preceded them from their work at the Wardian workshop. The OC was asked to pay a visit to the admin base at Sofafi Fort. Although they were army troops, rather than part of 30 Corps, they were persuaded to use their precious skills. On his return Peter Yates explained that a small tank repair workshop at Sofafi was overloaded with requests for vehicle spring replacements and welding work in general.

Spring!

The diverse experience of the company was again put to good use. This time the problem was springs. The desert took a heavy toll on the leaf springs which allowed fighting and supply vehicles to bounce their way across the rock strewn terrain around Tobruk.

Replacement springs were not among the priority supplies ordered from England. Spring steel was in short supply in North Africa. It required very special metal forging techniques involving heating and quenching the metal in order to impart to the metal the ability to flex without fracturing.

Wrecked Italian and British vehicles had been stripped of their useable springs but it was not long before this reservoir of spares was exhausted. The harvest of derelict vehicles had produced a quantity of particularly heavy duty spring steel of Italian origin.

The solution was to set up Harry Carr, a blacksmith in Doncaster, with a forge and a three ton truck. Four skilled blacksmiths with their muscular hammer-men extruded the metal to the desired dimension. At their peak thirty springs were flowing from this improvised production line each day.

The steel was heated using two small furnaces and shaped on formers constructed by the blacksmiths. The steel was then quenched at the right moment in the special tanks they constructed for the purposes. The Italian springs were wider than required for British vehicles. Harry had to soften the metal in the forge before he could cut them to width. When that was done the steel had to be re-tempered to turn them into tough springs. After a few weeks Harry had quite a stock of springs for both Bedford and Morris trucks and lorries. Then with his small team he began to take broken sets apart and replace the damaged leaf at leisure.

The demand quickly outran the supply of steel as this, their side-line, became even more widely known. Although spring steel was promised they were advised to scour the desert for wrecked vehicles and remove their springs. An expedition to harvest raw material was planned.

He would head north into the desert where they were told there were plenty wrecked vehicles from previous skirmishes. Most were Italian lorries from the previous winter's defeat. They had already been cannibalised for spare parts. Fortunately most were left to rot with their springs attached.

A blacksmith's striker is the hard working chap who swings the sledgehammer while the blacksmith holds the chisel to cut the spring to width. This was one of the most undesirable jobs in the workshop. In the desert, even in February, Harry's striker had a job that few would envy. To give the full time striker a break, on the rare occasions when field punishment was necessary, a few hours as the blacksmith's striker was salutary!

Sandstorm

Bob Borthwick decided to join one of Harry Carr's forays into the desert. They were told that there were some British wrecks to the south of the railway so the party set out to look for spare parts. An armoured car patrol had given directions to where they had seen these vehicles, both British and Italian, some twenty-five miles due south of the forty-eight mile marker. It was normal to give directions with relation to the railway.

Bob takes up the story. 'We set off in the morning, taking our lunch with us. After an hour's uneventful run first along and then away from the railway steering by sun-compass, we came across two Italian wrecks. To be more exact they were skeletons as they had been stripped of everything useful except springs. We decided to leave them for the time being and look for the British vehicles a bit further on. In fact we nearly missed them, having stopped to inspect an Italian Lancia lorry, it was decided to have our lunch in its shade before going on.

'While eating, one of the youngsters pointed to the west of our intended route to what he said looked like truck wrecks on the skyline, so we set off to investigate. They turned out to be two Bedford lorries abandoned one with a broken spring and the other with a half-shaft gone. Both delivered up their spring sets and other spare parts that might come in useful for our vehicles.

'The last of the springs had barely been loaded when there was a shout from one of the men and looking to the south. An amazing sight met our eyes. A huge, brown wall, stretching from horizon to horizon and reaching high into the sky, was gradually shutting out the sun in a golden haze. We all knew what it was even before hearing the increasing hissing sound of the approaching sandstorm, but obviously one outside our previous experience. We gazed at it in awe for a minute, it was truly menacing, before coming to our senses.

'Everyone leaped for the truck to put the canvas hood up while the driver started up, and drove off north for the railway line. The race was on. Harry in the back was shouting through to me that the storm was catching up. We were losing and when the sand struck, everything went dark, forcing the driver to slow down with visibility ahead becoming almost nil.

'We had two choices either to stop and ride it out or to keep going until we hit the railway to guide us home. Whichever was chosen, we were going to suffer from sand getting in everywhere but we would probably suffer less by keeping on the move. On the other hand it was impossible to see where one was heading, one could easily get lost and even go round in circles.

'Fortunately the storm was roughly moving north, the direction we needed to go. So we used it to navigate. This was one of those storms carried by the Khamsin, a wind blowing north from the equator over the Great Sand Sea, generated in the early months of the year, by a depression in the Mediterranean. If we kept going with the wind and sand in our rear we would eventually meet the railway.

'Another problem was soon encountered, without being able to see ahead, even travelling slowly, we were unable to see and avoid any soft patches of sand and consequently getting stuck. In the relative safety of the cab and in the back with the canvas drawn, there was still more than enough sand flying about, but nothing compared with outside. Nobody was volunteering to walk ahead to warn of soft patches. We just had to keep peering to the front and hope for the best. As it happened many of the soft patches of sand must have been picked up in the wind for we only became stuck once and that, we all agreed, was our most anxious time.

'It was soon evident our worries of being permanently stuck were unfounded, the rear wheel drive had taken the front wheels through and had settled in themselves. But the metal sand channels we carried soon had them out. The sense of relief on getting back on board was more due to leaving the unpleasant conditions outside than the fact that we could now begin to move again.

'Meanwhile with the sun about to set, although we could not see it, it was certainly getting darker and even more difficult to see ahead. We slowed even more but this was now causing the engine to overheat and it was not long before the driver insisted on an unscheduled stop to cool down. Up to then, running with the storm, the sand still managed to get inside everywhere, but this time when we stopped, it was to find a more disconcerting fact.

'Not only was sand getting into the cab but a very fine dust, evidently from the arid wastes to the south, was covering everything. Everyone was covered from head to foot, the dust getting inside clothing, nose and mouth and, had it not been for wearing sand goggles, into our eyes which could have been much more serious.

'These sand goggles, with the green shade, made famous by Rommel always pictured with a pair on his cap, were proving to be one of the more sensible items on issue. The dust gave me one more worry, although nothing was said, and that was the possibility of it getting through the air filter to the engine.

'After three hours or so crawling, it was with considerable relief when we eventually struck first the beaten track alongside the railway, and we nearly ran onto the lines. Guessing that we were west of the camp, the driver turned right along the track looking for the first mile marker. It seemed an unusually long time before I spotted one, with the poor visibility it was probable that it might have been missed, but stopping to look, it was the forty-nine mile marker. We were four miles west of the camp.

'By now it was quite dark but thankfully the storm seemed to be abating, the fury dying down to a more continuous rush of sand and although dark, the visibility had improved a little. The forty-eight and succeeding markers were found until we came to the sleeper crossing at the forty-fifth. Here we turned west of north across the railway but it was not possible to hold direction, after a couple of hours casting around it was decided it was better to wait for morning and we would settle down for the night. Despite the sand a meal of biscuits was eaten, washed down with water. It was impossible to brew tea and everyone settled down in the back of the truck to sleep.'

'Early the next morning everyone awoke with relief at the realisation that the sandstorm had passed and imagine our surprise when we peered out of the truck to see the camp over to the west just a couple of miles away. We must have wandered about gradually drifting east away from our destination.'

Four weary but thankful travellers, eager for breakfast, drove into camp to be welcomed like lost souls. This sandstorm was the worst experienced that season, although it heralded a whole week of storms. Very little work could be done, particularly on the pipeline.

At the end of February the sandstorms gave way to thunderstorms. They were not prepared for the downpour which flooded everywhere. The birs and the pump were flooded. They had obviously been well sited to trap these occasional rains. This was the second time they had experienced such rain. At Kabrit with the tents sunk into the sand they were once flooded. Although inconvenient, this flooding was universally welcomed. They had almost forgotten about rain. It was freshening. It was almost home.

Bill Harvey had a better introduction to the western desert. After the course he was picked up by Sapper Lewis. 'It was a very pleasant experience being away from all things military. We could feel like nomads travelling through the beautiful and immense desert, only briefly calling in at Cairo on the way. Lewis was a good companion and very proficient at brewing up and preparing meals from the adequate stores in his truck.

Sleeping out under the beautiful night sky was a joy in itself. As we neared the Tobruk area he said we would spend another night under the stars for the express purpose of seeing Mersa Matru, a resort on the edge of the Mediterranean, in the moonlight. It was indeed very beautiful, standing on the escarpment, looking across a vista of incredible magnificence with the white villas looking ethereal and almost ghostly, still and silent under the velvet darkness of the moonlit sky.'

In the middle of the subsequent clearing up, a train arrived at the crossing with three tankers of full of water for the bir. This was intended as a present for General Ritchie at Eighth Army HQ. The new supply of water was duly delivered by Tony Lumkin accompanied by Stan Fox, to receive the thanks of the General himself.

Further instructions were now given regarding pumping. It was to be controlled by telephone from bir to bir by the RASC at their water points. They were allowed a leakage allowance of one per cent a week. This happily turned out to be very generous thanks to the quality of the ancient architects and their modern counterparts. 'Despite severe restrictions on the use of water, generally in the desert, we always had more than enough.' Bob Borthwick was proud to recall. This particular numbers game had been won.

Apart from springs, the other pressing need continued to be replacement bearings as abrasive dust destroyed them. The dealing in Alexandria had yielded some two inch diameter phosphor bronze rod, a rare commodity and not officially available. This hoard was clamped under one of the workshop lorries, its existence a secret to all but a chosen few.

Obtaining the correct quality and quantity of certain engineering stores was an art. Alan Jones and Bob Borthwick were masters of this art. A great deal of repair work was necessary on the early pipeline as the heat of the sun and surging of the water buckled and broke the pipe. 'Our normal source was from the Railhead but this was not always reliable, so, with the experience gained at Alamein, I decided to send, not one lorry, but two lorries to Mersa Matruh with instructions to go on to Alexandria if necessary, to get gas.'

Two trucks would allow all the stuff that could be scrounged to be brought back. Spare space could be filled with life's little luxuries. The cover story for the two lorries was the old excuse that the two welding gases should not travel together for fear of explosion. On this occasion the extra stores consisted of bottles of beer

The company had been at Bir Habata since February and towards the end of March their busy but otherwise peaceful existence began to change. Rommel had begun his drive on the 8th Army from Ageila. Air attacks, particularly along the railway, became frequent. It was not surprising that the camp had its first straffing. It was all over in seconds. 'Despite our knowledge of the possibility, all I remember was throwing myself flat under the workshop lorry as soon as I heard the roar of the approaching plane. Somehow knowing instinctively it was not one of ours before it opened fire'.

Bob Borthwick recalls. 'Luckily it was a lone plane that let fly with his cannon at our line of tents, which, at that time of day, were empty. The mess tents and the cooks had a narrow escape and one line of tents was left full of holes. The OC and his office staff did not move as fast. They had not even left their marquee before it was all over. It was the first time for all of us, to be fired on in anger, but only the tents suffered.'

With the pipeline functioning efficiently it was with some relief that the company would be moving again. The sense of relief was short-lived. The move was to be forward not back, to join the sections of the company already in Tobruk. On the twentieth of March the workshop section moved off, leaving the HQ and the other three sections to complete the laying of two more pipe-lines and to prepare another bir at Magbiya.

The movement order arrived on 13 April but there was no transport available. Fifteen RASC trucks arrived early on 15 April. 566 Army Troops Company, just arrived from Britain, had come up to take over at the beginning of April and Peter Yates, with the rest of his men, arrived in Tobruk on the 16 April.

By this time, some of the company were digging in on the outskirts of Tobruk. This was the war zone, so full military defensive procedures had to be taken. Weapons were taken out and cleaned but there was still no sign of ammunition. Their journey had been eventful, not due to enemy action, but because the vehicles were so old. The cylinders were well worn and the spark plugs soon became covered in oil. The only solution was to undertake minor engine overhauls en route. Two days later they were joined by their stores and could get on with their real work.

Before the HQ Section left Bir Habarta they had a personal visit from the Chief Engineer of the Eighth Army on the 3 April. It was a special visit not only to thank the company for the work done on the pipeline, but the special services they had rendered to all comers. But special mention was made of the work carried out on the Alamein Line which as the fortunes of war began to swing again was being appreciated. He wished them well in Tobruk.

As soon as Alan Jones found out Bill had returned from the NCO course he sent his truck to take him into Tobruk to join the electrical contingent. Bill Harvey's luck had not changed. 'CSM Joe Beckitt sent me on the training course, with the half promise I would be promoted to sergeant on my return. However, when I rejoined the unit I found he had been posted away, with a commission and there was a new CSM in charge who had promoted the canteen corporal to the sergeant vacancy. So much for all my efforts. It was therefore a very embittered man who sat in the truck on the way into Tobruk.'

War news was not good for the Allies. The fall of Singapore in the middle of February did not surprise Bob Borthwick. He had served there and had read of the Japanese progress knowing that there were no significant defences against land attack. All the big guns faced out to sea. But Germany had declared war on America which brought the promise of extra manpower and resources in due course.

Their initial hope that the Russian campaign might sap support for the Afrika Korps had not been realised. News from Russia was bad. Hitler had turned on his former ally and was well on his way to Moscow. The two

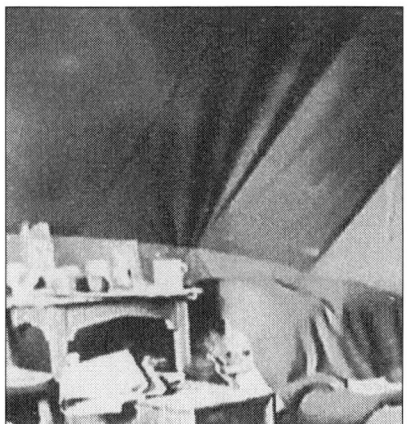

9.1
There was no need to be uncomfortable in the desert. Bob's corner has a table, chairs and china.

German battleships, the Scharnhorst and Gneisenau, whose existence had threatened the company's journey to Africa were no longer on the defensive. They had been penned in Brest but made an audacious break for their home port by sailing up the English Channel. Now Rommel was advancing again, having retaken Bengazi and just as the last of the company was moving into Tobruk.

Chapter Ten

Tobruk

Mid April – 21 June 1942

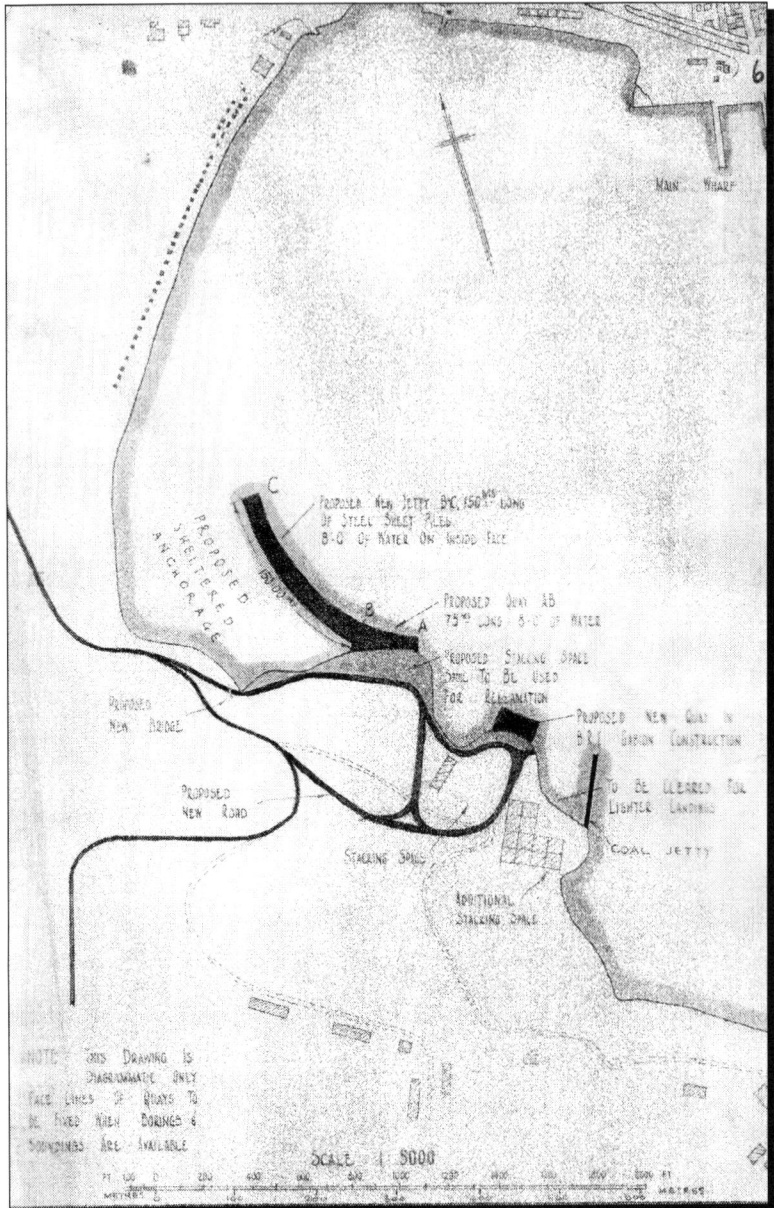

Plan of Tobruk Harbour

Considerable restoration work was required to make Tobruk into a usable supply port for the troops on the Gazala Line after the six month siege. Sadly, the towns defences were neglected and many of the mines had been removed to the new front line. *Reproduced by kind permission of the Public Records Office.*

Bill Harvey recalls his first impressions of the town. 'As we came over the escarpment, the town and harbour lay nestled along one side of the narrow bay. Much of the town, from this distance, seemed to be virtually intact. There were white villas at the higher level and I could see the outline of a white church. As we descended to a lower level there was plenty of evidence of the destructiveness of war. Half submerged ships lay in the waters near the docks and it was sobering to think of all the bitter fighting which must have taken place there during the siege. The epic struggle for survival had aroused deep feelings and admiration world-wide. Our task was to repair and get things back in working order.'

The company had their commando training at Kabrit interrupted to send an emergency team to build new jetties in January after the siege was lifted. Three months later, they were back in force to make Tobruk the forward base to drive the Axis powers out of Africa. That, at least, was the plan. The one section was already established in Tobruk when Bill arrived so they were well received and given a cup of tea each.

'This was my first taste of tea made with brackish water' Alan recalls. 'It was horrible and one thought how on earth one was going to survive with only that sort of beverage. As time went by, the cooks must have learned a local trick or two about producing a better brew. Perhaps I just became accustomed to it.'

The company had taken over a group of villas. The good news was that the buildings were spacious and in excellent condition. The bad news was that the neighbours were 1st Light Anti-Aircraft unit made up of lads from the Liverpool Irish Regiment. Every time enemy aircraft appeared, the noise was deafening as the captured Italian Breda on the roof opened up. The flat roof acted like a sounding board to amplify the staccato rattle. Whenever this happened, there was no point in 'being brave' and staying in bed as there was no chance of sleep.

They were able to equip themselves with the type of Italian cot used at Buselli. From the number available it was evident that every Italian soldier was provided with a bed unlike the tommy who had to make do with the floor or ground.

Alan established their workshop in the heart of Tobruk, on the eastern side of the harbour. The first section were there to build and repair the jetties. The base would be near the water distillery that would demand their constant attention. This facility was a priority target for the Stukas. Alan would watch the aircraft approach from the desert and begin their wailing, then screaming dive towards the harbour.

Alan was impressed by their accuracy and would observe the release of the bomb dispassionately judging its course and point of impact. There was time to take cover behind one of the substantial structures surrounding the harbour.

If they missed the distillery the bombs might hit one of the motor torpedo boats, MTBs, that moored just beyond.

The gunners from any ships plus the Bofors gun located on the habitual line of approach made an impressive din. But Alan never saw anyone hit a fast diving plane. Once the Stuka had released its load, the air brakes were slammed on as it levelled out. It should have been open season on the lumbering Stuka for the few seconds before it shot through the harbour mouth and banked steeply to the east.

Alan often wished he could have a go at one of the bombers as they turned for home. The cliffs that enclosed the harbour would make an excellent place to ambush the Stuka while it was low and the pilot distracted as he looked back to check what impact he had made. What they often left behind were unexploded bombs and a stack of these had been corralled a little too close to his workshops for comfort.

Bill Harvey also remembers the Stukas. 'However, I wouldn't want to leave you with the impression it was all beer and skittles as we were being subjected to daily bombing raids by flights of Stuka bombers, usually about twelve in a flight. They timed their run to coincide with the position of the sun so that they were on us before we could really see them. The target was normally the docks area and its installations. What with the banshee, blood-curdling scream of diving aircraft, the anti-aircraft barrage and exploding bombs it was a nerve-racking experience.'

'The biggest danger to us in the higher parts of the town was from falling shrapnel from our own anti-aircraft barrage. Pieces of shrapnel were anything between one to three inches in size and all capable of inflicting considerable damage to any unfortunate individual caught in the open. We soon found the most effective cover from this unfriendly rain of shrapnel was to dive under a lorry.'

Alan Jones explained Bill's first job was to install an overhead power line to the Navy House which was the local HQ. After the work at Buselli, they were experts at overhead line work. They needed to acquire one new skill.

'Along the way, we had adopted the Italian-style foot irons for climbing the poles. Each leg had a curved piece of metal with metal spurs on the inside edge. With these irons, climbing was easier and the climber felt more secure. However, in Tobruk it was often necessary to make a rapid descent whenever the Stuka appeared in order to retire rapidly to some shelter.' Descending was not the problem, Alan relates. The lineman could be on the ground within fifteen seconds of the distant throb of the approaching aircraft being detected. But the irons were very effectively strapped to the legs of the lineman and could not be removed in a hurry.

'The race to the security of the shelter was difficult. One had to run and keep the feet wide enough apart to allow the metal spurs to miss each other or they would certainly trip up the wearer.' The workers soon learned to run with the leg irons in place 'looking like ducks with very large, webbed feet' Alan recalls. 'We suffered no casualties from either the climbing irons or the bombers, shelling or gun fire.'

The ground was solid rock beneath a covering of dust so the navy had to use explosive to make holes big enough to plant the poles for the power lines. 'The only cable for the overhead lines Alan Jones was able to get was 19 stranded bare copper, making a cable about half an inch diameter. It was hard and heavy work to haul four cables of this size up each pole for a distance of about half a mile, and keep them parallel' Bill Harvey remembers. After the line work, Bill moved on to the hospital on the outskirts of the town which had sustained considerable damage during the siege. One incident brought the war very close for Bill Harvey.

'I had to accompany Staff Jones to the aerodrome, where there was a small hospital. While we were doing the small job we witnessed a Maryland plane trying to get down to the aerodrome with all its tail section ablaze. Later, in the ward there was a young Australian airman who was walking round, with a conical shield on each hand, attached to his wrists. In the course of conversation I asked him what injury held sustained. He showed me the inside of the cone and all that remained of his hands was a skeleton of fire-blackened bones. The doctors hoped that when he could be transferred back to proper hospitals they might be able to rebuild some resemblance of hand with flesh transplants. I wondered what his future life had to offer him.'

The military duties returned but there were opportunities to escape as Bill recalls. 'We had guard duties to maintain, usually at a desalination plant near the dock. In our off-duty time we went to the YMCA centre in the middle of the town, where we could get a cup and a bun and often a short Christian service. The centre was in close proximity to the church I had noticed when I first descended the escarpment into Tobruk but now I could see it was just a roofless shell, a casualty of war, with a pathetic beauty that outshines all man's destructive capabilities.'

The worst job was to be detailed to act as a stretcher-bearer at the hospital. Once the bombing resumed in late May there were always military and civilian casualties to recover. They returned to the billets, visibly upset, to unburden themselves.

Bill needed some soulful comfort. 'I was still harbouring the feelings of frustration and bitterness arising from not getting the promotion I had worked so hard to achieve and I thought of ways to get to another unit. I finally decided to apply for a trade training course to qualify for the status of a class 1 electrician, knowing such a course would take about 2/3 months and the possibility of then being posted to another unit.' When Alan Jones heard about this he was happy to recommend Bill be recognised as a first class tradesman from March 1942 in recognition of work done at Buselli thereby innocently scuppering Bill's latest attempt to earn a third stripe.

More jetties were needed to cope with the increased flow of material. Work also began on a slipway so that small ships could be repaired and sent back out of harms way. Of special importance was the fuel jetty which was positioned just a wingtip away from the habitual flight-line of the Stukas. No fuel barge could be caught there during daylight hours and no barge was to leave until all the precious fuel had been pumped out.

Such orders were simple to issue. They sounded good. They were undeniably logical but overlooked the lack of an effective pumping mechanism. Many nights, as the cargo was pumped ashore into thirsty browsers, valves would break, pipes burst, washers and seals improvised from available materials would announce their imminent failure with a fine spray of fuel, which would turn to a fountain very quickly if the pump was not shut down.

Nerves were strained by this nightly ritual, unrelieved by a soothing cigarette. Smoking was out of the question in such a volatile atmosphere. After the ordeal was over, the fuel so permeated fingers, lips and lungs that it would take most of the day to recover any sense of taste. But the fuel barges were always away before the sudden arrival of the desert dawn.

With their work on the pipeline complete the rest of the company were brought into Tobruk. Riding in the front of his truck Bob Borthwick had an even better view of their new home. The order to move arrived at 0300 hrs. Tents were dropped and they were under way by first light. He could see the partially submerged wreck of the Italian cruiser, San Giorgio, and several wrecked freighters resting in the harbour. Their convoy was well spaced because of the threat of air attack. When attack threatened they would move off the road so their vehicles would not be neatly lined up for straffing. Dispersed vehicles did not make an attractive target and this time they were unmolested.

Part of the journey was on the 'Axis' road built by the Italians at Rommel's request as a by-pass during the siege of Tobruk in the previous years. The alternative for the Germans was to bump across the desert which took a heavy toll on their supply vehicles.

Bob's journey to Tobruk took him down the escarpments leading from the desert down to the town. The final escarpment had been well fortified with concrete emplacements and barbed wire. Bob could make out the anti-tank ditches that had been cut and blasted but which the recent sand storms had filled. From his military training at Chatham, Bob knew that these fortifications, half filled with sand, were of little use.

When Bob arrived with the remaining sections fresh from pipe-laying, Alan Jones met them and led the workshop vehicles through the streets to their new base. Alan was about to perform the introductions when Bob recognised the man that had persuaded him to join the army. Reg Gunn lived across the road from Bob in Dover and had joined up a few years before. They laughed at the thought that their mothers were probably chatting away to each other and wondering where each of their sons were. He was now trying to run the power station. Bob also discovered that he had just missed meeting 551 Army Troops Company which he had helped form up at the outbreak of war.

During this time the mechanical staff was busy in the power house overhauling the diesel engines. They found a broken piston and the missing portion was located, submerged in the sump oil. Under normal circumstances it was unthinkable to weld a piston together and expect it to survive the stresses as it accelerated up and down inside the cylinders of the big diesel, but they went ahead and, to the amazement of all except their exceptional welders, the engine was successfully re-commissioned.

The other problem was to improve the quality of the tea brewed in Tobruk. The desalination plant had been damaged during the repeated attacks and over-extraction from the bore-holes and wells meant that the supply of water was now salty. This was fine for washing and some cooking but for drinking and cups of tea it was unpleasant. So important was this installation that orders came from on high that is was to be guarded with multiple rings of wire and a permanent armed guard to prevent sabotage.

Alan was joined on his first recce by the company officers, Major Peter Yates and Captain Bell whose section had been the first into Tobruk. The distillery was positioned at the heart of things so was in the line of fire. Bob noted the dump of unexploded Stuka bombs that the Navy had collected beside their workplace.

The main boiler was oil fired and could be made to work after some maintenance on the burners. The lining of fire-bricks had collapsed and would have to be rebuilt. None of the team had experience with oil furnaces although high-pressure steam was familiar territory among the railway engine builders. By improvisation and inspiration, the boiler was repaired and after testing steadily re-commissioned.

This was not a task to be undertaken lightly. A large boiler, with a working pressure of ten atmospheres could do enormous damage especially if it upset the pile of unexploded bomb beside the plant. 'Among our unit equipment was a hydraulic test pump and gauge so we were able to check the pressure vessels which revealed the need for some more repair work but step by step we were able to raise steam again' commented Alan as he recalls the tense moments as the pressure mounted.

The system worked by taking high-pressure steam from the boiler and passing it to some evaporators where the seawater was introduced. The evaporated water was then fed to condensers where it was cooled to provide vital drinking water.

The oil burners caused some anxious moments at the naval HQ who were in charge of activities at the harbour. Smoke stared to pour from the chimney and they were immediately ordered to shut down. Night time operation was allowed until the problem was identified and fixed. The smoke would make a good aiming point for enemy planes and guns.

The source of the smoke was quickly identified as oversized holes in the oil burners. These should have been replaced regularly. Some suitable metal was found for a replacement but the problem was the drill. The burner holes had to be very small to atomize the oil and prevent the smoke problem. The call went out for a suitable drill. Unfortunately, the owner of the only suitable drill in Tobruk could not be persuaded to part with it.

A compromise was reached and the corporal agreed to use his drill to make the holes himself. The operation had to be repeated regularly as the metal used was too soft and the hole was eroded by the flow of oil. But all these shut downs did not matter too much as the salt left behind in the distillation process rapidly filled the evaporators. The plant had to be shut down every three days to remove the accumulation. It took two full days to clear the salt and restore the still to an acceptable level of operating efficiency.

By taking parts from the various damaged stills, one working distillery was repaired in a couple of weeks and the output piped to the hospital and the airfield at El Adam along the new pipes they had laid. The small surplus headed for the troops teapots. This was completed just in time for Bob's birthday on 9 May. 'I was given one of my best parties ever. Looking back now I marvel at our optimism at that time.'

'In spite of all the many problems, we managed to produce 80 tons of potable water on good days. The staff worked twelve hour shifts, seven days a week. It was a prodigious effort' Alan recalls with pride. The flow of water was so important that the still was constantly tended to keep the temperamental machinery operating. The strain on the company was enormous.

After the thrust that had relieved the siege of Tobruk and taken the Eighth Army from Egypt into Libya at Christmas, it was time for a tactical pause. News of the attack on Pearl Harbour in December had opened another theatre of war. The British commander, General Auchinleck, had 2 Australian Divisions withdrawn from Africa to be sent to the Far East to help contain the Japanese threat. Supplies of tanks remained too low to replace the battle casualties his army had sustained.

As April turned to May, the lull in hostilities continued while both sides repaired their logistics and built up stocks after the surge that had retaken Tobruk. Those who planned the logistic build up had left the engineers short of supplies. There was an acute shortage of timber and wire. As ever, the company set about recycling and compromising to maintain progress.

By the middle of May, air-raids became a nightly event as Stukas attempted to destroy the flow of ships into the harbour bringing in reinforcements and stores for the Gazala Line. After each sleep-interrupted night there would be the inevitable repairs. It all added to the stress of those who were often working in a fuel-rich environment with a heap of unexploded bombs as their constant companions.

Alan Jones assumed that the army were still advancing and things were proceeding in an orderly manner. Tobruk was an icon and it would be held even if the tide of war ebbed in the desert war. But on 17 May there was a warning to expect a German parachute assault. Regular night patrols would be added to their day jobs. The North African campaign was about to recommence.

A set of defensive 'boxes', similar to those the company had started around El Alamein the previous year, were ordered to consolidate the gains. This became known as the Gazala Line, about 40 miles west of Tobruk. The water pipeline had been one part of the infrastructure constructed to support this defensive position. The Gazala Line would provide the base for the next move forward as soon as the necessary forces and logistics were in place.

But Rommel, the old adversary of 106 Company, was making his own plans to push the British back into Egypt and to retake Tobruk. Alarmed at the British preparations, he resolved to counter attack before the Allies could reorganise. The Gazala Line would also prove a forward base for the attack of his small, but capable, force. The military logic on both sides was sound. The British needed a pause to recover after their advance. The Germans, with their main base area under threat, needed to strike before the Allies could recover.

On the 24 May, the company was warned again to redouble its guards. Something was definitely about to happen. The threat was now seen as coming from the sea. The German attack was actually launched on 26 May deep in the desert. This event was almost welcomed at many levels of command. The direct assaults on Tobruk had been misinformation. They would not be in the front line.

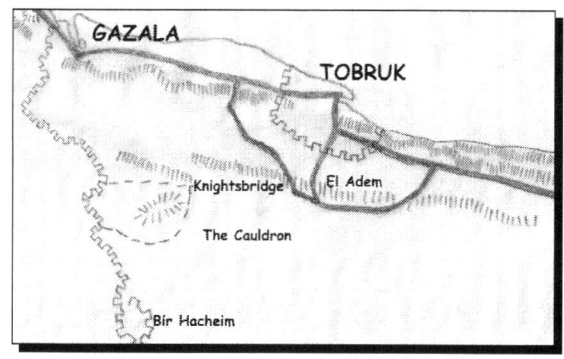

Map of the Gazala Line

The British high command was especially happy. Rommel's attack relieved the political pressure on Auchinleck. He was under instructions from the War Cabinet and Churchill personally to go on the offensive before the end of June. As an experienced commander he did not want to resume the advance until his force was ready just as Montgomery would demand later in the year as he prepared behind the lines of El Alamein.

The attacker is often wrongly perceived as being at a military disadvantage. The defender has chosen the ground to suit themselves and their weapons. The defender can lay minefields and build strong points forcing any attacker to pay a heavy price to dislodge them. They knew Rommel could not afford to pay the price. There was an impressive force of armour in reserve to destroy any German breakthrough between the defensive 'boxes.' Rommel would need to conserve his armour.

The ground was well prepared by the defenders. The sole weakness was the inability of each 'box' to support the others because of the area they had to cover. But after his initial assault on the Free French around Bir Hacheim, Rommel turned from attacker to defender. It looked like a victory for the Allies but this is where Rommel would earn the tile of 'the desert fox.'

The fierce battle that ensued earned the unnamed location between the defensive 'boxes' the title of 'The Cauldron.' Here Rommel's troops were able to destroy the armour sent to dislodge them. The German tactic was to lead with their tanks but then withdraw behind a screen of lethal, anti-aircraft guns that followed close behind ready for the Allied counter attack.

In May 1940, as he fought to stem the British attack near Arrass, Rommel, the would-be engineer, had appreciated that the high muzzle velocity of the '88' would punch through existing armour. Now these improvised German anti-tank guns were employed rather like archers against charging cavalry. The result was devastating.

Once they had weathered the counter-attacks which lasted two weeks in the cauldron, the Germans resumed their offensive. The battle of Gazala was lost. They had cut a hole through the middle of the defensive boxes and destroyed the Eighth Army's tank force. On 12 June the remaining Allied forces began to withdraw along the coast back into Egypt. The British had just 70 operational tanks.

By holding their position after the initial assault, the Germans were also able to conserve their limited stock of fuel and supplies brought through a gap cut through the defensive mine field. Military intelligence had observed this gap being prepared and optimistically interpreted it as the preparation of a possible escape route for the Germans.

The steady advance by the Germans across the desert began. Tobruk looked as if it would become an enclave once again. But that threat would emerge a week into the future. For the moment the company could continue with the routine of rebuilding the battered town and preparing the forward supply base for the next campaign.

It had been hard for the company to piece together the fortunes of the battle ranging to their south. Rommel appeared to be advancing, now being held and then apparently in retreat. The casualties and flow of damaged vehicles told of the intensity of the struggle.

The company was again called on to repair the tanks. This was no longer the clinical engineering task from their time at Alex. Now there was blood and worse to be cleared before the engineering work could be undertaken. Bob wondered about the broken bodies that had been taken from these tanks and if somebody was repairing them. Morale suffered. One NCO had to be disciplined for striking his men. Another incident affected a pair of twins in the company.

One twin was so disturbed that he was to be evacuated. His brother, working elsewhere, became so ill that the doctors decided that they would have to go out of Tobruk together. By good fortune a hospital ship arrived and the twins, plus all the nurses from the hospital, were evacuated. This was ominous.

'One incident stands out in my memory which concerned our section officer, Lieutenant Tony Lumbkin, who was billeted in the next villa to us. He sent for me one night and was obviously very distressed because he had just received news that his brother had been killed in Singapore. He wanted desperately to write a letter of condolence and comfort to his mother, but in his present state of mind he was unable to put pen to paper. All our letters home were censored by the section officers and he said that he had noted I always wrote very good letters and would I write one to his mother on his behalf. I duly complied and I've often wondered, in later years, whether it gave her any comfort.'

At this stage it became evident to Bill that the navy and air force were conspicuous by their absence. This confirmed rumours circulating about the breakthrough in the desert. 'We had no wish to be trapped in another siege and had pulled out. It was evident that Jerry had the skies to themselves' Bill recalls.

'As the days went by we continued to work at the hospital. The number of casualties arriving each night was increasing and we began to realise the tide of battle was turning against us dramatically. There were also a large number of tanks coming in, for repair at the ROAC workshop and our lads were helping out. Word began to circulate that fierce tank battles were being fought in the desert area, not so far away.

'Time became meaningless as we were being constantly turned out during the nights, in full battle order, to forestall any sea-based or parachute drops from German positions in Crete. It came as a pleasant surprise, on Sunday 14

June 1942 when the unit was ordered to pull back, along the coast road, to El Alamein. Everyone was quickly loaded onto their three ton trucks and we set off east.'

They joined the stream of vehicles heading east, bumping across the desert. As usual Bill Harvey found himself in a party of six to act as a rearguard. They had their own pick-up truck ready for their get-away which provided some consolation.

'There was still plenty of war noises but our thoughts were now geared up to the prospect of getting away from this benighted spot, and after a reasonable time had elapsed we set off to catch up with the main party. Much to our surprise, we caught up too quickly. The bad news was the company was on the way back into Tobruk.'

The company had been intercepted and told to turn back. Bill remembers an officer attached to the brigade staff confirming they had to turn round as the decision was that Tobruk was going to be defended. The staff officer, whose name Bill recalls bitterly, would have known that the German front line was already 100 miles south-east of Tobruk. But Rommel appeared to have swept past Tobruk in pursuit of the retreating Eighth Army. It looked as if the town might have time to prepare for another siege.

The following day all personnel not needed to defend a besieged Tobruk were again ordered out. The company was not on the new list of those to be evacuated. A formal decision to leave an isolated garrison was not made until 17 June. By then, any decision was academic as Rommel's tanks had reached the coast at Gamut cutting off any retreat or reinforcement.

The troops arriving from the Kensington 'box' brought more news and bolstered their confidence that the town could be held. But Bob and Alan recognised there was little or no chance that the necessary troops could be assembled to garrison Tobruk in time. They also that there was no time to repair the neglected defences. A decisive withdrawal, that had saved the company two years before in France, would not save them this time.

The bad news to turn back had been delivered to Alan Jones by a dispatch rider who had sought the company out among the retreating column. Alan had already reached the perimeter of the town leading the company convoy and joined a broad column of vehicles edging back along the coast towards safety. It was daunting and demoralising to have to turn the company round for a journey back to the billets against the flow of a retreating army.

Bill Harvey felt that they could have escaped again just as they had two years earlier. 'Our own commanding officer, Major Yates was in Cairo at this time but if he had been with us I'm certain he would have ignored the order as the captain wouldn't have been able to pull rank on him, most of our section officers were lieutenants. I'm afraid it was another glaring example of First World War mentality.'

The company nominally returned to their normal duties. But the sappers were aware that the situation was deteriorating. Thoughts of what might happen to them were never far from our minds. They did not need any newsletters to understand that the battle was not going well. Battle weary tank crews and infantry were being forced back and appeared in the town. Talk quickly turned to demolition and destruction to deliver a hollow victory to Rommel.

The excellent mine fields and defences prepared by the defenders in 1941 had not been maintained. Many mines had been lifted and moved forward to protect the boxes. Others were buried beneath a cushion of sand deposited by the sandstorms. The blown sand had also filled the anti-tank ditches blasted in the rock and would not hold back Rommel's troops.

There was serious confusion about Rommel's future intentions. Would he pursue the retreating army or turn on Tobruk? Tobruk had successfully withstood his repeated assaults during 1941. Would the memory of the fortifications protect Tobruk? The commanders hoped that the defences would hold again. In the event, the reversal of fortunes was too sudden to repair the situation.

On Friday, the assault on Tobruk began. The company woke to a terrific pounding. They watched waves of German Stuka bombers blasting a route through the minefield and the troops marooned there. Later the bombers turned their attention to the harbour although, apart from a few naval launches, the port was now empty. No ship wanted to be caught in the harbour during daylight hours. Bob Borthwick tried to keep the nearby workshop busy but the lookout he had posted on the roof brought regular warning of approaching planes. They passed most of the day in their shelter as raids of up to 90 aircraft prevented any significant military response around the perimeter.

Bob Borthwick had good reason to feel that he was in the firing line. General Rommel had identified the nearby desalination plant as a key installation in the survival of the town. The plant was, however, not on the target list as it was one of the prizes they hoped to capture. If there was to be another siege, he would certainly intend that those besieged should be thirsty so would doubtless target the plant.

The distillation plant, on which they had lavished so much attention, was put out of action. 'The plant's life was terminated when a quantity of explosive was detonated in the fire chamber of the boiler' Alan notes with some feeling. This singular action is reported to have so annoyed Rommel that he forbade the issue of water to the captives for a few days.

On Saturday 20 June, Rommel stood on the escarpment north-east of El Adem as the attack on Tobruk was pressed home. Stukas continued to dive-bomb the minefields and detonate the mines so their armour could advance.

Alan noticed the bombs had a long rod attached to the nose of each bomb. The bombs exploded above the sand the moment the rod touched the sand. The pressure created by the blast would set off any nearby mines.

Rommel had also pushed his engineers to the front line. He wanted the defensive ditches filled and his engineers completed the task under the cover of the intense aerial bombardment and a rolling barrage from his artillery, reminiscent of earlier trench warfare Bill mused. By 10 the tanks were able to breach the final line of defence.

The 60 panzers that broke through did not oblige the defenders by fanning out to attack their dispersed and well-sited positions but instead pressed on towards the town. The few anti-tank guns encountered were quickly dealt with. Most of the defenders looked on in frustration as they were by-passed by their attackers. Any attempt to re-deploy was disrupted by watchful Stukas. Before nightfall Rommel would know that he had secured Tobruk.

They were woken early on the Saturday by heavy gunfire and more bombing to the south-east. From the billets they could not see what was going on beyond the escarpment. They were still not unduly concerned as everyone expected the Germans to probe the defences. The consensus in the company was that Rommel would keep his troops in pursuit of the main force retreating along the coast, or attempt to cut them off by one of his dashes through the desert.

This assessment was wrong. Possessing Tobruk was more than a trophy. It would shorten German supply lines by 1000 kilometres. Rommel attributed his previous setback to a failure of logistics. In October the previous year he had written to Hitler explaining that once Tobruk had been captured, the enemy would not stand a chance. The port was vital to both sides. Without it, the Allies would have to fall back to the Delta to shorten their supply lines. This was a war in which logistics and engineers were as important as tanks and infantry.

After breakfast, everybody returned to normal duties. Alan Jones sent Bill Harvey and another electrician across to the hospital to check that all was still working. It was only a distance of 200 yards but they now found themselves under attack. It was a new and very unpleasant experience.

'A shell makes a terrifying and an awesome sound in flight and worse still when it explodes about twenty yards away. The ground was very rocky in this area and I noticed the shell had made a crater about three feet diameter and twelve inches deep. Forgetting about a stiff upper lip and casting dignity to one side, we dived into the shelter of the hospital.'

They were asked to set up an emergency operating room to cope with the flow of casualties. Lights were found and wired above the tables that would serve for the doctors. 'Making a last check to see everything was all right in the emergency theatre, we made our way to the main operating theatre to tell them the emergency set-up was available. On our way we noticed an artillery sergeant in full battle order, looking out across the bay, and he looked a bit forlorn. I asked him how things were going and he explained he'd been in charge of an anti-aircraft gun but had been shooting at advancing German tanks. Two of his crew had been wounded in the battle and he had brought them into hospital.'

He then pointed across the bay, where the road led up to the escarpment. 'That's a German tank and it will soon be all over' he said. The Germans were already through the defences and into the outskirts of the town. The lookout on Bob's workshop was reaching a similar conclusion. From the top of the building it was possible to see as far as Kings Cross, the name given to the junction of the El Adem and Bardia Roads.

Bill decided to take this information back to the billet and sought out their section officer but Lieutenant Lumbkin confessed he knew nothing of the situation. As the company gathered for lunch the alarming intelligence was shared. Their neighbours, the ack-ack gunners based next door, confirmed their worst fears. There had been a concentrated attack on the section of the perimeter held by the Indian Brigade and the panzers had broken through and were now at the innermost mine-belt.

Lunch continued and a disquieted workforce returned to work. From the roof of the workshop, the final act in the breakthrough was watched by the lookout. The Stukas began to blast the final mine belt, supported by a concentrated artillery barrage to disrupt any defences beyond the minefield. To the spectators on the roof who had no access to information about the battle it definitely did not have the feel of the successful counter attack of which they had been told by those in authority.

Bob Borthwick decided to pack up the workshop. Almost immediately a shout from the roof warned him that some tanks were driving down the road towards the cemetery. Bob rushed to the roof with his binoculars to confirm that the tanks had black crosses on their flanks. There was no mistake. It was time to move out.

Bob detoured via the power station to warn Reg Gunn. He had decided to stay and keep the power running for the hospital but had already placed explosives on the generators. They said a quick farewell and Bob returned to the company billets.

After some frantic telephoning on the gunner's phone next door, it was decided to withdraw in front of the advancing tanks. There was no line to their commanders. It was an anguished afternoon as they prepared, once again, to beat a disorderly retreat. There was the obligatory ritual of destroying paper work but most quickly prepared for their uncertain future.

There was no air-cover, little armour and few anti-tank guns or artillery to delay the attackers. The panzers broke through the weakened perimeter and began to destroy the many trucks that had taken refuge there. A small counter attack failed to drive the Germans out. With no prospect of support from the army retreating towards El Alamein or of an organised breakout, General Klopper, the South African commander of the garrison, surrendered that evening.

As dusk fell, everyone was again loaded into three ton lorries and they withdrew to the beaches about a mile away from the town centre. This was very much a last resort. They had been told that the navy had withdrawn all their support but remembered the little ships in 1940 and hoped for a similar miracle. With Bob Borthwick on 'Bitsa' this time in the lead, the lorries made their way through the streets, hurried along by intermittent shelling.

The journey was not without incident. On the way to the beach they picked up a man, with a shrapnel wound and took him along. They were not the first to have the idea of moving to the beach in the hope of rescue. There was already a crowd waiting. Bill Harvey identified a couple of medics from his time at the hospital that came and tended to the wounded man. 'The shrapnel seemed to have entered in the right shoulder area and passed through his body leaving at his left buttock, it was impossible to confirm what damage it had done on its way through' Bill recalls a lingering regret.

'It was dusk and I felt so helpless and ineffective. The hospital was probably already captured while this poor soldier lay losing blood. He died during the night. Looking back in later years I often wish we had loaded him into a truck and taken him back to the hospital, where he might have had a chance of survival and to hell with the consequences.' The man died just before dawn and Bob watched the melancholy ritual as one of the dog-tags was removed by the medics, the other being left for the burial party.

The sounds of war quietened during the night but a pall of smoke rose over the town. The smoke reflected a red glow from the burning facilities in the night sky.

'In that quiet, we had time to reflect on the futility of war that requires a man to die in those circumstances' Bill noted in his record of the conflict.

The section officers and senior NCOs discussed the option. There were no materials available for any rafts or boats. Some soldiers knocked the floor and side panel out of their lories to provide material but from their commando training they knew there was not enough for a single seaworthy craft. Their rations had been brought by the cooks so they were able to sort out some food and a brew of tea. Bob was struck by how the British tommy, of all ranks, was much happier once they had a hot drink.

The sounds of battle were audible around the perimeter but they seemed to indicate a mopping-up operation. There were no sounds of a fierce battle that might point to a British attack to counter the breakthrough. The town gradually fell quiet apart from the occasional tank shell that chased some fleeting target.

Following their conference, Bob expected to be captured and was worried about his ammunition. The two rounds that he carried for his revolver were made of lead unlike most bullets where the softer lead is covered in the harder copper. There had been rumours that the Germans had harshly punished anyone carrying 'dum-dum' bullets where the bullet had been modified to increase the injury inflicted. He fired his rounds into the petrol tank of 'Bitsa' and pushed her into the sea. The personal weapons that had been a rather useless but constant companion for the previous two and a half years were now wrecked. Bob's redundant revolver followed his beloved bike into the sea.

Huddled in their greatcoats after some desultory speculation, most fell asleep. The night had passed but no rescue came. The morning brought less talk of the possibility of a sea rescue. Some soldiers could still be seen gathering materials for rafts as the first light of dawn illuminated their plight. It was already far too late to contemplate any escape bid.

A gloomy, cloud-shrouded Sunday morning dawned slowly at first. There was a brief bombardment of one presumed stronghold in the harbour area. The shells fell mercifully short and did no damage.

'I was still only half awake when my dozing and dreaming was rudely broken by the fast approaching howl of a low flying fighter plane, closely followed by the sharp clatter from a nearby Bren gun. Jumping up, I joined in the general shouting at the Bren gunners for their idiocy' Bob recalls.

When the outcry died down, an officious artillery major appeared on the scene, waving his swagger stick and calling for defensive positions to be taken up in the dunes at the rear of the beach. 'He wants to recapture Tobruk' and 'You can have my Bren when the first tank appears' greeted his suggestion from those who were forming a low opinion of some of their leaders. Fortunately his plan was ignored by the other officers present.

The first sensible suggestion, 'Let's all have some breakfast', met with general approval and a move made to the lorries. With wood from the attempts at raft-building, a number of fires were lit and aroma of sizzling bacon and fried bread, drew everyone and their mess-tins towards the fires. 'I do not think anyone realised this would be our last breakfast of bacon for more than three years. It was certainly enjoyed considering the state of anticipation we were in' says Bill.

Alan Jones, like many others, had gathered some food and kept the two gallon water carrier that had served his crew during their stay in the desert. The stock of bully beef and the large, flat, flavourless biscuits were handed out.

The fighter plane that had flown over would have reported the group of troops on the beach and after breakfast they had visitors. From where they sat on the beach they were overlooked by the high rim of the escarpment, about

150 yards away. Over the bank, behind the dunes, there appeared a very large Panzer tank, which stopped well short. It began to swing its turret machine gun very threateningly. By midday two tanks were clearly visible on the rim just watching. They were surrounded by sand, sea and tanks.

'We all stood around for hour just waiting when, who should appear advancing towards the tank with a white handkerchief tied to his swagger stick but our little Artillery Major' Bob remembers. His act of surrender was wasted for the turret opened and a young officer appeared with a megaphone calling, in perfect English, for everyone to form up in front of the tank adding that all Tobruk had surrendered.

The Germans now took the initiative and advanced with white flags. One officer came walking forward from the direction of the tanks observed by the company. There were a few wise-cracks about whether they should let the Germans surrender. One of the sapper officers now improvised a white flag, went forward.

It was an anti-climax. Their active service in the army was over. Now it was just a matter of waiting to see what would happen to them next.

Alan had ensured the company had left their billets in Tobruk well prepared with water and rations which were now dispersed. 'We took what rations we could from the lorries' recalls Bob. 'I filled my coat pockets with packets of tea, milk and biscuits. Meanwhile the tank commander and two of his crew had dismounted and lined us up by rank, officers in front. We were ordered to lay down our weapons and ammunition and be prepared to march away. With some sort of order, we were marched off with the tank leading and the two crew following with machine pistols.'

Thus started a miserable trek through the town and up the road to the escarpment, made more depressing when they were overtaken by Bob's two workshop lorries driven away by their captors. To make matters worse their other lorries had been driven to the food store and were being loaded with NAFFI stock.

The one that got away

A few had managed to slip away as they awaited capture. Some of the Coldstream Guards escaped in their vehicles during the night. Earlier in the day one member of the company also had a lucky escape. The tanks plagued Lieutenant TK Brown's successful escape.

Saturday morning had been spent impotently watching the shelling and bombing that appeared well targeted on military facilities. During the morning, orders arrived that they were free to make a break for freedom if they could. He set off to find Captain Bell at the company billets in the villas which were now being shelled intermittently. By this time, the rest of the company had withdrawn and were nowhere to be found.

At about five thirty, Lieutenant Brown set off in a jeep for the jetty at the east end of the town where some vessels had been reported as still seaworthy. He met two naval ratings along the way who scrounged a lift. The jetty had about 400 personnel waiting around. Half were in navy uniform.

The shelling of the harbour began again and he decided to abandon the vehicle which seemed to attract the unwelcome attention. By very good fortune he found himself among a crowd, beside a civilian schooner that was preparing to leave. After a quick consultation with the skipper he supervised the loading for the navy with the help of an Australian army officer. As the cloak of darkness approached, they cast off. They could not wait until it was dark as they needed some light to navigate from the harbour.

A motor torpedo boat, MTB 260, had set out ahead of the small flotilla to lay smoke and provide some protection from the waiting tanks. This was a evidently an organised, if improvised, breakout. They all recognised that they would have to run the gauntlet as soon as they emerged from their moorings which concealed them from view of the tanks that overlooked the sea.

Their schooner was hit almost as soon as it got underway. It was not designed for combat and quickly began to sink. The MTB immediately came alongside and 50 people were able to scramble aboard. They continued to circle the schooner making smoke as the tanks did their best to sink both ships. Once the gunners had their range it was impossible to come alongside so attempts to take the schooner in tow failed.

As darkness fell, the MTB, loaded well beyond its limit, left the floundering schooner and made its way east and to safety. It was a lucky escape but he felt no elation. Lt Brown would in due course be called to testify to the courage shown by the skipper of the MTB at a Court of Enquiry.

The End

German soldiers marched them to an open area nearer the town where they joined many of those that had been rounded up the day before. From force of habit they kept with their own section. It was only about seven days since they were turned back towards Tobruk. 'Surely someone, somewhere should have known the true state of the desert battle and utter futility of contemplating another siege of Tobruk. I have even debated whether the captain had the authority to order us to stay' recalls Bill.

On 21 June 1942 Tobruk fell along with 29,000 men. It was another low point of the war. The blow was made worse for being so unexpected. At home, thoughts were of a victory in the desert. Instead, the desert army was in retreat. This time they would fall back to the defensive line at El Alamein where in a month of intense fighting would halt the Axis advance.

However, for 106 Army Troops Company Royal Engineers, the die was cast. 'We were in the bag, bewildered and apprehensive. We didn't know what would happen next. Needless to say everyone was deflated, uneasy and apprehensive as to what the future would hold now that we had started our journey into the unknown.' They were no longer masters of their destiny. They sat on the sand for three days. From time to time they would be reorganised by their captors and moved a short distance. The last of the season's dust storms added to their discomfort. There was no food or water. Conversation was limited but there was plenty of time to sleep.

Bill summarises his war in a few poignant words. 'At this point the unit's active participation in the war was over. It was a demoralising and heart-rending experience and the last thing we anticipated when we set off in September 1939. Up to this time, June 1942, we had been part of an army in a constant state of retreat and we had no battle honours to dwell on. Our claims to fame were being the first unit into France, and certainly one of the last to leave. Also the unit was the first to start the construction at El Alamein, before the world even knew such a place existed. All the work that we were called on to perform was carried out to a high standard of craftsmanship which brings great credit on the skills of the men concerned.

'I remember the 106 Army Trooper Company RE all with pride and affection. They were a great bunch of comrades.' They were just ordinary heroes.

For Rommel the reward was his appointment as a Field Marshall. For his troops the rewards were more material and captured dumps of food, sugar, beer and cigarettes.

On 13 August, Montgomery took over the Eighth Army and gave his famous order forbidding further retreat. Safely behind the lines, General Montgomery would not allow himself to be hurried by Churchill and held the position until he had received the troops and equipment necessary to break out and sustain an advance across the desert. From October 1942 until mid May 1943, the Eighth Army pushed Rommel back across the hard-fought desert in a campaign that would bring the North African campaign to an end.

The story of 106, Army Troops Company, Royal Engineers, is brought to a close on 15 July 1942 when they are officially listed as 'non-existent.' A few lucky ones had slipped away. Some, such as the OC and his driver were out of Tobruk. There were not enough left to continue or reconstitute the unit. The wartime history of the unit came to a close.

The men from Doncaster had been mobilised for a little under three years. It would be another three years before they would get home to Yorkshire. The stories are no longer of the unit but of the individual struggles to survive.

Chapter Eleven

Captivity Africa and Italy

June 1942 – August 1943

The first of many long marches into captivity finished at the top of the escarpment in the old Italian airfield. It was already crowded with prisoners, mostly South Africans, who crouched around little fires.

'We were directed to an area near the road and started gathering as many of the company around us. Alan Jones and I with Bill Richards collected Cliff Barron, Jack Hurren and Harold Crowcroft into a group' Bob recalls. 'The six of us agreeing to keep together for as long as possible. The rest of the company settled down around us in similar, small groups. It was then a case of sitting around waiting to see what would happen next. Would we be given food and water, when and how? There appeared to be thousands of us being herded by Italians with not a German now in sight.'

It was time to inspect the haversack Bob snatched from the wall in his billet during the rush to get away from the advancing tanks. 'I put all the oddments I had accumulated over the year. I was never sure what was in there and was gratified when I looked in to see what I could contribute to our group. There was soap, toothbrush and a new towel from my last parcel Wynne had sent. A box of fifty *Cape to Cairo* cigarettes from Mr Vye in Cape Town, and some two hundred or so Victory V cigarettes, the awful issue made locally in Cairo, which I only smoked when there was nothing else available. There were a couple of boxes of matches, a 'housewife' mending kit, two clean handkerchiefs and a packet of razor blades.' Each item greeted with a gasp of surprise among the group and thanks at Bob's unexpected fortune.

There were the tins of condensed milk and packets of tea that many had thrust into their greatcoat pockets. Between them they also had some bully beef and biscuits so the SNCOs were not so badly off when they sorted out what they had as a group. The soldiers around them were discovering similar treasures. Harold Crowcroft and Bill Richards were the heavy smokers and they had only a few packets. It was agreed that Bob would hold their supply and they would have three each a day, one after each meal. In the early hours of captivity they were still supposing they would get three meals a day.

'We had enough for a few days along with five tommy cookers, complete with fuel bricks that we normally carried in our mess-tins so we would be able to brew tea' Bob recalls. All this depended on a supply of water. Alan had made sure that everybody had filled their water bottles on the beach. The order was to keep their water bottles full until they could assess their situation. Alan had distributed many cans of water before the distillery was destroyed and these supplies were used to keep them going. A problem they quickly encountered was a lack of cooking utensils. Apart from their mess-tin they had no cups. They improvised as ever and used tin helmets to brew and drink tea which proved a great success.

'We were to learn later that Rommel had been so furious with the destruction of the fuel tanks and the desalination plant and other water

supplies that he forbade the issue of water to the POWs for the time being'
says Bob. 'Fortunately for us he left Tobruk to continue his advance and a
more liberal German command took over and we were eventually issued with
a cup of water each day. When the water trucks turned up, the Italian guards
made futile attempts to stop the rush and the fights that developed around the
water point until the officers appeared to restore order and form queues.'

On Monday morning, just after they returned with their water, they were
brought to their feet by the sound of approaching bagpipes. Coming down the
road were the Cameron Highlanders, led by their piper, and marching smartly
with their rifles at the slope. It was quite an emotional moment for the captives
and helped to hold off some of the looming depression. The Camerons held
out after the breakout on the southern perimeter, despite being surrounded. 'I
learned later from Jack Telfer, a Quartermaster Sergeant in the Camerons, who
joined me later in Germany, that they were told by a German officer with a
white flag, that they were the last of the Tobruk garrison to surrender and were
given the honour of marching into captivity. This was disputed by a
detachment of Coldstream Guards who came to the airfield after the
Camerons.'

There was much discussion regarding the fate of the Gurkha Battalion who
held the eastern perimeter on the coast. Only a few had filtered onto the
airfield and eventually they heard the story of their magnificent, desperate
defence. Outflanked, the Gurkhas fought off the Italians attacking the rear of
their position. With little opposition to their front, when ammunition ran low
most of them had eventually escaped along the coast.

'It transpired as we talked among the groups that General Klopper had
surrendered early that Sunday morning and the South Africans were the first
to be told' said Bob. 'Because they had not been engaged in any fighting, the
soldiers found it hard to believe that they had to surrender. It was rumoured
that tanks circulated the lines with South African officers on board to pass on
the word to surrender. Most of them had time to collect all their kit so they
were better prepared for captivity.'

'At the time, we had the impression that the South Africans gave up too
easily. Till the end of the war, it was maintained that we were not captured, we
were "Kloppered"' Bob recalls. 'This was unfair I realised later when the truth
was known. General Klopper had no alternative, nor had his troops, when the
breakthrough was made on the eastern perimeter and tanks descended on
them from the rear' Bob confesses.

These were tense times and there was too much time to contemplate who
was to blame. 'It also caused further resentment when we were moved
because the South Africans were separately moved. This may not have been of
any significance as most of the Indian troops were also moved separately' Bob
recalls, 'but is promoted gossip.'

Later on Monday morning, the Italians announced a water issue so they all queued up for over an hour to receive a cup of water in their mess tins. This was immediately brewed to make tea over their tommy cookers. A second issue of water was made in the evening accompanied by a couple of hard biscuits and a tin of Italian meat which was, at first, a welcome surprise. 'Later we were to learn that the enemy were only too glad to be able to give this meat to prisoners as they much preferred our bully beef, of which they now had plenty' says Bob.

When they sampled the Italian beef it was agreed that it tasted horrible. The small brown tins were labelled AM which they were told later meant 'Administratione Militari.' The Italians called it 'Arabo Morti', the Germans 'Alt Mann.' The tommys developed names ranging from 'Awful Meat' to 'Ancient Man' but 'Old Man' was the name agreed for all of the tinned beef and it was hated by everyone. It was probably tough horsemeat. Nevertheless some were glad to have it over the next few days, others felt it wise to eat whatever was on offer.

Bill recalls the unwelcome sensation of starvation to which they would become accustomed. 'We were so hungry. With my literary shortcomings I find it difficult to describe. I have often thought, since those days that normal, well fed people can live for about three weeks, without undue problems but after that the hunger gnaws at your mind and stomach, however brave a face you put on. Owing to the confusion at the time of capture, none of us had many possessions, just a few bits and pieces packed into a haversack.'

The pangs of hunger were beginning to bite. Bill recalls an amusing incident. 'Already some of the men were bartering their possessions with the Italian guards patrolling the wire. One pair of POWs had just reached the point of agreement when a German soldier approached and promptly kicked the Italian's backside. He then threw both the bread and the bartered watch back to the prisoner.' A good deal.

Tuesday was spent just sitting around, watching Italian 10 ton Lancia lorries with trailers loaded with prisoners packed together before heading west along the El Adem road. The selection of those to go was haphazard with a quarter of an hour's notice to move. None of the close-knit company were selected that day.

Early the next morning, Wednesday 24 June, an area around them was cordoned off and they were told to gather up their kit and be ready to move to the roadside. There was some hurried change of place so some of those separated from their pals attempted to re-group themselves. 'The five of us kept together to join some fifty on the roadside as we were herded by Italian guards' Bob remembers. A Lorry and trailers stopped with its tailboard right in front of the group. When they were told to board, Bob and Alan were first aboard. They made their way to the front which proved to be the best position.

With everyone standing, they had the cab to lean on and a good view of the road ahead.

Bob has pleasant memories of the journey viewed from his vantage point. 'As we approached Gazala there were signs of the fighting with wrecked tanks and vehicles strewn all over the desert and on the sides of the road. There was no stopping for lunch, but we convinced the Italian guards that we would like to satisfy the needs of nature and the whole convoy stopped.'

'After more than four hours of the same bleak desert under the hot sun, we approached the top of the escarpment overlooking Derna. Here we were given a most spectacular view of the coast stretching away to the west. Nearly a thousand feet below lay the most beautiful greenery we had seen in a long time. The town was neatly laid out with tree-lined roads, green grass, flowers and palm trees. The convoy halted for a short time to space each vehicle for the decent of the escarpment road. It was a hair-raising decent. The houses were neat little villas, similar to those in Tobruk but there was less damage. Each villa had its lawn and cascading bougainvillea.'

The convoy toured the outskirts to reach their destination to the west of the town. It was walled, about one hundred yards square, facing the dunes and the sea on one side and the road on the other. Many were of the opinion that it was an old graveyard. At the large iron gate stood the unmistakable figure of a Guard's sergeant major beside an Italian officer ready to greet them. They received an issue of AM and two biscuits. As they passed other POWs who scanned them for friends but nobody warned them to keep clear of the pit.

'There in the middle of the compound was a pit about ten feet long by four feet wide already filling with sewage. The smell was beginning to permeate the place and we new-arrivals had no choice but to settle nearby. Being the first lorry to unload, our little group were some yards back from the pit. This was our first taste of Italian sanitation. I was constipated and didn't use the pit in the two days we spent in Derna' Bob recalls.

Their first task was to brew some tea. The water in Derna was reported to be the sweetest in the whole desert, was drawn from a standpipe by the gate. During the journey they had been forced to drink from their water bottles and the temptation was to refill them direct from the standpipe. Nevertheless, they agreed to boil the water even though their fuel was running out.

The next day a group of German officers on the dunes, overlooking the wall, tried to take photographs of the prisoners. The response was to stand up and raise both arms in the Winston V sign. This was met with amusement by the visitors but not by their escorting Italian officer who, when his screams had no effect, drew his pistol and fired into the crowd. One bullet hit someone in the shoulder and a roar of rage arose from the camp. The German officers remonstrated with the Italian and hurried him away. A formal complaint was made by the sergeant major and the name of the officer concerned was eventually passed on to the Red Cross.

The next day the prisoners in the compound were loaded onto lorries for a further stage on the journey west with a parting gift of two biscuits and a tin of AM. Bob again secured a good view. 'We were treated to a pleasant journey through the greenery of this part of northern Cyrenaica. After climbing the escarpment out of Derna, palm trees and green bushes became more plentiful and we were soon in the lush green countryside which reminded us of home. We forked off the coast road and drove for the high ground seen ahead, the famous Jebel Akdar, the Green Mountains, covered in trees and greenery and showing little of the advances and retreats of Armies over the last two years of war. The countryside was populated by Italian colonists who had worked hard to turn it into a cultivated area of meadows, tomato plantations, and vegetable plots, all surrounding brightly painted little villas and farmsteads dotted the slopes of the surrounding hills.'

The road to Bengazi was a monument to the Italians who built it. They crossed long viaducts spanning green valleys and rounded hairpin bends on the steep mountain passes. Their destination was a tented camp alongside an airfield on the outskirts of Bengazi to awaiting shipment to Italy.

'By this time my constipation, although not yet uncomfortable, had become a worry. Dysentery had become widespread with a long queue for the medical tent. It was my first chance to see the medical officer. In the tent were two South African doctors and when it came my turn I explained. "Sir, I've been constipated for the last eight days." When he appreciated what I had said, a look of amazement spread over his face and turning to his companion he exclaimed "John, I have a staff sergeant here in the happy predicament of not being able to shit!"' Bob recalls as the medics burst out laughing along with the rest of the sick parade within hearing. Bob was offered a 'Number 9' pill with instructions not to take it unless it became necessary but in the event did not need it.

The next day they became aware that everyone had become infested. A new task became the inspection of all shirts and shorts seams morning and night. The lice were easy to catch and destroy but the eggs were more difficult find. The burning tip of a cigarette was the best weapon but these were already in short supply.

The Italians set up a table and some were able to fill in a card, giving particulars, apparently for the Red Cross. It looked a bit haphazard but Bill was particularly grateful for this opportunity. He had already imagined his wife Edith receiving a telegram reporting him missing. He knew how upset she would be and prayed that his capture card would be transmitted quickly.

The stay in Bengazi lasted four days. They observed that those nearest the towngate had the best chance of being shipped out. Near the gate, Bob was reunited with Reg Gunn who had arrived the night before having been captured in the power station as he was preparing to fire the charges.

During their stay at Benghazi the guards herded them, a few at a time, to a barber armed with haircutting shears. They received a very short, shaven look. 'I thought, why not? We were prisoners and we may as well look the part.' conceded Bill Harvey. However Alan Jones had a rebellious streak. 'Our staff sergeant did not fancy this and asked if we could cut his hair to look shorter so he could avoid the chop. Our efforts weren't particularly good and in the end he was pleased to go and have the convict cut.'

With a ration of four biscuits and two tins of AM a group of about one hundred marched through the town to the docks. The docks were large and busy and they marched past several ships before stopping at one of the smallest, one-funnelled tramp collier. This time those at the back of the group earned a place on deck which was preferable to a place in the hold into which most of the group had disappeared.

Bill was unlucky again. The covers were off the holds and he found himself looking down at a 30 foot dungeon. Access was down a rope ladder, secured at top and bottom to keep it taut. Buckets were placed at the stern for latrines but the hold cargo was not permitted to stay on deck but the trip provided some relief from the conditions below.

Once on board Bob traded his cigarette lighter for a bowl of macaroni soup with some meat served in the galley. The hot soup worked better than any No9 pill and Bob made desperate signs. The laughing crewman pointed as Bob hastily retired. Bob was lucky as many had to dump their dysentery over the sides.

Alan also found himself on the deck. There appeared to be plenty of lifeboats and rafts about so he began to talk to those around him how they might escape if their boat was torpedoed. The trick was to work out which coast was nearest. Should they head north to Italy, or south, back to Africa? Either way, the prospects would not be good. The journey was completed without any other ship or plane being sighted.

Bill was stuck in the bowels of the boat. 'As we set sail across the Mediterranean my only morbid thought, as we stewed in the hold, was of the possibility of our own submarines being on patrol' Bill recalls.

It was a pitiful lot that formed up on the dockside at Brindisi but two sergeant majors worked their magic. With a lot of shouting and a little pleading they were cajoled to smarten up before leaving the docks to march through the town.

Bill recalls one small positive. 'Eventually we were moved again and naturally that meant using our feet. One thing I do remember, with pride and pleasure, was that somewhere along the line we had acquired a Scottish regimental pipe major and when we had to march anywhere he proudly took up position at the head of the column and piped us along in good army order and not as a shambling mob. Everyone was proud of that man.'

It must have been a normal sight for the local inhabitants for, although they stopped to look, nothing was said or done. Bob recalls 'I must admit we did do our best to look cheerful and smart to create an impression.'

Bill recalls the experience. 'Lots of people were lining the roads to see the English prisoners, an experience we did not enjoy. At one point there was a young woman, rather brazen looking, who took a half smoked cigarette from her mouth and tossed it at me. I was pleased to be able to let it brush my shirt and fall to the ground where I crushed it underfoot. Being English we had to have some pride and at least she looked very startled.'

They marched into the country where marching deteriorated to a country stroll. There was an attempt at singing but nobody was in the mood so after a few half-hearted choruses a silent shuffle resumed until they found themselves rambling alongside turnip field.

After a brief hesitation there was a rush that started at the front, into the fields for turnips. The guards threatened to shoot but most were too busy picking and cleaning the turnips on the grassy roadside. Despite the shouts of the Italians attempting to stop the feeding frenzy, everyone soon returned to the road with at least one muddy turnip. After a meal of raw turnips they were soon singing merrily. 'I am sure the Italian guards thought we were mad, perhaps just maddeningly hungry!' noted Bob.

Prigioneri di Guerra

Approaching mid-day they arrived at a hutted camp behind barbed wire with a sign above the gate: Campo PG 85. Inside was a welcoming party of prisoners who said they were the cooks and cleaners with a hot meal ready. This was good news after nearly two weeks of AM meat and biscuits plus a fresh turnip. The meal was a spaghetti soup with some meat in plus a roll of bread. Then huts were allocated, everyone had a hot shower which was the first wash since capture. Deeply satisfied, they sat out in the sun searching their clothes for lice.

In the evening they had their first taste of ersatz coffee made, they all reckoned, from acorns. It was nearly black, tasting nothing like real coffee but was hot and not unpleasant. It was most welcome in the early morning after roll call.

Their huts had three-tier wooden bunks sleeping six with straw filled palliasses and two blankets each. After sleeping on the ground for the last fortnight, this was luxury.

Things got better. 'An interpreter came round later on the second day to tell us that in the morning we would be asked for our particulars for their records and to notify the Vatican and the Red Cross in Geneva so that our people at home would know what had happened to us' Bob recalls.

'I was concerned, not only about what the future held for me but also for the worry caused to my wife and family. Wynne received the normal War Office notification of 'Missing believed Prisoner of War' a week or two after our capture but the first official notification came from the War Office in August quoting a Vatican report. So those two months were a worrying time for her but she then knew what had happened.'

'After a good night's sleep, despite the lice, we gave our name, rank, age, with the name and address of our next of kin. We were not photographed. Our razor blades were useless so most had decided to grow beards. Some vowing we would not shave until released. Even at that time we were still optimistic about winning the war and being released, especially now that the Americans were in the war at last.'

Bob was still in a group of six. 'Three staff sergeants, Alan Jones, Reg Gunn and myself, with three sergeants, Cliff Barron, Jack Hurren and Bill Richards. Quite a number of the company were still with us. I remember Bill Harvey, Stan Fox and Bill Cracknell were with us. At Derna and Bengazi the selection of people for moving on was arbitrary and it was possible for groups to be split up if they did not stay together. That is how Harold Crowcroft was left behind in Bengazi.'

The following day, after a breakfast of a roll of bread and coffee, there was a short march to a little station where they were packed in cattle trucks for the first time. There was never room to lie down but each small group arranged to sit in turns. With only one small, barred window, set high in the door, there was little chance of knowing where they were going.

At midday they stopped and were given some hot soup plus a roll of bread in a siding at Foggia before the journey resumed until the early evening. 'As we disembarked we could see, not far away to the south, a volcano which we recognised as Vesuvius. So we were not far inland from Naples' Bob recalls. Packed into lorries, they soon dismounted outside a large, tented camp with a sign PG 66 Capua over the gate.

'A warrant officer appeared to tell us that this was a major transit camp. Most POWs passed through PG 66 at some time. He said our stay might last for some time as the Italians were busy sorting out permanent camps. What he did not tell them was that Italy did not have enough permanent camps but what he told us left us more optimistic despite the tents into which we were directed with a promise of coffee later' Bob relates.

They joined thousands of prisoners milling around, looking for friends or just walking endlessly round the perimeter. With no more food or smokes to share, they were now relying on the Italians for sustenance. News was another precious commodity and many inmates were searching for their desert comrades.

'It was evening and we were all weary and, as usual, very hungry but with little likelihood of anything to eat but we waited patiently for the coffee, before settling down for the night. There was a constant stream of visitors to see who we were.'

The next day they were issued a letter-card to send home but because this was a transit camp they were informed it was most unlikely to receive mail. 'I sent mine to Wynne just to say I was fit, a POW, and that I would let her know when we were permanently settled for mail. We were all looking forward to just getting a letter' said Bob.

Time was occupied in talking with the subject of food banned. The alternative to talking was walking and everyone spent some hours each day alone with themselves.

Bill recalls how their change of circumstances had affected their morale. 'I suppose we were still in a state of shock, to find ourselves POW after the pride of being a worthwhile army unit and all within about four weeks. The general uncertainty of not knowing what lay in store for us and how long we should be in this unwanted state was discomforting. One comforting thought was that we were still more or less together and we could sit or walk, yearning more than ever for things of home.'

The general boredom had started to get some down. Fights developed and twice someone ran to the wire and started to climb over. With cries of warning from prisoners and guards, the watch tower guards opened fire. The bodies were hurriedly taken away on stretchers. It was another lesson of prison life.

After a week, there was an outbreak of disease. Many reported sick with sore throats and soon several medical teams came into the camp and there was a roll call. 'We were directed to queue and we were told we were to be tested to sort out those who were positive to something or other. Later we learned it was for diphtheria. When the results were known the whole camp was sorted out into the two groups, those who were negative and a smaller group of those positive. Alan Jones, Reg Gunn and myself, had been pronounced negative.'

Bob continues, 'we assumed the others must have been positive because they were taken out of the compound and we never saw them again. The next morning there was a hurried sorting out and Reg Gunn and I were grouped together and marched out of the camp without Alan. We were piled onto a convoy of lorries and driven away eastward, all wondering what was to happen to us now.'

Gradually the company had been broken up. 'Circumstances gradually split the unit apart. I remember Sergeant Shaw's little speech before we left Tobruk that it was now every man for himself' remembers Bill. The future was just about survival.

Bob watched Vesuvius disappearing as they headed inland through some beautiful countryside for forty miles until the convoy stopped before a medieval Italian town lying in a valley against a backdrop of green hills. The guards seemed pleased by their admiration of the view and confided that this was Benevento, the centre of the tomato cultivation area.

Benevento

Bob takes up the story in his own words.

'We drove to a pleasant and prosperous town and what was obviously a newly erected camp of square, brown tents set in a large field on the green-pastured slope of the hills. The field was wired but with no sentry towers, huts outside for the Italian administration and two large buildings behind the tents.

'We dismounted and automatically fell in three ranks before a collection of Italian officers and NCOs, one of whom was the interpreter. He immediately shouted in a strong American voice for us to reform in ranks of five to be counted. This was the first time that they had taken the effort to count us. I was to discover later that there were exactly nine hundred and eighty seven of us.

'After the count, we were addressed by the Camp Commandant, a dapper major who evidently knew English but used his interpreter to shout out his instructions. Waving his two arms, in one hand holding a roll of bread and in the other, his Baretta pistol, he introduced himself by saying, when translated, he could give us this, holding up the bread roll, or this, waving the pistol! A typical Italian gesture, reminiscent of Mussolini, that we all had difficulty in keeping a straight face.

'One question he did have for our camp leader was to find a prisoner who could speak Italian. A suitable candidate was to report to a captain Bianci in the quartermasters store hut in the camp. With that the major marched back into his office with his minions, leaving the interpreter to answer any questions.

'Our reception over, we marched into the camp. There was no main gate but we came to know it as Campo PG 87. The entrance was blocked off by a crossed legged barbed wire contraption which two guards had to lift out of the way for us to march in. Still in our five formation, it was easy to allocate ten to each tent where we found a straw palliasse and two blankets each.

'Reg Gunn was our tent-senior and Stan Fox was the only other person I knew in our tent. The former broke the golden rule and spent most of his day talking about the meals he would order when he was back in Dover. He would describe the food at the Crypt Restaurant in Market St, did I know of it? Was it not the best for food? and so on, ignoring the fact that it was obviously the wrong sort of conversation in the circumstances. We were all as hungry as he was and we eventually persuaded him to shut up.

'Our first roll call that evening was chaotic. People were not sure if threes or fives were needed or which row of tents was which when we paraded out in the field. After a discussion everyone was told to fall in at their tent. After an excellent meal of macaroni soup with meat and tomatoes, cooked by our scratch team in the cookhouse, the camp leader came round searching for an Italian speaker.

'The next morning it transpired that no-one would admit to being able to speak Italian. It was announced that anyone who could speak French should report to captain Bianci after roll call. The pay on offer was an extra roll of bread each day, but for the sake of having something to do, I went along to the quartermasters office and joined the other half-dozen waiting there.

'When it was my turn I entered the office and, as a matter of courtesy, I saluted the Captain sitting there. He was a smart, youngish looking in his late twenties and clear featured, not swarthy and he rattled out in French for me to sit down. He first asked my name, where I lived, and where I learnt my French. I told him my name, that I had learned my French at school in Dover and had been over to France many times as I had friends in Calais. I also mentioned being in Rennes escaping from Brest, about why I wanted the job and what I intended to do after the war.

'Later that day I was told by the camp leader, accompanied by the Italian interpreter, that I was now the official camp interpreter. I was to deal directly with captain Bianci, his sergeant and the Italian interpreter. I was to get to know this interpreter well. He had come over from America to visit his grandparents in Naples when war was declared and was conscripted despite his passport. He was worried now that the Americans were in the war and did not know what to do about it. Before we left the camp, I wrote a note for him.

'Captain Bianci became a good friend not only to me but to the whole camp. He came from a good family somewhere near Turin. He regularly bought extras for the camp out of his own pocket. When I first reported to him, he introduced me to his sergeant and explained my duties were to report to him immediately after breakfast every day except Sundays, accompany him on his daily inspection of the cookhouse and store room, then to issue the daily bread ration with his sergeant. After the midday soup issue, I was to spend an hour or so in the office on ration returns. I was then free but we used this time to learn each other's language.

'Our ration was based on the field ration in the Italian Army in grams which didn't mean much to me but was quite small. Meat, even the dreaded AM, was in short supply and appeared once a week if at all. When I once commented on this to captain Bianci, he explained that AM tinned meat was only for front line soldiers. In Italy meat was scarce for everyone, including the Army.

'In the afternoons the captain would sometimes invite me to accompany him on a visit to Benevento to see what food was available. I thoroughly enjoyed these excursions. I was never asked to give any parole. The fields around the town were tomato plantations and the town had factories producing tomato puree and sauces. The captain ordered a supply for the camp and I always returned with tomatoes or fruit willingly given me by shopkeepers.

'Captain Bianci bought the prisoners some jam from the local jam factory where we began a tour of inspection for my benefit. They made a large selection of jams but no marmalade despite the availability of oranges. I enquired and the captain said he had heard of this particular English habit. I am fairly certain that he paid for this out of his own pocket for it was not our normal ration issue. I suspected that he also paid for some of the cheese as we always had more than was issued in other camps.

'The bread issue was a roll about the size of a fist, the official ration per day being 150 grams, nearly six ounces, although I don't think any of us bothered weighing them. The bread was issued after roll call. Two men from each group of one hundred came to collect their rolls in a blanket. I would toss the rolls into the extended blanket two at a time while the sergeant and I counted, he in Italian and I in English, I expect the two carriers also counted so there was no room for mistakes. After a few days I had picked up enough Italian to count with the sergeant to avoid confusion.

For the starving soldiers the bread ration was another vexing problem and continued all the time they were in Italy. Bill recalls: 'It was agreed that two men in rotation would take a blanket to collect the bread ration of 20 small bread cakes which could differ slightly in shape and size. To save any further dissension, the corners of the blanket were drawn up to form a bag and each of the twenty men, in rotating turn, was allowed to put his arm into the bag, without seeing the bread, and pull out the first loaf he touched. Woe betide any man caught fishing around for the biggest one. Any unfairness usually finished up with a fight. To the reader this may seem ridiculous and foolish but at the time it was happening it was very real and a serious business' Bill confesses.

'You must remember that at this time we had been in the bag about three months and were subsisting on very basic, minimum rations. I think we were still regarded as being in transit to a permanent camp but the hunger and conditions were beginning to bite very hard. There was no regular issue of Red Cross parcels and consequently everyone was changing from the cheerful squaddies of the army days into a miserable, morose mob' Bill remembers.

'Apart from the bread, jam and sometimes the cheese, the rest of the rations went into the soup of rice or macaroni, with vegetables, olive oil puree. The soup was cooked in the normal type of copper from which it was ladled into Italian Army dixies which held enough for fifty prisoners.

'The ladles used by the cook were standard Italian army issue that held the correct ration. At first, the sharing out the soup was haphazard. The troops used home-made tin cans and these always caused arguments. When macaroni was on the menu some groups even counted the number of pieces in their dixie. If someone was short, the person doing the ladling was in trouble and this caused more argument than any other.'

Bill was at the rough end of the ration distribution system and recalls how rations were distributed. 'Our daily menu was also soon established. About eight in the morning we received a drink of black liquid, unsweetened and milk-less, masquerading as coffee. At midday we received a bread ration, about the size of a small luncheon roll and a very small portion of cheese. 'Woof', two bites and it was gone.'

Bill continues: 'Between four and five we received our main meal of the day comprising a bowl of soup, prepared by our own people and naturally the only prisoners in the camp who looked well fed were the cooks. The soup (for want of a better name) was cooked over an open fire, in square cooking dixies. One dixie held the rations for 40 men i.e. two tents, so we had to share with the tent opposite ours. Our only utensils were mugs shaped from tins, definitely home-made, with a handle on the side.'

'In the absence of parcels everything connected with our daily rations had to be scrupulously fair and way above any suspicion' Bill recalls. 'As a corporal, I was asked to undertake the doling out of the soup for our 20 men. The dixie was collected from the cookhouse, by two men, one from our tent and one from the tent opposite and placed squarely between our two tents for everyone to see.'

'We agreed to line up in rotation and move up one each day, with the first of that day dropping back to the end next day. This was necessary because the soup was mainly vegetable, sometimes thickened with macaroni. Naturally the bottom of the dixie would be thickest, although we stirred it at regular intervals. Some days it was all thin so the rotation idea was still satisfactory. My own tin was carried by the man who slept next to me so that ensured I took my turn in the rotation' remembers Bill.

'So I stood at one side of the dixie with the serving tin at the ready, opposite the man from the other tent. Both serving tins were identical, with a mark to show we both served the same to each man. In the event of any soup being left in the dixie we had a separate roster. This worked well enough for our tent but a few days later there was an unholy row in the opposite tent and a deputation came to ask if I would do the issue for both tents, fortunately for my peace of mind we never had any further trouble' Bill recalls.

These problems over the fairness of food distribution threatened the peaceful operation of the camp. The solution was simple. Bob continues:

'After a few days captain Bianci obtained twenty more standard ladles to accompany each dixie and every man took turns to do the ladling. This reduced the grumbling although there were still those who counted their macaroni but then another problem arose. I discovered that there was often soup left in the cook house. To the delight of everyone this was distributed for each tent in turn. Two cooks were caught stealing rice and sugar to make themselves a rice pudding for which they were sacked. Food theft was considered by the prisoners as the most punishable crime but we had no means of punishment.

'I was asked by the camp leader to sound out captain Bianci on what was possible for us to do under the circumstances. He came up with an idea that offenders could be manacle to the wire as an example to others. The Italian version of the stocks! A committee of senior NCOs discussed the circumstances under which punishment was to be given and appropriate sentences. It was agreed that fighting was to be given one hour on the wire, two hours for stealing of property, and a minimum of four hours for stealing food.

'The accused person was, in serious cases, offered the choice of accepting the punishment or be in the camp leaders report for a court martial after the war. In the four summer months we were in Benevento there were only two cases of manacling to the wire, one for stealing cigarettes and one for stealing another's bread ration. I have often thought that the effectiveness of this type of punishment, with little physical hurt but the shame of being on show, was much better than a jail sentence.

'Not only were we always hungry, but smoking helped relieve the pangs of hunger and cigarettes were non existent. My original stock of cigarettes was shared and I gradually reduced my smoking habit. There were those whose hunger for nicotine was greater than that for food, and would barter their roll for Italian cigarettes. It was a common sight at the main gate to see half a dozen prisoners hanging about waiting for the Italian guards to throw down their cigarette butt-ends to laugh at the POWs scrabbling about in the dirt. It was a disagreeable spectacle.

'I vaguely remember it was August, two months since our capture when captain Bianci asked me what I knew about Red Cross parcels. I had to admit that although I knew of the Red Cross and the Geneva Convention, I knew nothing of parcels. He explained that Campo PG 87 had been registered with the Red Cross as a permanent summer POW camp and that their representative from Geneva would be visiting us at some time. I told the camp leader about the parcels that would be issued in the next few days who was as mystified as me. We both began speculating on what the parcels were and agreed that we should ask if we could go and see what they were before they were distributed.

'We now learned that they were food and cigarette parcels. The normal issue would be one food parcel and fifty cigarettes each but with the large influx of prisoners from North Africa, the issue would be one parcel between two. When the camp commandant announced the distribution next morning it engendered considerable excitement and speculation around the rest of the camp.

'After the morning bread issue, lorries piled high with brown boxes arrived. Each parcel was a brown cardboard box with the badges of the Red Cross and St John printed. The Italian guards were standing around looked bemused at the spectacle but I wondered what they really thought. The issue of the parcels proceeded without a hitch. It was the issue of the cigarettes and the choice of pipe tobacco that took time. It stands out in my memory that for the first issue we were not interested in the cigarettes. We wanted to get back to the tent and open that food parcel.'

Bill remembers it well. 'Every tin was punctured before issue, presumably to stop us from storing food for an escape. The issue was twice a week, one parcel between two men. They didn't completely quell our hunger but they were wonderful.'

Bob recalls his first parcel. 'It is difficult for me now to adequately describe the feeling at that time, just seeing Brook Bond tea and Nestles milk with all those other delectable foodstuffs in our state of starvation. Now at last we could have a cup of tea. From that day there was a feeling of contentment at any parcel issue and a silent blessing for the Red Cross and St John at the same time. But this first issue was something special.

'I was sitting in the tent with Reg Gunn pleasantly contemplating the contents of our parcel and enjoying my first cigarette for weeks when I realised two things. I was supposed to be at the weighing of the soup but much more important, how were we to brew our cups of tea? I rushed off to the cookhouse to tell them to prepare a lot of boiling water ready during the afternoon to meet the expected demand for tea.

'I was a bit embarrassed with my extra loaf which I usually ate in the office. But Reg Gunn did not smoke so we agreed he could have half my loaf for his twenty five cigarettes. Neither of us had any idea how such bartering would develop so I had the better bargain for the next few weeks. We would soon appreciate that there was a difference between parcels. Those packed in Scotland always had a tin of oatmeal and one English depot always had a tin of vegetables, which, was not much welcomed in Italy where vegetables were in plentiful supply. What we really needed were tins of meat and there was never enough meat, so the tin of meat stew was highly valued.

'It became essential that some means of individual cooking be arranged. Permission was granted for a limited number of fires in the corner of the field and a promise for a supply of wood. Bargaining also started as heavy smokers exchanged food for cigarettes. The Italian guards cast envious eyes on the parcels containing items they had not seen since the war started. Bartering among ourselves became common but the pricing of everything in terms of cigarettes had not yet taken hold. Each parcel had a bar of chocolate and a market came into being. Chocolate was exchanged with the Italians in clandestine deals mainly for bread. In our tent we had our fun with one guard who was keen to have some tea for which he was offering two rolls of bread. This was not considered enough for a packet of tea but a scheme was devised to get the bread.

'One advantage of having a fire to brew the tea rather than boiling water from the cookhouse, was that one could make 'tinkers tea.' This entailed putting the tea leaves into the cold water and bringing to the boil and pouring the tea off straight away without waiting for it to brew, the leaves are then boiled twice more for tea of slightly diminishing strength. After such treatment the tea leaves beceme pale but after drying in the sun we put them back in the packet, sticking the top down with condensed milk. The doctored packet was then thrown over the wire to the Italian guard for his two rolls. This deception only worked for a few times before the guard realised the tea was no good as no more rolls were forthcoming but he dared not do anything about it.

'On one occasion we received a batch of Canadian parcels. They were greeted with some excitement because they were different. They contained more bulk, bigger biscuits, a tin of spam, butter but coffee instead of tea, so they received a mixed reception. Next came a delivery of food parcels from the Argentine. As it was the first for the Italians, captain Bianci wanted myself and the camp leader to accompany him to the parcel store to find out what they contained. In the hut we found a stack of wooden crates, all stamped Argentine Red Cross but with the contents stamped in English.

'Rather than individual portions, there were crates of butter, sugar, tea, biscuits, powdered milk, chocolate and, of course, corned beef. It took us all day and the help of other senior NCOs and Italian guards to open the crates, inspect the contents and decide how it was to be issued. A complicated system of issue by tents of ten or twenty was devised which worked out to everyone's satisfaction and no complaints were heard. There was more bulk individually but less variety and the usual Red Cross cigarettes that came with the crates, allowed an issue of fifty each.

'There was an amusing sequel to this bulk issue. When the bars of chocolate were unwrapped they were found to be full of mites, probably due to storage. There was no doctor in the camp, we had to rely on the Italians to produce a medical officer who was asked if the chocolate was safe to eat. His reply was that it was not only safe to eat but the mites supplied the necessary protein we all needed to do us a lot of good!

'Reg and I shared our parcels and often joined others in the tent to brew tea and cook items in the parcels. The crates from the Argentine gave a welcome addition to the limited supply of wood from the Italians and the number of blowers of varying design increased. With only a few wood chippings and a forced draught from the blower, a bright fire burned quickly and efficiently for brewing tea.

'The mail remained one-way through the summer months. From July we were able to send cards home with the camp address in the hope of return mail. Wynne did not get my first card until the end of August and her reply, addressed to PG 87, eventually caught me up after Christmas.

'For my part our stay in Benevento was the most interesting of all the Italian POW camps. It had been a sunny summer so the tents were no hardship. As the end of September approached our desert drill kit was becoming threadbare. Parcels also become erratic. The issue of 'one between two' became persistent so everyone shared in groups of two or four. This grouping was a matter of necessity when any cooking was required.

'As the weather became colder and the rains came, many changed into Italian clothing and I accepted a pair of Italian boots which were a comfortable fit. A visit from the Swiss Red Cross was promised for the end of September and he promised British battledress. Italian promises were always 'domani', a tomorrow that never came.

'So in October, the Italians begin an issue their pantaloons, shirts and jackets to anyone who needed them but it was not a popular idea. Luckily I still had my greatcoat and had no desire to wear Italian uniform, although my desert 'brothel creepers' were getting badly worn and I would soon need boots. There were Italian boots on offer but no socks, instead one was expected to use the Italian army equivalent of two squares of cloth to wrap round the feet.

'Things became pretty miserable inside our tents with the rain and cold, so I began spending most of my time in the store and office where at least one could stand up and walk about. The sergeant was also not very happy because, when the camp shut down, he would be posted to North Africa. This did not appeal to him in the least and so he asked me to write him a letter to say he had been with us POWs and had treated us well. I felt sorry for him, with a wife and a large family. Like most Italians, not being interested in the war, he would give himself up at the first opportunity, so I wrote what he wanted.

'During November I contracted yellow jaundice along with several others. The Italian doctor thought it was due to the olive oil in the soup, so we were put on a special diet of soup without the oil and, at the same time, advised me not to use the margarine in our parcels for the time being. It was only a mild attack and after a couple of weeks the symptoms disappeared with no after effects.

'At the beginning of December we were officially warned of a move to a permanent hutted camp, although not even captain Bianci knew where. He was to be posted to Africa. I was sorry to part from the two of them. They were the only two good Italians I met. The rest seemed to enjoy their sudden superiority. No wonder they did not fancy being in the same position as we found ourselves.

'With little warning, in the second week in December we were all given a parcel and told we were to leave the next day. With very little to pack, everyone was ready next morning when the lorries arrived to take us to Benevento station where the cattle trucks awaited us. We travelled for about three hours and stopped, we thought for lunch, but were told to disembark.

'The station was Castelnouovo with no lorries. We marched round the outskirts of the town to a very new looking hutted camp, PG 68. Things seemed to be well organised with permanent British staff. The huts were new with double tier bunks, palliasses and two new-looking blankets. Best of all, there were two upright stoves for heating on which one could cook and brew tea.

Christmas 1942

'Two incidents of note occurred while in the camp where I was destined to spend three weeks over Christmas. A few days before Christmas we learned we were to be visited by the Papal Legate accompanied by a representative of the Swiss Red Cross. This was the first time that I had experienced a visit of the Red Cross and I was to learn that they took our welfare to heart. We were assured that the parcel situation was improving and that there would be a special Christmas parcel each and that British battle dress was on its way here. Mail, too, was catching up.

'The Papal Legate gave each of us a little diary for the year 1943 and an orange as Christmas presents with the Pope's blessing. The next day we were given a parcel each which I suppose the Italian authorities were shamed into doing. This was followed by an additional Christmas parcel on Christmas Day full of all the extra little delights such as a tinned Christmas pudding plus an extra roll from our captors. In our state it made a wonderful Christmas, even appreciating the Pope's blessed orange.'

Bill recalls the visit. 'One day great excitement swept the camp. Apparently a delegation of either Papal or Red Cross people had arrived and someone said they had seen packages that may be food parcels. Later that day we each received a gift of something like a square biscuit or maybe it was supposed to be cake. Whatever it was it was greatly appreciated, if only to stop the dogs of war growling in our stomachs.'

Bob continues the story: 'The next week, as a New Year present, the bales of battledress arrived and needless to say I was among the first in the queue to be fitted out with a blouse, trousers and a shirt but no boots or socks. Boot and sock did not arrive before I was among a large group detailed to move to another camp so my mail had some more catching up to do. In my last letter to Wynne I asked her send me some underwear and socks in her next, personal parcel. It had been over six months since capture and still no mail. Despite feeling depressed, I was keeping my fingers crossed for a flood of mail soon.'

Bill was a lot less optimistic. 'Our only entertainment was to walk round the perimeter of the camp. Misery, boredom and the general uncertainty of our future was the order of the day. We were still in the army desert kit that we had been captured in and autumn was settling in. We were reasonably excited by the recent move which provided a break from our monotonous existence and we thought we would be better off. What a vain hope.'

Bob continues: 'The selection for this move was as arbitrary as usual. The consequence was Reg Gunn and Bill Richards were left behind as was most of the rest of the company. I do remember Bill Harvey was in the group to move.

'Having no news from home, constantly on the move and now separated from one's friends, was enough to make a saint feel down. It was in deep depression that I boarded another cattle truck, with no friends, for what turned out to be a three days journey with countless halts. The first night was spent waiting in a siding in Firenza. Part of the second night in Bologna before reaching our destination the next morning.

'The railway yard turned out to be Modena, a town I had never heard of but evidently is in northern Italy. Lorries arrived and after an hour bumping along we drove through the town of Carpi to a camp on the outskirts with a notice board saying Campo PG 73. The hutted camp was on the main road out of town and appeared to be fairly new. Originally a tented camp, the former occupants of the tents which I believe included civilian detainees, were now housed in half of the new huts, named sector II.

'We would occupy the huts in sector I which had been built against the wire along the main road which divided the two sectors. At the far end of our sector there were four large huts, two of which, next to the cookhouse, formed the Hospital, the other two were empty. Our arrival had increased the camp numbers to nearly five thousand. It appeared, at last, this was our permanent prison camp. The only British officers were the three doctors manning the Hospital.

'It was now January 1943 and bitterly cold despite our new battledress and I was huddled in my greatcoat, one of only a few to possess one. Imagine our consternation when entering our new hut to find a minute stove in the centre with no fire. The hut remained cold for months. I never felt warm and most of my time was spent sitting on my bunk in my greatcoat. For the one time in my life I felt lonely.'

Bill remembers the winter. 'The bad news was that no more parcels were in store and we could expect some delay because winter makes transport difficult. So it was back to bedrock rations again. We were twice as miserable as before. The general environment was bleak and unattractive and we had reached a point where before, talking to each other had been a consolation, we now found there was nothing fresh in conversation so the tendency was to withdraw into our own shell and avoid contact with other people.'

But keeping warm made a good home for lice, Bill recollects. 'At this time we felt as low as we could possibly get but there was still a further stage in our downward path to degradation we had to endure, and from which there was no escape. We were all now lousy as cuckoos due entirely to the shortage of adequate food and this was the final straw. These body lice weren't little things you had to search for but ugly brutes which found the warmest part of the body. You could spend an evening examining all the seams of your clothing but next morning they would still be there. Since the war I have read books describing conditions for Jewish men and women in the notorious camps and they also spoke of these same lousy conditions.'

'With regard to our close intimate companions it was, and still is, my belief that if you are deprived of food for any length of time eventually you will be lousy. We were now in the middle of winter, nearing Christmas and it was bitterly cold, without any form of heating in the barracks. Don't let anyone delude themselves that it is always warm and sunny in Italy because the winters, in the northern part of the country are very severe. During these worst months of our early captivity the area of the camp was a virtual quagmire and it was normal to wake in the morning to see icicles, about six to eight inches long formed on the inside of the windows. I thought this six months, since we were captured, was one of the worst periods of my life but before the end of the war, worse was to come.'

'Everyone was now stretched as tight as a bowstring and very touchy. I had one friend, who when we were first captured suggested we should stick together until it was all over. It sounded all right and we kept together until one afternoon the subject turned to food, as always. We were talking of our favourite food. His dreams were of roast beef, Yorkshire pudding and lashings of vegetables and my thoughts were for a freshly baked brown loaf and a large chunk of cheese. Sounds harmless enough now, but somewhere along the line we got into a fierce argument and that finished our beautiful friendship. Following this experience I vowed never to enter into any close relationship.'

But for Bob, things were about to get better. 'Parcels were eventually delivered, one each per week. Fuel for the stove, although minimal, was issued regularly and further issues of battledress and overcoats were made.

The big surprise was that we were actually paid, admittedly in locally printed camp lira, but at least there was a shop in which to spend it. Minor items such as soap, cigarette papers, razor blades and pencils were available. It was the only camp we had been in where everyone was paid, why this was so, I have never discovered. Normally camp staff were paid a nominal sum, and other-ranks outside on working parties were paid, but otherwise it was "no work, no pay".

'Another surprise came in our second week when we were told that one hundred of us would be allowed a country walk. It appeared that this was a regular practice, one hundred men daily except Sundays, each hut taking it in turn. In my case this meant in the six months I was there, I went on three walks. It was a chance to get outside the wire, with guards of course, but it gave one a sense of freedom. At this time of year it was an opportunity to collect firewood. To see the men returning to camp after the walk, they looked so happy one might have thought they had been on a Sunday-school picnic.

'I needed something to do while sitting on my bunk attempting to keep warm. I have never been one to sit around doing nothing. It is not so much that I get bored. I get downright miserable. So one day, sitting thinking of something to do, it struck me. When I was eleven years old I sat for the eleven-plus scholarship to attend the grammar school. At the same time my headmaster entered me for a scholarship at the art school. I passed both and had to decide: Did I want to be an engineer or an artist? I wanted to be an engineer so I chose the grammar school. I joined the Army as a draughtsman.

'I could try my out pencil sketching and see if the talent was still there. Perhaps I might even earn something doing it. At least it was an occupation that could be carried out while just sitting, keeping warm. I needed warm fingers anyway. I jumped from my bunk and made my way to the camp shop to buy the necessary pencils and paper providing the latter was available and I had enough camp lira. The Italian soldier who ran the camp shop had only the normal HB variety and no paper. When I explained my needs, he promised to get me some H and B pencils and see what he could do about paper. When I mentioned cost and our lack of lira he told me not to worry, he would take cigarettes or chocolate.

'Some days later he produced a sketchbook with very poor quality paper and had been told of a shop in town where my pencils could be obtainable. So I decided to start with an HB pencil, a rubber and the sketchbook. My opening effort was the Royal Engineers badge with the 106 company's battle honours, dated 26 January 1943. Not very enterprising but it was the start. I needed to know I had not lost my touch and this was followed by a map of Italy.

'It was while I was sketching from a photograph of Table Mountain at Cape Town with our troopship the "Empress of Canada" in the foreground, that my neighbour on the bottom bunk became interested. He was a staff sergeant in the Ordnance and had been serving in the tank workshops at Tobruk, I have completely forgotten his name, but he did say he had served his apprenticeship at Rolls Royce. He had a photograph of his wife and asked if I would do an enlarged pencil sketch of it. It turned out to be a huge success, even though it was on the poor paper and he was so pleased that he became my salesman.

'Showing off his sketch soon brought a series of commissions of wives, sweethearts, sons and daughters which kept me busy through the late winter and into the spring and enabled me to buy additional pencils and better paper, ordered in the town. Payment for my sketches was in camp lira, cigarettes or a bar of chocolate. Cigarettes became the rate of exchange not only because of the regular ration from the Red Cross parcels but cigarette parcels now began arriving from home.

'My staff sergeant neighbour had become my "mucker", that is we "mucked in" by sharing our parcels which we found more convenient to stretch the food over a week. It was a matter of great trust to have a mucker when it came to that most important item, sharing food. The only way to get boiling water was from the cookhouse. This was one of the chores we shared, much as we disliked the walk to the cookhouse and hurrying back, trying to keep the tea hot. It was also wasteful as we could not get more than one brew from the tea leaves. But we had to have tea and urgent requests were made for some cooking facilities on a space inside the wire.

'In the spring, as the weather improved, an area was allotted for making fires for cooking. My mucker and I had paid someone who was making blowers. The country walk was an opportunity for collecting firewood although some guards tried to prevent it without much success. It was easy to pick up and pocket twigs which was all that was necessary for a blower.'

Early in March a deluge of mail arrived that had been following us wanderers. Bill remembers that letters 'now arrived intermittently but allayed our fears for our wives. At least they knew we were reasonably safe. I believe this god-send was arranged by the Red Cross.'

The POW post was slow. The last posting date for Christmas in 1943 was the end of July.

Bob was happy. 'There were several letters from Wynne including my first personal parcel containing underclothes and, best of all, two pairs of socks. From then on the mail became more regular. Later I received my first cigarette parcel. I had no knowledge that personal cigarette parcels were allowed but, thankfully, Wynne had been told of them at the Red Cross packing station she attended in Farnham. It appeared that she was allowed to send me, via an order on the manufacturers, a hundred cigarettes per month. She had chosen Players.

'I can't remember why, but my mucker and I had our photo taken outside the camp shop. I think it must have been the Italian running the shop, with whom I had become quite friendly. I sent this home to Wynne to let her see how well I was and within a month I received an anxious reply. Not that I looked other than well, but why were my toes protruding from my boots, were they that bad and couldn't I get Army boots? I had to write back and explain that I was wearing Italian boots that had some chalk on the toecaps, having been outside on a walk. It had been a trick of the light that gave the wrong impression. I had been wearing them since Benevento and they were comfortable but nevertheless I went and changed them for an army issue pair.

'On the bunk above mine resided a Welshman who, in common with most of his countrymen, was not only a good singer, but had studied music. His neighbour on the next top bunk had a piano-accordion and between the two of them they began to compose the hymn music for the choir they formed. With this going on above me all day, it was not long before I had some knowledge of the bass part and joined the choir.

'There was some ulterior motive. Padre Hullah, came on a Sunday afternoon from the nearby officers camp in Modena to conduct an open air service and after the blessing, finished his service with snippets of news from the officers' camp radio. Hence good attendance was maintained, even if it

11.1 Bob's boots:
The picture of Bob's dirty boots that got him into trouble back home. Modern technology allow images to be enhanced but on the original, his toes seem to be poking out of his boots.

was very cold, to share the news of the outside world. It was difficult to believe that the guards were not cognizant of what was being said, even if they had no understanding of English. Nevertheless, nothing was done to stop the padre's addendum so we were all kept up to date with news of the war's progress and particularly the slow advance northwards by the Allies. There was still a long way to go but we were ever optimistic.

'With the approach of summer, living conditions began to improve as parcels and mail became more regular and extra huts were made available reducing overcrowding. My mucker and I spent many pleasant summer days outside with our blower making tea, heating some food or just lounging in the sun. In my wandering there I came across Bill Harvey, the only remaining member of the 106 Company in the camp. He was a member of the embryo band being formed for a show but I have no memory of any show.

Bill takes up the story: 'I remember one day word percolated through asking if anyone still had the regulation mending kit and any aptitude for sewing, would they report to a hut designated as a recreation hut. It transpired that some four or five men had managed to retain musical instruments when they were captured and had also received help from the camp commandant with some further acquisitions. They announced that they wished to form a band with the idea of organised entertainment and they wanted ideas of a dance band uniform, as the camp commandant would also assist in providing materials. I was interested, especially as it would occupy my time and about six others who volunteered.'

The trousers were no great trouble. Bill asked for ten pairs of Italian army issue trousers which were three-quarter length, gathered into a band just below the knee. 'I proceeded to cut this band off and from another pair of trousers I secured pieces of the same material which I sewed on to the first pair so that I had normal, ankle length trousers in Italian olive green.'

'Soon the original volunteers vanished and I was on my own which I didn't mind because I was gainfully occupied and interested. Before completing the sewing up of the trousers I asked for and got some army underpants which were made out of strong white calico. From these I was able to form an eight inch V shape which I sewed into the side seams of the trousers giving a wide-bottom, Mexican gaucho appearance especially with the contrast of the white insert against the olive green main colour. All this took time, I felt like an old-fashioned tailor doing all this hand stitching.

'I was fully occupied with the band uniforms. I secured a further supply of the white calico underpants. By cutting and sewing I was able to make bolero short waistcoats, without sleeves, but with wide lapels and as a finishing touch, I cut out a treble cleft symbol and embroidered it on to the left lapel. I was quite pleased with the general effect, almost professional.' Events beyond the wire would prevent Bill's band uniforms being used.

'With the Allied troops slowly advancing north, the country walks would prove tempting to escapers. On my second walk a couple did get away into the woods without the guards suspecting anything. Even we knew nothing until our arrival back at camp. Then the fun started. It took the Italians several counts to be sure that two prisoners were indeed missing. Our continuous movement gave different numbers each time. The poor guards received a whipping from the commandants swagger stick in his fury and that was the end of our walks.' Bob remembers.

'The two escapers were not out long due to lack of planning and preparation. There was only one near successful escape throughout my stay. After its discovery, there was a buzz of excitement among otherwise resigned prisoners. It appeared that with the help of the escape committee a sergeant Hawith, dressed in a very good copy of an Italian officer's uniform, simply walked out of the main gate immediately after the change of the guard. Because he was not missed until the next day, no one, including the Italians, had any idea of how he had succeeded. However, the metal badge on his home made cap and metal collar stars were not good enough to pass muster in daylight and he was back in jail before nightfall.

'In August I started what was to be my last sketch, a photograph of the sailor son of a sergeant from another hut on which was written 'To Dad with love from Cyril'. It was unfinished when we were moved to Germany. I did not know the sergeant's name and he was not with those who came to Germany. The sketch remained in my sketchbook for years after the war, along with the photograph of Cyril. All attempts to trace the family failed.

'Years later Cilla Black started her programme on television with the 'help line' and I immediately sent off the sketch and photograph with an account of the circumstances. Both sketch and photograph appeared on the next programme accompanied by the initial remark "Does anyone know this sailor called Cyril." and a brief account of my search. The programme was seen by Cyril's sister who, recognising her brother, who then rang Cyril's wife to tell her about it. I received a call from the studio asking my permission to send the sketch and photograph to Cyril's wife who had written to them and of course I agreed.

'Some weeks later a lady was at my door asking if I was Mr Borthwick. She was Cyril's wife. She had come to thank me and presented me with an etching of Plymouth Hoe where she lived. Her husband had, unfortunately, died two years before and Cyril's father CSM Wright had died soon after the war, but she was overjoyed to get both the photograph and sketch as well as my story.

'On 8 September the Guards came, full of excitement, into the camp to tell us that the Italian Government had agreed to a separate armistice. It was not surprising. None of the Italians had their heart in the war and the guards were pleased that as far as they were concerned the war was over for them. We were not so sure of the effect on our situation. The camp leader, warrant officer Exall, told everyone to remain calm while he confirmed the news and discovered what our situation would be. Later in that day of rumour, padre Hulla came into the camp and was closeted with the camp leader.

'They confirmed the end of the war for Italy but our orders from the senior officer at the Modena were that we remain until the situation was clarified. This did not go down well with some of the prisoners, many of whom took immediate and hurried steps to prepare for escape attempts that evening. The whole of the night was taken up with the shouts of guards, searchlights blazing but fortunately no shots. It was probable that many did escape. The Italians were not really bothered by all the attempts to get through the wire and good-naturedly, escorted parties of would-be escapers back to camp.

'None of us had much sleep that night. In our hut there were some escapers returned but at least three disappeared. Imagine our chagrin the next morning when we discovered that the camp was surrounded by the Waffen SS troops. On the road outside our hut there were several armoured cars, the occupants of which were signalling for us to get back into our huts. We had been taken over.

'Within an hour we were being chased out of the huts by the black uniformed SS for a roll call, to find our late captors dejectedly lined up on one side of the field. We were addressed first by the Camp leader who stated the obvious. We were now prisoners of the German Army. An officer in black uniform stepped forward and in perfect English said that the Italians had been relieved of their responsibilities for the Camp. The troops who had taken over were our temporary guards, more permanent guards would arrive in a few more days and he hoped we would co-operate.

'The Italians, having refused to carry on under German control, were put into a separate compound so we felt some sympathy for them. It was not until they were moved out and the Germans sent in a stock of Red Cross parcels found, they claimed, in the Italian Barracks that we felt our sympathy had been wasted.

'The Waffen SS were replaced by some local garrison troops who began to sort out groups to be moved. A batch of about a thousand in the original sector II were ordered to prepare to move. This caused another rash of potential escapers. The new guards were not very experienced in dealing with POWs and were easily satisfied with roll count. Many of those selected just disappeared. This time most hid in the roof space as huts were emptied.

'The following days saw another batch of some two thousand from both sectors, again mainly other ranks with some sergeants, with more hiding in roofs. In the next two days, the rest of us, including all the senior NCOs, were assembled on the road to be loaded into lorries. While this was taking place a Feldwebel and a few guards left in the camp, began bringing out a number of those who had been hiding. Later we discovered that this Feldwebel beat those in hiding and shot three allegedly trying to escape. The post-war report say that attempts to find this Feldwebel have not succeeded.

'At the station in Modena, we were packed into the same old cattle wagons again. But this time I was sorted out with all the other senior NCOs, about fifty of us packed into a wagon at the front of the train behind the engine. The Germans issued each with a bread roll but we all had plenty of parcel food. Everyone travelled with a Red Cross parcel box, mine, tied with string, was slipped over the straps of my haversack. I still had the haversack. It carried all my possessions. Inside my rectangular mess tin, held all my small items such as toothbrush, hussiff, razor and blades. I had a towel, handkerchiefs, socks and not much else apart from my sketchbooks and pencils. As we left on that hot September day, I was carrying my greatcoat like everyone else on our long journey to, we assumed, Germany. Into the unknown and much further from freedom'

Chapter Twelve

Captivity Germany

August 1943 – June 1945

Portrayals of life as a prisoner of war in stories such as 'The Wooden Horse', 'Great Escape' and 'Colditz' provided one impression. But an important dimension has been omitted from the popular record of book, film and TV. The German system segregated officers from other ranks. Much of the existing fiction has been woven around the officers' camps.

The majority of POWs were other ranks and their story is not romantic. An accurate report would include forced labour and forced marches, survival, squalor and starvation, work and concentration camps. But their tales provide an monument to the spirit of those who spent some of the prime years of their young lives as captives.

These are the individual tales of some members of 106 Army Troops Company Royal Engineers. They provide four contrasting stories. Bill Harvey tells a tale that is typical of the majority of POWs. Alan Jones was in a small but strategically placed camp with a minority of Allied POWs that was not liberated by the Americans until the war was over. Ken Venables was put to work in the coalmines in Poland before a long walk home. Bob Borthwick spent his time as a German POW along with several thousand other senior NCOs in a 'model' camp. He provides an interesting and ultimately optimistic story which ends when he is finally released by the Russians after the Yalta agreement to repatriate the Ukrainian's who had fought with the German army.

As far as possible, the stories are told in the words of their subject. This is Bill Harvey's story.

Bill's story

'As I write of these unforgettable memories of the dark days we had to endure, the words seem so banal, and I dearly wish I possessed the literary skills to portray a more vivid picture of our total misery.

'These dark days seemed to last a lifetime without any glimmer of hope. Snatches of war news seemed to confirm that the Germans were still in control of events. I suppose looking back we didn't feel too much resentment against the Italians because they didn't seem too well blessed with food and the Germans seemed to despise them.

'As the weather improved in spring of 1943 so did camp conditions, especially when we were put on a regular supply of Red Cross parcels. It was still rationed out one parcel between two men, twice a week with all tins being punctured. Some items like condensed milk were difficult to split so in most cases one man would have the whole tin from one issue and his partner would have the next one.

'The ground gradually dried out from the muddy mess it had been all winter. Walking the wire again became the normal pastime. In the next few months the Red Cross managed to supply British army uniforms which made us feel infinitely better. I suppose as things improved, we began to feel better and were able to organise ourselves better.

'With the general improvement, mostly associated with the arrival of the Red Cross parcels, the body lice began to disappear to our unmitigated relief. I never thought a cardboard box of food, about the same size as a shoebox could make such a difference to a life.

'It was late in 1943 and rumours were circulating of Montgomery's victory in the desert and even of a possible invasion of Italy. Red Cross parcels kept arriving, although the basic rations never improved and altogether we felt almost cheerful. Once again another bombshell was dropped.

'Suddenly it was announced that some prisoners were to be transferred into Germany, which was a shock considering the optimistic thoughts we were having of being released by our own forces. I found out later that the Jerries had combed through the cards which we had filled in for the Red Cross. I remembered that in addition to the normal details of addresses and units we had been asked to state our trade and in our innocence, and the turmoil at that time we had put our civilian trades.

'Evidently the Germans must have been considering, even at that time that they might lose Italy. So one day a number of us, all tradesmen, were rounded up and taken to the nearest railway station. We embarked, not in seated carriages but long wagons which bore the inscription that they were meant to carry eight chevals (horses) or forty hommes (men) and they smelt as though horses had recently used them. All we could do was to secure a small area to sit in and hope for the best. We had no idea where we were bound for or how long it would take.

'Toilet facilities consisted of a narrow door at the end of the wagon and you had to hang on to make sure you didn't fall through onto the track. In other words a very lousy situation.

'On this journey I became quite ill, very cold and shivering uncontrollably. I felt absolutely terrible with a head like a bucket. I now know I had picked up malaria at the Italian camp and it wasn't a pleasant experience in those conditions. I dimly remember someone saying we were going through the Brenner Pass but I couldn't have cared less.

'Eventually we stopped and found ourselves at a place called Chemnitz, a town in the middle of Germany and by this time the shivering had abated and I was moving into the very hot stage, sweating profusely and some of my mates drew the guards attention to my condition and the next thing I remember was in the Krankenhausn or camp hospital.

'A couple of German doctors examined me and looked perturbed because malaria is virtually unknown in Germany. It was always said that it is no good telling a German doctor you feel ill unless you had a temperature. I was all right because I believe I touched about 103 degrees. I gradually came out of the sweating stage and although I was offered rations I felt too ill to touch them. I went through that day just feeling lousy and the next day I was into another attack and laid low again, with the same sequence of violent shivering followed by a sweating period. After this attack it went away and I thought I was cured and began to take notice of the new world around me.

'There were about eight other men in this ward and I found out most of them had been captured in the Dunkirk fiasco. Apparently they had been there sometime and had the impression they were to be repatriated, they all had some injury or other. One told me that in the early days of their captivity they were made to work and conditions were very harsh, until one day they were detailed to load ammunition and they refused, under the terms of the Geneva Convention.

'As a penalty they were lined up in front of a firing squad and, fortunately for the man who was telling me, one bullet hit one of his ribs and skidded round his chest and came out under his left armpit. Another bullet caught him just above his left eye and again the bone deflected the bullet. I suppose he could count himself lucky because most of the others were killed.

'The Jerries may have been a bit scared of what they had done and instead of finishing the survivors off with a revolver shot, they sent them to a hospital and eventually to this camp where they were told they were going to be repatriated. Whether it ever transpired I don't know.

'Being clear of malarial attacks the doctors decided I could travel to join the other people who travelled from Italy with me, and I learned they had been sent to a place called Brzeg (Brixlegg) known as Stalag 8B near the Polish border. I should add, we were a group of about eight people all who had been detained at Chemnitz for some reason or other. I know we had to line up and march to the camp some distance away. You will all have seen films of German prison camps and how horrible they looked and this camp was very typical, with its general air of dreariness.

'As usual all the camp was surrounded with barbed wire fencing plus lookout towers with lights and sentries. To the best of my remembrance there were about 12 barrack blocks, housing about 200 men in each. There was also a football field. We were all placed in the first compound, which was designed as a reception, a holding place for documentation, and held there for some time, during which I made new friends. But after a week or two I was struck again with malaria.

'The reception compound was near the main gates and I was hustled into the camp hospital where I shivered out the first few hours under a pile of blankets before passing into the sweating phase. There were about twenty beds in the ward and two New Zealand medical orderlies were in attendance, together with British doctors. Usually quinine was the only remedy for malaria but fortunately for me one of the British doctors obtained a new drug, I believe it was called "Nepacome" and after a few weeks it was judged to have cured me and now I would have to go back into the hell-hole.

'Before leaving, I must relate one very poignant and distressing occurrence. The day before I left the hospital the orderlies said the Jerries were bringing some prisoners in, who were to be repatriated. As we stood in the doorway watching, a line of soldiers came into view, walking single file and each holding the shoulder of the men in front. About 20 men and all blind, followed by about another 30 men on crutches, all with one leg only.

'In those few moments we could see all the futility of war, all youngish men who would live the rest of their lives with these dreadful legacies. I remember the1920's after the Great War when small groups of men with similar injuries used to walk the streets begging for a living and I could well imagine a similar situation after this war. Heroes today, are a nuisance tomorrow. It made me realise my mishaps were very trivial.

'As far as conditions were concerned, life was easier in Germany than the terrible hunger we encountered in Italy. The camp was better organised and we had potatoes, a bigger portion of bread and occasionally sauerkraut and a boiled barley concoction. All very filling.

'Being well established, Red Cross parcels were received regularly which made such a difference. However there I was back in the reception compound and my new-found pals were still there. They had already been chosen for a working party and although I was not forced to work, as an NCO, they strongly urged that I should go with them to give me a chance to recover from the malarial trouble. They pointed out that a lot of corporals regularly went out on working parties and if I didn't like it I could always ask to be sent back to the Stalag.

'So, feeling like a zombie, I finally agreed to give it a chance. The time was about July/August 1943 and we'd already had one year as a POW. From snatches of news we sometimes heard there seemed to be no heartening news to relieve the monotonous existence.

'We were mustered and proceeded to the working camp at a place called Blechammer, where apparently some kind of a chemical plant was being constructed. We arrived at the new camp in the late afternoon. It was like all the other camps with a high perimeter fence, armed sentry towers at frequent intervals and a number of brick-built huts and a parade-sports space.

'There was a wide river on one side and the camp which was not much higher than the level of the river. There was a sharp rise to the main gates so the German barracks gave the appearance of looking down and over the camp area. After reporting in at the German orderly room we were sent into the camp where a sergeant allocated us to various billets. I was very lucky in my allocation. In each billet there were two tables, lengthways, with double bunk beds and lockers round the walls of the room to house about sixteen to twenty men. About half of the men were army and the other half navy, which proved a very good mix. Although I was a stranger to them they made me very welcome. Most of them had been prisoners since the Dunkirk days, in fact the navy men were all from a submarine named Seal, which ran aground on some mud flats on the Netherlands coast and they had managed to keep together.

'The man in charge was a petty officer known as 'Happy Eckersley' from Scunthorpe who had been a boxing champion in the peacetime navy and he maintained a fair discipline. One army man, Harold Swift from Manchester, turned out to be a very good friend and helped me over a lot of the snags you encounter in this kind of experience. I was doubly fortunate in that he was constantly receiving gift parcels of 200 cigarettes and he was a very generous man. Everything was very well organised and the German rations were plentiful.

'We were allowed a day to organise ourselves and then we were included in various detachments and marched to the various locations to work. I was allocated to one group under the direction of a little man called Dickman, most unlike the usual blond haired blue eyed Teuton.

'Our job was piling. Suspended from a tripod and block-and-chain mechanism hung a long metal shaft ending with the steel earth scoop, about nine inches in diameter and about eighteen inches long with a cutting slot in the bottom. With the aid of two metal shaft sheathes, we could bore to about a depth of fifteen feet, when the scoop was removed and concrete was poured in to create the pile. Our secret was to contrive to drop a shovel or two of earth in without being seen, to break the bond. Usually we could complete about two piles a day which brought us to mid-afternoon and time to march back to the camp. When we arrived there the formality was a hand search, to make sure we hadn't secreted anything resembling a weapon, or bartered food with civilians.

'It was funny to see a man searched, with both arms above his head, and what the searcher didn't know was he had an egg in each hand. All clean fun to bring a smile to the face of a POW. My friend, Harold, seemed to always get back early because he had a meal prepared. Fortunately letters still arrived but it was a frustrating business because all letters were censored and it is difficult to pour your heart out when you know other people are reading them. But it was still a comfort to receive news of the loved ones although it didn't alleviate all our worries and fears.

'Saturday afternoon and Sundays were free time and under Happy Eckesall's direction everything was thoroughly cleaned to his satisfaction. Some of the huts were like pig stys. Life was certainly easier in the working camp than the Stalag, at least we were free from bed bugs, fleas and body lice, for which I was very thankful. It was distressing to see the Jews on the working site, little seven to ten year olds in the horrible striped garments they had to wear, although the youngsters seemed well fed and happy in their little worlds and I didn't see any actual brutality directed against them.

'The older ones had a much more worrying life. I saw one party coming on site one day and they were supporting a comrade who was evidently very ill and I, in my innocence, asked why they hadn't left him in camp. The answer, of course, was that anyone left sick in camp was immediately sent to one of the gas chamber death camps. So we knew these places existed before the world had heard of Belsen.

'Some Polish forced labour people seemed to have a more relaxed regime and even though their accommodation was near ours they weren't wired in or restricted. This brings us to the last group in this area, the Russian POWs. They had no Red Cross convention to protect them and they evidently didn't get enough food to keep them alive. It was a common sight to see them scavenging in the rubbish bins in the Polish area for anything edible. However badly the Russians treated the Germans in the later phases of the war it was no more than they deserved. Winter was now settling in and it looked as though I should be spending Christmas 1943 in this camp.

'On the site there were occasional air raid warnings although I never saw any planes and one of the defences was to flood the area with some kind of chemical smoke to create a mist which would obscure the building details. A truly obnoxious smell and it made your eyes water.

'As Christmas 1943 drew near, a feverish activity seemed to settle over the camp. Most of the men were drinkers and although they could buy some light bottled beer from something like a camp NAAFI permitted by the Germans, they were wanting something stronger to get them well and truly drunk.

'Some ingenious souls had contrived to make stills, consisting of a receptacle, usually copper, in addition to a filling valve there was an outlet at the top to which was connected a copper tube, shaped as a spiralling coil to increase the cooling area. To feed this contrivance a group would pool all the dried fruit such as apple rings, dried apricots or raisins usually a packet in each food parcel. This was put into a tub, concealed, under floorboards, or a bed and allowed to ferment, with the addition of sugar and yeast, bartered from the Polish workers on the working site. All the huts had a pot bellied stove for cooking and heating purposes and when the concoction had fermented long enough, the stove was stoked up after tea, when the camp was quiet and the distilling commenced.

'The spirit obtained was once tested by the camp medical staff and found to be over 80% proof which is quite potent. So we came to Christmas day and after dinner the binge started with a lot of the spirit followed by a chaser of beer. Soon it seemed that all the camp were in differing states of drunkenness. Fortunately about one third of the men in our hut were sensible drinkers and although merry, were still orderly. The Germans were evidently expecting the binge, maybe from previous years, and they locked the gates, after ration time and discreetly kept out of sight.

'The drunks gradually flaked out and we put them to bed and cleaned up after them, not a very pleasant task for a teetotaller. During the winter there was thick snow and ice everywhere and although they continued to send us to the construction site there was very little work done. At least it passed the days of our monotonous existence. Gradually we got through the worst of the winter and thankfully we still received letters from home. One morning, I think it must have been a Sunday because we were all in camp, there were shouts of excitement and we were called out to have a look.

'Sailing majestically across the high heavens in the brilliant winter sunshine there was a flight of about thirty to forty American Flying Fortresses, evidently on their way to some bombing mission, in a tight box formation. They flew on seemingly untroubled, until they faded from our sight. It was a truly awe-inspiring occasion and lifted our spirits no end.

'It made us feel for our safety in case they ever came to bomb the construction site about two miles away. We noted at the back of our barrack there was some brick built surface bomb-shelters and I remember thinking they wouldn't be much use in a raid. Spring comes early in these southern parts of the continent and by the end of February things were getting drier which helped to ease the general depression.

'However I decided I had had enough of working and made an application to be returned to the Stalag 8B. I remained in the camp for a week or two until they had sufficient men to make up a party. I knew life would be more difficult back in the Stalag but I had always felt a bit guilty about working when I wasn't forced to.

'My friends in the billet were very good and I eventually came away with a suitcase from one of them and Harold had put a few packets of cigarettes in as a gift.

'Eventually as one of a small group we were shipped back to Stalag 8B again and after a luggage search I was directed to one of the barracks, where I was allocated a bed space. It was mid-afternoon, nice and sunny and I decided to have a walk around and familiarise the layout of the camp. Being of a trusting nature I left my case on the bed as most of the people were out of the barracks. I really should have known better because when I returned, I found my case had been forced open and all the cigarettes, that Harold Swift had so kindly given me, had gone. It was useless to try and find the perpetrator so this was another painful lesson in my education as a prisoner.

'So in a very downcast mood I prepared for bed that night to renew acquaintances with the bugs and fleas that were lying in wait for me and it was certainly a painful night. Having been clear of them at the working party camp I suppose I could be regarded as fresh meat to them. A round swelling was a bug bite and an irregular swelling was evidence of a flea target area.

'I have known times when things got so bad we would dismantle the wooden framework, get a small fire going outside and pass each piece of wood through the flames to dislodge them but they would be back in a couple of nights.

'It was horrible to occupy one of the lower bunks because when the occupant above turned over you'd feel a plop on your cheek and that was a bed bug falling and when you crushed them there was a terrible smell. Body lice were not a problem in Germany and although we were never free from hunger pangs it was certainly an improvement on our starvation diet in Italy. There was even education courses available and in hindsight I should have taken lessons in German or French language but the dehumanising effect of prison life is not conductive to ideas of betterment.

'As one would expect there was some good footballers among our number and matches between respective barracks were often played much to our enjoyment. These enjoyments had to be offset by commonplace tragedies which kept occurring. Escapes from working parties were common and when caught they were usually brought back to the Stalag and confined in what was known as a punishment block i.e. solitary for a period of time. During that summer period of 1944 the German Commandant sent word around that although the game of escape had, up to then, been tolerated it had got to be stopped and punishment would be more severe. I have tried to keep this account factual and not weave a story into it, but there are some factors which occurred on which I must elaborate.

'On the point of escaping we were all in our own compound when we saw an escapee being escorted up to the Straff Lager, the Punishment Camp. The two guards didn't have him fettered in any way and they were walking one on each side. The gateway of our compound was immediately opposite a compound for RAF prisoners and as the prisoner and escort came level with the gateway, the prisoner dropped his bag and made a dash into the RAF compound. Fortunately the entrance to the barrack was near the fence and he was able to get inside the barrack before the escort could recover themselves. Loud cheers from everyone watching, as his chances of being found were very remote in a camp of that size, so everyone wished him well. However there was an unhappy sequel to the event.

'After a period of about six weeks he thought he was safe and went down to a room just outside the main gates where you collected the parcel and opened it for the Jerries. Unfortunately he was re-arrested and again two soldiers took the long walk up the road to the Straff. No one imagined he would be silly enough to try again but he did. Even sillier, instead of ducking and diving he chose to run down the side of the barrack, a distance of about 40 yards in the open. The guards were a bit more vigilant this time, one shouted a warning and then they shot him. What a wasted life but very typical of the type of Stalag madness that developed in some prisoners, especially those who had been prisoners since Dunkirk, nearly four years.

'Another unhappy incident occurred during the same period in our own barrack. The three tier bunks were situated to one side of the barrack, leaving an open space where we had tables for eating our food or recreation. It was midday and we were all gathered around waiting for the rations to come, when we noticed a middle aged South African man and he appeared to be ill with his blanket pulled up to his chin. We decided to check and when we turned the blanket back he was covered in blood. He had a razor blade and he had slashed his forearms. We got one of the table tops and pulled him and his bedding straight on it and four of us jog-trotted down the road to the main gate to get him into hospital. I think they saved him but I never saw him again so they may have kept him in for observation.

'I am thankful I never got in that state. I couldn't forget Edith and the children waiting for me to come home and look after them and this gave me the strength to survive.

'The last event I suppose, looking back down the years was two men returning from a working party to the Stalag. One was a Glaswegian, a rough looking hulk of a man and evidently one to keep clear of. The other one was a slim, very good looking young man. It came out later that his mother was French and possibly that's where his good looks came from. In manner and appearance he was nearly effeminate but he was detailed to our barrack and he was good to talk to.

'The Glasgow man came to visit him, from another barrack but it was evident the younger man wanted to be on his own and there was constant fallings out. I don't know the circumstances but one day they went walking round the perimeter wire and apparently another quarrel started and the outcome was that the big man hit the younger one with such force that it fractured his cheekbone. Following this unprovoked attack he turned to the perimeter fencing and forced his way through with the sentry in the watchtower telling him to go back, but he ignored the shouts so the sentry shot him. One more to the total of wasted lives, possibly with some poor woman or family in Britain waiting for his return.

'But worse was to come. One day word got round that some prisoners were coming in who had been wounded in an allied air-raid and we naturally congregated at the gate to meet them. Much to my surprise and distress two of the first were men who I had left behind at Blechammer and both had head injuries. There was worse news to follow, apparently it was a raid by an Allied fleet of Flying Fortresses and apparently one bomb fell on the camp and hit the billet that I had occupied during my stay there. The men had taken shelter but as I had noted the shelters were ineffective and to the knowledge of these survivors at least three men from my former billet were killed. They were injured themselves so didn't know the names of the casualties. It made me realise how lucky I had been to get away, but what a terrible end for men who had already suffered years imprisonment and ironically killed by our own people.

'This would be about September 1944 and up to this time I hadn't received a parcel from home, when suddenly I received one from Edith, a pair of good boots and a block of chocolate. Needless to say the chocolate was soon bartered for a loaf of bread, which cheered us up no end. From underground sources we were getting news of the Allied landings in France and the Russian advance towards Germany so our thoughts were very much on how long it would be before we were liberated and would it be Russians or our own people.

'To top that good news I received a parcel from the Plant Works POW fund, 200 Player cigarettes which made me quite popular with my mates. There was a general undercurrent of excitement in the camp as just after Christmas, 1944, we began to hear the sound of what was evidently an artillery barrage. It could only be the Russians and it raised our hopes of an early release, but as we got to know later the Russian advance was delayed by having to cross the river Oder, which gave the Germans time to move us.

'Word came round the camp that we were to move out of the camp at about five o'clock and we had the afternoon to pack our things. I shall always remember the day, January 15th 1945.

'It was the middle of winter and terribly cold. The word was that we were going to have to march to another camp at Breslau which we knew to be about forty or fifty miles to the north of us. I contrived to make a kit bag, with shoulder straps and an old haversack for my gear and knowing how extremely cold it would be, I rolled two blankets into the form of a horse collar which together made a very bulky amount of luggage to carry. About teatime, already dark, we moved out to the Stalag gates and to make matters worse we were each handed a Red Cross parcel and a bit further on half a loaf of bread and a piece of margarine. They wouldn't allow us time to stow these away so we had to start marching along a road which was already like a sheet of ice.

'They kept us going in these terrible conditions until about 11.30 pm and then parked us in a barn. If I slipped down once on that first stretch I must have fallen on my back, with a crash about twenty times. In the following days I was going to suffer severe pains in my back and shoulders due to muscle damage caused by the falls. In the barn we slept in the straw as best we could and next morning we moved out and on to the roads by about eight o'clock.

'I often thought that poor Edith must have felt a lot of joy in being able to send the pair of boots, but they had heel plates and toe plates as well as studs and it was like trying to walk across an ice-rink. We had already endured a lot of suffering but this was real physical hardship in the worst conditions of the winter. Fortunately one of my mates was able to pinch a child's sled from somewhere and they put my kit bag on this, which was a big help. I had already discarded the two blankets at the first nights stop to reduce the weight. I couldn't move my head or shoulders without pain. I have never known such misery.

'This daily routine continued for several days and we kept going in the ice, snow and bitter cold in the expectation we should arrive at another Stalag but then we were told we had changed direction to go deeper into Germany. I think if they had shot us and dumped us at this point and in these conditions it would have been a relief. Worst was to come because the change in direction to the west meant we had to cross the Sudety mountain range which was notorious for the extreme blizzard conditions in winter. In the barns at night we had to take our boots off to ease our feet and this meant the leather froze during the night, so the first hours march next day was in frozen boots.

'I had a towel which I wrapped around my head and face especially on this walk over the mountains where we faced snow driven by high winds. This must have been mid-February, nearly a month after setting out, the food in the Red Cross parcels had all been eaten and we were dependant on getting a bread allowance every three or four days, usually a loaf between six men. I clearly remember one morning, after a night in a barn, when we thought it was a bit warmer, but as we passed through a village a large thermometer attached to a building showed fifteen degrees centigrade below zero, not so warm.

'We had long since jettisoned as much as we could to lighten our loads, a trip to a toilet was in the open fields, with the knowledge we then had to catch up with the column. Washing and shaving were a luxury we couldn't indulge in and I remember long facial hair from the neck and chin being a source of discomfort. Still we carried on, no longer marching or even walking just shuffling along, the column of the damned. A horse and cart followed behind for those who collapsed through exhaustion or illness. I presume those very ill would be taken to a hospital somewhere. I was pleased my shoulders and neck were easing off.

'Towards the end of February the snow and ice began to thaw out and we had to jettison the sled and resort to carrying what gear we had left. To make matters worse we got into a barn one night, when an alarm broke out and it transpired one of our chaps had pinched a guard's loaf, from the back of a bicycle.

'The next thing we knew was that we were cleared out of the barn and hustled away to a quarry, where we were told we had to stay the night, as a punishment for the theft. A grim night where we could only huddle together, to mitigate the intense chill of the frosty night eating into our bones. Day followed day and we were beyond bothering about where we were or anything else. Gradually the thaw became a reality and the days really did become warmer. One day, must have now been into March we passed the outskirts of a town and we were told it was Chemnitz, which put us somewhere in the lower middle of Germany.

'I still had to experience another bitter disaster. One night we were put into a barn and as usual, put my boots near my head before going to sleep until we were roused by the Germans telling us to get outside. When I went to put the boots on I found someone had pinched the good boots Edith had sent me and I was left with some old ones. It was useless trying to find out who did it with the Germans rustling us out and getting very impatient, not forgetting there must have been over 500 men in the column.

'So I had a very painful day and I could feel the blisters developing. The next day was even worse and I must have fallen a long way behind. Then fortunately I encountered a medic who cut the blisters and put some sticking plaster on, what a relief. Without the blisters the days were more manageable and I kept going.

'Day in and day out we marched, now our only rations were a portion of bread every three or four days. In this situation, time has no measure but we were mighty pleased when one day the Germans left us in the same place, because at one end of the area there was a shallow stream and we had the luxury of a good wash and shave and the bliss of paddling our feet in the deliciously cold water. The weather now was almost summer like and the only water we could get was when we were near a stream, as long as there was ripples, showing running water, we drank. We also chewed sugar beet when we could find some.

'It was getting quite evident now that nobody seemed to have any idea where we were going, and even the guards had stopped pushing us. I remember one evening when we arrived on the outskirts of a town that was completely devastated, it must have been Magdenburg, but we could feel no pity when we could recall the damage done to English cities like London, Glasgow, Coventry etc. when the German Luftwaffe had control of the skies.

'The German officer passed the word back that we were going to change direction again, this time towards Berlin but we had only gone a short distance when we came to another farming village and the inevitable barn for the night I found out it was Horsingen. Next morning we were surprised when the guards withdrew into a huddle and there was no cry of "raus von beden".

'Suddenly an American truck arrived at the gate, loaded the guards in and took them away. Shortly after more trucks arrived and took us some distance to what had evidently been a school. There we were documented and eventually moved to an airfield. Dakotas were being used to trans-ship us. Some were lucky and were ferried direct to England but our flight took us as far as a channel port and we finished the journey on a ferry boat arriving in Dover about teatime.

'There were marquees to rest in and later on we were given a full dinner served by kindly women volunteers. I made a gallant effort to eat and then my stomach rejected it leaving me miserable through the night. They soon got down to business the next day, giving us new kit and a medical exam. The doctor looked at me and what remained of my stomach and said 'You've had it rough I'll give you a double leave (six weeks) and double rations.' All I wanted was to get home.

'We got started next morning and arrived at Doncaster in the mid-afternoon. It was trolley buses at that time with one service from the Co-op via Catherine Street and Hyde Park. The very kind and lovely conductress told me not to bother when I proffered the fare. I think she was the only person who thanked me for my soldiering.

'So there I was walking down Chequer Avenue to Edith and the children, I know we were liberated about the middle of May and here I was. One thing struck me as I walked. The march, I have described in earlier writing, started on January 15 1945 in Brzeg and we were liberated in the middle of May which meant we were walking the highways of Germany for four months and in that time, I don't recall receiving any hot food only the pitiful bread ration. In retrospect it seems unbelievable that we could have survived the ordeal.

'I walked into the kitchen and as usual in these precious moments there was a nosey neighbour evidently wanting to be in the re-union, the first time I had seen Edith since January 1942. Janet the little toddler I had left was now about eight to nine years and the baby Billie who I last saw in a pram, was now a little boy of six years. I remember kissing Edith but after that time apart we both felt rather strange with each other and I suppose in my rundown condition I would seem aloof and miserable. It was at least a fortnight before we could come together in the normal relationship of husband and wife, due entirely to my physical condition.

'I was in Group 26 for discharge so when my leave was up I was sent to Horsham in Kent, billeted in a school and as far away from home as they could find. There was nothing to do and it struck me as we occasionally walked through the town not a soul spoke to us. I suppose after the glamour of Americans, Free French and Polish troops we were just nondescripts. Our pleasure of being home and survival did not seem to have universal appeal, and my thoughts were somewhat bitter.

'The next move was to Halifax and the first night there an old man, passing the gate shouted "Goodnight lads" and we felt we were home at last.

'Then someone had the inspiration to send us to Ripon and an understanding captain explained that all he wanted from us was to do some maintenance work on some boats. A short while after this we were told Group 26 was due for discharge on November 5 1945 and on that day we went to Strensall Barracks, York for a demob outfit and our discharge. A free man at last and I received a post office draft to cover the financial settlement of a demob bonus, payment for time on leave and wages not drawn whilst a POW. The total was £130 which seemed a lot in those days, until I started work and found a lot of the Plant workmen had more than that in Post War tax credits.

'November 5 was a Monday. On Wednesday I reported to the Plant Works and asked when I could return to work. It was George Taylor, then Carriage Works Manager who promptly said as soon as I liked and it was agreed I would start the following Monday November 11.

'As I walked to work on that day my first rebuff was at the tobacconists shop, which I had patronised, before the war, where to my request for a packet of cigarettes I was told in no uncertain tones that cigarettes were only for regular customers. In the workshop the welcome didn't seem too over-enthusiastic and for some time I felt an undercurrent of resentment at our return which meant an end to the good times of high wages, doubled during the war, and unlimited overtime. A good start and a place to stop.

'My biggest regret was all the hardship and trouble I caused to my wife. Much to her credit she never reproached me to wonder if it was worth it or just an unmitigated folly.'

Bill's wartime narrative ends.

At its peak in 1944, Stalag VIIIB held 18,000 Allied POWs and supplied workers to 236 work camps in the area. This POW camp featured in the 1962 production *Badge of Courage* starring Dirk Bogard.

Alan Jones' story

Alan quickly decided that his job as a captive was to be awkward. This was not just his military duty but also helped to make life interesting. He would end the war running a camp with over 10,000 Russian and Serb prisoners in May 1945 as they awaited their liberators.

The mischief was manifest when he claimed he knew Morse code and was promptly shifted to Rome for interrogation. 'Quite what would have happened if they had asked me to send or read any Morse code, I don't know. I certainly didn't know a single letter.' The Italians wanted to know the meaning of certain key words. Alan was not able to help them and insisted that they could only ask about his name, rank and number. After a short, but enjoyable stay in Rome, he was escorted alone to rejoin the prisoners still ruffing it in a transit camp.

The next ploy was to volunteer as an interpreter. The trusting captors allowed the volunteers much freedom and this was used to explore possibilities for escape but they were a very long way from home. Alan went absent a few times but there was no alternative but to return and face the excited admonishments of his jailers. Meanwhile, much of the company had headed north.

Prison life was interrupted by another bout of the malaria Alan had contracted the previous Christmas. He was moved to a hospital at Perugia where he was well cared for but without any medicine his situation became critical. As his blood count tumbled he was handed to the religious sisters for terminal comfort and care. This was not the escape that Alan had planned.

Alan, however, recovered but was in no hurry to let his careful nurses know and enjoyed a few months in the scenic mountains of Italy. Rumours of rifts within the Italian government were widely reported. Those who had sought to join the Allied cause rather than the Axis in 1939 began to assert themselves. There was open talk of Italian capitulation.

Recovery sent Alan north to a new camp. Italians running the camp as well as those outside seemed sympathetic so escape would not be difficult. But with Germans moving through the area the risk outside the wire was significant. They were hundreds of miles north of the Allies whose advance had bogged down. The Germans were still in effective control of much of Italy and showed no sign of withdrawing.

Allan and fellow prisoners prepared a tunnel in case it was needed. The going was relatively easy through the clay. They cut slices with the knife that each man carried to cut their rations. The lumps of clay were placed on a piece of mat that was hauled back to the entrance-man who would unload it for other to disperse. The work was very hot and the shortage of air meant that even fit young men could only work for 20 minutes before replacement.

The aim was to emerge beyond the wire into a riverbank that would provide good cover for the getaway. The thirty-metre tunnel was ready by the 8 September 1943 but no immediate action was taken. As a newcomer, Alan was not privy to the discussions but the prisoners were getting mixed messages about what they should do. The capitulation of the Italians came and went. The following day the Germans had the camp surrounded.

It was disappointing, but not a crushing blow as Alan had not really been sure what was going on. The camp continued to run itself for a week. Then the Germans summoned a group of prisoners to fall in and they were marched away to a slow train heading north. There was some puzzlement back home why the Germans selected some soldiers to remove from the camps to take to Germany. Many prisoners would remain in their Italian camps but under new, German management. The best guess was that those the Germans had captured were repatriated to German. It had been Alan's misfortune to be captured by a German unit at Tobruk, unlike most of the prisoners at Tobruk whose surrender had been accepted by the Italians.

It was not a long train ride before Alan found himself being unloaded in a picturesque valley where the colours of autumn were just touching the Alpine treescape. The POWs were told that this was a transit camp. For Alan it would be home for the rest of the war.

In early in 1941 Markt Pongau had been prepared for 10,000 prisoners to provide a work force for the timber, stone and agricultural industries clustered around the railway marshalling yard in this alpine pass. There was extensive accommodation for 1000 guards. Originally designed as a camp for soldiers from Eastern Europe, the Red Cross reported to the Foreign Office that it was variously known as a Punishment Camp, a Discipinary Camp or the more sinister Special Camp.

The original occupants were Serbs and Poles captured during the expansive phase of the war. In 1942 they were joined by the French who were billeted in a new set of huts. Following the Russian campaign, a new north camp was constructed in four months by the prisoners and covered eight hectares. The Eastern POWs were concentrated there.

Each of the sub-sections of the camp had between twenty-five and thirty huts designed to hold up to 500 men. Each man was supposed to have a space in a three-tiered bunk. As crowding increased, the concrete floors were often covered with straw to take the overflow. When the floor was full, hundreds of prisoners were accommodated in tent lines even in the winter. Stalag XVIIIC (317) finally held about 30,000 prisoners of assorted nationalities.

The French POWs were the reluctant workers assembled from other prison camps. It was the German policy to concentrate those in special camps who it felt might cause them trouble. Some French agreed to work on farms and an escape network was in place. However, there were few home runs but escapes ensured that the guards could not relax. But like most POWs, the French contingent had now settled in for the duration. They produced a prison newspaper, had two cinema projectors, an orchestra, a jazz band and substantial quantities of sports equipemnt. On liberation, the US Army complained that it needed 26 trucks to remove all the French baggage.

The official history compiled by the Austrian government notes that 'regular beatings were administered to increase the work rate.' When the Russians arrived in the autum of 1942 'they were driven by SS Schergen under impacts and insults...which would persist to the end of the war. The Russian prisoners of war were considered as the inferior east people so their facilties were the worst. Forty Russians died of malnutrition and different diseases daily. Also Russian prisoners of war were shot. 3542 prisoners of war are buried near the prison.' It was to this camp that Alan was delivered in late September 1943

The site of the camp had been well chosen. It stood like a little island. On one side there was a fast-flowing river that carried the Alpine, spring melt-water from the mountains to Southern Germany and eventually on to the Rhein. On the other side ran a busy rail line. Its strategic location would make it a tempting target for attack. As well as watching the trains and the water, they had to watch the American Air Force apparently trying to seal this bottleneck by destroying the river bridges. Alan and the other prisoners would watch the icy trails of the approaching Flying Fortresses.

After a dozen incidents where bombers had killed allied POWs late in 1944. The worst incident was the one reported by Bill Harvey where twenty eight POWs had been killed on 2 December by a direct hit on their shelter. A major air reconnaissance effort was launched to identify all POW camps and the

12.1
In the closing year of the war, much research was done to map the precise location of all POW camps. These are the photos used to brief aircrew to ensure that they did not hit the camp when attacking the valley bridges. However, the POWs did not know this and watched helplessly as the bombs released from high altitude in daylight raids crashed into the hillside beyond the camp. *Reproduced by kind permission of the Public Records Office.*

associated work camps. All Allied air stations were issued with a set of the images identifying the location of POWs.

The USAF was not trying to destroy the bridges that threaded through the North and South camps. They were under strict orders not to bomb within a thousand yards of the camp. Furthermore, they were advised that columns of prisoners were on the move and should not be mistaken for retreating Germans whose movements they might be used to camouflage. Indeed in a special instruction to ground-attack aircraft, who were warned that the POWs in their greatcoats could easily be mistaken for the Hungarian Infantry fighting as German allies.

The daily routine of the camp that the small contingent of British and Commonwealth prisoners imposed on themselves was rigorous. Although they were not allowed to mix with the other nationalities or even the British 'other ranks', the 'seniors' set a fine example. They would parade themselves each morning. Jobs were detailed and done before any recreation activity was undertaken. Uniforms were always carefully cleaned and maintained aided by a good stock supplied through the Red Cross.

To provide the homely touch, wild flowers were picked for their barrack block. The eccentric flower picking served as a disguise for other activities that would not be approved of. Their weekly shower took them out of their compound and past the pile of coke that was used to take the chill off the water provided for the showers. They expected to return from their ablutions with a significant supplement to their fuel allocation.

Communications in a multi-lingual environment was tricky. The limited latin Alan had acquired as an alter boy and later at Retford Grammar School provided one basis for a camp lingua-franca. In pidgin latin, the Poles, Serbs, French and British managed to organise their affairs. Contact between the national groups was not easy or encouraged but it was possible to exchange men between compound to keep the roll-call numbers right.

Alan attempted to repeat his success as a radio ham at Kabrit where he had built a radio but to no avail. Reception in their Alpine valley was very limited. Even the well-established French did not appear to have contrived any means of keeping themselves in touch with the world by illicit radio. The limited flow of news was coaxed from the German guards and supplied by arriving prisoners.

Mid-October brought a fresh supply of prisoners and their news. Two hundred of those captured at Arnhem were dispatched to this tough camp at the other side of Greater Germany. They related the size of the airborne Armada that had assaulted Europe on D-Day and then with stories of the plan to take the Rhein bridges intact. The scale was hard to imagine for those who had been captured before the full might of the Allies had been mobilised.

Many of the Arnhem survivors were walking wounded and were still dressed in the uniform they had been wearing when captured in September. With stock of clothing now running low, the existing inmates managed to provide the newcomers with the vital items. It was a great boost to morale to discover that the Allies were poised to cross into the German heartland. Informed speculation was that the war could be over by Christmas. Their captors would find it increasingly hard to maintain control of this spirited group.

Collective punishments were regularly imposed and the British NCOs were moved to the North Camp with the Russians as a punishment when eight of their number absconded from a work party. When they did not appear to be taking their punishment seriously all sports' materials were confiscated. But that did little to break the spirits of the NCOs.

Parades at Stalag were regular, long and potentially tedious. While they and their accommodation were systematically searched they were not permitted to visit the latrines. One particularly unpleasant trick they played on their captors was to scribble a rude message on a scrap of paper. Alan or another volunteer would ask if he could relive himself and was allowed to fall out and go behind the ranks. He would wait until he had the attention of some guards before ripping the paper to shreds and covering it.

Amid much shouting the vigilant and ever suspicious SS would recover the scraps from the steaming pile. Imagining how their tormentors would react when they pieced the paper together would keep their spirits warm at night!

It is not surprising to read that Herr E Mayer of the Red Cross had little sympathy for the state of the British NCOs in his report of 22 February 1944. The German Commandant had reported that they were undisciplined and refused to work so could not expect favourable treatment when resources were short. He nevertheless noted that they had no heat, no light, no clothing issued for nine months and the straw in their mattresses had long since been burnt to produce some heat and destroy the bedbugs.

What Herr Mayer did not know was that the NCOs were an accomplished bunch of actors well able to put on a bad show for the Red Cross. After listing the more general shortages and the failure of any mail to arrive for three months, the pious representative of the ICRC put in a plea for more equipment to meet the spiritual and intellectual needs of the POWs who 'seemed to talk, and think, of nothing but food and the lack of news'.

Alan was taking good care of his own and others' intellectual needs. He was able to get hold of over 200 books. Prisoners gave some. Other came as a gift from the Royal family. Alan's other project was to complete a set of differential and integral calculus calculations. He had long been attracted to maths and during his time in the camp filled many exercise books with the worked examples which were then bound into volumes and survived as treasured possessions.

Shortly after the arrival of the paratroopers, there were other arrivals of prisoners singly or in small groups. Some were not brought into the camp but lodged in the guards' barracks. Rumours began to circulate that the camp was being used to concentrate some key prisoners that the SS could employ as bargaining counters when the war reached this remote corner of the continental war.

Among them were the nephew of the British queen, John Elphinstone: The nephew of the British Commander-in-Chief in the Middle East, Michael Alexander: One senior American officer and 16 survivors of the Warsaw rebellion in the late summer of the 1944.

In mid-October, a young Polish boy was brought into the camp. His name was Alexander Robinson, son of a Scottish diplomat and a Polish mother who had been caught up in the Warsaw Uprising. Alex had a keen interest in mathematics which would see him sponsored through college once repatriated to England where Alex often lived with Alan's growing family. After graduating, Alex migrated to the US to teach mathematics at Berkley in due course.

As the Second World War drew to a close in April 1945, the Allied prisoners of war in the camp at St. Johan im Pongau, watched refugee trains passing in both directions. Trains packed with German troops were heading back to Germany while a mixture of soldiers and civilians headed south to cross the Alps towards Italy. The small contingent of English-speaking prisoners had a good view of the railway line as the track was just the other side of the wire.

The train line was kept illuminated at night so allied reconnaissance would see that it was surrounded by prisoners of war. However, in the calculations of war, the junction stood close to Hitler's fortress, the 'Eagles Nest' at Berchesgarten, so the flow along it had to be destroyed to prevent the area being reinforced for a last stand.

But nothing went to plan. Two treeless areas on the surrounding mountains testified to the difficulty of bombing valleys. Not a single bomb fell in the camp or on the line. The trains continued to run.

On 23 April a column of about four hundred Allied prisoners from Wolfsberg and Graz arrived at the village of Markt Pongau about a mile from the camp. They had been moved east just ahead of the advancing Russians, loosely controlled by their guards. They fed themselves with food traded for cigarettes and chocolate from local farmers. It was an agreeable break from the routine of prisoner-of-war camp life. There was no more space in the camp itself and the influx from other camp of the Stalag XVIII group of camp grew to around thirteen thousand Allied POWs. They settled into the town and its surrounds, seeking what cover they could and living off the land.

By the beginning of May 1945 it was very clear that German military order was collapsing. The guards were no longer in effective control. Routines broke

As the war drew to a close, the running of the Stalag XVIIIC was left to the prisoners. The senior ranks took over. The captives wanted photographs and a local photographer was brought in to make this unique record.

12.2 *(top left)*
The British senior ranks that had posed the Germans so many problems. The poor quality of the block work behind testifies to the amateur who built the camp in 1940.

12.3 *(centre left)*
Alan Jones and an Australian SNCO who organised the trade with the town of Markt Pongau. Inside the camp there was a supply of cigarettes and chocolate to barter with the local town. In this rural area, there was an adequate supply of food and sufficient stocks in the camp itself to keep them going until the 101 Airborne Division arrived.

12.4 *(bottom left)*
The inscription in this copy of 'Boswell's Life of Johnson' is from the King and Queen as a gift to the prisoners of war at Christmas 1943. It formed part of the library run by Alan Jones. The two-volume work was brought back to England after liberation.

12.5 *(top right)*
Two prisoners doing some sign writing as the camp is reorganised under new management. A chalk inscription on the wall advertisers boots for sale. The camp was administered by the prisoners for a week before outside help reached them.

down and the guards withdrew to their bunker the south of the two camps. Civilians began to approach the wire to trade. Staff Sergeant Alan Jones was the senior British NCO and along with an Australian warrant officer, they took control of the camp.

The majority of the prisoners were unwilling to leave the confines of the camp in this anarchic environment. There was enough German currency and trade goods available to enable the prisoners to obtain food to sustain the camp for the fortnight it took for the Allies to reach and liberate the camp about a week after the war ended.

Into this uncertain situation, Hans Gallusser of the Red Cross was plunged on 7 May for a routine inspection. He reported that the south camp designed for about four thousand was housing 13000 prisoners. He noted that discipline was breaking down as the guards had withdrawn for their self-protection. Typhus had broken out. Trains were being stopped by prisoners and checked for food. Other prisoners, the number is put at 300, had even boarded one train south.

Into this sensitive situation, US bombers that had earlier delivered such destruction to the surrounding hillsides began a supply of food and arms flying at very low level. The following is taken from the diary of Ben Haller Jr, a Bombardier with the 461st Bomb Group. 'On May 9, there was a call for volunteers to fly cargo missions to drop supplies to Allied POW camps in Austria. The purpose was not only to get food and medical supplies to these people as fast as possible, but also to arm them so they could officially be in charge of their camps and adjoining towns before the Russians could race in and claim they had 'liberated' our people. My diary shows I flew on 9 May to the Americans held in the German prison camp at Spittal, Austria, northwest of Villach. Dropped twelve 350 pound cans of supplies from 1,000 feet.

'On May 10 or 11 I flew another one to Wolfsberg POW camp where the English fellows are. Saw streams of German trucks, guns and carts for miles pouring in to surrender to the Allied troops in this area. Dropped from 800 feet.

'I failed to make an entry for May 16 .... I can't recall the name of the POW camp but it was again in southern Austria, near the Villach and Klagenfurt area. The volunteer crews carried no gunners, of course, although I think a few guys were allowed to ride strictly as passengers to see from low level the landscape we'd been bombing from high altitude and to be able to say they took part in those historic flights that meant little to anyone else, but everything to the POWs on the ground.'

Urgent action was called for and Hans Gallusser, escorted by his German liaison officer Colonel Kadecke, set out for Munich along with a British medical officer identified as Major Lambie. Their aim was to obtain supplies of food and stop all air raids in the area. Unknown to them at three that morning, General Eisenhower had announced a cessation of hostilities.

The party reported to the German HQ in Munich. Here they were informed that it was now a matter for the US Army which was in the process of taking control. After a short wait they were taken to meet Colonel Robert Strayr (sic) who it was noted by the Red Cross representative as 'commanding a parachute regiment.' The 101 Airborne Division, through their newly appointed executive officer, accepted the job of looking after the POWs.

The food problem at the camp was solved by distributing supplies of American army rations. Accommodation was provided by tents while arrangements were made for the speedy evacuation. On 20 May a slick operation to move about twenty-five thousand Allied soldiers by lorry to the Salzburg airfield for flights to France where the RAF flew them to England.

Alan Jones was officially liberated on 25 May 1945 by the Americans of 101 Airborne Division who had earlier captured Hitler's Eagles Nest at nearby Berchesgarten. The war had been over for 18 days. 'It was an extraordinary time. One puzzling thing was that everybody seemed to want to have a photograph. We found a local photographer who was very happy to produce prints for the men in exchange for some of our goods.' This produced a unique set of images of life in POW camp and some haunting images of the unfortunate inmates of the North Camp.

12.6 & 12.7

These two haunting shots are of the prisoners in the north camp. They are lining up for food when this shot was taken. Alan Jones reports that it was common to carry the sick and even the dead to claim the extra set of rations. The two prisoners strapped together are evidently both alive in these images.

Much of the camp still survives as a timber yard and furniture factory. Not everybody left at the end of the war and the camp was refurbished. Serbian officers with royalist loyalties were afraid to join their soldiers and return home. With the agreement of the Americans they refurbished their accommodation and established the HQ of a Royal-Yugoslav Army. In October 1949 over five hundred refugees from the camp, among them 259 Serbs, were moved to America.

The role of the Red Cross

The role played by the Red Cross in the welfare of Allied prisoners cannot be overstated. To cater for their physical needs they supplied food, uniforms and medicine. The welfare needs of POWs were overseen with inspections, information flow, repatriations and the establishment and moral enforcement of codes of conduct.

The International Committee of the Red Cross, the ICRC, distributed nearly 400 million kilos to around two million Allied prisoners in Europe. Red Cross parcels were assembled from ingredients provided by the Allies. A shoe-box sized parcel always contained, tea, powdered or tinned milk – known as 'klim'- and sugar. The other ingredients varied but included dried fruit, biscuits, sweets and chocolate along with jam, meat paste, tinned margarine, vegetables, salmon or curry. At least one item for personal hygiene such as soap or toothpaste was inside the box.

These sturdy boxes had many other uses. It was tough enough to provide insoles for boots when the soles had worn so thin that the nails pricked the feet. Alan Jones used them to make hardback covers for the maths books he wrote while a prisoner.

The ICRC registered prisoners of war and communicated essential information about them to their families by using 'capture cards' and 'individual identity cards.' The Agency also undertook to forward prisoners' correspondence. During the six years of conflict in Europe the Agency completed around twenty-five million of these 'individual identity cards' and passed on some one hundred and twenty million messages, carrying news to and from prisoners of war and their families. Years later, Kathleen Jones would often express her gratitude for the Red Cross and Vatican Radio who had provided her with information on the whereabouts of Alan through the years of captivity.

The flow of information through the Red Cross office in Berne was two-way. Issues of promotion were important as they affected pay and also the camp in which prisoners were confined. There was a regular flow of information about substantive rank which their captors would accept as grounds for reclassifying a prisoner. There were conflicts of identity, and many missing and sick persons to be traced. Tragic confusions over names might mean joy for one family and desolation for another.

The ICRC also passed divorce papers and other legal documents so life at home did not entirely by-passed the prisoners of war. Ken Vanables, who had been repatriated from France in 1939 when he was found to be under-age, used the Red Cross to communicate with the legal system when reports of his wife's behaviour reached him. All correspondence was conducted through a prisoner know as the 'man of confidence' who was recognised by all parties.

Ken's story

Ken Venables had left the company when it was discovered that he was too young to be sent overseas. Once he reached his nineteenth birthday in February 1940, he was sent back to France but with another sapper unit. His military life would continue to run parallel to those in the company from which he had been separated until it also ended in capture outside Tobruk.

Ken was one of the sappers whose task was to mine the bridges to slow the German advance in May and June 1940. Separated from the rest of his company during one of their mining missions, his small demolition party headed west and reached Le Mans before they had to abandon their truck.

Ken began the first of his epic marches, this time heading west towards Rennes and his previous base with the company. Later he would learn that most of his unit had gone to the north coast where many were killed or captured. Only 40 of the original 400 strong squadron would muster in Chatham at the end of June.

After a day's slow progress amid the tide of French refugees the sappers realised that they would soon be overtaken by the advancing Germans. Most abandoned vehicles along their way had been left unserviceable or had run out of fuel. But Ken spotted a car that appeared to be serviceable. To the delight of his small party it ran once he connected the wires.

Progress towards the coast was now rapid. The tide of humanity sensed their approach and cleared a way as they motored west. There were no checkpoints to help or hinder them and they encountered no other military refugees along their way. 'It was pretty obvious that everybody had gone' Ken recalls. 'We passed through Rennes and it was deserted apart from the displaced people who were heading west like us.'

They reached Brest to find a solitary ship loading. Aboard they discovered the passengers were French soldiers with whom they shared an uneventful trip to Southampton. A bout of glandular fever earned Ken some home leave, perhaps not the best moment to enter a stormy marriage.

Ken set out for Africa as a Sapper with 7 Field Squadron in November 1940 and his fateful convergence with the company at Tobruk. He had earned two stripes but lost them in a dispute with a vindictive sergeant major following the return from his mother's funeral shortly before embarkation.

Ken had another brush with the arbitrary nature of justice when he was charged with buying a bunch of bananas during their stop in Freetown. The rules forbade the consumption of fruit that did not have skins. The army did not recognise the slippery outer layer of a banana as a skin and Ken enjoyed seven days confinement aboard the SS Franconia as she continued on her way to Durban.

Eighteen months of desert warfare came to an end on 20 June 1942 when, abandoned by the British armour and out of ammunition, the troops in the 'Knightsbridge' box surrendered to the inevitable. The path to Tobruk was open for the Afrika Korps.

'We were waiting to be relieved or evacuated. We had no idea that the main fighting elements were already withdrawing across the desert and along the coast. We stayed in our trenches for a couple of days waiting without any news. I saw truck loads of 25 pound shells arrive but they were sent away. I wondered 'why?'

'On the last day, one of the German tanks drove up from behind the box. An officer was sitting on the front and told us in English that the war was over for us.'

They were rounded up during the day by Italian infantry and the next day set out marching towards Tunis. Three long, hot days into the march they were met by Italian trucks. Much to Ken's relief there were cans of water inside. 'We must have survived on what we had with us but it was gruesome.'

'We lived under canvas and received a lump of bread and cheese in the morning and some soup at night.' There was no washing facility and water remained a precious commodity. Inactivity was the only option. 'It was annoying to deal with our captors. The Italians were worst. They thought that they were the Cock of the Walk which did not go down well with us.'

After three months Ken was moved with a lucky group of one hundred and fifty to another camp. 'The Italian officer in charge was much more sympathetic. There were still no facilities for washing in the camp but there were sulphur springs nearby. He took us in groups of a dozen to wash and shave. The curative effects of the water was amazing. The desert sores, septic bites and rashes quickly vanished.' Ken began to walk round the wire with the other captives to give themselves some minimal exercise. There was nothing else to occupy them.

Another three months passed in this improvised POW cage before a ship was provided to carry Ken to Italy. With no warning and little ceremony, they were packed into trucks one afternoon and transported to the harbour in Tunis and loaded into the hold of a ship. 'We were very afraid during the journey. The hatches had been battened down so if we were attacked we didn't stand a chance.' It took 12 hours to reach near Naples where they were moved to a deserted factory, again without any facilities apart from some bunks.

'We were still in our desert uniforms. The legs on the shorts could be rolled down but they were no match for the winter temperatures in Italy. They issued us with Italian army uniforms just in time. Our clothes were in tatters and it was getting cold.

'For the rest, it was then a case of doing nothing. You couldn't even stay clean as there was just one tap for two hundred men. Eventually showers were installed. That was the best part of being a POW having a hot shower.' After months without the means to wash or shave and clean their clothes, the regular shower was an unimaginable luxury.

'We were now taken out to work camps each day and brought back every evening.' This relieved the monotony and the walk was enjoyable. Winter months of inactivity gave way to a spring and summer of waiting around. A whole year of captivity had been bored slowly away.

'We were then moved to the north to work on farmland.' Deprived of the manpower to harvest it, the corn stood overripe in the fields. Ken learnt to cut corn with a sickle while the villagers bundled it. A hard day's backbreaking work brought the reward of a cob of bread. 'Some farms treated us much better. There was even an occasional meal' recalls Ken.

Morale received a lift when the Red Cross arrived with new battle dress for them. Rumours of the impending capitulation of the Italians began to circulate. Ken and some fellow prisoners realised that they were still deep inside German occupied territory. The captives had no illusions that the Germans would withdraw from their erstwhile allies land. Italy would just move from an Axis power to an occupied nation.

They resolved to get outside the wire to make sure they were not handed over to the Germans. When the capitulation of the Italians was announced, they tried to leave but guards would not open the gate. There were no instructions to release their new allies so they remained prisoners. The next day it was too late. The Germans arrived and moved them to Cremona.

A mass of prisoners had been assembled to be loaded onto a freight train which hauled them over the Alps through the Brenner Pass and on to the heart of wartime Germany. For seven days they travelled. Once a day the trucks were opened and they were let out for some soup. There was no sanitation along the way no ablution was permitted during their short excursion.

Ken's temporary home was Stalag 8B near Lamsdorf, Upper Silesia, close to the pre-war Czech-Polish border. This was the main holding camp and distribution centre for Allied prisoners. From this marshalling camp prisoners were dispatched to the surrounding work camps. Before Ken settled in, he was on the move again, this time a short trip with fifty POWs into Poland. They were unloaded and taken to some almost cosy accommodation.

'From the guards we learnt we were about twenty miles from Cracow. They also informed us we were going to work down the mines. Next day we were given a hard hat and some overalls.' Although from a mining area, Ken had no first-hand experience of the business.

'We went down the main shaft to a gallery. The overseer was a right bastard, half Polish, half German. He kept shouting "Now you work for us". He did not appreciate my Yorkshire humour when I demonstrated to him that he was mistaken. He had a range of threats which varied from locking me up to starvation. Most of the time he just waved his pistol under my nose.'

A 'modus vivendi' was arrived at but not before a few games of cat and mouse around the underground shafts and galleries. On one occasion the entire guard force was drawn into the mine and the POWs were able to return to the surface. 'There was some talk of escape' Ken remembers. 'But we decided we were too far away from anywhere and completely unprepared for the very cold weather expected. So we fell in as normal and marched back to barracks. When we got there they would not let us in. We were locked out of our prison camp! We were kept outside until our guards came rushing back.' There were no repercussions as it would be hard for the guards to explain how it had all gone so wrong.

Ken worked with two Polish miners who were in effect fellow prisoners. It was their job to cut the coal on their twelve-yard face which was about six feet high. Once the coal was cut it was the job of the three prisoners to shovel it onto a conveyor. The team had to stay till their day's work was done and the cut coal was cleared. A good relationship developed with their miners. The atmosphere underground became very friendly. From them they learned about the concentration camps and German atrocities. Friends and family had vanished to Auschwitz.

There were well fed by the standards of other POWs. There were no regular Red Cross boxes but the guards made sure their workers could keep up their work rate. The POWs also helped themselves. The dealing went on in the darkness of the mine where the Poles would exchange fresh food for soap, cigarettes and chocolate. Ken had done a successful trade for half a dozen eggs.

'A young guard, he looked about fourteen, decided to do a thorough search and discovered my eggs. He removed them and proceeded to pack them into his own hat which he placed carefully on his head. With a big grin he indicated that he would have a good tea tonight.' Ken lent forward and brought his hand down on the boy's hat. 'That'll be scrambled eggs' he announced to the other prisoners.

As the friendship developed Ken and some colleagues planned to escape. Ken loaned an army uniform to their Polish colleagues so they could prepare identification papers through their contacts with the resistance. The Poles also had a radio but it could only pick up a German station. They understood enough of the language but they only had the official German version of events. They learned of the allied landing and advance but only when they had crossed into Germany. Until then it was all about German victories.

In January 1945 any plans for an escape were thwarted. They were preparing to go down the mine when they were told they were abandoning the camp. They moved out with what kit they could carry and set off through the snow. They were in a hurry. The fit and well shod party covered forty miles on the first day and kept up this impressive rate for a week. Later they learned from an English-speaking guard that the Russians were just ten miles away when they deserted the camp. This guard was familiar with every racecourse in England which he had visited but remained very cautious in what information he revealed. 'Typical of a racing punter' thought Ken.

Throughout his captivity, Ken kept his own counsel. Life had its random brutalities and everyday uncertainties. The Germans did their best to disrupt the organisation of the prisoners' previous chain of command. The structure of his military life had been stripped away and the POWs were deliberately shuffled about. Camp organisation ensured that there was little opportunity to organise. Ken saw no camp entertainments, little sport or organised recreation. Forced labour was the only alternative to isolation and boredom.

Survival was now Ken's preoccupation. The pace and lack of food took its toll. Those too weak to continue were simply left by the roadside in the snow. 'Quite a few dropped out. The older ones in their late twenties and thirties had it very tough. This was a very selfish time. Survival was a challenge. It had to be everyone for themselves' Ken recalls with obvious regret.

The daily average dropped dramatically when the Red Cross caught up with their column. Twenty miles was set as the limit and after three days a day of rest was ordered. With this routine Ken reckons they covered about 1800 miles between January and May as they meandered towards the west, staying ahead of the Russians.

There was no formal feeding at any stage. They had to forage on the farms. The situation for the guards and their charges was one of survival. There was some cooperation in the hunt for food. At each night's stop they would move into a barn and consume whatever they found. The best find was a potato clamp. These could be spotted even under a mound of snow. Along with the guards, the foraged food would be gathered and cooked later. Boiled vegetables provided a welcome, warm liquid before another cold night. One farmer, as they passed through Czechoslovakia, killed his race horse which was divided among the prisoners and guards to cook. Some ate it raw but most kept it until they had a fire to cook.

On 13 February 1945 they were, as usual, herded into a barn at dusk about two hundred yards from a bridge across the Elbe. They heard, and then watched, the night bombers begin their devastation of Dresden. At first it was a spectacle but soon they were watching from an unsafe distance as their bridge was evidently a target. The following day the bombing continued but by then the guards had moved them away from the developing firestorm which is estimated to have claimed twenty five thousand lives.

They walked on but the routine was now variable. Ken's boots had just about survived the walk. He kept them on at night to dry them. Dry boots kept the cold out longer than wet boots and dry boots lasted longer. Keeping his boots on also stopped his blistered feet swelling. Ken soon learnt that it was difficult and painful to get a comfortable fit once they were removed. As everybody's boots fell to bits, even his flimsy footwear might be an attractive target for another survivor. They walked on for many weeks, the daily distances and direction varying.

Then one day, they stopped at a farm for few days where, unannounced by any distant rumble of guns, some tanks were seen moving towards them. As they drew closer they could see that US tanks were approaching. The tanks paused briefly before sweeping on. The German guards smiled and started shaking hands with the prisoners. Ken would have none of it. 'I had no desire to share this moment with those who had driven us like a herd of animals half way across Europe during the winter.'

A few hours later US trucks turned up to take them to Landschut aerodrome. 'They couldn't do enough for us. We were de-loused. I had got shot of them but most of the others were infested. We were given new military clothing. Once again we were told that the war was over for us.' This time it was welcome news. They were full of questions and were given briefings on the war news.

Once they had been fully processed they were flown to Rheims where they were handed back to the British army. 'We were quickly dispatched; thirty five to each plane and we were airborne. I wandered round the fuselage and went to the rear gunner who showed me how they were fired. I then went to the mid-upper turret to admire the view along the length of the Lancaster.'

The trip home returned Ken to Brize Norton, near Oxford. There was an efficient processing system that not only fed and clothed them but handed them a week's pay and the medals and medal ribbon earned. Ken was particularly amused to receive one for seven years service and good conduct.

The Women's Royal Voluntary Service ran a sleek system including a sweepstake on which of them would process their charges out of the centre quickest. Ken had the good fortune to be in the care of the winner and within two days of touching down, was on his way to Conisborough.

Looking back I think 'how the hell did I manage? It was a nightmare.' For some years he maintained a correspondence with Janek, one of the Polish miners who had run away to join the resistance. A local displaced Pole had settled nearby and acted as interpreter. When he left, the correspondence lapsed.

'I have never spoken of these things. Nobody seemed interested and few would understand. It was only thirty years on that I discovered Dave Robert with who I had passed my time in 106 company lived nearby.' Dave Robert had subsequently been selected as Alan Jones' driver.

Bob's story:

'Fortunately the Germans were efficient so feeding was organised en route. But there was not room for everyone to sit so one half would remain standing close together while the other half sat or slept for two hours at a time. It was impossible to eat packed so tight and standing up so it was arranged that those sitting would eat first. It was agreed that part of a floorboard in the corner of the wagon would be removed for a toilet.

'Around midday on the third day the train stopped at a siding in a wood. We were formed up to march out of the wood and there was our destination, a large POW Camp. As we marched beside the outer wire we met an awful, characteristic smell which we would get used to. The inmates were not shouting in English. On the south side was a Russian compound and further along there was a French compound. As we turned the corner at the western end of the camp, there was the main gate, an imposing structure with the words Stammelager IVB below a guardhouse over the gateway.

'Stalag IVB contained a mixture senior NCOs of allied nations from the army and RAF brought from Italy. As we marched through the gate the guards directed us into a small compound with three or four huts. Here we were met by the Camp Leader, WO1 Meyers of the Canadian Air Force and he, in turn introduced an SS Officer as Captain Konig, the Lagerführer. He explained this was the transit compound where we would be given a hot shower, our clothing deloused and records made before entering the camp proper. First we would be issued with bread and hot soup and he would talk to us again later.

'Thankful, we sank to the ground to await the meal while the guards sorted us into groups for showers and delousing. The meal consisted of potato soup, better than the Italian variety. The bread was one dark brown loaf between four, giving each three or four slices. This became our normal lunchtime meal, superior to what we had been used to but, still a limited ration. As the meal finished we were directed to one of the larger huts to strip and label our clothes in a bundle for the disinfector alongside and enter the hut for our shower. The weather was warm for September so waiting for our clothes was not unbearable and when they were returned at least they were warm.

'While waiting, I became involved in conversation with a Scot sitting by me, who seemed on his own like me. He told me his name was Jack Telfer and had been a quartermaster in the Camerons at Tobruk. During the conversation I brought up the subject that I knew nobody in particular and would he care to join me to 'muck in' when we moved into the camp. He agreed as he too, had lost contact with his friends. I was lucky to have had Jack Telfer as my 'mucker.' Jack and I mucked-in together until we reached England at the end and went our separate ways.

'Without any warning there was a shout and the guards started herding us back to the disinfector and telling everyone to strip again. It appeared that some people, possibly more as a matter of habit, were seen inspecting their clothing for the lice eggs. So we were deloused again. This time we all made sure that everyone understood, lice hunting was over.

'The rest of the afternoon was spent having a haircut although the Russian, with a huge smile on his face, operating a pedal machine sheared every hair from our heads. The outcome was, of course, hoots of laughter as each of us saw our neighbour. A more villainous crowd was difficult to imagine. We were taken to a hut for photographing and a registration card with the number 249069. I looked like a convict.

'Six hundred of us were marched up the main road to the army compound at the far end of the camp on the left. During this move we realised we were in a cosmopolitan camp with compounds for Dutch, Belgian, French, Russian and of course the commonwealth contingents in the RAF and army. We were to fill the last huts. Jack and I were almost the first into our hut 49B so we had a good choice of bunks. We chose the bottom two bunks of a block of six in a row of three against the far wall and nearest the stove which was adapted for cooking with a large steel plate in the top of the fireplace standing on an iron grid.

'The brick stove itself was six feet long by four feet wide and three feet high, with the fire door in the side below the plate, a foot off the floor. Leading from the stove was a brick chimney about two feet square, running most of the way down the centre of the hut before rising to the roof spreading heat through the hut and an ideal place for drying clothes.

'The coal issue was quite generous under the circumstances, being 75 kilograms per half hut daily. The coal shed was situated in the corner of the compound under one of the guard towers but nevertheless, always a target for some individuals to raid at night, usually with some success. There was an occasional issue of coal dust which was very acceptable to bank the fire overnight. Two volunteers always had water boiling for tea in the morning and midday, as well as a period in the evening for cooking. In the summer the fire was normally relit before roll-call and later tea was made using our improvised electric heaters.

'We were the last Army contingent from Italy, making over seven thousand British, including over two thousand RAF, to fill this corner of the camp for senior NCOs. There were already some two thousand French, one thousand Dutch with some Belgians, Serbs and Poles. There were many thousands of Russians occupying most of the south side of the camp. This area was out of bounds to the British for our own good, but the Russians were free to come into our compound to work or looking for food.

'As soon as the parcels were issued everyone made a dash for the stove with a variety of dixies for their first brew of tea. Jack had an old style half-moon dixie which had been replaced by the flat mess tins as a normal issue. I think he obtained it from an Indian soldier in his last Italian camp. It was more useful under these circumstances for cooking and especially for brewing tea. This first cooking session was somewhat disorganised but everyone soon got to bed after three days tiring travelling.

'The bunks with straw filled palliasses had two new blankets. Pillows were improvised. In my case I used my great coat and when the weather became colder I had a linen bag made, stuffed with my spare clothes to act as a pillow. We soon learned that we could say goodbye to the louse and welcome the German flea. It appears that fleas and lice are not compatible.

'This non-compatibility proved to be not strictly true, although none in our half-barrack suffered again from lice, the Russians were infected and there had been outbreaks of typhus. In March 1944 there was an outbreak of typhus and diphtheria, when quarantine was enforced. Later I learned that, before the British camp was set up, there had been a serious outbreak of typhus among the Russians and some thousands had died and were buried in a mass grave. Rumour had it that this grave was under the football pitch in the French compound.

'The camp lay about five miles east of the town of Muhlberg on Elbe, and the railway in the woods to the east of the camp was the main line north to Berlin from Dresden. We were about 120 km south from Berlin but only 60 km from Dresden. The guards were mainly soldiers who were no longer fit for active service. Most of them had been released from the Russian front after being wounded or having suffered from frost-bite. Several had lost an eye, an arm and many found it difficult to walk. To see them marching up the camp road to take post was a sight that brought a touch of pity among the British prisoners. I became friendly with some of the guards who would come, surreptitiously, to barter and examine our war-map.

'On the whole the guards treated the British with something approaching sympathetic respect but could not understand our fighting as allies of the Russians. They treated the Russian prisoners harshly explaining that the

Russians treated German prisoners even worse. They had no protecting power as Russia had not signed the Geneva Convention. They received no parcels and subsisted on a lower ration scale. There was a separate small compound in which resided a few Russians who appeared to be an elite, in smart khaki uniforms, perhaps warrant officers or merely camp racketeers. They appeared to be better fed, did not associate with the main Russian compound but kept to themselves. The French and Dutch also kept themselves as separate communities, sharing a cookhouse and were rarely seen visiting other compounds.

'In Stalag IVB my life was busy except on Sundays, so I had little time to spend on cooking or brewing tea. Jack on the other hand, although he became the camp quizmaster and general source of all sorts of information, did most of the work in the hut, so tea and meals were always ready for me and I did my bit on Sundays.

Jack was a former pupil of Fetty's College in Edinburgh and very clever. His main attribute was his photographic memory. Not only could he read a passage from a book and repeat it later, word for word, but he composed all his quiz questions from memory and carried the answers in his head. He composed a new quiz program every four weeks and toured the huts each evening except Sundays.

'Jack and I agreed to forego sugar in our tea, Jack did not normally have it and I wasn't bothered. Nor were we all that interested in chocolate which fetched a high barter price. Both items would be sold for meat and other items we required.

'We all were surprised and pleased that a shop had already been established, with a cigarette monetary system. The cigarettes for such transactions had to be what we called 'tailor made' from a packet, not hand rolled. When they become tatty with handling one could roll two from one 'tailor made.' Both of us smoked in moderation, something like ten a day, depending on how busy we were. Every smoker had a tin of some sort in which was kept the cigarette papers, obtained from the camp office, and their tobacco and butt ends. Nothing was wasted.

'The camp food situation was better than Italy. The soup was much the same but the potatoes and bread made the difference. The bread was a square brown loaf between four, which gave each about four slices, twice the Italian ration. The daily food cycle of ersatz coffee morning and evening, soup at mid-day issued with three or four potatoes cooked in their skins and bread in the late afternoon.

'Jack and I ate two slices with our evening meal and saved two slices for breakfast. Our evening meal usually consisted of the potatoes re-cooked in various ways with parcel meat and vegetables. Although cheese was not in the ration scale, it was sometimes issued with the bread and on rare occasions, sausage meat or meat paste when meat was not in the soup. The Germans seemed to be very short of meat.

'Potatoes appeared to be in plentiful supply locally, stored not only in a hut, but in a field of clamps outside the wire. It was an item of food that never ran out. The potato issue was delivered to the hut in weighed sacks where the hut leader divided them also by weight into twenty groups with a home-made steelyard. There were always a few left over in this division, so a careful record was needed on who got the extras, how many and when. There was little argument about this for it was seen to be as fair as possible, but when Jack had to share out his group issue to the ten of us, it needed the wisdom of Solomon because it had to be done by numbers (despite the variations in size), rather than weight. Luckily Jack was full of tact. One could hear arguments in some parts of the hut, usually two comparing the size of their potatoes, but I don't remember any fights, now we were not that hungry.

'We were settling down for the coming winter. Near the main gate there were three hospitals or lazerets, staffed by six doctors. However there was no dentist this meant the doctors pulled teeth. There was a shortage of anaesthetics so it was necessary to be accompanied by two companions to hold one down during dental operations.

'Soon after our arrival about two hundred senior Italian officers, mainly from the Balkans, who had refused to fight on with the Germans joined us. At first their arrival caused some amusement but when they diffidently came into our compound to volunteer to do our dobying, our feelings changed to sympathy. We had learned their reasons for being there and that, as officers, they had not been treated very well. Payment was in kind, mostly cigarettes and some food. They were soon moved out and replaced by a thousand Italian NCOs who lived in tents set up in the compound to which they were confined so we did not see anything of them. They disappeared later in 1944 to be replaced by Polish girls from Warsaw.

'I was appointed British camp electrician, working with the German electrician. He came to the theatre accompanied by the French Electrician with whom I was to cooperate. Our duties were not onerous, replacing 40 watt bulbs, soon to be reduced to 25 watt, replacing fuses, reporting faults and generally controlling the use of electricity.

'All staff were paid by the Germans as workers and I was informed that my pay was 0.7 Reichmarks per day, but I never saw any of it. There was no way of spending money, so it all went into the camp fund for the general benefit of the British. It provided cigarette papers, razor blades and matches on free issue to huts.

'Pickaxe Pete' was the Feldwebel Security NCO, was nicknamed because he carried an icepick on a leather thong as he searched huts for contraband. He would patrol the camp, accompanied by an armed guard, tapping the walls of huts while the word went round that he was on the prowl. The RAF were noted for pulling his leg. A wire was discovered leading out of one of the windows and disappearing underground.

'Pickaxe Pete set the guard to open a long trench to follow the wire until they came across a tin. Excitedly Pickaxe Pete broke open the tin to find a folded paper on which was written the German equivalent of 'Ever been had?' Pickaxe Pete, although discomforted at first, took it all in good part.

'His boss, Capt Konig, despite his command of English, never understood our sense of humour. As propaganda chief for the camp, his duty was to circulate copies of cartoons from British newspapers showing unflattering caricatures of Winston Churchill which Captain though were good propaganda for his side. He was at a loss when they were much appreciated by everyone. I think we eventually impressed him that they were indeed funny.

'The conversion of the hut next to ours to a theatre was proceeding apace and Harry Watson and I prepared our plan for electrical equipment. Harry, came from Haydon Bridge in Durham where his family owned a garage, had been a sergeant in the Ordnance Corps attached to an armoured unit when he was captured in the desert. He admitted he was not really an electrician, but had earlier used stage electrician as a cover for his involvement in the camp radio. On the move to Germany he and his colleagues carried the radio parts between them. They were split up so only a part arrived in IVB and that meant starting again.

'The story the radio began in Italy where Harry attended a class to learn about radio, run by Sergeant Henry Simmonds, Royal Signals, a radio expert in civilian life. The two soon got together with the intention of building a radio set, Harry, the fitter to make some of the parts, and Simmo to put it together and make it work.

'Simmo had already applied for some components for demonstration purposes in his class. To his surprise they agreed on the condition that they were only used for training. If used in a radio, the Fascista would have them shot. Harry became the stage electrician and requested a microphone, amplifier and loud speaker to allow those at the back to hear. Similar conditions were attached to their supply.

'Harry worked on a tuning condenser and a reaction condenser, the centre spindle for each being obtained from a brass tube cut from a bugle. Solder was melted out of parcel tins and the tinplate cut for the vanes, a copper rod for a soldering iron, and flux from a fiddler who had resin for his violin bow. A coil was wound on a shaving stick, the thin wire coil was insulated as well as stuck by immersing it, after some experiments, in hot soup.

'Condensers and resistors were bought from an Italian guard and the difficult task of obtaining batteries was solved by bribing the guards. The prototype managed to get a weak Overseas Service of the BBC. When the Italians surrendered, the guards became very helpful in supplying more valves and best of all, a rectifier. With the prospect of a move to Germany the parts were carefully divided among those in the know. Harry had the batteries, Simmo the valves and other took parts of the amplifier.

'With more improvisation, bribery and an earpiece from an American flying helmet, the first news was received on 19 December 1943. Batteries were difficult to obtain so it was felt essential to get onto the mains. A transformer was needed. The transformer provided, needed rewinding which took a fortnight in the cubby hole. The 6pm news from the BBC Overseas Service was first written down in shorthand by the listener with the ear phones then re-written. Two typed copies were produced in our camp office, one for the RAF and one for the army and sent on its journey round the huts. Each hut had a lookout while the news was read out. I normally heard the news from either Harry or Jack when I retuned after the show.

'Harry had a top bunk in the corner of his hut which was where we arranged to tap into one of the lights. He removed a ceiling board, ran two wires in a grove cut in a ceiling joist and connected the wire to two nails. His cap hung on one nail when the set was not in use. By February 1944 the Germans were becoming suspicious that there was a radio in the camp. Pickaxe Pete was the first German to see our map. It seemed pointless to hide it as everyone was talking about the 'invasion' and we guessed that Jerry knew we had a radio. Nearly every hut had a map and the guards puzzled at our interpretation of the war situation which differed from what they were being told. They switched off the lights in different huts to try and isolate which held the radio but we changed to the battery set. So they gave up.

'Both sets had two hiding places, one of which I knew about for the battery set was behind the stage front reached from our cubby hole. The other hiding place I knew nothing about until after the war when Harry gave me all the information. When not in use, the mains set was kept in a Red Cross parcel box tied with string and hung on a hook under the floor boards in the night toilet in Harry's hut.

'Nevertheless there were some anxious moments, usually when Pickaxe Pete was on the prowl. One time the set was being maintained when a roll call was called. Harry and Simmo hurriedly packed the bits into its box to join the tail end of the crowd with the Red Cross box under Harry's arm. This was not unusual, he was prepared to say he was a 'mosser', a hoarder who did not trust leaving his parcel in the hut. Fortunately there were others with their boxes so Harry escaped back to the hut without question.

'Altogether a team of four attended the radio and the other occupants of hut kept the knowledge to themselves. It would not have been impossible for some less trustworthy individual to curry favour with the Germans by reporting the radio.

'We were issued with one letter sheet and one card a week. The letter was similar to the air-mail letters in Egypt only I doubt if these went by air. My usual habit was a letter to Wynne every Sunday and send the card to my mother in Dover. When personal and cigarette parcels arrived, I sent cards of thanks to those in the family who sent me the parcels instead.

'Saturday and Sunday afternoons were earmarked for sport. There was a hut league on a Sunday but serious matches such as Army v RAF or England v Scotland were always on a Saturday. There were several professional footballers in each team and for the cricket matches there were some county players. It never ceased to amaze me what a complete cross-section of life existed in the camp.

'When the Americans came into the camp after the Ardennes we were given the chance to see American football played and make up teams for matches from among Canadians in the RAF. I cannot remember anyone attempting to play Rugby as there was no grass and the ground proved too hard. Apart from these spectator games there were always kick-about games going on in the compound during the week.

'The majority of us were keen to keep as fit as possible. For the really keen there was a keep-fit class as well as sports such as volley ball taking place in various corners of the compounds throughout the summer. Few sports continued in the winter when it was more important to keep warm by staying in bed.

'The Germans were asked for permission to start a school. They constructed and equipped a new hut in the corner of the RAF compound near the wire with four classrooms. The priority was the subjects of the School Certificate, Matriculation and the National Examinations but Art, Music, German and Shorthand were also popular. The school was soon filled every day and evening so teachers took classes in the huts or in the open.

'I had already asked Wynne to send me books and eventually some arrived from the Bodleian Library in Oxford, one of which, on Diesel engines, I brought home with me. On the subject of books, the only book I possessed when captured was the Army issue of the Gospels which I carried in the top pocket of my battledress. Not that I am particularly religious but I enjoy reading the Bible occasionally and this little red, hard backed book had other uses. Its pages made excellent cigarette paper. The experience of my imprisonment made me, after the war, an avid reader especially of books about the war I had missed.

'The Red Cross obtained authorisation for a list of examinations that the various bodies in the UK had agreed could be taken in the camp. I joined another six taking London external degree in Pure Mathematics. While I was struggling with mathematics exam, opposite me sat someone taking a music theory paper. Can you imagine the amount of concentration necessary with a constant humming coming from across the table? Sadly, none of the papers got through during the collapse of Germany.

'My maths tutor was a WO1 in the RAF, a navigator, who was an Oxford mathematics tutor before being called up and he proved to be an excellent teacher. His speciality was to set his students a mathematic puzzle for solution by the following week, the first to do so won a prize of ten cigarettes.

'The school hut had been built on low piers about a foot above the ground and in a corner of the RAF compound near the outside wire. I thought this was asking for trouble so when an RAF Sergeant approached me and asked about the availability of electric wire and light bulbs with holders, my suspicions were aroused. It struck me straight away that these items were essential for lighting a tunnel and I would not put it past the RAF to think of such an idea, even if Jerry hadn't.

'I told him he could get as much wire as he wanted the same way as I did. I removed the earth wire from the hut lighting. As for light bulbs and holders, I told him that we had an arrangement in the theatre to buy almost any items with cigarettes or chocolate, through a guard when the requirement was unofficial. I explained he would need permission from the Camp Leader and the agreement of the Escape Committee. He returned later with the necessary agreement and requested twenty low wattage bulbs and holders which he would pay for with cigarettes which I bought for him.

'Some weeks later something was in the wind. The camp was in a stir of excitement and the school was closed and a guard put outside. Then all the RAF were moved out of their compound into the transit compound. The rumour was of a tunnel that had reached the cornfield beyond the outer wire and been discovered. A tractor ploughed the earth between the outer and inner wire for a kitchen garden had collapsed the tunnel. Little fuss was made by the Germans.

'We all knew the school hut was the entrance when the Russians filled the tunnel with sewage. The smell hung around the school for months. Harry and I were on tenterhooks when Capt Konig asked us if any of our bulbs and holders were missing. We showed him what he expected to see although I had the feeling that he was suspicious, nothing further developed.

'Morning roll-call or appele was just after sunrise in the summer and later in winter. There were no bugles or whistles, just the passage of a guard through each hut, rifle slung, shouting raus and banging on each bunk with his bayonet. Then everyone had less than five minutes to get outside, usually with greatcoat over pyjamas, if one possessed any. On his way back through the hut, having checked for sick still in bed, the bayonet was wielded at those who had not yet left the hut. Standing at the door, the hut leader, reported to the guard his numbers including the krank or ill.

'Roll-call usually took about thirty minutes. We no longer took any pleasure in baiting the enemy by messing up the count as everyone wanted to get back for breakfast. There was rarely any delay on the morning roll-call and any miscount received a loud raspberry from those who had left their beds and were often freezing cold. Acorn coffee was brought from the cookhouse immediately after roll-call and, despite its awful taste, were glad to have it in the morning cold.

'Breakfast was two slices of the previous day's bread ration with either butter or margarine and jam. Before roll-call, every dixie, with a number on each lid and tea leaves in the water, was left lined up on the stove. With the fire going and everyone seated at the tables with their bread waiting in front of them, there was silence. All eyes were fixed on their plate and ears cocked waiting for their number to be called. There was room on the hottest part of the metal top for about half of the dixies, the rest queued. The water was brought to the boil, supervised by the fire attendant, to catch the tea just as it boiled, the mess tin was lifted off and the number called.

'Water could not be boiled without a lid. It was also the rule that no dixie was allowed on the stove if it had been cleaned on the outside, the point being that black absorbed heat so the water boiled quicker and fuel was saved.

'The camp leader, WO Meyers, who by now was known as 'Snowshoes' from his Canadian origin, started the sensible idea of a 'cleaning hour' after breakfast to give every half hut a clean out while getting everyone outside for exercise. Leafy branches brought in by the wood fatigue parties and all windows were opened for fresh air. This cut down on the muggy atmosphere created by two hundred bodies but in winter we sometimes opted to stay muggy but warm.

'Lunchtime saw the issue of potatoes and bread followed by 'skilly' which was the derogatory term for the soup. It was certainly enjoyed by the Russians when we gave them our soup ration at Christmas. I am sure our cookhouse did their best with the ingredients. It had vegetables and on rare occasions pieces of meat of unknown origin. When the turnips and vegetables ran out in the last months an awful concoction of millet was produced.

'Suppertime varied from summer to winter with ersatz coffee delivered to the hut after evening roll-call. In summer, supper was usually taken before roll-call so that one could get to the theatre or prepare for the hut entertainment. The fire attendants and hut leader decided when cooking would start. Jack and I contented ourselves with a daytime snacks and relied on the evening meal for a fill.

'The potato store, next to the French Theatre, was always in line for raiding, though the lowly potato had less attraction than extra coal but the potato store was an easier target. Just stealing from the Germans plus the adventure was the attraction for many. David Leslie told me the story of such an adventure he had been involved in.

'All Commandos, Parachute Regiment or SAS prisoners were deemed RAF and had one purpose in life as a POW: To harass the Jerry in whatever manner they could. Ten men, all with their bags nearly full, were disturbed by two guards entering by the front door. There was a mad rush for the side door and across the divide to the side door of the French theatre. The French had just finished a performance and were amazed when eight stalwarts, complete with swag, dashed across stage to escape back to their huts pursued by the shouts of the guard. Two were caught and sentenced to ten days in the cooler.

'A less risky hobby was 'tin bashing.' No tin can was thrown away but carefully washed and passed to your friends and large ones auctioned. Blowers were going out of favour as they were replaced by electrical heaters fabricated from two tins with tops and bottoms removed. The smaller tin fitted inside the larger with blocks of wood separating them. The resistance of the water to the passage of electricity generated heat. Soldering heaters was a major occupation of the theatre workshop.

'Control of these became my major concern as camp electrician from the point of view of safety and protecting the fuses. There were no socket outlets which meant connecting to the lighting in some way. There were six pendant lights in each half hut to which they could be connected. The German bulbs had screw fitting and many connection were made using the brass ends of broken bulbs until it was found that a wooden screw fitting plug was ideal.

'As the camp electrician I had to do some tests on sizes of tins used for a dixie of water and realised 40 watts was not enough. The hut fuse was a 10 amp fuse and calculated that we could use three boilers at a time in each hut and only in day time when the lights, and fire, were out. Restriction were set on the size of boilers. For some months they caused no trouble, but some people became more adventurous and I found fuses blowing, usually caused by a larger than standard boiler. One bucket-sized one was constructed for washing!

'Carving wood was also popular, although the knives used had to be hidden from Pickaxe Pete who would have confiscated them. The level of artistry was high. One product was a pendulum clock made from tins, bits of wood, string and a razor blade. I saw it working but cannot say how accurate it was.

'Camp newspapers appeared about once a month, the single copy distributed to each hut for one day only. I remember the 'News Flash' and the 'New Times.' The first was noted for its artistic production news and illustrations. Whereas the 'New Times' remains in my memory for the gorgeous pin-up that appeared in each issue. These drew admiring gazes from the lovelorn prisoners and guards. So professional were these wall-newspapers, mounted on boards, that everyone hoped they would be taken home after the war for display.

'A specialist wall newspaper which did survive was the 'Flywheel', a motoring magazine which had started in Italy and continued in IVB as a forum for the motor club run by Tom Swallow and all those who were interested in cars and motorcycles.

'There was a speaker circuit which made me realise how interesting other's lives were. One lecture, by the son of a London undertaker, was very amusing despite the macabre subject. Another gave away all the tricks of the second-hand car trade. There were visits from the Russian dancing troupe, all smartly dressed in their khaki smocks and calf boots, with a senior NCO speaking excellent English to introduce each dance and its history. There was no equality among these Russians. There seemed to be an elite in a separate compound among them were one or two who spoke good English, used as contacts and interpreters by our Camp staff. We all mucked in to feed them as payment which they thoroughly deserved.

'On the 6 June 1944 at the 7 a.m. roll-call there was an undercurrent of expectation among the guards who wanted to rush the count and were chattering among themselves. For some weeks we had been anticipating an invasion across the Channel although nothing had been said on our news. The guards had been hinting of an invasion at Calais. A guard had whispered that their radio had announced a landing near Cherbourg. Harry organised a radio watch. Towards mid-day a runner came round to give us a quick confirmation that both British and American troops had indeed landed in France.

'As we heard the first broadcast of the news we were surprised that the Germans already knew. The betting was that the invasion proper would be across the Straits of Dover so Cherbourg was probably a diversion. There was a lot of activity in the hut to make maps of the Channel coast. As I had lived in Dover and spent time with friends in Calais, I was at least able to contributed a rough map of what I knew.

'However, all this went up in the air when a runner came round with the evening news. It was a large landing and no diversion, on the coast of the Seine Bay east of the Cherbourg peninsular. Now contact was established with the French compound and the next day detailed maps produced by the newspaper artists from French information. By the end of that evening, our map was mounted on a board, updated from the evening broadcast with flags to indicate on the map what we hoped would be the advance into France.

'Soon there was a stream of guards, French, Dutch and the occasional Russian, coming to see the real situation maps. When new names were mentioned such as Averanche or Falaise the French were consulted and new maps produced. The relief of Paris caused wild scenes in the French compound. At the same time news was reaching us of the Russian advance into Poland.

'Through that July and August we were not only enjoying the marvellous weather, but our morale was on a high with the continuing news of the advances through France and Belgium. Towards the end of August we received our first batch of 400 D-day prisoners. In every hut there were eye-witness talks about the invasion, the Falaise trap of the trucks and panzers. Soon, these tales faded as news reached us of the battle for Arnhem and the Rhine bridges in September. The Germans made much of a defeat while the BBC stressed the capture of several bridges by the Americans. It was some months before some parachutists arrived so we could learn the whole story.

'At the beginning of November the small compound next to the RAF was filled with some three or four hundred young women and girls overnight. I went round at lunchtime, more from curiosity than to see some females in a male dominated camp. They were in their late teens and early twenties dressed in some sort of uniform. All looked dishevelled and weary, standing about with an air of uncertainty but looking back at us with equal curiosity.

'We were warned that the compound was out of bounds and any conversation banned, although that was difficult to enforce through the wire from the RAF side. It appeared they were from Warsaw and by the evening the guards had given up trying to stop any talking through the wire and food was being passed freely. There had been an uprising in Warsaw, started in the belief that the Russians would be arriving at any time in the city. The revolt had lasted for nearly two months with no sign of Russian help and when the rebels capitulated, the girls had been separated from the rest and brought here by train.

'This was as much as we knew at the time but for the next few days all of us were busy sorting out from among our few possessions, items of clothing such as socks and shirts for the girls who nearly all had overcoats. Food from our parcels was collected centrally for the girls, this time with the German agreement. Then they all disappeared overnight, rumour had it, to a factory near Dresden.

'At the end of the year hut life became a bit strained when we had an influx of three thousand Americans captured in the Ardennes. We were told that some were to be accommodated in our huts, one to each pair of bunks. Jack and I were allotted a Top Sergeant to sleep with us on our two bunks. It was an eye opener being the first American troops with whom we had such close contact. Our Top Sergeant was an experienced regular whereas the majority were new recruits and very green. He was a member of a Reconnaissance Unit, all well trained regulars like himself, who, after landing on D- Day, had very few casualties until they were given the task of spearheading the advance through the Hurtgen Forest.

'Even they were surprised at the strength of the German attack when it came and did their best to stay out of trouble. However, the rapid advance of the enemy tanks through, and around, their lines soon had the green infantry troops in a panic. 'Running around like a lot of rabbits' was how the Top Sergeant described the scene all about him. He and his Captain tried to break out but, when his passenger was shot and the jeep crashed, he was calmly told by a white coated Jerry 'Ami Kriegsgefangener.'

'Most had arrived from the States and were flung in to hold the line. They had a rough time travelling here. The Germans evidently having a problem in deciding where to put so many prisoners. As a result they were all in a sorry state on arrival, many suffering from pneumonic, dysentery and respiratory problems. The lack of drugs added to our high death rate in the camp now numbering over sixty.

'Most had not shaved and all complained of a lack of food. Our Top Sergeant was anxious for them to get settled down and smartened up. They had no gear so we all mucked in to help. Jack and I spent some time giving him the lowdown on how to exist as a POW and he passed it on in his own not very gentle style to his fellow Americans.

'When their first issue of parcels was made, we watched in amazement as, having opened the Canadian boxes and viewed with wonderment the contents, they mixed the milk powder, raisins, sugar and powdered biscuits into a cold water mess to be eaten with a spoon. It took a few days for them to be shown that cooking was not as difficult as might have been supposed. At least they did not need to be shown how to brew the Canadian coffee! After living on the 'ersatz' issue, the price of Canadian coffee began to soar.

'When one of their number was caught stealing potatoes from another POW, the Top Sergeant agreed that they would award punishment themselves. All of us British were intrigued and climbed onto our bunks as the floor of the hut was cleared. The Americans lined up in two rows facing each other and, releasing their belts and made the culprit run the gauntlet up and back, egged on by swinging belts. Charlie Phelps, on the bunk above me, who was by now the most perfect 'girl' in the theatre productions, gave a masterly performance of a very shocked lady at such male brutality.

'One disturbing aspect of being caged was the possibility of being shot for a perfectly innocent action. I had witnessed two incidents of a prisoner being shot in Italy neither of which was justified. In IVB there were four cases of deaths attributed to the guards.

'The first occurred at the end of March 1944. Flight/Sergeant Jones was shot by a watchtower sentry when observed leaving the coal-store hut by the window. A companion, who ran off, was also shot and slightly wounded. The Commandant ruled that the culprits had been stealing coal so the sentry was justified in firing. Stealing coal was accepted as a risky exercise by those who undertook it. We had two such in our hut and their efforts were much appreciated by us all. A few had been caught, mainly by Pickaxe Pete and their punishment was a few days in the German 'cooler.'

'There was a trip wire all round the camp, six feet inside the high double wire fence. It was well known that to step inside was an offence for which the sentries were entitled to shoot. But it was also accepted that a football could be recovered if permission was to be obtained from the nearest sentry. In June a Corporal Brown went to retrieve a football but forgot to seek permission and was shot by the sentry. The second shooting in June was a bizarre affair. It concerned Paratrooper Fittock, who was in the inner Strafe Barrack, awaiting trial and lodgement in the outside jail. He escaped from the hut and crawled under the single wire into the main compound. Later, he was shot and killed by a sentry as he returned to the cooler.

'The fourth killing was even more bizarre and witnessed by many. A JU88 from the airfield at Lonnewitz just north of the camp, would buzz the camp for a bit of fun. I heard the roar of a plane passing over our compound. The sound was louder than normal and I dropped what I was doing and ran out to see an aeroplane climbing away to the north. I joined the crowd at the wire to see a gathering of RAF in the centre of their compound. After a spate of rumours, it was confirmed that one RAF man was killed and another seriously hurt.

'Later we learned the plane had dived so low that a wheel caught the top wire of the fence separating our compounds. Catching this wire caused the plane to stagger, the left wing almost hitting the ground and hit the two men. The buzzing of the camp ceased.

'Rumours abounded in the 'sheisenhausen' where one normally sat in idle chatter with ones neighbour, whether you knew them or not. The stock phrase of 'have you heard' was the usual opening for the latest rumour, plans for escapes or other unlikely event. One such rumour I dismissed was of someone hiding in the roof of one of the huts. Not until the Russians arrived did I learn the full story.

'A New Zealander, Sergeant Fred Ward, who had been brought into the camp jail to be held for trail, accused of sabotage, possibly a capital offence. He was taken to the hospital, for a medical check where the doctor, Major Whyte, learned of his predicament. The doctor set in motion an improvised scheme to have the man spirited away. A medical orderly was sent into the Russian compound to collect lice in a matchbox and when shaken into Wards clothing. This allowed the doctor to report to the Germans that the arrival was still lousy. The two South Africans who ran the disinfector had been briefed so when Ward entered the shower room he was hidden in the tank room on the roof.

'The German guards waited but eventually they raised the alarm. An immediate search and an emergency roll-call was called and everyone was kept out until all the huts were searched. Ward was later successfully transferred to the roof of one of the huts. The occupants of the hut remained silent but the rumour persisted.

'From my point of view, the second and most fantastic rumour I caught a whiff of in the theatre. This one claimed that there was a woman secreted in one of the huts. It was so fantastic that I gave it little credence at the time, supposing that it might be one of the Polish girls, but that was unlikely given the efficiency of the German counting when they left. However events sometimes occurred which were beyond believe and this was one of them.

'The full story first appeared in the Daily Mirror in June 1945. In the 1930s, Florence Barrington, a widow with a teenage son, Winston, met and married a German photographer working in London. They moved to Germany in 1935 and Winston returned to England for school. When war was declared, her husband was called up in the Luftwaffe and shortly after Winston, in England, joined the RAF. Her husband was shot down and imprisoned in England. To avoid internment, Florence went to live on a farm in Trebsen with a forged identity card.

'In 1943 Winston was also shot down on a bombing mission and ended up in Stalag IVB. Previously from letters smuggled out by his mother, he knew his mother had been staying with friends in Trebsen. As luck would have it, and with his knowledge of German, he met a guard in the camp who came from that area. He managed to bribe the guard to get a message to his mother to tell her that he was in Stalag IVB Florence immediately moved to Muhlberg to try and make contact with her son and through the friendly guard sent him food.

'When Winston was warned that his mother risked arrest, he reported to the camp leader who agreed to smuggle her into the camp. The plan was for Florence to meet a party in the woods who were going out of the camp for medical inspection. Having cut her hair and bound her breasts and put on battle dress she joined the prisoners. At the local hospital she took the place of an RAF Sergeant who wanted to escape.

'The right number of prisoners returned and she was taken to the theatre where make-up expert, Bill Oxley, set about the task of changing her appearance and fitting her with an altered RAF tunic. She came under the supervision of the Camp Quartermaster, who had his office in the Red Cross parcels hut, where a tiny bedroom was made from crates for his female guest.

'Florence was able to see her son at irregular intervals over the next five months. Even on our march to Reisa none of us guessed there was a woman amongst us. Florence Barrington did not return to her husband but flew back to England together with her son, to disappear for some years until re-discovered by the Daily Mirror in 1971 and brought as surprise guests to a reunion of the Stalag IVB Ex-Prisoners of War Association in Edinburgh. Mrs Barrington died the next year 1972 and Winston in 1990.

'We knew we were expected to salute German Officers but we normally avoided saluting by pretending not to see them. This was usually followed by a shout and a torrent of German fired at the offender who stood with a perfect look of non-understanding, much to the exasperation of the officer concerned.

'Eventually, the Commandant summoned all the hut leaders and the camp staff to a meeting in the theatre. He opened the proceedings with the following statement: "The French walk about the camp as if they own it, the Dutch as if they would like to own it but you British do so as if you don't care a damn who owns it!" Everyone present managed to repress their laughter realising no humour was intended and he meant what he said. He explained that part of the Geneva Convention applied to saluting and in the German army, junior NCOs salute senior NCOs as well as Officers. The Camp Leader compromised and instructed everyone to salute just the officers.

'The RAF were not normally allowed outside the camp. The feeling of the German civilian population against the 'terror bombers', as the RAF were known, meant they were likely to be badly treated by the angry populace. There were a few in the RAF compound who were attacked and even one or two who were nearly lynched when caught. RAF staff, would be given Army battledress when they came out on staff walks with us.

'These staff walks occurred about once every two weeks on a Sunday. I had my turn every six weeks. Sometimes we walked north along the bank of the Elbe. Sometimes we walked south. But the most popular outing stopped at a beer garden on the riverside at Muhlberg. Either the Commandant or our Camp Leader, I never discovered which, gave the guards some money for us to have a drink and a pie. The drink was a local beer, very weak and sweet but none the less appreciated.

'In this relaxed state, we would attempt to extract information form each other. The guards claimed they were keen to learn English but were always asking about rhyming slang. We were told to play along but not to give any hint of back slang. This was a code used when any German was about. It was quite simple and with some practice one could talk normally and quite incomprehensibly to anyone who overheard not in the know. Cockney rhyming slang was just our cover story.

'We learned a lot from the guards on these walks. They were all classified as unfit for fighting units having suffered from frostbite or wounds on the Russian front. They had no time for the Russian prisoners and could not understand why we did not join them to fight against Stalin. Few had much love for the Nazis and began to appreciate we were anti-Nazi and not anti-German. At this time none of us knew anything about the atrocities and the extermination camps and it did appear that none of our guards knew of these.

'As we moved into 1945 the attitude of the guards was changing, coming into the huts to talk and bringing items that we required in exchange for cigarettes or chocolate. In January and February there were very heavy air-raids on Leipzig west of our camp but near enough to keep us all awake at night. In February there was the first air-raid on Dresden to the south and further away than Leipzig but the noise had us all awake watching the sky lit with explosions and widespread fires. In the morning we questioned the guards who blamed the use of the city as a reorganising centre for German troops retreating from Russia. The guards showed little resentment to this raid.

'Red Cross parcels started to dry up. More were promised in February but none arrived. By the end of February we were down to one between five with no stock and a promise of more in March which also never arrived. As the parcels faded the prices of food rose. Fortunately I had received my last cigarette parcels just after Christmas as mail, too, was petering out. I did get some letters at the beginning of February but they were all late. After I reached home, Wynne did tell me of further parcels sent but not received, including one containing a record player and records sent in November as my Christmas present.

'The Dutch came into their own at this time of shortage as they had always been the food hoarders of the camp and were still receiving their supplies. They did little business for most of us were equally short of cigarettes to trade. I determined to ration myself and prepare for the unknown future. Most of the prisoners, I suspect, myself included, did not fully appreciate this serious situation.

'The supply shortage seemed to affect the Americans more than us. They did not take kindly to being POW, whereas we were used to it taking things as they came. The Americans left in February so we were less crowded and it improved our ration situation. The ration of bread, potatoes and cabbage soup returned to normal and continued plentiful throughout March despite the BBC news predicting a state of chaos in Germany. The potato clamps outside the camp still covered a large area and we were told the Army stock of flour at the local baker was enough for a month or more.

'With better weather due we stopped lighting fires until the evening to conserve fuel. Brewing tea during the day had become a luxury few of us could afford. What sustained us was the certainty of victory and eventual release. The question during those months of March and April for us and our captors was, who was going to reach us first, the Americans or Russians? Our maps were actively subscribed to by our guards who were willing to plot the towns mentioned on the BBC news. Not wanting to be caught in the middle we were praying that the Americans would reach us first.

'Later in March, the approach of the Americans was heralded by the appearance of their new Lightning fighters busy to the west. One day when two Lightings flew low over the camp chasing a Jerry fighter, firing their cannons continuously as the Jerry pilot dived over the huts. The cannon fire ripped over the roof of our hut 49B and across the roof of the theatre next door. I was in the theatre at the time, fortunately on the stage when the shells ripped across the empty auditorium before we had time to dive anywhere. Later Jack showed me where the shells had pierced the roof and walls before hitting the ground outside without hitting anyone inside or out.

'We laid out a large POW sign on the football pitch and three Union Jacks on an army and RAF hut roof as well as the hospital. That was evidently a success as later fighters circled about and dived on the camp with wing waggles. Since the raid on Dresden in February there had been continuous day and night bombing in the west over Leipzig and over Berlin in the north where at night we could see the sky aglow. Quite often we would be out in the compound when, in the cloud above, cannon fire was mixed with the hum of bombers and the whine of fighters.

'Once, out of the clouds, came seven parachutes, almost over the camp, one landing in the field opposite our compound and the other six drifting further east towards the woods. We were loudly cheering the one in the field, calling him over but guards were pouring out to pick them all up. Soon there were seven new American prisoners in the RAF compound.

'Not long after we heard a bomber flying low over the camp at night. It sounded in trouble. The engines were coughing but even in the dark we correctly guessed it was British. They crash-landed somewhere nearby and in the morning the crew of a Lancaster joined the RAF compound.

'This busy air space witnessed a tragedy towards the end of March when a couple of American Mustangs, seeing our signs, decided to strafe the German quarters outside the wire. We started to cheer but the news soon spread that a wood fatigue party was about to come in and had been caught in the firing. Four Americans, one Russian and one German guard were killed.

'In April, a flight of Lightnings spotted a train in the sidings to the east of the camp normally used for unloading POWs. Each Lightning dived to attack and truck after truck went up in flames with several explosions destroying every truck before departing over the camp giving us a wing wave.

'A few days later a throbbing hum brought us all into the compound to witness the sight of over one hundred American bombers approaching from the west, almost filling the sky. Every plane released its bombs simultaneously which the RAF told us was used over industrial areas. One result was that the camp lost its electricity supply.

'Now in the middle of April the news from our battery radio set showed that the Americans were fast approaching the Elbe and much nearer than the Russians. So with our fingers crossed, we all waited in hope of being released to experience the reputed, fabulous American rations.

The Russians Take Over

'Life was in limbo. Our time was spent outside waiting to see what would happen next from our vantage point between two frontlines. There was small arms fire some miles away to north and south but very little action around this camp. There was a stream of refugees passing along the road to the south of the camp. With no transport other than a few carts, they had evidently moved out in a hurry. They were coming from the east and, I suppose, hoping to cross the Elbe to the relative safety of the Americans.

'On about the 20 April there was a lot of action in the air above the Elbe to our west, and consequence we had no delivery of bread from Muhlberg that day. The Germans offered to escort us over the Elbe. This was both surprising and suspicious and all the national leaders voted to stay. The Commandant handed over the camp administration to the British. There were several RAF officers in the camp awaiting transfer to an Oflag who now took over responsibility for the RAF compound and a newly arrived Lieutenant Jessop agreed to take over the Army compound.

'Early on the morning of the 23 April, an early visitors to the urinal started shouting that the Jerries had gone. Everyone made a beeline to the locked door which did not resist our battering. Even in the dawn gloom one could to see there were no German guards silhouetted in their towers or patrolling the wire. Soon the whole camp was awake lining the wire and chattering.

'The Camp Leader eventually restored some order and sent everyone back to their huts to dress and await events. Gathering some of his staff, including myself, we walked down the road to the main gate. Dawn was now breaking and a cosmopolitan crowd had gathered at the gate. There was no sign of any Germans outside the gate which had its chain and padlock in place.

'After a discussion with the French it was agreed that some would go out to the German huts when the gate was forced. I was lucky enough to go out with a group detailed to search a hut full of desks and filing cabinets. I soon found the file cards of the British prisoners, RAF and army. All were in alphabetical order so I was soon able to extricate my card and shouted out the door for the others to come and find theirs.

'The Germans had gone, probably across the river to give themselves up to the Americans rather than become Russian POWs. It must have been well arranged as everyone had left silently in the night. The betting was now that the Russians would reach us first.

'I shall never forget the date. 23 April 1945 and we were free. But what was to be done about it.

'Around mid-morning there was a shout and a lone figure, sitting on a little horse, his feet almost touching the ground, wearing a long grey coat with conical hat and a gun slung over his back. We all knew at once that our liberator was a Russian. Not the sight we had expected and we all burst out laughing until he was followed out of the woods by three more riders. Surely these were not the notorious Cossacks?

'As the first neared the wire, he was shouted at by some of the Russian POWs near us and received a shouted reply which none of us understood. He then swung off to the west followed by his fellows to make for the main gate. Soon they were galloping down the camp road surrounded by Russian prisoners who soon brought them to a halt with excited questions.

'Some thirty minutes later, with most of us still looking hopefully through the wire for the Americans, there came the sound of vehicle engines from the woods and out came a number of armoured cars and lorries. They all made for our back gate, pushed it down and entered the Camp. These new arrivals were all dressed smartly in khaki uniforms and were soon surrounded by their fellow countrymen.

'We retired discretely to our compound to await whatever our Russian deliverers would want us to do next. It was a kind of anti-climax, we had no feelings of freedom. At least we considered ourselves released but these Russians were an unknown quantity.

'The Russian prisoners returned to their compound as instructed but immediately broke down the outer wire and poured across the road to raid the potato clamps in the field opposite. They were welcome to a decent feed under the circumstances. Word was sent round that for the rest of the day we would remain in our respective compounds and not to leave the camp. Other troops had been sent for to take over the camp. Meanwhile a meal of soup and bread would be organised and the Russians would see to the food situation for the next few days.

'The remainder of that day, after some soup and a loaf between five, we were left alone to discuss the situation over cups of tea. The main subject of heated debate was whether we should risk crossing the river to join up with the Americans. The more sensible decided against something so dangerous. Eventually we all went to bed having decided that we would stay put until the Russians chose to hand us over to the Americans.

'The next morning a large convoy of lorries came down the road from the east along with more troops, the lorries entering the camp and turning into the Russian compounds. The troops started shepherding all the Russian prisoners onto the lorries, driving off as soon as loaded. A Russian officer, accompanied by a couple of NCOs, turned up at the camp office and told the Camp Leader, in excellent English, that all the camp was now his responsibility. A daily issue of bread was all he could promise us as his own troops would be living off the land for the time being. The Russian bread, when it arrived that evening, proved to be similar to the German bread but darker, tasting better and there was enough for three or four slices each.

'Therefore we would be allowed out of the camp to forage for vegetables in the fields and bring in whatever we could find. It was not long before chickens were being carried in. Cattle and sheep were being herded into the compound in ones and twos to end up being slaughtered by those who volunteered as butchers. The washrooms were covered with feathers and had all sorts of joints hanging from the ceilings. The huts themselves were being stripped of wood for fuel, the coal having disappeared the first day.

'The next day I was called to the office early and introduced to the Russian officer by the Camp Leader saying I was the electrical engineer and that I was to accompany him to find out why we had no electricity. The officer's name was so unpronounceable that I never did find out what it was, so from that time he was always "Sir". Speaking good English he ask about the loss of electrical supply so I told him of the recent air-raid on Torgau which was the probable cause. He nodded in understanding and asked that I should accompany him on a tour of inspection to try and remedy the situation.

'He asked what I thought of his American jeep, he was very proud of it and I had to explain that I knew nothing about them. It was a queer experience for me not only to be driven by a Russian officer to the stares of all on the road out of the camp, but to be spoken to quite normally in English. We headed in the direction of Muhlberg where he said we would visit the power station in the town as the overhead lines ran that way.

'The overhead lines led us to the power station on the outskirts of the town and to a sub-station into which our lines had disappeared. The place had been so hurriedly deserted that there was still food on the table inside. When the tangle of lines was sorted, I located our transformer and its overhead line which ran through the town towards the river. Following the line, we passed through the square where I questioned the officer regarding bodies still lying on the ground, all men in civilian clothes. He said they were the town officials, all Nazi functionaries including the local Gauleiter, all having been shot and left as an example to the citizens. The centre of town was deserted. Undisturbed he said 'They did the same in Russia.'

'At the river, the jeep turned north to follow the incoming line from Torgau. We began to see fields in front of us torn apart by bombing and soon we found a gap in the power line. The pylon had been hurled into a field from the road. We decided to turn back, 'Sir' saying that he would arrange for a priority repair. The town itself must have been in a mess, so I was not optimistic of getting our electricity back in a hurry. Surprisingly the electricity was restored in a couple of days. I began to realise the power our Russian officer.

'The renewal of electricity to the camp was celebrated a few days later by a unique experience. Everyone had been told to assemble in the army north compound, including the RAF, behind the theatre hut at 3 pm camp time. Not that camp time had meant much to us as there was roll call when the Germans decided. There was lunch time and lights out but rarely if ever can I remember being told to do something at a particular time. Many of us still had watches and Harry, with his radio team, were the only ones who kept their watches correct to catch the news bulletins and as a matter of course I occasionally checked my watch with his.

'Suddenly we were all startled by the sound of the chimes of Big Ben coming from a box on the roof of the theatre. The chimes were undeniable and initially caused a rising murmur. Then everyone fell silent as a voice announced 'This is the BBC Overseas Service. Here is the one-o-clock news.' I didn't hear what was said next for I must admit I burst into tears. I was not the only one, most were also openly crying, others had tears in their eyes. The emotion was terrific. We began hugging each other. Few heard the rest of the broadcast. It was certainly the most wonderful experience since my marriage to Wynne, just to hear Big Ben striking after more than three years.

'Harry later explained to me how it all came about. With some bribery a Russian soldier driving a small lorry was going to Muhlberg for bread, he and Simmo were given a lift to help him load the bread. In town they managed to liberate a loud speaker, some batteries and other useful items from a deserted electrical shop.

'The next morning a load of American cigarettes and chocolate was our first indication that the Yanks were just across the river. A jeep carrying an American officer arrived at the camp gate having heard of our existence. The American army had stopped at the River Mulde, some thirty kilometres west of the Elbe. We could not understand was why we were not being transferred across the ferry.

'It was not difficult to understand that with fifteen thousand of us foraging over the country east of the camp, and the Russians doing the same, within a week the countryside larder was bare. On 3 May we were warned to pack up ready to move out the next day. This was good news not only because food was scarce but with no Russians to empty the latrines, the sewerage was not being removed. The camp was beginning to have an unhealthy smell. The next day the army and RAF were moving out. The French and others were told to wait for instructions regarding their repatriation. We were told to take as little as possible because we would be marching south along the river to the town of Reisa, twenty five miles away.

'Every village we passed was occupied by Russian soldiers who had taken over the houses with red flags at every window. The more I saw of the Red Army, the more I was glad Jack and I had not foraged far from the camp. We were among the first arrivals at a deserted German Army panzer barracks. The Russian officer and his staff were there to meet us and, recognising me from our trip in his jeep, he told me to report to him in his office the following morning.

'When I reported to Sir the next morning, I was told there were British, prisoner working-parties at two camps on the outskirts of Riesa. One camp was across the river and he wanted me to be his liaison with them, to visit them alternately on each day to see if they needed anything and to tell them when they were to move. He admitted to me that we would be handed over as soon as possible but was waiting instructions to do so and gave no reason why we were still being held. He handed me a pass written in Russian which allowed me to be outside the barracks at any time and on the back he pointed out that he had written that I had permission to ride a bicycle. The pass was signed in red ink with a signature that was quite unreadable. I just hoped that an illiterate Russian would recognise the signature.

'I went off the next day on the bicycle to find the two camps and to see what chance there was to forage for food so I took an empty haversack with me. I had barely left the barracks before a Russian soldier stopped me wanting my bicycle. Not understanding a word he saying it was obvious what he meant, so I showed him my pass, particularly the bit on the back and the signature. He turned out to be one who could read and with a smile he waved me on. At the next stop I was not so lucky, the pass might just as well been written in English, for this one turned it all ways until I pointed to the red signature and shaking my head. He took the hint and let me go.

'This happened many times over the next few days mostly with non readers, and I developed an imperious look of command. Pointing to the signature always worked. Some years later, having kept the pass as a souvenir, I sent a copy to the Russian Embassy in London for a translation, telling them the story. The first thing I discovered was that it wasn't signed by Sir with his long unpronounceable name, but the red signature was of the Reisa Garrison Commander, a Lieutenant Gusev, with whose signature the local troops were familiar. This had made my passage easier than I expected. I also discovered that the date on the pass, 17 May 1945, was a mistake for it was issued to me on the 7 May 1945, two days before VE day and my birthday.

'The first camp had received no news of what was happening until I arrived. They were happy with their own resources for food so had no complaints except wanting to know what happens next. I left them carrying a gift of some butter and jam. The camp across the river also had two sergeants in charge with a hundred or so men working on farms. They filled my haversack with vegetables and cheese which made certain I would come again, and they gave me some good advice regarding where to forage.

'At one village I came across a cider brewery but the Russians had already taken all the bottles of cider but left some unfermented apple juice in the vats, so I spent some time filling bottles, leaving others to collect later. At one deserted farmhouse, the Russians had stripped it bare but had missed a larder full of freshly baked bread because the cupboard door was not obvious.

'The rail and road bridge over the River Elbe in Reisa had been destroyed by the retreating Germans. The Russians had built a pontoon bridge. Trains bringing all sorts of loot and food from Germany had to unload to pass over the pontoon bridge on lorries before reloaded for Russia via Dresden.

'One day I was given the tip by Sir that a train of foodstuffs would be arriving that morning and if I hurried down to the station yard I might be allowed to pick up some odd bits. Knowing the variable behaviour of the Russian soldier, I was not hopeful as I left on my bike with an extra empty haversack. At the station yard I found a number of trucks being guarded by a solitary soldier marching up and down. I stopped beside him with all the appearance of someone who knew what he was doing and presented my pass to him.

'He evidently could read and seemed impressed so I made signs of eating pointing to the wagons. To my surprised delight he took me down to a wagon with the doors open and signalled me to climb in which I did with alacrity. The wagon was half filled with cartons containing brown tins, many of the tins strewn on the floor so others had been here before me. I hurriedly filled my two haversacks with the tins and jumped down to the ground. As I did so I heard the same sentry shouting and when I looked, he was frantically pointing to an officer approaching further up the train.

'I jumped on the bike and started pedalling furiously in the opposite direction, while the sentry, to back up his shouting, fired a shot after me. The bullet whistled over my head, so I assumed he had made no attempt to hit me, although one never knew with the Russians, perhaps he was a bad shot. I did manage to escape back to the barracks, but then came the anti-climax when we eventually opened a tin to find it full of peas! A great disappointment hoping for meat, but we did enjoy peas for a change.

'The Russians were evidently trigger-happy. A military policewoman was on duty each day at the cross-roads outside the gate, wielding her red and yellow discs at the traffic very efficiently with her automatic rifle across her shoulder. One warm afternoon I joined the crowd watching her performing. She raised her red disc to an approaching lorry whose driver ignored the signal and drove on past. Without hesitation the policewoman dropped her discs, unslung her rifle and she let fly a succession of shots at the back of the lorry.

'The lorry stopped and out of the cab jumped a very irate Russian soldier who started to run back. He was met by a stern policewoman wielding a rifle and shouting at him. The soldier meekly backed his lorry and came to a halt behind her retrieved, upheld red disc.

'Individually, I found the Russians willing, friendly allies. In a group, however, they always acted suspiciously, not wanting to talk, especially if an NCO or officer was present so most of the time they tended to ignore us. I soon learned that if I wanted anything, I had to catch one on his own. The officer was definitely superior, in charge, and more feared than respected.

'Wednesday 9 May was my birthday. I was 30 years old and not expecting any sort of celebration. That is until I reported to Sir when he greeted me with the news that it was VE Day for the Russians, yesterday having been VE day in the west where the Germans had surrendered. There had been strong rumours of an armistice and cease fire for some days but we had no radio. News of VE Day spread like a wild fire through the barracks, everyone cheering and rushing about. Even the Russians troops were catching on and slapping us on our backs, they too, were happy with the news and probably thinking of going home just like us.

'When I mentioned to Sir that it was also my birthday, he disappeared into his office to reappear with a bottle of schnapps which he presented to me as a present. I took it to my room which I later shared with Jack and the others. I thought it tasted awful. The others thought it fine and soon finished the bottle. I never was a connoisseur of liquor nor of beer, but it served for our celebration of Victory in Europe.

'It was suicide to go outside that evening with the Russians going berserk with their celebration wandering and reeling about drunk, firing live rounds indiscriminately from every weapon they had. I felt sorry for those POWs who were lodging in town for most had not heard the news until they were caught up with the Russians and the stories of their narrow escapes were believed when we discovered there had been many casualties among the celebrating troops.

'It was time to press Sir for an answer. Next morning, WOI Meyers and Lt Jessop, came to the office while I was there and demanded to know more of what was happening. Sir told us we were to be handed over to the Americans when a convoy of lorries arrived with some Russian POWs and slave workers from the west. In other words we were being held more or less, as hostages, to be exchanged.

'What none of us knew was the agreement the allied leaders had made at the Yalta Conference to exchange all Russians for Allied POWs being held by the Russians. It was the Russians who had been fighting in the German Army that caused a lot of heart searching, knowing they would be shot when returned. Churchill realised that he had no alternative and agree knowing the Russians were holding thousands of British POWs, including me.

'There was a flow of refugees from the west, mostly Poles, heading back to their homes after being slave workers in Germany. Although still young, they looked old and weary, our sympathy and the odd gift of food went out to them. I was in the queue for my medical when five refugees approached. There were two boys almost carrying an 'old lady', we thought, with two other women helping. They wanted to see our doctor as the casualty had collapsed outside the gate. A couple of medical orderlies carried the 'old lady' inside while we tried to learn something from the others.

'One boy spoke a little English. It appeared that these five were all teenagers, Polish Jews from a camp to the west called Buchenwald. The name meant nothing to us, but these thin, aged youngsters looked terrible and the 'old lady' we were told was a girl of twenty three. They were on their way back to Poland though we all doubted they would make it in the condition they were in. We pressed them to stay with us for a little time for food and rest while the girl was under the care of the doctor. In the end they were taken into the barracks by some who were leaving after their medical and that was the last I saw of them, although I have never forgotten them.

'One day I was told to go and collect a number of boxes from a store in town. It seemed a strange request. A Russian truck took us into town to a building where some Russians piled some wooden crates on the truck for us to unload at the barracks. The crates contained German cigars which Jack was responsible for issuing the next day when we would be leaving. As we marched out of the barracks every man had to be smoking a cigar, whether they smoked or not. This all seemed very puzzling.

'Everyone paraded the next day, including quite a number from the houses nearby, to whom Jack issued the necessary cigar. Onto the parade ground marched a full Russian military band followed by two vans with cine cameras on their roofs. Given the order, we all lit our cigars, the band struck up and off we marched through the gates. The situation was so funny with the cameras focusing on us, that we all burst out laughing, which was probably just what the Russians wanted. Happy Allied Prisoners of War being released by their Russian allies, smoking cigars and being filmed for posterity.

'As we marched through the town all the German civilians had been turned out of their houses with red flags to wave to us. I don't think we looked quite so happy by this time, but at least we knew we were on our way home. On reaching the main Leipzig road on the outskirts of Reisa, one cigar just about finished, we found a long convoy of American lorries waiting. Without fuss we all clambered aboard, packed tight, but who cared, we were about to start our first leg of the journey home. We never did discover, or thought to ask the drivers, if they had brought Russians back from the west, I don't think we cared.

'The journey was uneventful. I remember noticing that the countryside was entirely free of sign of war. On our arrival at Halle we were welcomed by the Station Commander and told that a meal would be ready for us in three sittings. He warned us that the food was different to what we had been used to and to be careful of over-eating. Meanwhile we were allotted huts, many newly built behind the station.

'You have to imagine our bulging eyes when we saw the food stacked there.

It was impossible to choose a menu so he told us the others were having stew with tinned potatoes and peas followed by fruit and ice cream. We asked for the same but asked for white bread and butter before the ice cream. There is no need to say the meal was eaten quickly. It was nevertheless enjoyed, especially the white bread. It was out of this world after the brown stuff we had been used to over the years.

'After the feeding was finished we were advised to hurry over to the PX where everything was free to us and it would be closing soon. At the PX, the equivalent to our NAFFI Shop, Jack and I found everything that we needed laid out on tables. There were shirts, towels, soap and of course, American cigarettes and candy bars. We were expected to help ourselves to whatever we needed and given a plastic bag to put it in. It was difficult not to be greedy but they were so good about it that everyone restricted themselves.

'In the morning we would be issued with the day's issue of cigarettes and candy bars at breakfast, before boarding our plane for Brussels to be handed over to the British for new clothes. Looking back on that first night with the Americans I still cannot describe our feelings at the time. Of course we were happy but it was because we had again been released from a kind of imprisonment. We were in a mood of anticipation, awaiting the final arrival home. Each of us had been given the detail of our flights. I was in group six for the next day. Flights were leaving continuously all day. We had been hoping for a flight straight back to England but the Americans had made it plain that we were to be handed over in Brussels for the RAF to do the final flight home.

'Next day Jack and I ate early and what a breakfast. It was a 'help yourself buffet' of steaks, sausages, eggs, bacon, potatoes and more of that wonderful, white bread. Alongside each plate was a packet of Camel cigarettes and a bar of chocolate and with some real coffee it was all we had dreamed about for the last three years. We wasted no time at the breakfast table, it was out on the field to watch the first five flights take off. Then it was our turn to board a plane. There were bucket seats down each side of the fuselage but many were expected to sit on the floor.

'On the flight one of the crew gave us a running commentary and on arriving over Cologne the plane circled several times for us each to look at the devastation of the whole city with the Cathedral standing up apparently undamaged in the middle of the rubble. Another sight I shall never forget.

'We landed in Brussels some twenty minutes later, just in time for lunch we thought as we drove through the city in lorries. But no: We were dropped off in the courtyard of what had been an hotel to be greeted by a group of medical orderlies in white coats. Lining us all up, they proceeded to squirt a white powder down our necks and trousers. We were being disinfested again. This was followed inevitably by a visit to a clothing store in the basement where we gave our sizes and received new battledress, underclothing and boots before passing to a shower room. Here we gave up our old clothes to be burned, including my old greatcoat that I had had since leaving Scotland in 1941.

'After the shower and getting dressed in clean clothes, we returned to the courtyard to a room where necessities were laid out for us to take what was needed. All I decided I needed was spare socks and underwear, although I did take more cigarettes. I still had several packs of Camels but those on offer were Players, which I preferred. All of our meagre possessions could now be contained in a small kitbag.

'At last we were led to the hotel dining room for a late lunch, told of our room numbers where we were to stay for the night, and that we were free until the next day when we would be sorted out for the flight home. When given our room keys we were warned not to wander too far away in the city and recommended to go to the '21Club' in the square where we could get a drink without getting robbed. We pointed out that we had no money, nobody had thought of paying us. Would they take pounds?

'The sergeant at the desk laughed saying we were the first to mention money, but not to worry if we say we are ex-POW we will not be asked to pay, so off we went to find the '21Club.' A group of us found the club in the square and before we could tell the girl at the bar, she said that she guessed we were exPOW so what did we want. I think she expected us to order beers for she looked surprised when we ordered tea and buns.

'Attracted by the sound of jazz music some of us wandered into a hall where dancing was taking place and there we were standing in the doorway with looks of amazement on our faces. After a moment of surprise, our looks almost became those of laughter at the spectacle of ATS girls gyrating energetically round their gum-chewing Canadian partners while the said partner stood calmly holding the girls hand. The Canadians quickly took exception to our amused looks and came over to demand what we thought was so funny. They were sufficiently mollified by our explanation to explain the 'jitterbug.' To us, seeing it for the first time, I was worried in case this had become Wynne's idea of modern dancing,

'The next day we were lorried to the RAF airfield and aboard a transport plane. We all sat on either side of the fuselage, but when the navigator came to tell us we would be passing over Dover, I said my home was there and was told to go up to the cockpit. Whilst crossing the coast the pilot asked where was my house in the town. I explained about a mile up the valley running north west. My house was on the right of the main road. As we approached the harbour he dropped down, turning northwest to run up the valley and I pointed out the position of our house. He swooped down and up almost over the top of our house. Later, my mother said she did wonder why a plane swooped down. It gave me a thrill to be so close to home.

'We landed 'somewhere in England', near Oxford. We were herded to queue alongside tables where we gave our particulars and received some money, then to more tables with WVS ladies offering more 'necessities' which none of us really needed but I did take some chocolate and cigarettes. Another queue formed outside a medical tent with a large Red Cross for a medical inspection before being given a leave pass and sent home, I hoped.

'As soon as I stood in front of the doctor in my underpants he shook his head and asked me how I felt. Of course I said 'fine' but his next question was about my distended stomach which he began to tenderly press. Did I feel uncomfortable? Did I suffer from wind? The questions went on and I reluctantly agreed that I was not one hundred per cent fit. I told him about the bout of dysentery I had suffered with only condensed milk to help and he shook his head again. He thought it would be wise for me to go to a nursing home for a time, saying something about restoring the lining of my stomach, but when I demurred, he insisted it was for my own good.

'The outcome was that I found myself in an ambulance with another sergeant, who had been ill on the flight over. With just the two of us the ambulance we drove off to Seer Green near Beaconsfield where I was shown into a large airy room with four beds, all unoccupied, given some pyjamas, told to have a bath and get into one of the beds.

'I had clambered into bed, not feeling ill and wondering what would happen next when a nurse appeared to tell me that she would be looking after me and I would be staying in bed for the present to rest. I was put on a milk diet to renew my stomach lining, drinking Ovaltine, Horlicks and so on. I was to ring for her to bring the drinks whenever I wanted them while my nurse would also bring them when she thought I should have them. When I explained that my wife would not know that I was back in England and that they were not on the phone, she suggested I phone a telegram giving the address and phone number of the nursing home.

'That evening Wynne rang, on a neighbour's phone, to say she would be arriving the next day. I tried to calm her fears, saying she would see that there was little wrong with me. The same good neighbour drove her through the night and delivered her the next morning.

'I cannot now describe how I felt at the time just to see her. I had hardly slept in anticipation and we chattered until the nurse brought us both some lunch, the neighbour having gone into Maidenhead, would be back at teatime.

'Wynne managed a few more visits in the fortnight I was there and on 10 June 1945 I was discharged on indefinite convalescent leave and caught a train to Aldershot.

'I am often asked about those three years as a Prisoner of War and if they were wasted years. My first feeling as a POW was one of boredom. There was nothing to do and I wanted to do something. Not until I reached Stalag IVB could I settle down and become busy. The important gain was that of patience and tolerance. Everyone, with few exceptions, had an unshakeable belief in freedom when the war was won. This gave us all a feeling of stoicism and companionship.

'It amazes me how everyone managed to be so cheerful. One rarely saw any signs of depression, even when circumstances grew worse towards the end. There must have been some 'Dear John' letters but I heard of none in our hut or the theatre nor from other contacts. Our women back home were wonderful.

'My wife has often since, pulled my leg about my boast of being able to cook, and although this was in fun, even Wynne admitted that when I came home, I was much more useful about the house than she remembered and also more eager to get things done. I must agree life has been much more enjoyable since, perhaps I should put that down to appreciating what I now have.'

12.8
Bob outside his hut in Stalag IVB. The Germans had wisely concentrated the SNCOs in a few camps. The pool of talent made camp life not unpleasant as the relaxed smile on Bob's face indicates.

Postscript

106 Company Royal Engineers

106 Company Royal Engineers still exists. It is now based in Sheffield and is still a Territorial Army Unit.

Bob Borthwick

Bob stayed in the army and he and his wife, Wynne, brought up two children, while serving postings in Sierra Leone, Malaya and Hong Kong – always returning to Brompton in between. Bob lectured at the R.E. Military School of Engineering at Brompton for some of this time and his final posting was to Horse Guards in London, having an office overlooking the Changing of the Guard in Whitehall. He retired in 1961 and joined the Atomic Energy Authority as Site Services Engineer at Winfrith in Dorset and later, Culham Laboratory in Oxford-shire. He was persuaded to write about his experiences by his grandchildren and died at 83 years of age in 1998.

Alan Jones

Alan married Kathleen in July 1945. When the time came to sign the register, she discovered that she was marrying someone called William Jones. The nickname of Alan attached itself so firmly because of his habit of singing, in the style of the crooner Alan Jones, while he worked. He stayed in the army and raised three children. Following Kathleen's early death

13.1
Bob Borthwick

13.2
Wedding at Ripon Cathedral
7 July 1945.

he worked setting up hospital engineering centres around the globe until he finally retired at 80. As the book goes to press he is entering his ninth decade.

Bill Harvey

Bill returned to work on the railways where he became an inspector of facilities until his retirement. There was one more addition to his family.

Sadly, Bill Harvey died as the work was being completed. I chatted with Bill just before his last illness. When it was time to take my leave I realised that Bill understood this was to be our last meeting. He gently asked for a reassurance that I would publish this record. The smile that greeted my acceptance of this duty almost split is face. It was also an easy duty to provide a eulogy for Bill a few weeks later as he had provided the text.

Bill Harvey has the final word.

'Most people live worthy, dutiful lives which do not have to be recorded' he told me. 'Their deeds are recorded by family, friends and workmates. So they live on in their memories.

'But history chose to take a group of us away from home and put us in crucial places at critical times. All of this happened out of sight of those who knew them.

I want to record the deeds of these ordinary men'.

13.3a & 13.3b
During their delayed honeymoon, Alan and Kathleen Jones were shown round Paris by the Fortis brothers. Alan had worked with one of the brothers, Edmund, when they were prisoners.

13.4
Bill Harvey and Alan Jones meet again 60 years to the day after they were captured at Tobruk.

Glossary and Acronyms

Every attempt has been made to avoid military jargon but it has occasionally been left in as reported speech or for accuracy. The list is short.

ADC
Aide de Camp is a junior officer who invariably accompanies his superior to act as his personal assistant in a military capacity

Battalion
The normal infantry formation under command of a Lieutenant Colonel

BEF
British Expeditionary Force. This derivation of this quaint appellation is explained in chapter one.

Blitzkreig
Literally 'lightning war'. The method of modern warfare developed by the Germans and re-invented by the US as 'shock and awe' tactics.

Blower
An efficient cooker designed by POWs which required air to be forced, by some sort of bellows, past the fuel to produce quick, smokeless heat.

Box
A defensive and logistics area prepared during the desert war.

Bren gun
A light machine gun noted for its accuracy.

Commission
Along with any officer rank in the British army comes a Royal Commission which grants the right to give orders to the monarch's troops.

Company
A subdivision of an infantry battalion and sometime a part of a regiment

Cooler
Solitary confinement cell in a POW camp

Court Martial
A non-judicial court operating under martial law used by the military for breaches of its rules

COY
Abbreviation of Company

DC
Direct Current is the sort of electricity supplied by batteries and found in cars.

Dixie
An oval shaped cooking or serving pot with a lid and handle. Used by army cooks

Doby or dobying
Washing, probably derived from the Indian army.

Domestic supply is AC
Alternating Current

EFI
English Film Institute that took mobile cinemas to the troops

HMS
Her Majesty's Ship

Hussiff
Probably derived from 'House wife', a very small roll with thread needles and buttons to carry out repairs on army clothing

ICRC
The International Committee of the Red Cross

Lieutenant
The rank below Captain and the lowest commissioned rank. Many ranks are prefixed with Lieutenant which derives from the French for 'one who holds the job instead of' or place-holder.

LOC
Lines of Communication

Megger
A machine used to test the continuity and insulation of electrical circuits. In that era, a handle was cranked to generate very high voltages. Handled incautiously, the machine can deliver a memorable shock.

NAAFI
Navy Army Air Force Institute; the purveyor of recreational food and drink to service personnel.

NCO
Non Commissioned Officers: Corporals or Lance-Corporals.

OC
Officer Commanding of a company sized group. Not to be confused with a CO who typically has half a dozen OCs under his command.

OR
Other Rank. An ambiguous term as it can mean 'all the ranks and grade not already mentioned' but is often taken as synonymous with private soldieries and their junior NCOs i.e. Everybody below the rank of sergeant.

Parole
A system of trust where a POW agreed to abide by certain rules if granted some privilege.

Panzer
The German word for a tank. The etymology of both words is fascinating. The large, iron structures arriving on the Western Front were explained as tanks for some facility possibly related to gas decontamination or so went the cover story. The designers preferred the word Landship. The original compound German nouns for armoured fighting vehicles fell into disuse, as the term panzer (which denoted the armoured belly of the tank) was adopted for their armed, tracked vehicles.

Plant, The
Abbreviation for The Railway Plant, Doncaster where many famous steam locomotives were constructed and maintained.

Polder
The term used in the Netherlands for the land recovered from below sea level

POW
Prisoner of War an official status recognised in most civilised countries. POWs being the accepted plural. Their treatment is now governed by the Geneva Convention which came into force in October 1950.

PT
Physical Training

Puttees
A coarse bandage wrapped in the proscribed manor around the top of the boot and lower leg.

RASC
Royal Army Service Company used to be responsible for much of army transport and logistics.

SNCO
Senior Non-Commissioned Officers are any of the numerous ranks of Sergeant. Among the hierarchy the RSM Regimental Sergeant Major is at the top with CSM or Company Sergeant Major just behind.

Section
The smallest formation in the army organisation led by a Corporal

Serial
An entry on a list

Stalag
German wartime prison

VD
Venereal Disease now commonly called SDT or Sexually Transmitted Diseases

WO
Warrant Officer holds a warrant from the Sovereign to instruct

To gauge the size of an army the hierarchy read like this as you move from large to very personal.

Army
A very large force of 50,000+ with all the arms required.

Division
This has several Brigades and is led by a General.

Brigade
A combat formation with a mix of infantry, armour, artillery and support with a Brigadier in charge.

Regiment / Battalion
Life is too short to clarify the difference especially within the British army and led by a Colonel (or Lieutenant Colonel).

Many of the measures quoted in the book are in miles, yards, feet and inches.

Annexes

A. Reorganisations of the Territorials

Two of the Army Troops Companies deserve special mention. The Royal Monmouthshire Royal Engineers was formed from an ancient militia unit. This militia was the only unit to survive the reforms of 1908, 1920 and 1924, because of its special engineering role given to it under the Cardwell Reforms of 1877. This continuity has earned an honoured place as the senior territorial unit to this day. They provided the 100 and 101 Army Troops Companies during the war.

B. The prelude to war

War, when it did eventually start, should not have surprised anyone. The path to war was a series of small steps that led to that dreadful destination. Each step evoked conflicting opinions on a continent still erecting monuments and memorials to the fallen of the Great War. This might excuse the majority who ignored the emerging pattern of aggression.

War had been threatening for five years. Germany, under the Nazi Party, had been expanding its territory since Hitler became Chancellor in January 1933. It took him two years to consolidate the absolute power of the Nazi party and office of Chancellor, before the German government began to assert the rights of ethnic Germans in the surrounding territories.

Many ethnic minorities had been stranded within the new territories carved from Germany and Austro-Hungary by the Treaty of Versailles. The British Government had recognised that some of the new national boundaries were unworkable although it had accepted them reluctantly in 1919. France remained committed to the detailed treaty boundaries which encircled its continental rival, Germany.

Nazi news-management was particularly effective. They demanded the right of these people to determine their own fate. The new forum for international disputes was the League of Nations. It offered to resolve the boundaries by conducting plebiscites. They would ask the stranded population to which country they felt they belonged to.

These realignments began with the reoccupation of the industrial zones of the Saar. This area, bordering France, had been demilitarised under the treaty of Versailles. The Saar was reoccupied in March 1935 following a pro-German plebiscite and the withdrawal of the French army of occupation. The German army was once again facing the French. The buffer zone that allowed the Belgians to feel secure in their neutrality was also gone. The process of building the Greater Germany had begun.

The next occupation had no legitimacy. Just one year later, on 7 March 1936, the demilitarised Rheinland, including the industrial Rhur district, was occupied in defiance of the Treaty of Versailles. German troops now returned to the borders of the Low Countries. The lowland route taken by invading armies since Roman times was once again open.

German attention now turned to the south and east while their neighbours turned their attention to constructing border defences. They had no doubt about the growing menace of Germany. From 'Fortress Holland' in the west via the Maginot Line and the Czech border and along the Polish frontier on Germany's eastern boundary, substantial defensive works were prepared.

During 1937, the League of Nations was busy sounding opinions and organising plebiscites in the disputed zones. There was little agreement on which regions should be polled. Each region was ethnically mixed so what should become of the ethnic minorities, within the minority, if borders were redrawn?

There were no easy solutions and Hitler was impatient. Like most tyrants he liked simple solutions. If there was an ethnic German majority in any area it should join the Greater Germany. In March 1938 Austria was annexed after a period of subversion and Hitler's birthplace became part of the Greater Germany.

Czechoslovakia had been one of the successes of the Treaty of Versailles. It incorporated Poles, Hungarians, Slovakians and Ruthenians in addition to 3.2 million Germans. Collectively, these ethnic minorities were half of the Czech population. Dr Benes, the French delegate at the Versailles peace conference spoke of creating a new Switzerland where the ethnic balance would foster, if not guarantee, the country's neutrality.

It had been the industrial heart of the Austro-Hungarian Empire. It had emerged as a prosperous, democratic nation combining the substantial ethnic groups. Fifteen years of stability and prosperity had produced few ethnic pressures inside its boundaries to break away. However, the German media-manipulation succeeded in persuading much of the world's political establishment that the Sudaten-Germans were being denied their right to rejoin their motherland. The Czechs disagreed. Tension mounted.

In early September 1938, Hitler began to threaten to invade Czechoslovakia in order to obtain 'independence' for the Sudatenland. German forces were poised along the borders on 1 October. The Czech army occupied their border forts and prepared to fight. The British and French governments remained willing to appease Hitler. Neither country was militarily prepared to oppose him. The British Government had already tacitly accepted that European borders needed revision.

Chamberlain flew to meet Hitler at Munich. The result was a disaster. There was nothing to console the Czechs who were not present for the negotiations in Munich but expected better from their allies and friends. The Czechs felt they had no option but to accept the infamous deal. Ethnic civil war, backed by Germany, was the alternative.

The loss of the Czech army and armaments industry was a diplomatic coup for the Nazis. The country's formidable frontier defences were breached. The border fortifications designed to contain Germany were all located in the Sudatenland. This loss profoundly upset the balance of power in Europe. The containment plan written into the Treaty of Versailles was destroyed by Chamberlain's policy of appeasement.

Before returning to London, Chamberlain had a further meeting with Hitler. At that private meeting the two leaders 'agreed that the question of Anglo-German relationships is of the first importance for the two countries and of Europe. We regard the agreement signed last night *(the Munich agreement)* and the Anglo-German Naval Agreement as symbols of the desire of our two peoples never to go to war with one another again.'

'We are resolved that the method of consultation shall be the method adopted to deal with any other questions that may concern our two countries, and are determined to continue our efforts to remove possible sources of difference and thus contribute to ensure peace in Europe.'

This was the text on the paper that Neville Chamberlain waved as he stepped from his plane at Croydon. The press was unanimous. It was peace in our time.

Strategically, the moves against the Czechs and Austrians removed any threat to German territory from the south. The alliances constructed by France to contain the growing might of Germany were systematically shattered. The French felt themselves isolated, facing the might of the German army alone. Only the Poles and Soviet Empire blocked further expansion of Nazi Germany.

The remaining provinces of Czechoslovakia were occupied just six months later. Most people were finally convinced that another war with Germany was inevitable. Appeasement had not worked and most people privately acknowledged it. The flow of refugees from the occupied lands began to warn of the true nature of the Nazi party.

The Allied Governments were able to wriggle out of the guarantee they had given to the Czechs when its borders was redrawn at Munich. This time the pretext was the ethnic Slovaks' desire to assert their independence within Czechoslovakia. Hitler maintained his momentum. In March 1939 he annexed the Czech provinces of Moravia and Bohemia that he had already occupied to create the notionally independent state of Slovakia.

German diplomats helped sell their latest coup to world opinion by sacrificing a small part of Czechoslovakia, populated with ethnic Ukrainians, to neighbouring Hungary. The Germans claimed to be outraged when the Poles pre-empted their annexation of the Sudatenland by taking a chunk of

Hungary for itself along with its ethnic Poles. As spring came to central Europe, populations were on the move. Few Czechs wanted to join Greater Germany while ethnic Germans left Poland and headed west.

Hitler's resolution for 1939 included bringing the port of Danzig back under German control. It served the political purposes of the victorious allies to isolate Prussia from the main territory of Germany. The Treaty of Versailles re-created the nation of Poland. The new landlocked Poland demanded access to the sea so, after a plebiscite, Danzig was placed within the Polish custom's area. A rampant Hitler now demanded the return of the port plus a corridor for access to Prussia. The Polish government would not consider this.

It is one of the ironies of these final days of peace that Hitler demanded that the British and French put pressure on their new ally. It had worked with Czechoslovakia. As war loomed, Hitler was portrayed by his propagandists, and the world media, as an advocate of peace tidying up the mess created by the Treaty of Versailles.

Hitler himself was under pressure from the military High Command. They were frustrated by his indecision. They had been kept waiting on each disputed border while their commander vacillated. Their military plans had become increasingly confident and sophisticated with each confrontation.

The military were becoming frustrated at their marginalisation and the repeated success of their political master who they had hoped to control. The timetable for the Poland attack, they claimed, permitted little flexibility. Hitler gave in and signed the 'Directive No. 1 for the conduct of the war' after lunch on Thursday. Poland would be invaded on Friday morning.

While these events were unfolding across the Channel, the cautious attempts by the British Government to increase military spending had met with defeat or reduced majorities at half a dozen Parliamentary by-elections. The public might recognise the danger but they were not yet willing to countenance the cost of armed conflict.

C.   'Maginot Mentality'

Plans for strong border defences were conceived after the Great War. France had suffered two major attacks across its frontier in 1870 and 1914 from the newly emerging nation that had become Germany. The French reluctance to engage in an active war was a consequence of the losses they had suffered in the 1914-18 war. A quarter of the young men had been killed. A fortified line was politically and militarily attractive.

The Germans had demonstrated during the war how difficult it was to breach their well-situated and fortified defensive line in 1916 and 1917.

Constructed behind their front line during 1915, The Germans withdrew to the Hindenberg line while the Allies had spent millions of men's lives capturing the forts and elaborate defences. The military lesson appeared clear.

The Maginot Line was a set of fortifications in depth which ran from the Swiss frontier to Luxembourg. The configuration covered the likely invasion routes and protected the industrial regions of the North East. It was never envisaged as a continuous defensive line although this myth was propagated. The termination of the Maginot Line near the Belgium frontier was neither a naïve nor an incompetent oversight.

There were many reasons for not extending the line. The terrain of the low lands could be protected by demolishing bridges over the numerous waterways that crossed the land. Flooding was also seen as a valuable weapon to be used against any invasion and was indeed used to help protect the evacuation beaches in May and June 1940. The water-table itself would render the engineering task of excavations and fortifications difficult and expensive.

There was a political reason not to extend the Maginot line along its common border with Belgium. France enjoyed good relations with this constitutionally neutral land where half the population spoke French. To extend the line could be interpreted as abandoning Belgium or inviting Germany to violate Belgium neutrality in the future. Gestures and politics were at the core of French military strategy.

The French had been unable to persuade the Belgians to extend their line which would strand many of their kin on the German side of the line. When challenged to explain this chink in their defensive armour they had a well rehearsed answer. They would meet any attack in Belgium. Marshal Petain, who became Minister of War when Maginot died in 1932, advertised the ability of the French Army to move swiftly into Belgium in case Germany chose that route again. They had more and better tanks than the Germans.

Propaganda played a significant strategic role in promoting static defence as the panacea among the victorious allies. The line, it was claimed, was so well concealed that it could not be seen. A popular myth was created that the Maginot Line did indeed run all the way to the coast but was so well concealed. Even experienced military experts such as Liddle-Hart reported in 1937 that the line ran to the coast. It was an understandable mistake. The Maginot Line was not a continuous wall but a series of fortresses. These were well situated to dominate all lines of approach. The positions were well concealed exploiting the concealment offered by the terrain.

The propagandists did not have to massage reality too much to allow the claim to be made that the line extended to the coast. It was another comfortable piece of self-deception. The French public were persuaded they were safe behind their line and would not need to come out and fight. Any war would be fought on German territory. If some Germans did penetrate the

Line they would be repulsed by the best equipped tank units in the world.

The Germans were, however, the decisive victors in this propaganda war. German strategists observed this formidable obstacle with a professional eye. They were well informed about the construction details of the Maginot Line and had already commissioned the Krupp works to design a weapon that could destroy the Line's gun emplacements.

The Germans then went on to wage a propaganda war of their own. They needed to protect themselves while their armoured divisions were engaged in the East. Hitler commissioned the 'West Wall' in early 1938. It was a set of earth works, mine fields and obstacles in depth. This was not designed to be concealed. The most visible parts were the rows of 'dragons teeth' anti-tank obstacles that wound their way across the country as a very expression of Germany's claimed vulnerability. The construction work was well publicised and contemporary film was spliced together with shots of the annexed fortifications built by the Czechs to protect themselves from a German invasion. The trick worked by reassuring the German people that their borders were secure and probably played a part in discouraging allied interventions into Germany during the first nine months of the war.

The propaganda war continued when the Blitzkrieg was launched in 1940. Just one fort on the extreme left close to Montmedy was taken using flame weapons. However, newsreels broadcast round the world purported to show that the whole of the Maginot Line had been captured. In fact the Line surrendered only when told to do so by the French Government.

But the decisive victory was in the mentality engendered. The Maginot mentality did not prepare the French for a fight. It encouraged the myth of invulnerability that seemed to sap the will to resist when the myth was exposed. The weakness of a strategy based on a static defence is obvious now and just as clear to many observers at the time. Churchill visited the Maginot Line in 1937 and observed the enervating effect it had on military thinking.

The German High Command knew better than to rely on such defensive lines. Unlike the French, who challenged attackers to overcome the fortification, the Germans had the realistic aim of slowing an attacker while mobile reserves assembled to confront and repair each breakthrough.

When the BEF was dispatched in 1939 the Secretary of State for War, Hore Belisha, sent X Force of Royal Engineers to complete the line along the French-Belgium frontier. They managed to construct over 400 pillboxes and associated defences in the months available only to abandon the line when Belgium was attacked. The Maginot Mentality that encouraged the military to sit behind fixed defences would soon be discredited.

Just as a tracer bullet works both ways, pointing back to the firer as well as allowing the impact to be observed, so the Maginot Line's stiffest test came when it was assaulted by the American forces in November and December

1944. Patton's 3rd Army only succeeded in capturing the line because the speed of the advance and shortage of material prevented the German army from occupying the line as planned. Even attacking from the 'wrong direction' the fortifications proved an effective obstacle to the best equipped army in the world.

Perhaps the German offensive in early 1918 should have warned the French Generals that a fixed defence would not work. The German High Command employed small scale, fire and manoeuvre to drive the Allies from their trench defences to fight in open country with improvised defences. The successful Allied counter offensive supported by tanks should have reinforced this lesson of mobility for post war military strategists. In Germany and Britain, tanks and manoeuvre warfare were discussed and new tactics developed.

The Germans experimented and developed armoured divisions where motorised infantry would support their tanks. Britain was moving in the same direction although the concepts remained theoretical. The lack of tanks meant that any final decision about their organisation and employment could be postponed. In France, however, in 1920 the tank was designated as an infantry support weapon and the infantry now inhabited fortifications.

The harsh surrender terms insisted on by France had included the disbanding of the institution of the German Military Staff. Ironically, the new generation of German generals might not fight in the conventional way advocated by staff colleges. They could not be relied upon to launch massive attacks against prepared defences in a repeat of the trench war.

Guderian, whose division would lead the assault on France in May 40, began to teach tank tactics in 1928. He based his ideas on the manual used by the British Tank Corps. He had this and other foreign articles translated and published at his own expense. He argued for the need to integrate tank units with infantry, artillery and logistics units so that they could manoeuvre together. He reasoned that tanks working without the support of infantry could not hold territory. Support for a new way of conducting warfare was hard won in the reconstructed German Military Establishment. Guderian's reward came in October 1935 when he was given command of the 2nd Armoured Division when still a colonel

D.   The Phoney War

The phoney war was recognised by all participants. For the French it was 'la drole de guerre' (the boring war) while the Germans coined the ominous phrase Sitzkrieg (sitting war) although Churchill employed the term 'Twilight War'. The term 'Phoney War' was coined by American journalists and imported.

Hitler was anxious to replace the Sitzkrieg with Blitzkrieg. He set 25 October 1939 as the date for an attack in the west. He wanted to forestall attempts by the Allies to build up their defences or to bring the Netherlands and Belgium into their alliance. This date slipped as it took too long to replace the divisions that had invaded Poland with garrison units.

A new date of 12 November was set in spite of fierce opposition from the army. The commander in chief of the Army High Command, von Brauchitsch, offered his resignation when his advice was ignored but it was angrily rejected by Hitler who nevertheless postponed the assault blaming the weather.

A new date of 17 January was then selected. However, this plan too had to be changed when the plans for Operation Yellow were compromised. On 10 January a Luftwaffe Major, Helmut Reinberger, accepted a lift when summoned from his base in Munster to a meeting in Cologne. The plane got lost and the pilot, in a panic, accidentally cut the fuel supply and they crash-landed on Belgian soil. The alert border guards took the prisoners and the partly burnt secret papers away for interrogation. Reinberger later attempted to thrust the papers into a stove but they were retrieved by a Belgian officer.

The Belgians released enough of the information to the British and French to alert the Germans to the fact that key aspects of their plans had probably been compromised although the appalling weather was once again blamed for postponement.

The Allied response to the captured information was confused. There was a risk that this plan was a bluff dreamt up by German Intelligence. If it was a trick, there was a significant political risk that such a spoof might drive the Belgians to abandon their neutrality and join the Allies.

The Allied plans were not modified. Belgium remained neutral. The BEF remained in France, poised to move forward into unprepared position along the Dyle if Germany attacked. No French armour was moved north to block the proposed route of the invasion through Belgium. It remained dispersed behind the Maginot Line.

This latest pause was used effectively by the Germans. It gave them the motive to do more than simply postpone the attack. They began to rethink their plan to sweep through the Low Countries in a repeat of the first phase of the First World War. Instead, they returned to examine a previous plan to attack further south.

Eric von Manstein was the author and salesman for the Ardennes attack. He would have been aware that Marshal Petain had frequently ruled out the possibility of an armoured attack through this hilly and forested area. Consequently, no armour had been posed to oppose a thrust from this direction which could slide round the northern end of the Maginot Line.

The state of preparation of the British would have been well known to the Germans as the Belgian border remained open with workers crossing the frontier daily. The Germans certainly plotted the progress of pillboxes and anti tank ditches as well as the arms and equipment they would have to face.

The view of the influential papers and politicians was that Hitler 'had missed the bus.' Their comfortable view was that if Hitler could not achieve dominance and impose favourable peace terms before the end of 1940, he would lose the war.

Meanwhile ill-equipped and under-trained units continued to move to France. It is tempting to believe that those sending them saw them as little more than cannon fodder in a war of attrition rather like the High Command twenty years earlier. Battles were won by big battalions. It was the type of warfare they understood. The new generation of generals would not assume command until the BEF had been driven out of France.

The superior supply of men and material that helped defeat the German's in 1918 was being created. The military planners were content to sit and wait. Conventional wisdom was that time was on their side. It was better for the troops to be bored than to risk fighting. The French strategy was clear. They would wait. As they provided 90% of the soldiers, their view prevailed.

E.   9 and 10 May 1940

On the domestic front however, the Allied Governments were losing the confidence of their people. The Germans were making progress in Scandinavia and the Nazis were winning the propaganda war.

In Paris, Daladier, the French Prime Minister, had been toppled in March and replace by Paul Reynaud. On 7 May, Leo Amery, a former cabinet minister employed the words originally spoken by Oliver Cromwell when he dismissed the Long Parliament. Now these forceful words were addressed to Chamberlain. 'You have sat here too long for any good you have been doing. Depart I say. Let us be done with you. In the name of God, go.' Chamberlain sought in vain to muster support, feeling that the impending crisis might rally critics to his support. But on 9 May he bowed to the inevitable and resigned.

Concurrently, Reynaud had resigned having failed to topple Gamelin as head of the French army with his policy of waiting for the Germans to attack.

On Thursday 9 May everybody in Britain was looking forward to the Whitsun holiday weekend after the struggle to mobilise during a long cold winter. In Germany Hitler was preparing his Order for the Day. In the evening his message went out to the troops. The divisions in the Ardennes were about to launch his second blitzkrieg. 'Soldiers of the West Front! The hour of the most decisive battle of the future of the German nation has come.' At dawn on Friday 10 May, the battle for the west began.

Back in London, Chamberlain met Churchill and Lord Halifax before attending the King to present his resignation. Churchill, in the Cabinet as Lord of the Admiralty, was not popular with King George VI as he had been an ally of his brother, now the Duke of Windsor, during the abdication crisis. The King would therefore have preferred Halifax as his Prime Minister. Halifax had told Chamberlain that he did not want the job. By default Churchill was invited to become the Prime Minister just as the panzer divisions crossed into Luxembourg, Belgian neutrality was about to be breached.

F.   Dunkirk

Operation Dynamo, the plan to bring the BEF home from Dunkirk, began on 26 May. Preparations for this remarkable evacuation had been ordered by the Cabinet on 20 May. The German advance made it probable that some of the BEF would have to be taken out of Belguim as that country was overwhelmed by the advancing German divisions. The initial decision to assemble a naval force supported by the small ships was not the first part of a military withdrawal from the continent.

Churchill's flying visit to Paris on 16 May had left him few options. He was stunned to discover that the French 7th Army, originally designated as the counter-attack force, had already been committed when the blitzkrieg was launched. Instead of waiting at the northern end of the Maginot line it had advanced towards Holland when Belgian and Dutch neutrality were breached.

In his history of the second world war, published just four years after the end of the European war, Churchill describes the failure to maintain a reserve or, *masse de manoeuvre* as 'one of the greatest surprises I have had in my life.'

It was vital to impart this vital intelligence back to the Cabinet and Military planners in London so they too knew that the army they thought was protecting their back had vanished. Among the small party that had flown to Le Bourget aboard their escorted Flamingo aircraft was the Head of the Military Secretariat to the War Cabinet, General Ismay. He had served much of his career with the Indian Army. With no secure communications Churchill's telegram was translated into Hindustani by Gen Ismay before telegraphing it to London.

The new French Prime Minister Reynard confided that the battle for France was lost. The sight of French official papers being burnt left Churchill in no doubt that the French Government was unlikely to offer significant resistance. Plans to recycle the evacuated troops back to France stuttered and then stalled. The amount of reorganisation required to achieve this was overwhelming.

Even the many French and Belgians, snatched from behind the front line, could not be reconstituted as fighting units when they were returned to France and were sent on leave.

Not only had the departure of the BEF removed the reason for the logistic infra-structure constructed over the previous eight months but it had removed their protective screen-force. The infantry, artillery and armour minus their equipment had been evacuated to Britain. Their vehicles and weapons lined the roads and fields of Flanders. Even the trucks that had enabled the BEF to fall back from Belgium to the coast had been abandoned although a few had performed a final service as a jetty constructed by a team of sappers on the Dunkirk beach at low tide.

The new French commander Gen Weygand decreed that the line of the Seine/Aisne would be held. The British sector in the north would be commanded by the LOC HQ at Rennes. Neither the French or British armies were in a position to resist the inevitable onslaught when it came. Few of the local commanders had any illusions about the precarious tenure of the LOC.

Winston Churchill made three visits in order to inspect the situation. His last was on 13 June. He was anxious to keep a foothold on the continent and to so keep the French in the war. When the Weygand line was breached and the Seine crossed the plight of the Lines of Communication troop seemed to be sealed.

As a fallback, he was initially keen on an idea suggested by the staff of the LOC that Brittany could become a redoubt. Churchill was attracted to the idea, later advocated by General Weygand, that the X French army and British troops should maintain a bridgehead in Brittany with Rennes as the notional front line. The idea was not as fanciful as it sounds, as the German defenders held various pockets on the Brittany Peninsular when the Allies returned to Europe in June 1944 and held out until the war ended. But that was four years in the future.

Churchill might have tried to persuade his new military commander General Brooke that Brittany, the home of 106 Army Troops Company, could be fortified and held. Brooke replaced General Gort as Commander of the British and Commonwealth troops in France on 12 June. When Brooke arrived on the morning of the 14 June and realised that the situation was untenable even though the 52 Highland and the First Canadian Divisions had recently landed. The day before Churchill already seemed to have appreciated the predicament and made the first of his memorable wartime speeches remembered for its promise of 'blood, tears, toil and sweat.'

General Brook knew the enemy he faced. He had faced them during the withdrawal to Dunkirk. He had no illusions about their capability. His advice to evacuate the remaining Allied troops was unambiguous. 'I would not be surprised to see a party of German armoured cars drive up to our front door'

Brooke noted in his diary on the 15 June as he pondered the lack of any reconnaissance units.

Churchill was persuaded that a foothold in France was untenable. He accepted General Brooke's appraisal and on the evening of 14 June he agreed to a complete withdrawal. The BEF was no longer under French command. The idea, already agreed with the French Prime Minister Reynaud, for a 'Torres Vedras Line' in Brittany came to nothing.

As this plan crumbled, the French Government still led by Reynauld, persuaded his cabinet that they should make their stand in North Africa. But the next day the appeasers within the French cabinet pushed the case for negotiating with the Germans. The appeasers argued that if terms were harsh, they could fight on from their North African bases. But the Germans might be persuaded to offer lenient terms to avoid taxing their overstretched logistics.

Churchill anticipated that making any peace overtures would destroy the morale of the French army. He was right. On the 16 June Reynault resigned and was replaced by Marshall Petain. The order for the French to stop fighting would follow the next day. Bob Borthwick noted that French soldiers were already heading home.

The Royal Navy began to plan for the evacuation of the 140,000 British troops still in France as the Dunkirk operation was drawing to a close. Plan *Aerial* would need to repeat the miracle of Dunkirk. This time it would need bigger boats. Naval vessels for escort duty were in short supply. Approximately a third of the Naval vessels had been crippled or sunk.

.

References

This was not intended as a work of scholarship or reference. However, the work has taken me to several excellent original sources. Some of the papers studied have been listed below with any relevant notes or discussion. Unless otherwise stated, the references are to the Public Reference Office, Kew.

There were many references that did not contribute anything to the story and are not recorded. Three quarters of the documents checked yielded nothing for this story but provided many tempting distractions. I have noted some storylines that came from a particular reference as this might benefit of any others who want to revisit this story. My hope is that this imperfect outline will be of some assistance.

Copies of the diaries of Bill Harvey and Bob Borthwick have been lodged with the Imperial War Museum, London. The taped material is yet to be found a home but it is hoped to put them in an accessible archive.

The loss of the war diary at certain critical times means that there are some gaps in the official record of the company but these periods are well covered by the personal accounts. However, it does illustrate the danger for anybody recording history. History records what it can. It has to make do with what is available. By happy chance, the declassification and release of private diaries and the availability of much German material allowed some of the gaps in the record to be plugged and several events to be understood.

I would again express my appreciation to the patient scholars who staff our national archives. This book would not have been possible without their advice and help.

Chapter One
Mobilisation plans WO 33/1433 WO 168/888.
The Story of Plan W Brig. LA Hawes *Army Quarterly Review* July 77 pp 445–456.
Getting the BEF to France WO 197/1 /2 /32 Army Plan W.
War diary 106 ATC June–Aug 39 & Sept–18 May WO 167/930 /931.
Rommel's Papers edited by Liddel Hart.

Chapter Two
Propaganda during the Phoney War - From Pillar of Fire by Ronald Atkin.
Le Mans Region papers WO 167/54.
Public Relations WO 167/45.
Entertainment WO 167/46.
Pilferage WO 167/54.
Rennes HQ Nov–June 39/40 WO 167/86/ /88.

Chapter Three
Evacuation of troops and equipment WO 197/89.
Investigation of loss of equipment in Brest WO 197/108.
Events in the LOC from 16–18 June 1940 WO197/108.
War Diary CRE Rennes WO 167/91.
Accounts of evacuation complied in Aug 41 WO197/34.
Plan Aerial – Brittany evacuation WO197/105.
Churchill's enquiries into the conduct of the evacuation CAB 120/248.

Basil Karslake 1940 The last Act isbn 0850522404 This work of scholarship by the son of the man who was held responsible for the losses during the final evacuation from France and amply exonerates him. A study of the war diaries and contemporary records also reveals a heart warming story of senior staff, deprived of effective communications, moving among the retreating forces maintaining order and morale.

'Reports of the speed of the enemy's advance were, as at Brest, greatly exaggerated and this led to a decision to hasten the end of the evacuation. At 11 a.m. on the 18th twelve ships sailed in convoy with the last troops and by early afternoon the operation was ended, except for the usual search for stragglers by small craft. Again the end was premature and again much more transport and equipment could have been saved had we possessed accurate intelligence of the enemy's movements.'

Information about the surrender of Brest is recorded in their civic history. German military plans show no significant advance to support the capture. The assumption has been made that the small parlay group recorded in the civic record, took possession of the city and would have moved to the fort overlooking the naval dock from where they would have been unable to observe the civilian quay or exert any control over the town. The Germans did not enter Brest in force for some weeks to judge from the deployment maps inspected.

Chapter Four
The records for this time are very thin. It is possible that more information exists in local authority records. There were other priorities. The following shed some light on the defensive preparations undertaken.
Air 40/228
WO 201/661
WO 167/86
WO 106/3243
WO 199/2883 /2872 /74 /2883
The minutes of the Corporation of Glasgow City Council provide an over-detailed record of the problems when the wartime, military culture encountered the civic pride and traditions.

Chapter Five
Convoy organisation ADM 237/1619.
WO 106/3245 Defence of Crete Sept–Nov 1940.
On 22 April 1941 Churchill is personally writing to Wavell to warn of an airborne invasion. The Middle East HQ felt that Cyprus or Syria were possible targets for the untried tactic of aerial invasion.
Reading this file one is tempted to think that the Germans were privy to these secret signals because they were able to strike in the way, at the time and at the places identified as the most vulnerable. The Germans also provided a flow of false intelligence to support the suspicions of the military staff in the Middle East and leave Crete unprepared.

Chapter Six
WO 169/1314 CRE Alexandria reports
on the labour troubles at Buseli.

Chapter Seven
Major Ops and policy Mid East
Defensive construction policy
WO 201/152.
Mid East Ops planning WO201/371.
CRE Defensive planning WO 201/680.
A.8A/3021/1/RE 'Low priority of
defensive work'.
Lists all RE units in Mid East but 106
ATC is not listed although there are
other ATCs in the list.
Middle East Defensive Plans
WO 201/673.
Road construction WO 201/668.
Defence of the coast WO 201/462.
Cyrenia plans 1941 WO 201/418.
Mid East 'Q' ops including jerry cans
and springs stories WO 201/370 /479.
WO 201 /661 /665 /675 /681.
The Official History of the Royal
Engineers mentions the work of 106
ATC at El Alamein but the source of
any plan is not recorded.

Not a single reference to the
construction plans at El Alamein
was traced. Apart from the electrical
section, sent to Buselli, there is no
mention of the activities of the unit.
In the light of their next posting to
provide the engineers for the Special
Forces brigade being planned, it is
possible that the work at El Alamein
was just a holding operation for the
Company until the plans for what
became the SAS were ready.

Chapter Eight
Company sent to Kabrit for training
WO 200/78196.
Employment of engineers
WO 201/665 /666.
106 ATC war diary WO169/5265.
Plans for advance including logistic
plans March 41 WO 201/644 /639.
Escape of the Sharnhorst
ADM1/11782.
Operation Bootjack WO 201/719.
Operation Buckshot
WO 201/639 /640.
L Detachment WO 201/721.
Landing Dernia WP201 724.
Operations Fire eater & Flipper
WO 201 /684 /720.
Use of special forces to stop pilferage
WO 218/158.
WO 201 /358 /359 /365 /368.

Chapter Nine
Deal with water supply
WO 201/379 /479 /666.
Move to the desert from Kabrit
WO 169/5265.
Emergency repairs in Tobruk Dec 41
WO 201/661.

Chapter Ten
Harbour rebuild plans WO 201/661.
Fall of Tobruk WO 201/418 /429.
The capture of Tobruk from the
German perspective obtained from
prisoners debrief WO 201/382.
106 ATC declared 'non existent'
WO 201/690.

Chapters Eleven & Twelve
The Imperial War Museum has a
collection of the POW magazine which
was first published in May 1942.

Movement of POWs Feb-Apr 45
WO 219/1462.
POWs in Italy
WO 224/179 /202 /205 /230.
POW moves to Germany
WO 224/179 /202.
Dachau district FO 916/244.
POWs in Germany 41-42 916/25 /257.
Other Foreign office papers FO
916/581 /584 /585 /907 /912.
Identity of locations and FO relations
with Red Cross FO 1038/34.
Bombing of POWs Air 916/1648 Given
the frequency with which attack by
allied aircraft have been reported
recently, the official record cannot be
taken as complete although it does
tally well with the reports of those
who feature in this book.
Photo of camps and actions to prevent
bombing Air 14/1240 /228 /229.
Stalag 317 Red cross reports
WO 224/47.

Printed in Great Britain
by Amazon

78362007R00179

métrique, de l'arrangement immobile des forces, du syllogisme, du raisonnement. Du matériel, du logiciel. Supprimez un pied du trépied, tout s'écroule, biffez une thèse, un terme, tout s'évanouit. Tout tombe justement sur les pieds de l'athlète, les conviés sont estropiés. On crie au miracle, et le miracle est bien que le même écart se conserve entre les petites énergies et les grandes, que le monde réel soit donc compréhensible. Que la parabole du parasite et la paralysie de l'hôte soient, précisément, parallèles. Demain, l'athlète ainsi que bien des invités se jettent de côté, bancroches. Un pilier leur manque, il y faut un bâton. Comme au vieil Œdipe de la Sphinge. Comme à Héphaïstos. Les boiteux sont découvreurs, l'inclinaison est le début du monde.

On ne loue jamais trop, voici la liste de l'excès, du défaut, de l'écart. Il apparaît dans la logique du raisonnement, dans le calcul, le compte des bilans, il apparaît dans le langage, les mots et le poème, dans la parabole et la paraphrase, il apparaît dans l'ordre, le plan et l'espace, il apparaît dans l'échange et dans la monnaie, le dû et le gré, le salaire à nouveau doublé, le paiement du poète et des dieux, part maudite, il apparaît à l'extrémité de la poutre, au sommet du pilier menaçant, dans le porte-à-faux et l'entablement, il apparaît maintenant aux systèmes physiques, dans l'équilibre difficile de la pierre et du marbre, il apparaît enfin aux systèmes vivants, marcher, courir, comme des estropiés, lutter, jumeaux, jusqu'à ce

d'aujourd'hui, poètes ou lutteurs, connus ou inconnus, le gré arrive après le dû, le festin après le paiement : peut-être qu'il eut peur de perdre, outre son dû, le gré de la louange. L'échange est premier, les festivités, comme on dit, suivent si elles peuvent. Pour les dieux, à l'inverse, le gré passe avant le dû : les Gémeaux apparaissent, miracle, tous deux rendent grâce, d'abord, au poète olympique, et pour prix de ses vers, l'avertissent de tel danger qu'il va courir bientôt. Échange mot pour mot, éloge pour avis. Merci, nous parlons ensuite de remboursement, c'est bien le monde renversé. Il tourne dans un sens, l'histoire va son économie, où l'échange est fondamental, cela est nommé le sens de l'histoire. Il s'arrête un peu, il repart dans le sens inverse, et dans cette histoire, nouvelle, l'échange est produit, après un état antérieur, où tout allait de gré à gré. Cette histoire n'est pas nouvelle, au contraire elle est archaïque, perdue au noir de la mémoire, elle est celle des dieux. Je comprends maintenant pourquoi ils passaient tout leur temps à table, à boire et banqueter. Je comprends maintenant pourquoi le festin fut interrompu. Par le basculement de l'histoire. Par une catastrophe dont je n'ai pas l'idée, encore. Les sociétés du gré ont disparu, on les croyait déjà divines dans l'Antiquité. Elles ont laissé place aux collectifs du doit et de l'avoir. L'histoire du gré n'a laissé que des traces méconnaissables, dans les textes et les monuments. Nous courons, depuis lors, l'histoire économique, le temps à calcul d'échanges, et le rattrapage des tares. Y a-t-il un extérieur à cette histoire ? C'est exactement le sujet de ce livre. Je n'ai pas fini. Quand l'histoire et le temps sont mesurés par le calcul d'échanges et ramenés à lui, je crains fort qu'il y ait, ici et là, des insolvables. Qui n'aient plus à donner que leurs enfants, leurs muscles et leur corps. C'est le temps de la mort, une histoire de mort. Qui n'aient plus à donner que leur vie et leur corps, morceau par morceau. Combien de fois est monté des hommes, à la table des dieux, un chaudron rempli de membres épars? Je n'ai plus à donner que mon approche de la mort, je n'ai plus de change que mon courage de cette ombre, je n'ai plus à écrire que son immédiate proximité. Ce temps, cette histoire s'invaginent au voisinage du néant. Il faut un zéro à leur calcul, il faut un néant à leur métaphysique. Je comprends tout à coup pourquoi les dieux, aux yeux des hommes, passaient pour immortels, je crois savoir au moins ce que l'ambroisie ne contenait pas.

Revenons au festin des hommes, toujours ainsi interrompu. Qui sont les dieux, encore? Ceux qui ne sont jamais interrompus dans leur repas. L'immortel est le convivial continu. Voici donc Simonide, au banquet, il mange et boit son gré, en position, exactement, de parasite. Il s'empiffre et s'enivre pour le gré de ses vers, il a payé en mots les convives choisis et la grande chère. Mais quelqu'un troubla la fête pendant qu'ils étaient en train. A la porte de la salle, ils entendirent du bruit. Le Simonide détale, mais nul autre ne le suit. La cohorte n'en perd pas un seul coup de dent. Elle a tort, car elle va mourir.

Pour la première fois nous savons qui fra[porte, qui fait du bruit derrière l'huisser. dieux. Qui font avis qu'on doit déloger, car le tomber sur les têtes. Les Dioscures détalent, . nide le suit. Voilà : ils se jettent à côté.

La parole se fait chair. L'écart se fait statique. pilier manque, il se jette à côté. Tout se jette à cô bientôt : la parole-parabole, l'exemple et l'éloge, dû et le gré, le poète et les dieux, la colonne e l'entablement. Nous calculons toujours le trop. Le trop et le para. Parabole, parasite. Celui-ci paie en paraboles. Ici la liste des écarts, leur dénombrement, rubrique ou recueil.

Un pilier manque et nous passons du logiciel au matériel, du verbe à la chair, à la pierre, de la parole au référent. Qui se venge? Le divin, le poète ou la chose même? On n'habite pas longtemps le langage, les mots, sans qu'une fois l'objet revienne, sans que manque un pied soudain. Sans que le réel tombe sur la tête. J'imagine une salle triangulaire, un plafond à trois architraves, cimaises, travées, cela est prévu par le calcul de statique, par le verbe, le logiciel. Que le triclinium ait été carré, la faute d'une colonne pouvait ne pas être un irréparable malheur, le porte-à-faux peut résister. Un pilier manque et le plafond ne trouve plus rien qui l'étaie. Il était à trois poutres comme l'éloge, sur trois pieds, trois appuis, tro' thèses, comme le discours. Deux pour les die' jumeaux, une pour toi, mortel, qui un jour, u nuit, ou un soir, nous manque. Deux color stables, une instable. Triangle : maille élémer de l'équilibre statique, de la distribution de l'e de la disposition des sites, de la topologie qu'un des deux piliers de cette lutte manque, et fasse un vainqueur, un vaincu, paralytique de corps et paradigme élémentaire du groupe social au combat.

Je compte cette impressionnante avancée comme une construction savante du réel, telle que l'âge classique en faisait souvent l'œuvre.

Le préfixe *para* est compté, calculé, à la tare, dans son écart à l'équilibre. Mais il est aussi posé, situé. Quand la colonne tient la poutre, une ligne, dans son dessin, va au bout de la deuxième ligne, ici, la verticale joint le bord de l'horizontale. Cela fait angle droit au sommet. En tout cas, cela fait un angle, cela fait un sommet. Décalez maintenant le pilier, marquez un porte-à-faux, tare ou écart, *para*. Dans le schéma, la ligne ne va plus au pied de la seconde ligne, mais en un lieu autre, sur le parcours. Le parasite a relation non point à la station mais à la relation. Et il la met en porte à faux. Le schéma le plus simple apparaît. *Static*, en anglais : parasite.

En un mot, non point, en un préfixe seul, tout le texte et toute l'histoire. Il faut comprendre alors et alors seulement qu'elle est une origine à l'art de la mémoire. Le discours, le parcours est d'une simplicité canonique : il est déductif, il construit la réalité, il construit le réel à partir de l'écart. Dans une variété ensemencée de flèches simples, l'écart tient lieu d'inclinaison.

Picaresques et cybernétiques
La nouvelle balance

Le parasite est invité à table d'hôte, il doit, en retour, égayer les convives de ses histoires et de ses ris. En toute exactitude, il échange de bons morceaux contre de bons mots, il paie son repas, il l'achète en monnaie de langue. C'est le plus vieux métier du monde. On en trouve trace dans les témoignages les plus anciens. Autour de cette loi de justice, mille variations, simples rarement et souvent compliquées, sont connues, pratiquées, dans le quotidien familial, tribal, amical, sociétaire, comme dans la comédie la plus archaïque ou le récit le plus enfoui. Par exemple, il arrive que l'écornifleur paie en monnaie de morale, et que l'hôte donne, par ce devoir imaginaire et lourd qui le remplit de culpabilité. La morale est un discours parmi tant d'autres, ou une variété d'espèces, de numéraire convertible. Chaque société donne cours à une monnaie langagière qu'on peut échanger, avantageusement pour l'estomac. Les groupes forts et influents diffusent ainsi un lexique forcé. Il est économique aujourd'hui, de même qu'il était humaniste naguère, voltairien autrefois, ou religieux jadis.

Un chemineau, mourant de faim, se trouva, un beau soir, à la fenêtre des cuisines d'un restaurant hautement réputé. Les odeurs y étaient délicieuses. Il s'en emplit, cela calmait un peu sa douleur de famine. Un marmiton s'aperçut du manège, et sortant brusquement, exigea de lui le paiement de ce qu'on pouvait nommer un service. Le passant et le cuisinier en venaient presque aux mains, sur ladite contestation, lorsque survint un tiers qui proposa de les départager. Donnez-moi une pièce, dit-il. Le miséreux la tendit, renfrogné. Il la posa sur le pavé de pierre, et du talon de son soulier, la fit sonner un peu. Ce bruit, dit-il, comme sentence, est le paiement de l'odeur des bons plats. Le rôti est la chose qu'on mange, or il s'en dégage un fumet. La pièce est chose qu'on échange, or il s'en dégage un son. Si la pièce vaut le rôti, alors le bruit de la première vaudra bien l'odeur du second. Et il rendit au passant sa monnaie. Justice était rendue.

Vieux racontar qui met une sagesse en place. Nous sommes creux et vides, ce n'est pas de vent et de voix que nous avons à nous remplir; il nous faut de la substance plus solide à nous réparer. Deux places ou deux ordres : substances et solides ici, et là, les vents et la voix. Cette sagesse veut que si l'on échange, on le fasse dans le même ordre. C'est la philosophie, la justice de l'estomac. Solide pour solide, substance pour substance et repas pour argent comptant, et ailleurs, si on veut, vent pour voix, voix pour vent. Il y a les infrastructures, c'est du sérieux, il y a les superstructures, où on vend du vent. Le consistant et le diffus. Chaque auteur, chaque langue dit ce partage à sa manière. Les philosophies lourdes le consacrent.

Le parasite invente du nouveau. Parce qu'il ne mange pas comme tout le monde, il construit une logique nouvelle. Il croise, il diagonalise l'échange. Il ne troque pas, il change de monnaie. Il cherche à donner de la voix contre de la substance, du gazeux contre du solide, ou bien de la superstructure contre de l'infrastructure. On rit, on l'expulse, on se moque de lui, on le bat, il nous trompe, mais il invente du nouveau. Il faut analyser cette nouveauté-là. Ce son, ce fumet, cette odeur, passant pour pièce d'or ou rôti de gibier.

Un paralytique se traînait sur les coudes et les genoux. Était-ce notre athlète, blessé? A quatre pas d'un repas gras, on peut mourir de faim, Tantale, si on ne peut se déplacer. Il crevait de misère et pourrissait dans un coin noir. Un beau jour, il vit un aveugle qui trébuchait sur mille obstacles et risquait à tout coup de se rompre le cou. Il peut mourir de tomber dans un puits si la margelle est basse et paraît une marche, et si les bras tendus ne touchent que du vent. L'immobile l'appelle et lui offre un contrat. L'aveugle est le porteur, et l'estropié le guide. Ils font un normal à eux deux.

Vieux racontar qui chasse la sagesse de place. Vous avez ri du parasite, et vous ne riez pas de l'échange des pieds contre l'œil. Et pourtant. L'aveugle donne du solide, la force, le transport, une puissance calculable en calories, et produite par tel ou tel mets, du repas. Je veux dire une énergie à l'échelle ordinaire. Que donne, en échange, le cul-de-jatte dans ce nouveau tableau à la mode d'Orion? Il dit, et voilà tout. Il annonce l'obstacle, il veille, il propose la direction. Juché sur les épaules d'une force noire, il la clarifie, l'illumine. Bientôt, il faut dire qu'il la dirige, qu'il lui donne des ordres. Après tout, il n'a pas proposé à l'aveugle un autre contrat que le pacte parasitaire. Car il paie en information, en énergie d'échelle microscopique. Il donne des mots contre de la force, oui, de la voix, du vent, contre une substance solide. Pis encore, il prend le pouvoir, il gouverne.

Le parasite invente du nouveau. Il capte une énergie et la paie en information. Il capte le rôti et le paie en contes. Deux manières d'écrire le nouveau contrat. Il établit un pacte injuste, au rapport des vieilles balances, il construit un bilan neuf. Il dit une logique jusqu'à ce jour irrationnelle, il dit une nouvelle épistémologie, une autre théorie de l'équilibre. Il diagonalise les ordres des choses, les états de choses, solide et gazeux. Il évalue l'information. Ou plutôt : il découvre l'information sous la voix et les bonnes paroles, il découvre l'Esprit dans le souffle et le vent. Il invente la cybernétique. L'aveugle et le paralytique, association croisée du matériel et du logiciel, échange du solide contre la voix, c'est la fable la plus ancienne en théorie du gouvernail. Et si l'éclair gouverne l'univers, l'éclair, ici, c'est le regard, et la sollicitation d'obliquer. Le boiteux est l'inclinaison. Il est l'écart et il l'annonce.

Il y a là plusieurs balances fines. D'abord toutes les voix ne valent pas information, tous les vents n'apportent pas ici de nouvelles. On n'invite pas n'importe quel diseur de bons mots, les brillants causeurs se distinguent des vantards assommants ou des ergoteurs opiniâtres. Le roi de Prusse pouvait choisir, il préféra Voltaire, et la tsarine Diderot. Ils n'auraient pas invité Jean-François Rameau, dérisoire. Il y a un marché de la bonne parole. Un cours forcé, parfois. La mauvaise monnaie y chasse la bonne, souvent. Mais cette balance est évoluée, sophistiquée, inutile d'abord.

Revenons au paralytique, c'est-à-dire au gouverneur. Celui qui a les énergies, le producteur de mouvement, peut distinguer parfois, dans les voix du vent, le message utile. Sa cécité, pourtant, lui interdit à tout jamais d'en contrôler l'utilité. Le cul-de-jatte, juché en haut de son regard aveugle, peut le précipiter dans une basse-fosse. Il faut bien qu'il fasse confiance. Et, sans doute, à n'importe qui. Car il ne peut choisir son cornac. C'est l'estropié qui le voit et l'appelle, et il vient à sa voix. Il entend, il écoute, déjà il obéit. Bien sûr, il saura distinguer un message d'un bruit, mais son absence de contrôle fait qu'on peut lui mentir à loisir. Je te garderai de tous les obstacles et je t'emmènerai aux lieux de tes désirs. Alors il vient comme un mouton.

Dès lors, celui qui veut rester assis sur les épaules d'un athlète n'aime pas qu'il soit clairvoyant. Dès lors, celui qui aime à commander peut, s'il le veut, rester assis, à une seule condition. Il faut crever les yeux aux producteurs. Aux énergiques, aux forts. Il faut que ceux de l'énergie n'aient pas d'information; alors, ceux de l'information peuvent se dispenser de l'énergie. L'information est d'autant plus précieuse qu'elle est rare. Il faut donc provoquer cette rareté. L'aveugle et le paralytique avaient déjà établi ces théorèmes-là, et cette nouvelle balance. Ils ont commencé par une symbiose, elle a duré le temps des roses. Le parasite est tout aussitôt revenu.

La balance de rareté fonctionne en perfection dans un espace ou un milieu vides d'information. Ici, le premier signal apparu vaut tout l'or du monde, il vaut la vie. Premier éclair qui s'incline dans le chaos. Première branche d'olivier, au bec de la colombe, sur la plaine diluvienne. Tout le sens, par après, s'ensuit. Et l'histoire est aussi tributaire de cette étincelle. Il faut commencer par la boîte noire, il faut commencer par la nuit, par l'aveuglement.

Il faut donc commencer par retirer aux travailleurs, aux producteurs, toute source de renseignements. On dresse bien les étalons en leur apposant des œillères. On place bien les veaux, les poules dans le noir, à l'école, comme s'ils étaient de simples petits d'hommes. Il faut donc commencer par diviser, comme on dit, le travail. Le travailleur manuel doit être aveugle par rapport au paralytique intellectuel. L'homme de barre ne dispose pas de hublot, il entend la voix de son maître, il écoute, il répète, et il obéit. Comme tout à l'heure, aveugle, il vient à la voix. L'un fournit l'énergie, l'autre l'information. L'un donne la force de travail, l'autre les

directives. La substance et la voix. Cet échange est
encore inique, mais il fonctionne dans l'histoire et
pas seulement dans la comédie. On a dû trouver très
sérieuse la diagonale parasite. On a dû trouver intelligente la nouvelle balance. Car le partage rebondit,
fait système très vite : le producteur intellectuel est
tout aussi aveugle par rapport au paralytique administratif et aveuglé par lui, et ainsi de suite. Cette
cybernétique se complique répétitivement, fait
chaîne, puis réseau. Elle est pourtant fondée sur le
vol de l'information, chose simple. Il suffit d'éditer
des lois et d'en retirer la connaissance au plus grand
nombre Si bien que le pouvoir, à la limite, n'est rien
d'autre. Il se mesure à la balance dite. Il est le rapport, et, à la lettre, le fléau, entre les lieux où l'information est stockée, et les lieux d'où elle a été ôtée.
Qui a crevé les yeux de qui ? Où le savoir est-il placé,
de quel espace est-il absent ? Il est assez vrai que le
partage des fonctions manuelles et intellectuelles
recouvre bien le vieux rapport ville-campagne, par
exemple, ce que les rats font voir.

Ce pouvoir, qu'on peut dire bureaucratique, me
paraît plus fort et plus stable que celui de la force,
jamais assez forte, ou que celui du droit, jamais assez
juste. Il repose sur le savoir et sur la connaissance,
pis encore, sur l'information, sur le signal, presque
au niveau réflexe. Pourtant sa genèse est paradoxale. Celle des pouvoirs forts est simple, il s'agit
de violence et de mort, de moyens guerriers,
muscles et stratégie. Celle des pouvoirs justes est
simple, également, il s'agit de foi et de sacrifices, de
martyrs et de fanatiques. Rien que de l'ordinaire, du
fréquent ou du dérisoire. Ici, l'ancêtre est parasite.

Il est ridicule, il est bafoué. Il prétend échanger de bons plats contre des mots risqués. Mais on n'entend que lui, à table. On ne voit que lui, sur les planches de Plaute. Lui, ses éclats de voix. Tout le monde rit. Par quel miracle, tout à coup, tout le monde pleure-t-il, déjà? Entre-temps, le maître de céans a perdu le pouvoir de l'exclure. Il est là, bien enraciné. Ruine le père, baise la mère, éduque les enfants, régente la maison. Nous ne pouvons plus nous en passer, il est notre système même, il commande, il a le pouvoir, sa voix est devenue celle du maître, il parle de telle sorte qu'on l'entend de partout, nul ne peut plus placer un mot. De la table d'hôte au tableau d'Orion, le voici maintenant sur les épaules, dominateur, jupitérien. Comment une telle chose est-elle possible? Quelle foudre a frappé les yeux des producteurs, quel aveuglement, tout à coup?

Le producteur joue le contenu, le parasite joue la position. Celui qui joue la position battra toujours celui qui joue le contenu. Celui-ci est simple et naïf, celui-là est complexe et médiatisé. Le parasite bat toujours le producteur. Celui-ci, attentif au jeu des choses mêmes, suppose que l'autre ne triche pas, puisque les choses elles-mêmes sont fines, mais loyales, comme disent les physiciens.

Celui qui joue le contenu joue l'objet. Il est artisan, il est savant aussi, et c'est ou ce n'est que la maîtrise du monde, subtil, rusé, mais non fraudeur. Celui qui joue la position joue les rapports entre sujets, il gagne donc la maîtrise des hommes. Et le maître des hommes est le maître des maîtres du monde.

Il y a ceux du feu, il y a ceux du lieu. Ceux dont la parole est de feu, ceux dont la parole est de lieu. Ceux du lieu sans feu sont les maîtres, froids. Ceux du feu sans lieu brûlent éperdument, si fort qu'autour d'eux les objets se transforment comme dans un four ou autour d'une forge. Langue de feu dans le lit du vent, le vent vient d'où il veut, souffle où il veut, pour attiser le feu. Ils ne sont pas les maîtres, ils peuvent être esclaves, mais ils sont les débuts. Ils sont le bruit du monde, la rumeur des gésines et des transformations.

Jouer la position, jouer le lieu, c'est dominer la relation. C'est n'avoir relation qu'à la relation même. Jamais aux stations d'où elle vient, où elle va, ni par où elle passe. Jamais aux objets comme tels et sans doute jamais aux sujets comme tels. Ou plutôt à ces points comme opérateurs, comme sources de relations. Et c'est là le sens du préfixe para dans le mot parasite : il est à côté, il est auprès, il est décalé, il n'est pas sur la chose, mais sur sa relation. Il a des relations, comme on dit, et en fait un système. Il est toujours médiat et jamais immédiat. Il a relation à la relation, il a rapport au rapport, il est branché sur le canal.

Il y a ceux des sources et il y a ceux des canaux.

Toute la question du système est maintenant d'analyser ce qui y est un point, un être, une station. Ils y sont traversés d'une étoile de relations, ils sont carrefours, échangeurs, triage. Or n'est-ce pas cela même, analyser : dire que cette chose est à l'intersection de plusieurs séries. Dès lors, la chose même n'est rien d'autre qu'une tête de relations, ce carrefour, ou ces passages. Elle n'est rien que position, situation. Et le parasite a gagné.

La Pentecôte

Et factus est repente de caelo, il se produisit tout à coup venant du ciel, sonus, tamquam advenientis spiritus vehementis, un bruit comme celui d'un vent impétueux, ἦχος ὥσπερ φερομένης πνοῆς βιαίας, a sound from heaven as of a rushing mighty wind, et replevit totam domum ubi erant sedentes, et il remplit toute la maison où ils étaient assis. Et apparuerunt illis dispertitae linguae tamquam ignis, et ils virent apparaître des langues séparées les unes des autres qui étaient comme de feu, διαμεριζόμεναι γλῶσσαι ὡσεὶ πυρός, cloven tongues like as of fire, une distribution de langues comme de feu, des langues bifurquées, divisées, bifides comme des flammes, seditque supra singulos eorum, et qui se posèrent sur chacun d'eux; et repleti sunt omnes Spiritu Sancto, καὶ ἐπλήσθησαν πάντες πνεύματος ἁγίου, et ils furent tous remplis du Saint-Esprit. Et ils commencèrent à parler diverses langues, et coeperunt loqui variis linguis, λαλεῖν ἑτέραις γλώσσαις, to speak with other tongues, selon que l'Esprit-Saint leur donnait de s'exprimer, dabat, καθῶς τὸ

πνεῦμα ἐδίδον, as the Spirit gave them utterance,
leur donnait, dabat, ἐδίδον, gave them.

Des langues advenues à partir du vent et du bruit.
Parler en langues après le feu, après le bruit. A la
porte de la salle, ils entendirent un grand vent.

Il y avait à Jérusalem des juifs pieux, de toutes les
nations qui sont sous le ciel. Facta autem hac voce,
convenit multitudo, après que ce bruit se fut fait
entendre, ils accoururent en foule, γενομένης δὲ τῆς
φωνῆς ταύτης συνῆλθεν τὸ πλῆθος, now when this
was noised abroad, the multitude came together,
hac voce, φωνῆς, ce bruit, this was noised, voix ou
bruit, l'accord se casse tout à coup, et le rythme et le
sens, mais les deux se mélangent, et c'est la voix et
c'est le bruit, c'est le message et c'est le parasite, et
chacun les entendait parler dans sa propre langue,
audicbat unusquisque lingua sua illos loquentes,
every man heard them speak in his language,
ἤκουον ἕις ἕκαστος τῇ ἰδίᾳ διαλέκτῳ λαλούντων
αὐτῶν. Parthes, Mèdes, Élamites, Mésopotamiens,
ceux de Judée, άe Cappadoce, du Pont et de l'Asie,
de Phrygie, Pamphylie, Égypte, Libye, Cyrène,
Romains, étrangers, juifs et prosélytes, Crétois,
Arabes, entendons parler en nos langues les merveilles de Dieu, mirabilia, wonderful works,
μεγαλεῖα, merveilles.

Le sens nouveau distribué partout à partir du vent

et du bruit. Non point une langue unique traduite
en plusieurs langues, mais plusieurs émises et plusieurs entendues en même temps.

La suite des événements est exacte, vue de nos
rationalités. Tout à coup, brusquement, d'une
manière inattendue, le bruit, un bruit venant du
ciel, un son comme fait le vent lorsqu'il souffle avec
force. Il se produit localement, dans une direction
singulière, et bientôt il remplit le lieu, tout le lieu.
Peu prévisible, il passe du local au global. C'était un
bruissement, c'est une rumeur. C'était un événement dans un coin du système, il pénètre, envahit,
occupe toute la maison. Il était entendu, il est vu. Ils
virent apparaître. Le bruit est un hasard, un
désordre, et le vent est un flux. Ce qu'ils virent est
d'abord une distribution, une dispersion, mais aussi
une division. Ce qu'ils virent est aussi ce qui est
généralement ouï, comme le bruit. Des langues. Des
langues divisées, ou distribuées. Mais des langues de
feu. C'est le feu qui pousse le vent, c'est la chaleur
qui produit les souffles de l'air, c'est le feu qui cré-
pite, qui produit le hasard pétillant, grésillant, c'est
le feu de la force et c'est le feu de la clarté, de
l'énergie, de la lumière, de la puissance et de
l'information. Le bruit se fait message avant que le
verbe se fasse chair. Il était bruissement, rumeur, il
est le feu de langue, il est, de la langue de feu, le
sens. Le sens qui bifurque, incliné, divisé comme la
fourche de l'éclair, le sens illuminé. Vers la déclinaison et par la flamme qui s'annonce à la vue et à

l'ouïe. C'est le commencement et la transformation, c'est ainsi fort communément que les systèmes changent d'ordre. Une fluctuation, un bruit, une étincelle de hasard et l'état de choses change d'état selon cette séquence juste. J'ai changé de voix et ma langue bifurque, je parle en langue rationnelle.

Quel changement? Supposons une multitude, la voici, elle s'assemble, attirée par les bruits et les voix. Elle n'a aucune unité : venus de Pamphylie, de Phrygie, de Judée, de l'Asie et de Cappadoce, ils sont là, Méditerranéens et Persans. Le bruit, le vent, la rumeur, les voix sont reçus. Mais les langues? Autrement dit, l'événement local envahissant le lieu provoque momentanément la multitude. Un système se forme, seulement pour les grains, les points, les unités, les éléments. Ce n'est pas encore un système. Comment faire communiquer ces monades, Mèdes et Parthes, Élamites, Romains? Quelqu'un se lève et parle. Il parle araméen, grec ou latin. Qu'a-t-il dit? Le traducteur s'avance. D'abord le traducteur persan, puis le truchement assyrien et ainsi de suite. Le schéma est en place. Voici.

Voyez le caducée d'Hermès. Deux serpents s'y croisent, répétitivement. La maille élémentaire du dessin ressemble à un sablier. Un sablier met en relation deux ensembles ou deux multitudes, par l'intermédiaire d'un goulot très fin. On l'imaginera si fin qu'un seul grain y peut prendre place. C'est la place du locuteur. Il parle seul. Il parle seul à quelques-uns, qui, à leur tour, parleront à d'autres, et ainsi de suite. La hiérarchie est installée. Le premier qui parle ou bien le plus fort, etc., impose sa langue au lieu du goulot. C'est le schéma d'Hermès, et c'est aussi le schéma de n'importe quel commerçant. Il met, lui seul, en relation, un ensemble hétéroclite de sujets, de pratiques, et un ensemble hétéroclite d'objets, de marchandises. Il en discute ou fixe le prix. L'important est qu'il ait la place isolée, unique, à l'intersection, au nœud, au goulot des deux tasses du sablier. Celui qui tient ce lieu dessine, à partir de lui, divisions et dichotomies. Celles de la traduction, par exemple : le latin qu'il énonce est traduit en grec, le grec en araméen, le latin, de nouveau, en perse, et ainsi de suite. C'est le schéma naïf des langues qui bifurquent, des langues divisées, clivées, translatées, qui se posent sur chacun de nous. C'est l'organigramme usuel de toutes les archies. Filet de divisions qui remontent vers un point commun. Le bruit, le vent du Paraclet renversent et transforment ce système, le remplacent par un autre, nouveau. Improbable et miraculeux.

Le sablier, maille élémentaire du caducée porté par Hermès, figure des rapports multiple-un-multiple. Beaucoup de langues, un seul orateur, une foule de langues ; un ensemble d'objets, un commerçant, un groupe de clients, etc. Supposons maintenant que n'importe quel émetteur parle en sa propre langue et que tout récepteur le comprenne en la sienne, quelle que soit la langue et quel que soit le lieu. Les relations alors peuvent être dites multiple-multiple, et le réseau qui les dessine est décentré. Sans échangeur ni carrefour. On n'a jamais vu pareil graphe. Sur ses chemins, Hermès agonise, l'échangeur a défait ses nœuds.

Le traducteur se tient au centre ou au foyer du sablier, ou de n'importe quel sous-sablier. Ainsi le commerçant, ainsi le démon de Maxwell. Ils transforment les flux qui passent au sein de l'échangeur. Ils facilitent le passage, ils le contrôlent, ils ont rapport au un-par-un. Une langue pour ce récepteur, une molécule reconnue plus lente, une marchandise pour telle cliente. Tout transite par les mains d'Hermès. Il est placé aux bons endroits, il y a donc de bons endroits. Tout passe par ses mains parce que, peu ou prou, tout se transforme entre ses mains. L'échangeur est aussi un transformateur. Au moins par changement de direction, au moins par division du flux, par bifurcation, au moins par semi-conduction, sens uniques et sens interdits, au moins par aiguillage. Hermès est bien le dieu des carrefours, il est bien le dieu dont Maxwell a fait un démon. Le message, donc, transitant par ses mains, au lieu de l'échangeur, se change. Il n'arrive pas pur ni invariant ni stable. Je veux bien qu'il s'y améliore, mais cela reste un jugement. Et s'il s'y dégradait? Je ne sais, je n'en décide pas. Ce qui demeure sûr est que le message se charge, et qu'il arrive ainsi chargé. En termes propres, il est parasité. Le parasite s'est branché aux lieux les plus profitables, à l'intersection des relations. La maille élémentaire de son activité singulière était d'avoir rapport à une relation, il améliore de beaucoup ses performances aux lieux où plusieurs relations se croisent ou se coupent. Il est aux nœuds de la régulation, et tout à coup, il a rapport au collectif. Celui qui réussit un rapport multiple-un, le forme et le fait fonctionner, celui-là est le politique et il a trouvé le pouvoir. Comme on dit souvent, il tient les lieux de décision : bien sûr, puisqu'il est aux coupures. Ici, aux intersections.

Si l'orateur est entendu tel quel, le réseau se décentre, même localement : il n'y a plus d'intercepteur, il n'y a plus de carrefour, il n'y a plus d'intermédiaire, il n'y a plus de ville, Hermès, père de Pan, est mort le jour de Pentecôte. C'est un miracle, disent-ils, cela n'arrive pas. Je peux dire et ouïr de l'Ouest à l'Est, les murailles s'écroulent sur le coup de vent, sous la rafale de musique. Je puis avoir rapport directement à quelque objet sans qu'un intercepteur s'interpose, j'ai relation ouvertement à l'autre sans qu'un intermédiaire s'intercale ni pour intercéder, ni pour interdire. L'absence de parasite, est-ce si rare ? L'immédiat serait-il si miraculeux ? Faut-il que la parole soit toujours parabole, c'est-à-dire toujours décalée ? Non. Si ce n'est pas miracle, pouvons-nous construire cela ?

Je recommence. Le premier système connu de communication est le système de Leibniz. Il est radical, il est simple. Nul n'a rapport à rien ni à personne, portes et fenêtres non pas fermées seulement mais absentes, tout a rapport à tout par l'intermédiaire de Dieu. Unique médiateur, il est donc tout connaissant et tout puissant. Quels sont les mes-

sages échangés par Dieu entre les monades, c'est
une autre question. Ce système est parfait, il est
mathématisable de part en part, en droit et en fait.
Inversement, cette mathématique est de communication optimale. Tout parasite y est réduit à presque
rien, grain de sable ou de sel, septième. Le problème du mal est ramené à l'harmonie par calcul
d'optimum.

Le deuxième est celui d'Hermès. Il est polythéiste
ou multicentré, chaîne de sabliers, réseau de telles
chaînes. Les anges qui passent, dieux ou démons,
tiennent les carrefours : nœuds d'échanges, de
changement, coupures, bifurcations de décision,
fuseau, faisceau où le multiple vient en une main
unique. Début du politique. Les messages, les flux
transitent selon les énergies et les interceptions. Ce
qui est reçu c'est ce qui est émis, plus ou moins les
parasites. Il arrive que la différence soit considérable : ce qui parvient, parfois, est quasi nul. Les
intervalles ruinent les affamés. Le système de Leibniz est une limite de celui-ci.

Ce réseau peut demeurer en équilibre, pour un
temps, mais il peut fondre, aussi, d'un coup, sous
l'action d'une forte chaleur. Le feu ramène le
désordre. On n'entend plus que du bruit. La
rumeur du vent. En ce commencement nouveau est
la distribution.

Le troisième connecte le multiple au multiple, sans intermédiaire. C'est l'invention du Paraclet, le jour de Pentecôte. Le multiple s'autorégule. Cela est très nouveau, si nouveau qu'on croirait un effet-miracle. Dans le second réseau, les démons et les dieux sont nombreux et connus, roitelets locaux et caïds, petits chefs et petits proxénètes, d'argent ou d'idéologie, de chantage ou d'information, despotes singuliers de rackets régionaux. Dans le premier, tout se passe aux limites, le local file vers le global, et le pluriel vers l'un. Au centre, est sis le Roi, j'entends le Roi-Soleil, le Soleil. Dieu, c'est le nom que Leibniz lui donne. Il est l'universel des communications, il en est la commune langue, l'espéranto, le volapük, la musique, l'algèbre, la caractéristique universelle, ou le *calculus ratiocinator*. Il est le calcul qui, en se faisant, fait le monde. Communiquer ici est calculer, c'est-à-dire coder. Or cet universel peut aussi se nommer l'argent, autre code, autre équivalent général. A chaque dénomination un échangeur, un change unique pour l'ensemble du réseau. Si vous parlez théologie, vous l'appellerez Dieu, si vous discourez comme un économiste, vous direz l'argent, si vous adoptez le langage philosophique, vous traduirez ou plutôt vous expliquerez en usitant des termes comme code, comme équivalent général, et ces traductions laissent tout inchangé, même et surtout lorsqu'il dit : Raison. Nous vivons plutôt dans un univers de rationalités. Ceux qui changent ainsi de langue se battent d'autant plus entre eux qu'ils affirment la même chose.

La question est bien de savoir si on peut construire un réseau sans contraintes de carrefour, sans échangeur, sans intersection où se branchent les parasites. Où un élément quelconque peut avoir rapport à un autre élément sans contrainte de médiation. C'est le schéma de Pentecôte. Il faut décidément écrire une philosophie sans échangeur. Je viens de commencer.

L'ancienne et vénérable théologie du Paraclet recouvre avec quelque bonheur partie de l'anthropologie de l'échange. Quand le Saint-Esprit vient, adviennent les dons. Il est le donateur, *munerum dator,* et ses dons sont sept, *septiformis munere, sacrum septenarium.* Les voies du vent ne sont pas réversibles, le lit remonte vers un point de la rose, le flux n'y revient pas. Le don a une source, elle n'est pas un pôle de réception. Il n'y a pas d'échange. Ce qui en advient est la Sagesse, la Science, l'Intelligence, le Conseil, la Force, la Piété, la Crainte de Dieu. A éliminer de la liste ce qui est proprement divin, restent les caractéristiques de ce que nous nommons l'information.

Le feu, d'où vient le vent, qui vient du bruit, d'où adviennent les dons, est paradoxal. Il réchauffe : *fove quid est frigidum, ignem accende,* il brûle ; mais il refroidit : *dulce refrigerium, in aeste temperies.* De cette source, de cette bouche, soufflent le chaud et le froid.

Les plus usés des mots du monde portent parfois un faste inouï. Nul échange, nul don ne passerait, au moins dans les langues que j'ai ouï parler, si, au bout de la ligne, le récepteur final ne disait merci. Le terminal rend grâce. Le mot n'est qu'un coup de vent, il est pourtant indispensable. Il jette cette grâce dans le bilan du gré. On a connu, sans lui, des cas de guerre : les ingrats contre les magnifiques, les parasites contre les évergètes. A quoi servirait de donner, je vous le demande, si cette reconnaissance minime ne reconnaissait pas le superbe et le géné-reux ? Celui qui remercie, d'autre part, se dégage du poste dernier, un peu difficile à tenir. Avoir le der-nier mot, c'est laisser à l'autre la place finale et sau-ter à la pénultième. Aussi l'hôte ou le donateur se hâtent de répondre : « Avec plaisir, je vous en prie, à votre service », et ramènent, gentiment, le comblé à sa place.

Je n'ai jamais compris ce supplément de révé-rences, avant d'avoir eu l'occasion de l'échanger en grec. Dans les autres langages, le machinal l'avait laissé en noir.

En prononçant merci, l'hellène dit : eucharistie. La bonne grâce. Tout s'éclaire. Ce mot pour cette chose et ceci est mon corps. Je ne sais si ce tour en complément d'échange explique ladite transsubs-tantiation, ou si, inversement, le mystère illumine le quotidien, mais je suis sûr, depuis le rire clair de la paysanne crétoise, qu'il s'agit du même acte et de la même opération. Eucharistie, cette parole vaut la chose, le logiciel descend dans les secrets du maté-riel, Eucharistie, Dieu est dans notre rapport, notre relation est Dieu même, sous des espèces incarnées,

Eucharistie, l'échange finit en prière, et quand nous prions en commun, le Christ est en tiers parmi nous. Eucharistie, le verbe se fait chair et le pain se fait verbe. Εὐχαριστῶ πολὶ.

Παρακαλῶ est, comme on sait, la réplique de fermeture. Je vous en prie, je vous prie et je vous invite. Oui, vous êtes la bienvenue. Je vous appelle, j'appelle, je prie. Qui est l'invité, le prié, l'appelé? Dites son nom, dis ton nom, dis un nom. Παράκλητος, le Paraclet, le nom commun du Saint-Esprit, la troisième personne. Il intervient, il interrompt, il entre en passant les murailles, au milieu du repas ou de la réunion, il intercède et il procède et du Père et du Fils. Il est le vent, l'être du vent, le souffle, celui que les juifs nomment *Ruagh*. Il est don, l'être du don, le donateur universel. Tu dis à celui que tu pries parce qu'il a reçu, qu'il est celui qui donne. Le feu vole au-dessus de l'échange et du groupe, saute de la dernière place à la toute première, boucle la chaîne irréversible, constitue la communauté. Le parasite Paraclet devient l'hôte. A la porte de la salle, ils entendirent du bruit, ce jour-là. Divisé en langues de feu sur les têtes, le tiers, inclus, est désormais à toutes les places. Il est possible que ce feu apporte quelque lumière dans la boîte noire du nous. Hermès est mort, un jour d'interférence.

Eucharistie et Paraclet, la deuxième et la troisième personne ensemble, dans des paroles usagées de la conduite quotidienne : le schéma précédent était, sans qu'on le sache, trinitaire. Et les dieux sont ici.

Sans doute savons-nous, peut-être un jour connaî-trons-nous les choses du monde. Nous ne saurons jamais si elles sont créées ni qui les a créées. Ce mystère est tout à fait hors de nos prises. Il n'est pas du tout sûr que le religieux ait quelque chose à voir avec le monde. Je veux dire avec la physique. Derrière l'épaisseur des choses, celui qu'on nomme Dieu est presque infiniment caché. Nos classiques l'avaient caché sous les conditions à l'infini de la pensée exacte. Cette distance est aussi longue, dans le sujet clair que dans l'objet ombreux.

Je désire dire qu'il y a du divin dans ce monde-ci, des choses divines. Ce que je dis est posé à l'écart de la question directe : Dieu est un substantif, un nom, divin est adjectif, jeté à côté. Le monde est divin, il est plein de choses divines. Cette mer, cette plaine, ce fleuve, la banquise, l'arbre, la lumière et la vie. Je le sais, je le vois, je le sens, j'en suis illuminé, brû-lant. La mer vineuse et la vie divine. L'adjectif, posé à côté, tout à l'écart des noms et des notions de la philosophie, me suffit, comme parabole. Oui, le divin est là, je le touche, ces choses-ci sont des miracles improbables, je n'ai jamais cessé d'aimer le monde et de voir qu'il est beau. Oui, ma philo-sophie est adjective, elle est émerveillée. Le réel n'est pas rationnel, il est improbable et miraculeux.

Nous ne saurons peut-être jamais ce qui passe et se passe dans notre collectif. Ce qui passe est l'objet ou le mot échangé. Que se passe-t-il, à la fin du don ? Les dieux descendent lentement dans cette boîte noire, l'adjectif Paraclet, l'invité donateur, l'illumine d'un jet de flamme. Il n'est pas du tout sûr que le religieux n'ait pas tout à voir avec nos rap-

ports intersubjectifs. Dieu est perdu derrière la physique, Dieu est perdu derrière la logique, Dieu est
perdu derrière les objets, Dieu est perdu derrière le
sujet, intelligent ou pathétique, de la connaissance
ou du sentiment. Celui que mes pères disaient le
Père, infiniment caché, demeure absent. Les
preuves canoniques, par le chemin du monde ou le
fonctionnement de la rigueur, sont hors terrain.
Quand la philosophie n'est pas dans l'objet ni dans
le sujet, ni dans leur rapport désuet, le religieux n'y
est pas pensable. J'ai perdu pour toujours la puissance et la gloire, la toute-connaissance et la surabondante création.

J'habite parmi ces choses, divines, et je suis
plongé dans le groupe, obscur. Elles sont plus faciles
à connaître que lui, je ne dis pas plus simples, car
elles sont exquisément complexes. J'ai du bonheur
dans ce divin des choses elles-mêmes, elles me
poussent vers le panthéisme ; je souffre souvent de
ce groupe et de l'obscurité, dans mon intelligence
et ma vie. Bientôt, pour éclairer le collectif, j'appellerai la notion de quasi-objet. Il circule, il passe
parmi nous. Je le donne, je le reçois. Merci, je vous
en prie. Eucharistie et Paraclet. Nous sommes
seconde et troisième personne, immergés dans
l'incarnation et dans le vent de Pentecôte, laissant le
Père à l'infini, pour l'éternité. La grâce passe dans
le flou entre mots et choses, elle passe entre les
canaux où fluent les nourritures substantielles et les
voix sonores, elle passe entre les échanges d'énergie
et d'information, espace intermédiaire, espace
d'équivalence où naît la langue, où naît son feu, où
elle fait apparaître les choses dont elle parle, écart

instable de l'extase et de l'existence, de l'incarnation et de l'ascension, du pain et de l'oiseau.
J'avance dans la boîte noire, un peu. J'entends l'invitation à demeurer ensemble, dans cet espace où
matériel et logiciel s'échangent. Le troisième apparaît, le tiers est inclus. Peut-être est-il chacun de
nous.

Nouveaux repas interrompus
Technique, travail

Repas de rats

Diode, triode

Le rat de ville se régale avec le rat des champs, l'histoire ne se raconte pas de deux rats seulement. Quelqu'un trouble la fête, interrompt le repas, intervient. Qui est ce troisième homme ? Il fait du bruit et c'est l'ordinaire leçon. Il est assurément une prosopopée du bruit. Le bruit est une personne, c'est la leçon de Pentecôte, il est bien la troisième personne.

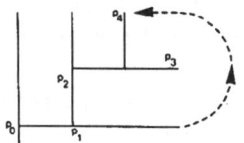

Le banquet en train est une relation des deux rats, relation présentée, presque théâtrale, sur le tapis, et la porte au fond, trouant le décor, mais relation réelle, où l'on croque de l'ortolan et où l'on se fait fête, une relation, croyez-moi, parmi les excellentes possibles. Et le troisième l'intercepte, il la parasite au moyen d'un bruit parasite. Il la fait cesser.

Tout n'est pas dit, pourtant, par ces premières figures. Ce troisième, probablement, était le parasité.

Le maître de céans, tiré de son sommeil par la
course des rongeurs et leur dent sur la carcasse des
oiseaux, revient sur les lieux du festin où traînent la
vaisselle sale et les restes épars. Le système, jadis dessiné, se ferme, soudain. Sur la série gigogne des vam-
pires, le premier, comme à la main chaude, saute en
dernière position et supprime d'un coup les intermédiaires, qui détalent, éperdument. Un beau coup
de feed-back, la gifle sur la joue d'où les moustiques
s'envolent : anéantissement, aplatissement du système. Il n'était rien, ou presque. L'hôte contre-para-
site ses hôtes, non pas en prélevant sur eux sa nourriture, premier sens, mais en faisant du bruit, second
sens. Théorème : si le premier devient dernier, alors
les intercalaires s'annulent.

Question : mais comment se fait-il que le bruit
fasse peur aux voleurs ? Et que les vers, les rats
besognent dans le secret, le silence et la nuit ? Que
cela ne se dise pas ? Obscur rapport entre la chose à
prendre, substance, et les vents et les voix. Noire
épouvante, angoisse, la seule qui ait fait lâcher la
plume à Rousseau, qui ait interrompu ses confessions. Le parasite a peur, l'hôte le sait. Donc il joue
sur l'alarme, il équipe ses pertuis de signaux d'alerte.
Il ne cesse pas de donner le signal. Ainsi chante le
rossignol, aboie le chien, pour définir leur niche et
leur propriété. Le signal et la chose ne sont pas si
coupés l'un de l'autre qu'on dit. Le *Cratyle* se joue à
la fuite des rats au premier bruit du bâtiment. Que la
porte craque un peu et je lâche la pomme. Nul ne
met les pieds en des lieux assourdissants, pleins
jusqu'à la gueule de pierres précieuses. Le signal
d'alarme est d'autant plus fort que le coffre vaut

cher. Voix des dieux, sur les montagnes, dans les éclairs et le tonnerre. Le plus nominaliste de mes contemporains ne peut refuser aux oiseaux d'éloigner de leur nid les coucous, et crie si on le vole. Rapport d'alarme entre chose et signe.

Le système s'annule quand le parasité fait du bruit, en feed-back. Or ce signal ne dure pas. On ne peut passer sa vie à chanter, on ne peut la consacrer à protéger son bien, puisqu'il faut acquérir, réparer, travailler. Faute de quoi, la bise vient et on danse devant le buffet. Le bruit cesse donc un moment, il est fonction du temps, même la cigale s'arrête. Un signal qui ne cesserait pas cesserait par là de paraître un signal. Et donc le troisième homme se retire. Le système, aussitôt, se remet en place. Rats en campagne. Au premier bruit, le système s'annule ; si le bruit s'annule, tout revient en l'état. Cela montre au moins que les parasites sont toujours là, en l'absence du signal. Seul le signal distingué les annule. Ils sont inévitables, comme le bruit de fond. Le bruit de fond est le fond de l'être, le parasitisme est le fond de la relation. Le bruit de fond est l'espace de fond, le parasite est le fond du canal tracé sur cet espace. Le parasitisme n'est qu'un bruit linéaire. Le système est oscillant, on peut aisément le construire. Il existe entier, il retourne au néant, selon le bruit, sa longueur et son temps. Le bruit, par sa présence et son absence, le clignotement du signal, produit le système nouveau, c'est-à-dire l'oscillation. Il oscille deux fois dans le texte d'Ésope, La Fontaine, visiblement, ne cherchait pas cela.

Il y a cependant une condition à cette stabilité variable, à cette invariance par instabilités. Le rat de

ville réinvite le rustique. Si celui-ci accepte, le système se réinstaure, comme j'ai dit, jusqu'au prochain bruit. Or il n'en est rien. Le rat des champs se
défile, c'est assez de ce signal-là. Et il détale à la campagne où le rat de ville ne le suit pas. Donc c'est le
rat des champs qui, maintenant, interrompt le repas.
Ce n'est plus le bruit, puisqu'il a cessé. L'invité
devient alors l'interrupteur. Le parasite au premier
sens le devient au second, car il coupe la relation, il
ne veut pas entendre le message d'invitation. Le
montage du système est un peu plus complexe que
prévu.

   Pour qu'il demeure aussi simple que ladite oscillation, il faut que le rat des champs ressemble au rat
de ville, qu'il apprenne les bruits, qu'il se domestique. Toute l'oscillation provoquée par le bruit tient
à l'égalité des rats, peut-être à leur gémellité. Ils se
ressemblent, ils sont des rats, ils ne sont pas
jumeaux, ils ne sont pas égaux. Mettez cela en équa-
tion, rien n'est plus facile, et le système est construc-
tible. Comme ils sont inégaux, un autre système
s'ajoute au premier. Le rat des champs devient
l'interrupteur, comme le bruit. La relation rompue
est celle du rat de ville et de l'hôte, celle du rat de
ville et du bruit. Car le citadin, mithridatisé aux
agressions de ce calibre, s'écarte un peu et retourne
au repas. Il ne mangerait pas sans cette accoutumance. Il a donc relation continue aux interruptions, elles lui sont familières, il sait les apprivoiser, il
est lui-même acclimaté. Il est vacciné, par les parasites. Son invité du soir rompt tout à coup ces habi-
tudes. Dès lors, le parasite change de place. Qui est,
disais-je, le troisième? C'est le bruit. Certes, et, de

plus, c'était l'hôte, le maître de céans. Maintenant, c'est l'hôte, au sens de l'invité. Le troisième, c'est le second, le second devient le troisième. Le système oscillait, maintenant son montage même se change.

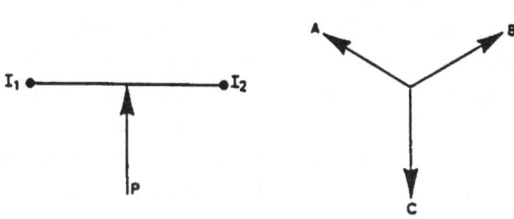

Soit donc deux interlocuteurs et le canal qui les relie. Le parasite, branché sur le flux de la relation, est en position tierce. Jusqu'à présent, le schéma suffisait, c'était la maille élémentaire du système. Or, les positions changent, maintenant. Qui était l'invité devient interrupteur, qui était bruit devient interlocuteur, qui était du canal passe à l'obstacle, et inversement. Les questions : qui, où est le troisième homme ? ont des réponses fluctuantes, en fonction du bruit, en fonction du temps, et aussi en fonction du nouveau rapport, d'égalité ou de similitude, entre les termes. Le même et l'autre changent leur site avec le tiers. Logique bien tranchée, depuis le Platon du *Sophiste*, depuis *le Villageois et le serpent*. Il faut un diagramme à branches indéterminées, où les tranches ne sont pas spécifiées.

Autre exemple. Les rats se ressemblaient un peu,

étant de même espèce, sinon de même lieu, le troisième interrompt la fête. Ce jeune homme, Socrate,
a le nez camus, comme toi, les yeux à fleur de tête,
comme toi, il te ressemble de visage et de corps ;
quant au second, il est ton homonyme. Celui-là, que
je te présente, est un étranger. Ou une étrangère.
D'Elée, de Mantinée, d'ailleurs, non du même dème
comme nos ancêtres l'étaient. Les analogues et
l'hôte, ceux d'ici et ceux de là-bas, ceux du *Banquet*,
ceux qui troublent la fête, celle qui la fait réussir, les
homologues avec l'étranger venu. Pas d'entretiens
sans parasite, obstacle ou dopant. Celui de Xénophon est trop grimacier. Il est grimacier, il est mime.

Or, Simonide est au banquet, il est interrompu,
comme les rats. Il court à la porte, et nul ne le suit.
Le voici, épiphanie, en la présence des divins
Gémeaux. Pollux et Castor se ressemblent à s'y
méprendre. Et la situation, qui fluctuait dans la salle
au tapis de Turquie, se retourne complètement.
Deux rats festinent, un tiers est à la porte et fait du
bruit ; un poète festine, deux hommes, à la porte,
font du bruit ; les rats détalent, Simonide déloge, les
animaux sont analogues et les dieux jumeaux. Les
diagrammes sont antisymétriques. Le rat de ville s'est
trompé : le premier craquement peut précéder la
catastrophe.

Pour l'éviter, le rat des champs fait tourner le
schéma lui-même, et l'invité devient l'interrupteur.
Par la grâce des dieux, le même schéma se retourne
complètement : les interrupteurs sont deux, et semblables, comme des interlocuteurs. Tournent les
positions, changent les rôles et contrôles, mieux vaut
se donner un diagramme à tranches indéterminées.

De nouveau, qui est Simonide? Un invité parmi les autres. Il participe à une communication festive, au festin. Or, poète en odes triomphales, il a payé de mots sa place à table, gré ou dû, je ne sais, il est donc parasite. Est-il du canal, de l'obstacle? Cela ne se décide pas, cela se tranche. Et chacune des branches peut prendre toutes les valeurs. Autrement: Alcibiade interrompt le banquet, fait grand vacarme à la porte de la cour, d'une voix avinée crie à tue-tête, accompagné d'une joueuse de flûte dont on entend la voix, aussi; jeunesse dorée, parasitaire autant qu'on veut, d'économie, de politique, de beuverie, et ici, très finement, sur les opérations de communiquer. Ces bruits désordonnés vont induire dans le système en train une désorganisation, puis un nouvel ordre. Mais les invités de ce symposium sont en train de payer de discours, voix et vents, leur participation à la fête. Ils sont parasites, comme Simonide. Je ne sais plus très bien comment dire, sinon: le parasite parasite les parasites. Autrement dit, n'importe quelle position sur le schéma ternaire est, *ad libitum*, parasitaire. Qui est le troisième? On. Le bruit cesse, *on* se retire. On, à la fois formel et aléatoire.

Logique du flou

Qui donc fait ce vacarme à la porte ? Les dieux, ici venus pour sauver d'un risque mauvais celui qui a commerce au divin par le style. Les bienfaiteurs, les bienveillants, les messagers, les anges. Qui fait ce bruit, ce vent, ces voix, ces langues ? Le Saint-Esprit, le Paraclet, le donateur. L'interrupteur est un intercesseur, favorable.

Non. Dire non aux puissances du bruit pour s'écouter enfin, s'entendre et se comprendre. En arrière, Satan. Éliminer les parasites du canal pour que transite le message, optimalement. Impératif de purge. Exclure donc le tiers, le Démon, prosopopée du bruit. Si nous voulons la paix, si nous désirons un accord au sujet de l'objet, l'objet apparaissant ainsi au moment même de l'accord, à la Cène de même qu'au laboratoire, au dialogue comme au tableau noir, nous avons à nous mettre ensemble, à nous rassembler, à nous ressembler, contre quiconque trouble nos relations, l'eau de notre canal. Il est sur l'autre rive, le rival. Il est notre ennemi commun. Notre collectif est l'expulsion de l'étranger, de l'ennemi, du parasite. Les lois de l'hospitalité deviennent lois d'hostilité. Quelle que soit la taille du groupe, de deux au multiple, et à l'humanité, comme on dit, la condition transcendantale de sa constitution est l'existence du Démon.

Diable ou Bon Dieu ? Exclusion, inclusion ? Je ne sais. Mais je sais, en tout cas, ces questions archaïques. Les luttes à deux ne sont jamais que de théâtre : apparence, représentation, décor, morale, amusements. Dès que nous sommes deux, déjà nous sommes trois, ou quatre. Nous l'avons appris depuis très longtemps. Le dialogue, pour réussir, demande un tiers exclu, notre logique aussi le requiert. Peut-être exigent-ils aussi un quart inclus. Cette leçon ne cesse plus, elle est partout écrite. Saint Georges en face du dragon fait le fort contre son contrefort, tous deux sont associés de fait pour couper en morceaux les corps qui croulent sous l'arche stable de leur pont. Ces logiques à deux, ces batailles à deux, ces dialectiques ne servent qu'aux affiches, aux vignettes, à la montre, à la publicité de ceux qui s'y montrent. Le loup et l'agneau, seuls, chacun sur une rive, peuplent leur espace de chiens, de bergers, de familles, de rois.

Diable ou Bon Dieu ? Exclusion, inclusion ? La thèse ou l'antithèse ? La réponse est un spectre, une bande, un continuum. Nous ne répondrons plus jamais par oui ou par non aux questions de l'appartenance. Dedans ou dehors ? Entre oui et non, entre zéro et un, une infinité de valeurs apparaissent, et donc une infinité de réponses. Les mathématiciens nomment floue cette rigueur nouvelle : sous-ensembles flous, topologie floue. Qu'ils soient remerciés : nous avions besoin de ce flou depuis des millénaires. En l'attendant, nous avions l'impression, avec notre logique raide et nos concepts grossiers, de jouer du piano avec des gants de boxe. Enfin, nos moyens s'affinent et se multiplient. Mon livre est, désormais, rigoureusement flou. La géométrie a fait sa paix avec la finesse.

Le maître et le contre-maître

Le maître et l'esclave, jamais, ne sont face à face. Le maître est assez rusé pour éviter une confrontation qui mettrait en jeu, à chances douteuses, sa maîtrise et sa possession. Cette ruse est la maîtrise même et sa conservation. Le maître a quitté la bataille, aussitôt la victoire acquise. Le maître n'est pas là. L'esclave le cherche sans cesse, le cherche partout et ne le trouve pas. Nul n'a jamais tué un adversaire absent. Le maître est perdu dès lors qu'il est trouvé, repéré. La lutte est rare, elle est un cas exceptionnel, celui où le maître s'est laissé trouver, elle est la figure la plus optimiste de l'histoire. En fait, le maître a peur, il vit comme traqué, il se terre, et se cache. Il expédie des émissaires, il envoie des lieutenants pour se battre à sa place. Que gagne le tenant-lieu et le maître a gagné, qu'il perde et ce n'est pas le maître qui a perdu. Dès que le maître est maître, il a peur de la mort et il vit avec elle, réalité de son pouvoir.

Il a raison d'avoir peur de la mort, car il est assez seul parmi une population rare de maîtres. L'esclave est foule, il est en nombre, il est toujours le plus

grand nombre. Comment très peu de gens asser-
vissent le plus grand nombre, toute l'humanité à ce
très peu près, c'est là le miracle, c'est là l'exception à
toutes les lois. Ainsi est-ce une erreur grossière de
poser le rapport du maître à l'esclave comme le rapport d'un à un, deux héros singuliers en lutte dans la
lice, objet en jeu ; leur rapport est au moins celui de
l'un au multiple, sinon de l'un à la quasi-totalité.
C'est pour avoir conçu ce rapport comme celui
d'individus, ou de singularités, quel qu'en soit le
symbole, que l'inventeur de cette lutte a dessiné là
une figure maximalement optimiste de l'histoire. S'il
y avait toujours ce rapport un-un, il y aurait deux
sous-ensembles équipotents, celui de la maîtrise et
celui de la servitude, qui échangeraient sans cesse
leur jeton, et il n'y aurait ni miracle, ni exception.
Ce ne serait jamais la servitude, mais l'image d'un
titre mis en jeu chaque automne et décerné chaque
printemps, l'illusion d'une gloire sportive, à changements de titulaire. Ainsi la philosophie donne-t-elle
depuis deux siècles le spectacle d'un tournoi médié-
val ou de jeux olympiques, l'opium.

Or il n'en est jamais ainsi. L'oppresseur est rare,
l'asservi est myriade ordinaire. La relation du maître
et des esclaves est toujours une relation de l'un au
multiple. Les classes ne sont jamais équipotentes et
ce n'est presque pas un partage de classes : plutôt le
nombre et la rareté. Le maître exploite, de cet
immense nombre, la puissance positive de vie,
l'énergie et le temps, la production de forces, le travail, et ainsi de suite. La foule produit, le petit
nombre décide et canalise le mouvement. Exploiter
signifie préparer l'espace, décider, canaliser, etc., en

spécifier les stratégies. Les grandes colonnes de fourmis se déplacent, à heures et jours fixes, le long des
routes et des rues, et se distribuent à leurs postes
prévus. Le maître est toujours d'abord géomètre,
topologue, un savant de l'espace, l'empire est pre-
mièrement grand. Le maître sait toujours où passe,
où va passer l'esclave, il a marqué les guichets, il a
signé les passeports. Il arrive pourtant que, parmi les
fourmis innombrables, une rumeur de révolte se
lève, et qu'apparaissent d'autres énergies que celles
qui acceptent de se trouver canalisées vers le travail.
Les esclaves, alors, entrent en lutte avec le maître. Et,
parfois, le forcent à paraître.

Il arrive que la foule se rue. Qu'elle saccage tout
sur son passage. Cela est rare cependant. Il semble
qu'on ait peur de cela. Pourquoi, je ne le sais, mais je
sais qu'on a peur. Et que beaucoup de choses sont
montées pour éviter ce qu'on nomme plutôt un
déchaînement. Cela n'est pas mal dire. En général et
en réalité, le grand nombre *délègue.* Il se lève, parmi
les esclaves, en même temps que la rumeur, un ou
plusieurs héros individuels qui représentent, comme
on dit, la foule en colère ou la classe en lutte. Ils sont
directement produits par les énergies qu'on pourrait
appeler négatives de la masse, non celles de travail,
mais de rébellion. Le maître parasite les unes, et ces
héros sont produits par les autres.

Ils entretiennent, alors, avec leur classe propre,
des relations un à multiple, les mêmes, formellement
d'abord et très vite concrètement, que celles
qu'entretenaient les maîtres et les esclaves. Cet
esclave-là devient maître, c'est vrai, mais loin de
devenir maître du maître, il devient un autre maître

des esclaves. En tant que tel, en tant que représentant des esclaves, il entre en lutte avec le maître. Et celui-ci le reconnaît. Celui-ci alors se laisse trouver. Dès lors, il n'y a plus, entre eux, de relations un à multiple, mais bien la relation un-un, du combat individuel, du tournoi, de la lice. Le maître et l'esclave s'affrontent, à chances égales, ou, au moins, douteuses, Horaces et Curiaces, sous les clameurs des militants, des militaires enrôlés. L'esclave peut alors devenir, tantôt, le maître du maître, et ainsi de suite. Il est, précisément, un contremaître. Un autre maître contre le maître. Opposé à lui et tout près de lui. Dans le flou de son voisinage.

Et c'est ainsi que le maître, jadis, avait commencé sa carrière.

Nouveau repas de rats
Machines et engins

On peut construire avec des bouts de bois, des brins de jonc ou des cordages en chanvre, de petites machines simples qui ont un rapport exquis à l'affaire. Une tortue, boiteuse et lente, comme toute tortue de sa taille, et, de plus, chargée de maison, lasse de ramper sur des parcours petits, voulut voir du pays. Deux canards aiment le projet, ils forgent un engin volant pour transporter la pèlerine. Dans la gueule, en travers, ils lui passent un bout de bois qu'ils saisissent chacun par une extrémité. Serrez fort, disent-ils, décollage immédiat. Le schéma formel se dessine, vu d'ici, à trois mille pieds : les deux oiseaux jumeaux et le parasite, dents accrochées au milieu du bâton. Miracle, disent les badauds, la philosophie, relations et diagrammes, passe très haut sur notre tête. Au-dessus de vos têtes, sots, reprend la passagère, qui lâchant le lien pour jaser, tombe et crève aux pieds des passants. Le parasite doit se taire, même si le bruit de la foule porte sa position aux honneurs suprêmes. Profiter des canards, des pigeons et des dupes, mais n'en jamais dire un seul mot, sous peine de tomber des nues, dans la rumeur désordonnée de la foule disséminée. La machine à babil est mortelle. Et le tiers imprudent ou sottement bavard en est exclu. Et mis à mort d'autant plus cruellement qu'il est très différent des interlocuteurs qui, entre eux, se ressemblent. Engeance aérienne ou pédestre reptile, voyageurs d'air ou d'eau et casanier à maison ambulante, vue globale et plongeante, myopie basse. De quoi se mêle ce troisième ?

Il n'est pas inintéressant de remarquer ici que la machine bien montée ne mime pas le corps des animaux, leur système organique, mais les relations que nous entretenons entre nous. Peut-on concevoir une origine intersubjective des machines simples ? du levier ? de la balance ? de la technique en général ? La réponse à cette question est affirmative. Elle est encore affirmative, pour les machines plus que simples.

Les canards, on s'y attendait, construisent un engin à parasites acoustiques. A varier sur le logiciel, le matériel se change. Par sa parole, la tortue interrompt le canal, c'est-à-dire, ici, le voyage. Cette machine marche si le tiers ne dit rien. Les oiseaux, quant à eux, criaillent et nasillent autant de couacs qu'ils veulent. Mais le milan. L'oiseau de proie rencontre une machine à parasites ordinaires, ceux qui recherchent bonne chère. Une grenouille donc voulut manger un rat, il faut bien, pour arriver là, que ces histoires soient des fables. Soit un rat gros et gras, obèse et sans régime, parasite qui réussit et sans interruption. La grenouille l'invite à dîner, l'histoire prend de l'intérêt : on y mange partout, on y mange toujours, le festin est gigogne : le rat mange sans carême, la grenouille mange le rat, et le milan, bien avant qu'elle le fasse, les mange. Venez chez moi, dit-elle. Mais il faut nager dans le marécage. D'où la machine, l'engin nouveau, le lien. Relation souple, et non raide comme un bâton, un brin de jonc en fait l'affaire, la grenouille et le rat sont liés patte à patte, la première le tire au fin fond des roseaux. Et, déjà, veut le dévorer. Pour cela, fait d'abord, du bruit, brekekekex. Le festin change d'hôte et l'invité de rôle, de sujet du banquet, le rat devient l'objet, de parasite il devient chère. Mon corps n'est que ceci. Est-il vraiment rare qu'on mange l'hôte? La peur, l'angoisse du passant dans l'antre du satyre, est-ce le souvenir de vieux abus anthropophages? Toutes ces histoires recouvrent-elles un oubli du cannibalisme? Et ces banquets interrompus n'ont-ils interrompu que la manducation du semblable par le semblable? Bref. Tout à l'heure, les canards, analogues, laissaient tomber une tortue bavarde et maintenant les reliés, très différents, si différents que, tenus par le pied, ils en viennent aux mains, voient fondre sur eux le troisième. Au lieu d'être exclu, il arrive. Au lieu de crever, il les tue. Et le diagramme est symétrique. Qui est hostile, qui est hospitalier? Tout le monde. Vue du tiers, la chose est toujours double, chacun est bien chair et poisson, hôte dans les deux sens, et ennemi, en outre. Le tiers est exclu, le canal est bon. Le canal est mauvais, le troisième est le maître. Mais, déjà, nous savons comment un sujet peut à la rigueur devenir objet. Or si cela se produit pour l'un, cela aussitôt se produit pour l'autre. Et pour la relation aussi bien. Ceci est mon corps, ceci est mon sang.

Et, tout à coup, je ne sais plus si nous avons
construit un schéma, si nous avons réalisé, de bois ou
de jonc, un modèle de relations, ou si nous avons
découvert, dans cette pratique, l'origine de la technique, de l'outil, du moyen. Ce moyen si bien
détourné. Ces médias qui, toujours, se mettent entre
nous.

Pour une fois, rare il est vrai, Ésope est au-dessus
de La Fontaine. Sa morale naïve amène une déesse
et sa justice et sa balance, et le fléau de la balance, le
joug, l'équilibre du joug. Mais j'en ai vu déjà l'équipage : le milan tient bon au milieu du fléau, la grenouille et le rat sont liés par ce joug. Ainsi de la tortue avec les deux canards. Qui ne voit, dans le ciel,
passer la barre de traction ? Laissons là un moment
balance et justice, morale au sens reçu. Revenons à
l'action, comme on dit. Ou revenons plutôt à toutes
les actions ici rapportées, dont mille se rapportent
depuis que le monde est monde, c'est-à-dire depuis
l'histoire. La relation en jeu n'y est jamais simple,
canal ou chemin, bâton ou canal entre deux
canards, ou n'importe qui. Toujours vient se brancher le parasite. Le parasite est toujours là, il est inévitable. Il est en tiers sur le schéma trivial, sur l'étoile
à trois branches. Voici la relation inanalysable,
j'entends par là qu'il n'en est aucune plus simple.
Voici comment commence l'intersubjectivité. Le
tiers est toujours là, dieu ou démon, raison, rumeur.

Il existe un troisième avant le deuxième. Il existe
un tiers avant l'autre. Comme dirait le vieux Zénon,

je dois passer par un milieu avant que d'arriver au bout. Il y a toujours un médiat, un milieu, un intermédiaire. Et, dans ce jeu à trois, le moyen terme peut tomber sur l'un des trois, selon et selon. Si c'est un homme, il est esclave, il est serviteur, il est domestique ; ou roi, ou proie, ou sacrifié, ou mangé, ou exclu, ou vainqueur triomphal. Aimé, haï ; divinisé, chassé aux enfers ; obstacle ou adjuvant ; cela ne tourne pas forcément deux par deux. Il est l'être de la relation, il en procède, et elle procède aussi de lui. Ses rôles ou ses avatars sont fonction de la relation, la relation en est fonction, en causalité circulaire, en loupes de feed-back.

S'il est un homme, il est tout cela, tortue crevée ou milan à la fête, lion sans rival ou devenu vieux, s'il est un homme, il est tout le règne animal, par ses fabuleuses métamorphoses. Si vous ne reconnaissez pas le parasite, c'est justement qu'il court la fable et qu'il court le système, qu'il se transforme féeriquement. Ainsi le Saint-Esprit parle toutes les langues et chacun le reçoit dans la sienne propre : c'est la métamorphose absolue de l'être de la relation. Il est tantôt légion de rats qui font du bruit dans le grenier, tantôt entourage de roi, et roi, dans les palais où on s'incline. Citrouille et carrosse, souillon et princesse. La fable seule dit cela. Seule la fable et sa métempsycose me permettent de voir le même troisième homme à la niche, dans la cave, à ma table et sur le trône. S'il est homme, il n'est rien, comme un élément neutre, un joker, il n'est rien que ce pouvoir étrange de grimace et de grimage. Ce matin, il défend les humbles, la justice ; à midi, on n'entend que lui, ce soir il prend tous les postes et demain il est roi. Ou autrement. Et ce pouvoir est simplement issu de ce qu'il est la relation et qu'il n'est pas fixé dans l'être, qu'il n'est pas fiché dans une station, qu'il est dans le fonctionnement des relations en ce qu'il est plongé dans leur fuseau, en ce qu'il est relationnel, et donc en ce qu'il est multiple et collectif. Comme il est, sans savoir clairement ce qu'il est, dans la boîte noire du sociétaire, on l'en voit ressortir sous des apparences variées. Il est sophiste et politique. Il a intérêt que tout un chacun soit fiché à sa place et fixé dans son être. La relation mobile cherche à pérenniser la permanence de l'Être. S'il est homme, il est comédien. Il monte les tréteaux, il plante les décors, invente le théâtre, impose le théâtre. Il est tous les visages de l'écran. S'il est homme, il est à l'origine de la comédie, de la tragédie, du cirque et de la farce, des réunions publiques où il recueille le vacarme des légitimités. S'il est homme, il est le joker des systèmes gratuits de collectivités. Il est la technique sociale, il sait jouer à la maîtrise des hommes et à leur domesticité.

S'il est animal, il est domestique. Il fut un temps, dit la fable, un temps qui n'est pas fabuleux, où il n'y avait pas tant de festins ni tant de noces. On ne mangeait pas tant, ni si bien, ni surtout ensemble, avant ce néolithique si miraculeux où furent inventés l'agriculture et l'élevage. Pas de banquets, pas de montures, pas de festins, pas de bêtes de somme. La Fontaine dit en parallèle ces choses dont le parallèle nous instruit aujourd'hui. La noce résulte, bien sûr, de la domestication et de la basse-cour ; où seraient, sans cela, les agneaux, les veaux, les couvées, les poulardes ? Pas de festin sans parasite, disions-nous. Cela s'entend deux fois. Dont la deuxième est bien que l'élevage est, justement, parasitaire. L'écornifleur n'est pas toujours celui qu'on pense. C'est l'invité, c'est l'inviteur, c'est le convive, c'est l'éleveur. Tous nos résultats ensemble, à nouveau. Or donc, un cheval haïssait un cerf et courait après lui, à l'inverse de la grenouille qui, par désir, attirait le rat. Ne le rattrapait point, les cerfs font vite ce qu'ils font. Il appelle l'homme qui se met en selle, qui invente, disons, la chasse, et qui ne libère pas l'étalon après l'hallali. Le même diagramme ne cesse pas son efficace. L'homme en tiers maîtrise le lien, du cheval au cerf. On remarque aussitôt que la chasse n'est pas primitive, on le soupçonnait. Avant la chasse à courre, il faut bien élever des coureurs. Chevaux et chiens, lisez Xénophon au sujet des derniers. Et le parasitisme est bien fondamental, premier dans l'acquisition de ces nourritures indispensables à l'histoire. Le cheval meurt aux écuries où il traîne son lien, ce lien qui s'est changé de haine en servitude, ce lien qui se réoriente du second, le cerf, au troisième, l'homme. L'homme qui invente de toujours jouer le troisième pour devenir le maître. Maintenant, il peut avoir rapport au cerf, parler de chasse et de gibier, puis dire du cheval qu'il est en position troisième. S'il est un animal, il est domestiqué. Il est aux écuries, à l'étable, à la basse-cour, à la porcherie, bref dans une école.

Et s'il est un objet, c'est un objet technique. Depuis quelques moments, je ne parle que de technique : sociale, biologique, c'est-à-dire exercée dans ou sur des systèmes complexes, où la pratique aveugle paraît précéder, de très loin, toute théorie.

Mais cette distinction ou cette précession n'a peut-être aucun sens. Elle est sans doute relative, elle est sans doute dominée par des catégories culturelles étroites. Bref, c'est la même chose, exactement, que de découvrir l'origine et le fonctionnement de la servitude ou de la domesticité, de la domestication ou de l'élevage, et de l'outil ou de l'engin. C'est l'objectivation croissante de nos relations intersubjectives.

Dans ce champ de recherche, théorie de la connaissance, histoire des pratiques, on ne considère jamais que l'ensemble des rapports du sujet, personnel ou collectif, à l'objet, local ou global. Sur ces relations, directes ou inverses, on n'a jamais formé que des écoles ou des sectes, munies d'affiches et de noms, de cuirasses et d'armes de guerre, on n'a jamais trouvé que des contradictions ou des impossibilités, de l'harmonie, des miracles ou des illusions. Ou des banalités vulgaires, comme le prolongement des organes en marteau, lunette ou tenaille. Légèrement obscène. Et naïf : comment cette philosophie de la houe rend-elle compte, je ne dis pas encore d'un ordinateur, mais simplement d'une machine simple ?

Voici, découvert, le moyen. J'entends d'abord par là l'intermédiaire, le milieu. Un tronçon, la queue et la tête : le tronçon de la relation entre tête et queue. Le milieu, le médiat. Ce qui est entre, ce qui existe entre. Le terme milieu, le moyen terme. Le moyen donc, et le moyen pour une fin. Le moyen et l'outil ; l'outil et l'usage ; le moyen et l'usage.

Le moyen, le milieu

A la porte de la salle, ils entendirent du bruit. Que s'est-il passé? Le maître est là, il trouble la fête des rats. Pourquoi? Il dormait, pesamment, sur une digestion d'ortolans, un peu lourde. Soudain, il se réveille. Il a perçu du bruit. Inquiet, anxieux, il se lève, à tâtons il ouvre la porte. Personne. Les rats ont détalé. Un rêve, un songe, il se recouche. Qui donc a fait du bruit? Les rats, tout justement. Un festin fait du bruit. Voici les invités, sur leurs petites pattes, on dirait un tonnerre au-dessus du plafond. Voici les grincements de dents et les grattements des rongeurs. Cela réveille. Le bruit, donc, était appelé par le bruit. A la porte de la salle, il entendit du bruit. Se relève, les rats détalent... Changement de site pour l'observateur.

Autrement. Au festin, les paroles volent. A la porte de la salle tinte un bruit, l'appel du téléphone. La communication coupe la conversation, ce bruit interrompt ces messages. Dès que j'engage le dia-

logue avec le nouvel interlocuteur, le brouhaha
reprend du côté du banquet, il devient bruit pour le
nouveau nous. Le système a basculé. Que je me rapproche de la table, et la rumeur, peu à peu, redevient la conversation. Dans le système, bruit et message échangent leur rôle, selon, par la position de
l'observateur et l'action de l'acteur, mais ils se transforment aussi, l'un dans l'autre, en fonction du
temps, du système. Ils font de l'ordre ou du
désordre.

Ce cas, comme celui des rats, est plus intéressant
qu'il n'y paraît. Dans la salle, il y a deux systèmes, le
festin et le téléphone. Un bruit donné, la rumeur
des paroles, est bruit pour la conversation que je
tiens avec mon interlocuteur au bout du fil, mais il
est message pour mes invités. Inversement, pour eux,
ma conversation solitaire est bruit pour leur rumeur.
Cela dépend de la position de l'observateur. Ce
résultat est connu. Mais d'autre part le signal de la
sonnerie a rompu la conversation de la table : ce système de message s'est effondré dans le bruit. Inversement, il annonce l'échange de message au téléphone, et le bruit ouvre un nouveau système. Cela
ne dépend plus de l'observateur, cela ne dépend
que du temps. Le bruit est la fin d'un système et la
formation d'un nouveau. C'est tout à fait l'apologue
des rats. Le festin est interrompu par l'hôte, et au
redépart les conditions se trouvent transformées
pour le repas ordinaire à la ville et le banquet courant à la campagne. Le bruit les sépare, habitude ou
horreur, et forme un système complexe à deux festins différents. Le bruit est signe de croissance de la
complexité. On suppose que la séparation de la ville

et de la campagne fut décisive dans l'histoire. Il y eut des rats simples et des rats de complexité.

Le bruit est un joker. Il a au moins deux valeurs, comme le tiers : une valeur de destruction, une valeur de construction. Il faut l'exclure, il faut l'inclure. C'est l'histoire des rats, c'est la description d'un système complexe. L'informatique et l'anthropologie sont ensemble sur le même front. Est-ce à dire que l'une, par son intervention technique, va toucher aussi profond que l'autre l'indique, par ses analyses ? Ou est-ce à dire que la science objective ce que les contes de bonne femme disaient depuis si longtemps ? Tout peut se dire en ce nouveau rationalisme qui travaille d'un coup et l'exact et l'humain.

Où suis-je en ce moment ? Je me déplace entre le festin et le téléphone. J'ai trouvé une zone juste, où, à une très faible vibration près, de part ou d'autre de la crête, les bruits se font messages et les messages bruits. Bien entendu, la crête est dentelée, hasardeuse, stochastique. Qui m'observe dans mes déplacements croirait voir voler une mouche. Je me guide au son. Je suis sur les dents de scie de la montagne, aux frontières des bruits. Non point l'écho, non point au centre de tout comme un écho sonore, mais aux marges des messages, aux naissances des bruits. Cette randonnée parcourt exactement les chemins de l'invention. Ces bords sont aussi bords communs aux sciences exactes et humaines. Diode, triode, méthode[1].

1. Cf. *Randonnée, à paraître.*

Les topiques à deux valeurs se perdent en ces lieux. La valeur de l'appartenance passe par l'espace, par le spectre qui sépare ou unit les deux vieilles valeurs. La mathématique du flou explore ce milieu, ce moyen, ce médiat.

Autrement. Tel système est en place. Le festin des rats ou le nôtre, ou n'importe quelle autre organisation. Cela fonctionne et cela fait du bruit. Cela s'use et cela vieillit, cela dérive vers le bruit. Mais le fonctionnement ordinaire est un ensemble de messages. Voyez la conversation du banquet, voyez une machine classique, voyez un circuit de communication, voyez l'organisme vivant. Le couple bruit-message est du système, et son rapport est un indice juste de la bonne marche et de l'âge dudit équipage.

Ce couple et ce rapport sont prélevés par un observateur sis dans le système. D'une certaine manière, celui-ci majore le message et minore le bruit, s'il fait partie du fonctionnement. Il refoule les parasites pour mieux émettre ou recevoir les communications, pour les faire circuler de manière distincte et opératoire. Ce refoulement est aussi bien l'excommunication religieuse, l'emprisonnement politique, l'isolement des malades, l'enlèvement des ordures, l'hygiène généralisée, la pasteurisation du lait, etc., que le refoulement au sens analytique. Mais il s'agit d'histoire aussi, et d'histoire des sciences en particulier : qui fait partie du système en perçoit d'autant moins les bruits et les refoule d'autant plus qu'il est opératoire dans le système. Il ne cesse d'être dans le bon, le juste, le vrai, la nature, la norme.

Tous les dogmatismes vivent de ce partage, aveugle ou décidé.

Il suffit de sortir soi-même du système pour qu'apparaisse évidemment le couple, et pour que le message soit minoré brutalement. On peut s'extraire du système de plusieurs façons : par sa propre différence ou par le geste d'exclusion que je viens de nommer refoulement. Cela n'est pas si simple. Si les systèmes étaient univoques ou mononormés, cette description suffirait. Il n'en est rien. En fait, ils fonctionnent à plusieurs normes à la fois. Preuve en est qu'on y parvient parfois au centre en jouant la périphérie. Autrement dit, on peut jouer le jeu de l'exclusion sans sortir du système et, au contraire, en s'y enfonçant plus avant. Ou inversement : le meilleur moyen d'y faire carrière est de le prendre à contre-pied. Autrement dit : la contre-norme n'est jamais un bruit de la norme, elle est la même norme inversée, je veux dire jumelle. Si vous faites tourner un moteur à l'envers, vous ne le cassez pas, vous fabriquez un réfrigérateur. Depuis Bergson, qui a inventé toute cette affaire d'ouvert et de clos, d'intérieur et d'extérieur, les systèmes se sont mithridatisés en se faisant plus complexes. C'était prévu. Ils se sont renforcés en devenant plus tolérants. Ils sont acclimatés au révolutionnaire, au fou, au déviant, au dissident... Un organisme vit très bien avec ses microbes, il vit mieux, il est aguerri par eux. A la cruauté des systèmes à une norme et à leur geste d'exclusion, il faut ajouter l'implacable pouvoir des systèmes à plusieurs normes, à plusieurs variables groupant chaque fois une norme et sa contre-norme, et leur fonctionnement d'inclusion. D'un côté on tue, de l'autre on châtre. D'un côté on enferme, de l'autre on décore. La tolérance est de la panoplie de l'intolérance. Le génie, alors, ne défait jamais le système, il le généralise, il y introduit une variable supplémentaire, munie de sa contrevariable. Il ne met jamais la science en question, mais un de ses paradigmes ou avatars, et c'est cela, dit-on, la science, la suite rompue de ces avatars. Il ne met jamais la raison ou l'histoire en question, mais l'un de ses moments, ou états, ou cas singuliers, car c'est cela, dit-on, l'histoire ou la raison, la série discontinue des moments. Récupération du simple par le complexe. Mais ce n'est pas, je crois, parce que c'est plus complexe que ce n'est pas la même chose.

Ces descriptions ou ces phénoménologies, parfois logicisées, souvent topologiques[1], répétées depuis presque un siècle sous une multiplicité d'apparences, expriment le système. Elles sont les voix du système. Elles font voir comment le transformer pour le renforcer. Comment utiliser l'exclusion ou la contre-norme pour enrichir une complexité. Supposons un observateur mobile. Il perçoit tout d'abord l'ensemble des messages opératoires, la conversation du banquet. Il s'approche de la frontière. Il a, de plus en plus, la voix du refoulé. La frontière qu'il traverse n'est pas linéaire. A l'extérieur, il

---

1. Ces notions d'ouvert et de clos, de clôture et d'enfermement, qui, depuis Bergson, servent d'opérateurs à la rhétorique d'histoire, ne sont souvent que des représentations dans l'espace, des projections dans une topologie à la Jordan, de la dialectique hégélienne. Au lieu de parler logiquement, on décrit un espace. Mais rien n'est changé par la transposition.

n'entend que du bruit, le brouhaha que font les invités, le grignotement des dents des rongeurs. La frontière est large, elle est la couronne, le tore du renversement. Elle va du message à bruit refoulé au bruit à message refoulé. Le couple fluctue dans le tore. Le tore est l'espace de transformation du bruit en message et inversement, pour l'observateur.

Il en est de même pour tout banquet, pour tout système. Je me suis éloigné de la table (des dieux), j'écoute au téléphone mon nouvel interlocuteur. Auprès de l'écouteur, dans telle ou telle condition, notre message refoule, expulse, la rumeur du repas. Si je m'éloigne, la rumeur se redresse en conversation et le nouvel intervenant devient inaudible. Nouvelle couronne autour du système, nouveau tore, nouvelle bouteille, nouvel espace de transformation. Le festin des rats fait du bruit pour l'hôte, l'hôte fait du bruit pour les rats. Le bruit des uns tire l'autre du rêve, le réveil de l'autre tire les rats de leurs agapes. Je veux dire par là que les systèmes interfèrent.

Les philosophies dont je viens de parler jouent à ce monde imaginaire où il n'y a qu'un seul système, et où celui-ci n'est construit que sur une norme ou un principe uniques. En fait les systèmes sont tous très complexes, en fait, il y en a plusieurs. Elles jouent à ce monde idéal de lumière et d'ombre où il n'y a qu'un extérieur et qu'un intérieur, une ténèbre seulement et seulement une clarté. Ce monde imaginaire est sur la lune. Sans atmosphère, un écran sépare l'espace en noir et blanc, fournaise et glacière, éblouissement aveuglant et opaque nuit. Dans les deux cas, nul n'y voit goutte. Or l'atmosphère, l'air, le milieu, font se diffuser la lumière, elle contourne les obstacles, elle éclaire l'envers des murs, festons autour des sources, dentelles au hasard. Il faudrait habiter au site ponctuel singulier de la source pour n'avoir que la lumière. Ou ôter le milieu. Faire le vide d'air, je ne sais. Dès que le milieu intervient, le rayon cherche sa fortune dans le monde, il court sa randonnée de force chaude et de hasard. On n'y voit jamais que parce qu'on y voit mal. Ça ne marche jamais que parce que ça marche mal. Tout système est un ensemble de messages, pour n'entendre que le message, il faudrait ne faire qu'un avec l'émetteur. Dès que l'amour fuit, reflue le bruit. Dès que le discours d'amour baisse, Alcibiade est à la porte, criant à tue-tête avec sa joueuse de flûte. Dès que nous sommes deux, il y a un milieu entre nous, le rayon s'y perd dans les lames de l'air, le message se perd dans les interceptions, il n'y a qu'espace de transformation. Le tore, la couronne dévorent le système. Il n'est pas besoin de s'en éloigner grandement pour qu'apparaisse le couple fluctuant message-bruit. Peut-être même je n'entends le message que parce que le bruit répand sa rumeur.

Tout à l'heure, je croyais qu'entre les systèmes, dans leurs intersections ou leurs interférences, dans un espace conditionnel où ils se trouvaient tous plongés, les transformations fondamentales s'opéraient. Je croyais que ma méthode était une randonnée dans l'espace transcendantal de plongement. Qu'elle suivait les crêtes stochastiques, la dentelure des sierras, le cheminement capricieux du partage message-bruit. A un très faible déplacement près, j'entends une rumeur ou un message inchoatif, donc la crête est assez aiguë, mais pour demeurer sur elle, il faut beaucoup se déplacer dans la couronne ou dans le tore, ou dans l'intersection de ces volumes.

Ma méthode était bien une randonnée capricieuse, au sens que j'ai donné à ce mot ancien et nouveau, dans l'espace préjugé transcendantal où les systèmes sont plongés.

Or les systèmes eux-mêmes ne sont pas si différents de ce milieu lui-même. Le milieu n'est que le prolongement d'un système particulier. Le transcendantal n'est que le prolongement dans le conditionnel d'un système de singularités. On peut appliquer au transcendantal une analyse de l'espace de plongement. L'espace conditionnel n'est pas si différent de l'espace systématique. Et il est tout aussi relatif.

Espaces de transformation

Lieux singuliers, catégories ou phénomènes, pratiques ou objets ouvrés, placés ensemble sous le patronyme d'Hermès, tels étaient les espaces de transformation rencontrés d'abord.

L'interférence est un phénomène pour l'ouïe, le regard, la physique, c'est une métaphore et un art d'inventer. L'échangeur est un immeuble où les mobiles, invariants, sont triés quant au sens, par cela seul qu'ils se déplacent, une sorte de van à plusieurs trémies, où la transformation n'est que cinématique. Au carrefour, les morales branlent autour du col de décision, parfois des meurtres sont commis, et la bifurcation, d'espace et de logique, monte soudain au fantastique, et se charge de vieilles histoires où la parole est au plus près de sa naissance : on y change sa raison de vivre, on y change aussi de raison tout court. Le discours parle du parcours et suit ses erres. Le puits, le pont, le labyrinthe... sont vignettes ou figurines, jeux, stratégies, hasards et chances, circonstances, monuments bâtis ou construits, phénomènes aussi puisque la mort vient rôder dans la suite, mais fantasmes encore et pourtant théorèmes

exacts de changements de phase. Riche série
d'espaces divers, séparés, pour multiples transformations, peut-être la plus riche ou la plus baroque. A
l'inverse, l'espace nu et chaotique de la lande nor-
mande, à Lessay, perd un peu, perd beaucoup des
attributs trop définis d'un dieu trop déterminé
quoique mobile, pour devenir simple, à la fois formel et concret. Comment passer la lande aux chemins obliques et aux références perdues? Comment
passer la mer? Qu'est-ce que passer la mer? Images.
L'espace de transformation comme tel émerge de ce
bric-à-brac d'abondance, dont le mérite reste d'avoir
pris en écharpe, en traverse, en diagonale, bien des
distinctions usuelles et sottes de la philosophie. La
traduction est, à la fois, une pratique et une théorie,
la turbulence un phénomène stable-instable, où le
fluide passe et demeure dans une forme hasardeuse-
ment fixe, l'organisme, mon corps, est maintenant,
un échangeur de temps. Sur le stigmate du présent,
plusieurs chronies se nouent. Je n'avais jamais rencontré, peut-être, que des espaces de transformation,
lieux singuliers ou variétés étales. Dont la plus
simple, absolument, est le vide, le vide où les atomes
tombent, où, tout à coup, claque l'éclair du clinamen : soit un ordre amené à son état élémentaire,
éléments de distribution pour un élément d'ordre,
vide purgé de toute détermination, soit un transformateur amené à son état élémentaire, soit un
opérateur minimal, différentielle d'angle, le plus
petit des changements de sens. Alors paraît un
deuxième ordre, volume dans la chute de fond
amorcé par une volute petite accrochée à l'étincelle
éclair de hasard. L'espace de transformation est ici

amené aux premières simplicités, presque à l'état
zéro, dans le théorique et dans le concret; de là,
pourtant, se forme un système global, un monde
parmi l'univers des mondes. L'écart de performance
est aussi large que l'origine est voisine de rien et la
phase finale proche de la totalité. Soit la séquence :
une distribution, un signal, un système. Le bruit de
fond-chaos, un clin d'œil, le monde. Ainsi l'espace
de transformation revenait à la physique et à des
phénomènes usuels pour le regard ou l'ouïe.

Les états changent de phase, les systèmes
changent d'état, par des transitions de phases ou
d'états. Mais à considérer le système lui-même, il
n'est jamais stable. Son équilibre est idéal, abstrait,
jamais atteint. L'état, au sens premier du mot, est
hors le temps. L'état est le contraire de l'histoire,
celui-là tente de bloquer, de figer celle-ci. L'état est
l'adversaire mortel de l'histoire. Et il peut la tuer.
Nous n'en sommes pas loin. Le système, au sens premier du mot, est rare dans le temps. Il s'avance
comme la poutre sur le mur décharné quand les
vents se déchaînent et que la terre tremble. Il tombe,
il ne tombe pas, il se redresse, il tombe. Il s'use, il se
dégrade, il est délité par le flot. Agrégation, il perd
comme un vase tissu de fissures. Un miracle réunit
ses fragments et fait flamboyer sa synthèse, le temps
le désagrège lentement. C'est cela exister, faire face
à la mort, être en écart perpétuel à l'équilibre. Ces
flux, ces flots, ces fleuves ne cessent jamais de courir
ces terres lacunaires. Pour les dévorer, les parasiter,
les nourrir et les faire vivre. La chute nous tue et
nous crée. Nous dérivons sans faute vers le bruit,
mais nous venons du bruit. L'oxygène alimente la

chaleur de nos vies, mais le vieillissement est une oxydation. Ça marche parce que ça ne marche pas. Le système est très mal nommé. Peut-être n'y a-t-il pas, n'y a-t-il jamais eu de système. Dès que le monde est né commence sa transformation. Le système en lui-même est un espace de transformation. Cela est général. Il n'y a que des *métaboles*. Ce que nous prenons pour équilibre n'est qu'un ralentissement des processus métaboliques. Mon corps est échangeur de temps, il est parcouru de signaux et de bruits, de messages et de parasites. Il n'est pas exceptionnel dans le vaste monde. Cela reste vrai de l'animal et de la plante, de l'air et du cristal, de la cellule et de l'atome, des groupes et des objets construits. Transformation, déformation d'information.

Je croyais que les échangeurs étaient des intermédiaires, que l'interférence était à la frange, que le traducteur se plaçait entre les instances, que le pont reliait deux rives, que le parcours allait de la source au but. Il n'y a pas d'instances. Ou plutôt les instances, systèmes, rives, etc., sont à leur tour analysables en échangeurs, parcours, traductions et ainsi de suite. Il n'y a d'instances ou de systèmes que des boîtes noires. Lorsque nous ne comprenons pas, lorsque nous remettons notre science à plus tard, lorsque la chose est trop complexe pour les moyens du jour, lorsque nous plaçons tout dans une boîte noire temporaire, nous préjugeons qu'il s'agit d'un système. Quand nous pouvons enfin ouvrir la boîte nous la voyons fonctionner comme un espace de transformation. Il n'y a de systèmes, d'instances, de substances que de nos ignorances. Le système est le non-savoir. L'autre côté du non-savoir. Le non-savoir a un côté chaos et un côté système. Le savoir ponte ces deux rives. Le savoir comme tel est un espace de transformation.

Toute cette question est fractale.

Leibniz avait déjà dit le réel fractal, formé d'étangs et de poissons, pleins, à leur tour, de poissons et d'étangs, cela ne cessant pas. Mandelbrot le redit du monde, en inventant le mot et, sans doute, la chose. Je le dis du procès de la connaissance.

Repas de lune

Qui est le meilleur, le plus fort et le plus rusé, du renard ou du loup? Je crois, quant à moi, qu'à jouer à ce jeu de compétition, qu'à jouer au plus fin, au plus puissant, au plus cruel, ces espèces ont disparu et vont laisser les hommes seuls à jouer encore à ce même jeu, de la destruction. Mais avant qu'il n'y ait plus de loup ni de renard, on pouvait se poser la question de l'intelligence. Cette question, tout justement, a tué les renards et les loups. Ésope a élu le goupil et La Fontaine élit le loup, les professeurs aiment cela, classer. Je les crois bien équivalents, et je crois que cela dépend. Tantôt c'est Achille, tantôt c'est Ulysse, tantôt penche la balance dans ce sens, tantôt elle change ses poids, vire au guindeau dans l'autre sens. Ce jeu est une machine qui va et vient, comme une pesette oscillante. Et c'est notre fléau.

Nous savons tous que, nue, la vérité réside au fond des puits. C'est là qu'il faut l'aller chercher, dit-on. Ce fut, un soir l'avis de Renard, après Thalès ou l'astronome. Penché sur la margelle il vit, pâle dans l'eau, la lune, ronde et pleine, qu'il prit pour fromage. Affamé, il saute dans un seau qui dégringole, dans un vacarme de ferraille, et qui efface le fromage dans un petit réseau de risées. Sa famine s'attise de cette stupide illusion. Comme la vérité s'enfuit des lieux où on la croit blottie! Bref. Renard meurt de faim pendant une petite semaine. Un beau soir, par le télescope à vue directe sur le ciel, il voit Maître Loup sur la même eau penché. Voyez le beau fromage, lui dit-il, j'en ai mangé un morceau de quartier, je vous invite à manger l'autre. Sur un tapis aquatique, le couvert se trouve mis. Prenez donc le deuxième seau par quoi vous ferez le voyage. Le loup descend par la machine qui remonte et sauve Maître Goupil. Qui était le plus bête? Voyez donc la balance : le renard la semaine passée, Maître Loup aujourd'hui. Bête? Que non pas. Qui croyait dur comme fer, et plus dur que l'autre, que la vérité pure et nue se trouvait là où on le lui avait enseigné? Cela fluctue, cela oscille.

Je ne veux plus jouer. Ni au jeu du plus fin, ni au jeu de la vérité. On y meurt de faim, de froid, de noyade. Je veux manger du bon fromage. Non pas du meilleur, ni du vrai, racontés aux miroirs de l'image. Et je veux être sage. Et je veux ma petite part du banquet, l'objet.

Ils sont trois. Le goupil, malin, et le loup, stupide. Ils sont trois, deux idiots et la lune. Qui est le plus fort, qui est le plus sot? La réponse à cette question tourne comme le treuil. Pendant que la balance branle, pendant que le trébuchet change et varie, douteux, pendant que la lutte à chances égales, à meurtres partagés, à issues réversibles, guinde l'histoire vers sa fin, pendant la durée de l'échange, l'échange d'armes et de ruses, de mérite, d'argent, de coups, de pouvoir, de paroles, de blessures, d'injures, de victoires et d'écrasements, de cadeaux, de lauriers, de caresses, de sang, de horions et d'assassinats, pendant l'échange qui n'en finit pas, pendant que le renard pendu vire le loup au haut et que le loup, niais dans le seau, guinde en haut le goupil, pendant que les sujets jouent à la balançoire, à se tuer de faim, à s'enterrer vivants, l'objet-fromage, lentement, monte au ciel ou descend au puits, devient une illusion, une image, une idée. On ne mange pas une image, on se combat jusqu'à la mort pour une idée. Plus la lutte fait rage, et plus longtemps elle dure, plus disparaissent les objets. Dans un monde blafard de lumières et d'ombres, la guerre continue. L'histoire.

Ils sont trois. Deux symétriques et en rapport de forces, en alternance, en phase, comme la lune. Le maître et le quartier-maître. Qui donc croyait qu'en manœuvrant le treuil, tantôt dessus, tantôt dessous, ils finiraient par assécher le puits aux chaînes de la vérité? ou l'histoire, par leur tourniquet dialectique? Non, ce sont des dragueurs de lune.

Échange sans usage, et sujets sans objet.

Valeur d'abus.

Autrement. Les deux sujets du même désir sont infiniment éloignés de l'objet. Autrement. L'objet disparaît, illusoire, par clignotement des sujets, ou par leur meurtre réciproque. Autrement. C'est un festin, c'est un banquet interrompu. Autrement. Ce rapport entre les sujets peut être infini. On n'a jamais vu un seul treuil dont la chaîne soit infinie. Lorsqu'elle est déroulée, il faut, à nouveau, l'enrouler. Lorsqu'elle est enroulée, il faut la dérouler. Cela tourne, éternellement. Comme la lune. Autrement. Plus il y a guerre, plus il y a représentation. Inversement. Plus il y a représentation, plus la lutte fait rage. Autrement. La dialectique est la logique de la phénoménologie. C'est-à-dire de l'apparence. Lune, images de lune.

Autrement. Deux parasites parallèles n'ont à manger que d'illusions. Enfin : hyper-enfer des Danaïdes où les condamnées-sœurs se placent dans le seau.

Repas du seigneur au paradis

Je veux, pour un moment, parler du paradis. Soit un carré d'oignons, d'oseille, d'aubergines. Je dis mon goût, je tiens que le gourmand a ceci de commun avec les habitants du paradis persan qu'il aime le jardin, le jardin est son rêve. Il est facile, quasi vulgaire, d'aimer les sucres et les viandes, d'aimer les fruits et les gibiers. Mais la fève, le pissenlit, le haricot et le navet! Le haut goût est légume. Le reste est l'entourage, l'accompagnement, la cour de la reine aubergine. Je m'égare. Voici le jardin et alentour des plates-bandes, l'espace était aménagé pour les fleurs de Margot, le bouquet dans sa tête, et la senteur des draps. Oignons et jasmins, la table et le lit, une seule fête, peut-être un seul jardin. Je m'égare encore, mais il s'agissait d'un festin.

Quelqu'un de nouveau a troublé la fête, c'est le repas interrompu. Le lièvre mange la laitue. Je soupçonne le bon La Fontaine de vouloir dire, outre ce qu'il dit, que le rongeur dévaste les carrés, ce que je dis aussi, savoir qu'en un repas, la viande et même le gibier dérangent un peu bien le légume. Laissons cela. Qu'il dérange aussi l'amour à Margot. Laissons

cela, vous dis-je. Il faut exclure le gêneur. Il est parasite, parasite de la relation du jardinier à son jardin,
à son légume, à sa Margot. Il faut chasser le parasite.
Le lièvre prédateur qui fait le parasite, comme un
homme.

C'est le bon emploi du verbe chasser. Pousser
dehors, débusquer, déloger. Congédier, purger,
refouler. Nous refoulons ce qui nous gêne. Ce qui
est refoulé, mais qui reste et demeure, parasite
encore la communication. Il faudra bien revenir là-
dessus. Le lièvre est en tiers, il doit être exclu. Il doit
être chassé. Je crains qu'on ait ici une origine de la
chasse. On ne chasse, je crois, que ce qui doit être
chassé. On chasse, au second sens, les animaux
qu'on chasse, au premier. Au fond, il y a deux sortes
d'animaux, ceux qu'on invite et ceux qu'on chasse.
Les hôtes et les expulsés. Les domestiques et les sau-
vages. Le loup et le chien, au col pelé par le collier.
On dit de l'hyène et de la grue qu'elles furent
domestiquées puis chassées de céans. Pourquoi ? Je
ne le sais, mais l'hyène, a-t-elle appris à cette occasion des conduites parasitaires, charognardes ? Il y a
les bêtes que nous parasitons, et celles qui risquent
de nous supplanter, que nous chassons, que nous éliminons par conséquent.

Ce refoulé me revient, il parasite ici mon propos.
Telle force vient en tiers, que je refoule. Ce peut être
mon père, ma mère, mon enfant, nous avons appris
à tourner sans arrêt sur l'étoile à trois branches. Ce
peut être ceci qui rompt la communication. Ce peut

être un parasite au sens de la biologie, cet enfant que le père élève, nourricier, qui mange à la table du maître, qui gazouille gracieusement; que la mère a porté, qui suçait le cordon et le sein, que la théorie charge des péchés du monde. Qui veut tuer son chien dit qu'il a la gale. Acarus ou sarcopte parasitaire. Pervers polymorphe, assassin de papa, violeur de sa mère : c'est le massacre des Innocents. Cacher l'Abraham par l'Œdipe, le bélier par l'enflure des pieds. Ce peut être le parasite au sens acoustique, fauteur de lapsus et de cuirs. La théorie analytique, obscurément, cherche, elle aussi, à rendre cohérents les trois sens de notre concept. La santé serait-elle silence des organes? Et la maladie fait du bruit. Ça parle tout le temps, ça fait sans cesse du bruit à la porte pendant que nous sommes en train, ça ne cesse de gratter dans le grenier pendant notre sommeil, on se lève, on y va voir, il n'y a rien, on se recouche et ça recommence. La fête est troublée, le repas interrompu, toujours. Allons, déplaçons-nous à la campagne, où l'angoisse n'a rien corrompu encore : déplacement vers un lieu purgé de parasites. Hélas! ce sont les rats qui s'y déplacent, et cela recommence. Le parasite est bien ce refoulé, ce chassé qui revient toujours : voyez les rats, voyez le lièvre. En campagne tout aussitôt. L'autre se rit des pièges, des pierres, des bâtons. Expulsez-le, il retourne en ce lieu, inévitable. Sans doute, je trouve là une définition forte de la fonction parasitaire. Elle est inéluctable et comme nécessaire. La force qui l'exclut se renverse aussitôt pour la ramener. Ce qu'on refoule est toujours là.

Vous ne pourrez en fait le chasser qu'à la condi-

tion d'un autre parasite. Un parasite chasse l'autre, il
le supplante. Le seigneur parasite Miraut qui chasse
le bouquin. Cherchez le parasite qui rétablit la santé
altérée. Altérée par un autre. Théorie ou pratique,
ensemble de discours parasites, et parasités.

Que nous étions heureux, Margot, t'en souviens-tu, quand nos problèmes, comme on dit,
n'étaient pas résolus.

Cela est général. Il n'y a jamais de silence, pris à la
rigueur. Le bruit de fond est toujours là. Si la santé
se définit par le silence, la santé n'existe pas. La
santé demeure le couple message-bruit. Les systèmes
marchent parce qu'ils ne marchent pas. Le non-
fonctionnement demeure essentiel pour le fonctionnement. Et cela peut être formalisé. Soit deux stations et un canal. Elles échangent, comme on dit,
des messages. Si la relation réussit, parfaite, optimale, immédiate, elle s'annule comme relation. Si
elle est là, si elle existe, c'est qu'elle a échoué. Elle
n'est que médiation. La relation est la non-relation.
Et c'est cela, le parasite. Le canal amène le flux, mais
il ne peut s'effacer comme canal, et il freine le flux
peu ou prou. Or la communication parfaite, réussie,
optimale, ne tiendrait plus compte d'aucune médiation. Et le canal disparaît, dans l'immédiateté. Il n'y
aurait plus, nulle part, d'espaces de transformation.
S'il y a des canaux, alors il y a du bruit. Pas de canal
sans bruit. Le réel n'est pas rationnel. La relation
optimale serait la relation nulle. Par définition elle
n'existe pas ; si elle existe, elle est inobservable.

C'est le paradoxe du parasite. Il est tout simple,

mais de grande conséquence. Le parasite est l'être de la relation. Il est nécessaire à la relation, inéluctable par le renversement de la force qui tente de l'exclure. Or cette relation est la non-relation. Le parasite est être et non-être à la fois. Non pas être et non-être qui sont des noms (ou des non-noms) de stations; mais flèche et non-flèche, relation et non-relation. D'où ses métamorphoses, et la difficulté de le saisir. L'ancienne topique s'appuyait sur une ontologie, celle-ci est de la pure, de la simple et de la seule relation. *Le Sophiste* et *le Politique* sont intérieurs au fonctionnement des *Dialogues*. De même le *Banquet*, l'ancien, et celui-ci, aussi. Pardon : le sophiste et le politique sont intercepteurs de toute relation en général, ils sont la relation même et, je l'ai dit, le collectif. Le parasite est être et non-être, relation et non-relation. Ainsi le politique, par exemple. Rien n'existe plus que lui, puisqu'il est toujours là, dans nos relations et le système où nous vivons, et pourtant rien n'existe moins que lui, puisqu'un certain bruit le fait immédiatement disparaître, au-dessus du seuil de son accoutumance et de la nôtre. Il est lui-même un bruit du système qui ne peut être supplanté que par le bruit. Ainsi le bruit, je passe ici des sciences humaines aux sciences exactes et inversement, mon discours demeurant invariant, ainsi le bruit est chute dans le désordre, ainsi le bruit est le début d'un ordre. J'y reviendrai, inévitablement.

Nous repartons au paradis, en persan, l'enclos du seigneur. Il faut en exclure le lièvre, il faut en chas-

ser nos premiers parents, qui ont mangé, tout justement, le fruit à l'arbre du seigneur. Banquet interrompu, le tout premier festin. Ils sont déjà tous là,
en groupe, à l'aube de l'histoire. Les deux, bientôt
nus, de la relation, où l'autre est tellement même
qu'il est tiré de la côte du même, le tiers intervenant.
Les hôtes parasites sont chassés. Il faudra revenir au
paradis perdu, où les tiers sont Diable et Bon Dieu.
Que je sache, eux y sont restés. Je connais maintenant le chemin pour y revenir, il n'est plus ni perdu
ni promis. Ce lièvre est sorcier, dit le demi-manant à
son seigneur à lui, roitelet du bourg, demi-bourgeois
et demi-hobereau, roitelet du bourg mais surtout de
la chasse, il est sorcier, vous dis-je, il se joue de ma
force, il se rit de mes ruses. Il est sorcier, le mot est
bon. Il est Diable, nous y voici, nous voici revenus en
des lieux connus. René Girard nous a enseigné comment le chassé devient Dieu, comment il devient
Diable aussi. En équilibre sur la crête, pas encore
expulsée, devant l'être bientôt, pas encore victime et
se gobergeant à loisir, à plaisir, en attendant la mort,
le lynchage dans la foule et le tintamarre, la bête est
à la fois Dieu et Diable : sorcière. Elle est en tiers,
elle est le moyen terme entre le jardinier demi-
bourgeois et son jardin ou sa Margot, et elle a les
moyens, la capacité, le pouvoir de tenir tête à ses
assauts. Elle a un pouvoir thaumaturge. Qui ne peut
être supplanté que par un autre pouvoir thaumaturge.

Je reprends plus haut, en feed-back. Soit deux stations et un canal. Elles échangent, comme on dit, des messages. Or le nécessaire du canal, c'est le tiers. La relation est là, en troisième, et elle est là, première. Il n'y aura d'échanges possibles qu'à la condition, évidente, d'instaurer une relation. Donc le troisième homme est bien préalable à l'échange. Antérieur et conditionnel. Le parasite précède l'échangeur, le cambiste, je ne sais comment le nommer. La relation parasitaire précède l'échange en général. Il y a toujours un lièvre dans le jardin. Il y a toujours eu un lièvre, même lorsque le clos était en friche, que Margot était vierge, et que personne n'était là. Pour la simple raison que celui qui ramasse l'herbe pour les lapins est un lapin aussi, et que le jardinier bourgeois et manant est aussi un lièvre, en quelque manière. L'un fait des trous et l'autre des sillons. Et c'est pourquoi la relation d'échange est toujours dangereuse, que le don y est un dommage, et qu'elle peut croître jusqu'à la catastrophe. Elle passe avant tout sur un terrain miné. Les choses échangées transitent sur un canal déjà parasité. La balance de l'échange est tarée, elle est montée sur un fléau. L'échange est toujours calculé, compte tenu d'une relation sans échange, abusive. Le terme abusif est un terme d'usage. L'abus n'empêche pas l'usage. La *valeur d'abus*, consommation complète et sans retour, précède les valeurs et d'usage et d'échange. C'est simplement la flèche dans un sens et un seul.

Donc, le Quirinus des laitues, parasité par le Jupiter des bouquins, thaumaturge, va quérir aussitôt le Mars du château proche, le suzerain de son enclos.

Où l'on voit se constituer la théorie des trois fonctions où chacune, je crois, parasite le rapport des deux autres. Elle est montée sur notre diagramme à trois tranches. Je n'en suis pas très sûr encore, faute d'avoir examiné assez ce qu'est un producteur. Un producteur, est-ce un reproducteur ? Il ne serait aussi que parasite. Il y a là encore toute une ruche de questions. Mars arrive aussitôt que requis, l'ange à l'épée de feu, c'est son métier de chasser, aux deux sens de ce mot. Va-t-il se jeter, à la course, rapide et léger, sur les traces du lièvre ? Lisez Xénophon l'admirable, vous y verrez, surprise, les nobles grecs courir le lièvre, à pied. Courir après un tel coureur, je voudrais voir mes contemporains, cuirassés comme pour Azincourt, et armés jusqu'à la moustache, pour exterminer ce qui est déjà mort, Tartarin plus le Bourgeois Gentilhomme plus Tintin au Congo quand il s'agit de safaris, je voudrais enfin les voir courir derrière l'antilope, la gazelle ou le phacochère. Ils deviendraient joueurs d'échecs et ne saccageraient plus notre monde. Je m'égare, toujours courant à la suite du parasite. Non, le seigneur ne bouge pas, tout aussi peu que le chasseur français. Il lance Miraut sur le lièvre. Tiens, le chasseur est parasite. Et il est parasite, d'abord. Non pas seulement le chassé, mais le chasseur, vous dis-je. Il fait faire au chien (respectivement au faucon, à l'épervier) ce qu'il ne sait ou peut pas faire. La chasse est tout d'abord un art cynégétique. Le mot le dit : conduire des chiens. Des chiens, une meute, des chevaux, des oiseaux de proie. Chiens, chevaux et valets, tous gens bien endentés. Le seigneur, le chasseur, est un Mars pour la frime, ou plutôt Mars n'est que la guerre par esclaves interposés. Comme le chasseur a des chiens, le guerrier a des hommes. On ne les appelle hommes que dans ce cas. Taïaut! Miraut. Debout, les morts!

Deuxième festin. Le premier, je l'ai dit, était de légume. C'était celui de Quirinus. Je crains que ce n'ait été aussi celui de Caïn, cultivateur du sol, et donateur sacrificiel de prémices florales. Végétarien. Le deuxième est de viandes, pour Mars : on fricasse — de quand sont vos jambons ? — de viandes et de vins. Abel est passé là, l'élevage a supplanté l'agriculture, on offre en sacrifice les prémices du troupeau. Quirinus est double, au moins. Ici, se rapproche de Mars, sanguinaire mangeur de viandes. Ce repas ne sera pas interrompu. Le seigneur est, pour le moment, le parasite le plus fort.

Le seigneur parasite Miraut pour attraper le lièvre, parasite le jardinier pour caresser Margot, parasite la production pour manger à sa guise. C'est bien la parabole du cheval s'étant voulu venger du cerf. Il commande chez l'hôte. Toujours ce beau mystère de l'invité du maître qui devient le maître du maître.

Entendez maintenant pourquoi la chasse à courre a besoin de musique, et pourquoi le cor sonne faux. Il annonce à grands fracas au gibier apeuré que ce n'est pas l'homme qui chasse, mais les chiens, les chevaux, les faucons, bêtes mieux éduquées. Il annonce de loin son tintamarre parasite. Allons, disons le mot, il paie de mots, de sons et de signaux. Il paie de logiciel son bénéfice matériel. Comme la mouche, il fait du bruit. Excite les chiens et chevaux de la voix, souffle au sifflet pour le faucon, et donne de la trompe et du cor, pour que détalent, rapides, les rats.

Je dirai, nous aurons à dire ce que signifie propre, lorsque nous possédons une terre, un jardin, une niche. Il faudra dire aussi après Rousseau ce que signifie le clos et l'ouvert. Le jardinier possède un jardin propre et le clos qui le jouxte. Il ne fut pas le premier, je le crois, à fermer cet espace et à dire ceci est à moi. Ceci est à moi parce que c'est fermé. Ceci n'est plus à moi, est moins à moi s'il y a un trou dans la haie, non pas un trou mais une plaie. Ce jardin est un peu mon corps, ou le prolongement de mon corps propre. Il est en ordre, et il ne sera plus à moi, il sera moins à moi dans un état piteux. Il faudra revenir sur ce propre.

Le jardinier propriétaire fait croître ses légumes pour le potage et ses fleurs pour le sein de Margot. Je dirai plus tard que si l'éleveur est parasite de la faune, de partie de la faune, l'agriculteur parasite, à son tour, partie de la flore. Ou mieux il est parasite de leur reproduction. La production des systèmes vivants est leur reproduction. L'agriculture et l'élevage sont des pratiques parasitaires de la reproduction des vivants. L'arbre et la vache nous ont dit que l'homme jamais n'avait rendu ni reconnu les dons de flore ni de faune. Il en use et abuse, il n'échange pas avec elles. Il donne à manger aux bêtes, dites-vous? Oui-da, il donne de la flore à la faune, de la faune à la faune, de l'inerte à la flore. Que donne-t-il, de lui? Se donne-t-il lui-même à manger? Celui qui le fera, dira une parole immémoriale. Une parole unique, d'hôte. Ou d'hostie?

Le jardinier n'a que son corps et les prolongements de son corps, comme on dit en philosophie, je veux dire en classe. Il jardine, le potager pour le potage, il élève cochons et poulets, pour les jambons et pour la fricassée, il garde Margot près de lui. Je ne sais plus qui est Margot, maîtresse ou fille. Le jardin de Vénus, ou le jardin de mon père, les lilas sont fleuris. Je suis perdu, dans ce carillon de jardins. Il court le lièvre, il le court comme il bêche les planches ou appelle le coq. A la main, à la voix. Au moyen de bâtons et de pierres. Il fouaille le terrier, lapide le bolide qui boule. Cette chasse, directe, est inefficace. Il le chasse au moyen de pièges. Si j'ose dire, aux pieds. Le piège est pédieux, on le sait. Œdipe. Je n'ai pas le temps d'en parler tout de suite. A suivre. Pourquoi ces chasses ne sont-elles pas efficaces? Parce que le manant ne dispose ni de Miraut, ni de chiens, ni de chevaux, ni de valets, comme en a le Bourgeois Gentilhomme. Le seigneur chasse-t-il? Je ne sais pas, non plus. Je ne sais ce que c'est que chasser. Qui sonne et crie dans le grand tintamarre à courre? La trompe et le cor. Qui galope? Le cheval. Qui force et mord? La meute. Qui organise la battue? Les valets rabatteurs. Celui qui chasse enfin fait donc tout sans rien faire. J'aime de plus en plus les élèves de Xénophon. Qu'échange le chasseur avec les chevaux et les chiens, les valets, les sonneurs, les piqueurs et les louvetiers? Avec les fauconniers? Que fait-il ici, le seigneur? Ce que fait le jardinier. Mars et Quirinus seraient-ils jumeaux?

Le seigneur et le jardinier ne sont pas si différents qu'a voulu nous le faire croire, à l'école primaire qu'elle avait fondée pour que nous y croyions, la bourgeoisie toute-puissante. Elle nous pousse encore à prendre la Bastille, les châteaux et les évêchés, pour que nous n'ayons pas l'idée simple de prendre son pouvoir absolu et ses coffres-forts. Le jardinier demi-manant est un demi-bourgeois ; le seigneur est du bourg, demi-bourgeois et demi-noble. Ces demis se rapportent ou s'additionnent. Quand naîtra le bourgeois, il agitera le noble (et le clergé) comme leurre au nez des manants. Il jouira en tiers de leur lutte inutile. Il parasitera un combat vain parce qu'achevé, archaïque, entretenu par lui, et mis par lui au-devant du décor. Il peut donc arriver qu'une classe dominante jouisse en paix d'une lutte des classes. Jeu à trois où l'un fait jouer les deux autres.

Ici l'intersection seigneur-jardinier n'est pas vide, ils sont tous deux bourgeois ensemble. Je recommence : le jardinier parasite les choux, de cela le seigneur s'abstient. La noblesse ne serait-elle ni potagère ni légumière ? Le jardinier, toujours, parasite cochons et poulets, le seigneur les chevaux et les chiens, tous animaux dans les deux cas, comestibles ou non comestibles. La différence, ici éclate aux esprits, elle est dans la médiation et la médiation seulement. Chevaux et chiens sont des médiats, des médiateurs, que sais-je. L'homme des jardins est de l'immédiat. Les choux venus vont à la soupe et les cochons gras au saloir. Belle, déjà, la médiation de leur attente. Il faut déjà différer le désir, pour cultiver, pour élever. Il faut déjà différer de manger, pour choisir la semence ou croiser les races, biner,

repiquer, nourrir et châtrer. Le jardinier, comme
parasite, est déjà l'homme du médiat. Mais du
médiat portant directement sur ce dont il s'agit à
table. Le porc et le chou pour plus tard mais tout de
même le porc et le chou. Morale de la fourmi, non
de la cigale. La cigale vient d'échouer, elle n'a pu
payer, de son chant d'été, mouche ni chou pour passer l'hiver. Danger de jouer le médiat sur le médiat.
La cigale est expulsée, comme parasite reconnu. Or
le seigneur chante, lui aussi : sonne de la trompe et
du cor, siffle ses chiens, excite ses chevaux, tout un
tintamarre étonnant. Il est seigneur des médiations.
Et c'est pourquoi d'abord il laisse les légumes. Que
faire avec la flore, sinon aller au but, directement,
sans boucle : manger. Le maître diffère de manger à
un degré de plus que le jardinier. Il diffère de différer. Celui qui diffère est toujours le maître. Voici le
moment des cigales, voici le temps venu où la cigale
gagne. Où le mot, où le bruit, où la voix, où le cri
vont l'emporter sur la substance et sur la chose. Le
seigneur a le temps, il attend. Il ne stocke ni porc ni
oseille, ni le chapon ni l'aubergine, il forme des
meutes, il peuple l'écurie. Le chien va où le maître
dit, le chien revient, porteur de la perdrix, le cheval
court, il saute, il galope et trotte, le maître siffle, crie,
chante, appelle, nomme. Nuit et jour, à tout venant,
il chante, ne vous déplaise. Il expérimente la puissance du logiciel. Il dresse, il dompte, il mate. Il
dresse les chevaux et les chiens qui dressent les
oreilles. Il dresse les valets et les gens les uns contre
les autres. A la voix. Le jardinier a la main, le seigneur a la voix. Que sont les chevaux ou les chiens
par rapport aux bêtes de basse-cour? Des relations.

Plus forte est la voix, plus longue est la relation. Chevaux et chiens la multiplient parfois jusqu'à l'inaccessible : je veux dire le monde. Le jardinier met la
main à la pâte de l'immédiat. Le seigneur fait porter
sa voix à distance de médiat. Le jardinier ferme son
clos où tout est à portée de main. Le seigneur troue
la haie pour que passent les chiens, pour établir des
relations, pour sortir du jardin à cheval. Maître de
l'enclos, maître de l'ouvert. De quoi fut le vrai fondateur le premier qui, ayant troué une haie qui fermait
un enclos, s'avisa de dire : ceci est mon passage, et
trouva des jardiniers assez faibles pour le croire, et
pour le laisser faire, voire pour l'appeler ? Opposition du voyageur et du casanier, du pasteur et du
paysan, du droit de passage et du droit de propriété.

Mais il y a deux agricultures. La deuxième est celle
des fleurs, si la première est celle du potage. On diffère encore de manger, pour un autre motif, plus
doux. Le bouquet de Margot, le jasmin, aussi, est
une relation. De nouveau, elle est assez proche, bientôt elle est immédiate, elle est l'immédiateté même.
Il y a deux agricultures, mais il n'y en a qu'une, au
bout de tous les comptes. Cela s'appelle la culture.
La nappe et le drap.

Mais il y a deux élevages. Deux élevages irréduc-
tibles. Celui de la basse-cour et celui de la chasse à
courre. Pour manger, pour courir après celui qui
sera mangé. Celui de la basse-cour et celui du travail.
Pour manger, pour préparer de quoi manger. Il y a
deux parasitages. Le premier, plus direct, quoique
très astucieux et retors, le second, plus médiat, thé-
matise la relation, la complique, l'élève aux relations
de relations. Comme si on inventait là le para-para-

site, comme si on décalait le décalage, comme si on s'écartait encore de l'écart. Ruse première, et ruse de la ruse, cela bientôt n'en finira pas. Faire d'abord, puis faire faire. De la main à la voix, de l'aveugle au paralytique, le redoublement passe au logiciel. Cybernétique, de nouveau. Tout à coup, je vois qu'il n'y avait pas de travail avant qu'il n'y ait eu un commandement. Le jardinier jouit, sans son seigneur, il jouit de l'oseille, il jouit de Margot. La fruition du fruit. Bien sûr, cette valeur d'usage est totalement idéale, elle est exactement paradisiaque. Il faudrait, pour qu'elle ait lieu et temps, la fermeture absolue du système. Or il est ouvert, puisque le lièvre est advenu. Qu'il y ait toujours un lièvre au jardin, un pou de vigne dans les pampres, ou un serpent au paradis prouve qu'ils sont ouverts. Il faudrait ôter toute relation, monade sans trou ni porte. Encore ne ferait-elle pas d'usage, puisqu'elle n'aurait plus aucun rapport avec cela dont elle jouit. Elle tirerait tout de son fond. Cela dont on jouit, on a rapport à lui, donc on le parasite. Le revenu, le fruit du jardinier, ne revient jamais à qui l'offre. C'est un beau mensonge que de le nommer revenu. C'est un abus de mot, et c'est l'abus des choses. L'originelle relation est d'abus. Elle ne cesse pas. Elle est contemporaine de la relation, elle est la relation même, et l'ouverture du système. Pour entrer au jardin, de quel droit, je vous prie, le lièvre et le serpent ont-ils pratiqué une porte? Par ce trou est passée l'histoire. Par ce trou sortent le cheval et le seigneur. Par cette porte-plaie sont sortis nos premiers parents, éveillés blessés de leur réjouissance éternitaire, tombes de leur envol supralapsaire. Le système est ouvert, c'est

le seul réel, il y a toujours des relations, et des parasites. Le trou, la médiation, pour aller loin, avec les
chiens, sur les chevaux.

Je suis ici, seul, dans mon jardin. Mon carreau et
ma planche sont ma page blanche, ma houe est ma
plume, j'aligne des sillons pour l'ensemencement. Je
suis cultivateur, comme mon père, à bureau fermé, à
champ clos, nous ne faisons de mal à personne. Vouloir faire du bien est si cruel, souvent. J'avoue n'avoir
jamais travaillé, j'ai cette chance inconcevable,
inouïe et miraculeuse, d'ignorer le travail. Là,
croissent à plaisir l'intuition et la joie. Un bonheur
de plume, parfois, faire un bouquet pour sa fête à
Margot. Je n'ai jamais cherché plus loin que le
potage, un cordonnier pour les enfants et du dessert
pour le dimanche. Beau, mon beau doux jardin de
ferveur, de prière continuée, mon attente de l'aube
et l'espérance de lumière. Avant le jour, je suis tendu
vers la révélation, blanche. Le temps est dense,
incandescent. L'espace est transparent. Je vois le sourire innombrable du monde. Je ne travaille pas, je
voudrais être au paradis. Mais la haie fourmille de
plaies. J'écris. Par exemple, il faut bien que je
nomme, comme Adam les premières bêtes. Et le tintamarre commence, messages et bruits. Le tohu-
bohu d'où tout est venu n'a jamais cessé. Il traverse
l'espace et le temps. Le désordre engendre l'ordre et
le traverse. Nous ne bougeons pas, ni moi ni Margot,
et pourtant mille seigneurs sont là, que nous n'avons
point appelés, qui nous proposent de chasser le
lièvre du désordre. A la porte de ma salle, ils font du
bruit, interminablement. Ils traversent à cheval cette
page, lancent leur meute dans mes mots, leurs bat-

teurs, leurs sonneurs, leurs piqueurs dans mes phrases. Du coup, je travaille. Et je travaille à mort pour qu'il reste du transparent dans tout ce gâchis, pour sauvegarder un peu de lumière dans ce salmigondis. Je suis chassé du paradis, je travaille, je vais mourir, noyé par le désordre, j'accouche au milieu des douleurs, j'ai perdu l'immortalité.

Le travail

Qu'est-ce que le travail? Sans aucun doute, il est lutte contre le bruit. Si nous laissons faire sans intervenir, les écuries s'encombrent de fumier, le renard vient manger les poules, et le phylloxéra traverse les mers pour assécher les feuilles des sarments. Le canal se charge de vase. Vous voyez bien, à basse mer, ce port comblé de sable. Bientôt, les vaisseaux ne passeront plus. Les choses se mélangent, n'agitez donc pas, ne tournez pas la cuiller, le sucre fond dans l'eau, inévitablement. Il y a, parfois, des mélanges qui nous arrangent, mais la plupart sont obstructions ou embarras. Travailler, c'est trier. Le démon de Maxwell est inévitable, tout autant que le parasite. Hélas! ils sont peut-être des jumeaux. Il existe un fondement objectif du travail. Sans lui, la dérive temporelle vers le désordre ou la complexité serait plus rapide. Contrairement à tout ce qu'on dit, en philosophie classique et contemporaine, les hommes ne sont pas les seuls à travailler. Nous ne sommes jamais si exceptionnels. Les animaux travaillent, les organismes vivants aussi bien. Je veux dire que la vie travaille. Qu'elle est vie par la lutte contre la tendance à la mort, par le tri, par l'activité du démon de Maxwell. L'organisme reçoit de l'ordre et de l'énergie, les triture, les trie, les classe et reforme son ordre propre et sa propre énergie en éliminant les déchets. Un meunier fait-il autrement? Le traitement des granulats de fleuve est-il une autre activité? Qu'est-ce donc qu'une production quelconque, en usine? On dira que nous projetons dans un système naturel notre propre organisation du travail. Peut-être. J'ai tendance à penser que nous ne trouvons pas ici une cause et un effet, mais deux effets parallèles ou un cercle de cause-effet. Bref. Je ne vois plus la différence entre l'abeille et l'architecte.

L'œuvre, tout à l'heure, coule de moi comme du miel, comme le fil de l'araignée, je ne sais de quel ordre externe j'ai nourri cet ordre second, mon corps est un transformateur de soi, mais aussi un transformateur pour cette cire de langage, sécrétion longue issue de mes cinq doigts, je travaille comme une bête, je ne travaille pas, ça vient à loisir, à plaisir, comme je me doute qu'une bête fait quand elle est conduite par son instinct, quand elle est, comme on dit, une bête à ceci, une bête à cela, je m'extravase, exactement, et c'est l'extase, l'écart à l'équilibre tout ordinaire du vivant. Je suis une abeille ou une araignée, un arbre. Je ne vois plus la différence entre l'œuvre et la sécrétion. Mais le bruit est aussitôt là. Dans les actes mêmes où un ordre se pose et se range. Le tohu-bohu de l'état zéro, avant le jour premier, perdure le long de la semaine, et traverse le paradis même. La toile d'araignée perd les angles de ses spirales, les carrés d'oseille et de choux sont écornés par le lièvre, il n'y a pas de miel sans cire ni de discours sans de l'obscur. Mais, de nouveau, il ne s'agit pas même de cet état second. La fabrication même de l'ordre, la sécrétion, l'organisme même qui se charge de la production sont en lutte, pour exister, contre une rumeur qui ne cesse pas, contre un entraînement vers la mortelle fortune des mélanges. Travaillent donc éperdument à déplacer vers un amont de cet entraînement le point d'application des forces en jeu.

Les systèmes vivants sont en travaux, sont des travaux. L'acte d'écrire ce livre et la vie de celui qui l'écrit sont une seule et même action. Cette écriture même et ce corps. Porter l'aussière sur la bitte amont par rapport au fleuve qui coule. Travail mécanique : déplacer le point d'application de la force ; thermodynamique : remonter l'entropie ; informationnel : pouvoir distinguer les deux points. La vie, le système organique, est cette page même, la vie est ce carré de choux, ces ruches et ces toiles, ordres fragiles, frêles, prêts à se déliter, qui refusent la déjection. La mort est toujours d'accepter la mort. La mort est la fin de l'œuvre. La vie est œuvre, simplement, et l'œuvre est la vie même.

Certaines ombres errent, pâles, cadavres sans œuvre, dans un monde semblant aux arrière-mondes, quasi déjà morts, et d'autant plus avides, assoiffés, du sang frais de ceux qui produisent une œuvre. Innombrables aspioles, brucolaques sans nombre, attachés en paquets grouillants sur les corps assez rares des ouvriers, de ceux qui ouvrent. A chaque œuvre majeure est rattachée la descente aux enfers comme indice sûr qu'il y a œuvre. Dès qu'apparaît un Homère, un Virgile, un Platon, leur corps odysséen traverse les champs blêmes où les âmes boivent le sang. Tous sont des hôtes. Ils se donnent eux-mêmes à manger ou à boire dans leurs propres écrits. A leurs contemporains et à leurs successeurs. La vie a tant besoin d'œuvre qu'il faut, pour survivre, ou la faire soi-même ou la chercher ailleurs. On peut accepter d'être tributaire. C'est ainsi que le parasite se condamne lui-même à mort, se condamne au moins à disparaître si Ulysse ne passe pas. Celui qui fait une œuvre a rapport à la vie, marche entre ciel et sol, sort des abîmes infernaux quand il le décide, connaît le chemin qui délivre des souterrains, le chemin de l'œuvre. Les grands corps pâles sans œuvre, rivés à la mort, attendent, sous les plaques de marbre, que les vivants passent à leur portée. Ils organisent un enfer tout à fait policé, où ils condamnent des populations entières à vivre sans œuvre, ils les condamnent donc à mort, et ils condamnent les vivants, tout liés à leur œuvre, à leur donner leur chair et leur sang. Ils ont accepté la mort, la leur et celle des autres. On peut toujours accepter que les veines s'envasent, comme les ports et les canaux. On peut accepter que la communication se tarisse. Dès que Prométhée dépose le feu, un aigle lui déchire le foie. La mort est toujours un suicide. Les démons de Maxwell suspendent leurs travaux.

La vie travaille, la vie est œuvre, la vie est travail, énergie, puissance, information. Il est impossible de transposer la description en un discours éthique. Il en est ainsi, en effet, doit-il en être ainsi, je ne sais. Le travail de la vie est une œuvre et un ordre, mais il ne se fait pas sans emprunter ailleurs de l'ordre. Il fait de l'ordre ici mais en défait un autre là. Et il renforce le désordre et le bruit. C'est un travail considérable de chasser le lièvre de son jardin, pour que l'ordonnance des laitues soit améliorée, mais le seigneur fait du dégât, ce qui veut dire qu'il s'installe à demeure, pour faire sa cour à Margot, dévorer les jambons, supplanter l'amateur du jardin. Il s'y installe comme un lièvre, mais comme un lièvre carnassier. Un parasite chasse l'autre, comme un désordre chasse l'autre. Le seigneur ne pillera pas l'oseille, mais la cour et la basse-cour. Le parasite remplaçant change de registre. Il change d'ordre, il ajoute une médiation. Il mange les poules qui picorent le grain. Il dévore la faune qui dévore la flore. Non qu'il change de lieu dans le jardin même, mais il ajoute une boucle de plus dans le système parasitaire. Il en accroît la complexité. La Fontaine évalue en nombre cette mutation. Une heure du second vaut un siècle de toute l'espèce. Comme si un individu était une espèce, comme si l'unité de son temps valait l'histoire : un siècle, une ère, une époque d'histoire, de l'espèce à quoi il est comparé. On change d'ordre au sens que ce mot prend lorsqu'on dit ordre de grandeur. Le parasite humain est d'un autre ordre par rapport à ce parasite animal : celui-ci est un, celui-là est ensemble, celui-ci est temps, celui-là est histoire, celui-ci est jardin, celui-là est province. Détruire un jardin ou détruire un monde.

Les choses ne sont pas encore morales, mais elles deviennent sérieuses. Cultiver son jardin, mais tout d'abord ne pas détruire le jardin, ne pas laisser le jardin se détruire. Le mot grec pour dire l'ivraie, ou la mauvaise herbe, est le mot zizanie. Introduire la zizanie, la mauvaise herbe, le lièvre enfin. Ce livre, on l'a compris, est le livre du mal, le livre du problème du mal. Ne chassez pas le lièvre, il vous y faudrait toute la compagnie Saint-Hubert. Ne chassez pas le lièvre, vous finiriez comme saint Julien. Qui fut chasseur, puis hospitalier. Qui, à force de chasser tous les animaux, se mit à inviter les hommes. Qui, à force d'exclure, se mit à inclure. Bonjour, le lièvre, reste ici. Tant qu'on a la chance d'avoir un lièvre, de n'avoir qu'un lièvre dans son jardin, autant faire bon ménage avec lui. On n'extermine pas les microbes, voilà une sagesse, on en fait du fromage, on ensemence le lait de ces pestilences pour en tirer l'ambroisie des dieux. Le lièvre est un sorcier, un diable, mais — que diable — un bon diable. Tous les autres sont pires, je crois. La tolérance commence dès ici, et la morale, peut-être bien. Jupiter, Mars et Quirinus étaient interchangeables. Ils ne savaient que chasser les parasites.

Je voudrais savoir qui détruit le jardin. Décidément, il y aurait deux types de travail. Les moralistes de la société du travail deviennent, ces jours-ci, dangereux.

Que nous étions heureux, Margot, t'en souviens-tu, quand nos problèmes, comme on dit, n'étaient pas résolus...

Nos parents ont été exclus du paradis. Je l'ai quitté aussi, nous avons tous été chassés. Plus nous chassons, plus nous sommes chassés. Plus nous excluons, plus nous sommes exclus. Or, nous passons notre vie à exclure.

Nos parents ont été exclus du paradis. Tu travailleras, tu accoucheras, tu mourras. Répétitions ou redondances.

Le petit d'homme né ou naissant est chassé par sa mère. La naissance est une exclusion, l'accouchement est un congé. Ostracisme, quarantaine, bannissement. Puissent les dieux faire que tout exil soit une naissance, et tout renvoi un accouchement. Le petit parasite protélien est éliminé par sa bonne hôtesse. Il est chassé du paradis.

Le vieillard, le mourant, l'accidenté, l'agonisant quittent le festin de la vie. Voici qu'ils remboursent au cycle de l'azote, au milieu, à l'environnement les quatre atomes de base qu'ils avaient empruntés, plus quelques terres rares, dont ils étaient pétris. Retour au monde et seul paiement. Revenir aux poussières élémentaires, cesser brusquement de parasiter le banquet vital. Le moribond est exclu alors de l'hôte-monde. Il est chassé du paradis.

Entre ces deux congés, entre ces deux repas, nous ne cessons de travailler comme j'ai dit : exclure le mildiou pour boire le vin de la vigne, exclure le lièvre pour manger l'oseille au maigre ou au gras, ôter le désordre et le bruit des choses pour imposer notre ordre à nous. Ne cesser de chasser des êtres de leur paradis, ne cesser d'en être chassé par les autres.

Répétitions et redondances. Il n'y a jamais eu qu'une seule malédiction. Elle recommence, indéfiniment.

Etre chassé des abords de cet arbre. Etre exclu du savoir. Un interdit est ce qui est dit « entre », au milieu du canal. Le parasite est toujours là, entre l'être et l'acte de connaissance. Le serpent indéfiniment déroulé, enroulé, entre nous et le monde.

Je quitterai la vie comme je me suis levé mille fois de table. J'aurai perçu un bruit, à la porte, il interrompra le festin, je le reconnaîtrai. Je ne sais pas si une cloche sonne ou si une voix retentit, je ne sais si un souffle de vent fera le signal. Je sais que je comprendrai.

Il faudra que je me retourne, un moment. Avant de suivre cet éclat, chercher des yeux mon hôte, et lui sourire, être courtois, ne pas quitter les lieux sans avoir dit merci à qui m'a invité.

Ai-je été, à mon tour, un hôte convenable? Ai-je assez payé cette chance, d'être ici assis, dans le jour et la nuit, par quelques paroles volantes, par des notes allègres, par des mots ou des sons tenus? Ai-je assez soutenu la conversation? D'un coup, maintenant, je peux tout rembourser, peut-être. Vite, un instant court où la voix vaut la vie.

Merci à qui? Où êtes-vous, mon hôte? Qui donc m'a invité ici? Je ne vois que des étrangers, comme moi, tout autour de la table, que des dîneurs qui vont, ce soir, rentrer chez eux. Vide, absente est la place du maître de céans. A qui donnerai-je enfin l'instant d'équivalence dense?

Mon dernier détour de regard est fini. Jamais plus, jamais plus je ne pourrai dire merci. Jamais je ne dirai assez merci. Merci pour les hasards, merci pour ce miracle, pour la mer turbulente et l'horizon flou, merci pour les nuages, pour le fleuve et le feu, merci pour la chaleur, la ferveur et les flammes, merci pour les vents et les sons, pour la plume et pour le violon, merci pour ce repas immense de langage, merci d'amour et de souffrance, pour la douleur et la féminité... non, je n'ai pas fini, je commence, je commence à me rappeler qui je dois remercier, je commence à peine mon chant de réjouissance et mon tour de table est fini.

Je suis l'éclat, le bruit, le vent. Aveugle, ébloui, assourdi. Je commençais à peine, en larmes, à dire le merci, l'équivalent de grâce.

Je vous en prie, souffle le bruit, le vent, le son, qui résonne derrière la porte. Je vous prie et je vous invite, soyez le bienvenu.

Repas d'insectes

Aventures de la cigale au guichet clos de la fourmi. Elles sont archaïques par rapport à celles du lièvre et à celles des rats, et peut-être à toutes les autres, préhistoriques même. L'échange du chant et du grain y est évoqué, mais y est impossible. On y reste à la distinction des substances propres à nous réparer quand nous sommes vides et creux, les solides, et les vents, et les voix. Au lieu de chanter, amasse des vers. La fourmi n'entretient pas à sa table une joueuse de flûte ou un chanteur de folk. De ces voix qui ne cessent d'occuper l'espace. Elle exclut donc le parasite. Cette histoire est d'un classicisme imprenable. Le congé donné à ce parasite ne coûte rien. La chasse au lièvre coûte le seigneur, c'est-à-dire l'asservissement. C'est follement cher. La chasse à la cigale coûte un mot, c'est presque gratuit. Vous pouvez, dit le sauvage, reprendre votre chemin. Un geste. Le passant ne s'accroche pas, la cigale ne colle pas. On ne sait pas encore le retour du refoulé. Le nettoyage est encore naïf. Nul ne vient remplacer, nul ne vient supplanter la cigale qu'on envoie danser. Autrement dit, la fourmilière est un système propre. Le réel de

la fourmi est rationnel, peut être rationnel de part
en part. Le coût du travail est nul. Le travail est tout
bon et seul bon, il fonde une morale. La fourmi est,
bien sûr, un démon de Maxwell. La fourmi exclut les
cigales et elle inclut les vermisseaux. On pourra
dire : l'éthique de Maxwell. La morale est gratuite.
Elle est morale sous cette présomption de gratuité.

La fourmi est chez elle, la fourmi est rationnelle et
la fourmi travaille. Elle travaille en chassant le
désordre. Elle a constitué de l'ordre, elle a classé les
grains, les mouches, les vermisseaux, elle a chassé
chanteuses et danseuses, elle a bâti la cité collective
par sa propre collecte et par ses collections : grandes
villes bien administrées, gérées à la perfection. On
remarque aussitôt l'équivalence du travail à la police.
Le démon de Maxwell trie les laissez-passer, il est
douanier. Éliminer le bruit est bien le but des deux
activités. Toute société fondée sur le travail et sur
l'économie est policière, ce n'est rien de dire qu'on
le sait depuis Ésope, l'homme le sait depuis la
fourmi, l'hominité le sait depuis l'effondrement
d'élan vital de certains animaux collectifs dans l'instinct mécanique de la vie sociétaire. Ouvrières et soldats. La fourmi qui parle à la cigale, ici, est de la sol-
datesque, mais elle porte en avant la morale de
l'effort, du stockage et de l'ordre. Gérer un stock,
c'est à la fois travailler à un ordre et exclure. C'est
aussi remonter le temps de l'hiver à l'été.

Les cités animales n'ont plus que des consomma-
teurs, des soldats et des ouvriers. C'est une société
rationnelle de part en part. Ésope a-t-il su qu'il
représentait ainsi le travailleur dans son geste exact,
l'économie dans sa bestiale essence ? Travailler, c'est

toujours chasser la cigale ou chasser le bourdon, amasser, stocker, gérer, organiser les flux, cela se ramène en dernière analyse à éliminer les cigales. Nous devinons ici notre horizon, l'entrée dans les ténèbres de la termitière parfaite, l'effondrement dans le rationnel animal. Animal raisonnable, animal politique, animal en tout cas. Retour à l'archaïque fabuleux, retour au préhistorique rigoureux. Économistes, policiers, travailleurs, tous définis d'un coup comme des éboueurs.

La fourmi travaille, la fourmi est chez elle dans la raison pure. Elle a formé un système ou une cité, en fabriquant de l'ordre. Cela n'a pas de fin, il faut éliminer le désordre, pour cela travailler. Non, la fable n'est pas naïve, elle saisit la fourmi en instantané, en un instant donné, dans le cours de son geste. Le travail ne cesse pas, il faut des armées de soldats pour éliminer les cigales, des armées d'éboueurs pour ôter les déchets. C'est-à-dire des travailleurs, et des économistes pour optimiser l'ensemble de ces gestes. On espère que le système sera propre, à force d'éboueurs. Un jardin assez propre et le clos attenant. Nous serons chez nous, enfin, quand il sera bien propre. La théorie stercoraire de l'origine du droit de propriété le prévoit. La propriété collective doit être propre comme l'œil. On travaille jusqu'à l'épuisement pour enfin habiter chez soi. Le monde est habitable quand il est propre. Approprié à nos us et mesures. La philosophie a pour but de rendre le monde habitable. Elle ne parle donc plus que de l'ordre et du désordre, du travail, de l'économie. Combien faut-il d'énergie à ces démons formiques de Maxwell pour éliminer les chanteuses et les danseuses ? Combien consomment-ils, ces soldats revêtus de chitine noire, pour exclure les ordures ? Tant et tant qu'ils produisent beaucoup de bruit, donc beaucoup de désordre à éliminer. La fourmi qui mange et ne parle, parle pourtant pour chasser la cigale. Elle produit des parasites en les éliminant. Il y a du mouvement perpétuel dans le travail et l'appropriation du monde, et c'est pourquoi il passe, dans les philosophies traditionnelles, pour moteur de l'histoire. Demain dimanche, vous serez chez vous dans la terre promise, où le miel et le lait circuleront à suffisance. Chez vous, c'est-à-dire au pays de vos propres ancêtres. Pourquoi donc ce détour immense, puisque là étaient nos parents ? Je vous l'ai dit, voyons : ils en avaient été chassés. Sans doute par quelque éboueur. Tout à coup, le travail n'est plus gratuit, le travail a un coût, un coût d'énergie, de puissance, de temps. Et de déchets. Un coût de travail. Il faut travailler pour pouvoir travailler. La morale, donc, se déplace, et toutes les questions.

La fourmi travaille, la fourmi sera chez elle, la fourmi est rationnelle. Je voudrais bien savoir ce qu'il en est de la raison, à ce compte. La raison pure est en inflation. La pureté, inaccessible, accroît ses prix.

Énergie, information

Si tout le mérite, tout l'honneur et toute la gloire sont rendus généralement à la population noire de la fourmilière, il arrive parfois qu'ils soient rendus aussi au peuple des cigales. Il suffirait, paraît-il, d'en introduire assez dans le système pour que nous puissions enfin être heureux. Comme à l'accoutumée, le bien et le mal se partagent, et le jeton correspondant est donné soit à la travailleuse, soit aux chansons. En assouplissant le système, on le rend plus complexe, plus dynamique, on le sauve, on lui rend la vie, on le multiplie, le voici à la dimension d'un ensemble de fourmilières. On est plus avancé, le savoir est plus fort, mais les contraintes sont encore plus féroces dans leur souplesse.

La musique a été la moitié de ma vie. Je ne concevais pas de vie sans la musique. Je commence à la détester, maintenant. Elle m'attend partout, et me piège en tout espace. Je savais que nous étions à l'ère des moteurs quand les bruits venaient d'eux et remplissaient tous les volumes. Il n'y avait plus d'espace sans moteur. Dans les coins les plus retirés des campagnes, la tronçonneuse aiguë comme une fraise de dentiste remplaçait les cigales. Je veux dire par là que la fourmi avait compris, qu'elle avait lu enfin toutes les fables, elle qui en était restée à leurs premières lignes. Elle avait compris que le producteur ne peut se saisir du pouvoir que s'il prend aussi la place du parasite. Alors, le moteur a rempli l'espace, phénomène expansif, expansé, qui, je vais le dire bientôt, fonde le fait de la propriété. Le bruit est stercoraire, il rend insupportable l'occupation d'une étendue, et donc se l'approprie. La cigale contre-attaque. A distance de la fourmilière, elle chante, elle comble l'espace. La fourmi ne peut pas évacuer ce cri. Voici un parasite inéliminable pour une fourmi. Le parasite doit trouver un phénomène contre lequel le producteur ne peut rien. On ne chasse pas un bruit, on le couvre. Dès lors, la fourmi fait des moteurs pétaradant dans les espaces. La cigale contre-attaque et y place des haut-parleurs. Haute fidélité, pleine puissance, et casque à oreillettes, le moteur est battu. La culture de la musique, j'entends des communications, vient de battre à plate couture ladite révolution industrielle, celle des productions. Les petites énergies chassent les grandes. Un parasite chasse l'autre. Un pouvoir chasse l'autre. Un propriétaire chasse l'autre. Une expansion chasse la précédente. Ce qui compte c'est bien de changer le milieu. Avoir le moyen de changer le milieu. Hélas, oui, je hais la musique.

Le parasite gagne le pouvoir, moins parce qu'il
tient le centre que parce qu'il remplit le milieu. La
cigale occupe l'espace. Les médias. Le milieu, l'environnement, l'espace est sa propriété, au sens où le
propriétaire émet un phénomène expansé dans le
lieu.

Le pouvoir, naguère, tendait ou tend à occuper le
centre. Pour qu'il émane de ce centre, qu'il soit efficace jusqu'aux périmètres, pour qu'il soit porté aux
périphéries, une condition nécessaire est qu'il n'y ait
aucun obstacle, que l'espace soit homogène autour
de son action. Bref, il faut que l'espace soit déparasité. Pour être obéi, par exemple, il faut être écouté,
il faut être entendu, il faut que le message d'ordre
passe le silence. Il faut obtenir le silence. Il faut chasser les parasites. La fourmi s'y emploie, elle envoie
crever de faim les cigales. Elle tourne autour de son
chez-soi, la chanteuse est à tout-venant. D'où je
reviens aux trois fonctions, que je ne sais plus distinguer, dont je ne vois plus que les analogies. Le titulaire de la fonction juridique et sacrée purifie
l'espace, il élimine les ordures par la porte stercoraire, au temple de Vesta, il découpe des temples et
les lustres de sang ou d'eau jusqu'à leurs bords. Le
profane est dehors, le mal court, le saint est dedans,
jusqu'au centre, le saint des saints. L'espace intérieur est assez homogène, isotrope, déparasité. Le
chef de la fonction martiale garde les bords, défend
les portes et frontières de son épée de feu, il dispose
la mort tout autour du jardin. Dans les deux cas, vio-

lence pour la paix. Or les actifs de la fonction de
production organisent le travail et l'économie de la
même façon, en formant de l'ordre et en excluant le
désordre, comme j'ai dit. Geste qui n'est pas différent de ceux de ses deux co-dieux. Tous les trois
Mars par la violence, tous les trois Jupiter par l'exclusion, tous les trois Quirinus... ils forment des espaces
propres, d'autant plus propres qu'on va vers le
centre, des espaces centrés, fermés, entourés d'un
désert barbare inconnu, où le mal court, où peuvent
toujours chanter et danser les cigales. Trois dieux, la
religion, trois concepts, la métaphysique, ou trois
fonctions, l'histoire, en tout cas, trois pouvoirs, un
pouvoir, et le même schéma, où la même activité
s'organise. La même fourmilière. L'activité commune aux trois travaux est de déparasiter une loca-
lité spatiale finie. C'est le plus vieux dessin de tous
nos héritages, c'est le plus répété de toute notre histoire, c'est le plus reproduit de nos institutions, de
nos cultures, de nos sciences. Découper, centrer,
purifier. Vous le retrouverez de l'agriculture à l'axio-
matique. Peut-être est-ce le schéma, la structure fon-
damentale des cultures de producteurs. Comment
cheminer en avant, à partir du centre ? Laisser stable
le bord, un temps, puis le promouvoir. Le pouvoir,
au centre, organise, à partir de là, un espace clos qui
s'étend, un ordre qui avance, un monde en expansion. Production, ou la marche en avant. Nous
sommes décidément tous des Indo-Européens. Car
c'est cela même la production, cette croissance.
L'avance de la clôture dans le jardin à la Rousseau.
Conquérir l'espace progressivement, pas à pas, et
absorber peu à peu le désert. Informer le chaos,

changer le désordre en information, transformer la face de la terre. C'est cela même la production au sens indo-européen, il y faut bien les trois fonctions, ou un seul dieu sous des avatars trinitaires, un seul dieu en trois personnes. Et c'est exactement cela notre histoire. L'Empire romain (ou perse, ou grec, ou anglais, que m'importe) et la dialectique : thèse, le jardin sous-ensemble ; antithèse, le complémentaire ; synthèse, le jardin et le clos attenant.

Avons-nous quitté cet ancrage et cette progression, d'un coup, d'un seul, d'un coup de maître ? Les fourmis productrices traînent leurs processions lentes dans l'espace fini. La cigale chante, elle passe l'espace. La fourmi travaille dans le temps, elle traverse en caravanes, chargées de tissus, de parfums et de poteries, les déserts qui entourent l'espace fermé de murailles temporaires. Elle se traîne dans l'espace, elle décélère le temps. Elle se hâte avec lenteur. La cigale occupe d'un coup, en un éclair, tout l'alentour. Elle n'a pas besoin de temps pour combler un espace. Non, elle n'est pas productrice, elle est un tout autre pouvoir. Ni Jupiter, ni Mars, ni Quirinus. Autre chose. Où es-tu ? Je ne sais. Où vas-tu ? Que m'importe. Elle erre, à tout venant. Autrement dit, les émetteurs peuvent être distribués au hasard. Le centre perd sa place, sa fonction et son importance. Par où passes-tu ? Partout. L'espace entier baigne dans le pouvoir. Le parasite est partout. Sa voix se répand et s'expanse, où qu'il soit, où qu'il aille. La voix, le vent, le bruit et la rumeur. C'est le règne du Paraclet. Le règne de l'esprit, Hegel enfin réalisé. Le règne des Beatles, c'est-à-dire

des bouffemerde. Ceux qui mangent l'ordure éva-
cuée par les fourmis.

Cigale et fourmi, le jardin clos des travailleurs en
partance pour l'impérialisme, et l'espace occupé
d'un coup par la fulgurance des voix, par le tintamarre des cors. Cigale et fourmi, le Roi-Soleil, je
crois. Le centre ici, et le rayonnement expansif qui
remplit le monde, dès l'aube. Nous avons changé
tout cela. Il suffit de l'expansion désormais. Vous
pouvez vous passer du centre. Il suffit d'émetteurs
circonstanciels. L'empire mondial d'IBM, demain,
l'empire absolu de la relation. La fin de la substance.
Le substantialisme, c'était encore et toujours le
refus des voix et du vent. Nous ne nous réparons
plus désormais que de relations. Nous ne buvons
plus que des ondes.
Il faut donc chercher ce qui se répand, qui
s'expanse. Les bruits, les odeurs et les ondes. Peut-
être, aussi bien, la Raison. La Raison, *ratio*, le logos
hellénique, je retrouve la voix. La Raison se répand
par la voix. Par le calcul et la mesure, qui supposent
de longues chaînes de raisons. Les vieilles chaînes
cartésiennes étaient lentes, et hyperboliquement
déparasitées. Aujourd'hui les chaînes courent la
vitesse de la lumière, les parasites les ont en main.

Ce texte fabuleux mis au début comme une
pierre. Chanter n'est pas échangeable, chanter n'est

pas d'usage, chanter c'est se condamner à mourir de faim. Platon exclut les poètes de la cité en vertu de la stricte justice. Parler n'est pas manger. Solide et vent. Le parasite est chassé, le fabuliste est invité à danser devant le buffet.

Tout le reste sera la revanche ou la vengeance des cigales. Ceux qui viennent quêter l'hospitalité, ne les rejetez pas, ce sont des dieux. Vous serez métamorphosés. La cigale se venge. Métamorphosée en renard, elle transforme le corbeau en phénix des hôtes. La cigale n'a pas caressé la fourmi, elle ne lui a pas dit qu'elle était superbe, elle ne l'a pas écorniflée, elle ne l'a pas encore fait chanter. Vous chantiez? Non, dit la cigale, en revenant sur ses pas, vous, chantez! Du coup l'oiseau croassant lâche le fromage. Ils ne sont pas prêteurs? Ils seront donneurs. Le retour des cigales ne va plus cesser, le retour des exclus, le retour des refoulés, des poètes, des fabulistes, des parasites à la table du château de Vaux.

La première fable est bien archaïque. Elle est une exception. Tout le reste du fabuleux annonce notre monde.

Les dieux, l'hôte perpétuel

D'un geste exact, d'une sûreté imprenable, notre maître choisit, dans *les Métamorphoses*, celle des hospitaliers. Philémon et Baucis vont s'immortaliser, comme saint Julien. Non sans avoir été l'occasion ou la cause d'un déluge de violence : tout le bourg disparaît, animaux, habitants sont entraînés, sans choix, par la crue, la recrudescence, la crise, comme sont massacrés, sans choix, dans le vallon, les bêtes du chasseur. Peut-être est-ce la peste vue avec les yeux de l'âne.

Les deux petits vieux, retirés, misérables, sont les seuls à ouvrir la porte à Hermès, précédant Zeus soi-même. Fardés en pèlerins, les dieux n'avaient trouvé nulle place à l'hôtellerie. Personne, dans le voisinage, ne leur avait été secourable. Ne pas trouver de place à l'hôtellerie : un dieu va-t-il naître ? Un hôte tel que nul hôtel ne peut le recevoir.

Philémon et Baucis préparent le festin, pour leurs hôtes.

Lait, fruits, sobres et pauvres dons. Les voyageurs ont soif, les hôtes versent, du vase, l'eau de la source, mêlée de vin. Repas interrompu, interrompu par un miracle. Plus le vase versait, moins il s'allait vidant. Deux miracles.

La Fontaine. Elle verse toujours, elle coule en surabondance, elle est inépuisable. Divines fables, plus l'auteur en écrit, plus encore il en reste à écrire. La production ne saurait tarir. Ce n'est pas un miracle, c'est vrai, peut-être le seul vrai mouvement perpétuel. Plus on écrit, plus on écrit. C'est toujours avoir soif et c'est toujours donner à boire. Immortalité de l'œuvre, festin d'immortalité. Repas ininterrompu, enfin.

Miracle parasitaire. Plus vous me donnez à manger ou à boire, à moi qui suis un dieu, plus vous obtiendrez de ces fables dont je ne manque pas, dont je ne manquerai jamais. Payer du vin en mots, payer de la substance en information, est si bon marché, si gratuit, que je ne manquerai jamais de monnaie. Par conséquent, le mouvement est bien perpétuel. C'est cela le miracle, mais c'est cela aussi tout miracle. D'un mot dit, la chose se fait. Cela ne coûte que paroles d'acquérir telle chose. A ce prix, rien ne cesse, rien ne s'épuise. Si l'information valait de l'énergie, nous serions des dieux. Miracle au sens de la puissance, miracle au sens de la physique. Mais ce geste impossible, l'invité l'accomplit. C'est le miracle journalier du parasite. C'est toujours, c'est encore la table d'hôte, et le phénix des hôtes. Le parasitisme ne cesse pas. L'hôte, indéfiniment, renaît de ses cendres, de ses cendres expulsées par la porte stercoraire. Asseyez-vous à la table d'hôte, il aura toujours préparé le repas. Il est là pour ça. L'hôte resurgit de sa consommation, de sa consomption par le feu, le vin rejaillit de son épuisement. Cela marche indéfiniment. Il n'y a jamais d'équilibre : la table où l'on sert est bancale, il lui manque un appui, elle penche, on la rétablit un peu, tout justement par un débris de vase. Et la table verse toujours. Verse le vase, verse la table, verseau des vers surabondants.

Le versement de l'hôte est infini. Sa dette est inépuisable.

S'il est inhospitalier, il est condamné à mort, et son cadavre est entraîné par le déluge. S'il est hospitalier, il paie à perpétuité. Il verse, en continu.

Autant de vin à boire que d'hommes à tuer au fond du vallon, dans le bourg, sous les eaux. Ou bien : autant d'eau versée du vase que d'eaux déversées des nuages, pour le déluge.

L'hôte venu, étranger, à la table, ne parasite pas un individu, mais la reproduction des individus. Non leur production, exceptionnelle et rare, mais leur reproduction, commune. Cela, justement, ne s'arrête pas. Tel parasite la vie de l'autre, sa vie ontogénétique, parfois, sa vie phylogénétique, toujours. Ce qui verse toujours, c'est la phylogénèse. Ils se reproduisent pour ça : chair à canon, chair à tuer, chair à travail, chair à manger, chair à instruire et

commander, chair qui accouche. Oui, la vie est inépuisable. Et les dieux en ont soif.

Que seraient les fables sans métamorphose ? Il faut
bien, d'un coup de baguette, changer les hommes
en bêtes. Et comment cela se peut-il ? La métamorphose dans la fable, voilà le secret de la fable. Il s'agit
d'un miracle d'hospitalité. Ou de l'infinité des relations parasitaires.

INTERLUDE

Portrait en pied du parasite

Repas confessés

La plume me tombe des mains... Elle ne tombe pas des mains de Rousseau pour n'importe quelle raison. Il avoue avoir tort, en d'autres occasions, de la prendre peut-être sans nécessité. Raison de la prendre, raison de la perdre. Il ne la perd jamais d'avouer sa sexualité morose, ni d'être surpris à montrer quelque chose aux filles près du puits. Là, il la garde bien en main, pour l'enchantement des commentateurs, si ravis de prendre la place des filles. Courage, maintenant!... La plume me tombe des mains.

Il vient d'être surpris à voler des pommes. Non pas, bien sûr, par effraction de la porte de la dépense où elles étaient entreposées, faisant main basse, hardiment, sur la proie, mais en cherchant à les faire passer par un petit pertuis, par une jalousie. Pour un exploit de ce calibre, il a besoin d'outils. Une broche à gibier, une latte, un couteau. Observez maintenant la chasse du maître, celle du gibier, celle de la broche, et ce que Rousseau nomme la chasse aux pommes, en détournant le mot de son sens. Il est vrai que cette réserve, la réserve du maître, contient les produits de la chasse du maître et ses armes et ses outils. L'apprenti donc détourne à son profit et le gibier, ou la cueillette, et la broche à gibier. Le maître est prédateur, cela reste à voir, et le manœuvre est parasite. Il n'est jamais question de conquérir le jardin des Hespérides ni de mettre à mort le dragon, l'entreprise est de manger sur lui, furtivement.

Broche trop courte, broche allongée, pomme qui se refuse, et ouverture trop étroite, couteau qui tranche, et dragon qui ne dort que d'un œil, angoisse enfin d'être surpris la main loin dans le sac, c'est la fête au psychanalyste, d'autant plus que, tout justement, la plume me tombe des mains. D'autant plus qu'il s'agit d'un jardin, de ce jardin précisément que la petite Savoyarde, à la neuvième promenade, porte devant elle, en éventaire, pour désir aigu des petits Savoyards. Traduire ici serait tomber dans le banal. Et donc, directement, il s'agit de pommes, de ces fruits qu'on mange, de ces fruits qu'on mange quand on a faim, et quand le patron vous a renvoyé au tiers du repas, au moment où on sert le meilleur à sa table. Cela rend fripon et friand.

J'aime à manger, dit-il, sans être avide : je suis sensuel, et non pas gourmand. Trop d'autres goûts me distraient de celui-là. Je ne suis jamais occupé de la bouche que quand mon cœur est oisif; et cela m'est si rarement arrivé dans ma vie que je n'ai guère eu le temps de songer aux bons morceaux.

Voire. Il faut toujours croire ce qu'il dit, ne jamais croire ce qu'il dit qu'il dit. Car enfin, à toutes les pages ou quasi, lesdits bons morceaux apparaissent.

La question est toujours de savoir où ils passent. Pour le moment, les pommes restent où elles sont.

Mais les asperges. Que je sache, une asperge est un autre morceau qu'une pomme. Or ici le vol demeure impuni. J'allais tous les matins moissonner les plus belles asperges. L'intérêt, je viens de le dire, est de voir où elles passent. Rousseau ne les mange pas, il les rend. Il les rend au profit d'un tiers, qui est le fils de la propriétaire (à nouveau le jardin, le jardin de la mère, la fête continue, et un jardin d'asperges, et savez-vous que l'homme se nommait Verrat?), fils qui, lui-même, partage le produit de la vente avec un autre camarade. Le jeune apprenti n'est plus parasite, il est parasité. Le schéma des pommes s'inverse. Tout à l'heure, le maître, qui, très précisément est l'hôte, comme ici la mère est hôtesse du fils, accumulait des biens, par tel ou tel moyen productif, cueillette ou chasse. Et l'apprenti les détournait. C'est ce détournement qui est décrit avec ce luxe de détails et de circonstances, grande broche et petite broche, la latte et le couteau, le tout et les parties, le trou de jalousie, c'est le circuit parasitaire, toujours en détours de ruses, toujours complexe et dupliqué, toujours muni d'excentriques et d'épicycles. Un producteur, un prédateur, est toujours un simple. Que si vous rencontrez un homme compliqué, demandez-vous à quelle table il mange. Ou lisez des traités de science et vous admirerez les somptueux détours, les ruses baroques des parasites. A croire que ces bêtes sont intelligentes. A croire que l'intelligence fut un jour inventée par ces bêtes-là. *Parasitus sapiens.* Bref, dans l'affaire des asperges, Rousseau est dans une position symé-

trique : il ne mange pas les marrons, il les tire du feu
pour un autre. Pour un autre qui est dans son dos et
le dirige, et qui détourne, à son tour, la cueillette, la
chasse. (Entendez, par ce dernier mot, la chasse
botanique, à la Rousseau ; pomme ou asperge, enfin,
que fait le narrateur sinon herboriser ?) Deux histoires couplées, elles n'en font qu'une. Dans le
schéma complet, le voleur surpris et le voleur volé
occupent deux positions intéressantes, inverses ou
symétriques, par rapport à qui vole ou à qui sur-
prend. Il existe toujours un tiers, au désir, voyez
l'Héloïse, comme en science, où il était exclu. Mais
nous n'en sommes pas à ces traits généraux, encore.
Il s'agit de manger, simplement, de survivre, peut-
être. Me voici et voici la pomme. Et voici le tiers qui
prend position. Il est, là, source de pommes, il est,
ici, à l'embouchure des asperges. Je suis l'embouchure des pommes, je suis la source des asperges. Du
coup, la bonne position apparaît, elle se découvre
par la comparaison des deux histoires : il faudra s'y
tenir, ne jamais se laisser supplanter. D'où les essais
et les erreurs, comme méthode. D'abord voleur volé,
après voleur surpris, le progrès s'annonce, sensible.
On a récupéré la bonne position. Reste que
l'apprenti, pour ses coups d'essai, reste un apprenti.
D'abord il se contente de quelque bribe, sans toucher au vin, puis, décidément, n'obtient rien, il ne
croque pas un quartier de pomme. Cette leçon ne
sera jamais oubliée. Si importante, assurément, que,
pour la seule fois des *Confessions*, la plume tombe de
ses mains, comme la broche à petit gibier. Cette
leçon qui vaut tous les fromages. (A propos, dans

l'Émile et à ce vers de La Fontaine, Rousseau note : la
pensée est très bonne.)

Fromage. Départ à Turin : j'imaginais des festins
rustiques, sur les arbres des fruits délicieux, sur les
montagnes des cuves de lait et de crème. A Turin
même, le réflexe est un peu bien conditionné : en
même temps que la sonnette du viatique me faisait
peur, la cloche de la messe ou de vêpres me rappe-
lait un déjeuner, un goûter, du beurre frais, des
fruits, du laitage. Le viatique est la nourriture
emportée pour la promenade, pour une promenade
spéciale, tout à fait solitaire, celle de notre mort.
Pour la dixième promenade, inachevée. A deux pas
de la Contrà Nova, non loin de la table, et du sein,
de Mme Basile : avec du laitage, des herbes, du fromage (je n'y tiens plus, décidément, cette gastrono-
mie du laiteux, du crémeux, du mammaire est peu
évoluée, infantile sans doute, protestante peut-être,
et anglo-saxonne, depuis; mais pour l'honneur des
lettres françaises, Rousseau ne déteste pas le bon
vin), du fromage, dis-je, du pain bis et du vin passable, on est toujours sûr de me bien régaler. Le
régal n'est pas autonome, le verbe n'est pas prono-
minal. Oui, la position est parfaitement prise. On est
sûr. Qui est sûr ? Celui qui me régale. Celui qui
m'invite à sa table. Celui qui me nourrit. Mon hôte.
Voici, pour information, mon menu, à vous qui me
lisez, à vous qui, éventuellement, pouvez, un soir,
m'avoir à votre table. Couvrez-la donc de crème. Et
pour boire ce vin passable, pourquoi ne point rêver à
la coupe célèbre à qui le plus beau sein du monde
servit de moule ? Le meilleur parasite est-il le moins
sevré ? Certes, il est question de Jean-Jacques, de

Maman et de la gouvernante, du laiteux et de
l'enfantin, de l'orphelin de mère et du maître d'éducation qui conseille aux mères d'allaiter leurs
enfants. Certes, il s'agit de cet individu qui a manqué
d'un sein et le cherche, et qui perd ses enfants pour
n'avoir personne à nourrir, c'est-à-dire pour conserver ce que j'ai appelé la bonne position. Mais cet
individu se montre, nous dit-il, dans la vérité de la
nature. Je ne forme aucune hypothèse sur une
affaire aussi controversée que la nature humaine.
Mais je crois n'avoir pas rencontré d'homme parfaitement sevré. Ils me paraissent tous munis de
pompe ou de suçoir, invisible ou visible. Parasites et
mal sevrés, je ne sais lequel est la raison de l'autre et
je soupçonne que chacun est la cause et l'effet. Mal
sevré à coup sûr : Rousseau se nomme le Petit, tout à
côté de sa Maman[1].

L'usage des grandes tables n'a point altéré, dis-je,
la simplicité de mes goûts. Du lait. Mais surtout pas
de maître d'hôtel, ni valet, ni laquais. Tout le monde
voit là le bon républicain, poète et paysan. Non. Qui
a été valet connaît parfaitement la position. Elle est,
tout justement, la bonne. Le vrai concurrent de
Rousseau est ici en situation de le supplanter.
Exemple : ce laquais appelé Dupont, qui écrivait très
bien, et à qui je payais dix écus, tirés de ma poche,
qui ne m'ont jamais été remboursés. Dupont, copiste
ou écrivain ? deux fois le double du modèle. Aveux,
plus loin : La raison pourquoi mes goûts restent

---

1. Mon petit ménage, mon petit babil, mes petites affaires. La
France du petit remonte à Rousseau, la France du petit repas, de
la petite plage et du petit vin de chez nous. Elle était, avant lui, le
pays du grand et de la grandeur.

simples, c'est que toute association inégale est toujours désavantageuse au parti faible. Soit, et vive l'égalité, nous ferons ou nous avons fait la Révolution pour cela. Entrons un peu dans le détail. Vivant non loin de l'opulence, je me vois forcé d'imiter les mœurs des gens riches. Ils ont leurs serviteurs, je n'ai pas de valet. Or, l'hospitalité du maître fait de moi un autre maître des mêmes serviteurs. Si quelqu'un sait parfaitement que je ne suis pas maître, c'est justement le serviteur. Derrière moi, il rit : rogue, fripon, alerte, le coquin. Il faut payer cette arrogance. D'où les étrennes infinies, dans la maison et hors de la maison, aux laquais, aux porteurs, aux cochers, cela n'en finit plus. Sans compter le linge ni le barbier. Dites, vingt-cinq écus pour ne coucher que quatre fois chez Mme d'Houdetot, c'est insensé, voyons. (Mme d'Houdetot est le grand amour de sa vie.) En fait, le désavantage de l'association inégale ne vient pas directement des grands, des riches ou des princes, mais des petits, du menu peuple, situés en dessous. En position de grippe-sous. C'est insupportable. Je rendais mille petits services aux domestiques, je n'ai jamais reçu les leurs qu'à la pointe de mon argent. Alors que les grands étaient, toujours, à mon service, pour avoir compris mon petit babil. Les grands sont haïssables en raison des petits, les riches sont infréquentables en raison des pauvres, autour. Adieu, Révolution. Bref, le parasite n'a qu'un ennemi : celui qui peut le supplanter, en position de parasite. Donnez-moi à manger, mais service compris[1].

1. La haine de Rousseau pour les valets et les laquais est implacable. Il faut lire dans *la Nouvelle Héloïse* comment ils sont

Revenons au départ vers Turin, un peu avant : j'allais trouver des festins (encore), des amis prêts à me servir, des maîtresses empressées à me plaire. Voici ma suffisance et ma modération : un seul château bornait mon ambition. Favori du seigneur et de la dame, amant de la demoiselle, ami du frère et protecteur des voisins, j'étais content; il ne m'en fallait pas davantage. L'ironie, certes, colore le schéma, mais elle n'en adultère pas l'exactitude. L'aveu demeure, dans l'humour. Et c'est si vrai que la vie, comme le roman, tentera d'approcher cet état. En attendant, des paysans de connaissance m'accueillaient, me logeaient, me nourrissaient, voyez donc la lettre à Julie où les paysans valaisans, et leurs compagnes aux gros seins, donnent gratuitement leur hospitalité au voyageur philosophe, au promeneur amoureux. Service compris — le service est assuré par lesdites femmes, placées derrière.

Le schéma projeté se construit peu à peu. Premier hôte de qualité, M. de Pontverre, descendant des gentilshommes de la Cuiller. Ce nom fameux, dit-il, me frappa beaucoup. Je suis enchanté, moi aussi, de ce verre et de la cuiller. Il me donne à dîner, c'est inévitable. Les choses, désormais, sont sérieuses, c'est la guerre de religion, curés contre ministres. Jean-Jacques sort de l'éducation du ministre et il dîne chez le curé. On dispute de théologie. Je trouvai, dit-il, peu de chose à répondre à des arguments qui finissaient ainsi (entendez : à table), et je jugeai

---

traités pour voir l'infamie du paternalisme. On sait que la Révolution française coupa la tête de ces gens : ils forment le groupe social qui eut le plus à souffrir de la guillotine.

que des curés chez qui l'on dînait si bien valaient tout au moins nos ministres. J'étais trop bon convive pour être bon théologien : ma supériorité (dans l'ordre théorique) ne valait pas le prix de son vin de Frangy. Un dîner vaut bien une messe. D'autant qu'une messe, après tout, est un autre festin, une cène. L'abjuration va venir : elle se négocie à table d'hôte. Il changea de religion, dit Émile, pour avoir du pain. La voix intérieure ne sait point se faire entendre à celui dont l'estomac crie. Revenez encore à cette même lettre à Julie, où Saint-Preux raconte comment on s'enivre sans payer chez les vignerons du Valais. Le vin y est violent et bon, et l'hospitalité requiert qu'on n'y refuse pas ce fendant. D'où ceci : ne pouvant payer un écot de ma bourse, je le payais de ma raison. La raison pour du vin, le culte pour du pain, l'échange reste eucharistique. Voici donc une première profession de foi, aux *Confessions*, en terre savoyarde : je ne songeais point à changer de religion, je me laissais circonvenir, je faisais la coquette à la manière des honnêtes femmes (ici, le mot ne manque pas d'exactitude : une chaste coquette offre et ne donne pas, obtient sans rien payer, il faudra bien revenir là-dessus), la faim pourtant me talonnait. Il faut vivre. Adieu, ministre, je suis curé. Pardon, vicaire. Qu'il est intéressant ce terme de vicaire — et le rôle indiqué par lui. Vicariant, suppléant, remplaçant ; et situé en dessous du curé, au dernier échelon. Il n'y a personne sous le vicaire et cependant il peut remplacer le curé. Vicaire est un mot d'échange, comme vice versa. Et c'est un mot de voie et de passage, comme on dit un agent voyer. Un mot de promenade. Voici donc que le bon curé de Pontverre est muni d'un vicaire, d'un suppléant, ou plutôt d'une suppléante, Mme de Warens. Qui elle aussi vendit sa foi pour le roi de Sardaigne et quelques centaines de livres de rente, et chez qui la canaille va vendre sa foi.

Le parasite détourne. Exemple : ce bon jeune homme, maintenant pensionnaire (?) chez le vicaire savoyard, voit transiter entre les mains du prêtre l'argent de la charité, qui va du bienfaisant à l'assisté. Il cherche à se brancher sur le canal. De cet argent, il demande une part. Il a, nous dit-il, cette lâcheté. Il est vrai que c'est plus facile, quoique plus fin : de la sorte, il n'est pas un pauvre qui demande l'aumône et à qui on la fait, mais il détourne un flux, selon sa règle de conduite ordinaire. Le vicaire aussitôt refuse et lui donne son argent, à lui, dont il n'a pas pourtant à sa suffisance. Le don est alors direct, sans détour ni détournement, sans vicariance ni remplacement. Nul n'est supplanté. Cette leçon, paraît-il, ne fut pas perdue. Encore.

Le parasite se détourne. Je ne comprends pas encore pourquoi. Vers Annecy, le voyage est d'un jour, j'en mis trois. J'errai de gauche et de droite, de château en château, à l'aventure, et je chantais sous les fenêtres. Ceci, tout à coup, devient très sérieux. Voyage, oui ; promenade, déjà ; c'est un début de randonnée. Dont les règles sont d'irrégularité : ne jamais prendre le chemin le plus court, tirer à gauche, venir à droite, exode, hors de la route, se confier à ses goûts, les châteaux, se laisser aller au hasard, l'aventure, et chanter, ne vous déplaise. Ceci est un chemin, mais non point *le* chemin. Pourquoi le bon, le vrai chemin, serait-il maximalisé, comme superlatif : le plus simple, le plus facile et le plus droit ? Question : il est accordé que la méthode est le chemin ; comment, alors, faire discours de la méthode, si on a quitté *le* chemin ? Je donnerai plus tard la réponse à cette question.

Arrivée impromptue chez la Maman de vicariance. « Allez chez moi m'attendre ; dites qu'on vous donne à déjeuner. » Pour causer à loisir, elle me retint à dîner. Ce fut le premier repas de ma vie où j'eusse manqué d'appétit, et sa femme de chambre, qui nous servait, dit aussi que j'étais le premier voyageur de mon âge et de mon étoffe qu'elle en eût vu manquer. Cette remarque, qui ne me nuisit pas dans l'esprit de sa maîtresse, tombait un peu à plomb sur un gros manant qui dînait avec nous et qui dévora lui tout seul un repas honnête pour six personnes. La présentation me paraît réussie. Ne pas manger, ne pas même avoir d'appétit, c'est précisément s'effacer comme parasite. Ce n'est pas moi, c'est lui, le gros, le bâfreur, le vorace. Il me supplante, ce manant, de qualité au-dessous de la mienne, et qui, donc, par sa position, reçoit tout et ne donne rien. A Turin, d'ailleurs, il me dépouillera. Le parasite est l'ennemi. La guerre de tous contre tous se traduit ainsi : parasites contre parasites. Ici : Maman me nourrit, elle nourrit son Petit, que fait-elle d'autre que sa fonction et que son rôle ? Attention : il n'est pas naturel, il est vicariant. Maman est la vicaire savoyarde. Et je crois bien que ce mot de vicaire et que le titre d'invité ont une seule et même racine.

Changeons de table et passons à Turin, chez
Mme Basile. Jolie, coquette, enchantée aussitôt du
petit babil. Le parasite mange, mais il amuse l'hôte,
en retour. Il porte dans sa bourse du vent : le babil,
le talent, le paiement de paroles. Son malheur est
qu'il parle assez mal en public (il ne sait pas tirer
parti de sa figure mignonne), il se trouble, il bégaie,
il dit n'importe quoi. Et c'est un peu l'échec de sa
tactique : il est aussi contradictoire de vouloir devenir parasite en demeurant muet, que gigolo en res-
tant vertueux et puceau. Il reste l'écriture, vicariante
de la conversation. Il faut dire qu'en cette monnaie,
il va bientôt payer un écot abondant, sinon retardé.

Bref, le M. Basile, en voyage, a laissé un Egisthe
auprès de la brunette qui, maintenant, aguiche un
peu bien notre faux naïf, dont le discours torrentiel
de vertu voile gentiment la pratique ordinaire des
picaresques. Le triangle se met en place, dont on sait
qu'il abonde partout : Claude Anet chez Maman,
puis le fendeur de bûches, M. Basile chez Madame et
le flûteur Egisthe en son absence, soit le vicaire de
Monsieur, autres doubles vivants ou fantastiques,
masculins de l'inséparable, auprès de l'Héloïse. Le
troisième homme est parasite, pour l'instant.

Ne fermons pas encore le triangle : quelqu'un a
relation à un autre ou à quelque chose. Un tiers survient, qui n'a aucun rapport aux êtres ou aux choses,
mais qui n'a de rapport qu'à leur relation même. Il
se branche sur le canal. Il intercepte le rapport. Il
n'est pas médiation, mais intermédiaire. Il n'est pas
forcément utile, sauf, bien sûr, à sa propre survie :
cette relation à la relation lui permet d'exister. Or, le
danger qu'il court est immédiatement visible : il peut

être exclu par une association groupant les deux sujets dont il parasite la relation, ou par un seul sujet qui veut se réserver l'exclusivité de l'objet. Ce risque d'exclusion, il le connaît dès qu'il se met à table, il le connaît dès qu'il a faim. Risque de mort. Il a toujours dans les oreilles cette sonnette du viatique, cette sonnette qui fait peur, l'annonce du dernier repas, de la dernière cène interrompue, avant le trépas. Il a toujours su qu'il était un tiers, il a toujours su qu'il n'était qu'en tiers, il a toujours connu que la règle implacable était celle du tiers exclu. Il s'y connaît en exclusion, errant, hors de la ville aux portes closes, il n'est pas de ce monde. Il s'y connaît en persécution : me voici donc seul sur la terre, proscrit par un accord unanime. Proscrit par un combat, par la volonté générale. Je n'ai désormais que moi seul pour ressource. Peut-il survivre ainsi ? Peut-on s'autoparasiter ? Rêveries : n'avoir que moi pour me nourrir. Non, non, c'est impossible. La mort survient fatalement alors qu'il écrit de sa mère vicariante, et le dernier mot de sa vie est le mot de sa règle de vie : l'assistance que j'avais reçue. Cette assistance est irrémissible, jamais rendue, jamais effacée, impardonnable, comme une relation sans réciproque et sans converse. Toujours aux enfants assistés. Faut-il continuer d'écrire l'histoire véridique du parasite et du paranoïde ? On peut dire ainsi ou ainsi, comme on veut, l'essentiel est de conserver le préfixe. *Le Tigre et le Pou* n'était pas une fable, c'était une parabole [1].

---

1. *Critique*, n° 375-376, pp. 730-741.

Allons, passons à table, nous perdons notre temps à discourir de théorie. C'est le dîner du jacobin. Voyez les parasites pulluler autour de la nappe : le moine, confesseur, Egisthe, l'espion, et moi, le narrateur des confessions. C'est bien le cas de dire qu'ils payent de paroles. La table ne se trouva pas suffisante, il en fallut dresser une petite, où j'eus l'agréable tête-à-tête de M. le Commis. Commis est comme vicaire, le lieutenant du commettant, le mandataire. L'espion est mari vicariant. Figurez-vous donc deux niveaux, la grande et la petite table, comme on dit le haut bout, le bas bout. De la haute table vers la basse table coule le flux de mets, dans ce sens, non dans l'autre. Au tête-à-tête de M. le Mari suppléant, je ne perdis rien du côté des attentions et de la bonne chère. J'étais dans le bon sens et dans la bonne position. Il y eut bien des assiettes envoyées à la petite table dont l'intention n'était sûrement pas pour lui. L'espion voit passer les masques, c'est la fête. Quand, tout à coup, ciel! mon mari! Basile rentre avec fracas. Le roi dit : qui est donc ce petit garçon? et fait quelques demandes qui montrent la traîtrise de l'espion. Egisthe, parasite de Basile, supplante Rousseau, parasite de la brunette. Le roi est plus haut que la reine, l'espion est plus bas que le joli cœur. Qui, le lendemain, se retrouve dehors, à battre le pavé. Exclu, expulsé, chassé. Me voici donc seul sur la terre...

Il faut peut-être s'arrêter de lire dans le bon sens, et revenir sur la lecture, et remonter aux souvenirs d'enfance les plus hauts. Si le même dessin se répète souvent, jusqu'à devenir loi, suivons la récurrence de son geste. Nous devons en découvrir un modèle archaïque, un schéma primitif. Voici l'horrible tragédie, la grande histoire du noyer de la terrasse. Mon oncle le fit planter pour avoir de l'ombre. Soit dit en passant, qui lui avait soufflé une pareille idée ? L'ombre du noyer, c'est connu, est mortelle. Bref, la chose se fit avec quelque solennité. Or, mon cousin et moi voulûmes aussi planter, sans partager un tel mérite avec quiconque. Une bouture de saule fit l'affaire, elle prit place à huit ou dix pas de l'auguste noyer. Mais pour arroser la bouture, pas d'eau. On ne nous laissait pas courir assez pour en prendre nous-mêmes. D'où l'invention industrieuse de l'aqueduc souterrain, fait de boîtes et de planches, qui amenait au saule, qui détournait vers lui l'eau de l'arrosement destiné au noyer. Voici le bon modèle botanique, et la botanique, nous le saurons assez bientôt, est la reine des sciences, de tous les détournements parasites. Le bassin au noyer, percé, communique au creux du saule, en contrebas. La grande table et la petite table, le haut bassin et le bas creux, laissent couler entre eux un flux alimentaire. Le saule (pleureur ?) parasite l'arbre fruitier, aux feuilles d'ombre. Tout à coup, tragédie. Ciel ! mon oncle ! Frappé de voir se partager entre deux bassins l'eau du noyer (Jean-Jacques a dit : résolus de nous procurer cette gloire sans la partager avec qui que ce fût), l'oncle prend une pioche et fait voler l'aqueduc en éclats. Il y a toujours quelqu'un pour surprendre le parasite branché sur le canal. Mais le texte poursuit sur la gloire de cette affaire. D'avoir inventé ça, je me jugeais mieux que César : quand il visite le pont du Gard, il est là, seul, au beau milieu de l'aqueduc. Nul ne l'a détruit, celui-là. Et que ne suis-je né romain[1] !

Le dessin, peu à peu, s'affine, se clarifie, se fixe et se construit. De la grande à la petite table, les envois de Mme Basile emmènent plats et bons morceaux, jusqu'à ce que le mari interrompe le flux. Du haut bassin, au pied du noyer, vers le creux bas, au pied du saule, un flux d'eau coule à nourrir la bouture, jusqu'à ce que l'oncle interrompe le flot. Le parasite est un interrupteur, l'hôte interrompt l'interruption. Nous raisonnons, je crois, par récurrence. Allons donc tout au bout du texte, nous sommes à l'île Saint-Pierre. Bonheur d'être logé, nourri, abrité, protégé par un receveur. Receveur dont je soupçonne le métier d'être analysable de même façon. Les meilleurs hôtes seraient-ils les meilleurs parasites ? Cette logique est imprenable, elle est inscrite dans la langue, où le mot hôte a les deux sens. Nulle difficulté ici puisque la relation se retourne. On retrouve ici le fermier général, les rats et la cascade. C'est le livre douzième ou la cinquième promenade. Voici le lac, bassin de forme ronde qui renferme deux îles en son milieu, une grande, habitée, cultivée, une petite, déserte, en friche. Tout recommence. La première est un paradis, je veux dire un réservoir : plantes, animaux, poissons. Thérèse et moi, dit-il, nous faisions un plaisir de partager avec la receveuse et sa famille la récolte des fruits et

---

1. On dispute de l'étymologie du verbe « supplanter ». On se doute que ma préférence va vers l'idée de planter en dessous, planter au niveau bas. Ainsi le noyer de M. Lambercier se trouve supplanté par le saule.

légumes. L'aveu est d'importance : je me demande si l'hôtesse remerciait, je la suppose débordante de reconnaissance. Bref, avec autant de solennité qu'autrefois on plantait, ici on peuple. De la grande à la petite île, passent par bateau des lapins. Jusqu'à ce que les autorités de Berne interrompent cette peuplade. Et chassent l'herboriste.

Mais ici, tout à coup, les choses se retournent. La petite île sera détruite à la fin par les transports de la terre qu'on en ôte sans cesse pour réparer les dégâts que les vagues et les orages font à la grande. C'est ainsi que la substance du faible est toujours employée au profit du puissant. Que s'est-il passé ? Quelle circulation, dans l'autre sens ? Quelle révolution ?

Grande table, grande île, noyer auguste, les grands. Les grands de ce monde, entendez la noblesse. Hauts de naissance, de qualité, parfois de fortune. Le citoyen est bas de qualité, de naissance et de bourse, mais il est gonflé de mérite : pensez, il est professeur de philosophie. La rêverie, la promenade, l'imagination, cette fois, nous ramènent au château. Souvenez-vous du programme insouciant, désinvolte, aimable, souriant, de celui qui nous avouait qu'il ne pouvait aimer que des demoiselles, jamais de ces filles du peuple, si mal tenues : favori du seigneur et de la dame, amant de la demoiselle, ami du frère et protecteur des voisins. L'amant de Julie est justement sur le point de réussir le coup. Il tient la mère, ou à peu près, la fille, sûrement, comme le frère est mort, Claire et milord Édouard en sont les vicariants, il est aimé, fêté, choyé de tout son monde. Il devient le protecteur de Fanchon et de Claude Anet, le bien

nommé. Tout est en place, y compris le refus hau-
tain de l'argent qui aboutit, par une sûreté tactique
inégalable, au doublement des sommes proposées[1].
Jamais le petit saule ne s'est trouvé mieux arrosé,
jamais saule pleureur ne fut dans un si beau jardin,
jamais la petite table n'a été couverte de si bons morceaux, jamais la petite île ne fut si bien peuplée. On
se demandera longtemps quel est le beau mérite de
cet anonyme pour qu'il suscite un tel remue-ménage
autour de sa personne. La philosophie? On n'a
jamais vu ça. L'amour, voyons, l'amour, vous dis-je,
l'amour issu de la nature et non des conventions,
l'amour qui régale, qui aplanit les différences de
niveau, l'amour aux entrailles de qui la Marion vaut
la demoiselle. Peut-être, mais pourquoi ne pouvez-
vous aimer que des demoiselles? pourquoi faites-
vous chasser la Marion, pourquoi Fanchon reste-
t-elle à sa place, pourquoi la sauver à tout prix de ce
monsieur bien riche?

Écoutez : elle écrit mal. Je laisse là mes préven-
tions et ma froideur critique; oui, pour un style
pareil, je donnerais vingt quartiers de noblesse, châteaux et parcs, pouvoir et fortune, toutes les inégali-
tés. Sauf, peut-être, le lit de Margot. Il faut que l'aris-
tocratie française ait aimé le langage et l'ait mis
au-dessus de tout. A juste titre et à bon droit. Elle
abandonne ici sa différence pour une liasse de

---

1. *La Nouvelle Héloïse*, 1ʳᵉ partie, lettres 15 à 18.

lettres écrites au parfait de la diction. Oui, le parasite
la paie de mots. Mais son royaume pour ces mots,
pour des mots de ce vol. Ce penser mâle des âmes
fortes, qui leur donne un idiome si particulier, est
une langue dont il a la grammaire. J'aurais été Julie,
Claire, Édouard, vieux ou jeune, femme ou homme,
roi ou Fanchon, j'eusse été aussi à genoux. Faut-il
que les hommes de lettres, Grimm ou Voltaire,
moins nobles ou ignobles, en aient été jaloux!
J'échangerais, je crois, ce discours contre toute inégalité. Cependant, il ne dit que des petitesses.

L'amour, voyons, l'amour, vous dis-je, l'amour
caché, enfoui et souterrain. Et tout à coup, l'horrible
tragédie. Ciel! mon père! il voit tout, il a tout
reconnu, découvert, il maltraite sa fille, il lui porte
des coups, elle tombe et, dans sa chute, elle saigne.
Je suppose qu'elle a tant saigné qu'elle en a perdu ce
qu'elle appelle son doux fruit. Mort de l'enfant,
expulsion de l'enfant, mort du jeune saule sous les
coups de pioche, un aqueduc! un aqueduc! Les
parents découvrent l'échange des lettres ou le flux
de l'eau. Ciel, mon oncle! Ciel, mon mari, M. Basile!
Ciel, le père noble et brutal. Ciel, le gouvernement
de Berne. L'amant est expulsé, l'auteur est expulsé,
l'enfant est expulsé, le parasite. Celui qui est branché sur la descente, non pas celui qui parle, qui dis-
court de l'inégalité, mais celui qui en fait l'expérience, qui en dessine les niveaux, qui la connaît
assez pour en tirer parti. « Dès l'instant qu'un
homme eut besoin du secours d'un autre, dès qu'on

s'aperçut qu'il était utile à un seul d'avoir des provisions pour deux, l'égalité disparut, la propriété s'introduisit, le travail devint nécessaire... » Qui est donc ce deuxième qui puise dans les provisions du premier, quel est donc ce besoin de secours?

Nous raisonnons, je crois, par récurrence. Il faut passer à la limite, au tout premier moment de la vie, sans mémoire. Je coûtai la vie à ma mère. Au moment de l'expulsion, celle qui donne vie la perd, et l'expulsante est expulsée, l'hôtesse originelle meurt. Il ne sera jamais sevré, celui dont la naissance est le sevrage même. Il n'a plus de logis, ni de nourriture, ni de chaleur. Le parasite tue son hôte, comme il peut arriver, parfois. D'où cette généalogie intéressante, cet arbre où les aqueducs sont brisés. Je n'eus jamais de mère, morte dès l'expulsion. Je n'eus pas de père, ou quasi : expulsé du pays pour une affaire où le nez d'un capitaine saigna. Je n'eus pas de frère ou quasi : libertin et fugueur, il s'enfuit, disparut tout à fait. C'était l'homme des escapades. Je n'eus pas de femme, ou quasi, je me mariai sur le tard avec celle que je nommai ma gouvernante. Donc je n'eus pas, je ne pus pas, je ne dus pas avoir d'enfants. Pas de père, pas de mère, pas de frère, pas de femme et, par conséquent, pas d'enfants. Pas d'amont, pas d'aval, nous détruisons les aqueducs. La chose est déductible et nécessaire. Ce n'est pas un événement de la vie, mais une suite de sa règle. Les cinq enfants sont expulsés, comme tous, comme père et mère, comme moi, comme doivent l'être ceux qui risquent de me parasiter. Ils auraient vécu à mes dépens, à mes crochets, ils m'auraient mis à la place de l'auguste noyer. Je veux demeurer saule, arrosé, pleureur et sans ombre.

Détruire l'aqueduc, détruire le canal, défaire les liens généalogiques, ou supprimer la dépendance. On définit ainsi une insularité. Le paradis de l'île Saint-Pierre, ou le peuple de Corse, qui n'est pas usé par la législation, qui est un peuple neuf. Moi, une île. Je suis unique, inengendré. Ma mère est morte à ma naissance : la nature a brisé le moule dans lequel elle m'a jeté. Mon entreprise n'eut jamais d'exemple, et son exécution n'aura pas d'imitateur. Pas d'amont, pas d'aval, pas de père, pas d'enfants, pas d'origine, pas de suite. Théorie générale de l'agénésie. *Sine patre, sine matre Melchisedec*, je suis de l'ordre des grandes figures messianiques. Jean-Paul Sartre ne manquera pas, dans *les Mots*, de répéter le même geste, la même découpe généalogique.

Du coup, toute ma famille n'est composée que de vicaires. Ma mère disparue, Mme de Warens est maman vicariante ; mon père expatrié, mon oncle le remplace ; mon frère en escapade et je me jette au cou de tous les Bâcles du monde, et partout les triangles, à foison, restitueront des inséparables ; ma femme, indigne de mon égalité, n'est que ma servante, et je la rembourse du titre de gouvernante. Donc je dépose mes enfants aux Enfants trouvés, Sophie, Émile en seront les vicaires. Famille de mots, enfants de papier. La logique de la vicariance est une généalogie du sacré.

La plume me tombe des mains, surpris à piquer, de la broche, une pomme. Pourquoi, maintenant, ai-je pris la plume? Pour confesser l'affaire du ruban. Le péché, ici avoué, demeure le même, invariant. J'ai accusé Marion, j'ai dit que Marion m'avait donné le ruban. Non, Jean-Jacques n'a pas menti, car on ne ment jamais, vu d'une certaine manière. Il a mis la petite Marion dans la position d'avoir été voleuse, prédatrice, pour se mettre aussitôt dans sa position ordinaire, celle du parasite. Marion m'en a fait cadeau. Il avoue, et il avoue la vérité vraie, en mentant. La honte, cette honte qui n'a jamais cessé de peser sur sa vie, venait de s'être dévoilée. Le désir de m'en délivrer a beaucoup contribué, dit-il, à la résolution que j'ai prise d'écrire mes confessions. Il prend, dès lors, la plume, et il ment. C'est maintenant qu'il ment. Il est bizarre, mais il est vrai, dit-il, que mon amitié pour la fille fut la cause de mon ignominie. J'avais Marion en tête, car je voulais lui donner le ruban. Dès ce moment, je l'accusai. Menteur! as-tu jamais rien donné à personne, as-tu jamais eu l'intention de donner? J'étais babillard, menteur et gourmand. J'aurais volé des fruits, des bonbons, de la mangeaille. Non, jamais je n'aurais donné ce ruban à Marion. Je n'espérais vraiment qu'une chose, c'est le recevoir de ses mains. Ce n'est pas moi, c'est le Xénophon du *Banquet* (encore un repas), qui définit le philosophe comme proxénète ou entremetteur. Celui qui se place au milieu d'une relation de désir, pour la parasiter. Exemple canonique : un jour, à table, au moment qu'elle avait mis un morceau dans sa bouche, je m'écrie que j'y vois un cheveu : elle rejette le morceau sur son assiette;

je m'en saisis et l'avale avidement. Le schéma est ici ramené à sa plus abstraite simplicité. Ou à sa nomination : quand elle me présentait une assiette, j'avançais ma fourchette pour piquer modestement un petit morceau de ce qu'elle m'offrait. Pique-assiette.

Jean-Jacques, juge du législateur

Il a soixante ans. Il vit seul, ou presque. Il copie, le matin, de la musique à tant la page. L'après-dîner, il se promène, alentour de Paris, solitaire. Il écrit, quelquefois, juste pour affirmer qu'il n'écrira plus. Il est sombre, méfiant, soupçonneux, il se dit bon et nul. Ils disent qu'il est fou. Et l'histoire dira qu'il est devenu fou. Est-il fou, en effet? Je crois pouvoir résoudre cette question.

Il a eu contre lui tous les grands polémistes d'Europe, à une époque où le venin était de qualité. Il a connu les déménagements furtifs aux petites heures de l'aube, décrété de prise de corps, comme on disait alors, en France, à Paris, à Genève en Suisse, à l'île Saint-Pierre dans le lac de Bienne. Dès le voyage en Angleterre, où il se réfugie, on parle du délire de persécution. Il y a là erreur d'optique, erreur de temps, surtout : les attaques contre le pouvoir en place n'étaient pas encore devenues d'efficaces leviers pour la prise des places et des pouvoirs. Le martyr ne risquait pas seulement une promotion. Rousseau avait de quoi, vraiment, se croire et se trouver persécuté. Ce n'est pas là, pourtant, le principal.

Ce principal peut être lu en clair dans les minutes d'un procès où Rousseau lui-même est en position de juger Jean-Jacques. Trois cents pages de fièvre où dialoguent un avocat et le ministère public, non plus devant le tribunal des *Confessions*, mais au-devant d'une plus haute instance, si possible le roi, sinon Dieu, le Juge suprême : ce pourquoi l'auteur cherche à déposer l'avant-dernier de ses livres sur le maître-autel de Notre-Dame. La grille étant fermée, il se trouve à nouveau exclu de ces législatures.

Son histoire à nouveau. C'est le malheur d'un homme seul face à l'humanité rassemblée, unanime et méchante. On sourit, méprise et range le livre au rayon des monuments de psychiatrie. Une minute, je vous prie, avant de le classer. De quoi s'agit-il donc, à travers le pathétique, la peur et le soupçon, la souffrance et le semblant, l'œil en coin et le noir théâtral ? De ce que peut savoir un homme de ce que les autres pensent de lui. Et de ce que les autres pensent tout court et font ensemble. Avant donc que d'examiner l'acte par lequel les autres pensent ou disent, il serait bon d'examiner l'acte par lequel les autres sont les autres.

Il faut supposer d'abord, et logiquement, cet individu indépendamment de toute relation. Sans cela, les autres, de son point de vue, ne seraient pas tels. Voici donc une description de l'isolement, de la singularité insulaire. Du bonheur à l'île Saint-Pierre à la tombe dans l'île aux Peupliers, à Ermenonville, l'île est toujours présente y compris dans la théorie, pour la constitution de la Corse. L'île se définit par ses bords ou, mieux, toute définition est une île. Elle est déterminée par ce qu'elle nie ou refuse, terre haute sur l'eau, le long du rivage. Rousseau n'emploie dans ces derniers dialogues que des mots du même ordre : il est environné, il est circonvenu, il se trouve entouré comme d'une barrière, il vit dans une étroite enceinte, il est dans une cage. Il n'est pas sûr qu'il y soit malheureux, puisqu'il souhaite vivre en prison, il n'est pas sûr non plus qu'il y soit heureux. En tout cas il y est, il dessine cet isolat.

Or, par un cas unique depuis que le monde existe, tout Paris, toute la France, toute l'Europe, tout le monde a fomenté complot contre un seul. Un seul qui, depuis lors, est seul sur cette terre.

Je dis que la chose est intéressante du simple point de vue de la logique. Il existe un singleton bien défini, moi, moi seul, il n'en existe qu'un, seul, seulement moi. Hors ce cas insulaire unique, il n'en existe pas d'autres, il ne peut en exister d'autres, parce que les autres forment un ensemble bien défini, compact et uniforme. Qui suis-je ? Seul. Seul n'est pas ma manière d'être, seul est mon être même. Qui sont les autres ? Tous. Attention : non pas tous moins un, mais tous absolument parlant. Tous sans exception et seul sans rémission.

Tous. Les grands, les auteurs et les gens de lettres, les médecins, les puissants et les femmes, les corps accrédités, l'administration, le gouvernement, les opinions publiques (bienheureux temps où ce terme était au pluriel), les commerçants, les badauds, les passants. Les visiteurs, les mendiants. Ceux qui écrivent des lettres, ceux qui envoient des manuscrits. Ceux qui me vendent bon marché, ceux

qui me vendent cher. Ceux qui sont gentils patelinent, ceux qui sont durs m'insultent. Ceux qui me
regardent m'inspectent, ceux qui font semblant de
ne pas me voir me méprisent. Toujours intéressant
du point de vue logique. La totalité vient de la réunion : d'un sous-ensemble et de son complémentaire. Ceux qui font ceci et ceux qui ne le font pas.
Ceux qui pensent ainsi et ceux qui ne le pensent
pas. Donc tout le monde. Lorsqu'on met la main sur
l'affirmation et sur la négation ensemble, on a toujours raison.

Tout le public, toute la génération, tout le genre
humain.

Il n'y a pas de particulier, il n'y a pas d'individus,
il n'y a pas de singuliers dans cet ensemble. Cela n'a
aucune importance que tel y soit auteur, que tel
autre y soit médecin ou administrateur. Cette totalité n'est pas l'agrégation de nombreux éléments
divers, c'est une somme de forces qui ne peut naître
que d'un concours. D'où la dénomination constante
de la ligue, de la secte, du complot, qui, par un
concours unanime à son exécution, met tout le
monde d'accord pour un mouvement concordant et
un assentiment universel.

Rousseau a reconnu de l'extérieur l'existence
d'un contrat social. Il décrit en fait à la fin de sa vie
ce qu'il avait posé en droit et abstraitement dans son
exercice de philosophie politique. Les autres en
bloc ont ensemble un pacte. Et ce pacte est issu de
l'animosité générale, qui est la perversion ou la dérivation de l'ancienne volonté générale. Jean-Jacques
dédoublé récrit le *Contrat social.* Le *Rousseau, juge de
Jean-Jacques* est son second traité de droit politique.

Il est environné de ténèbres, d'une triple enceinte de ténèbres. Il ne sait rien, il ne peut rien savoir de ce qu'on veut de lui, de ce dont on l'accuse, et du complot formé par ses persécuteurs. Pourquoi, comment? demande-t-il sans cesse en ces trois cents pages. Lorsqu'il écrivait du pacte social, nulle contradiction ne le gênait, tout lui semblait clair, lumineux. Il lui paraissait transparent de remonter à une convention première, il lui paraissait évident qu'un acte d'association puisse produire un moi commun ou une personne publique. Aujourd'hui, ceux du complot, ceux de la ligue forment, dit-il, un corps indissoluble dont chaque membre ne peut plus être séparé. Au sens politique, ils forment donc une république. Rousseau voit de l'extérieur se constituer ce qu'il avait prévu, il voit un ensemble dispersé faire une unité, un concours unanime de forces, et il trouve cela ténébreux. La vérité, c'est qu'il a raison, la vérité c'est qu'il a fait un progrès décisif en politique, la vérité, c'est que sa théorie n'était pas aussi claire qu'il le prétendait, que nul ne sait, que nul n'a jamais su comment se formait un concours unanime parmi des individus séparés. Que cette question est encore et toujours une question noire, ténébreuse. De la théorie, Rousseau descend à la pratique, du clair il en vient à l'obscur. Qu'est-ce que le collectif? La politique est l'ensemble des discours théâtraux tenus par des illusionnistes qui veulent nous faire croire qu'ils le savent clairement.

Cependant il existe au moins une réponse claire à la question. Et les professionnels de la politique la connaissent, d'ordinaire. Pour qu'apparaisse dans un groupe l'unanimité, il suffit parfois de faire naître justement l'animosité générale contre qui portera le nom d'ennemi public. Il suffit de trouver un objet de haine et d'exécration. Les grands succès de librairie ou d'élection se remportent ainsi. La volonté générale est rare, elle est peut-être théorique. La haine générale est fréquente, elle est de pratique. Non, Rousseau n'est pas fou, il reste un écrivain politique. Il passe à l'expérience, tout simplement, il passe de l'abstrait au concret. Non seulement il voit, de l'extérieur, naître un pacte social, non seulement il constate la formation d'une volonté générale, mais il observe, à travers des ténèbres épaisses, qu'elle ne se forme que par l'animosité, qu'elle ne se forme que parce qu'il en est la victime. Pourquoi ? Je n'en sais rien, il n'en sait rien, personne n'en sait rien, cela n'est pas clair, ne sera peut-être jamais clair : il reste que c'est ainsi. L'union se fait sur l'expulsion. Et c'est lui l'expulsé.

Est-il fou ? La réponse est simple et facile. Celui qui souffre du délire de persécution mime, tout simplement, une pratique politique. Cette politique a besoin de martyrs, elle en consomme abondamment, elle n'en manquera jamais, elle trouve assez de volontaires : les martyrs, en effet, ne sont que des rois, des princes, à peine inversés. Des ambitieux ratés, qui vont réussir. Voyez, au *Contrat Social*, le chapitre du « Législateur » : Rousseau, déjà, y jugeait Jean-Jacques. L'homme supérieur, le sage, celui qui est capable de transformer chacun en partie d'un grand tout, c'est évidemment l'auteur du *Contrat Social*. Il est hors les passions et les connaît à fond, il est hors le contrat, le prévoit et le forme.

Il est unique, il est presque un dieu, et le voici donc seul sur la terre. Il aura travaillé sous Louis XV et il jouira sous la Convention. Alors tout se retourne et l'inverse est encore vrai. Cette pratique politique mime, tout aussi bien, un délire du même genre. Le Moïse de Vigny, le Mahomet de Goethe, l'homme providentiel de Rousseau, avant ou après lui, ou lui, n'est, à tout prendre, qu'un beau paranoïaque. Le document de psychiatrie et le texte de philosophie politique sont tous les deux écrits de la même encre et par la même main. Avec les mêmes mots et pour le même sens. Et les mots — fou et politique — n'ont plus de sens propre, pour avoir le même.

Résultat profond et considérable. Les malades mentaux ne sont pas tous aux Petites-Maisons, comme on croit. Ils pullulent aux palais des rois, dans les grands postes et les hautes fonctions. Mais, à tout prendre, nous le savions depuis longtemps, l'expérience en est usuelle. Ce que nous ignorions, que nous apprend Rousseau, par sa vie théorique et ses livres vécus, est qu'un discours politique peut être un délire, et réciproquement. Autrement dit : puisque nous ignorons tout du fonctionnement collectif, la théorie qui en donne raison est cruellement délirante. Les torturés, les affamés, les morts le savent ou l'ont su dans leur chair.

Encore une classification qui s'effondre. Le *Contrat* s'étudie dans les instituts de sciences politiques et les *Dialogues* dans les écoles pour psychiatres, alors qu'il s'agit d'un seul et même écrit. Faisons faire à ces beaux messieurs des études communes : fous et politiques font une seule population, d'étudiants, d'étudiés. Angoisse, tout à coup :

l'évidence tirée de Rousseau, j'ai idée qu'elle est générale. Oui, ces maladies sont des politiques. Oui, ces politiques, théories et conduites, ne sont que maladies.

Bruits

Nous sommes ensevelis en nous-mêmes, nous émettons des gestes, des signes et des sons, indéfiniment, inutilement. Personne n'écoute personne. Chacun parle, nul n'entend, la communication directe ou réciproque est en échec. Celui-ci professe doctement, il est ennuyeux comme son dernier cours, il se moque absolument qu'on l'entende ; tel autre, jovial, tient un rôle fort, qu'il s'acharne à ne pas lâcher, il arrose l'écoute de sa belle humeur ; le troisième, colérique, dressé sur les ergots de sa petite taille, terrorise son entourage ; ils jouent de leur instrument préféré, qui s'appelle de leur nom propre. Tout cela devrait faire une cacophonie, cela fait du bruit, je l'avoue. Et Leibniz a raison, les monades sont fermées, elles ne s'entendent ni ne s'écoutent. Et pourtant, quelquefois, un accord. La chose la plus étonnante du monde est qu'il y ait parfois du concert. De l'entente, de l'harmonie. Leibniz supposait Dieu pour cette loi-miracle.

Il disait : voici un orchestre. Chaque musicien joue de son instrument comme s'il était seul au monde. Il n'aime que son cor anglais, ce cor anglais c'est lui, c'est lui-même en personne. Il fait sa partition et quand il a fini, tout au bout de la page, il pose sa dépouille et il sort du théâtre. Seulement pour mourir. Comment se fait-il que le premier alto soit en consonance avec lui, alors que le premier alto, encore, n'a jamais pensé qu'à ses quatre cordes? Leibniz répondait : Dieu a créé l'alto de telle sorte qu'à ce temps préfixe bien déterminé, il produira la note préformée harmoniquement à celle du cor anglais, au même moment. Dieu prévoit l'harmonie et Dieu est l'harmonie. L'histoire est programmée, chacun a une partition. D'autres disent qu'ils sont plongés ensemble dans le même bain de langue, dans le même bain de la même langue. Il faut bien que les mots se trouvent puisqu'ils sont dans le même ensemble. Et c'est la même solution : il existe un chef d'orchestre ou il existe un texte commun à jouer. Quelqu'un ou quelque chose précède toujours.

Cela n'est pas résoudre le problème, c'est se donner la solution. Se la donner sous forme de personne ou bien sous forme de prétexte. La probabilité de l'harmonie est faible dans la distribution multiple des émetteurs et la faiblesse qualitative de la réception. L'harmonie n'est pas une loi, elle n'est pas la régularité, l'harmonie est la rareté même. Elle est, très précisément, un miracle. J'appelle miracle une très haute improbabilité. Quand le miracle vient, d'une entente improbable, elle produit un chant nouveau, rare si hautement, qu'il est exclu que la répétition ait jamais eu lieu, aussi longtemps qu'ait duré le temps avant la rencontre. Cet accord est néguentropique, il est producteur, il est peut-être la production même, dans sa définition et son dynamisme.

En tout cas, la répétition est la mort. Elle est la chute dans le semblable, comme l'identité figée du trop-connu. S'il n'y avait jamais concert que du déjà écrit, le monde serait vite un enfer blême où flottent des ombres. Il en est ainsi souvent, je sais. Mais que la vérité, que le réel ne soit jamais que du prescrit transforme tout en sépulcral. Le toujours déjà n'est qu'un cimetière, où l'entropie va pourrissant. Par bonheur il y a du rare, l'exception se produit, la nouveauté paraît, le miracle improbable. Par cette rareté, le monde advient à l'existence, nous sommes des vivants, nous pensons. Ces trois événements sont improbables, et néanmoins sont là. Le préformé, le toujours à reprendre est ce texte de mort qui porte disparition du réel. Encore un avatar de la philosophie thanatogène qui cherche à transformer le monde en statue de sel, en plaine où gisent les cadavres. S'il y a un texte, déjà, s'il y a un chef de l'orchestre, s'il y a eu bien des répétitions, alors le monde est un enfer et nous ne sommes que des ombres. La mort a gagné la partie, assistée, dans ses œuvres, de la philosophie.

De la cacophonie usuelle. Les composants émettent ici même des sons à peu près canoniques, ils produisent, parfois, du sens. La somme ou le produit ou la composition de ces sources est ouï comme caricatural, inaudible, insensé. Ce repas, hier au soir, était ordinaire. Le jovial parlait haut et récitait fort, le docte pérorait, suffisant à soi-même, le doctrinal criaillait la vérité entière et pleine, le colérique tonnait le pouvoir, le vaniteux racontait sa toute belle voix, le profond se taisait, sombre, guettant la fatigue globale pour ramasser le dernier mot. Parmi le tohu-bohu, je faisais passer le fromage. Disons que j'étais l'hôte et que le chavignol était délicieux. D'une main à l'autre, il se divisait, mais il restait seul identique à soi-même, jusqu'à l'évanouissement. L'assiette contenait le stable prêt à disparaître, l'air vibrait de bruit et de brouhaha. Il eût été hors de coutume que la jovialité entendît la doctrine ou que le vaniteux écoutât le docte, il eût été miraculeux qu'un seul accord se produisît. A supposer une épiphanie de cet ordre, nous aurions à coup sûr résolu quelque difficulté ancienne ; un théorème, un texte, ou une chose, même, serait entré tout à coup dans la pièce, comme un vent propre à courber nos têtes, et se serait posé sur la table, au milieu de nous, douce-ment. Quand une monade fermée entend une monade close, quand un sourd écoute un muet, il arrive qu'ils produisent ensemble un vivant tout nou-veau, qui n'est jamais une répétition. Cette naissance est une preuve. Notre naïveté, j'entends le né nou-veau qui vient à la lumière, est une preuve, et déci-sive, de la néguentropie fantastique des accordailles. Il y va, tout à coup, de la production. Il n'y a de nou-veau que la naïveté. Il n'y a de nouveau que le mira-culeux. Or ce miracle est de l'entente.

Soyez naïf, vous serez l'enfant de la nouveauté. Mais aussi, écoutez, vous ferez des enfants. Voici venu l'enfantement dans la beauté, au milieu du banquet.

Nous ne connaissons rien à la composition, au produit, à la somme, à l'intégrale des monades ou des individus, de quelque nom qu'on nomme leur société ou leur association. Nous ne savons rien des opérations les plus simples, ou directes : additionner, multiplier, composer, combiner, quand il s'agit de nous. Hélas, nous ne pouvons que soustraire, analyser, tuer. Le collectif est une boîte noire. L'ensemble fait du bruit, est rumeur. Même si chaque élément joue juste ou émet du sens, la mise ensemble produit une clameur, fausse, hasardeuse, insensée. Le collectif est le bruit de fond même, nous ne savons aucunement ce qu'est un orchestre, comment un chœur s'accorde. Le collectif n'est pas une harmonie préétablie ou bien, ce qui revient au même, le toujours déjà là. De la boîte noire, sort le bruit. Le noir et le charivari.

Le politique fait semblant de comprendre. Le savant, le théoricien, fait semblant de comprendre. Le religieux fait semblant de comprendre. Le militaire, l'inspecteur, le militant font semblant de comprendre. Chaque fonction sociale est une variété connue et repérable de la méconnaissance noire déguisée intelligemment en expertise blanche. Mais le renversement du bruit réel en une harmonie théâtrale, de la tuerie du sens et du son en un accord au moins représenté, n'est pas ici le seul des bénéfices. Chaque fonction sociale, du juge au professeur, et de l'artiste au président, chaque fonction classée ou classable dans une théorie quelconque des classes ou fonctions, chaque fonction, dis-je, mange et vit de ladite méconnaissance. Elle apparaît tout aussitôt qu'il faut fermer la boîte noire. Et cette opération se paie, elle se paie assez cher pour que le détenteur de la clé en vive grassement. Qui détient une clé ne détient pas forcément un savoir, il peut garder aussi

une serrure et défendre qu'on l'ouvre. Chaque fonction sociale est gardienne d'une porte de l'arche, et
d'une porte dangereuse, croit-on.

Nous ne comprenons rien du collectif, ni de
l'ensemble. Nous devons avouer que cette arche
n'est pleine que de ténèbres et que d'elle ne sort
qu'une rumeur intraduisible. Qu'il n'y a pas de site,
hors de la boîte ou hors de l'arche, d'où quelqu'un
puisse entendre ou traduire ou voir. Que nous
sommes dans l'arche : et si nous sommes hors, nous
ne sommes plus nous. Le collectif n'est pas un objet
ordinaire, il n'est susceptible ni de définition, ni de
découpage, ni d'extériorité. Il n'est pas, non plus, un
sujet : qui le serait, parmi nous ? Qui serait-ce nous ?
Qui est-il ? Que dit-il ? Où est-il ? Cet ensemble n'est
pas un sujet, il n'est pas un objet, il est donc hors du
fonctionnement de la connaissance. Nous ignorons
ce que signifie nous, ce qui le constitue. Nous ignorons ce qui passe entre nous et ce qui se passe entre
nous. S'il n'y a pas de connaissance, comment pour-
rait-il se faire qu'il y ait une volonté ? Cette volonté
générale est un automorphisme, j'entends par ce
mot la projection ou la reproduction de ce qu'on
croyait qui se passe en moi dans ce nouveau sujet
mythique, le nous. Elle est une égologie retraduite.
Qui assure que le nous a les mêmes attributs, les
mêmes facultés que le je ? Une pensée, une intelligence, une volonté. Pourquoi pas des désirs, des
appétits ou une sexualité ? Nous avons commis la
même erreur sur le collectif que sur Dieu, nous
l'avons fait à l'image du moi. De mon âme parfois,
quand on lui donne volition, intellect, pouvoir de
décision, quand on passe du *cogito* personnel au *cogi-*

tamus ou du *volo* monadique au *volumus*, mais de mon corps souvent : gros animal, corps mystique, Léviathan, modèles biologiques, la Bête. Non, nous ne savons rien du nous que ce que nous croyons savoir du moi, corps et âme. En somme, nous ne savons rien et, de nouveau, le collectif est noir et fait du bruit.

De quoi ne discute-t-on point ? De quoi n'y a-t-il pas de dispute ? Sur quoi nous accordons-nous immédiatement ?

Sur un point de droit, il y a contrat. Le droit est notre existence assez stable, la politique est notre histoire instable (en principe, car, en fait, les professionnels s'empressent de la stabiliser à leur profit). Le contrat social théorique est écrit en lambeaux dans les textes de droit. Mis ensemble, ils renvoient à un texte non écrit qui, s'il était écrit, nous apprendrait ce que signifie être ensemble. Or ce texte n'est pas écrit et, peut-être, ne peut-il l'être. En tout cas, nous ne discutons pas sur le droit, sauf à la marge des jurisprudences. Nous ne discutons pas sur lui, à cause du gendarme. Nous avons peur de la force sur quoi il est fondé. Nous sommes d'accord, un peu, et nous obéissons, beaucoup. Car nous avons peur. Peur du noir.

Le droit organise notre vie concrète de groupe, de la famille aux relations entre les peuples. Il est plein de détails et de sens. Il varie d'une culture à une autre, des spécialistes cherchent à connecter les différences ; tous ces efforts, différences et ressem-

blances, fluctuent par les circonstances de l'histoire.
L'accord se perd.

Il existe, deuxièmement, tout un corpus devant
lequel l'accord se fait, comme par miracle, c'est le
corpus mathématique. On n'en discute qu'à la
marge, entre chercheurs, à propos de pointes avan-
cées. Pour tout le reste, on ne dispute point. On
peut être antidarwinien, contre la relativité généralisée, nul ne peut, sauf à se retirer de la communauté,
mettre en doute les quatre règles. On peut truquer
la balance au marché, on ne peut falsifier l'addition
ni la soustraction ; le partenaire peut vous tromper
sur le change, mais il ne peut tricher en rendant la
monnaie. La mathématique est l'accord entre nous.
Le cercle a un centre, l'ellipse en a deux, que voulez-
vous redire à cela ? D'une certaine manière, la
mathématique est un nous. Elle ne l'est plus, assurément, dans les cercles fermés où s'élabore l'invention, elle le reste, cependant, à mesure qu'elle est
comprise. Elle est un nous assez nouveau, inventé
par les Grecs, infusé par eux dans l'histoire, avec
d'immenses conséquences, dont celle de nous
peindre un portrait commun, idéal. Illusoire ? Nous
nous accordons au moins sur les nombres.

J'insiste. L'accord ne porte pas sur la monnaie,
mais sur les unités, puis les opérations. La monnaie
renvoie au texte de droit, l'imprimé sur le cuivre, le
laiton, l'or, l'argent, le papier reste une convention,
un contrat, fondé, en dernier recours, sur la force,
fondé, en dernière instance, sur la mort. L'économie
repose, évidemment, sur la violence. On voit sans
peine que l'accord sur les nombres est d'une autre
nature et d'une autre portée. Il est translinguistique

et transculturel, vous ne pouvez rien à cela. Il se peut que nous acceptions de nourrir indéfiniment des savants, dans la reconnaissance où nous sommes qu'ils aient bâti ce pont fragile entre nous autres; peut-être unique, en vérité. Il ne circule entre nous que des signaux mathématiques. Ils sont les seuls à traverser en paix l'épaisseur d'incommunicabilité qui nous sépare, et que ne traverse, cruellement, que la force armée, hurlante, mortelle.

Non, ce train de signaux ne fut que le second. Il fallait un train, tout d'abord, il fallait des signaux. La condition de l'accord sur un sens, fût-il minime ou univoque, est l'accord, pur et simple, parfait. Pour que se réalise une entente, à propos d'une chose ou à propos d'un mot, il faut une entente, une ouïe.

Je suis seul ce matin, comme à l'accoutumée, penché sur mon travail, dans un silence blanc. Sans doute mes oreilles ne sont-elles sensibles qu'à ce bruit de fond vague, indispensable à la survie. D'un repli de l'espace, comme d'un creux du monde, me parvient une onde audible. Elle est impure, elle crie, elle crisse, elle criaille, donc je fuis; je me recroqueville au foyer de mon attention, dans l'apex de ma solitude. Je cherche d'instinct un lieu haut inaccessible à cette attaque. J'ai peur. J'ai peur du grincement, de la stridulation et du charivari. Ma peau en a horreur, elle se creuse et se hérisse. Que croisse l'intensité de cet éclat qui occupe l'espace, je perds bientôt ce refuge en moi et je perds conscience.

Peut-être est-ce le ciel qui tombe sur ma tête, tonnerre, volcan, tremblement de terre, inondation soyeuse ou tsunami roulant. Je fuis. Peut-être est-ce l'autre qui hurle. J'ai peur. J'ai peur du cri, du braillement, de ce stentor qui lance la foudre de Dieu. Donc je fuis. Les rossignols ont peur des rossignols qui chantent et qui délimitent ainsi leur niche de puissance. La mélodie qui nous enchante est un inaudible criaillement, pour eux, on doit le supposer. Le bruit nous sépare, nous individualise, comme la fureur nous disperse. Le mur épais qui existe entre nous est construit de clameurs et de cacophonie. La monade n'a ni porte ni fenêtre, nous sommes sourds et, pour autrui, muets, parce que, le plus souvent, ce qui parvient à nous, à notre réception toujours ouverte, l'ouïe, nous est insupportable.

Nous sommes plongés dans le bruit. Et ce bruit est inextinguible. Il est extérieur, il est le monde même, et il est intérieur, produit par notre corps vivant. Nous sommes dans les bruits du monde, nous ne pouvons fermer la porte au reçu de cette clameur, et nous évoluons, roulés dans cette houle incalculable. Nous sommes chauds, brûlant de vie, et les foyers de cette extase temporaire émettent le tumulte sans trêve de leur innombrable fonctionnement. Que ces sources se taisent et la mort est là, sous forme d'ondes plates. Plates pour l'enregistrement, plates pour les oreilles closes. Au commencement est le bruit, le bruit ne cesse pas. Il est notre aperception du chaos, notre appréhension du désordre, notre seul lien à la distribution éparse des choses. L'ouïe est notre ouverture héroïque au trouble et à la diffusion, les autres récepteurs nous assurent de l'ordre, ou, s'ils n'en donnent pas ou n'en reçoivent plus, se ferment aussitôt. Que nous soyons plongés dans la fluctuation, que nous en soyons pleins, le bruit nous en assure. Et il nous chasse du chaos, par l'horreur qu'il nous en inspire, il nous ramène, il nous rappelle à l'ordre.

Le réel me paraît stochastiquement régulier, comme de la similitude ou de l'homogène, jetés au hasard.

La monade n'a pas de porte, elle n'a pas, non plus, de fenêtre, ceci pour se défendre du malaise mortel. Si nous percevions tout le bruit du monde, si nous souffrions notre propre bruit, l'évanouissement nous ferait glisser vers le plat. Aussi la monade ferme à double tour ses orifices, elle finit par les supprimer tout à fait, en raison de ce danger physique, de la mort par inondation. Elle a plus vite fait, somme toute, de tout tirer de son propre fond.

Or la solution leibnizienne, par un paradoxe qu'on n'attendait pas, est maximalement pauvre, pour minimiser le désordre. L'ordre a tout envahi, reste le grain de sel des septièmes devant le flot de l'harmonie. La dépense n'est, certes, pas grande, mais la diversité demeure faible. L'accord parfait n'est point, que je sache, le comble de l'art, peut-être n'en est-il que la misère. L'harmonie ne serait-elle pas une variété, un peu excitée, de plat? Ne serait-elle pas une antichambre de la mort? Cet ordre, dont on chasse au maximum la dissonance parasite, cet homogène, ce semblable courant vers l'identité, cette répétition, cette ligne droite optimalement courte, ce plat, n'est-ce pas ce vers quoi nous glissons quand nous perdons l'acuité, la conscience, la vie? Je crains que l'harmonie parfaite ne soit qu'un flonflon lourd pour tête qui n'appète qu'à répéter. Le monde autour de nous, en nous, se défend victorieusement contre cette sottise par le miraculeux torrent d'inattendu. Ce qui demeure intelligent dans le cursus des sciences est ce qui est devant, qui échappe à la loi. Le meilleur en moi se retourne, il n'est pas seulement chassé par le bruit, par le chaos et le désordre, il est chassé par la règle, et le plat, et la mort. Le meilleur, c'est-à-dire le moins cadavérique.

La pauvreté suprême du système de l'harmonie nous est connue enfin non seulement par la nature des choses, comme on aimait à dire, mais par les établissements collectifs. Dieu chez Leibniz monte chaque monade, qui n'a de singulier que son site. Ce qui circule dans le système est un message unique, la loi, différentiellement codée par la position des individus. La seule nouveauté qui puisse intervenir dans l'uniformité, dans l'ordre, est ma situation. Le patron ne commande pas au vice-président comme à celui qui tient la position infime. Toute l'horreur d'une société sans espérance est contenue là : qu'il ne s'y dit qu'une chose, vite sans intérêt, mais qu'elle ne se dit qu'en se modulant par le site du récepteur. J'imagine qu'il s'agit là d'une collectivité animale. Je l'imagine seulement, car ce que nous savons des bêtes nous indique finalement qu'elles sont, par rapport à nous, plutôt des génies de la politique. La métaphore par la bête est souvent une flatterie.

Le bruit détruit et fait horreur. Mais l'ordre et la répétition plate sont voisins de la mort. Le bruit nourrit un nouvel ordre. L'organisation, la vie et la pensée intelligente habitent l'adhérence entre l'ordre et le bruit, entre le désordre et l'harmonie parfaite. S'il n'y avait que l'ordre, si nous n'entendions que des accords parfaits, notre sottise tomberait bientôt vers un sommeil sans rêve, si nous étions roulés toujours dans le charivari nous perdrions haleine et consistance, nous nous éparpillerions au milieu des atomes dansants de l'univers. Nous sommes, nous vivons, nous pensons à la frange, dans le probable alimenté d'inattendu, dans le légal nourri d'information. Il y a deux façons de mourir, deux façons de dormir, deux façons d'être bête, la plongée tête nue dans le tohu-bohu, l'installation stabilisée dans l'ordre et la chitine. Nous sommes assez bien pourvus, de sens et d'instinct, contre le danger d'explosion, nous sommes dépourvus devant la mort par ordre ou l'ensommeillement par règle et harmonie.

Notre chance est sur la crête. Notre parcours vivant et inventif suit la courbe frangée, capricieuse, où la plage simple de sable rencontre le déferlement bruyant de la vague. Une méthode simple et droite ne donne aucune information, son inutilité, sa platitude est enfin calculable. L'intelligence, on le savait, demeure inattendue, comme l'invention, ou la grâce, elle n'excède pas le surprenant vers le n'importe quoi. La rigueur n'est jamais dans le simple qui tend vers l'identique, elle ne serait rien sans réunir, tenir ensemble ce qui ne devrait pas être associé. Il n'y a de nouveau que par injection de hasard dans la règle, que par introduction de la loi au sein du désordre. Une organisation naît des circonstances, comme Aphrodite sort de l'onde.

Musique

Il est intéressant que le mot choisi par les musiciens pour leurs textes écrits soit le mot partition. Il est intéressant qu'on en ait une définition rigoureuse, depuis que l'ont choisi les mathématiciens. Ce n'est pas la première rencontre entre ces deux groupes, ces deux fonctions et leur langage. Sans le savoir toujours, ils sont toujours ensemble. Ils sont nés sous le même ciel et au même moment, jumeaux, ils sont nos compagnons sous les mêmes orages. Eux seuls savent, parmi nous, ce qu'est un accord et comment le réaliser. Il faut bien s'accorder, pour jouer ensemble, pour calculer ou pour déduire ensemble.

Ils découpent un ensemble ou une collection d'objets quelconques en parties ou sous-ensembles deux à deux disjoints. Nulle de ces parties n'empiète sur nulle autre. Et leur intersection est vide. Aucune note du violon ne peut être jouée sur la flûte, et ainsi pour tous. Ainsi pour la partition de l'écu où tout espace est séparé. Je veux dire que le texte est adapté à l'instrument, nul ne doit jouer sur hautbois ce que le violoncelliste doit lire. Tout est paradoxal ici :

pour jouer ensemble au plus juste, il faut que la dis-
jonction soit parfaite et stricte. Il n'existe pour personne un texte commun. Seul le chef a sous les yeux
le recouvrement de l'ensemble.

Comment, pourquoi Rousseau avait-il choisi pour
métier de copier de la musique à tant la page ? Comment, pourquoi cette pratique le fascinait-elle, au
point d'y consacrer ses plus longues heures de vie ?
Au point de compter, à loisir et pour le plaisir, les
milliers de pages qu'il avait couvertes de notes. Pourquoi, comment suivre ainsi les notes, presque aveu-
glément ?

Je crois que Jean-Jacques a vécu, sans la voir
devant lui, évidente, la relation parasitaire. L'exigence de revoir sa vie, en la confessant, est venue
d'avoir à chercher ce qui manquait aux écrits théo-
riques, ce que la théorie cachait, loin de le manifes-
ter clairement.

Rousseau construit progressivement, comme ce
livre-ci l'essaie, le champ des sciences humaines ou
sociales, comme on dit par abus de langue. Non lesdites sciences, dans leur contenu positif, mais leur
champ, dans les conditions. Il est assez clair qu'il
faille commencer par une théorie des relations,
qu'en ce commencement l'hésitation soit imman-
quable entre une théorie locale ou globale, et
qu'enfin cette hésitation soit intégrée dans le problème. Dans un petit groupe fermé, le jardin de
Julie, un ménage à trois raffiné châtre le nouvel Abé-
lard, dans un groupe plus rare encore, un élevage

attentif laisse un orphelin vert; en face, le *Contrat social* dit la volonté générale et trace la face du législateur. Local, global. Les *Dialogues* font enfin voir la vue aveugle de l'écart, en l'exaspérant : je suis seul et les voici tous. Le local se minimise jusqu'à la solitude et le global se maximise vers l'universel quantifié. Je vois enfin, dans les ténèbres, ladite volonté générale. Et la chose est atroce. Peut-être le législateur est-il quelque fou dangereux ou quelque innocent sacrifié. Mais en même temps, les *Confessions* cherchent obscurément, au voisinage de la monade solitaire, où va, où se fixe, comment se constitue la relation. Elle tend vers zéro, elle va s'évanouir dans les îles, au milieu des lacs.

Jean-Jacques meurt et sa dernière phrase s'enchante de rendre à la femme l'assistance qu'il en a reçue. Son dernier mot confesse qu'il n'a jamais rendu. La vérité sous la dernière boucle de la plume, il meurt peut-être sans savoir qu'il a découvert ce qu'il cherchait, enfin. La chaîne simple, moi, mon frère, mon prochain, mon ami et ma société demande un enchaînement, et il manque. Non, il ne manque pas, il est la flèche simple, atome logique, atome relationnel, vécu, obscur, dans la vie chez l'hôtesse. Mais moi, détaché d'eux et de tout, qui suis-je moi-même? Celui qui a toujours reçu, et qui, à l'article de mort, se souvient tout à coup qu'il avait, à loisir, résolu de rendre. Le parasite. Détaché, oui, je ne suis rien qu'un pauvre fou dans les ténèbres, mais mon premier attachement est la dérivation, l'ente, la greffe, l'installation dans un petit hôtel, muni de mon petit ménage. Petit.

Il abandonne ses enfants. Le bilan moral de l'affaire m'est indifférent. Que m'importent faute, punition, culpabilité, serments, réparations feintes ou vraies! Ces adhérences visqueuses répugnent. Pourquoi, de quoi défendrais-je Rousseau? Pourquoi l'attaquerais-je? Faut-il toujours l'éthique et le combat, pour former un théâtre et passionner les spectateurs? Tout cela est lassant. Que m'importe qu'il ait été mauvais ou bon, que m'importe la pincée de cendres grasses au fond d'un pot du Panthéon. Quittons le cirque. L'éthique y est laissée. Ce qui compte est, presque, l'herbier, je veux dire le symptôme vital, comme le signe de l'espèce, la biologie enfin, l'histoire naturelle. Voici : un parasite, jamais, ne nourrit ses enfants. Il serait, sinon, à la place de l'hôte. Un parasite se défend d'être parasité, la chose est là, dans sa simplicité. Je coûtai la vie à ma mère, hôtesse, et, symétriquement, je laissai mes enfants, je ne suis pas un hôte possible. Nul ne saurait me supplanter. L'Assistance publique est un hôtel possible. Voyez cet animal pondre ses œufs dans un magasin convenable ou un vecteur éventuel, les descendants vont s'y développer, alimentés au gîte, où ils mourront, comme leur grand-mère. Curieuse dénomination que cette Assistance publique : et si les enfants de Rousseau avaient été abandonnés à la Volonté générale?

Peut-être aurais-je aimé dire : épiphyte, cet herbier aussi me poussant. Je ne sais ce qui me retient, le mouvement sans doute. La promenade.

Des îles de cohérence apparaissent, qu'on n'apercevait pas. La théorie est moins dans les lieux désignés pour elle qu'elle n'est dense dans l'obscur des textes confessés. Le philosophe y cherche d'expérience, il faut suivre sa randonnée. Elle fait émerger la vieille tradition culturelle, à nouveau, celle qui associe à nos valeurs d'abus la vie de quelques plantes et de certaines bêtes. Les hôtels rencontrés, les attachements, l'abandon instinctif des enfants, la botanique même, la maladie, ces éléments épars se concertent, non pas tant dans une nature qu'autour d'une fonction mieux, d'une relation. Le jardin de Julie est exubérant de plantes parasites, c'est l'herbier-paradis.

Du coup, il est aisé de courir aider la victoire, de voir que ce qui manque à cette tradition est justement ce geste laborieux qu'à longueur d'heure et de journée Rousseau ne cesse pas de faire. Pourquoi tenait-il tant à gagner sa petite vie en copiant des notes, éperdument? Réponse : en raison du bruit. Réponse : il complétait l'aire du parasite.

Il pouvait vivre de son œuvre. Je m'arrête un peu. Qu'est-ce qu'une œuvre? Elle mange son ouvrier, elle dévore sa chair et ses heures, elle se substitue, peu à peu, à son corps. Cet envahissement fait peur. Qui suis-je? Ceci, là, écrit noir sur blanc, fragile, et ceci est mon corps, a pris la place de mon corps, frêle. Ceci est gravé de mon sang, j'en saigne, et ne s'arrêtera qu'à sa dernière goutte. L'œuvre parasite l'ouvrier, non, bientôt, il n'existe plus. Il en meurt. Et il n'y peut rien. Il en vit. Je mange mon travail et de lui, je bois cette production ruisselante par la longueur des jours, je dors sous la tente de son tabernacle dans la largeur de son espace, j'existe enfin dans l'ombre de ses volumes-fruits. Qui suis-je? Ce corps, réuni dans sa casse, je ne serais rien sans ceci. L'œuvre me parasite et je la parasite. Bientôt, peut-être, serons-nous des convives sages. Bientôt, espérons-le, serons-nous adaptés l'un à l'autre, en un banquet joyeux, léger, perpétuel, où nous partagerons l'ambroisie. Oui, je le sais, ma vie devient symbiote. Fin de la parenthèse, elle n'était pas un bruit, tout à fait.

Il copie des grappes de notes, alors qu'il pourrait vivre de son œuvre, se nourrir d'elle. Non. Il ne peut vivre, comme vous et moi, que de ce qui fait vivre, on sait de quoi il a fait dépendre sa vie. De vérité. Vivre de vérité, voilà tout. Or, il n'a pas dit le vrai dans le champ de l'économie, dans celui de la politique, ni celui de l'éducation, dans les conditions générales, contractuelles, de la vie sociétaire. Non qu'il ait menti. Mais il n'avançait que par abstractions. Il revient donc à l'expérience, il médite, il confesse. Émerge alors le sens compact, la vérité relationnelle recherchée. J'ai vécu à la table des autres, qui suis-je donc?

Qui suis-je, assurément? Me voici seul, sans relation. Réduit à moi seul, je me nourris de ma propre substance, elle ne s'épuise pas, je me suffis, quoique je rumine à vide, mon imagination tarie et mes idées éteintes ne fournissent plus d'aliments à mon cœur. Qui suis-je, encore? A la lettre une partition. Je ne suis pas un élément d'un ensemble social, famille, groupe, humanité, tous ont délié mes appartenances ou inclusions, j'ai perdu toute relation. Je vis dans le disjoint, autour de moi les intersections restent vides,

eaux calmes, agitées, alentour de l'île. Qui suis-je ?
Une partition.

Cette méditation, cartésienne, retrouve, sourde-
ment, les solutions de Leibniz. Elles sont présentes
dans la musique, elles y sont comme ensevelies.
L'harmonie recèle de soi le recouvrement des parti-
tions sans relation aucune. Autant s'asseoir, du
matin jusqu'au soir, en leur présence assourdissante.
J'écris, je fais le quart depuis l'aube, en attendant et
pour attendre un feu qui jaillira un jour, l'écriture
de feu, en haut du mur, au-dessus du banquet sou-
dainement interrompu, ou les langues de feu volant
sur les nuques raides, ouvrant l'écoute, enfin. Il fait
le quart à la musique, dès les petites heures, il attend
la réponse cachée dans le fouillis des notes et des
clés, la réponse simple aux questions, dans leurs
traces noires.

Je suis la partition, voici la partition. Qu'est-ce que
l'harmonie, la musique, enfin ? Comment s'établit
cette composition ?

Il est dans les ténèbres et nous y sommes avec lui,
nous voyons clair enfin de voir cette nuit-là. Le collectif est une boîte noire. Que peut-on voir des relations, qui les voit ? Les hommes parasitent les
hommes, l'hôte est l'hôte de l'homme, et c'est
encore un théorème noir. La relation parasite la
relation, la relation soi-même est parasite, ces
logiques sont obscures et elles se renversent, floues.
Je ne dois plus chercher dans l'épiphanie transpa-
rente d'une théorie pauvre ce qui demeure noir
dans l'épaisseur de l'à peine observable.

La volonté générale était une abstraction, l'animosité générale est concrète, vécue, soufferte. Sur le

chemin des conditions, nous ne pouvons plus arrêter la requête.

Comment se sont-ils accordés? Je ne sais. Comment s'accorder, non pas pour ou contre tel ou tel autre, ce n'est plus, désormais, la question, mais comment s'accorder, maintenant et ici, de manière quelconque?

Au courant de la vie banale, telle qu'elle est à confesser, les interceptions vont et viennent. Invitations par-ci, par-là, chez la marquise et le vicaire, chez le lion, le seigneur et le rat, branchements astucieux, vols furtifs, petits bruits, la plume, tout à coup, mais sérieusement pour le coup, la plume tombe de mes mains. Les petits bruits, les interruptions croissent jusqu'à la crise, jusqu'à la catastrophe. Le plafond tombe sur la table. Les eaux du déluge ennoient la vallée. Craquements, rumeurs, chaos.

Hors de la salle, Simonide. Hors du naufrage, les vieux hôtes arborescents. Ils entendent le vacarme, ils sont amis des dieux. Ou inversement, la catastrophe est Pentecôte, le tiers est seul dehors, il ramène le vent et le son. Jean-Jacques est seul dehors, il voit les ténèbres, il entend le chaos et le tohu-bohu. La victoire est aux mains des bruits parasites.

Je parle à plusieurs voix. De Rousseau, œuvre et vie, parcours, achèvement; de tout ce qui précède, aux festins de ce livre; des Actes des Apôtres et des récits gréco-latins; de la *Répétition*, au milieu de l'orchestre, chez Fellini, mon texte parallèle, en images et sons. Il faut recommencer, parmi la salle inondée de décombres, dans une obscurité inquiète, parmi les morts et les vivants, au risque des bruits qui ne manqueront pas de revenir très vite. Les parasites vont se multipliant jusqu'au tonnerre et la fureur. La relation d'abus n'arrête pas sa crue. La simple flèche va, elle n'a pas de frein. Jusqu'à un seuil où le bruit, l'abus ou la flèche ne sont plus tolérés. Simonide est devant les morts, Philémon devant le déluge, Rousseau en face de la nuit, le troisième hors la salle close. Que faire?

Ce qui nous désaccorde, ce qui nous interrompt, celui qui mange notre pain et qui interdit nos messages : le parasite. L'invité devient maître et il produit un bruit terrible. Nous y sommes, je suis cet invité. Il faut partir de lui, du bruit, de moi. Qui suis-je? Le parasite. Et je suis dehors, seul, au milieu de l'île et dans la nuit. Écoutez. Ouvrez les oreilles. Les mots font entendre les solutions. Suivez les mots. Le parasite désaccorde, il bruisse. Je suis une partition. Je suis seul, isolé, solitaire, disjoint. Seul sans aucune relation, ou muni d'une relation qui ramène vers moi, qui brouille les messages. Dès lors, je suis exceptionnel pour l'étude que je me donne. Je suis une exception au nous, ce qui rend impossible ce nous. Or, cette exception est universelle. Qu'est-ce donc qui nous accorde? Suivez le mot, le son, le vent : l'accord.

Pas de théorie, je vous prie. La note. Suivez la note. La musique nous sauve, et les notes nous sauvent. Les notes nous apaisent et la musique apaise. Agrippez-vous aux notes, suivez-les. Elles seules. L'accord.

L'accord. Sur quel objet, à quel sujet? Plus tard, plus tard. Mais, au moins, sur un sens. Plus tard, vous dis-je. Sur le son même, tout d'abord. Si tu ne fais pas trop de bruit, j'essaierai de cesser le mien, si je sonne assez juste, tu évolueras vers cette paisible justesse. Avant d'échanger un seul mot, avant de s'accorder sur le code, au moins faut-il émettre un son ensemble. Ici, on peut émettre et recevoir en même temps. Oui, mon signal est seul au monde, et ma voix crie dans le désert, dans le désert pierreux de mes criailleries. Cailloux spécifiques, individués. Otons ces pierres parasites; en rabotant ces épines de son, l'un vers l'autre nous avançons. L'accord sonore et musical est l'archaïque accord des accordailles. Ensemble. Vibration à plusieurs voix. Jouissance. Le collectif, au minimum, est utopie sonore. Hermès requiert des traductions. La Pentecôte chante, sonne et vente, les langues fondent à ce feu, la musique a parlé en langues. Elle est pure de parasites. Langage universel d'un contrat enfoui.

Comme un invité affamé se fascine au buffet d'un festin, Jean-Jacques garde la musique. Là gît, manifeste et enveloppée, la solution. Cette solution l'inclut et l'exclut, elle l'inclut comme partition, elle l'exclut comme parasite. Qui suis-je? La condition de la musique, de l'accord, son empêchement.

Il la copie, l'écrit, la conserve, la garde, la donne. Il l'échange et la vend. Il a toujours su résoudre sa question : non pas en ce qu'il dit, mais en ce qu'il fait, qui est plus clair que la lumière des concepts, qui est plus aisé à entendre que la langue de bois de la philosophie.

Et en ce qu'il fait, quand il dit.

Si jamais une plume laissa sur le silence blanc de son aire de caresse un frémissement, un envol, si jamais quelqu'un entendit, pour écrire de la sorte, des voix célestes ou les bruits de l'enfer, ce fut le gardien de cette musique. Pure de parasite, pure, pure, pure de soi-même, absolument purgée de moi. Plus j'écris et moins je suis moi. Enfin délivré de ce bruit.

Chaque ligne s'écarte, se sauve, de l'avancée aléatoire du tohubohu, de la lave des volcans, des zébrures qui hachent la terre quand elle tremble, elle vole au-dessus des ouragans, elle apaise les bêtes hurlantes, les jaguars qui rugissent et les loups affamés, elle arrache l'amoureuse aux enfers, elle avance, courageuse, au voisinage des rumeurs, elle fait face au bruit, un accord y résonne, non pas simple, non pas sot, naïf, repris ou piétinant, mais, à chaque pied, tout nouveau, nourri longuement de désordre et d'inattendu et posé doucement aux limites, dans la frange, la marge où le cristal pur des fontaines coule entre toi et moi, dansons en attendant que les bêtes se rafraîchissent. La langue nous accorde sous le sens, et le sens, souvent, nous disperse.

Écrivez, comme lui, sur la distribution d'un jeu de cartes, sur le dos noir et ténébreux des faces du hasard, écrivez sur l'envers-endroit que vous montrez aux autres en cachant votre jeu et votre partition, ne cessez pas d'écrire à l'envers du hasard, du désordre, du bruit, à l'envers de vos circonstances propres et à même leur chair, une petite musique-harmonie, pour l'autre et avec lui.

Vaches grasses et vaches maigres

Économie

Repas de salade
Origine stercoraire du droit de propriété

Rousseau n'a pas voulu nous dire comment s'y était pris le fondateur de société civile pour enclore son terrain. Il a fiché des pieux ou creusé un fossé, paraît-il. Dès l'aurore du jour suivant, les premiers furent arrachés ou le second fut, à coup sûr, comblé, non par un philosophe égalitaire passant là, mais par ceux qui voulaient se mettre à la place du propriétaire. L'un de ces successeurs est sur les lieux très vite, si vite que je le crois contemporain du premier occupant. Aux primitifs labours des murailles de Rome, on distingue assez mal deux jumeaux, celui qui enclôt le terrain, celui qui transgresse la fermeture. Ils sont, tous les deux, des premiers *ex æquo*, dans ce temps d'origine. Et ils s'entre-tuent. Trouver des simples qui vous croient n'est pas trop malaisé, se sauver de la jalousie est une entreprise sans espoir. Le premier qui, ayant enclos un terrain, s'avisa de dire : *Ceci est à moi*, fut un homme mort, il suscita tout aussitôt son assassin. Au commencement est le meurtre, les vieux textes le disent, le raisonnement nous le montre. Romulus ne labourait que pour enterrer, profond, Remus.

Il existe pourtant des choses closes, j'entends de la propriété. Quelle est l'origine, quel est le fondement de la propriété? Je n'ai jamais cru que mes semblables et moi fussions des anges, mais nous ne sommes pas assez bêtes pour n'arrêter jamais la guerre, pour ne jamais nous ménager des instants de tranquillité. Les théories de la guerre sans trêve sont généralement conçues par les concurrentiels de la conquête et de la gloire, bourrés jusqu'à la gueule de cette *libido dominandi* qui en fait de grands hommes. L'humanité serait si paisible sans ses grands hommes, vrais ou faux. Le combat continu est leur stratégie propre et leur jouissance privée. Non. Tout le monde n'est pas ainsi. Je le répète, ceux qui tiennent cette philosophie sont si connus, si gonflés de puissance et de gloire, qu'ils se sont mis du côté des dominateurs, qu'ils sont représentés par une classe dominante, laquelle a besoin, justement, de ladite philosophie. Allez voir les panneaux géants où ils sont peints, en rouge et rose. Non. Quelques-uns jouissent aussi des autres variétés du plaisir. De la tête et du sexe, pour faire bref et unitaire. Si la propriété n'était fondée que sur le meurtre, l'histoire ne serait pas tout à fait ce qu'elle est, un fleuve en crue de supplications, de sang et de larmes, elle ne serait pas, ne serait pas du tout, se serait achevée faute de combattants depuis l'aube des temps. Dans la guerre il y a des lâches, au moins les dominateurs, justement, qui la font faire plutôt qu'ils ne la font. D'où ceci que des temps morts l'arrêtent. Il y a de la paix. Nous ne serions pas là, sans elle, pour le dire.

Il y a du privé. J'ai souvenir de livres qui le nient. De fait, une fouille minutieuse, brusquement décidée par une police en lieu clos, révèle vite le caractère très commun de ce que tous désirent cacher comme propriétés personnelles. Chaque sac ne contient que des choses publiques et le sous-vêtement tombe dans le banal. Tout a été payé au grand magasin. J'ai appris, en ces circonstances, qu'il n'y a pas de langage privé, je veux dire de mots ni de choses privées. Tout au plus, rendons-nous propre le commun.

Cette thèse est d'autant plus juste qu'elle avantage immodérément les polices du monde entier, tous les pouvoirs totalitaires, les puissances d'argent et d'idéocratie. Nul ne détient de la monnaie privée, inutile et inéchangeable, nul ne peut inventer d'idées, hors du four banal, et si oui, nous l'enfermerons.

Elle serait juste infiniment qu'il faudrait pourtant la réputer fausse, par un certain goût de la liberté, par une horreur certaine de la chute dans le bestial. Par goût, par odorat. Cette thèse du gros animal est une idée qui n'a pas de nez. Je m'explique, en répondant à la question : comment rendons-nous propre le commun?

Qui a été pensionnaire longtemps, donc en groupe, jusqu'aux actes les plus secrets, où le privé n'est jamais sauf, a souvenir de qui ne pouvait souffrir de partager le plat de salade. Quand arrivait le saladier, il crachait dedans, et l'herbe lui restait. Elle

était toute à lui, nul ne la disputait. Il avait résolu,
comme cent mille autres, le problème de Rousseau.
Il crache dans la soupe, dit-on. Du coup, elle est à
lui. Nouveau repas interrompu.

Nul besoin de fossé ni de pieux, ici le crachat
éloigne sans retour la concurrence famélique. Vous
haïrez cet homme, sûrement, car vous aimez, vous
aussi, la salade, mais aussi sûrement, vous ne touche-
rez pas une feuille de celle qu'il a su faire sienne.
Vous le tuerez, peut-être, mais un dégoût irrépres-
sible retire votre langue au fond du palais. Il y a du
privé. Tout à coup, il est stable. Comme si le jumeau
jaloux avait brusquement disparu.

Il marque son territoire, dit-on d'un chien qui
pisse et qui compisse une racine d'arbre. Le terrain,
tout à l'heure, était une salade, il est ici la niche de la
bête. L'objet varie, de la nourriture à l'écologie
générale. Ce qui ne varie pas est le phénomène usité
pour chasser le voisin, le concurrent jumeau, pour
transformer le public en privé, ou le commun en
propre. Il faut trouver un processus, issu d'un lieu,
d'un point, capable de remplir quelque espace alentour, il faut créer une expansion quelconque.
Qu'est-ce donc qu'un milieu, mon milieu, son milieu
ou celui de la bête? Simplement l'étendue pleine du
phénomène, le volume rempli par ledit processus.
Première, archipremière occupation des lieux. Il
faut trouver de l'expansé. Il faut qu'il soit un son, il
faut que ce soit une odeur. Il faut qu'il frappe les
oreilles, ouvertes, il faut qu'il pénètre le nez, ouvert,
sous le vent. Ces phénomènes sont communs aux
récepteurs toujours ouverts.

Nous aurons à nous souvenir, demain, avec quelque peine, de notre monde remuant, sonore et enfumé, de l'air puant, irrespirable, des moteurs. Quelque chose est en train de mourir, sous la brume. Cette clameur avait conquis l'espace, avait délogé même le silence et la paix ruraux. Dans cette combe verte, friche, prairie, ruisseau, haie, seule la guerre avait porté un tel fracas. Aujourd'hui, le jet, le bull et la tronçonneuse percent l'oreille comme la fraise attaque la dent d'un éclair de douleur, je l'ai dit. Cette guerre n'a pas lieu qu'à Troie, dans la ville, mais elle est partout, nous avons perdu nos anachorètes, on n'entend plus les bœufs patauger à la source, on ne sent plus l'ordure animale ni la fragrance de l'été, le pain, le lait, la pêche et la tomate ont perdu le goût, le moteur a pris l'ouïe et l'odorat, bruit et puanteur. D'anciens pouvoirs s'en tenaient à nos âmes, celui-ci s'en prend à nos corps. Rien n'est plus profond que les sens. Mais la chose est en train de mourir, dans le tohu-bohu. La rumeur des médias l'a couverte.

Le moteur devait remplacer la peine des hommes. Il n'a été en fait que l'objet substitut du travail. Combien de temps et où aura-t-il été un outil? On peut le dire : ici et là, dans des occasions telles et telles. Mais nous aurons travaillé aux moteurs autant et plus que grâce à eux. Ils nous ont déplacés, voilà tout.

Ils produisaient un travail calculable. Mais ils faisaient du bruit, en produit dérivé. Il n'est pas certain que le bruit soit un dérivé : peut-être est-il le but direct. Nous en discuterons, si cela vaut la peine. Mais, en tout cas, tout le monde le sait, celui qui détient le pouvoir est celui qui détient la source et l'émission du son. Qui a la voix forte et haute a toujours raison. C'est la raison du verbe le plus fort. Stentor qui assourdit commande ou en tient lieu. Et qui dispose des trompettes est suivi de l'artillerie. Nul ne va plus vite que la musique. Platon le savait, le disait déjà, et l'État français, platonique, garde la haute main sur les chaînes qui diffusent vacarme et charivari. Qui a le pouvoir? Celui qui a le son, le bruit et qui fait taire. Il n'a même pas besoin de la parole, il lui suffit d'intercepter. De dire n'importe quoi, mais d'empêcher de dire. Il suffit de tonner. Le pouvoir n'est jamais que l'occupation de l'espace. Il n'y a pas beaucoup de techniques pour conquérir, envahir le lieu et le terrain, d'ici vers l'universel. La première, peut-être, celle du rossignol, du coq ou du lion, est voix, son, cri, ébranlement sonore. Etre chez soi, d'ici à là, volume privatif. Et puis, de là, prendre le plus possible d'espace. Le pouvoir n'est qu'une variété de tintamarre.

Oui, bien sûr, c'est là l'origine des supports de discours. Voici la variété des langues, les accents qui marbrent la carte. Ici les étrangers ne comprennent rien, les signaux ne sont pour eux que parasites. Le signal propre est bruit pour un tiers, celui-ci est exclu. Oui, bien sûr, c'est là l'origine du point central, de la centralisation du pouvoir. Le son, comme l'odeur, vient d'une source ponctuelle. Quand la sirène, à la mairie, a remplacé la cloche, à l'église, nous avons su que le pouvoir n'avait pas changé. Ainsi quand la radio remplace la sirène. Même chose enfin dans le champ du goûter : vos recettes sont infectes et les nôtres sont délectables. Nous ne sommes pas hôtes de n'importe qui. Le même train d'ondes est signe ou sabbat, la même matière est puante ou parfumée, le même aliment détestable ou exquis. Tout cela définit un espace réticulé, qu'on peut appeler pascalien, où chacun, pour un temps, est maître de sa niche, où tout centre, distribué, produit son pouvoir local, par identification à l'intérieur, expulsion à la frontière, où chaque groupe se retrouve en son lieu, où l'équilibre instable des rapports de force fluctue, espace maillé où ce qui se retourne du pour au contre quand on traverse un fil de réseau n'est pas seulement le précepte de morale ou la valeur de vérité, mais tout ce qui enchante le corps ou lui donne de la répugnance. Parole en deçà des Pyrénées, parasite au-delà. Son en deçà, tintamarre au-delà. Leur langue n'est que bruit, borborygme barbare. Clarté cisalpine, ombre transalpine. Passée la limite de la langue d'oc, l'huile pue et dégoûte, si délicieuse ici sur du pain aillé. Sous ladite relativité des mœurs, institutions et lois, gît la diversité des langues, antérieure, dirait-on, à l'origine même des langues, puisque l'espace vaut pour les voix et les cris, pour le vautour et pour le coq, gît le couple message-brouillage, la nuit du bruit et le soleil du sens, gît la double réponse des sens, goût et dégoût, plaisir, douleur, accueil et expulsion. Il n'est pas très intéressant de chercher si le corps s'imprègne de culture ou si celle-ci émane des corps. Il l'est, au contraire, de constater que la même situation se distribue partout. Qu'elle est d'anthropologie, qu'elle est de religion : le profane et le sacré sont du même espace, généralisé de Pascal. Qu'elle est de religion, qu'elle est de politique. Toutes les sciences humaines, tous les quasi-savoirs et toutes les pratiques reconnaissent une logique de ce type. C'est, peut-être, la condition générale de toute communication.

Or cette condition est formulée par la physique même. C'est le théorème d'ambiguïté. Ceci, maintenant et ici, est une information. Ceci, vu de là, entendu de là, situé là (mais sans doute aussi : senti de là, goûté de là), est un bruit. N'est qu'un parasite et doit être exclu. De ce principe, j'ai tiré jadis une origine du langage, en traversant le corps vivant de part en part. Cela traçait un chemin de la biophysique à la parole articulée[1]. Nous retrouvons la même circonstance dans l'exercice de nos sens, la formation du collectif, la culture à l'état naissant. Dans nos rapports aux aliments, aux excréments, aux clameurs, à l'espace et aux autres. Les sciences humaines, pour parler un peu vite, savent construire cette carte. Or les sciences exactes la construisent aussi. Les deux savoirs sont ici au concours. Nous parlons, à plusieurs voix, une même logique, en ce détroit entre deux océans. Le passage du Nord-Ouest, que nous avions déjà reconnu, en d'autres circonstances, est à nouveau ouvert[2].

Le rossignol couvre, de sa voix musicale, sa niche privative. Que nul n'entre ici, sans cette harmonieuse géométrie. Sûrement toi aussi tu en es, ton

1. *Hermès IV. La distribution*, pp. 259-272.
2. *Hermès V. Le passage du Nord-Ouest*, préface et *passim*.

accent te trahit, homme de Galilée. Ou : je te
reconnais, enfant de la Gascogne. Danger, tranquillité.

La privatisation commence ainsi, par l'émission
d'un phénomène qui s'épand. Ensuite on enchaîne
un pays en s'appropriant tous les émetteurs. Oui, les
médias remplacent les moteurs. Preuve que les bruits
ne sont pas des produits dérivés. L'espace est plein
de haut-parleurs. Le système du son franchit les différences, de l'Ouest à l'Est. Partout et toujours, la
voix de son maître, pour lui devenu chien.

Cette bouche est ouverte, elle émet. A l'entour de
la source, l'espace est saturé de ce qui en émane.
Elle montre sa belle voix, dit-on. Non. L'horreur
atroce de son bruit, la puanteur de son crachat.
Volume-niche de la bouche, que nul ne viendrait
lécher. En cette appartenance, tout ce qui est bon à
manger, à baiser ou à boire est réservé à cette
bouche. Elle pue le fromage. Il faut être un renard
pour aimer cela. Elle chante, elle avale. Elle parle,
elle paît. Elle crache et se gave.

Et le parasite apparaît. Il est invité, ou non, chez
un hôte. L'hôtel, l'oustal, maison du maître, est
ouvert au passant morfondu. Table ouverte, dit-on.
Le privé tombe, pour un temps, au domaine public,
et le propre de l'hôte dans le commun qui passe. A
la faveur de l'ouverture entre le parasite. En activité
immédiate, il cherche à s'approprier ces communs
temporaires. Pour lors et pour cela, il parle. Ce n'est
même pas nécessaire, il résonne. Il fait du bruit

comme les rats qui rognent. Il produit des toxines,
des inflammations, de la fièvre. Bref, il excite le
milieu. Il l'excite thermiquement, ce qui fait du
bruit, ce qui donne la fièvre. Il intervient dans les
réseaux, interrompt les messages, parasite les transmissions. Voilà, son nom est cohérent et son acte
unitaire. Le phénomène d'expansion est son affaire
propre. Son appropriation.

Parasite. Le préfixe *para* qui signifie voisin, à côté
de, mesure une distance, comme un écart léger. Le
sitos est la nourriture. Dans cette bouche ouverte qui
parle et qui mange, ce qui est à côté de manger,
comme sa fonction proche, est ce qui, justement, fait
l'émission du son. *Para* mesure une différence entre
une réception et, au contraire, une expansion.
Celle-ci rend propre ce qui est commun, et ce qui va,
bientôt, être plus propre encore, le corps vivant. Elle
mange déjà l'espace.

Ce n'est pas le seul phénomène expansif, issu du
corps propre. Qui crache dans la soupe ne crie pas
pour autant. La bouche mange, parle, elle vomit
aussi. George Dandin, au bout de sa passion, sent de
la gueule, il pue le vin à pleine bouche. Nous appro-
chons le stercoraire, l'expansion des odeurs.

Ne venez plus désormais porter votre merde chez
moi, m'a dit naguère un patron philosophe, quand il
crut voir que j'étais adulte. Il avait la tête colère et la
langue fleurie. Les cambrioleurs, paraît-il, laissent
dans l'appartement saccagé, au milieu des objets
délaissés par le vol, d'effroyables traînées. La privati-

sation du commun, l'appropriation de l'espace n'ont pas lieu seulement par le cri ou par le crachat, l'excrément y suffit souvent. Le chien a compissé sa niche, où le philosophe vomit. Voici qu'ils marquent leur terrain. Ceux qui voient partout du public manquent d'odorat, voilà tout. Dès que vous le souillez, cependant, il est vôtre. Ainsi le sale est-il le propre, et tout est dit. Le premier qui, ayant conchié un terrain, s'avisa de dire : *ceci est à moi*, trouva tout aussitôt des gens assez dégoûtés pour le croire. Ils s'écartèrent de chez lui, sans guerre ni traité.

Qu'est-ce donc que le propre ? C'est ce qui n'est pas sale. Qu'est-ce qui n'est pas sale ? Mon propre, justement. *Stercus suum bene olet :* voici le fondement de la propriété, que sa propre fiente sent bon. Non, ce n'est pas un jeu de mots, c'est, simplement, le même mot : le propre, c'est le propre, et la propriété n'est que la propreté. Cette chose horrible pour vous, c'est la mienne en tant que je suis seul à n'en pas concevoir exécration ni répugnance. Vous sortez, je reste, chez moi. Si vous en vomissez, je crois bien que votre intention est de vous réapproprier cet espace. Celui qui a vomi sur la racine d'arbre s'approprie, quelques livres plus tard, sa généalogie : c'était déjà fait. Nous connaissons tous des personnes propres, elles détachent leur milieu de leur appartenance fragrante, elles savent, hôtesses, recevoir l'étranger. Il entre, il peut entrer en ce terrain banalisé. Se laver reste un acte social, purifier son espace est un geste d'accueil, religieux, amoureux, collectif, hôtelier. Plus le corps propre est sale, plus la niche est breneuse, plus la personne est attachée à sa propriété. L'hôte est propre, le parasite est sale, je

veux dire par là qu'il n'est propre que pour soi. Le
pour soi pue, c'est bien fatal. Vous pouvez manger,
dormir, faire l'amour et mille choses, dans l'hôtellerie désodorisée, vous ne fermez pas l'œil, vous ne
touchez pas une miette, dans la saleté borgne. Elle
est la propreté d'un seul. Aimerez-vous les ortolans
après avoir chassé le rat des champs ? Mais le rat de
ville se remet en campagne aussitôt. Il est chez lui,
plus que chez le maître.

   Coup de génie : l'argent n'a pas d'odeur. Il est à
moi, c'est un petit cumul de bran, il ne sent pas, il
est à tous. C'est du propre et il est échangeable. Je
peux donc tout avoir pour de l'argent. Par le travail,
j'arrose le terrain de sueur, il est mien. Il garde mon
odeur.

   L'harmonie rassemble ceux que les bruits tenaient
épars. Quel parfum unira ceux que séparent les
odeurs ? Leibniz a écrit l'accord musical préalable au
contrat social, mais Rousseau le cherchait aussi
quand il s'occupait de musique. Peut-on écrire
encore un tel préalable au sujet des fumets ?

   Vous aimerez l'odeur des autres.

   Voilà une théorie stercoraire. Elle fournit un fondement, si j'ose dire, à la propriété privée. Celle-ci
n'est pas vol, elle est l'ordure, simplement. Elle dessine un espace centré à partir de ce lieu d'émission.
Comme tout à l'heure, autour du haut-parleur. Plus
on approche de ce lieu, plus on est voisin du privé.

Inversement donc, si on s'en éloigne. Je médite sur
le parasite : le préfixe *para* mesure toujours la distance, il évalue le voisinage. *Sitos*, en grec, signifie,
parfois, l'excrément.

Distance périnéale, voisinage périnéal. Le sexuel
est si privé qu'il est mon propre, au maximum. Rien
n'est si proche des lieux mêmes de l'excrétion. Entre
les fèces et l'urine, nous ne naissons pas seulement,
nous aimons. Trésor gardé par les dragons. La distance est minime entre mon privatif et ce sale pour
autrui qui veille sur mon propre. Elle n'était pas
longue non plus pour une bouche qui mange et
parle, qui avale, qui crache et crie. Le même organe,
ici, est de relation, de rejet. Il attire et repousse. Il
enclôt son terrain et il invite l'étranger. Il est hôte, il
est parasite. Non. Il est hôte et hôte, comme il est
propre et propre. Et chaque fois dans les deux sens.
Invitant, invité, propre pour soi et sale pour autrui.
De bouche et de sexe, le préfixe *para* évalue distances et voisinages entre les deux fois deux fonctions, comme le mot hôte et le mot propre évaluent
différences et identités. Nous sommes ouverts, haut
et bas, sur deux bifurcations différentielles.

Les barbares avaient des amours parasites, ils
confondaient arrosage et ensemencement. Ils pre-
naient possession du terrain, ils avaient sali une
hôtesse, elle était leur chose privée, ils avaient souillé
un espace hôtelier, ils devenaient propriétaires. Que
d'usages suivent de là. Ces foireux parlent fort et ils
aiment leur sale, ils ne jouissent donc que d'appropriation. Ils ont une femelle propre et taciturne,

effacée. Inversement, il leur arrive, à elles, d'occuper un espace immonde qui avertit de n'avoir pas à pénétrer. *Et caetera.*

L'hominité adviendra aux barbares d'apprendre la bifurcation de sexe et de langue. La merveille des amours gardées, le miracle des amours libres et de la parole éperdue.

Annulez cet écart : l'amour est excrétion, la nourriture est crachat, vomissure, et la femme est un bien, comme la parole. C'est la même équivalence et le même bilan d'échange. La philosophie s'est-elle beaucoup délivrée, même récemment, de ces archaïsmes ? De ce corps propre/sale et du rêve commun d'appropriation ?

Le théorème fort de tout idéalisme s'écrit : le monde est ma représentation. Cela peut se traduire : le monde est mon territoire marqué, le monde est ma foire. Dans les bons idéalistes, les objets privilégiés sont ceux qui sortent de leur corps. La salive, le sang, l'urine, la sueur, le vomi et le sperme, d'autres défécations réjouissantes. Ces déjections, qui marquent le terrain de leur encre, les font propriétaires impérialistes. L'idéalisme est stercoraire, et la théorie stercoraire découvre l'idéalisme.

Non. Le monde est là, sans moi, avant moi, après moi. Je ne suis, privatif, que mon sexe et ma langue, feux sans lieu.

Repas de satire
L'échange et l'argent, l'exact et le flou

Il ne sait rien faire et il est exigeant. Je vais analyser cette phrase avec précision, avec la plus fidèle exactitude. Comme s'il s'agissait d'entomologie. Sans passion, froidement. Mais je ne peux faire que cette phrase ne soit pas un souvenir. Elle me revient, comme on dit. Mieux, elle ne m'a jamais quitté. C'est peut-être mon étonnement fondamental, premier, originaire. J'étais encore petit, je faisais déjà les problèmes ou je traduisais les versions pour quelques cancres bien vêtus, bien nourris, souliers vernis, fine chemise, gras. Ils ne savaient rien faire, assurément, mais ils étaient d'une autre nature. Il fallait déjà protéger les faibles. J'étais entouré de crevards. Tout le monde savait, j'étais aussi persuadé, que je me débrouillerais toujours et partout. Qu'avec trois noix et une couverture, je survivrais, sans cesser jamais de donner du bon lait tout autour. Serviteur. Mon monde était constitué de choses dures, de cailloux à casser, de manches de pioche, ou de brins de fourche. Nous faisions des routes, elles étaient très lisses en surface pour que les carrosses y glissassent commodément. Mais profondes comme des tom-

beaux, en dessous, et bloquées de notre sueur. Les
ingénieurs venaient, une heure ou moins, de temps
en temps, pour crier. Ce n'était jamais parfait. Ils ne
savaient rien faire, ils étaient terriblement exigeants.
Je n'ai jamais cessé de rencontrer ces cancres, ces
faibles, ces chefs, ces puissances. De les considérer
comme plus astucieux que moi. Ils ont toujours
l'argent, les places, les honneurs. Ceux qui sont incli-
nés, courbés, fléchis sous la rafale violente de l'intuition, ceux dont la vie est interrompue, intermittente,
par la sujétion à l'outil, ceux-là n'ont jamais le temps
des médiations. Celui qui transforme est dessous, il
agit sous le blocage de la route. Elle le recouvre. Et
les autres courent dessus, la plante des pieds à l'aise.
Je me suffis et cela me suffit, c'est vrai ; du papier, un
crayon, de la lumière, un brasero, je suis content,
laissez-moi seulement un moment de silence. Je vis
dans l'immédiat. Au contact dur du référent, du
métal dans la gangue à transmuter en or. Dans
l'immédiat du monde. Dans le bonheur de l'immédiat. Dans une bouleversante allégresse. Je ne peux
pas m'en détacher. Je suis lié à mon travail plus sûrement que par des chaînes. Je n'ai pas, je n'ai plus,
n'ai jamais eu de temps. Je n'ai pas le temps de courir l'étendue. Ils ne savent rien faire et donc ils ont le
temps. Marchent, voient, comparent, jugent, savent
assurément où se trouve la bonne soupe. Examinent,
mesurent, critiquent. Ils sont les hommes de la
médiation. Du choix, du jugement. Ils occupent
l'espace, ils savent où se placer, où placer tel autre
qui cherche, à son tour, une place. Le discours de la
place occupe l'espace. Il annule tout le discours dési-
gnant quelque chose. Il ne parle que stratégie,

occupation savante et envahissante des lieux, il n'est que stratégie. Le propos du lieu dévaste les lieux, occupe les lieux, ravage les lieux, crée les lieux. Il parasite de son bruit le rapport inventif au brut. Le parasite du médiat parasite tous les canaux. La rumeur des chercheurs de la bonne soupe couvre la campagne de son ramage. Elle empêcherait même le travailleur de produire. Paradoxe : alors que les uns vivent de son produit, voici qu'il lui faut se cacher, pour ne pas entendre tout ce vacarme. C'est que la production, l'invention, consiste à injecter de l'information dans du plat pour le changer en rare. Comment en de l'or pur le vil plomb s'est changé ? Par cette injection inventive. Or ce rapport ne saurait se constituer au milieu de la foire d'empoigne. L'artisan ne quitte pas l'échoppe dont l'ouverture demeure un peu sombre et voit, parfois, émerveillé, passer les impuissants. Ceux-là courent couper la rue, noircir la place, frayer l'espace de leurs voies et s'asseoir sur les trônes. Ils ne savent qu'être exigeants. Ils trouvent tous les points où se décide l'important, ils ont entre les mains la foudre, la puissance et la gloire. Cherchent le rare, et font du rare leur commun plat.

Il est vrai, je l'avoue. Je n'ai jamais été exigeant. Je n'ai jamais cessé d'être agissant. J'ai besoin de connaître et de comprendre cet écart. Cet écart d'existence dont j'ai déjà éclairé un peu la notion statique, autour de l'équilibre. Ici l'écart est dynamique, puisqu'il s'écrit : l'action.

Jamais exigeant, sauf sur la réalité sans exemple de l'invention.

Il ne sait rien faire et il est exigeant. Il mourrait de manger de la chère médiocre. Il est drogué de rareté. Il exige quelque chose plutôt que rien. C'est là son existence et c'est là sa raison.

Exiger, qu'est-ce à dire? A voir le mot, il s'agit d'agir, plus un décalage, plus un écart vers l'extérieur. L'*exigere* latin, de même formation, n'est pas exactement de même sens. Il est plus instructif, il nous pousse, peut-être, dans le dos. Il signifie d'abord (et en plus par rapport à notre exigence) : pousser dehors, chasser, exclure. Il est vrai que *agere*, l'agir latin, dans son premier sens, physique et concret, signifie déjà l'expulsion. Il n'est pas inintéressant de prendre conscience de ce qu'était l'action pour nos ancêtres immédiats. C'était la purge, c'était le bannissement, l'éviction, le rejet, l'élimination. Il n'est pas étonnant que le terme action soit, chez nous, tout aussitôt monté sur le théâtre. La tragédie aux pieds de bouc expulse le bouc émissaire, la victime au sens de Girard. L'action tragique est une expression quasi suffisante. Mais nous le savons bien, nous aussi : la satire, la fable et la comédie, autour du parasite, parlent essentiellement d'exclusion. Au commencement est l'action, c'est-à-dire le crime.

Or l'exigeant ne se contente pas d'agir, il ne se contente pas de l'action. Il va jusqu'à l'exaction. *Exigere* signifie donc aussi : faire payer. *Exactor* est le percepteur tout autant que celui qui bannit, *exactio* est le bannissement et la rentrée d'impôts. Mais nous n'avons pas à l'apprendre; chez nous, aussi bien, les impôts sont exigibles. Il n'est pas inintéressant de comparer cette exigibilité à l'exaction : cette violence par laquelle l'impôt excède ce qui est dû. Comment l'excès se rabat sur la norme, comment l'existence finit par tolérer l'écart insupportable, comment l'équilibre dans le mouvement récupère la tare statique, voilà des lois paradoxales qui sont pourtant les ordinaires lois. L'exaction devient exigible, comme l'excès devient normal. Non, l'existence n'est pas stable. Exister, c'est déjà un excès ou une exception.

Nous sommes passés, peut-être un peu vite de la purge à l'impôt, de l'exclusion à l'exaction, de l'espace à l'argent. Ce qu'on pousse au-dehors, ce n'est pas seulement le roi sacrificiel ou l'épouse répudiée, c'est aussi le flux des marchandises produites et excédentaires. *Exigere* signifie bien écouler ces produits, c'est-à-dire les vendre. Écouler n'est rien d'autre : le flux se dirige vers l'extérieur, nous ne disposons pas d'autres métaphores. La vente serait-elle une autre forme de l'expulsion ? N'échangerait-on que cela même qu'on chasse ? Il est vrai que Joseph, autre évincé hors d'une autre aire culturelles fut aussi vendu par ses frères. Sommes-nous ici à l'origine même de l'échange ? N'écoule-t-on jamais que ce dont on ne veut plus ? Les fruits vont se gâter, les grains vont pourrir, les parasites vont dévorer le stock, il faut vendre. Il faut s'en débarrasser, dit-on. Chasser, vendre, exiger un impôt. A prix sacrifiés, dit-on. S'il est vrai, l'argent est substitut de la victime. L'argent est la trace de l'exclu. L'argent est le symbole du banni. Le signe du sacrifice. L'argent est religieux, il est Dieu, Marx le dit sans détour ; il est aussi, je l'ai montré ailleurs avec Freud, le stercoraire comme tel. Cela se comprend sans écart, s'il est le substitut de l'expulsé. Cela ne serait rien, encore, si l'on ne comprenait qu'il est exactement le substitut du parasite et le parasite lui-même, l'expulsé qui revient toujours.

Ce résultat n'est pas inattendu. Ce flux de marchandises ou de fruits offerts était autrefois dévoré au cours du festin. L'invité le payait de mots, le payait de signes. L'échange du logiciel contre le matériel est d'invention parasitaire. Le parasitaire est là, aux premiers temps de l'échange et du don, du don et du dommage, il aiguille les changes entre ce qui n'est pas équivalent. A l'évidence, logiciel et matériel ne sont pas équivalents. Et il les rend équivalents. Il est donc l'équivaluateur le plus général. Il est l'argent soi-même. Le signe en écart par rapport à la nourriture (para-site), le signe en écart par rapport aux biens. C'est-à-dire la mobilité même de l'échange, son écoulement. J'ai décrit naguère le parasite comme la puissance de métamorphose. C'était l'équivalent général, justement. Et c'était celui que l'hôte latin pouvait battre (et couvrir d'injures) pendant le festin.

Résultat non inattendu, par un autre chemin. Toute relation entre deux instances demande un chemin. Ce qui est déjà là, sur ce chemin, facilite la relation ou lui fait obstacle. L'écran devient aide, souvent, et l'adjuvant, parfois, se place à la traverse.

L'amour interdit qu'on s'aime, la parole assourdit les oreilles, la langue est la meilleure et la pire des choses, ce n'est pas moi qui invente la loi, qu'il n'y a pas de loi. Entre ces deux pôles, tout est possible, sauf le tiers exclu. Le tiers est, par nature et fonction, la population qui se tient sur le canal. Nous la nommons parasite, on le sait. Or nous avons préparé sa logique : l'algèbre des sous-ensembles flous. Les sous-ensembles flous se trouvent exactement sur ce chemin, sur ce canal.

On sait que l'argent peut se substituer à toute relation. L'argent est encore le tiers, il occupe tout le canal de sa monnaie liquide, il est le canal des liquidités. Nous y sommes. L'argent est Dieu, l'argent est le Diable, il est l'Être et il est le Néant, il est le précieux et l'ordure, il est l'exclu, il est l'inclus, inévitable en tout chemin, et barrant le chemin à toute relation. Il est là comme substitut général. J'ai dit : le parasite revient toujours, vous le chassez, le voici qui regagne la place. Écoulez donc les fruits, en fait vous les vendez, ils reviennent sous forme d'argent. Ce que vous excluez, vous l'incluez par cet équivalent. Donc vous ne pouvez pas discourir de l'argent au moyen d'une mathématique à deux valeurs. Donc tous vos modèles d'économie mathématique sont disqualifiés. Marx s'est trompé, Freud s'est trompé, Zola s'est trompé, je me trompe, les économistes se trompent. La seule mathématique applicable à l'économie est la théorie des sous-ensembles flous. L'algèbre floue et la topologie floue. Inversement,

qui parle flou parle d'argent, comme Ésope parlait
la langue, la meilleure et la pire, et, mieux, tout ce
qui se passe entre le meilleur et le pire, entre le faux
et le vrai, le certain et le non-probable, l'extérieur et
l'intérieur de l'appartenance, entre Dieu et le
Diable, la merde et le précieux, l'Être et le Néant. La
mathématique du flou procède, en fait, de la même
intuition que celle proposée ici. Ce que j'échange
revient : est-il hors de mon appartenance ou dedans ?
La question ne se décide ni ne se tranche. Elle est
exactement une question spectrale. On parlera
demain d'économie spectrale, de théorie floue du
flux. Elle est simple, on le voit, jusqu'à la redondance. Elle n'est un modèle qu'à l'ancien sens :
l'économie, réellement, l'imite.

Tous les échecs de l'économie ordinaire sont là.
Et, je le crois, son avenir. J'y reviendrai, quand
j'aurai du loisir, et que m'intéressera autre chose
que cette relation que j'entretiens avec quelqu'un, et
qui refuse, indifférence, la substitution par l'argent.
De l'amour lui-même, nous irons parler, dans quelques minutes de temps. En attendant de ne plus
aimer, ce qu'à Dieu ne plaise, avis aux spécialistes :
votre mathématique de base est floue. Travaillez
donc, je peux très bien ne pas venir. Si je viens à
l'économie, ce sera au milieu des larmes, j'aurai
passé le temps d'aimer. Bien sûr, la langue, ici, fonctionne comme l'argent. Il est trop clair que toute
aire sémantique est un sous-ensemble flou. La

science du sens a désormais trouvé son formalisme.
Si je viens à la linguistique...

Où en étais-je? A exiger. Le mot latin signifie
encore achever, aller au bout de son travail, non, de
son œuvre, la parfaire. Aussi bien parfaire sa vie,
l'œuvre des œuvres, dont la mort souveraine est la
dernière main. Nous disons, en ces lieux, exact. Il
faut être content que les sciences exactes prennent
ici la place, non loin du coût et de l'impôt, de
l'échange et du flou, de l'expulsion, de la violence.
Que nul n'entre au laboratoire s'il n'est géomètre.
On sait qu'*exigere* signifie mesurer, peser, examiner,
juger, régler, voici bien la métrique exacte, l'expérience quantitativement précise. Cette expérience
coûte — de l'énergie, de l'argent, de l'information
— elle augmente l'entropie du laboratoire isolé
fermé. Quant au voisinage immédiat de l'exactitude
et de l'exaction, elle permet de dire un mot de l'activité rationaliste de la physique nucléaire. Qu'est-ce
que le travail, ici, de la chose ou du concept? Ce
n'est pas une activité, non. C'est un petit écart à
l'actif ou à l'acte, qui la rend exacte. Comme si quelque chose hors de l'activité s'ajoutait au travail. Quel
est donc cet écart d'exigence?
La réponse est physique et métaphysique à la fois,
puisque la physique, ces jours derniers, s'interroge
sur un écart que le préfixe *méta* interprète (ou *méta-*,
ou *para-* ou *ex-*). J'ai dit ailleurs, et récemment, que
l'existence avait pour raison le plutôt de son principe, la raison inclinée. Nous retrouvons ici le même

écart, au travail de la science. Son rapport au réel est
de le retrouver : l'exactitude, ici, est l'existence, là.

Il ne sait rien faire et il est exigeant. Cela se dit
tout simplement du villageois de La Fontaine : il faut
à ce gourmand et du lait blanc et du veau et des
noix, alors que l'herbe suffit à la vache et que
l'humus suffit à l'arbre. Il faut à l'un et il suffit aux
autres. Les flèches de la relation ne sont pas tour-
nées dans le même sens. On voit tout aussitôt que,
dans le vaste monde, l'herbe est plus fréquente que
les veaux ou le lait, qu'il y a plus d'humus que de
noix. En termes comptables, que la matière première dépasse en quantité les produits transformés
ou finis. Le transformateur, producteur, inventeur,
puise dans le commun, qui est toujours à suffisance.
Le parasite est en quête de rareté.

Être exigeant, dès lors, signifie choisir. Ce choix,
ce filtre, implique une élimination, nous revenons,
pour ordre et cohérence, au premier sens, chasser,
pousser dehors. Celui qui examine sépare, celui qui
juge exclut, celui qui choisit partage les choses et les
populations. En tout cas, ils produisent de la rareté.
Non, ils n'en produisent pas, ils la sélectionnent
lorsqu'elle est déjà là. Le producteur la promeut à
partir du commun, quand elle est absente, il la
remet au parasite. Le feu cuit les marrons, d'une
patte prudente et précautionneuse, Raton, écartant
la cendre, escroque les mieux cuits, derrière lui Bertrand les croque. Le singe avait placé entre lui et le
producteur, qui est toujours l'homme du feu, un gui-

chet. Le guichet de la rareté. Le lieu du tri. Raton
choisit, Raton ne mange pas, Raton parasité, Raton,
au guichet : voici le démon de Maxwell. Tout y est :
le feu, les éléments-marrons, le choix, et, derrière,
celui qui croit au paradis perpétuel. Au mouvement
perpétuel : plus le vase versait, moins il s'allait
vidant, Philémon reconnut ce miracle évident. J'ai
déjà dit le festin divin de Baucis. Une servante vient :
Bertrand, avec Raton, détale. De même qu'autrefois,
ils entendaient du bruit à la porte du poêle. Un parasite chasse l'autre, le mouvement perpétuel s'arrête.
Le démon est exorcisé. Chassé, poussé dehors,
délogé du guichet. Où l'on voit que ce qu'on appelait littérature est une réserve de science.

Le parasite court l'espace et l'ensemence de guichets. Pour prélèvements de la rareté. Le plus
souvent, il sait les disposer en cascade, pour que la
rareté soit relative, pour en créer encore, et pour
qu'il y ait de l'histoire. Il place les guichets en structure d'ordre. D'où une autre illusion du perpétuel.

A la petite porte du guichet, une population passe,
élément par élément. Un par un. En grec, cela se dit
catena, la chaîne. Ces longues chaînes de raisons
toutes simples et faciles supposent, d'abord, un guichet. Elles y passent, maillon après maillon, pour
choix, rejet, acceptation : épreuve. Le guichet peut
être, doit être maximalement étroit. Je rejetterai
tout, etc. Hyperboliquement étroit, pour jouer
immédiatement le dernier guichet de la toute-puis-
sance. Tout y est, de nouveau : le feu, le démon,
l'exorcisme, le toujours du perpétuel, Dieu, etc.
Bref. L'exigence installe des guichets : exigus, cela va

sans dire puisque le mot le dit déjà. La rareté se fait
d'autant plus rare que le guichet se fait chas.

Un par un : il suffit de peu pour s'assurer la peau
d'un seul. Or la passion mimétique de la rareté
pousse la population au goulot d'étranglement,
devant le guichet, où elle s'écrase, où elle se bat, se
piétine et se hait avec allégresse. Elle s'offre,
exsangue, au couperet de quelques-uns. C'est la
genèse du pouvoir, la solution au paradoxe de La
Boétie : comment si peu de gens commandent au
plus grand nombre ? Je me demande parfois si la
mort, différée ou non, du bouc émissaire n'est pas
une variante singulière de ce schéma. Genèse du
pouvoir, genèse de l'économie : elle sélectionne,
aussi, de la rareté. Ce n'est pas tellement que le pouvoir politique soit fondé en dernière instance sur le
fonctionnement économique. En fait les deux instances fonctionnent pareillement, de manière struc-
turalement isomorphe.

La passion folle des guichets assure l'émergence
des rois et des élus, des biens précieux, de ce qu'on
cherche, sans doute aussi de l'exactitude scienti-
fique. De l'exigence : exact, exigu, exaction.

En attendant qu'on ait loisir de démontrer toutes
ces choses à notre aise, on peut jouir, pendant
l'entracte, de la cinquième *Satire* de Juvénal. Le festin, la table du riche, du grand, du roi, du maître, y
fonctionne comme un guichet. Mais le repas lui-
même est dit rare, et il y a concours pour la place.
Les loqueteux se pressent à l'envi pour être l'invité

du troisième lit. C'est le plus bas, et il y avait un manquant, il faut boucher un trou. On se bat. En haut, le patron s'abreuve de vins millésimés, en aval, le parasite n'a que la piquette. Le roi boit une coupe d'ambre rehaussée de béryl, surveillée des voleurs par un esclave policier, la piquette pourrit dans une tasse fêlée. Beau serviteur coûteux, coureur de peu de prix à la mine patibulaire. Farine moisie et compacte, molle fleur de froment. Poisson monumental, petit crabe. Lamproie de Corse ou de Sicile, anguille des cloaques. Huile vierge fine, carburant de lampe. Au bas bout, les reliefs puants, sur le haut bout, les truffes, les foies gras, les sangliers, la scène belle des écuyers tranchants, le théâtre envié de la rareté. Toute la question, l'angoisse jalouse et la vie gâchée, consistent à passer le guichet. Comment parvenir au rare ? Ce n'est pas Hegel, c'est déjà Juvénal qui formule ceci : comment devenir maître, ou plutôt le roi de son maître ? Non pas comment l'esclave devient-il maître du maître, mais comment le parasite peut-il devenir hôte de son hôte. L'hôte du maître ou le maître de l'hôte. Il faut avoir quatre cent mille sesterces, dit Juvénal au Bourgeois Gentilhomme, on ne saura plus, lors, qui est le Turc et qui est ridicule. Il faut avoir une femme stérile qu'on peut offrir sans risque de suite. Maquereau. Parasite et maquereau.

Decimus Junius Ethicus propose une morale. Elle est simple et naïve : rien n'est plus frugal que le ventre. On ne manque jamais du peu qui lui suffit. Un quai, un pont, une natte en lambeaux, un pain grossier, le sage est à la cloche. Le clochard est bon

philosophe et le guichet le pervertit. Retour aux
routes de l'enfance.

Bergson aimait modéliser son élan vital par une
gerbe d'eau qui fuse. Elle s'élève, elle parvient à son
acmé, elle retombe en pluie sur les côtés, autour de
l'axe, de la colonne presque dure de poussée. Geyser, ce vieux fidèle, qui promeut une évolution qui se
casse et chute en répétition. D'où vient-elle, quelle
est sa force vitale, quelle est son énergie spirituelle?
C'était peut-être le geste de Dieu.

Je dessine la gerbe dans l'autre sens. Dans le bon
sens, j'ai dessiné naguère une flamme[1]. C'était pour
le temps de l'information et ses flammèches au
hasard, imprévisibles. Je dessine un geyser, comme je
l'avais fait pour rendre clair Lucrèce. Tout tombe et
va vers l'équilibre. Vers la stabilité, vers la mort. Nous
n'avons plus besoin de l'élan vital. Voici la coulée
torrentielle, qui suit les lois de la nature, simplement.

J'ai marqué les turbulences qui festonnent, çà et
là, le laminaire qui ne se maintient pas. Ces turbulences sont fractales, comme le monde. Elles sont
le monde. Je marque aujourd'hui leur écart par rapport à la chute plane et les étapes des chemins, des
voies intéressantes par lesquelles le retour à l'équilibre est différé.

1. *Hermès V., Le passage du Nord-Ouest.*

L'axe principal, les génératrices laminaires sont de statique. A l'écart, l'existence. Quelque chose existe plutôt que rien. L'angle est formé, il varie, son espace est flou. Il fluctue.

Tous les vocables usités ici participent de cet écart. Exact et exaction, par rapport à l'action (à la moindre action), abus par rapport à l'usage, parasite et parabole (ou parole) par rapport à l'action de manger ou de dire. Tout se déduit de lui, ainsi que les échanges. Nous sommes emportés par le flux et le flou de l'existence, ses fluctuations et ses circonstances, l'avancée de sa production.

Repas entre frères
Théorie du joker

> *Putiphar abandonna entre les mains de Joseph tout ce qu'il avait, il ne se préoccupa plus de rien sauf de la nourriture qu'il prenait.*

Genèse, XXIX, 6.

Il paraît illogique ou il est scandaleux de jeter de la nourriture. On le fait cependant. On expulse, on exclut très exactement ce qui est en écart à la nourriture (le terme para-site le dit), son excès ou son excédent. Les prémices, parfois, ou la fleur, le meilleur, s'il est question d'un sacrifice. Chasser le parasite signifie aussi bien bouter hors, écouler ce qui est à côté, ce qui est voisin de la nourriture. Ce n'est pas forcément l'être qui la dévore. Cela peut être justement son excès ou son excédent. Et tout ce qui précède est nécessaire comme métaphysique de l'excès. Comme à l'habitude, cela même qui est exclu revient.

Sacrifice : les frères de Joseph désirent le tuer. Ils le chassent. Ils montrent à leur père une tunique à

longues manches trempée dans le sang du bouc
émissaire. Joseph est victime sacrificielle. Tout le
mythe est marqué de substitutions. Le meurtre n'a
pas lieu, mais a lieu l'expulsion. L'expulsion n'a pas
vraiment lieu, la vente la remplace. La tunique
pleine de sang est un substitut faux, les vingt pièces
d'argent sont le substitut vrai. Les Ismaélites ont
payé, l'argent est la présence de Joseph en Canaan,
et son premier retour. En Égypte, Joseph, sorti de sa
prison, interprète les rêves de Pharaon : vaches
grasses et vaches maigres. Il va devenir ministre de
l'Économie et des Finances.

Voici peut-être le premier traité d'économie politique. Vaches grasses, années d'abondance, vaches
maigres, moissons de disette. Quand la récolte est en
excès, l'usage est de se débarrasser de cet excédent,
en ôtant la barre. Du coup, on meurt de faim, aux
années où les vaches sont maigres et où les épis sont
brûlés par le vent. Comment faire autrement ? Il faut
revenir à ces pratiques paysannes simples d'où toute
la culture est née. Voici des fruits en surabondance,
des légumes, du lait, du vin, du froment. Les fruits se
gâtent, le lait tourne à l'aigre, et le vin au vinaigre,
ces légumes pourrissent, le stock de blé se remplit de
rats et de charançons. Tout fermente, tout se cor-
rompt. Tout change. La pourriture, la peste ne sont
pas seulement des symboles de la violence, elles sont
aussi des référents réels et singuliers, qui n'ont pas
besoin d'autre chose que d'eux-mêmes pour engendrer des conduites connues et repérées. On se
débarrasse de l'excédent parce qu'il est périssable.
En fait on expulse le pourri, on écoule une marchandise qui, elle-même, est en risque de couler.

L'échange naît de ce changement-là. L'échange est à ce change ce que l'excès ou l'excédent est à la suffisance, ou l'exaction à l'action, et ainsi de suite. L'échange ne veut pas que ça change. Il veut stabiliser la fuite. Contrairement à tout ce que l'on pense de lui, l'échange ne mobilise pas les choses, il les immobilise, il les coule, Πάντα ῥεῖ, tout coule, certes, tout meurt, tout pourrit, si le grain ne meurt. On écoule ce qui coule, on échange ce qui change. Cela revient en stabilité. L'idée toute simple de l'équilibre des échanges est ontologique. Par le mouvement même de l'échange ce qui change ne change plus. Cela menaçait de pourrir et c'est devenu de l'argent, sonnant, trébuchant, incorruptible. Que l'argent soit de l'ordure n'est en aucune façon un symbole ni un fantasme. Il est exactement le substitut du pourri expulsé, l'équivalent de l'écoulement par corruption. C'est ainsi ou il en est ainsi. Le coup de génie fut bien sûr d'aller chercher le stable dans l'instable, ou le repos dans le mobile, d'aller chercher dans l'échange ce qui s'oppose au changement.

Ce n'est pourtant pas la seule solution. On peut écouler l'excédent, on peut aussi stocker. On peut le stocker sous forme d'argent, on peut le stocker en nature. Alors la pourriture est là et les parasites sont à demeure. Dès lors, il faut aller au bout du processus de décomposition : faire du vin, des liqueurs, du fromage, du pain. J'avais jadis tiré philosophie du fromage. Elle trouve ici sa généralité.

Revenons à Joseph. Si Canaan est pauvre, c'est qu'il ne stocke pas. Si Joseph et l'Égypte sont riches, c'est qu'ils stockent. Les deux procédés se font face.

Rivaux jaloux, les frères de Joseph ont décidé de s'en débarrasser. Tuons-le, disent-ils d'abord, et jetons-le dans la citerne. La décision dérive, on ne fera que le jeter dans la citerne. Qu'est-ce qu'une citerne? Elle est un lieu, artificiel, construit, de conservation, de stockage. Dans l'aire indo-euro-péenne, *cista*, latin, est un coffre ou une corbeille, spécialement une corbeille servant aux sacrifices. Tibulle la chante comme confidente de mystères sacrés. Le grec κιστοφόρος, porteur de corbeilles sacrées, désigne une monnaie d'Asie Mineure sur laquelle de tels coffres sont gravés. Ciste est un sarco-phage de pierre, un tombeau mégalithe, où le cadavre est enterré avec l'ensemble de ses biens. Sa fortune est là, déposée, avec le corps même. Or, dans l'aire sémite propre, le mot hébreu usité ici, très voisin du mot puits, trou à eau, outre citerne, signifie le trou dans lequel on tombe, mais surtout le trou des ordures, où l'on jette les débris et les détri-tus, pourritures, décompositions. L'union de ces deux aires exprime notre thèse : ce lieu, où on se débarrasse d'un excès pourrissant, a trait au sacré, il a trait à la mort et au sacrifice, mais il a tout à coup des connexions avec les biens, les trésors échangés, l'argent et la monnaie. Enterré, jeté dans la citerne, Joseph est exclu, sacrifié, pesteux, mais il est tout aussi bien conservé, stocké, de même que l'eau qu'il remplace. La citerne régule années humides et années sèches, comme les greniers égyptiens, bien-tôt, réguleront années de vaches grasses et récoltes maigres. Joseph dans la citerne, situation énigma-tique et ambiguë : le stock en prévision de l'échange prochain. Il est expulsé, il est conservé. Il est sacrifié, il est vendu. Fondement mortuaire et sacrificiel de l'échange. Ruben a conseillé la solution dans le but avoué de garder son frère et de le ramener au père. Déjà la décision d'exclure fait voir des adhérences : un retour éventuel, peut-être une conservation. Comment expulser tout en gardant, comment chasser en conservant, comment laisser varier tout en sauvant un invariant ? Cette question est économique.

Le repas commence, au voisinage des lieux de l'action. Celle-ci se décale un peu. Au fond du décor apparaît une caravane. Des Ismaélites avec leurs chameaux portaient de la gomme adragante, etc., des marchandises, du pays de Galaad vers l'Égypte. Cette interruption induit Juda, qui a levé les yeux, comme ses frères, vers ce spectacle, à l'idée de vendre. Mais cette vente sera faite encore par des intermédiaires. Les substituts ne cessent pas, ni les vicariances. Des marchands madianites passent, ils retirent Joseph de la citerne et le vendent vingt pièces d'argent aux Ismaélites. Mais le texte dit que ce sont pourtant les Madianites qui le revendent en Égypte. Il faut observer qu'Ismaël, fils d'Abraham et d'Agar, la servante égyptienne, fut un frère chassé, exclu, au même titre que Madian, fils d'Abraham et de Qetura. Au moment d'expulser Joseph, apparaissent en fond de scène, dans l'espace, en fond d'histoire, dans le temps, les frères exclus. Ceux-ci sont devenus marchands, ils trafiquent des marchandises. Le rapport de l'exclu à l'échange apparaît déjà comme référentiel de l'histoire. L'argent circule assez mal, il ne circule même pas : Madian a vendu deux fois.

Jacob reçoit alors la tunique tachée par le sang du bouc égorgé. Joseph est la victime et il est innocent, il est son substitut, il est son vicaire.

L'histoire de Joseph s'arrête un moment, parmi les pleurs du père en deuil, elle fait un brusque détour sur Juda, celui précisément qui a eu l'idée de la vente. Il part de Galaad, vers Adullam, où il a trois enfants d'une femme, Er, Onan et Shéla. Er épouse Tamar, et meurt. Tamar, survivante, est donnée à Onan, son beau-frère. Celui-ci, on le sait, laissait perdre sa semence à terre lorsqu'il s'unissait à Tamar, pour ne pas donner une postérité à son frère.

Mettre le petit frère dans la citerne, dans la corbeille, ne pas le mettre, le retirer de la citerne.

Yahvé, mécontent de l'onanisme, fait mourir Onan. Il reste à Tamar le dernier fils, Shéla. Il est d'abord trop jeune et puis, devenu grand, on omet de le destiner à Tamar. Tamar est veuve, Tamar s'unit sans enfanter, Tamar est oubliée. Elle se couvre alors d'un voile et attend. Juda passe et la prend pour une prostituée. Elle négocie le prix de la passe : un chevreau. Elle demande un gage. Et Juda lui donne son sceau, son cordon et sa canne.

L'histoire de Juda contient l'histoire de Tamar et elle est contenue dans l'histoire de Joseph. A la querelle violente des frères, des meurtres et des exclusions, en bref du sacrificiel, se substitue tout à coup un échange curieux. Tamar est promise aux trois frères qui lui sont successivement ôtés de façon différente : par la mort, par l'onanisme, par l'oubli. Elle a, elle n'a pas. On l'a, on ne l'a pas. Puis elle passe au père par vente et prostitution.

Or l'équivalent de Joseph sacrifié fut un bouc égorgé. L'équivalent de la femme Tamar est encore un chevreau. Cela conduit encore au sacrifice. Or il est sur le point d'avoir lieu. Lorsqu'on dit à Juda : ta belle-fille est enceinte par son inconduite, il ordonne qu'on la pousse dehors et qu'on la brûle vive. Tamar est donc bien la victime. Comme Girard l'a montré, de nouveau, elle est innocente, et, de nouveau, jumeaux seront ses fils, concurrents dès l'heure de la naissance, tout comme Esaü et Jacob. Rivaux du fleuve maternel. Maintenant, elle montre à Juda le sceau, la canne et le cordon : tu es le père, c'est marqué. Elle est juste, plus juste que moi, dit Juda, car je ne lui ai pas donné Shéla, mon troisième fils.

Tamar est la victime, au même titre que Joseph. Celui-ci est vendu, frère exclu, vingt pièces d'argent à des frères exclus, devenus marchands. Tamar est en face de lui, en position quasi duale, comme objet sexuel des frères et du père. De frères tout aussi ennemis entre eux, puisque Onan use de sa pratique pour priver son frère de postérité. Tamar glisse de l'un à l'autre, toujours la même et transformée : femme toujours, et due et désirée, mais veuve après avoir été une épouse, mais stérile quoique féconde par le mésusage d'Onan, promise et non donnée, prostituée mais vertueuse quoique incestueuse, mère pour finir et restituant au temps ce qu'elle en avait reçu, des rivaux. Métamorphoses et stabilité, variations de l'invariante, ou circulation de l'équivalente. Elle est adaptée à toutes les places, et peut passer de place en place, soumise aux lois de la circulation. Elle est déjà, peut-être, un équivalent général.

Qu'elle vaille un chevreau marque en elle la victime, le sacrifice. Elle est voilée, alors, cachée derrière un voile. Ainsi Joseph disparaissait loin de sa
tunique baignée de sang. Il y a report du sacrificiel.
Joseph n'est pas assassiné, le bouc est son substitut,
en ritualisation du sacrifice d'Abraham. Tamar n'est
pas brûlée, mais, par un nouveau tour, il ne va plus
être question du chevreau. Il y a report de la mort du
chevreau. Et le gage suffit : le sceau. L'écriture,
stable, comme promesse. Demain, je paierai. De
nouveau, rendre stable ce qui est instable. Je suis lié
par le cordon, et je suis engagé par le gage tracé. Le
passage au symbolique est assuré par un objet que les
Grecs, justement, nomment symbole. Un jeton de
reconnaissance. Le symbolique est le report de la
tuerie. L'échange serait-il un report de meurtre ?
Tamar fait déjà voir ce qui va se passer au cycle de
Joseph.

Généalogie des jugements synthétiques.
Ceci est autre chose.
Tamar est une épouse, Tamar est une veuve,
Tamar est délaissée, Tamar est stérile, Tamar est la
prostituée du carrefour, Tamar est la victime, Tamar
est mère, Tamar est juste. Dévoilée, voilée, dévoilée.
Promise, non donnée, donnée. Non fécondée par
Onan, fécondée par le père, non marquée par
Onan, et marquée du sceau. Tamar n'est pas fixée
dans son identité, alors que Juda est Juda, que Jacob
est Jacob. Elle n'est pas, longtemps, reconnue, elle
n'est pas connue dans sa justice, elle est celle qui a le

malheur de s'unir à Onan. S'unir, c'est-à-dire ne pas s'unir. Qui couche avec Onan couche et ne couche pas.

Il n'est pas sûr non plus que Joseph soit Joseph. Il reçoit de Pharaon l'anneau et le collier, comme Tamar a eu le sceau et le cordon, Pharaon lui impose un nom, Joseph est Çophnat-Panéah. Il est esclave, il est majordome, il est emprisonné, il est l'intendant du geôlier, il est oublié par le grand échanson, il est le ministre de Pharaon et le dominateur de ses frères. Joseph n'est pas fixé dans son identité, alors que Ruben est Ruben, que Jacob est Jacob. Il n'est pas, longtemps, reconnu, il n'est pas connu dans sa justice, il est maître et esclave à la fois.

Tamar et Joseph sont victimes sacrificielles. Dans la citerne et promise au bûcher, le bouc est le substitut de l'un, et le chevreau la suppléance de l'autre. Joseph est le bouc, Tamar est le chevreau. La victime n'est pas tuée, la victime n'est pas victime. Face au meurtre, le geste se décale et dérive la décision. L'action bifurque et la tautologie se met à prédiquer, elle glisse, elle saute à autre chose. Elle ne dit plus : *a* est *a*, elle substitue et se met à dire *a* est *b*.

La victime n'est pas fixée dans son identité, la victime est n'importe qui, le sort tombe sur le plus jeune et le hasard sur le premier venu. Qui est-il, qui est-elle ? Celui-ci car c'est lui, celle-ci car c'est elle, ici et maintenant la fille de Jephté, Iphigénie ou le fils d'Idoménée, parfaitement déterminés ; mais choisis au hasard, tirés au sort, tout à fait indéterminés. La victime est celui-ci même, et pourtant celui-ci est un autre. Peut être un autre.

Émerge en cette circonstance une logique souveraine qui demande une explication, qui est l'explication soi-même. Il n'y a pas de commencement de raison sans un enchaînement de la forme : ceci n'est
pas ceci, ceci est autre chose. Cet enchaînement
rompt avec la redondance, l'identité ou la répétition. Il faut bien trouver un objet dont on puisse parler ainsi. Ou un sujet, n'importe. Il est alors d'expérience vitale qu'un enfant rejeté ne soit jamais
soi-même. Il est aussi de contrainte culturelle qu'une
femme doive se métamorphoser. Il est enfin d'expérience sociale que l'être sacrifié soit n'importe qui.
Mais il est surtout d'invention judaïque, nouveauté
fulgurante par le croissant fertile, que l'être sacrifié
soit substitué, que la victime soit, soudain, autre
chose : un bouc, un chevreau, mais aussi le début
d'une série tout autre.

J'appellerai cet objet un joker. Le joker est
souvent un fou, on le sait. Il est sauvage, dit-on en
anglais. Il n'est pas difficile d'y voir le double du roi
sacrificiel, issu de la fête des fous, venue des Satur-
nales. Cet objet blanc, comme un domino blanc[1],
n'a aucune valeur pour les avoir toutes. Il a bien une
identité, mais son identité, son caractère singulier, sa
différence, comme on dit, est d'être, indifféremment, telle ou telle autre singularité d'un ensemble
donné. Le joker est roi ou valet, il est l'as ou le sept,
ou le deux, à loisir. Joseph est un joker, Tamar,
reine, juste, méprisée, putain, est un joker encore.
a est *b, c, d,* etc. Flou.

---

1. Voir mon analyse de *Thérèse Raquin.* Je suppose que le
domino blanc a valeur de joker ; ce n'est pas toujours vrai, au jeu
des dominos.

Ce joker-là est un objet logique indispensable et fascinant. Placé en milieu ou en bout de série, d'une série munie d'une loi d'ordre, il lui permet de bifurquer, de prendre une autre allure, une autre direction, un nouvel ordre. La seule distinction énonçable entre une méthode et ce qu'on appelle un bricolage est, précisément, le joker. Le principe du bricolage est de faire quelque chose au moyen d'autre chose, un mât de barque avec une allumette, une aile de poulet avec un tissu destiné à la cuisse, et ainsi de suite. De même que le modèle de méthode le plus général est le jeu, de même le bon modèle de ce qui est nommé — par déception — le bricolage, est le joker.

Le joker Tamar fait bifurquer tant de fois la série que, l'inceste accompli, elle revient au commencement, la toujours neuve rivalité fraternelle. La suite fait un cycle, une circulation, mais avec supplément, vers David et vers le Messie. Ainsi du joker Joseph, pourtant plus complexe.

Joseph est expulsé, non tué. Il est exclu. Ruben ne le voulait pas, qui ne l'a mis dans la citerne que pour le conserver, pour le ramener à son père. Il est mis au rebut et il est mis en stock. En ce lieu singulier, il est rejeté à la fois et gardé. Joseph est exclu, Joseph est inclus. En tant qu'il est joker, l'exclu est inclus. Le joker, d'abord, est à deux valeurs ; qu'elles soient contradictoires n'ajoute rien à cette affaire. Ou, mieux encore, c'est parce qu'il est exclu et inclus que Joseph devient un joker. Il s'en va, il est toujours là. Vous l'avez rejeté, il ne cesse d'être présent dans votre histoire. Vous l'envoyez, par la caravane, au pays d'Égypte, vous ferez une caravane pour l'y rejoindre. Il est parti, mais il ne vous quitte pas, il s'attache à vos pas. Il reverra son père, vous reviendrez à lui. Le mouvement, l'hésitation, la vibration, la double frénésie de l'exclusion et de l'inclusion constituent le joker en une multiplicité de valeurs floues, en une multiplicité d'appartenances, en un spectre de possibilités. Il change, il est là, stable. La marchandise, périssable, risquant de se transformer en ordure, revient sous la forme d'argent. L'argent est le plus joker des jokers, celui qu'on a nommé l'équivalent général. A deux valeurs, exclu-inclus, puis à une multiplicité floue de valeurs et d'appartenances. Intuitivement, c'est ainsi qu'ont dû être constitués les deux côtés de la pièce d'argent, de cuivre ou d'or, pile et face, et qu'ils ont dû, dès l'origine, être les opérateurs du hasard. Inversement, la victime n'est pas tirée au hasard, elle est pile et face, elle est la pièce à deux valeurs, elle est le flou des probabilités. De l'argent, il est toujours possible de dire : ceci est autre chose. Principe nouveau : l'association du tiers exclu et du tiers inclus.

Le joker change, il est jeton d'échange, il est multivalent, et d'abord bivalent. Tamar et Joseph changent et ils sont échangés. Sujet, indifféremment, et objet de l'échange, Tamar, chevreau, victime, et enfin sceau, paiement. Et Joseph, vingt pièces d'argent. L'argent du blé d'Égypte est remis dans les sacs de blé à destination de la Palestine. Les frères ont laissé l'argent, mais l'argent ne les quitte plus. Exclu, inclus. L'argent est toujours présent, dans l'échange.

Ceci est autre chose. J'ai rêvé d'une gerbe de blé, du soleil et de onze étoiles. Cette gerbe n'est pas une gerbe, elle reste pourtant une gerbe, et la gerbe, c'est toi. La lune est votre mère, les étoiles sont votre fraternité. Le blé se prosterne comme une lune, le soleil pose son front à terre, dans le champ de blé. Ceci est autre chose. Je suis étoile et gerbe de blé, tu es gerbe et soleil, au commencement est la haine.

Ceci est encore autre chose. Tu as rêvé d'un cep de vigne et de trois sarments, de trois corbeilles de gâteaux, sur ta tête. Et moi je dis à l'échanson, je dis au panetier : les paniers sont des jours, les gâteaux sont ta chair et ton corps, les sarments sont des jours; les jours sont des sarments et ils sont des corbeilles. Voici le sens : ceci est encore autre chose. Au milieu, l'asservissement, la vie et la mort.

Ceci est toujours autre chose. Pharaon a rêvé de vaches et d'épis, les vaches maigres ont mangé les vaches grasses, les épis grêles et brûlés de vent ont englouti les épis mûrs et abondants. Je lui dirai le sens, ceci est toujours autre chose. Les vaches sont des ans, les épis des années, le temps est une vache, il est divisé en bouquets de graines, comme tout à l'heure en sarments ou corbeilles. Si la gerbe était gerbe, si l'étoile était une étoile et la vache une vache, il n'y aurait pas eu de sens, de clé, d'explication, ni d'interprète. Ni raison, ni devin. Il faut bien que ceci soit toujours autre chose. Enfin une logique

de lumière, nous mangerons enfin à notre faim.
Nous renverrons vers la Terre Promise des caravanes
de grains et de fruits.

Tous ces colliers de mots fourmillent de jokers.
Soit une série quelconque dont les maillons sont
bien identifiés, où une loi court, explicite. Le même
s'y diffuse le long des différences, il constitue l'axe,
rigide ou souple, de la suite. Tout à coup, un joker.
Puis-je le lire? Assurément. Il suffit que je
reconnaisse la loi de la suite amont, et les lois des
suites aval. Le joker, au lieu de la bifurcation, la rend
possible par le confluent des valeurs qu'il assure. Il
est, à la fois, ce qui est déjà dit et ce qui va se dire. Il
est à deux, à trois, ou à plusieurs valeurs, selon la
complexité de la connexion. La ramification du
réseau dépend du nombre des jokers. Mais je soupçonne qu'il existe un seuil à ce nombre. Lorsqu'il y
en a trop, on doit être perdu, comme en un labyrinthe. Que serait une suite où ne figureraient que
des jokers? Que pourrait-on en dire?

Les logiques du rêve me semblent de cet ordre.
Multivalentes à loisir, à plaisir, parce que serties de
jokers. Connexes *ad libitum*. Le temps est la vache, le
temps est l'épi, le temps est le sarment et la corbeille. La vache est un épi, ceci est autre chose. La
vache est un joker, le panier, l'épi, d'autres jokers
encore. Au-delà d'une certaine densité, d'un certain
nombre d'éléments à multivalence, les séries sont
méconnaissables. La question n'est jamais tant d'y
trouver une clé, ou deux, ou trois, ou *n* clés, mais de
parler une langue qui tienne compte des jokers.
Joseph, Daniel disent le sens, la clé, ils déterminent
les séries indéterminées, ils durcissent la logique

molle. Freud, au contraire, a découvert une langue à équivalent général. On comprend que Popper lui en veuille, et Popper aurait indéfiniment raison si le rêve n'était tissé de jokers en série. Freud traduit, en sa langue pauvre, un fait d'une grande simplicité, reproduit en cinq ou six autres lieux de culture : la polyvalence. J'ai longtemps fait confiance à Popper, je crois désormais que Freud se tire bien du critère d'extériorité. La preuve est la suivante : essayez donc de rendre l'argent falsifiable. Dans les lieux peuplés de jokers, il ne peut y avoir de faux-monnayeurs. Marx et Freud sont passés par là, simplement. Ils manipulent sans arrêt des contenus à multivalence, ils écrivent des langues à équivalent général. Qu'ils n'aient pas soupçonné un instant le risque de la chose, c'est vrai, Popper a raison d'imposer le critère. Mais qu'ils aient découvert des équivalents généraux, ce n'est pas douteux, et Popper, lui, ne l'a pas vu. Ce n'est pas seulement parce qu'elle est toujours vraie qu'il faut répudier une théorie. Elle marche toujours pour une autre raison : elle est dans l'équivalence générale. Elle est hors de vrai, hors de faux, elle indique des contenus-jokers. La *cosa*, disaient les algébristes italiens de la Renaissance, la *cosa*, la chose dite l'inconnue, l'inconnue = *x*, multivalente, dont on peut dire, indéfiniment, qu'elle prend toutes les valeurs. Ceci est autre chose. Vous avez observé au passage un nouveau passage du Nord-Ouest.

Et c'est pourquoi l'histoire de Joseph, notre premier traité d'économie, est aussi un traité de l'interprétation des rêves. Citerne-capital et citerne-inconscient.

La distribution des jokers.

Soit donc l'univers du discours. On peut ordonner ledit univers selon la distribution des jokers. S'il y en a peu dans une coupe ou dans une séquence, la détermination est forte et la contrainte règne, on est assez voisin de la monosémie. On peut imaginer, aux limites, un discours sans aucun joker. Il se réduit au principe d'identité, je suppose. Ainsi l'univers en question est-il minoré par *a* IQ *a*. Faites croître maintenant, quand vous quittez ce minorant, le nombre des jokers, ou leur pourcentage dans une série, une coupe ou une séquence. Allez au maximum, allez à saturation. La polysémie envahit l'espace, la multivalence, l'équivocité. Au voisinage de la fin, c'est le monde du rêve. Bourré de polyvalences jusqu'à la gueule. Aux limites du rêve, aux limites de l'univers, le discours composé exclusivement de jokers est l'argent. Quand il n'y a que des jokers, c'est le capital, c'est le compte en banque, c'est l'équivalent général. Ils sont les majorants de ce monde.

Curieux univers, logique pourtant, où les rêves adhèrent à la finance, où l'or est le voisin des songes.

L'univers du discours, quant à la distribution des jokers, est minoré par le principe d'identité ou des indiscernables, il est majoré, au plus près voisinage des rêves, par la circulation de l'argent.

Cet univers a la forme d'une corne d'abondance. De l'étroite singularité aux largesses de l'équivalence (étroite et large pouvant ici changer de position). L'univers du discours surabonde, perpétuellement.

Les parasites, bruits et mangeailles, grouillent en foule autour de cette trompe.

Judas est innocent. Éloge de Judas.

Ceci est autre chose. Tamar : ce chevreau est mon corps. Tamar : ce cordon est mon corps, le cordon, le bâton et le sceau. Le joker n'est plus dans le rêve, il circule dans nos échanges. Cet objet qui change, qu'on échange, est le corps. Celui de Tamar la bru, de Tamar la prostituée. Joseph est délivré de sa citerne : vingt pièces d'argent, ceci est son corps.

Judas est innocent du sang de ce juste. Ceci est autre chose, et ceci, ce pain, est mon corps, cet épi, ce froment et cette farine. Ceci est autre chose et ceci est mon sang, le cep de vigne et le sarment. Judas présent voit se constituer un autre joker. Il entend, il comprend que c'est le substitut du sacrifice. Il est juif et donc, dans son milieu et sa culture, il entend ce qu'il doit entendre, qu'il faut arrêter le sacrifice, qu'il faut un substitut et qu'il faut un joker. Et donc il fait le geste de Ruben, de Juda l'ancêtre, le geste qui sauve. Transformer la victime en argent. Reprendre simplement le geste fondateur des échanges. Vendre Joseph c'est justement ne pas le sacrifier, ne pas le tuer, le garder de la mort, pouvoir un jour le ramener au père. Judas est innocent, il faut enfin dire l'éloge de Judas et réconcilier à jamais les juifs et les chrétiens, faire sauter la racine antisémite la plus profonde, l'arracher enfin de la méconnaissance. Judas raisonnait justement, il faisait glisser, bifurquer la série fatale, il réorientait le meurtre en autre chose et l'évitait ainsi : Judas était un juste. L'accuser, le noircir est un déni de notre justice, c'est déjà un texte de persécution. Judas est innocent comme Œdipe l'était. D'où son désespoir lorsqu'il voit que la vente a raté, qu'elle a contribué au sacrifice et qu'elle ne l'a pas évité. Et il jette l'argent. Et il est la victime, l'autre victime.

Repas de marrons
Le soleil et le signe

Bertrand le singe avec Raton le chat sont commensaux, dit La Fontaine. Commensaux pour le plat qu'ils ont formé entre eux, comme on disait dans la marine, mais parasites malfaisants du même hôte et du même maître : voleurs et destructeurs, tout se perd, tout se gâte et tout coule autour d'eux. Nous verrons bientôt ce qu'il en était de ladite commensalité.

Un mot lève le doute, si le doute demeure : le chat délaisse les souris, si le logis lui laisse le fromage. Tel devient prédateur s'il ne peut plus parasiter personne. Tout le monde, au fond, sait cela : pour le ramener à la chasse aux rats, il suffit d'affamer le chat. La prédation, la chasse demandent plus d'énergie et de finesse que l'écorniflerie. Celle-ci est donc plus probable. On pourrait traduire, aussi bien : plus répandue, plus naturelle ou plus originaire. Si ces traductions nous répugnent, la haute probabilité nous suffit. C'est la figure d'équilibre.

Si le chercheur est dans sa niche, s'il a sa méthode, sa tasse de thé, son groupe de pression, il s'arrête de produire pour reproduire. Il ne sort plus, il ne va plus vers le noir du grenier, ses moustaches ne frémissent plus à un signal imperceptible, il s'endort aussitôt dans le berceau du même. Voulez-vous découvrir? Laissez donc les fromages.

Bertrand et Raton jouissent de leur niche. L'histoire d'aujourd'hui essaie les relations, comme on dit d'un essayeur d'or. Nous l'avons mesuré pour la chasse. Elle n'est que l'écart affamé du parasitisme. Dès qu'elle le peut, elle revient à la figure d'équilibre. Tentons la commensalité. C'est une relation égalitaire, où chacun donne et reçoit tour à tour. La relation parasitaire est léonine et inégale : celui qui prend ne donne, celui qui donne ne reçoit jamais rien. Quelle est donc la figure d'équilibre? Voyons Bertrand avec Raton. Ils regardent le feu où cuisent les marrons. Loin, tous deux, d'escroquer leur maître commun, ce qu'on aurait pu attendre de commensaux égaux, ils se placent comme en série et se parasitent l'un l'autre. Raton tire et choisit les marrons, Bertrand tout aussitôt les croque. La figure d'équilibre de la relation est bien toujours la même. Ce n'est pas moi, c'est aujourd'hui le fabuliste qui tire de là non point une comparaison politique, mais très exactement la genèse de ce pouvoir. Le premier mot du texte est singe, le dernier mot est roi. Il s'agit de ce prince, flatté, qui s'échaude, pour le profit du roi. Le singe le plus singe est le dernier chaînon de la série parasitaire; le roi, sans pouvoir au-dessus de lui, est le premier chaînon de la série de gloire et de puissance. Il faut penser, parce que cela est vrai, que ces deux séries sont les mêmes. Le sommet du pouvoir est le fond du puits attractif, de cet équilibre relationnel. Il est le point bas le plus bas de ces figures d'équilibre. La quête du pouvoir et la lutte pour lui ne sont que séries ou cascades, c'est la chute parasitaire sans fin. Et comme toute loi répétitive, elle ne produit pas d'information.

La figure de la pyramide est d'une tromperie sublime. On croirait voir les populations donner l'assaut et s'échiner pour se hisser vers le sommet, où seul le fort arrive, après expédition des rivaux dans l'abîme. La figure est à retourner comme un gant. Comme dirait Thom, ce serait plutôt un puits de potentiel, comme dirait Platon, une caverne. Les souris? non, le fromage. Les marrons? non, Raton. La lutte avec les rats? La lutte avec le feu? La concurrence avec Raton? Non. La loi de la relation est de se placer en aval d'un autre, pour que les marrons tombent sans obstacle. En aval, plus profond, plus avant dans le puits ou le long du ruisseau. Gagne qui regagne le poste aval. Celui qui est à l'embouchure, c'est un bon mot, sera le roi. Au fond de son antre où les animaux entrent, il les dévore tous, et personne n'en sort. Bertrand avec Raton ne sont pas commensaux. Ils ne sont pas liés contre l'hôte. Ils ne se disputent point les marrons. Ils ne sont pas égaux. Ils ne sont pas rivaux. Ils ne sont pas face à face, chacun sur une rive du ruisseau. Car la loi du courant, la loi du potentiel, la loi de chute, les fait tout aussitôt se décaler. S'ils étaient commensaux, s'ils étaient rivaux, il faudrait beaucoup d'énergie, un état excité, un meurtre peut-être, un partage sans doute. Le plus simple est de se décaler, pour que les marrons roulent au plus bas, tous ensemble. Mange qui regagne le poste aval. Et le loup le sait bien, qui dit, dès l'abord, à l'agneau qu'il trouble l'onde pure en amont de sa position. Celui qui joue le prédateur, celui qui jouerait aussi bien le rival, justifie d'abord son action par la loi d'airain du parasitisme.

La rivalité n'est qu'un spectacle, elle est l'état de l'apparence. L'équilibre est phénoménal, et l'écart est réel. La loi d'opposition est de phénoménologie, la loi d'irréversibilité ou de chute aval est réelle. Derrière toute représentation.

Reprise du repas des rats. Ils entendent du bruit à la porte, et ils fuient, la cascade parasitaire s'effondre, elle casse. Le parasite-bruit chasse le parasite-bête, je crois le premier plus fondamental, plus bas, plus abîmé au fond du puits. Moins il y a de sens au discours, plus il est proche du pouvoir. Derrière l'embouchure, derrière la bouche, la plus vaste bouche à tout avaler, il n'y a plus que l'immense clameur de la mer. Le chaos, le bruit, le désordre. Le fond de l'être. Ce parasite-là chasse tous les autres. Derrière le pouvoir, derrière la dernière puissance, derrière l'appétit universel, à leur voisinage, à leur bord, la rumeur, le vacarme ensemencent l'espace. Le fond du puits est noir, le fond de la caverne est sombre, l'onde pure enfin est amère. Toute relation, figure sur fond, ne s'inscrit que sur du désordre. Voici enfin la théorie pure de la relation : elle suit, ordonnée, le fleuve qui tombe, elle est irréversible, elle ne revient pas sur soi. C'est la première des relations, justement la relation d'ordre. Alors, derrière elle, comme son fond, le bruit. Le désordre. Au bout du ruisseau, la mer. Ce parasite-là est fondamental. Il tombe des flèches simples dans un bruit de chute d'eau.

Les rats reviennent au festin quand cesse le bruit. On ne dit pas si la servante qui intervient se retire. Le chat n'y reviendra pas, se dit-on. Il est échaudé, semble-t-il. Mais le rat des champs le fut tout autant. Le singe et le chat marquent un progrès : les deux rats sont de vrais commensaux. Tôt ou tard, leur relation aurait pris figure sérielle. C'est pour cela que le rustique part. Il voit tout à coup que la ville vit des marrons que les paysans tirent de leurs arbres, que la ville mangera toujours jusqu'à la mort des cultivateurs. Les deux rats ne sont plus commensaux, ils seront en série tout comme le singe et le chat. Raton n'est pas content, le paysan se retire à jamais. Derrière lui, l'humanité festine, il la nourrit, elle le tue. Il avait peur jadis, il avait bien raison de craindre. Nous vivons aujourd'hui l'événement universel annoncé par la fable, non seulement la fuite de l'homme rustique, mais sa mise à mort. L'agriculture, vieux parasitisme primaire, est éliminé par les parasites de rang supérieur, habitués au bruit, ceux de Mégalopolis. Les rats de ville ont dévoré les rats des champs. Comme les vaches maigres mangent les vaches grasses. Sans deviner, les imbéciles, ce qui arrivera quand auront disparu les rustiques.

L'équilibre d'un vivant dans son milieu ressemble fort à celui que réalisent enfin et où parviennent ensemble parfois l'hôte et le parasite. Après bien du tracas, des maladies, des morts, des catastrophes, l'un favorise, par exemple, le transit intestinal du premier, celui-ci le nourrit en retour. Au bout de

tous les comptes, le parasite n'a pas intérêt à tuer
son hôte nourricier. Nous avons intérêt au monde,
aux autres et aux objets.

Ainsi la relation, d'abord, est un abus, elle finit,
parfois, par un commun usage. Elle est une flèche
simple, elle cesse de l'être assez rarement. Elle
commence par l'irréversible, elle demeure ainsi
orientée. La simple flèche irréversible est l'élément,
l'atome de relation. Cet atome local peut s'enchaî-
ner à d'autres pour former un fleuve local, un flux
de sang, de larmes et de meurtres. Les vaches
maigres mangent les vaches grasses et font ainsi couler le Nil, le loup mange l'agneau et fait ainsi couler
l'onde sanglante du ruisseau. Dans le sens de l'histoire. La relation fait vivre et tue, elle entretient
quelqu'un de la survie de l'autre. Le parasite vit de
l'hôte, par lui, avec lui, et en lui, *per ipsum et cum ipso
et in ipso*, il a fait de lui sa demeure, sa tente, son
tabernacle, il s'y reproduit et pullule, jusqu'à l'inévitable seuil où l'hôte meurt. L'hôte devient hostie,
victime, et les invités du repas sont ennemis mortels.
Cela se dit en plusieurs langues, de l'histoire naturelle à l'histoire des religions, à l'histoire tout court.
Tout commence par ce que j'appelle valeur d'abus.
La relation d'économie première est d'abus. Mais
quand la flèche ne tue pas, quand l'abus ne passe
pas le seuil, il peut arriver que la relation évolue vers
un autre équilibre. Cela est aussi rare qu'un équilibre qui passerait, qui transiterait vers un autre équilibre, à puits moins profond. Les fleuves restent dans
leur lit, à l'ordinaire, ils cherchent rarement une vallée plus haute que leur talweg. Il y faut des écarts, il y
faut des fluctuations. Cela est assez rare, cela finit

pourtant par arriver. L'information acquise est,
alors, formidable. Cette rareté, quelquefois, se
nomme justice. Effort difficile, exceptionnel, miraculeux, humain.

Naissance d'un échange. Le parasite adopte un
rôle fonctionnel, l'hôte survit à ses abus, il survit
même au sens littéral de ce mot, sa vie découvre un
équilibre renforcé, comme un suréquilibre. Une
réversibilité se voit sur fond d'irréversible. L'usage
succède à l'abus, l'échange suit l'usage. On peut
imaginer un contrat. Le contrat n'est pas originaire,
il est un nouvel équilibre obtenu, fragile parce que
plus haut placé, plus rare que l'abus, plus exceptionnel, plus riche en information. Contrairement aux
schémas reçus, le pouvoir court vers le bas du talweg
et la justice s'en écarte, le pouvoir descend le cours
de l'abus, le contrat fluctue vers un autre équilibre.
Ces deux forces sont absolument différentes. Qui
veut prendre le pouvoir pour faire accroître la justice ment ou se trompe ou nous trompe. Il ne fait
qu'accélérer les valeurs d'abus. Il ressemble à qui se
hâterait de descendre le fleuve pour mieux monter
sur les collines alentour. Dans l'entraînement torrentiel de l'irréversible et de l'abusif, l'équilibre contrac-
tuel est une singularité. Il n'est d'histoire humaine
que de chercher à la produire. Cela est assez rare
pour que nous ne soyons humains que dans l'exceptionnel de nos actes.

On pourrait concevoir plusieurs séries de doubles
flèches. Au moins trois. Un contrat physique entre
nous et notre milieu. Nouveau, inimaginable. Un
contrat social entre nous. L'espoir insensé en la fin
du parasitisme. Un contrat gnoséologique entre le

sujet, d'une part, et l'objet, d'autre part : seule une flèche simple les unissait jusqu'à ce jour.

La théorie des relations émerge peu à peu. Nous connaissons maintenant la série. La série parasitaire est une chaîne irréversible, elle descend la pente, comme la rivière, comme une bille sur les parois du puits. Nous connaissons la loi de la série, de la chaîne, du ruisseau ou du puits. Nous pouvons l'énoncer, nous pouvons la décrire. Nous connaissons la fin du processus, le désordre, le bruit, la clameur, le chaos, la mer.

Je veux remonter la série vers sa source. Le fabuleux me cache un peu le chemin de cette ascension et ses marques. Derrière la porte de la salle, elle me dérobe qui se retire, après être venu. Qui est là ? On raconte parfois que la mort elle-même survient dans le courant du banquet volé. J'ai peur de me lever pour aller voir, dans ce noir. Si ce n'était que la servante. Si c'était la servante ? Je me lève, pourtant. Je remonte la chaîne du singe et du chat. Devant Bertrand, Raton ; devant Raton, les marrons ; devant les marrons, les flammes dansantes. Peut-on aller au-delà du rideau de feu ?

Le noir de la porte, la brûlure rouge. La remontée fait peur. Celui qui dépasse la peur, la boîte noire et la flambée de la caverne doit nécessairement déboucher un matin au soleil. Le producteur est celui dont nous mangeons les reliefs, les marrons. Il est devant. Il est un feu local. Et il est un signal. Il n'y a jamais de production humaine que par feu et signe. Que par une énergie et une information. La matière est une énergie, la forme est une information. La production demande un soleil local et une mémoire, j'entends la matrice, la topologie de la forme, le creux et le relief tracés. Toute production est donc une énergie, la grande et la petite. La grande pour la force, la petite pour la rareté. La production est donc solaire et rare.

A mesure que je remonte la chaîne parasitaire, le fleuve irréversible de plus en plus troublé, je vais vers le soleil de feux locaux en feux locaux, je saute, comme pendant la nuit de la Saint-Jean d'été, les flammes hautes où se grillent les mangeurs de marrons accroupis, j'ouvre les portes noires des boîtes de la rareté. Le rouge de l'énergie, le noir du signe peu probable, chromatisme du producteur, sont les couleurs de l'œuvre. La lumière flambe dans les boîtes noires, quand la nouvelle intuition paraît, foudroyante, quand le nouvel objet sort des mains qui l'ouvrent. Et croît la solitude, dans un monde nu, de plus en plus simple, où il faut se suffire de peu et laisser en aval ses vieilles exigences. Ici la rareté multiplie les idées sous la traversée du soleil.

La chaîne est simple, elle va du soleil à la mer.

A l'entour du soleil et du noir de l'espace autour, ceux du feu et du signe travaillent; pourquoi ne pas les nommer des archanges? Ils se cachent, on les voit peu, on peut les chercher, au grand jour, avec une lanterne sourde. Ils ne font aucun bruit. Mais il est sûr que la série, gigogne, se forme irrésistiblement derrière chacun d'eux, jusqu'au dernier, le roi, celui de la gloire bruyante et des pleines puissances. Le long de la suite le bruit s'accroît, il devient formi-

dable sous les pieds du roi, au voisinage de la mer
pure des clameurs. Le fleuve est bien de plus en plus
troublé, jusqu'à l'embouchure des sablons et des
vases. Le roi, plongé dans le limon et dans la fange,
grouille, dans sa souille, de parasites, de rumeurs. Le
soleil en tête de ligne est le commencement physique et la mer à la fin est une fin physique. La
chaîne des vivants est entée sur elle, irréversible
comme elle, on peut jouer à la nommer avec des
noms communs. Elle va sûrement des producteurs
de nouveauté aux mangeurs d'ordure.

Dans les théories de Bergson, ou de ses parasites
récents, jusqu'à Thomas Kuhn, le nouveau advient
de l'extérieur. L'extérieur n'est pas forcément le
négatif. La nouveauté n'est pas forcément le
contraire de ce que dit le père, comme l'ont cru
quelques fils de bonne famille. Le négatif n'est ici
qu'une redondance qu'on distingue mal de ce
qu'elle répète. Le nouveau est imprévisible, tout simplement. Il est à l'extérieur, avec le fou, le génie, le
héros et le saint. Comment est-il possible qu'ils
soient là?

Quiconque réside au-dedans des clôtures survit,
mange le stock, parasite ce qui justifie qu'on ferme
le système. Il est clos pour et par les parasites. Quiconque en est exclu n'a plus de prévu à manger, il
n'a plus de garde-manger. Il faut qu'il se suffise de
ce qu'il trouve, cherchant fortune dans le monde.
Ou il meurt, ou il devient fou. Ou il devient fou à
lier, ou il tente les voies du génie. Et devient produc-

teur. Avec ce qu'il ramasse sur le sol et qui n'a retenu l'attention de personne, avec les résidus des divisions et des cellules, avec les ordures trouvées dans les champs d'épandage, avec les miettes du festin des maîtres, il réussit à faire une œuvre. Ou il meurt. L'œuvre est pour lui une question de vie ou de mort. Il devient producteur en mettant sa vie tout entière dans lesdites matières premières. Je l'ai nommé archange par la double raison qu'il porte de l'information, du nouveau, des nouvelles, et qu'il est forcément à la tête de ligne, par rapport à la chaîne parasitaire. Tête de série ou hors clôture, c'est la même image, à une ou deux dimensions. Sa nouveauté à lui est d'avoir injecté sa vie dans l'objet produit, au lieu de tirer sa vie de l'objet choisi. Il n'y a de nouveauté que ma vie improbable.

L'exclusion n'est pas un petit malheur. Nous sommes les enfants d'un couple exclu du paradis. Ce paradis perdu est celui du parasitisme. Tous animaux, tous végétaux bons à manger y étaient à portée de la main. Dehors, il faut produire, mourir ou produire, mourir et produire, mourir et travailler, inventer forcément du nouveau, par exemple l'histoire, hors des stabilités de ce premier jardin. Bientôt, inventer un nouveau jardin, s'installer en terre promise, où le parasitisme reprendra, dans le miel et le lait.

Quand l'exclu a produit, la clôture à l'abri de laquelle dorment, repus, les parasites, s'ouvre, lance des pseudopodes pour inclure cette œuvre, où elle trouve un sang nouveau qui la fait se perpétuer. A l'intérieur, tout dort, en effet. La production est impossible puisque l'activité tout entière y est de

jugement ou d'exigence, de contrôleurs et guiche-
tiers. On note justement que cette activité fait des
exclus, parmi lesquels des morts, et, rarement, des
producteurs. D'où le processus recommence.

Nous venons de passer, tout à coup, au parasitisme
collectif, aux structures parasitaires sociales. Il n'est
pas étonnant que Bergson ait découvert un schéma
de cet ordre, en traversant le religieux, venant du
vivant, pour aller vers le collectif et l'historique. La
modernité, histoires de toutes spécialités, y compris
celles des sciences, n'a fait que parasiter cette découverte.

Qu'est-ce que le capital? Il est ce lac de retenue,
en amont du barrage, cette mine de fer, de charbon,
de manganèse ou de tungstène. La poche de
pétrole. Il est stock d'énergie, de matières premières, il est une île de néguentropie. Ce capital, je
l'ai nommé ailleurs le réservoir. C'est une appellation optimiste : conserver, préserver ce qui peut res-
servir. En fait, le réservoir, la réserve, est une poche à
temps. C'est de la matière et ce n'est que du temps.
Le temps géologique, immense, qu'il a fallu pour
l'amasser, le temps technique, foudroyant, qui suf-
fira pour l'épuiser. Le temps technique, court, qu'il
a fallu pour dresser le barrage, et le temps, long, de
son exploitation. Renouvelable ou pas, le réservoir
est une fonction concevable du temps.

Qu'est-ce que le capital? Une ville, une classe, un
groupe, une nation. Nous.

Qu'est-ce que le capital? Un trésor, une liasse, une

banque. On appelait cela de l'argent. L'argent n'est plus, ou guère plus, l'or et l'argent. Il tend de plus en plus vers le signe. Par le papier-monnaie, le chèque, la carte de crédit, c'est-à-dire un nombre gravé (imprimé en relief ou magnétiquement écrit) sur un rectangle de plastique, c'est-à-dire de l'information.

Le capital, serait-ce un nombre, un très grand nombre? Assez grand pour un tas, l'entassement et l'accumulation, le réservoir, la cité, la fortune, lac ou carrière, foule compacte, et compte largement approvisionné, mais assez grand aussi pour pouvoir désigner un individu : chaque objet a son matricule, chaque sujet en a plusieurs. Chaque chose a son spectre en bandes noires et blanches, nous sommes revenus à l'aurore des philosophes, nous sommes redevenus des pythagoriciens, toutes choses sont nombres. Que l'idéologie qu'on a tirée de là tire du côté des masses ou de l'atome, de la matière et du social ou de l'individuel, reste qu'il y va toujours du grand nombre, et c'est toujours la même chose. Il en est encore de même du côté de l'information. Voyez ici pourquoi les sites antagonistes se ressemblent. Le grand nombre est masse, mais il faut un aussi grand nombre pour l'individu.

Qu'est-ce que le capital? C'est un stock d'écritures. L'ancien support précieux, devenu banal, tend à s'évanouir. Comme le support banal de naguère. Il ne reste vraiment que le nombre, le matricule de l'individu (ou de la société) à qui l'on attribue tel nombre de numéraire. Il s'agit là de la monnaie électronique, signaux échangés entre terminaux d'ordinateurs. Le capital, maintenant, est à la mémoire. L'argent, dès lors, n'est plus qu'un cas particulier, il y a d'autres écrits à la mémoire. Ceux des livres et des bibliothèques, des listes et registres, des rubriques et répertoires, des fastes et des greffes, des obituaires et des sommiers, des codes et des cotes. L'encyclopédie s'enrichit et se miniaturise. Les vieilles encyclopédies n'auraient pas imprimé les horaires de poste, les fluctuations de la bourse, ni l'état des cyclones, ce jour, sur la mer Égée. L'individuel, le circonstanciel entre, avec le général, à la nouvelle banque. La banque des données, voici le nouveau capital, où l'argent n'est qu'un sous-ensemble de signes. L'équivalent général est, désormais, la donnée en général. Écrite au réservoir des signes.

Professeur et savant, prêtre et artiste, prêteur et banquier, assureur et tribun politique, publicitaire et journaliste, administrateur, magistrat, chanteur, danseur et policier, tous ces professionnels, ramenés, par le code, à un même langage, ramenés, par le nombre, à la même mémoire, amenés, à la banque, autour du même capital, se regroupent dans la même fonction.

Nous savons depuis trois millénaires qu'ils font le même métier. La fonction jupitérienne est celle du signe. La technologie informatique amène enfin la banque des données. C'est moins un progrès que le dévoilement simple de la vérité de nos systèmes. On ne découvre là, on ne construit là que le stock des stocks, j'entends le stock commun à tout ce qui était bibliothèque, cadastre, enlistement. Et apparaît le groupe des groupes, le Jupiter commun à la circulation des signes. Curieusement, le monde, après-demain, par une sophistication formidable, est déjà lisible comme primitif. Cela prouve sans doute que nous ne parlons jamais que du nôtre. Rien de nouveau, rien de nouveau sous le soleil, sous le soleil du signe.

Nous courons donc, ici, vers une banque des données.

Revenons au premier capital : lac, mine, poche, ces fonctions du temps. Le barrage réserve l'eau issue des glaces et des neiges, des vents, des nuages, enfin du réchauffement et du froid. Coke, pétrole ou chute, c'est, en tout cas, de la chaleur en stock. Tout à l'heure, la collection des capitaux convergeait vers la pierre faite de signatures, ceux-ci, à nouveau, vont ensemble vers un seul lieu. Ils dérivent du soleil ou vers le soleil. Ces réservoirs ne sont que des sous-soleils. Leur source, amont, dernière instance, est le soleil. Le capital, réel, ultime, est le soleil. Sous-capitaux fonctions du temps, mais notre temps est au soleil. Notre temps cosmogonique, notre temps astronomique, notre temps d'énergie, d'entropie et d'information, le temps cyclique et réversible, aussi bien que les temps irréversibles de désordre et de mort, de vie et d'ordre aléatoirement inventé, tous ensemble se nouent au soleil. En matière de matière, en matière d'énergie, seul transforme et crée le soleil. Tous les matérialismes, et surtout ceux qui cherchent à rendre compte du mouvement réel et du dépassement, se joignent en ceci aux énergétismes et peut-être aux idéalismes, qu'ils sont, au bout de tous les comptes, des sous-cultes du soleil.

Et donc notre savoir, les ingéniosités de nos pratiques dures sont bandés aujourd'hui vers la repro-

duction du soleil. Lors de l'érection d'un barrage,
lors de la percée d'un forage, on ne voyait pas bien
encore qu'il s'agissait déjà du soleil. L'eau était trop
froide, quoique haute, la houille trop noire, bien
que détonante, les huiles trop lourdes, encore
qu'inflammables. Des ombres. Dans l'enceinte
magnétique de la fusion, où l'étoile paraît léviter, au-
dehors, l'éblouissement n'aveugle plus notre intuition : nos travaux inventifs n'ont jamais qu'imité le
soleil, ou d'abord imité des imitations de soleil, nous
le construisons désormais avec fidélité, aux noyaux
secrets de sa flamme. Épiphanie, enfin, de la plus
vieille idée du monde. La vieille hyperbole platonicienne sort de sa métaphore, vieille caverne de
voleurs métaphysiciens, elle est, aujourd'hui, fabri-
quée. Nous sommes encore un peu en deçà de cette
hyperbole, nous n'avons pas rejoint l'au-delà de
l'essence, ils sont pourtant au bout d'une stratégie
droite. Non seulement nous regardons en face le
soleil, nous ne le représentons plus, mais nous le
produisons. Ce n'était pas, hélas, la merveilleuse
transcendance attendue : simplement le bout d'une
histoire. La métaphysique descend, elle perd son
préfixe.

Dans un mois, dans trois jours, dans vingt ans,
nous aurons amené le soleil sur la terre, nous
l'aurons établi, nous l'y aurons fixé, nous aurons
ménagé pour lui sa demeure. Il nous échappe
encore un peu, il se meut, il y clignote seulement.
Nous aurons annulé sa distance et rattrapé son
temps, réduit sa transcendance. Comment
nommera-t-on cette révolution, je ne sais. Elle sera
nouvelle, un successeur de Galilée, de Copernic, lui

donnera son nom, elle ne sera pas nouvelle, cependant. Car c'est là même que nos chemins, depuis longtemps, conduisent. Réserve d'amont, source en dernière instance, pour le fonctionnement de nos moteurs. Il y a des morceaux de terre qui étaient des soleils, déjà.

Nous avons lancé, nous lancerons encore des satellites de communication, couplés avec la banque des données, pour que fonctionnent sans entraves nos moteurs informationnels. Comment s'appellera cette révolution, astronomique encore, je ne sais. Un successeur de Ptolémée y pourvoira, de son nom propre. Elle sera nouvelle et ne le sera pas.

Nous aurons achevé un parcours sur une voie connue. La maîtrise, la manipulation de ces soleils et de ces satellites, de ces deux capitaux, feux et signaux, de ce nouveau système de notre ancien monde exprimeront, expriment nos virtuosités sur les hautes et sur les basses énergies, sur la matière à transformer, sur les langages à comprendre. Notre monde était de production, de traduction. Il faisait s'entrebattre deux philosophies pour s'établir enfin sur leur accord.

Un chapitre de nos raisons est en train de se clore. Mais nous en connaissons déjà la fin, nous en savons les conséquences. En arriver au capital-soleil ou à la banque des données, aux deux réservoirs concentrés de feux et de signaux, à l'universel concret des projets de production et des trajets de traduction, ce n'est qu'extrapoler sur le système en place, aller au bout de ses tendances, faire confiance à ses dérives, placer la nouveauté dans la conservation. Et donc le compléter, presque le faire naître, le faire apparaître dans sa perfection épurée. On croyait à un double progrès, au sens d'une double révolution : ce n'est qu'une simple croissance. Elle nous donne à voir dans sa pureté pleine cela même qu'impliquent dès leur naissance nos savoirs, nos performances, nos luttes, notre histoire et son temps. Le système nait sous nos yeux, il était déjà là : le mammouth mondial, le dinosaure gigantesque dont les gigantismes achevés sont des préliminaires, le Léviathan, le gros animal, déjà connu et baptisé, bien nourri d'énergie abondante et d'information normalement acheminée. La vieille philosophie s'applique de nouveau, comme on dit des mathématiques dans les sciences exactes. Nous savons désormais construire ce schéma, puisque nous en avons la force solaire et la donnée informative dans notre compte en banque.

Que peut faire de plus qu'un animal très gros le plus gros animal ? Et peut-on concevoir un animal plus gros que cette bête-monde, un soleil entouré de planètes de signes ? Je devine que ce système doit être assez fragile, toute variété d'une telle taille courant vers la disparition et la mort. Est-ce, une fois encore, la fin des grands sauriens, la fin des grands empires ? Sur la chaîne sans fin de la concurrence, de la force et du gigantisme, sur la relation d'ordre du plus fort, du meilleur, du plus grand, existe-t-il un seuil, une borne ou une limite ?

Vivants mangeurs de vivants, nous survivons, inégalement bien, dans le torrent issu du soleil. Bruyants et intercepteurs de signaux, nous survivons dans le torrent qui court vers le lac des données. Beaux parleurs invités à la table du monde, nous tentons d'échanger des signaux légers contre les objets du soleil.

Ce festin d'injustice et de mortalité sera-t-il un jour interrompu?

Les vaches montent du fleuve
Les stocks

> *Il se tenait auprès du Nil et il vit monter du Nil sept vaches.*
>
> Genèse, XLI, 2.

Le fleuve Jaune est vu de bas en haut, à partir de la plaine, alors qu'à peu près tous les fleuves de la terre coulent dans un lit creux. Depuis le début de nos temps, depuis que le cultivateur s'est mis à façonner la face de la terre, depuis qu'ils ont besoin d'irriguer les rizières, les paysans chinois sont là, sous le fleuve, surplombés par le fleuve, à boire l'eau du Houang-Ho, à se défendre à mort contre les eaux du Houang-Ho. Source de vie, péril majeur de destruction.

Le fleuve Jaune est un transformateur géologique énorme. Il déchire ses hauts, violemment, jusqu'à, parfois, capter des tributaires d'un bassin voisin, si travailleur, si inventif qu'il peut se jeter hors de ses équilibres homéorrhétiques, aller chercher des chutes et des pentes hors de sa pente, il dévore le sol, il mange le relief, il charrie des montagnes fon-

dues, et, plus aval, les dépose, restitue le loess
dérobé, enlise ses bas, épaissit le fond de son lit,
l'épaissit tant qu'il peut perdre ses rives et vaguer au
hasard, par la plaine. D'amont à la mer, très souvent
à l'écart des contraintes courantes, par son énergie
fluctuante, il redessinerait son lit. Modèle superbe
de trajet méthodique plus informationnel que
redondant, modèle complexe de randonnée, au sens
que j'ai donné ailleurs à ce mot.

Depuis longtemps, il s'élève, terrifiant, sur la
plaine. Il est un sillon, comme tous les fleuves, il est
une muraille de rives hautes, de remblais vertigi-
neux. Il ne déborde pas seulement, comme la
Garonne, il se rompt. Il est un canal suspendu, il est
rivière et pont, fleuve et digue. Ce qui est, pour
nous, souterrain, est, pour les Chinois de la plaine,
élevé, exhaussé, comme en lévitation, coule en l'air.
Et les eaux qui se ruent y sont déjà les eaux du ciel.
Tout le cours du fleuve inférieur est barrage, les paysans chinois vivent et dorment au bas de sa muraille,
à la merci d'une fissure. La moindre lézarde, la plus
petite fêlure, la cascade se mue en cataracte, et, par
sa débâcle, soudain, le déluge passe.

Vaguant parmi la plaine, il irrigue tout seul, il suffit de l'attendre. Mais on peut mourir de l'attendre.
Il ne vient pas, il vient, énorme, inattendu, il noie
plutôt qu'il ne féconde. Mieux vaut donc le canaliser, le régler, construire un réseau de rigoles tout
autour du tronc majeur. Par déblais, dragages, remblais, tassements, le génie civil se déploie. Rationalisation des hasards, ou normalisation du stochastique, les Chinois déjà se rendaient maîtres,
possesseurs de la nature. Ils ménageaient un réser-

voir, mais ils suspendaient, en même temps, une épée lourde sur leurs têtes. Au milieu des talus, le Houang-Ho, semaine après semaine, déposait des tonnes de loess et montait. Alors on élevait encore les remblais, glacis et talus. Et ainsi de suite. Que faire d'autre? Le modèle est, de nouveau, superbe. Et terrifiant. Quand vous montez une muraille, l'eau croît derrière la muraille, alors vous élevez encore la muraille, l'eau croit toujours derrière la muraille. Et s'élargit. La solution d'une question déniche dix problèmes, et cela recommence.

Travail sans issue, aux rendements décroissants. Ce n'est pas le travail d'Hercule; celui-ci est optimiste. Lorsque le héros grec chassait les parasites, monstres ou fumier, l'espace en était enfin purifié. Je ne sache pas que la mythologie ait imaginé leur retour. Le retour du virus de la varicelle en virus du zona, cinquante ans après. Le fumier d'Augias disparaît, le loess du fleuve s'accumule.

Nos sciences, nos technologies, notre culture occidentale : travail au pied du Houang-Ho ou le détournement du fleuve Alphée ?

L'agriculture, en Mésopotamie, en Égypte ou ailleurs, aux bords du fleuve Jaune, par exemple, a ouvert, au néolithique, un univers tout neuf, dont nous sommes les vieux enfants. Comment peut-on se mettre à cultiver la terre ?

La cueillette précède, à ce qu'on raconte. Déjà, nous ne savons rien faire, déjà nous sommes exigeants. Nous choisissons. Nous refusons, par là, d'autres espèces végétales. Nous les éliminons. Le geste d'exclusion, le geste d'expulsion est là, au début, le guichet.

Tout à coup, je le crois radical; rigoureusement, à la lettre, radical.

Nous avons l'usage d'exclure les mauvaises herbes, de trier le bon grain de l'ivraie. Cela n'est pas possible, au temps du blé en herbe. La purge donc, la sacralisation d'un espace donné, d'un *templum*, d'un jardin, commence par l'expulsion totale, radicale de toutes les espèces. Et pas seulement du lièvre advenu. L'agriculture n'a pas pu commencer avant la dénudation complète de certains lieux du sol. Avant qu'il soit fait place nette ou table rase du manteau végétal. Le champ, c'est d'abord un lieu d'où tout est arraché. Champ de bataille, champ de ruines, toute chose a levé le camp. Et lorsque je dis radical, je dis bien que les racines mêmes sont éradiquées, qu'on a porté le soc de la charrue assez profond pour détruire jusqu'aux radicelles les espèces expulsées. Il ne s'agissait pas de féconder la terre par labour, il s'agissait d'extirper, de supprimer, de bannir. De détruire. Le couteau de l'araire est un couteau sacrificiel. Tuer totalement les plantes et tenter une place nette. Tout ce qui pousse ici est exclu. Pas seulement ce que nous appelons maintenant les mauvaises herbes, tout. Nettoyage par le vide. C'est bien l'acte premier du religieux et ce fut, par chance, acte agricole. Même geste, même travail, même saccage. Même appropriation, propreté ou propriété.

Le soc de la charrue est un couteau sacrificiel manipulé frénétiquement, au comble de la fureur meurtrière. Le couteau tue, homme ou bête. Abel ou l'agneau, Isaac ou le bouc émissaire. Il est un coupe-gorge. Il tranche. Il ne décide plus, il tranche. Non plus en deux, en trois. Il découpe l'espace. Il dessine une ligne fermée : à l'intérieur le sacré, à l'extérieur le profane, à l'intérieur le temple, à l'extérieur le vague où le mal court. A l'intérieur la ville, entourée de murailles, et la campagne à l'extérieur. Le soc de la charrue a fondé la ville, et au creux du sillon, un frère a tué son jumeau. Le soc est le couteau qui sacrifie le frère. Il a coupé la gorge, il a découpé l'espace et la terre. Ce couteau, ce soc, ne s'arrête pas. Pourquoi s'arrêterait-il ? Il continue follement, il coupe tout, il déborde la maîtrise des apprentis sorciers. Non pas un sillon continu et ferme, mais un sillon, deux sillons, trois, dix mille, pour que toute la terre soit découpée, que l'espace soit partout tranché, que plus rien ne résiste à son mouvement fou, nulle herbe, nulle plante, nulle racine, rien de ce qui est là. Quand la fureur de ce couteau s'apaise, tout est labouré, en poussière fine. Hersé. Réduit aux éléments. Analyse.

Le premier travail était un meurtre frénétique, jusqu'aux atomes obtenus. Jusqu'à ce qu'on ne puisse plus couper, jusqu'à ce qu'on ne puisse plus trancher. L'assassinat, jusqu'au découpage de la victime en morceaux menus.

Ainsi est née l'agriculture.

Elle obtenait un espace nu, un domino blanc.

Il y fallait attendre un hasard, une graine. Et sa mort, naturellement.

Or le labour, sitôt, ne fut pas possible. Cette dénudation se fit toute seule aux bords du fleuve en crue.

L'inondation arrache tout sur son passage, arbres, arbustes, plantes, mousses, racines. Elle purifie tout, elle fait naturellement le geste culturel attendu. De cette rencontre ou de ce court-circuit improbable, l'agriculture naît sur les rives du Nil, du Tigre, de l'Euphrate ou du Houang-Ho. L'agriculture naît du fleuve Alphée qui nettoie, qui purifie tout le fumier des rois.

Reste un carré de sol nu, d'où tout le manteau végétal disparaît. Cela fait un écart formidable à l'équilibre des vivants. Par cette faille peut passer, par cette faille passe la prolifération verticale d'une espèce donnée ensemencée là, par hasard. Le problème, ainsi résolu, ne requiert, pour sa solution, que l'opération simple, élémentaire, d'expulsion.

Un parasite chasse tous les autres. Les hommes chassent la vie d'un endroit donné. L'inondation n'était pas souhaitée, le labour n'était pas exécuté, pour irriguer ou pour semer, tout était fait ou subi pour le nettoyage. D'où cette déchirure, d'où cette catastrophe, par où pouvait passer la multiplication du blé, du riz, ou du maïs, selon les lieux, les hasards et les circonstances.

Tout à coup se levait une autre inondation ; une aubaine, des stocks de nourriture inespérés.

Le parasite humain se multiplie aussi par cette faille à l'équilibre, par cette catastrophe. Il allait à son tour inonder le monde. Croissance contre croissance, l'inondation de riz luttait par des murailles contre l'inondation des eaux du Houang-Ho. Épidémies contre épidémies, logiques d'ensembles.

L'invention d'un espace vide, sa découverte sous les eaux ou sa constitution à la sueur de nos visages, ouvrent une déchirure dans le tissu du monde, font une catastrophe, un écart, une faille par où se rue, non plus la multiplicité exclue, mais la multiplication folle de l'unité la plus chanceuse ou la mieux adaptée. L'équilibre antérieur était tissé de différences. Or, dans le blanc local que nous produisons, l'homogénéité paraît. La crue. Le stock.

On imagine que ces carrés appropriés, rangés, bien limités, où rien ne paraît plus que la boulbène brune, sont des performances récentes d'une agriculture instruite et civilisée. Je crois qu'on aurait avantage à penser l'inverse. L'instauration du champ nu, vide, et, de nouveau, vierge, est le plus vieux travail du monde humain.

Le premier qui, ayant enclos un terrain ou un champ, s'avisa d'exclure tout ce qui était là, fut le vrai fondateur de l'ère historique suivante.

L'agriculture et la culture ont la même origine ou le même carré de base, un lieu blanc, qui réalise une rupture d'équilibre, un lieu propre constitué par l'expulsion. Un lieu de propreté, un lieu d'appartenance.

Le joker se change en domino blanc.

Il convient de comprendre cet espace blanc, apparu dans les savanes ancestrales, cette déchirure au milieu de leur fluctuante stabilité. Avons-nous jamais produit d'autres objets dans les moments où, d'un coup, l'histoire bifurque?

Voici que je comprends une nouvelle fois l'origine de la géométrie, voici que je comprends, à nouveau frais, les histoires qu'on raconte d'elle. Le Nil, en

crue, déborde et ravage les champs alentour. Les
harpédonaptes, prêtres ou philosophes, sages, agrimenseurs, redistribuent aux paysans ou aux propriétaires les parcelles dont l'inondation vient justement
d'effacer les limites. L'interprétation de ce dire tra-
ditionnel mesure exactement la culture agraire de
nos grands-parents. Les harpédonaptes, disaient-ils,
sont les premiers des géomètres, parce que les Égyptiens avaient pris pour juges de leurs disputes de bor-
nage ceux qui savaient obtenir les superficies par des
opérations sur les longueurs. Ils avaient le cordon,
l'unité, la mesure, l'écriture et le prestige. Voilà le
géomètre expert qu'on prend chez le notaire au
chef-lieu de canton quand le voisin, sournois, a
déplacé les bornes ou les a dépassées. Ne rions pas
trop vite, car tout est pourtant là, sous nos yeux. Non
l'expert, mais le prêtre. Le prêtre, c'est-à-dire celui
qui fait le geste d'expulsion, de découpage du *templum.* L'agriculteur a fait le même geste. Le fleuve et
sa crue ne s'opposent pas aux actions conjuguées du
prêtre et du cultivateur, mais les aident en cette
affaire, font mieux que les aider, agissent à leur
place et leur lieu. Ce n'est pas seulement la limite
que le fleuve efface par l'excès de sa crue, c'est la
population entière des choses qui existait dans cet
espace ou dans ce champ. Tout en est arraché,
expulsé, l'espace est blanc, homogène et couvert de
lise. Ce carré lisse apparaissant à la décrue, qui vient
le limiter ? L'agriculteur, le prêtre et le géomètre.
Trois origines en trois personnes en un seul geste, au
même instant. Le champ, le temple, et l'espace
métrique. Démocrite et mes aïeux disaient le juste, il
suffisait de les entendre. L'espace découvert par le

Nil, le Tigre, la Garonne ou le Houang-Ho, c'est le domino blanc, le lieu vierge des tiers exclus, la déchirure d'équilibre. Cette étendue, parce que vide, est homogène, elle est isotrope, elle est mesurable. C'est le champ de l'agriculture, en basse vallée, c'est le *templum* au sens de Mircea Eliade, au sens de l'étymologie comme au sens du sacré, mais c'est en même temps l'espace abstrait de la géométrie. Espace abstrait, d'où tout fut soustrait, d'où tout fut arraché, d'où tout fut éloigné, d'où tout fut extrait. Lisez maintenant avec attention les textes où Platon cherche attentivement à définir l'espace ou la figure, ils sont tous négatifs, ou tous exactement apophatiques. Le philosophe agit comme le prêtre ou l'agriculteur, il extirpe de là tout ce qui pourrait risquer d'y réapparaître. Y compris la couleur, jusqu'aux limites, justement. Il obtient à nouveau un domino blanc. Donc une déchirure dans la culture, donc la folle prolifération d'une variété, qui n'a jamais cessé de croître, jusqu'à nous. Et c'est la même solution que ma toute première, celle du tiers exclu. Celle-ci était dialectique, elle n'appropriait pas un espace. Il faut unir les deux pour rester chez les Grecs. Partout ailleurs où l'agriculture naquit, seule la géométrie des agrimenseurs était née. C'est-à-dire tout, sauf la science.

Quelques dominos blancs déchirent çà et là le manteau végétal, surtout dans les deltas et dans les embouchures. Quelques dominos blancs déchirent le langage en ce qu'on a nommé les idéalités, les réalités de l'intelligible. L'âge classique ne nous paraît instaurateur que par la reprise, en un autre lieu, de ce même geste. La méditation cartésienne élimine,

expulse, bannit tout, hyperboliquement. De nouveau
table rase et place nette, en tonalité religieuse
majeure, et cette table et cette place forment en fin
de compte une étendue dont je suis maître et possesseur par la pensée. Le je pensant chasse les parasites,
chasse en prosopopée le plus malin de tous qui
revient, qui risque de revenir toujours et partout,
chasse donc tout, absolument parlant, il découvre,
en un autre lieu, le monde, le blanc de notre dominance. Vierge cire. Dans la déchirure ainsi pratiquée
passent infiniment les chaînes de raison toutes
simples et toutes faciles, se multiplient le simple et
l'unitaire, le rationnel et le technologique. L'histoire
bifurque encore, ce n'est pas douteux. La maîtrise et
la possession commencent.

La constitution d'un espace vierge que la lumière
baigne, non plus comme idéalité, mais comme objet-
monde, fait une rupture si considérable dans l'équilibre culturel que, par la faille de l'écart, va se précipiter le rationnel moderne, la multiplication proliffé-
rante d'un certain type de même. A chaque
apparition de ce blanc, un buissonnement de
simples remplace l'ancienne multiplicité de
complexes. A chaque apparition de ce blanc explose
la reproduction.

Le blé, le riz. Les hommes. Les mathématiques. La
technicité, la rationalisation du monde. Les
hommes, à nouveau. L'histoire, souple, suit ces
blancs et ces geysers.

La multiplication de l'espèce parasitaire qui les

produit bondit, sitôt après le flux issu de ces espaces blancs.

La question de l'origine aboutit constamment à des solutions décevantes parce qu'il n'y a rien à l'origine que ce lieu blanc et vide. L'origine est toujours cet ensemble vide. Comme on dit, on part de zéro. L'histoire est comme la suite des nombres, et la datation est d'essence.

Mais toute la question est de produire le zéro. Par exclusion totale en un lieu donné. L'histoire commencerait au déluge, si celui-ci ne laissait voir un reste, Noé, l'arche et ses animaux, échappés à l'inondation. Le reste est moteur de l'histoire suivant un état sans reste. Et donc, dès les premiers versets de la Genèse, l'esprit de Dieu planait sur les eaux, c'était bien le premier déluge, l'inondation sans reste, d'où, fatalement, devait suivre la création *ex nihilo*. Le travail de limitation, de division commence, et bientôt les eaux sont séparées des eaux. Tout — je veux dire par là le monde — est bien issu de la première inondation, de la première opération qui supprime tout, et sans reste.

Nous commençons ainsi à comprendre le sens, qui paraissait si mystérieux, de cette création à partir de rien, *ex nihilo*. Même pas un tout petit point sur la graine, le hile, même pas ce à partir de quoi un brin d'herbe pourrait pousser. Rien, il ne reste rien après la crue, il ne reste rien dans le champ, rien dans l'espace intelligible où les sens pourraient accrocher, rien après l'épreuve du doute, le travail du négatif a pris fin avant tous les commencements. Discours de l'origine radicale, très improbable et donc porteur d'une surabondante information.

Les vaches, l'une suivant l'autre, montent du Nil en crue. Chacune d'elles est une crue, un stock, une fécondité, une abondance, et chacune nourrit ceux qui vont pulluler de la bifurcation qu'elle annonce. Le prêtre, tour à tour, le cultivateur, le protogéomètre, le maître et possesseur de la nature, le philosophe du discours radical...

De cette chaîne monte un vertige d'éradication. Du Nil montent les vaches, les stocks, nos hasards et l'histoire. Du Nil : est-ce l'Alphée, est-ce le Houang-Ho ? Avec reste ou sans reste, c'est toute la question. Le héros fait le vide et tout est commencé, ou il reste indéfiniment limon, lise, vase, loess. Je ne sais pas quelle est la voie.

Je ne peux croire que l'animal dévastateur d'une portion d'espace savait d'avance le produit final de son action, ou de son exaction — *overkill*, surtuerie —, et purifiait ou nettoyait ce lieu dans ce but. Ce travail a réussi, au-delà des espérances (quand il a réussi) pour de tout autres raisons que ses motifs. Rien ne change quand on passe des pratiques à la théorie.

Cette histoire n'aura pas de fin si elle va de carré local en carré local. Mais sa logique même, celle de l'éradication, n'amène-t-elle pas, nécessairement, à un global, sans reste ?

Les vaches mangent les vaches
Théorie de la queue

> *Sept autres vaches montèrent du Nil, laides et maigres, et se rangèrent à côté des premières sur la rive du Nil. Et les vaches maigres dévorèrent les vaches grasses. Et le Pharaon s'éveilla.*
>
> Genèse, XLI, 2-6.

La chaîne du parasitisme est une simple relation d'ordre, elle est irréversible comme le flux du fleuve. Tel se nourrit de l'autre et ne lui donne rien. L'asymétrie est locale sur un chaînon, elle se propage globalement le long de la série, par transitivité. Les parasites font la queue, en festins gigognes. La chose est, en réalité, plus complexe. Et la théorie des queues, on le sait, va plus loin. Nous en restons, pour le moment, aux éléments de relation. Car le parasitisme est une relation élémentaire, il est même l'élément de la relation.

Elle s'introduit comme un coin dans les équilibres, elle les fait dévier. S'il existe, s'il a existé, quelque jour, quelque part, un quelconque équilibre, l'introduction d'un parasite dans le système provoque aussitôt un écart, un déséquilibre. Le système, tout de suite, change. Il dérive. Le temps a commencé.

Le changement vient d'une rupture dans des échanges équilibrés. Le changement est le déséquilibre des échanges.

On peut donc introduire un parasite microscopique dans un milieu pathologique équilibré, un parasite de taille honnête dans un ensemble économique stable, ou un parasite bruyant dans un message dialogué, une histoire, en tout cas, s'ensuivra. On a cru pendant longtemps que ces histoires étaient très différentes.

Les questions évoquées plus haut sont plus ou moins des questions d'origine. Elles ont été résolues, toutes, par le parasite. La solution était aisée, puisque sans parasite, c'est-à-dire sans asymétrie ou sans déséquilibre, l'irréversible n'a pas lieu, n'émerge aucune chaîne, le temps est inconnu.

La commensalité au sens strict est éternitaire. Les Grecs ne s'y sont pas trompés, qui nous font voir les immortels ne cessant pas de festoyer, de boire l'ambroisie, de rire, inextinguiblement. Nous savons tous, parfaitement, de quoi l'ambroisie se compose, quels sont les ingrédients du nectar, boisson d'immortalité. Nous savons tous, parfaitement, où est le paradis, et comment produire l'absence d'histoire. Nous savons qu'il suffit de rompre la chaîne asymétrique, la série des abus, nous savons qu'il suffit de ne pas manger celui qui nous précède, dans l'ordre. Nous savons qu'il suffit d'échanger de la

nourriture, en boucle, pour échapper au changement, au temps et à l'histoire. De s'asseoir au festin
et d'être commensaux. D'annuler tout écart par rapport au *sitos*, ou de chasser, en nous, le parasite. Le
paradis est là, tout de suite.

L'ambroisie est, sans doute, autant chez les Hin-
dous qu'ici, la bière brassée qui sauva les groupes
humains du croissant fertile et des pays plus à l'est
de l'Eden encore, de certaines maladies infectieuses
courant les sources et les marigots. La bière, le vin et
le pain, aliments de fermentation, de bouillonne-
ment, nourritures de pourriture, sont apparus
comme des sauvegardes contre la mort. Ce furent
nos premières grandes victoires sur les parasites, nos
concurrents, obtenues, on s'en doute, pour des raisons et par des intentions tout autres que celles qui
les firent triompher de fait. Nous célébrons, depuis
les Olympiens de toutes langues jusqu'à la Cène
récente, cette victoire à laquelle nous devons la vie,
l'éternité de la phylogénèse, et nous la célébrons à
son lieu naturel, à table.

Ici la question découvre son modèle. Je ne mour-
rai plus de manger du pain, mon fils ne mourra plus
de boire, par le vin ou la bière des dieux. Dans notre
dos est abolie la chaîne qui nous dévorait. Prenez à
la lettre ce mot : vos ancêtres ont bu l'eau du puits
de Jacob, ils sont morts. Ils en sont morts, l'eau
n'était plus potable. Buvez l'eau changée en vin et le
vin changé en boisson d'immortalité, vous serez
saufs des parasites. De la putréfaction mortelle. Il

faut passer alors du modèle au système. Nous ne sommes pas différents des animaux qui nous mangeaient, des animaux petits qui nous tuaient. Nous nous mangeons, nous nous tuons les uns les autres. Quand les vaches sortent du Nil, elles se rangent les unes à côté des autres, le long du fleuve, en ordre, et elles se mangent les unes les autres, en ordre, en suivant le Nil, et selon la loi d'ordre, comme nous autres. Plaçons-nous autour de la table et faisons circuler notre nourriture, pratiquons un échange parfait, devenons commensaux. Et c'est l'équilibre immortel.

Bien sûr, ce n'est pas si simple. Dans toute l'aire indo-européenne, un étranger, voleur, vient se saisir de l'ambroisie, le système a un trou. Et dans l'aire sémite, en ce même festin, quelqu'un se donne à dévorer, le système est troué encore. Tout de même, on y transforme bien le logiciel en matériel.

Avant même de parler d'histoire, le temps a commencé par la déviation des systèmes. Nous aurons à y revenir, mais nous y sommes venus déjà, par Lucrèce, par la physique ancienne et contemporaine.

On dit que tel parasite, par la complexité de ses performances, par la sophistication de son cycle, est un miracle de l'évolution. Parfois on dit aussi que notre activité commence à peser lourd dans cette évolution. Je me demande tout à coup si l'évolution elle-même n'est pas, d'un certain point de vue, l'œuvre des parasites. Si, entre évolution et parasitisme, il n'y aurait pas, plutôt, des cycles de causes et d'effets, en circuits ouverts, en feed-back. L'évolution produirait le parasite qui produirait l'évolution. Je me demande tout à coup si l'étude, non pas locale et singulière, mais globale, formelle et opératoire de la fonction parasitaire ne serait pas comme déplacée, un peu à part et décalée, comme réflexive, par rapport aux sciences exactes, naturelles et humaines, comme un lieu de passage, où elles ne pourraient pas être dissociées.

La théorie de l'évolution se ramène à deux termes : mutation, sélection. On sait assez exactement sur quel ensemble agit le premier. Ce n'est pas tout à fait une métaphore que de dire d'abord qu'il s'agit d'un message écrit sur un support. Partie de ce message est changée par mutation, par absence, substitution ou décalage d'éléments. Ce n'est pas tout à fait une métaphore que de prétendre qu'il s'agit de l'intervention d'un bruit dans le message. Bruit au sens de désordre, et donc hasard, mais bruit aussi au sens d'interception, interception qui change l'ordre et donc le sens, si on peut parler de sens. Mais qui change l'ordre en tout cas. L'interception est parasite, on le devine. Le nouvel ordre apparaît par le parasite troublant le message. Il déconcerte l'ancienne série, la suite, le message, il en concerte de nouveaux.

L'introduction d'un parasite dans un système équivaut à celle d'un bruit. L'ordre du monde, chez Lucrèce, venu de la déclinaison sur un champ laminaire, est un ordre par fluctuation. Cette fluctuation est un bruit, elle est parasite. Le temps ne commence pas sans son intervention. L'irréversibi-

lité n'apparaît jamais sans ce facteur d'asymétrie.
L'ordre au sens de l'ordre des choses comme l'ordre
au sens des structures d'ordre ne peuvent émerger
sans cet élément de relation d'ordre. Le parasite est
un élément de relation, il est l'atome de relation,
l'atome sagittal, l'élément de flèche. La flèche volant
au hasard dans la clarté du jour. L'apparition du
sens.

La théorie de l'être, ontologie, amène aux atomes.
La théorie des relations amène au parasite.

L'introduction d'un parasite dans un système
équivaut à celle d'un bruit. Premier cas. Je parle à
plusieurs voix. Le message plonge dans le non-sens,
dans le bruit pur, dans le désordre, le système
s'écroule, tout meurt. La peste annule une population. La mutation fait avorter le foetus. Du coup, le
parasite, assassin, se suicide. L'écornifleur retombe
au ruisseau après avoir ruiné son hôte. De la théorie
de l'information à l'anthropologie, des signaux à la
vie, singulière ou nombreuse, la dynamique est
stable, invariante, elle amène partout les mêmes
résultats.

L'entrée de Tartuffe ou de l'abbé Faujas dans une
famille tranquille produit la comédie, la tragédie,
bruit et fureur, violence, prison, meurtre, incendie,
une histoire. Comment le système dérive-t-il et pourquoi ? Chez Zola, tout finit au spectacle du feu, dans
les cendres, par l'effusion du sang. L'arrivée de Tartuffe induit dès le début de nouveaux messages en
circulation. C'est le désordre, la cour du roi Pétaud.

Nul ne peut plus parler que Mme Pernelle, la circulation va d'elle aux autres, sans retour. L'hôte
revient, n'écoute pas et ne demande qu'une chose.
Tartuffe est parasite au sens matériel du festin, il fait
couler le flux de nourriture vers sa bouche, le « et
Tartuffe » est un parasite au sens logiciel du message, il fait couler le flux de sens dans un seul sens. Il
rompt le dialogue, il l'interrompt, il le redresse, il
fonctionne comme un redresseur. Le bruit, ce bruit
particulier, redresse le sens et le fait circuler dans un
sens unique. L'émetteur n'est pas troublé par le
parasite, le récepteur, lui, est troublé. Ainsi apparaît
le deuxième cas, ou, peut-être, la loi de la dérive. Le
système, tout à coup, s'oriente. Le système, tout à
coup, décline. Le système, tout à coup, a un sens. Ce
bruit-là est un redresseur, il filtre un sens, il crée un
sens. On voit maintenant pourquoi et vers quoi le
système dérive. Introduisez donc une impureté dans
tel ou tel cristal, vous aurez, d'aventure, produit un
transistor. Un semi-conducteur.

On a compris, dès lors, la sélection. Le parasite est
redresseur, il crée une circulation irréversible, il crée
un sens, il fait du sens. Comme on l'a vu plus haut, il
construit des guichets par sa haute exigence. Un guichet, que je sache, est encore un semi-conducteur.
La sélection est aussi, est encore, semi-conduction.
L'activité du parasite est parallèle au fonctionnement de la sélection. Ce sont deux opérateurs de
même structure. Il est intéressant de mettre en évidence des opérateurs et des opérateurs seulement.
On n'aura pas besoin d'une téléonomie à très
longue portée. Ici se crée un sens, pour favoriser
localement telle vie parasitaire. Les orientations,

nombreuses, différentes, se composent, et voilà tout. La pression globale de sélection est la composition globale de ces sens, localement créés, l'intégration des exigences.

L'évolution est de structure parasitaire. Elle ne favoriserait pas autant les parasites si, peu ou prou, elle n'était favorisée par eux. Émerge avec elle un ordre, une structure d'ordre, une dérive, par le bruit et par le guichet sélectif, par le bruit redresseur, et par le guichet redresseur, par le redressement qui est lui-même une relation d'ordre, un décalage ou une asymétrie. Si l'évolution est un ordre, le parasite est bien son élément. Il interrompt une répétition, il fait bifurquer la série du même.

On ne peut pas penser l'évolution sans penser, en-deçà des formes évolutives, en-deçà des permutations du codage, en-deçà des deux mécanismes considérés ou repérables, mutation, sélection, la temporalité irréversible, ce flux de fond asymétrique et lent, ce sens global qu'on se détourne de penser. Il faut tenter de penser ce temps.

J'ai dit ailleurs que les organismes vivants sont des bouquets ou des gerbes de temps, qu'ils sont des échangeurs de temps. Que la vie, sûrement, n'est autre que du temps, mais que cette proposition n'est pas simple. Et que nous en connaissons trois, au moins, si divers qu'on peut les dire contradictoires : le réversible, datable par les équilibres longs du monde, les deux irréversibles, celui de l'entropie et celui, justement, de l'évolution darwinienne. Le premier nous protège et il définit notre niche, le second nous fait mourir en une agonie plus ou moins durable, et le dernier nous perpétue, espérant dans le génie de nos filles et dans la beauté de nos fils. La vie serait le nœud de ces trois chronies séparables[1]. Je laisse un brin libre, flottant autour, cette espérance inconsolable dans la transparence de nos œuvres laissées.

Reste à comprendre leur entrelacement. S'il existe du réversible, il existe du répété, de la redondance. Elle est bien là, au système du monde — les éclipses et le retour des syzygies sont indiscernables de droit —, elle est là, dans la stabilité profonde d'un message qui ne jette jamais la reproduction sexuée hors de son espèce. Nul n'a jamais vu un homme et une femme engendrer un jaguar. Nul n'a jamais vu un cristal de neige prendre, tout à coup, en émeraude verte. Il existe de la redondance. Il existe du $a \equiv a$, le long d'un temps que cette identité enchaîne. Rien de nouveau sous l'éblouissement solaire du même. Redondances logicielles, équilibres mécaniques, invariants génétiques, stabilités matérielles.

Nous voici de retour à la chute blanche, ou à la redondance laminaire. Rien n'est discernable au sein d'un univers tel, tout y est réversible, échangeable. On aimerait à dire ce mobile immobile. Les deux trinquent et rient dans l'espace fixe des éclipses et des syzygies, on comprend qu'ils rient sans parler, qu'ils trinquent pour le bruit, que l'ambroisie soit inépuisable, en retour éternel. Plus le vase versait, moins il s'allait vidant.

---

1. *Hermès IV. La distribution*, « l'Origine du langage ». *Hermès V. Le passage du Nord-Ouest*, « Espaces et temps ».

Le temps irréversible commence avec le bruit parasite, avec la fluctuation, avec le *clinamen,* il s'écoule dans un seul sens. Le temps irréversible n'aurait pas commencé sans l'ensemencement du désordre dans la redondance. Dans l'espace blanc dont j'ai parlé plus haut, un atome de désordre, un atome de relation, suffit à ce que la dérive commence. De cet espace blanc, tout surgit à la condition de ce quark de bruit.

Le temps irréversible du vivant commence avec la vie parasite, sa double activité de bruit et d'exigence. Elle intercepte et canalise. Cette double opération est, au fond, unique, il s'agit d'un redressement, il s'agit de produire l'unicité d'un sens et d'une direction. L'écart à l'équilibre est en place, l'enlacement du redondant et de l'irréversible est saisi en son point de bifurcation. Cette déclinaison, cet angle, dont on ne connaissait que l'allure géométrique, nous en reconnaissons désormais le fonctionnement.

On comprend mal comment les deux chronies ou temps irréversibles s'enlacent à leur tour. Comment l'un dévale vers la mort et la destruction, alors que l'autre affine sans cesse différences et nouveautés. Le parasite enfin permet de comprendre cette divergence maximale. Sa haute exigence le fait se déplacer toujours vers l'aval, par constitution de guichets successifs, et la loi de sa vie est de ne jamais se laisser supplanter. Du coup, il expose tout système à la ruine, il tend à épuiser les réservoirs, il peut tuer tout ce qu'il rencontre. Mais du même coup il multiplie la complexité qui, elle-même, peut être étouffement ou nouveauté, il excite la production, il exalte,

il accélère les échanges de ses hôtes. Il est boltz-
mannien et darwinien à la fois. Il est dangereux, il
est si dangereux qu'il peut tout éradiquer alentour
(et, par ce pouvoir d'éradication, nous reconnaissons que nous sommes des parasites, du labour à la
philosophie), mais il exalte ici et là des multiplica-
tions productives. Il mène parallèlement l'opération
de nouveauté radicale et de destruction par éradication.

Ce résultat inattendu n'était cependant pas imprévisible. Nous savons depuis quelque temps que
l'intervention parasitaire au milieu d'un canal peut
être en même temps adjuvant et obstacle. Que le
parasite est un tiers inclus. Qu'il est en tiers dans une
relation et qu'il y entre. Qu'il a souci que d'autres
parasites n'y entrent pas, qu'il l'évite, qu'il ne l'évite
pas. Qu'il obéit donc à deux logiques, celle du tiers
exclu, celle des tiers inclus. Et qu'il traverse le
spectre du flou. Qu'il est donc producteur, induc-
teur, non pas d'un sens, comme je viens de le dire,
mais exactement d'une direction, et, sur cette direction, de deux sens opposés. La même direction,
excluant les autres, inclut le sens qui amène à
l'effondrement du système et à son renouvellement
perpétuel. La même direction amène le désordre et
la haute complexité, la haute complexité, parfois,
fait désordre, le désordre, parfois, fait complexité.
L'enjeu des polémiques sur le second principe est
un enjeu flou, et la polémique est à tiers inclus.
Boltzmann et Darwin tiennent les deux bouts d'une
chaîne, mais la chaîne est unique, c'est la chaîne
parasitaire.

Le parasite est l'opérateur actif et l'opération logique de l'évolution, du temps irréversible de la vie.

Le temps physique irréversible commence d'un parasite ensemencé dans une redondance. D'un bruit, ou d'un désordre, aléatoirement venu dans un espace blanc, lui-même, sans doute, apparu au hasard. Ce bruit, ce parasite produisent une pente, un écart, un déséquilibre, et la pente produit le bruit; le processus, entretenu, ne va plus s'arrêter tout de suite. Il part chercher fortune dans le monde. Elle peut être immense ou médiocre, ou nulle. Le désordre local tire l'ordre local vers une asymétrie. Le parasite est un opérateur, il est un *clinamen* généralisé.

Le temps irréversible du vivant commence avec l'introduction d'un parasite. Au voisinage commun de ce qu'on nomme inerte et de ce qu'on appelle vivant, tel virus se reproduit de manière parasitaire. Il n'est pas inintéressant qu'on l'ait baptisé phage. Le long de la classification et le long de l'évolution, le parasite est là, protozoaire, métazoaire, comme présent partout pour entretenir la continuité du cours. Les vaches qui se mangent les unes les autres, alignées sur la rive du Nil, font couler le Nil. Et les fleuves de Babylone. Elles tirent le temps vers l'aval. Temps de festins et de famines.

Le temps irréversible de l'histoire commence avec l'introduction de l'homme parasite. Depuis l'agriculture, au moins, et depuis l'élevage. Peut-être encore avant, parmi les arbres, nul ne sait. Le temps de l'histoire est commencé dès lors qu'une espèce parasitaire au sens de l'évolution se met à intercepter des messages et devient parasite au sens logiciel, dès lors que le sens du mot se complète, dès lors que l'animal mange à la table d'hôte, inventant d'échanger avec lui le logiciel du sens de son appellation contre le matériel. Quand l'homme devient homme pour être un pou bavard, un rat loquace ou un phage à babil.

Revenons encore à la chute blanche. Au vent de la voix, au cri, au flux ouvert sonore des voyelles. Appel ou plainte, fleuve uni, souffle laminaire. Le langage articulé commence avec l'ensemencement des consonnes. Or les consonnes sont les interruptions de la voix. La rupture, l'arrêt, la bifurcation de ce flux. Oui, les consonnes sont parasitaires. Elles bloquent le souffle, le coupent, l'interdisent, le ferment, le propulsent, l'aident, le modulent. Elles sont des obstacles et des adjuvants, comme des parasites ordinaires. Elles multiplient les inclinaisons et les angles dans le cours de la voix, elles multiplient les barrages et les chicanes, elles codent, du coup, la nappe blanche, elles multiplient les sens, tout à coup, produisent le sens. Les langues articulées sont des souffles parasités. Comme on le disait à l'âge classique, la voyelle est une âme, c'est-à-dire du vent, la consonne est un corps, savoir une limite et la prison temporaire de l'âme.

La voyelle est ouverte, la consonne, muette, est fermée. Il faut voir la topologie du canal. Quelle que soit sa forme, le passage est libre pour la première, contraint ou encombré pour la deuxième. La voix est emprisonnée dans une bureaucratie compliquée

de lacis, de guichets. L'articulation est un ensemble
d'étranglements, les consonnes étranglent les voix.
Elles les serrent.

Le parasite faisait la queue, la chaîne. Il est élément quelconque d'une chaîne quelconque. Et
maintenant il fait le goutte-à-goutte. Στράγξ, la
goutte, le flux étranglé. Le στραγγεῖον est un bis-
touri propre à tirer le sang, à l'intercepter, à interrompre un flux, pour le capter. La goutte est le pho-
nème. Le flux un peu visqueux est détourné,
contraint à des chicanes, à des soupapes, à des semi-
conducteurs à valves temporairement fermées ou à
lumière très étroite, et, par ces torsions, ces inclinaisons, ces étranglements, se distille. Comme si le pho-
nème goutte était une unité de strangulation. Une
poire d'angoisse vide. Stricte aux deux bouts. Serrée.

Les consonnes rendent péristaltique la progression des voix. L'articulation est l'ensemble des
nœuds d'interdits temporaires où se presse le
souffle. Chaque langue les distribue à sa façon.
Chaque langue est un ensemencement singulier,
une distribution originale de parasites. Il suffit, en
rêve, de les chasser pour obtenir la langue universelle, et c'est pourquoi la voix du Paraclet n'est
qu'un son, ou un vent. Voyelle de l'oiseau de feu.

Parfois, les vents, les souffles, ensemble composés,
s'inclinent les uns les autres sans intervention de
valves, de consonnes. Oui est une torsade, une tresse
de voix. Un peu libre, un peu lâche, défaite, sans
l'angoisse de l'étranglement. Oui, sans le pullulement des parasites. Oui, dans le vent du Paraclet.
Oui, dans la chevelure turbulente du fleuve. Oui,
enfin, se desserre.

La définition la meilleure

Le parasite est un excitateur thermique.

A table d'hôte, il s'efforce de plaire, il est invité dans ce but et dans cet esprit. Le climat convivial est changé par ses gestes, son bégaiement et sa grimace; il fait rire; il prend, il donne, il reprend, il oriente la parole, il communique à l'assemblée un petit frisson chaleureux, celui qui nous assure que nous sommes ensemble. Sans lui, le festin n'est qu'un repas froid. Son rôle est d'animer l'ambiance, mauvais mot pour dire milieu, mais on n'emploie ici que des mots noirs, milieu n'étant pas meilleur. Son rôle est sociétaire et, par là, théâtral. Parfois professoral, quelquefois pastoral. Un clerc à table, beau diseur, fait deviner où le comique a pris Tartuffe. Et pourquoi on le nomme ainsi. Quand les parasites pullulent, croissance foudroyante si la soupe est bonne, ils assurent la splendeur des évergètes (est-ce là, encore, un bon mot?) ou des généreux donateurs. Le riche paie en vin des légions pour chanter sa grandeur. Naissance de la publicité, sonnez, trompettes de la renommée. Leurs applaudissements, à mains maigres, font le succès des masques et des chefs. Par eux, la représentation n'est pas un four. Il reste vrai qu'il n'est pas de grands hommes sans eux. Et c'est ainsi, parfois, qu'ils deviennent grands hommes, pour être experts en cette stratégie.

Il entre dans les corps, il infeste. Son pouvoir infectieux se mesure à sa capacité de s'adapter à un ou plusieurs hôtes. Cette capacité fluctue, et sa virulence varie, et sa production de substances toxiques. Elles sommeillent, s'exaltent, s'exaspèrent, peuvent se perdre longuement.

Comment, pourquoi? Nous l'ignorons en général, notre savoir se distribue en cas d'espèces. La parasitologie est un savoir exubérant et parcellaire, à l'image de ses objets, un savoir local, spécifique, j'allais dire historique, au moins dans le vieux sens d'histoire naturelle, où le global, il faut le dire, est décevant. On peut y découvrir beaucoup encore, les synthèses conceptuelles y sont malaisées. Peut-être est-ce une science plus médicale que biologique, en chemin vers la biologie. On y connaît les ou des parasites, leur distribution, leur cycle, leurs effets, on peut parfois les combattre efficacement; sait-on en général ce qu'est un parasite? Quelle est, en général, son action, fluctuante et variable?

Pourtant elle peut changer la face de l'histoire. On l'a montré, au moins vaguement. Les parasites-hommes n'envahissent pas l'Amérique sans être précédés de ceux qu'ils portent. Le fait se reproduit assez souvent pour qu'un protocole apparaisse. On y lit autrement les actions, les relations humaines. On y reconnaît les premiers éléments d'une théorie des transformations.

Le parasite est un excitateur. Loin de transformer un système, de changer sa nature, sa forme, ses éléments, ses relations et ses chemins (mais qui accomplit cette performance, quel ensemble, quelle force la réussissent, que veut dire concrètement « transformer le monde », qu'est-ce que le travail, enfin?), il en fait, différentiellement, changer l'état. Il l'incline. Il en fait fluctuer l'équilibre ou la distribution énergétique. Il le dope. Il l'irrite. Il l'enflamme. Cette inclinaison, souvent, n'a pas d'effet. Elle peut en produire, par enchaînement, par reproduction, de gigantesques. Immunité ou crise épidémique.

Excitation, inclinaison, je varie le sens du préfixe, en plus ou moins, droite ou gauche, froid ou chaud, écart mesuré en tout cas au préfixe *para*. Le parasite intervient, il entre dans le système comme un élément de fluctuation. Il l'excite ou l'incite, il le met en mouvement ou le paralyse. Il change son état, il change son état énergétique, ses déplacements, ses condensations. Par actions spoliatrices, comme les ascarides ou les sangsues, par actions toxiques, comme les tiques ou les punaises, par traumatismes, comme les bilharzies ou les trichines, par infection, comme les amibes dysentériques, par obstruction, comme les filaires de l'éléphantiasis, par compression, comme les formateurs de kystes, par irritations, inflammations, prurits, démangeaisons irrépressibles (mes deux parasites ensemble mangent et font se démanger).

Le parasite nous entraîne au voisinage de l'opérateur le plus simple et le plus général de la variance des systèmes. Il les fait fluctuer par écarts différentiels. Il les immunise ou les bloque, les fait s'adapter ou les tue, les sélectionne et les anéantit. Faut-il dire de lui, en généralisant le mot, ce que Claude Bernard disait, dans sa leçon inaugurale, des agents toxiques : véritables réactifs de la vie ? C'est que le parasite nous amène à proximité des équilibres fins des systèmes vitaux, de leurs équilibres énergétiques. Il en est la fluctuation, l'ébranlement, l'essai, l'entraînement. Est-il l'élément de métamorphose, j'entends par ce vieux mot le mouvement transformateur de la vie même ? Ce mouvement commence au phage, il me semble que je le voie encore dans l'histoire même de l'homme.

L'homéostase fait comprendre les retours à l'équilibre. L'homéorrhèse fait comprendre ces retours dans le mouvement même. Il faut dire *parastase*, circonstance, pour l'ensemble des fluctuations qui écartent les systèmes de leur repos, il faut dire *pararrhésis* pour le mouvement improbable, hasardeux, complexe, déchiré, foudroyant, dansant comme un rideau de flammes, que la vie fait voir.

Le bruit des bravos réchauffe la salle, les saillies du beau diseur avivent le courant chaleureux. Ce n'est pas nécessairement une manière de parler. Les applaudissements ne reproduisent pas trop mal le bruit d'agitation thermique, celui que produisent, de soi, les molécules excitées. A supposer qu'elles le soient beaucoup, le brouhaha qu'elles font recouvre aisément un message qui passe. Le parasite, le brouillage du sens ou des voix, la dissolution des signaux dans le brouillard de la rumeur, est donc cette excitation même, ou celui qui l'obtient. Le parasite est toujours un excitateur.

Il n'est pas inintéressant d'obtenir tout à coup un opérateur unitaire. Il chauffe la salle, il donne la fièvre, il accroît l'agitation, le désordre thermique. Soit un système en général, ici social, puis vivant, inerte ou matériel enfin, des hommes ensemble, un organisme, les molécules d'un canal : l'opérateur excite le système.

Les rats s'invitent et cela fait du bruit. Je laisse à penser la vie que firent les deux amis. L'hôte, qui dormait, s'éveille; ou : il n'était pas là, il vient; son corps change de phase et de position, il s'avance et il pousse l'huis. La porte craque, ou le plancher, la partie de plaisir se casse, la conversation cesse, on se tait. Plusieurs figures certes, mais un seul parasite et la fin d'un état.

L'excitation thermique est minime, elle est différentielle. Cette affaire paraît avoir lieu la nuit, dans le silence et dans le noir. Tout y est très petit : grattement sur fond de calme, petite conscience au réveil, petit craquement, petite course au refuge et retour immédiat. Le parasite produit de petites oscillations

du système, de petits écarts : parastases ou circonstances.

L'invitation d'amis ou de relations à dîner a lieu
en supplément d'un bilan d'échanges. On peut dire
à la fois qu'elle n'est rien dans le bilan et qu'elle est
le bilan soi-même. Elle ne le fait pas bouger beaucoup, mais elle fait voir une finalité profonde et
directe de l'échange. Bien des récits racontent que
les invités sont des dieux qui nous sauvent d'un
grand péril quand nous savons les reconnaître, une
fois le repas offert, préparé, cuit, déposé sur la table.
Ils sont aussi des passants dangereux... C'est qu'ils
changent l'état du collectif qui les reçoit. Ils ne transforment pas le système collectif comme tel, mais ils
en font varier l'état. Non, ce n'est pas une révolution, ce n'est pas même une réforme, c'est un petit
écart, une action minime. Philémon et Baucis
s'aimeront plus encore, Alceste et Admète aussi,
après avoir été des hôtes généreux. Mais les voisins
du temple seront noyés sous le déluge, et la bonne
hôtesse est tirée des enfers. Excitation minime, effet
à peine perceptible, ils se sont toujours tant aimés.
Excitation minime et inverse, à côté, pour des effets
catastrophiques. Attention, cette logique est capitale.
Nous l'oublions sans cesse et ne comprenons rien. Il
faut apprendre à moduler le poids des causes et
celui des effets. Sans cela, pas d'histoire. Le changement différentiel d'état assure le groupe dans son
équilibre. Oui, ce n'est qu'un frisson, comme si
l'ensemble tremblait autour de sa stabilité. Qu'il est
spirituel, ce parasite, il nous rend conscients que
nous sommes nous, bien ensemble — nous étions,
ma foi, en train de l'oublier. Peut-être allions-nous

mourir de cet oubli. Le petit réchauffement du système réassure l'état ou, au contraire, annonce un
changement complet, un peu comme, dans un équilibre stable ou instable, l'écart s'annule promptement ou s'accroît de façon foudroyante, sans qu'on
puisse le rattraper. D'où la peur de l'écart : petit
bonheur ou catastrophe, conservation ou changement profond, stabilité ou aventure. Oui, vraiment
cette bouche souffle chaud et froid, j'ai enfin
compris que ce mot valait explication. Par de petites
énergies, par cette information émanée de la
bouche, le système renforcera son équilibre ou se
transformera de fond en comble. C'est l'affaire,
toute calculable, du vieux Tartuffe.

Ces logiques en basculement autour d'angles
minimes sont à l'œuvre aussi bien dans les autres systèmes. La parasitologie, on va le comprendre, utilise
le lexique de l'hôte : hostilité ou hospitalité.
D'abord, le parasite y est toujours petit, jamais il ne
dépasse la taille des insectes ou des arthropodes. Les
plus nombreux sont des protozoaires, même. Des
microbes ou des virus. Leurs effets petits sont le plus
généralement bien supportés des organismes, qui retrouvent assez vite leur santé, savoir le silence, au
moins relatif. Cet équilibre, bien recouvré grâce aux
systèmes de défense mis en place, est plus solide que
le précédent. A l'expulsion de Tartuffe, la famille
d'Orgon est mithridatisée contre un dévot prochain.
C'est la vaccination. Le poison peut être remède et
inversement, cette logique à double entrée devient
une stratégie, un soin, une cure. Le parasite donne à
l'hôte les moyens d'être sauf de lui. L'organisme
renforce sa résistance, il accroît son adaptabilité. On

l'écarte un peu de son équilibre et il le retrouve affermi. Les hôtes généreux sont donc plus forts que les corps sans visites et la génération accroît la résistance au beau milieu des endémies. Du coup, le parasitisme contribue à la formation d'espèces adaptées du point de vue évolutif. Du même coup, il fait disparaître, par épidémies terrifiantes, les espèces inadaptées, on peut même en écrire l'histoire. Petit écart et retour à une stabilité renforcée ; petit écart, multiplication foudroyante, innombrables ravages. Peste et déluge. Endémies, épidémies ; variations de la virulence, toujours de petites causes pour des effets quasi nuls ou immenses, à gauche ou à droite. Le tiers qu'on exclut, quand on exclut ces logiques-là, c'est l'histoire, tout simplement.

Il se multiplie follement de sa petitesse, il occupe l'espace de son imperceptibilité.

Il ne faut pas beaucoup chauffer le filament pour que croisse le bruit. Cette excitation interdit le message qui passe. Or elle permet, parfois, que le message passe, il ne peut transiter sur un canal non excité. Je n'entre pas dans le détail des techniques de dopage. Le bruit de fond est la condition du passage (du sens, du son et du bruit même), et le bruit est son interdit ou son interception. Le bruit, de nouveau, ou le parasite, est aux trois sommets du triangle, émission, réception, passage. Chauffez un peu, j'entends, j'émets, je collationne, chauffez un peu plus, tout s'effondre. L'accroissement minime, dans un sens ou dans l'autre, peut transformer, du tout au tout, le système de communication.

La théorie du parasite nous amène à des valuations ultrafines des changements d'état. Elle installe des chaînes inattendues où de petites causes ou des écarts très fins sont suivis d'effets nuls ou d'effets de retour et de meilleure résistance, ou d'effets immenses et catastrophiques. Où d'énormes rapports de force peuvent être suivis d'effets à peine perceptibles — s'ils s'enlisent sur le canal.

Du coup, on imagine sans effort des transformations de système où les phénomènes produits peuvent changer d'échelle, dans l'observable. Cette chose est très simple. Une inclinaison informationnelle, ensemencée circonstanciellement, peut engendrer parfois des effets gigantesques, à l'échelle entropique. Il est difficile de penser le changement, dans l'inerte, la vie, ou l'histoire, sans nous aider de cette idée. Cependant, nous ne l'avions pas. Dans les sciences humaines, au moins, le vieux modèle mécanique est toujours dominant, même chez ceux dont le discours bruit de le rejeter.

La guerre n'a pas lieu.

Il mange chez un grand — et le plus grand possible. Il nourrit en retour sa grandeur. Il jouit de l'appartenance. Il vit dans une secte, il pense dans une opinion, une idéologie, une règle. La vérité l'entoure comme d'un bouclier, il ne craint plus les terreurs nocturnes. Il est enfin spécialisé, il a une méthode. Il ne livrera plus bataille. Entouré d'amis, opiniâtres à sa façon, dévorant le même gruau à la même écuelle, ses ennemis ne sont que les ennemis de son genre et de sa différence, mais ils sont assez loin et ils n'ont pour fonction que d'assurer le groupe de pression dans son existence ou la spécialité dans sa pérennité. La division du travail, des partis, des idées, de la science, des religions, des pays mêmes, de tout espace en général, produit de petits roitelets locaux qui tiennent table ouverte où mangent, entre amis, ceux qui militent à longueur de pensée sans se battre jamais. Inversement, la partition en îles, classes ou sphères fermées, disciplines, se produit, simplement, sous la pression de ceux qui refusent la lutte. Elle transforme l'extérieur en intérieur. C'est le réseau du risque minimum. Il est assez stable. Sclérose.

Il est généralement spécifique. D'un animal, d'un organisme, d'un organe même. Au cours de son cycle, il peut se transporter d'un vecteur à un autre, mais le parcours, assez improbable et bien sélectionné, reste constant, c'est alors le chemin qui est spécifique. Il vit abrité dans le corps de son hôte (à la rigueur, à sa surface) qui lui sert de milieu. L'extérieur, pour lui, est l'intérieur d'un autre. Son extérieur est un intérieur. Du coup, le parasite compte peu d'ennemis, pour la raison élémentaire qu'il en rencontre rarement. Pour éviter l'hostilité de l'hôte, il lui arrive même de mimer, au lieu de fixation, quelques cellules du tissu d'accueil. Il minimise donc ses risques en changeant cette hostilité en hospitalité, en transformant légèrement son propre corps, en troquant l'externe contre l'interne. C'est qu'audehors, il rencontre des concurrents, il peut être détruit par le climat, variable, par l'histoire, improbable, il peut mourir enfin de l'absence d'hôtes, intermédiaires ou définitifs. L'ensemble de ces contraintes, mortelles, finit par le précipiter dans un autre type de relations. Le parasite pullule et se développe en quittant la bataille. Il invente la vie à risque minimal. Assez stable.

A quoi bon opposer mot pour mot, article pour article et antithèse contre thèse, son contre son, ou idée contre sens, alors qu'en se glissant dans le canal, on perturbe à loisir le son, le sens, la thèse et le système? Peine perdue, risque enfin épargné. Je l'ai dit ailleurs, le stratège avisé n'est pas dynamicien, il se moque des forces, il est topologue, il connaît les chemins, les canaux, le relief. Bref, il est géographe. Que l'ennemi survienne avec cent divisions, des blindés lourds et de l'artillerie, s'il le veut, je le fais passer par le marécage, il s'enlise, il se noie. Le parasite des réseaux ne livre plus bataille, nul message n'a plus d'importance, il se perd dans le brouhaha. Le bruit est distribué où le sens est rare, ondes chaotiques basses d'où émerge, pointu, le message. Rien n'est plus facile à produire que ces petites vagues, rien n'est plus stable à conserver. Le vieux combat, les deux lutteurs ensemble, disparaissent dans ce brouillard.

Quand disparaît la brume, on les aperçoit tous les deux, amis, associés, liés, ils n'ont plus d'ennemis que la brume.

Le parasite a déposé les armes. Il a ainsi gagné la lutte pour la vie. Le théâtre des opérations a changé de lieu.

Le parasite est un opérateur différentiel de changement. Il excite l'état du système : son état d'équilibre (homéostase), l'état présent de ses échanges et circulations, l'équilibre de son évolution (homéorrhèse), son état thermique, son état informationnel. L'écart produit est assez faible, et il ne laisse pas prévoir, en général, une transformation, ni quelle transformation. L'excitation fluctue, ainsi la détermination.

Quand existe un sujet de cette opération, son risque est faible et sa dépense minimale. Son risque croît avec la transformation, si et quand elle a lieu.

Les molécules, excitées, se mettent à circuler plus vite. Chaudes, elles sont rapides, froides, elles sont lentes. Elles tourbillonnent.

L'organisme, excité, réagit. Les flux s'accélèrent, les ganglions gonflent, le système défensif est mobilisé, la fièvre croît. Cesse le silence des organes, sous ce trouble de santé.

La soirée, autour de la table, est assez chaleureuse, les langues se délient et vont vite, chacun intervient à son tour, la conversation devient générale, spirituelle, un peu vertigineuse même.

Chaleur, bruits, tourbillons.

Le parasite était inévitable. Je venais du feu, des questions thermodynamiques. Je venais des eaux et des turbulences, des fluences fluides. Le parasite est une inclinaison au trouble, au changement de phase d'un système.

Il est un petit trublion.

Il était là, nécessaire, sur mon chemin. Comment transformer l'état des choses mêmes ?

De la maladie en général

Une tradition à reprendre appelait la santé silence des organes. Le corps muet, si léger qu'il lévite, inspire, il est vrai, une extase angélique. On aurait cru d'abord que la santé n'était que le silence des sciences médicales, toutes bruissantes du parler de pathologie. Le normal se dit peu ou ne se dit pas, la norme est une ligne perpendiculaire à l'horizon couché, l'orthogonal, debout, ne fait pas d'ombre, aussi peu que le soleil à midi juste. Que dire alors de l'angle droit et de sa force, sinon que son efficace est au maximum ? Le normal, comme beaucoup de nos concepts, est une crête, un concept optimal : force maximale et discours minimal. On ne parle jamais que des ombres.

Revenons au malade, oublions le discours médical. La maladie est un bruit. Nous disions une ombre. Métaphores ? Non pas. Ce bruit, est-ce la douleur, qui produit la plainte, est-ce la peur, l'angoisse ou l'étranglement qui font hurler ou délirer les fous ? Oui et non. La maladie, quelle qu'elle soit, intercepte un fonctionnement, elle est un bruit qui brouille les messages dans les circuits de l'organisme, elle parasite leur circulation ordinaire. Je doute qu'on en puisse donner une définition plus générale. Elle vaut du cancer à la névrose, de l'infarctus du myocarde à la sclérose en plaques. Les interceptions peuvent, en effet, avoir lieu le long des filets nerveux, de la circulation sanguine, dans les espaces synaptiques, entre les membranes de cellules voisines, sur la chaîne du code génétique, et ainsi de suite. La maladie, en général, est parasite. Et ce parasite intervient à tel ou tel niveau. Je ne doute pas que la douleur et le cri, que l'angoisse et le hurlement soient des traductions diverses de ces bruits nombreux. Le langage en est une autre, sûrement, qui associe, dans sa source, les vocalises de plaisir induites par la silencieuse santé. La maladie est un bruit parasite. Et le médecin mange de traduire ce bruit.

Il arrive, en particulier, qu'une maladie infectieuse soit provoquée par l'arrivée d'un parasite, virus, protozoaire, métazoaire ou champignon. Introduit de façon permanente, ou temporairement, dans l'organisme de son hôte qui lui sert, dès lors, de milieu, il en intercepte les flux, il les accélère parfois, il les détourne en sa faveur, de nouveau, à tous les niveaux. Tel est un spécifique — dans le circuit digestif — de la cavité buccale ou du transit intestinal, tel autre de la circulation sanguine, ici ou là, tel encore des glandes sébacées, j'arrête une énumération qui occupe, en fait, des volumes. La somme ou un synopsis de ces vivants et de leurs performances nous indiquerait, je suppose, qu'il n'y a pas de canaux, de transits ou de flux qui n'aient, en principe, leurs intercepteurs. Chacun a son créneau, comme on le dit dans le commerce, peu de créneaux restent inoccupés. Qui a un créneau, inversement, est parasite.

Nous avons coutume d'appeler parasites des êtres qui survivent et qui se multiplient selon ce mode seulement et de réputer infectieuses des maladies qu'ils induisent de cette façon. Nous ne pensons jamais à rapprocher l'interception du bruit et cette activité des précédentes parce que, dans un cas, des vivants sont à l'œuvre et que, dans l'autre, il faut concevoir un rapport. Si le vecteur est différent, l'opération est la même, pourtant. Les systèmes vivants sont des systèmes de communication en général, il s'agit, en tout cas, de la déclinaison locale d'un flux.

Leriche dit : la maladie ne nous apparaît plus comme un parasite vivant sur l'homme et vivant de l'homme qu'elle épuise. Nous y voyons la conséquence d'une *déviation*, initialement minime, de l'ordre physiologique. Elle est, en somme, un ordre physiologique nouveau ; la thérapeutique doit adapter l'homme malade à ce nouvel ordre. Admirable.

Appelons dérévolution, avec Paul Scheurer, ces découvertes simples et globales qui font dériver l'une de l'autre deux pensées dont l'une a fait nouveauté par rapport à l'autre. L'histoire des sciences est pleine de ces dérévolutions. Les querelles sont produites par les œillères.

Qu'est-ce qu'un parasite ? Un opérateur, une relation. Cette flèche simple intercepte. Elle intercepte les messages organiques en un lieu du système vivant. Bruit, peut-être, langage aussi bien, vivant souvent. Tous les médecins font un seul et même métier, on le voit. Qu'ils parlent, qu'ils tranchent, qu'ils piquent... ils vivent et mangent d'un seul métier. Qu'est-ce qu'un parasite? Une déviation, minime en commençant, et qui peut le rester jusqu'à s'annuler, qui peut croître jusqu'à transformer un ordre physiologique en un nouvel ordre.

Toute maladie, toute médecine, est parasitaire en ce nouveau sens. Ce que je voulais démontrer.

Banquets nocturnes

Société

Repas de l'imposteur
Analyser, paralyser, catalyser

Intermède comique parmi les travaux. Molière, par la bouche de Valère, dit de Tartuffe : « Le fourbe qui longtemps a pu vous imposer. » Le mot n'est pas sans saveur. Tartuffe est un imposteur, c'est le sous-titre de la pièce. On n'y entend que tromperie, le fourbe en impose. Mais c'est le même mot et c'est le même sens qui nous apprendraient qu'il retient, qu'il perçoit ou qu'il capte un impôt. L'hypocrite nous en impose, et ceci pour nous imposer. Pour intercepter la fille et la femme, la cassette et l'héritage, la signature et le dépôt. Pour prendre, comme il est d'usage, les mots, les femmes et les biens. Tartuffe — la truffe en italien, tubercule, champignon souterrain — est parasite, il détourne, et il capte. Il est même le canon, l'exemple, le modèle excellent du parasite. L'étonnant est qu'il soit devenu l'hypocrite en personne. Et la chose est si étonnante qu'elle pose problème. Autrement dit, l'imposture a superbement réussi. Car le terme imposture a pu faire oublier son lien avec la perception d'impôt, avec ce que nous appelions l'exaction. L'imposture fait dévier l'attention vers la fourberie, vers la cagoterie religieuse, et couvre l'opération économique de détournement. Pourtant la religion n'y est pas essentielle. S'il fallait aujourd'hui récrire un *Tartuffe*, il serait un idéologue, un moraliste politique, un intellectuel d'avant-garde qui se remplit les poches et accède au pouvoir en défendant les droits de l'homme ou en jouant au sacrifié. Si Tartuffe m'était conté, j'en ferais un économiste, un spécialiste des finances et de l'imposition. Oh! je n'y suis pour rien, dit-il des exactions de mille sortes, c'est la nécessité de la croissance, de la monnaie ou de la productivité. Le ciel, simplement, a changé de lieu, la stratégie est invariante. Un Tartuffe efface toujours son exaction locale dans une théorie globale.

Tartuffe est entré démuni en une famille tranquille, où il prospère, sa conduite y est exactement parasitaire : il détourne en sa faveur le testament, la femme et la fortune, il chasse tout le monde pour s'installer céans. Il impose le dilemme : exclure ou être exclu. L'hypocrisie n'est là que seconde, elle y est un moyen, elle y est une méthode. Qu'est-ce que l'hypocrisie ?

Pour éviter les inévitables réactions de rejet, d'exclusion, tel parasite animal fabrique ou sécrète, aux endroits de contact de son corps à celui de l'hôte, un tissu identique à celui de son hôte. Le corps parasité, abusé, trompé, comme on le voudra, ne réagit plus, il accepte, il agit comme si le visiteur était son organe propre. Il consent à l'entretenir, il se plie à ses exigences. Le parasite joue le mimétisme. Il ne joue pas à être un autre, il joue à être le même.

Je ne sais pas si le mimétisme est tout entier parasitaire, mais il est une ruse nécessaire au voleur, à
l'étranger, à l'invité, il est un déguisement, un
camouflage aux couleurs du milieu, quand le milieu
est l'hôte, qu'il est l'autre. Pour festoyer aux noces
chez le maître, il est convenable de revêtir ladite
robe nuptiale, sous peine d'être jeté dans les
ténèbres extérieures, au milieu des cris et des grincements de dents. Je prends pour commencer l'action
mimétique au sens du caméléon, de l'ours blanc ou
du lièvre polaire dans les neiges arctiques, du papil-
lon qui fait la fleur, du ver qui fait la branche, ou de
la truffe noire sous la terre, dont j'ignore ce qu'elle
mime Notre groupe, cette boîte noire. C'est un effa-
cement de l'individuation et sa dissolution dans le
milieu, c'est une bonne protection dans la défense et
dans l'attaque. Je suis oiseau, voyez mes ailes, je suis
souris, vive les rats Je suis un autre, *a* et *b*, de nouveau, jugement synthétique, et genèse du joker, du
domino blanc. Nous revenons aux logiques précédentes. Je est un autre. Ulysse est un mouton, quand
il sort de chez Polyphème. Qui dira ce que l'ego cartésien serait devenu, si le malin génie, dans le poêle,
s'était, soudain, montré dangereux, à la mort. Il ne
s'agit plus de l'animal et de son monde, c'est-à-dire
du caméléon sur le tapis vert, mais de l'animal et de
l'autre, du parasite et de l'hôte-autre. En cette
conjoncture, il ne s'efface pas dans l'horizon, mais
dans le milieu qui est l'autre lui-même. Il est alors le
frère, le jumeau, l'*alter ego*, l'autre doigt d'une seule
main, le semblable et parfois plus parfait que lui-
même. Tartuffe n'est pas seulement le pharmakon
de la famille, celui qui, en définitive, sera expulsé

des lieux, sacrifié par le prince et enfin démasqué,
pour le bonheur des fils et pour le collectif du
groupe, il est surtout la narcose d'Orgon, son homo-
logue narcissique et gémellaire. Et c'est ainsi
qu'Orgon ne le sent pas. L'hypocrisie n'est qu'un
concept moral, dégradé par rapport à l'action mimétique, elle-même une stratégie ordinaire par rapport
à l'hôte dans sa relation parasite. Oui, mon frère, je
suis... Or l'hôte parle, il est homme, loquace. Le parasite humain parlera comme lui, ou sera silencieux.
Pendant deux actes, pas de Tartuffe. Il rôde, il est là,
il se terre, il se tait. Sous la crise, sous le seuil décisif.

Je note au passage que la torpille dite dans le
Ménon pour qualifier la question de Socrate est un
poisson de mer dont le nom est celui de l'action
d'endormir, la narcose. Le pharmakon est à la phar-
macie ce que le narkon est aux narcotiques. L'un est
du collectif, l'autre de l'individuel. L'effet foudroyant du poisson est une drogue parmi les
drogues. Admirons que les Grecs aient déjà montré
l'intuition d'une action pharmaceutique derrière un
effet de magnétisme ou d'électricité qu'ils n'igno-
raient pas. Que leur langue, d'autre part, ait associé
ces phénomènes physiques et quasi médicaux ou
quasi chimiques au mythe de Narcisse, qui est le
nom propre de ces noms communs, est une
deuxième merveille. Les Grecs connaissaient déjà le
passage du Nord-Ouest, comme les pêcheurs
basques savaient l'Amérique, bien avant que Colomb
en dise officiellement la découverte pour l'histoire et
les rois. La question de Socrate nous réveille pourtant, l'image de Narcisse nous révèle. Mais la narcose
nous endort. Tartuffe est le narcotique d'Orgon, il

l'endort, dit la sagesse populaire, il l'endort et le
suce comme un vampire (il l'endort comme Socrate
endort tout son monde au *Banquet* d'où il sort se
connaître soi-même), il le révèle comme son double
et son jumeau, il le réveille enfin au voisinage de la
mort. Tartuffe est une truffe et Orgon est un ogre.
Prédateur ou parasite, ce n'est plus la question.
Jumeaux comme Narcisse? Qui mangera qui? La
question dépasse la pièce, je crois.

Du même coup, qui en même temps est un coup
de génie, la stratégie de mimétisme dédouble
l'action scénique. Qui peut savoir que le parasite est
un parasite, malgré ou par le mimétisme? Les obser-
vateurs extérieurs. Et ils sont sur la scène. Ils sont les
spectateurs de la comédie que se donnent ensemble
et Orgon et Tartuffe. La salle est sur les planches.

Orgon rentre, oyez, maintenant, éclater le génie.
Les trois sens du mot parasite, bruit physique, bête
vivante et relation humaine, se mettent tout à coup à
battre ensemble, comme au même rythme, dans les
mêmes sons.

Tartuffe est ici l'invité, l'imposé par Orgon, troisième sens. Or un hôte, attaqué par la bête,
deuxième sens, reçoit d'elle, au cas général, des
effets tuméfiants ou toxiques. Donc, Madame
l'hôtesse eut la fièvre avant-hier, avec un mal de tête
étrange à concevoir. Nul ne voyait d'où pouvait venir
le malaise.

Bruit : et Tartuffe? Premier sens. Le parasite ici
redresse le dialogue, tel un semi-conducteur. La

fonction de redresseur est prévue par Molière : que le ciel, dit Mme Pernelle de l'animal, l'a céans envoyé pour redresser à tous votre esprit fourvoyé. Car il contrôle tout, avait dit Dorine de lui. Tartuffe, directeur, conduit les flux sur les chemins, la métaphore court partout dans les dialogues. Elle décrit de près un intercepteur sur des voies. Et c'est le sens unique des trois sens, une personne en trois fonctions. Et c'est toujours l'asymétrie, l'opérateur asymétrique.

Le « et Tartuffe ? » est un redresseur, et le redresseur accomplit sa fonction, la personne comme son nom, le nom comme signal. Le parasite-animal redresse les flux en sa faveur, le parasite-signal redresse le canal en sens unique, et le Tartuffe religieux redresse les pécheurs sur le chemin du ciel. Mais, du coup, et sans qu'on le voie, le redresseur répond à la question : d'où vient le malaise d'Elmire ? L'hôtesse est enfiévrée de l'introduction de la bête.

Bête qui, nous dit-on, se porte à merveille, gras, la bouche vermeille. Vermeille est un mot merveilleux, c'est la couleur du sang que la bouche a sucé ; or, cette couleur rouge sang est celle d'un ver, du vermisseau nommé cochenille, qui donne l'écarlate. Tartuffe, un peu vampire, a la bouche rouge. Il est gros et gras comme un ver, comme un vermicule. Vermeil.

Encore un coup, l'imposture a gagné, le parasite est bien caché derrière son mimétisme, derrière sa représentation. L'opération de captage s'est évanouie derrière l'activité de simulation. Tout le monde voit l'hypocrite et aperçoit l'aveuglement de l'hôte. Tout le monde est aveugle de ne voir que l'hypocrisie, de ne voir que le mimétisme. Du coup, nul ne comprend ce que donne Dorine à comprendre, qu'Elmire est malade, simplement, de Tartuffe. Qu'il est un ver, qu'il est un champignon dans l'organisme de Madame[1].

« Et Tartuffe ? » est un bruit qui annule une réception et qui ramène à l'émission, c'est le redresseur du dialogue vers l'asymétrie, vers le sens unique. Dorine boucle la circulation, elle restitue l'autre sens. Elle est l'opérateur de la symétrie. Le parasite vole, elle est le don. Elle connaît les lois du don et de l'échange, et ne peut être dupe ni du vol ni du change. Elle est le don, Dorine est, proprement, son nom.

Donc, Madame, en dégoût, ne put toucher à rien. Le parasite lui, dévore deux perdrix, où vous reconnaîtrez Madame et Mademoiselle. Baise la mère, épouse la fille. Vous vous souvenez de Rousseau : favori du seigneur et de la dame, amant de la demoiselle, etc., j'étais content. Il peut.

Elle ne dort, il dort. Elle se résolut à souffrir la saignée. Pour réparer ce sang, il but quatre coups de vin. La question est bien résolue : ce que l'une perd, le second le gagne, et c'est la loi.

Mais, tout à coup, la loi dit autre chose. Dans le bilan d'échange, ou dans le flux à sens unique, l'hôtesse perd du sang et Tartuffe gagne du vin. La bouche vermeille ne reçoit pas exactement ce que l'organisme a émis. Entre sang et vin, entre vin et

---

1. On ne sait pas très bien si cette truffe noire est symbiote, commensale, ou vraiment parasite.

sang, un nouveau processus apparaît que la tradition nomme transsubstantiation.

La question du Tartuffe, tout à coup, se retourne, comme elle s'était déjà retournée : que vient faire ici la religion dans la relation parasitaire ? La religion n'est pas le sujet de la pièce, elle est le problème de cette comédie.

On a dit la fin du *Tartuffe* bâclée, gauche, artificielle, et l'intervention du roi aussi absurde et arbitraire que celle d'un dieu qui descend, tout suspendu à sa machine. On croît l'hôte perdu, et l'exempt, qui vient exécuter un ordre, assigne l'ordre opposé, tout à coup. Sa bouche souffle chaud et froid. Pourtant, il est l'officier d'un M. Loyal. On voudra bien le supposer tel. Absurde, qu'est-ce à dire ?

Toute la question de la pièce est la question parasitaire. Deux commensaux ou deux symbiotes vivent ensemble, convives, par échanges de bons procédés. Ici le mouvement est irréversible, tout va du maître à l'imposteur, et sans retour. Comme Orgon n'est pas infini, le processus va vers un terme. Et ce terme est le vide. Plus le vase versait, plus il s'allait vidant, aujourd'hui, malgré les prières, il n'y aura pas de miracle. Plus d'argent, plus de fille, plus de coffre, le vide, le nettoyage par le vide. Tartuffe absorbe tout, y compris le propriétaire. Dehors ! Le formidable du parasite, c'est que, peut-être, il est, lui, infini. Toute la question de la pièce est là : qui va décamper ? qui

Pour la première fois nous savons qui frappe à la porte, qui fait du bruit derrière l'huisserie. Les dieux. Qui font avis qu'on doit déloger, car le ciel va tomber sur les têtes. Les Dioscures détalent, Simonide les suit. Voilà : ils se jettent à côté.

La parole se fait chair. L'écart se fait statique. Un pilier manque, il se jette à côté. Tout se jette à côté, bientôt : la parole-parabole, l'exemple et l'éloge, le dû et le gré, le poète et les dieux, la colonne et l'entablement. Nous calculons toujours le trop. Le trop et le para. Parabole, parasite. Celui-ci paie en paraboles. Ici la liste des écarts, leur dénombrement, rubrique ou recueil.

Un pilier manque et nous passons du logiciel au matériel, du verbe à la chair, à la pierre, de la parole au référent. Qui se venge ? Le divin, le poète ou la chose même ? On n'habite pas longtemps le langage, les mots, sans qu'une fois l'objet revienne, sans que manque un pied soudain. Sans que le réel tombe sur la tête. J'imagine une salle triangulaire, un plafond à trois architraves, cimaises, travées, cela est prévu par le calcul de statique, par le verbe, le logiciel. Que le triclinium ait été carré, la faute d'une colonne pouvait ne pas être un irréparable malheur, le porte-à-faux peut résister. Un pilier manque et le plafond ne trouve plus rien qui l'étaie. Il était à trois poutres, comme l'éloge, sur trois pieds, trois appuis, trois thèses, comme le discours. Deux pour les dieux jumeaux, une pour toi, mortel, qui un jour, une nuit, ou un soir, nous manque. Deux colonnes stables, une instable. Triangle : maille élémentaire de l'équilibre statique, de la distribution de l'espace, de la disposition des sites, de la topologie, de la métrique, de l'arrangement immobile des forces, du syllogisme, du raisonnement. Du matériel, du logiciel. Supprimez un pied du trépied, tout s'écroule, biffez une thèse, un terme, tout s'évanouit. Tout tombe justement sur les pieds de l'athlète, les conviés sont estropiés. On crie au miracle, et le miracle est bien que le même écart se conserve entre les petites énergies et les grandes, que le monde réel soit donc compréhensible. Que la parabole du parasite et la paralysie de l'hôte soient, précisément, parallèles. Demain, l'athlète ainsi que bien des invités se jettent de côté, bancroches. Un pilier leur manque, il y faut un bâton. Comme au vieil Œdipe de la Sphinge. Comme à Héphaïstos. Les boiteux sont découvreurs, l'inclinaison est le début du monde.

On ne loue jamais trop, voici la liste de l'excès, du défaut, de l'écart. Il apparaît dans la logique du raisonnement, dans le calcul, le compte des bilans, il apparaît dans le langage, les mots et le poème, dans la parabole et la paraphrase, il apparaît dans l'ordre, le plan et l'espace, il apparaît dans l'échange et dans la monnaie, le dû et le gré, le salaire à nouveau doublé, le paiement du poète et des dieux, part maudite, il apparaît à l'extrémité de la poutre, au sommet du pilier menaçant, dans le porte-à-faux et l'entablement, il apparaît maintenant aux systèmes physiques, dans l'équilibre difficile de la pierre et du marbre, il apparaît enfin aux systèmes vivants, marcher, courir, comme des estropiés, lutter, jumeaux, jusqu'à ce qu'un des deux piliers de cette lutte manque, et fasse un vainqueur, un vaincu, paralytique de corps et paradigme élémentaire du groupe social au combat.

Je compte cette impressionnante avancée comme une construction savante du réel, telle que l'âge classique en faisait souvent l'œuvre.

Le préfixe *para* est compté, calculé, à la tare, dans son écart à l'équilibre. Mais il est aussi posé, situé. Quand la colonne tient la poutre, une ligne, dans son dessin, va au bout de la deuxième ligne, ici, la verticale joint le bord de l'horizontale. Cela fait angle droit au sommet. En tout cas, cela fait un angle, cela fait un sommet. Décalez maintenant le pilier, marquez un porte-à-faux, tare ou écart, *para*. Dans le schéma, la ligne ne va plus au pied de la seconde ligne, mais en un lieu autre, sur le parcours. Le parasite a relation non point à la station mais à la relation. Et il la met en porte à faux. Le schéma le plus simple apparaît. *Static*, en anglais : parasite.

En un mot, non point, en un préfixe seul, tout le texte et toute l'histoire. Il faut comprendre alors et alors seulement qu'elle est une origine à l'art de la mémoire. Le discours, le parcours est d'une simplicité canonique : il est déductif, il construit la réalité, il construit le réel à partir de l'écart. Dans une variété ensemencée de flèches simples, l'écart tient lieu d'inclinaison.

Picaresques et cybernétiques
La nouvelle balance

Le parasite est invité à table d'hôte, il doit, en retour, égayer les convives de ses histoires et de ses ris. En toute exactitude, il échange de bons morceaux contre de bons mots, il paie son repas, il l'achète en monnaie de langue. C'est le plus vieux métier du monde. On en trouve trace dans les témoignages les plus anciens. Autour de cette loi de justice, mille variations, simples rarement et souvent compliquées, sont connues, pratiquées, dans le quotidien familial, tribal, amical, sociétaire, comme dans la comédie la plus archaïque ou le récit le plus enfoui. Par exemple, il arrive que l'écornifleur paie en monnaie de morale, et que l'hôte donne, par ce devoir imaginaire et lourd qui le remplit de culpabilité. La morale est un discours parmi tant d'autres, ou une variété d'espèces, de numéraire convertible. Chaque société donne cours à une monnaie langagière qu'on peut échanger, avantageusement pour l'estomac. Les groupes forts et influents diffusent ainsi un lexique forcé. Il est économique aujourd'hui, de même qu'il était humaniste naguère, voltairien autrefois, ou religieux jadis.

Un chemineau, mourant de faim, se trouva, un beau soir, à la fenêtre des cuisines d'un restaurant hautement réputé. Les odeurs y étaient délicieuses. Il s'en emplit, cela calmait un peu sa douleur de famine. Un marmiton s'aperçut du manège, et sortant brusquement, exigea de lui le paiement de ce qu'on pouvait nommer un service. Le passant et le cuisinier en venaient presque aux mains, sur ladite contestation, lorsque survint un tiers qui proposa de les départager. Donnez-moi une pièce, dit-il. Le miséreux la tendit, renfrogné. Il la posa sur le pavé de pierre, et du talon de son soulier, la fit sonner un peu. Ce bruit, dit-il, comme sentence, est le paiement de l'odeur des bons plats. Le rôti est la chose qu'on mange, or il s'en dégage un fumet. La pièce est chose qu'on échange, or il s'en dégage un son. Si la pièce vaut le rôti, alors le bruit de la première vaudra bien l'odeur du second. Et il rendit au passant sa monnaie. Justice était rendue.

Vieux racontar qui met une sagesse en place. Nous sommes creux et vides, ce n'est pas de vent et de voix que nous avons à nous remplir ; il nous faut de la substance plus solide à nous réparer. Deux places ou deux ordres : substances et solides ici, et là, les vents et la voix. Cette sagesse veut que si l'on échange, on le fasse dans le même ordre. C'est la philosophie, la justice de l'estomac. Solide pour solide, substance pour substance et repas pour argent comptant, et ailleurs, si on veut, vent pour voix, voix pour vent. Il y a les infrastructures, c'est du sérieux, il y a les superstructures, où on vend du vent. Le consistant et le diffus. Chaque auteur,

chaque langue dit ce partage à sa manière. Les philosophies lourdes le consacrent.

Le parasite invente du nouveau. Parce qu'il ne
mange pas comme tout le monde, il construit une
logique nouvelle. Il croise, il diagonalise l'échange.
Il ne troque pas, il change de monnaie. Il cherche à
donner de la voix contre de la substance, du gazeux
contre du solide, ou bien de la superstructure
contre de l'infrastructure. On rit, on l'expulse, on se
moque de lui, on le bat, il nous trompe, mais il
invente du nouveau. Il faut analyser cette nouveauté-là. Ce son, ce fumet, cette odeur, passant
pour pièce d'or ou rôti de gibier.

Un paralytique se traînait sur les coudes et les
genoux. Était-ce notre athlète, blessé ? A quatre pas
d'un repas gras, on peut mourir de faim, Tantale, si
on ne peut se déplacer. Il crevait de misère et pourrissait dans un coin noir. Un beau jour, il vit un
aveugle qui trébuchait sur mille obstacles et risquait
à tout coup de se rompre le cou. Il peut mourir de
tomber dans un puits si la margelle est basse et
paraît une marche, et si les bras tendus ne touchent
que du vent. L'immobile l'appelle et lui offre un
contrat. L'aveugle est le porteur, et l'estropié le
guide. Ils font un normal à eux deux.

Vieux racontar qui chasse la sagesse de place.
Vous avez ri du parasite, et vous ne riez pas de
l'échange des pieds contre l'œil. Et pourtant.
L'aveugle donne du solide, la force, le transport,
une puissance calculable en calories, et produite par

tel ou tel mets, du repas. Je veux dire une énergie à
l'échelle ordinaire. Que donne, en échange, le cul-
de-jatte dans ce nouveau tableau à la mode
d'Orion? Il dit, et voilà tout. Il annonce l'obstacle, il
veille, il propose la direction. Juché sur les épaules
d'une force noire, il la clarifie, l'illumine. Bientôt, il
faut dire qu'il la dirige, qu'il lui donne des ordres.
Après tout, il n'a pas proposé à l'aveugle un autre
contrat que le pacte parasitaire. Car il paie en information, en énergie d'échelle microscopique. Il
donne des mots contre de la force, oui, de la voix,
du vent, contre une substance solide. Pis encore, il
prend le pouvoir, il gouverne.

Le parasite invente du nouveau. Il capte une énergie et la paie en information. Il capte le rôti et le
paie en contes. Deux manières d'écrire le nouveau
contrat. Il établit un pacte injuste, au rapport des
vieilles balances, il construit un bilan neuf. Il dit une
logique jusqu'à ce jour irrationnelle, il dit une nouvelle épistémologie, une autre théorie de l'équilibre. Il diagonalise les ordres des choses, les états de
choses, solide et gazeux. Il évalue l'information. Ou
plutôt : il découvre l'information sous la voix et les
bonnes paroles, il découvre l'Esprit dans le souffle
et le vent. Il invente la cybernétique. L'aveugle et le
paralytique, association croisée du matériel et du
logiciel, échange du solide contre la voix, c'est la
fable la plus ancienne en théorie du gouvernail. Et
si l'éclair gouverne l'univers, l'éclair, ici, c'est le
regard, et la sollicitation d'obliquer. Le boiteux est
l'inclinaison. Il est l'écart et il l'annonce.

Il y a là plusieurs balances fines. D'abord toutes les voix ne valent pas information, tous les vents n'apportent pas ici de nouvelles. On n'invite pas n'importe quel diseur de bons mots, les brillants causeurs se distinguent des vantards assommants ou des ergoteurs opiniâtres. Le roi de Prusse pouvait choisir, il préféra Voltaire, et la tsarine Diderot. Ils n'auraient pas invité Jean-François Rameau, dérisoire. Il y a un marché de la bonne parole. Un cours forcé, parfois. La mauvaise monnaie y chasse la bonne, souvent. Mais cette balance est évoluée, sophistiquée, inutile d'abord.

Revenons au paralytique, c'est-à-dire au gouverneur. Celui qui a les énergies, le producteur de mouvement, peut distinguer parfois, dans les voix du vent, le message utile. Sa cécité, pourtant, lui interdit à tout jamais d'en contrôler l'utilité. Le cul-de-jatte, juché en haut de son regard aveugle, peut le précipiter dans une basse-fosse. Il faut bien qu'il fasse confiance. Et, sans doute, à n'importe qui. Car il ne peut choisir son cornac. C'est l'estropié qui le voit et l'appelle, et il vient à sa voix. Il entend, il écoute, déjà il obéit. Bien sûr, il saura distinguer un message d'un bruit, mais son absence de contrôle fait qu'on peut lui mentir à loisir. Je te garderai de tous les obstacles et je t'emmènerai aux lieux de tes désirs. Alors il vient comme un mouton.

Dès lors, celui qui veut rester assis sur les épaules d'un athlète n'aime pas qu'il soit clairvoyant. Dès lors, celui qui aime à commander peut, s'il le veut, rester assis, à une seule condition. Il faut crever les yeux aux producteurs. Aux énergiques, aux forts. Il faut que ceux de l'énergie n'aient pas d'information ; alors, ceux de l'information peuvent se dispenser de l'énergie. L'information est d'autant plus précieuse qu'elle est rare. Il faut donc provoquer cette rareté. L'aveugle et le paralytique avaient déjà établi ces théorèmes-là, et cette nouvelle balance. Ils ont commencé par une symbiose, elle a duré le temps des roses. Le parasite est tout aussitôt revenu.

La balance de rareté fonctionne en perfection dans un espace ou un milieu vides d'information. Ici, le premier signal apparu vaut tout l'or du monde, il vaut la vie. Premier éclair qui s'incline dans le chaos. Première branche d'olivier, au bec de la colombe, sur la plaine diluvienne. Tout le sens, par après, s'ensuit. Et l'histoire est aussi tributaire de cette étincelle. Il faut commencer par la boîte noire, il faut commencer par la nuit, par l'aveuglement.

Il faut donc commencer par retirer aux travailleurs, aux producteurs, toute source de renseignements. On dresse bien les étalons en leur apposant des œillères. On place bien les veaux, les poules dans le noir, à l'école, comme s'ils étaient de simples petits d'hommes. Il faut donc commencer par diviser, comme on dit, le travail. Le travailleur manuel doit être aveugle par rapport au paralytique intellectuel. L'homme de barre ne dispose pas de hublot, il entend la voix de son maître, il écoute, il répète, et il obéit. Comme tout à l'heure, aveugle, il vient à la voix. L'un fournit l'énergie, l'autre l'information. L'un donne la force de travail, l'autre les directives. La substance et la voix. Cet échange est encore inique, mais il fonctionne dans l'histoire et pas seulement dans la comédie. On a dû trouver très sérieuse la diagonale parasite. On a dû trouver intelligente la nouvelle balance. Car le partage rebondit, fait système très vite : le producteur intellectuel est tout aussi aveugle par rapport au paralytique administratif et aveuglé par lui, et ainsi de suite. Cette cybernétique se complique répétitivement, fait chaîne, puis réseau. Elle est pourtant fondée sur le vol de l'information, chose simple. Il suffit d'éditer des lois et d'en retirer la connaissance au plus grand nombre Si bien que le pouvoir, à la limite, n'est rien d'autre. Il se mesure à la balance dite. Il est le rapport, et, à la lettre, le fléau, entre les lieux où l'information est stockée, et les lieux d'où elle a été ôtée. Qui a crevé les yeux de qui ? Où le savoir est-il placé, de quel espace est-il absent ? Il est assez vrai que le partage des fonctions manuelles et intellectuelles recouvre bien le vieux rapport ville-campagne, par exemple, ce que les rats font voir.

Ce pouvoir, qu'on peut dire bureaucratique, me paraît plus fort et plus stable que celui de la force, jamais assez forte, ou que celui du droit, jamais assez juste. Il repose sur le savoir et sur la connaissance, pis encore, sur l'information, sur le signal, presque au niveau réflexe. Pourtant sa genèse est paradoxale. Celle des pouvoirs forts est simple, il s'agit de violence et de mort, de moyens guerriers, muscles et stratégie. Celle des pouvoirs justes est simple, également, il s'agit de foi et de sacrifices, de martyrs et de fanatiques. Rien que de l'ordinaire, du fréquent ou du dérisoire. Ici, l'ancêtre est parasite.

Il est ridicule, il est bafoué. Il prétend échanger de
bons plats contre des mots risqués. Mais on
n'entend que lui, à table. On ne voit que lui, sur les
planches de Plaute. Lui, ses éclats de voix. Tout le
monde rit. Par quel miracle, tout à coup, tout le
monde pleure-t-il, déjà? Entre-temps, le maître de
céans a perdu le pouvoir de l'exclure. Il est là, bien
enraciné. Ruine le père, baise la mère, éduque les
enfants, régente la maison. Nous ne pouvons plus
nous en passer, il est notre système même, il
commande, il a le pouvoir, sa voix est devenue celle
du maître, il parle de telle sorte qu'on l'entend de
partout, nul ne peut plus placer un mot. De la table
d'hôte au tableau d'Orion, le voici maintenant sur
les épaules, dominateur, jupitérien. Comment une
telle chose est-elle possible? Quelle foudre a frappé
les yeux des producteurs, quel aveuglement, tout à
coup?

Le producteur joue le contenu, le parasite joue la
position. Celui qui joue la position battra toujours
celui qui joue le contenu. Celui-ci est simple et naïf,
celui-là est complexe et médiatisé. Le parasite bat
toujours le producteur. Celui-ci, attentif au jeu des
choses mêmes, suppose que l'autre ne triche pas,
puisque les choses elles-mêmes sont fines, mais
loyales, comme disent les physiciens.

Celui qui joue le contenu joue l'objet. Il est artisan, il est savant aussi, et c'est ou ce n'est que la maîtrise du monde, subtil, rusé, mais non fraudeur.
Celui qui joue la position joue les rapports entre

sujets, il gagne donc la maîtrise des hommes. Et le maître des hommes est le maître des maîtres du monde.

Il y a ceux du feu, il y a ceux du lieu. Ceux dont la parole est de feu, ceux dont la parole est de lieu. Ceux du lieu sans feu sont les maîtres, froids. Ceux du feu sans lieu brûlent éperdument, si fort qu'autour d'eux les objets se transforment comme dans un four ou autour d'une forge. Langue de feu dans le lit du vent, le vent vient d'où il veut, souffle où il veut, pour attiser le feu. Ils ne sont pas les maîtres, ils peuvent être esclaves, mais ils sont les débuts. Ils sont le bruit du monde, la rumeur des gésines et des transformations.

Jouer la position, jouer le lieu, c'est dominer la relation. C'est n'avoir relation qu'à la relation même. Jamais aux stations d'où elle vient, où elle va, ni par où elle passe. Jamais aux objets comme tels et sans doute jamais aux sujets comme tels. Ou plutôt à ces points comme opérateurs, comme sources de relations. Et c'est là le sens du préfixe para dans le mot parasite : il est à côté, il est auprès, il est décalé, il n'est pas sur la chose, mais sur sa relation. Il a des relations, comme on dit, et en fait un système. Il est toujours médiat et jamais immédiat. Il a relation à la relation, il a rapport au rapport, il est branché sur le canal.

Il y a ceux des sources et il y a ceux des canaux.

Toute la question du système est maintenant d'analyser ce qui y est un point, un être, une station. Ils y sont traversés d'une étoile de relations, ils sont carrefours, échangeurs, triage. Or n'est-ce pas cela même, analyser : dire que cette chose est à l'intersection de plusieurs séries. Dès lors, la chose même n'est rien d'autre qu'une tête de relations, ce carrefour, ou ces passages. Elle n'est rien que position, situation. Et le parasite a gagné.

La Pentecôte

Et factus est repente de caelo, il se produisit tout à coup venant du ciel, sonus, tamquam advenientis spiritus vehementis, un bruit comme celui d'un vent impétueux, ἦχος ὥσπερ φερομένης πνοῆς βιαίας, a sound from heaven as of a rushing mighty wind, et replevit totam domum ubi erant sedentes, et il remplit toute la maison où ils étaient assis. Et apparuerunt illis dispertitae linguae tamquam ignis, et ils virent apparaître des langues séparées les unes des autres qui étaient comme de feu, διαμεριζόμεναι γλῶσσαι ὡσεὶ πυρός, cloven tongues like as of fire, une distribution de langues comme de feu, des langues bifurquées, divisées, bifides comme des flammes, seditque supra singulos eorum, et qui se posèrent sur chacun d'eux; et repleti sunt omnes Spiritu Sancto, καὶ ἐπλήσθησαν πάντες πνεύματος ἁγίου, et ils furent tous remplis du Saint-Esprit. Et ils commencèrent à parler diverses langues, et coeperunt loqui variis linguis, λαλεῖν ἑτέραις γλώσσαις, to speak with other tongues, selon que l'Esprit-Saint leur donnait de s'exprimer, dabat, καθὼς τὸ πνεῦμα ἐδίδον, as the Spirit gave them utterance, leur donnait, dabat, ἐδίδον, gave them.

Des langues advenues à partir du vent et du bruit. Parler en langues après le feu, après le bruit. A la porte de la salle, ils entendirent un grand vent.

Il y avait à Jérusalem des juifs pieux, de toutes les nations qui sont sous le ciel. Facta autem hac voce, convenit multitudo, après que ce bruit se fut fait entendre, ils accoururent en foule, γενομένης δὲ τῆς φωνῆς ταύτης συνῆλθεν τὸ πλῆθος, now when this was noised abroad, the multitude came together, hac voce, φωνῆς, ce bruit, this was noised, voix ou bruit, l'accord se casse tout à coup, et le rythme et le sens, mais les deux se mélangent, et c'est la voix et c'est le bruit, c'est le message et c'est le parasite, et chacun les entendait parler dans sa propre langue, audiebat unusquisque lingua sua illos loquentes, every man heard them speak in his language, ἤκουον εἷς ἕκαστος τῇ ἰδίᾳ διαλέκτῳ λαλούντων αὐτῶν. Parthes, Mèdes, Élamites, Mésopotamiens, ceux de Judée, de Cappadoce, du Pont et de l'Asie, de Phrygie, Pamphylie, Égypte, Libye, Cyrène, Romains, étrangers, juifs et prosélytes, Crétois, Arabes, entendons parler en nos langues les merveilles de Dieu, mirabilia, wonderful works, μεγαλεῖα, merveilles.

Le sens nouveau distribué partout à partir du vent

et du bruit. Non point une langue unique traduite
en plusieurs langues, mais plusieurs émises et plusieurs entendues en même temps.

La suite des événements est exacte, vue de nos
rationalités. Tout à coup, brusquement, d'une
manière inattendue, le bruit, un bruit venant du
ciel, un son comme fait le vent lorsqu'il souffle avec
force. Il se produit localement, dans une direction
singulière, et bientôt il remplit le lieu, tout le lieu.
Peu prévisible, il passe du local au global. C'était un
bruissement, c'est une rumeur. C'était un événement dans un coin du système, il pénètre, envahit,
occupe toute la maison. Il était entendu, il est vu. Ils
virent apparaître. Le bruit est un hasard, un
désordre, et le vent est un flux. Ce qu'ils virent est
d'abord une distribution, une dispersion, mais aussi
une division. Ce qu'ils virent est aussi ce qui est
généralement ouï, comme le bruit. Des langues. Des
langues divisées, ou distribuées. Mais des langues de
feu. C'est le feu qui pousse le vent, c'est la chaleur
qui produit les souffles de l'air, c'est le feu qui cré-
pite, qui produit le hasard pétillant, grésillant, c'est
le feu de la force et c'est le feu de la clarté, de
l'énergie, de la lumière, de la puissance et de
l'information. Le bruit se fait message avant que le
verbe se fasse chair. Il était bruissement, rumeur, il
est le feu de langue, il est, de la langue de feu, le
sens. Le sens qui bifurque, incliné, divisé comme la
fourche de l'éclair, le sens illuminé. Vers la déclinaison et par la flamme qui s'annonce à la vue et à

l'ouïe. C'est le commencement et la transformation, c'est ainsi fort communément que les systèmes changent d'ordre. Une fluctuation, un bruit, une étincelle de hasard et l'état de choses change d'état selon cette séquence juste. J'ai changé de voix et ma langue bifurque, je parle en langue rationnelle.

Quel changement? Supposons une multitude, la voici, elle s'assemble, attirée par les bruits et les voix. Elle n'a aucune unité : venus de Pamphylie, de Phrygie, de Judée, de l'Asie et de Cappadoce, ils sont là, Méditerranéens et Persans. Le bruit, le vent, la rumeur, les voix sont reçus. Mais les langues? Autrement dit, l'événement local envahissant le lieu provoque momentanément la multitude. Un système se forme, seulement pour les grains, les points, les unités, les éléments. Ce n'est pas encore un système. Comment faire communiquer ces monades, Mèdes et Parthes, Élamites, Romains? Quelqu'un se lève et parle. Il parle araméen, grec ou latin. Qu'a-t-il dit? Le traducteur s'avance. D'abord le traducteur persan, puis le truchement assyrien et ainsi de suite. Le schéma est en place. Voici.

Voyez le caducée d'Hermès. Deux serpents s'y croisent, répétitivement. La maille élémentaire du dessin ressemble à un sablier. Un sablier met en relation deux ensembles ou deux multitudes, par l'intermédiaire d'un goulot très fin. On l'imaginera si fin qu'un seul grain y peut prendre place. C'est la place du locuteur. Il parle seul. Il parle seul à quelques-uns, qui, à leur tour, parleront à d'autres, et ainsi de suite. La hiérarchie est installée. Le premier qui parle ou bien le plus fort, etc., impose sa langue au lieu du goulot. C'est le schéma d'Hermès, et c'est aussi le schéma de n'importe quel commerçant. Il met, lui seul, en relation, un ensemble hétéroclite de sujets, de pratiques, et un ensemble hétéroclite d'objets, de marchandises. Il en discute ou fixe le prix. L'important est qu'il ait la place isolée, unique, à l'intersection, au nœud, au goulot des deux tasses du sablier. Celui qui tient ce lieu dessine, à partir de lui, divisions et dichotomies. Celles de la traduction, par exemple : le latin qu'il énonce est traduit en grec, le grec en araméen, le latin, de nouveau, en perse, et ainsi de suite. C'est le schéma naïf des langues qui bifurquent, des langues divisées, clivées, translatées, qui se posent sur chacun de nous. C'est l'organigramme usuel de toutes les archies. Filet de divisions qui remontent vers un point commun. Le bruit, le vent du Paraclet renversent et transforment ce système, le remplacent par un autre, nouveau. Improbable et miraculeux.

Le sablier, maille élémentaire du caducée porté par Hermès, figure des rapports multiple-un-multiple. Beaucoup de langues, un seul orateur, une foule de langues; un ensemble d'objets, un commerçant, un groupe de clients, etc. Supposons maintenant que n'importe quel émetteur parle en sa propre langue et que tout récepteur le comprenne en la sienne, quelle que soit la langue et quel que soit le lieu. Les relations alors peuvent être dites multiple-multiple, et le réseau qui les dessine est décentré. Sans échangeur ni carrefour. On n'a jamais vu pareil graphe. Sur ses chemins, Hermès agonise, l'échangeur a défait ses nœuds.

Le traducteur se tient au centre ou au foyer du sablier, ou de n'importe quel sous-sablier. Ainsi le commerçant, ainsi le démon de Maxwell. Ils transforment les flux qui passent au sein de l'échangeur. Ils facilitent le passage, ils le contrôlent, ils ont rapport au un-par-un. Une langue pour ce récepteur, une molécule reconnue plus lente, une marchandise pour telle cliente. Tout transite par les mains d'Hermès. Il est placé aux bons endroits, il y a donc de bons endroits. Tout passe par ses mains parce que, peu ou prou, tout se transforme entre ses mains. L'échangeur est aussi un transformateur. Au moins par changement de direction, au moins par division du flux, par bifurcation, au moins par semi-conduction, sens uniques et sens interdits, au moins par aiguillage. Hermès est bien le dieu des carrefours, il est bien le dieu dont Maxwell a fait un démon. Le message, donc, transitant par ses mains, au lieu de l'échangeur, se change. Il n'arrive pas pur ni invariant ni stable. Je veux bien qu'il s'y améliore, mais cela reste un jugement. Et s'il s'y dégradait? Je ne sais, je n'en décide pas. Ce qui demeure sûr est que le message se charge, et qu'il arrive ainsi chargé. En termes propres, il est parasité. Le parasite s'est branché aux lieux les plus profitables, à l'intersection des relations. La maille élémentaire de son activité singulière était d'avoir rapport à une relation, il améliore de beaucoup ses performances aux lieux où plusieurs relations se croisent ou se coupent. Il est aux nœuds de la régulation, et tout à coup, il a rapport au collectif. Celui qui réussit un rapport multiple-un, le forme et le fait fonctionner, celui-là est le politique et il a trouvé le pouvoir. Comme on dit souvent, il tient les lieux de décision : bien sûr, puisqu'il est aux coupures. Ici, aux intersections.

Si l'orateur est entendu tel quel, le réseau se décentre, même localement : il n'y a plus d'intercepteur, il n'y a plus de carrefour, il n'y a plus d'intermédiaire, il n'y a plus de ville, Hermès, père de Pan, est mort le jour de Pentecôte. C'est un miracle, disent-ils, cela n'arrive pas. Je peux dire et ouïr de l'Ouest à l'Est, les murailles s'écroulent sur le coup de vent, sous la rafale de musique. Je puis avoir rapport directement à quelque objet sans qu'un intercepteur s'interpose, j'ai relation ouvertement à l'autre sans qu'un intermédiaire s'intercale ni pour intercéder, ni pour interdire. L'absence de parasite, est-ce si rare ? L'immédiat serait-il si miraculeux ? Faut-il que la parole soit toujours parabole, c'est-à-dire toujours décalée ? Non. Si ce n'est pas miracle, pouvons-nous construire cela ?

Je recommence. Le premier système connu de communication est le système de Leibniz. Il est radical, il est simple. Nul n'a rapport à rien ni à personne, portes et fenêtres non pas fermées seulement mais absentes, tout a rapport à tout par l'intermédiaire de Dieu. Unique médiateur, il est donc tout connaissant et tout puissant. Quels sont les mes-

sages échangés par Dieu entre les monades, c'est
une autre question. Ce système est parfait, il est
mathématisable de part en part, en droit et en fait.
Inversement, cette mathématique est de communication optimale. Tout parasite y est réduit à presque
rien, grain de sable ou de sel, septième. Le problème du mal est ramené à l'harmonie par calcul
d'optimum.

Le deuxième est celui d'Hermès. Il est polythéiste
ou multicentré, chaîne de sabliers, réseau de telles
chaînes. Les anges qui passent, dieux ou démons,
tiennent les carrefours : nœuds d'échanges, de
changement, coupures, bifurcations de décision,
fuseau, faisceau où le multiple vient en une main
unique. Début du politique. Les messages, les flux
transitent selon les énergies et les interceptions. Ce
qui est reçu c'est ce qui est émis, plus ou moins les
parasites. Il arrive que la différence soit considérable : ce qui parvient, parfois, est quasi nul. Les
intervalles ruinent les affamés. Le système de Leibniz est une limite de celui-ci.

Ce réseau peut demeurer en équilibre, pour un
temps, mais il peut fondre, aussi, d'un coup, sous
l'action d'une forte chaleur. Le feu ramène le
désordre. On n'entend plus que du bruit. La
rumeur du vent. En ce commencement nouveau est
la distribution.

Le troisième connecte le multiple au multiple, sans intermédiaire. C'est l'invention du Paraclet, le jour de Pentecôte. Le multiple s'autorégule. Cela est très nouveau, si nouveau qu'on croirait un effet-miracle. Dans le second réseau, les démons et les dieux sont nombreux et connus, roitelets locaux et caïds, petits chefs et petits proxénètes, d'argent ou d'idéologie, de chantage ou d'information, despotes singuliers de rackets régionaux. Dans le premier, tout se passe aux limites, le local file vers le global, et le pluriel vers l'un. Au centre, est sis le Roi, j'entends le Roi-Soleil, le Soleil. Dieu, c'est le nom que Leibniz lui donne. Il est l'universel des communications, il en est la commune langue, l'espéranto, le volapük, la musique, l'algèbre, la caractéristique universelle, ou le *calculus ratiocinator*. Il est le calcul qui, en se faisant, fait le monde. Communiquer ici est calculer, c'est-à-dire coder. Or cet universel peut aussi se nommer l'argent, autre code, autre équivalent général. A chaque dénomination un échangeur, un change unique pour l'ensemble du réseau. Si vous parlez théologie, vous l'appellerez Dieu, si vous discourez comme un économiste, vous direz l'argent, si vous adoptez le langage philosophique, vous traduirez ou plutôt vous expliquerez en usitant des termes comme code, comme équivalent général, et ces traductions laissent tout inchangé, même et surtout lorsqu'il dit : Raison. Nous vivons plutôt dans un univers de rationalités. Ceux qui changent ainsi de langue se battent d'autant plus entre eux qu'ils affirment la même chose.

La question est bien de savoir si on peut construire un réseau sans contraintes de carrefour, sans échangeur, sans intersection où se branchent les parasites. Où un élément quelconque peut avoir rapport à un autre élément sans contrainte de médiation. C'est le schéma de Pentecôte. Il faut décidément écrire une philosophie sans échangeur. Je viens de commencer.

L'ancienne et vénérable théologie du Paraclet recouvre avec quelque bonheur partie de l'anthropologie de l'échange. Quand le Saint-Esprit vient, adviennent les dons. Il est le donateur, *munerum dator*, et ses dons sont sept, *septiformis munere, sacrum septenarium*. Les voies du vent ne sont pas réversibles, le lit remonte vers un point de la rose, le flux n'y revient pas. Le don a une source, elle n'est pas un pôle de réception. Il n'y a pas d'échange. Ce qui en advient est la Sagesse, la Science, l'Intelligence, le Conseil, la Force, la Piété, la Crainte de Dieu. A éliminer de la liste ce qui est proprement divin, restent les caractéristiques de ce que nous nommons l'information.

Le feu, d'où vient le vent, qui vient du bruit, d'où adviennent les dons, est paradoxal. Il réchauffe : *fove quid est frigidum, ignem accende*, il brûle ; mais il refroidit : *dulce refrigerium, in aeste temperies*. De cette source, de cette bouche, soufflent le chaud et le froid.

Les plus usés des mots du monde portent parfois un faste inouï. Nul échange, nul don ne passerait, au moins dans les langues que j'ai ouï parler, si, au bout de la ligne, le récepteur final ne disait merci. Le terminal rend grâce. Le mot n'est qu'un coup de vent, il est pourtant indispensable. Il jette cette grâce dans le bilan du gré. On a connu, sans lui, des cas de guerre : les ingrats contre les magnifiques, les parasites contre les évergètes. A quoi servirait de donner, je vous le demande, si cette reconnaissance minime ne reconnaissait pas le superbe et le géné-reux ? Celui qui remercie, d'autre part, se dégage du poste dernier, un peu difficile à tenir. Avoir le der-nier mot, c'est laisser à l'autre la place finale et sau-ter à la pénultième. Aussi l'hôte ou le donateur se hâtent de répondre : « Avec plaisir, je vous en prie, à votre service », et ramènent, gentiment, le comblé à sa place.

Je n'ai jamais compris ce supplément de révé-rences, avant d'avoir eu l'occasion de l'échanger en grec. Dans les autres langages, le machinal l'avait laissé en noir.

En prononçant merci, l'hellène dit : eucharistie. La bonne grâce. Tout s'éclaire. Ce mot pour cette chose et ceci est mon corps. Je ne sais si ce tour en complément d'échange explique ladite transsubs-tantiation, ou si, inversement, le mystère illumine le quotidien, mais je suis sûr, depuis le rire clair de la paysanne crétoise, qu'il s'agit du même acte et de la même opération. Eucharistie, cette parole vaut la chose, le logiciel descend dans les secrets du maté-riel, Eucharistie, Dieu est dans notre rapport, notre relation est Dieu même, sous des espèces incarnées,

Eucharistie, l'échange finit en prière, et quand nous
prions en commun, le Christ est en tiers parmi
nous. Eucharistie, le verbe se fait chair et le pain se
fait verbe. Εὐχαριστῶ πολί.

Παρακαλῶ est, comme on sait, la réplique de fermeture. Je vous en prie, je vous prie et je vous invite.
Oui, vous êtes la bienvenue. Je vous appelle,
j'appelle, je prie. Qui est l'invité, le prié, l'appelé ?
Dites son nom, dis ton nom, dis un nom.
Παράκλητος, le Paraclet, le nom commun du Saint-
Esprit, la troisième personne. Il intervient, il interrompt, il entre en passant les murailles, au milieu du
repas ou de la réunion, il intercède et il procède et
du Père et du Fils. Il est le vent, l'être du vent, le
souffle, celui que les juifs nomment *Ruagh*. Il est
don, l'être du don, le donateur universel. Tu dis à
celui que tu pries parce qu'il a reçu, qu'il est celui
qui donne. Le feu vole au-dessus de l'échange et du
groupe, saute de la dernière place à la toute première, boucle la chaîne irréversible, constitue la
communauté. Le parasite Paraclet devient l'hôte. A
la porte de la salle, ils entendirent du bruit, ce
jour-là. Divisé en langues de feu sur les têtes, le tiers,
inclus, est désormais à toutes les places. Il est possible que ce feu apporte quelque lumière dans la
boîte noire du nous. Hermès est mort, un jour
d'interférence.

Eucharistie et Paraclet, la deuxième et la troisième
personne ensemble, dans des paroles usagées de la
conduite quotidienne : le schéma précédent était,
sans qu'on le sache, trinitaire. Et les dieux sont ici.

Sans doute savons-nous, peut-être un jour connaî-
trons-nous les choses du monde. Nous ne saurons
jamais si elles sont créées ni qui les a créées. Ce mystère est tout à fait hors de nos prises. Il n'est pas du
tout sûr que le religieux ait quelque chose à voir
avec le monde. Je veux dire avec la physique. Derrière l'épaisseur des choses, celui qu'on nomme
Dieu est presque infiniment caché. Nos classiques
l'avaient caché sous les conditions à l'infini de la
pensée exacte. Cette distance est aussi longue, dans
le sujet clair que dans l'objet ombreux.

Je désire dire qu'il y a du divin dans ce monde-ci,
des choses divines. Ce que je dis est posé à l'écart de
la question directe : Dieu est un substantif, un nom,
divin est adjectif, jeté à côté. Le monde est divin, il
est plein de choses divines. Cette mer, cette plaine,
ce fleuve, la banquise, l'arbre, la lumière et la vie. Je
le sais, je le vois, je le sens, j'en suis illuminé, brû-
lant. La mer vineuse et la vie divine. L'adjectif, posé
à côté, tout à l'écart des noms et des notions de la
philosophie, me suffit, comme parabole. Oui, le
divin est là, je le touche, ces choses-ci sont des
miracles improbables, je n'ai jamais cessé d'aimer le
monde et de voir qu'il est beau. Oui, ma philosophie est adjective, elle est émerveillée. Le réel
n'est pas rationnel, il est improbable et miraculeux.

Nous ne saurons peut-être jamais ce qui passe et
se passe dans notre collectif. Ce qui passe est l'objet
ou le mot échangé. Que se passe-t-il, à la fin du
don ? Les dieux descendent lentement dans cette
boîte noire, l'adjectif Paraclet, l'invité donateur,
l'illumine d'un jet de flamme. Il n'est pas du tout
sûr que le religieux n'ait pas tout à voir avec nos rap-

ports intersubjectifs. Dieu est perdu derrière la physique, Dieu est perdu derrière la logique, Dieu est
perdu derrière les objets, Dieu est perdu derrière le
sujet, intelligent ou pathétique, de la connaissance
ou du sentiment. Celui que mes pères disaient le
Père, infiniment caché, demeure absent. Les
preuves canoniques, par le chemin du monde ou le
fonctionnement de la rigueur, sont hors terrain.
Quand la philosophie n'est pas dans l'objet ni dans
le sujet, ni dans leur rapport désuet, le religieux n'y
est pas pensable. J'ai perdu pour toujours la puissance et la gloire, la toute-connaissance et la surabondante création.

J'habite parmi ces choses, divines, et je suis
plongé dans le groupe, obscur. Elles sont plus faciles
à connaître que lui, je ne dis pas plus simples, car
elles sont exquisément complexes. J'ai du bonheur
dans ce divin des choses elles-mêmes, elles me
poussent vers le panthéisme ; je souffre souvent de
ce groupe et de l'obscurité, dans mon intelligence
et ma vie. Bientôt, pour éclairer le collectif, j'appellerai la notion de quasi-objet. Il circule, il passe
parmi nous. Je le donne, je le reçois. Merci, je vous
en prie. Eucharistie et Paraclet. Nous sommes
seconde et troisième personne, immergés dans
l'incarnation et dans le vent de Pentecôte, laissant le
Père à l'infini, pour l'éternité. La grâce passe dans
le flou entre mots et choses, elle passe entre les
canaux où fluent les nourritures substantielles et les
voix sonores, elle passe entre les échanges d'énergie
et d'information, espace intermédiaire, espace
d'équivalence où naît la langue, où naît son feu, où
elle fait apparaître les choses dont elle parle, écart

instable de l'extase et de l'existence, de l'incarnation et de l'ascension, du pain et de l'oiseau. J'avance dans la boîte noire, un peu. J'entends l'invitation à demeurer ensemble, dans cet espace où matériel et logiciel s'échangent. Le troisième apparaît, le tiers est inclus. Peut-être est-il chacun de nous.

Nouveaux repas interrompus
Technique, travail

Théorie du quasi-objet

Hoc memorabile est; ego tu sum,
tu es ego; uni animi sumus.

PLAUTE, *Stichus*, v. 731.

Ce que c'est que de vivre ensemble. Qu'est-ce que le collectif? Cette question, maintenant, nous fascine.

Le malheur des méditations qui précèdent est de ne pas dire assez distinctement si elles sont une philosophie de l'être ou de la relation. Être ou avoir rapport, c'est toute la question. Elle n'est sans doute pas exclusive. Je ne décide pas toujours si le parasite est relationnel ou réel, s'il est un opérateur ou une monade.

J'ai désir de penser que ce bruit que j'entends sans cesse à la porte est produit par un être que j'aimerais connaître. Je peux penser tout aussi bien que celui qui mange de moi ou qui mange à côté de moi le pain, le vin que je lui porte n'est qu'une figure commode pour penser l'âge adulte, ma fatigue du jour, les explosions, les pertes, les occultations de puissance, et les dégradations ou les éclats de message dans les réseaux. Ce bon et mauvais Hermès est un dieu, le dieu qui a préparé ma vieillesse et ne s'est pas substitué à celui qui a réjoui ma jeunesse, un dieu comme l'amour, fils de fortune et de passivité, un dieu, oui, c'est-à-dire : un être ou une relation? Le vrai Dieu, en classique théologie, est Celui en qui la relation produit l'être, en qui l'amour produit le corps, chez qui le verbe, le logos, le rapport, se fait chair.

Je ne disais pas assez si le parasite est être ou relation. Il est, d'abord, la relation élémentaire.

Qu'est-ce que, de nouveau, vivre ensemble? Qu'est-ce que le collectif? Je ne sais, je doute qu'on le sache. Je n'ai jamais rien lu qui me l'apprenne encore. J'ai vécu, quelquefois, certaines circonstances qui faisaient du clair dans cette ombre. Et à table, parfois, à côté de celui qui mangeait de moi ou d'un autre. Cette catégorie noire du collectif, groupe, classe, caste, que sais-je, est-ce un être, à son tour, ou une grappe de relations?

Le furet pue un peu, il pue comme un putois, auquel il est croisé souvent. Il occupe ainsi l'espace. Nous revenons à la propriété. Il est vampire du lapin, il le poursuit dans son terrier, il se jette sur lui, le mord au museau ou au cou, il lui suce le sang. Nous avons réduit le furet à l'état domestique, nous n'en connaissons plus la variété sauvage. Nous le faisons courir pour nous, comme l'autour, comme le faucon crécerelle, nous les parasitons. Nous muselons le furet avant de l'introduire dans le système du terrier, le lapin, affolé, sort par une autre issue, où le filet, enfin, l'enveloppe. Encore un beau détournement de flux, dans un réseau.

Le long d'un cordeau tenu entre les mains, nous avons tous joué au furet... le furet du bois, mesdames, il court, il court le furet, le furet du bois joli. Celui qui est surpris le tenir dans la main a un gage. Le furet le désigne. Tel ou tel est marqué du signe du furet. Condamné, il va au centre, il voit, il regarde.

Quel est cet objet, le furet?

Ce quasi-objet n'est pas un objet, mais il en est un, néanmoins, puisqu'il n'est pas sujet, puisqu'il est dans le monde; il est aussi un quasi-sujet, puisqu'il marque ou désigne un sujet qui, sans lui, ne le serait pas. Qui n'est pas découvert le furet dans la main est fondu, anonyme, dans une chaîne monotone, où il ne se distingue pas. Il n'est pas un individu, il n'est pas reconnu, découvert, découpé, il est de la chaîne et dans la chaîne. Il court, comme le furet, dans le collectif. Le fil entre les mains est notre simple relation, l'absence du furet, sa course font notre indivision. Qui sommes-nous? Ceux qui font passer le furet, ceux qui ne l'ont pas. Ce quasi-objet, en courant, fait du collectif : s'il s'arrête, il fait l'individu. Si celui-ci est découvert, il est mort. Qui est sujet, qui est je, ou qui suis-je? Le furet, mobile, tisse le nous, le collectif; qu'il s'arrête, il marque le je.

Un ballon n'est pas un objet ordinaire, puisqu'il n'est ce qu'il est que si un sujet l'a en main. Posé là, il est nul, il est bête, il n'a pas de sens, ni de fonction, ni de valeur. On ne joue pas tout seul au ballon. Ceux qui le font, ceux qui le gardent ou, comme on dit, le monopolisent, sont de mauvais joueurs, bientôt exclus du jeu. On les dit personnels. Le jeu collectif n'a aucun besoin de personnes. Considérons celui qui le tient. S'il le fait tourner autour de lui, c'est un maladroit, un mauvais comédien. Le ballon n'est pas là pour le corps, c'est le contraire exact qui est vrai : le corps est l'objet du ballon, le sujet tourne autour de ce soleil. On reconnaît l'adresse de balle à ce signe qui ne trompe jamais, le joueur la suit et la sert, loin de la faire suivre et de s'en servir. Elle est sujet du corps, sujet des corps, et comme sujet des sujets. Jouer n'est rien d'autre que de se faire l'attribut de la balle comme substance. Les lois sont écrites pour elle, sont définies par rapport à elle, et nous nous plions à ces lois. L'adresse de ballon suppose une révolution ptolémaïque dont peu de théoriciens sont capables, accoutumés à être des sujets, dans un monde copernicien, où les objets sont des esclaves.

De même que le furet, la balle circule. Meilleure est l'équipe, plus rapide en est le transfert. On a dit parfois que cette balle est une braise rouge qui brûle si fort les doigts qu'il faut s'en débarrasser au plus vite. Apprécions au passage la métaphore, que Rudyard Kipling n'a pas méprisée : la fleur rouge écarte les tigres, et le rameau d'or n'est pas loin. La balle est le sujet de la circulation, les joueurs n'en sont que les stations et les relais. Le ballon peut se transformer en témoin de relais. Témoin, cela, en grec, se dit martyr.

Dans la plupart des jeux, l'homme qui tient la balle est d'attaque, toute la défense va s'organiser en raison de lui et de sa position. La balle est le centre du référentiel, pour le jeu mouvant. Sauf exception — le football américain, par exemple —, on n'est autorisé à défendre que sur qui détient le ballon. Ce quasi-objet, que volontairement je nomme au masculin-féminin, le désigne. Tel est marqué du signe de la balle. Haro sur lui !

L'attaquant, porteur du ballon, est signalé comme victime. Il détient le témoin et il est le martyr. En ce lieu, en ce moment, sur lui précisément, tout l'important se passe et précipite. Le ciel lui tombe sur la tête. L'ensemble des vitesses, des forces, des angles, des chocs et des pensées de stratégie se noue ici et maintenant. Or, tout à coup, ce n'est plus vrai, ce qui devait se décider n'en découd point, la balle fuse, le nœud actuel se défait, par le déplacement. L'histoire et l'attention bifurquent. Le témoin n'est plus là, le furet court, brusquement muselé, il va quérir un autre lapin dans le réseau des galeries, le ballon est hors de portée, le sacrifice n'a pas lieu, il est différé à plus tard, le martyr n'est pas tel, il est tel autre, et encore tel autre, et pourquoi pas tel à nouveau. Tous. Le jeu est cette vicariance. Il est le graphe des substitutions. Prêtres, victimes, en habit bleu, rouge ou vert ? Non. Strictement, des vicaires. Vicaires par la mobilité des suppléances, par la vitesse des substitutions. Sacrificateur, maintenant, et très vite victime, vite neutralisé, rapidement changeant par la balle en course, dans ce terrain, délimité comme autrefois un temple. Le sacrifié a tout loisir, par son astuce ou son habileté, d'envoyer tout de suite son voisin au casse-pipe en son lieu et place, et le voisin a ce loisir et ainsi autant qu'on voudra. Dès lors, par le ballon, nous sommes tous des victimes possibles, nous nous y exposons et nous y échappons, et plus la balle court, plus le clignotement de la vicariance est rapide, plus l'émotion est suspendue. La balle navette, comme le furet, tisse le collectif en mettant à mort virtuellement chaque individu. Ce pourquoi la victime apaise la crise est ce savoir imprenable que nous portons tous, sous la voix qui dit je, que cette victime peut être je tout aussi bien, et au hasard. Le ballon est ce quasi-objet, quasi-sujet par qui je suis sujet, c'est-à-dire soumis. Tombé, mis dessous, piétiné, plaqué, jeté de haut en bas, assujetti, exposé, puis substitué, tout à coup, par cette vicariance. La liste est celle des sens de *subjicere, subjectus*. La philosophie n'est pas toujours aux lieux d'ordinaire prévus. J'apprends plus au sujet du sujet en jouant à la balle que dans le poêle cartésien. Où pourtant rôdait quelque mise à mort.

Pendant que Nausicaa lance la balle sur la plage à ses compagnes, Ulysse, jeté bas par la vague et par le ressac, arraché du naufrage, apparaît, nu, sujet, dessous. Enfant de la lame, enfant des passes de la balle.

Ce quasi-objet marqueur de sujet, comme on dit marquer un agneau pour l'autel ou pour la boucherie, est un étonnant constructeur d'intersubjectivité. Par lui, nous savons comment et quand nous sommes des sujets, quand et comment nous ne le sommes plus. Nous, qu'est-ce à dire? Nous sommes en précision ce clignotement fluctuant du je. Le je est dans le jeu un jeton qu'on échange. Et ce passage, ce réseau de passes, ces vicariances de sujets tissent le collectif. Je suis je maintenant, sujet, c'est-à-dire exposé à être jeté de mon haut sur le sol, exposé à tomber, à être mis dessous la masse compacte des autres, puis tu prends le relais, tu es substitué à je et le deviens, plus tard c'est lui qui te le rend, son travail fait, son danger assumé, sa part de collectif construite. Le nous se fait par les éclats et les occultations du je. Le nous se fait par les passes du je. Par échange du je. Et par substitution, et par vicariance du je.

Cela paraît tout de suite aisé à penser. Chacun porte sa pierre et le mur s'élève. Chacun porte son je et le nous se construit. Cette addition est imbécile et ressemble à un discours ministériel. Non. Tout se passe comme si, dans un groupe donné, le je comme le nous étaient non partageables. Il a le ballon et nous ne l'avons plus. Ce qu'il faut arriver à penser, pour calculer le nous, c'est, justement, la passe. Or elle est abandon du je. Peut-on donner son propre je? Il y a des objets pour le faire, de quasi-objets, quasi-sujets, dont on ne sait s'ils sont des êtres ou des relations, des lambeaux d'êtres ou des bouts de relation. Par eux, le principe d'individuation peut se transmettre et se gommer. Il y a là quelque chose et quelque geste qui ressemble à un abandon de souveraineté. Le nous n'est pas une somme de je, mais une nouveauté produite par légations du je, par concessions, désistements, résignations du je. Le nous est moins un ensemble de je que l'ensemble des ensembles de ses transmissions. Il apparaît brutalement dans l'ivresse et l'extase, anéantissements du principe d'individuation. Cette extase est aisément produite par le quasi-objet, dont le corps s'est fait serviteur ou objet. On se souvient comment il tourne autour de lui, comment le corps suit le ballon et lui donne le gouvernement. On se souvient de la révolution ptolémaïque. Elle montre que nous sommes capables d'extase, d'écart à notre équilibre, que nous pouvons placer notre centre hors de nous. Le quasi-objet se trouve investi de ce décentrage. Dès lors, qui le tient a le centre et gouverne l'extase. La vitesse de la passation l'accélère et lui donne existence. La participation est cela même et n'a rien à voir avec le partage, au moins pensé comme une division des parts. La participation est la passation du je par la passe. C'est très exactement l'abandon de mon individu ou de mon être dans un quasi-objet qui n'est là que pour circuler. C'est rigoureusement la transsubstantiation de l'être en relation. L'être est aboli pour la relation. L'extase collective est abandon des je sur le tissu des relations. Ce moment est un danger extrême. Chacun est au bord de son inexistence. Mais le je comme tel n'est pas supprimé pour autant. Il circule toujours, dans et par le quasi-objet. On peut oublier cette chose. Elle est par terre, et qui la ramasse et la garde par-devers lui devient le seul sujet, le maître, le despote, le dieu.

Sur la guerre, la lutte, le combat et l'opposition, derechef. Le meurtre est un principe. Le crime est un principe. La guerre de tous contre tous n'a jamais eu lieu, n'a pas lieu, n'aura jamais lieu. Le combat un contre un, la lice, la lutte trois à trois, Horaces et Curiaces, sont de surface et de spectacle, tragédie, comédie, théâtre. Tous contre un est la loi de toujours. Trois Curiaces contre un Horace, quand l'apparence est déchirée comme un décor et qu'il faut en venir au réel. L'issue est toujours certaine et la guerre est asymétrique. Les parasites arrivent en foule et ils ne prennent aucun risque. Il arrive, bien sûr, que la situation, miraculeusement, se retourne, qu'Horace soit vainqueur. On en parle, alors, on en fait l'histoire, et cela fait croire, mieux encore et plus, à la phénoménologie de la guerre. Horace était plus fort que chacun des trois autres, blessés à mort. La loi est invariante.

Ici, le processus est encore plus fin. Le jeu est si profond qu'il faut y revenir sans cesse. Le combat de tous contre un seul est différé par le vol de la balle, la vicariance et la substitution détournent sans arrêt l'issue obligée. Elles font diverger l'attention vers le beau combat de spectacle où règne une glorieuse incertitude, et la morale est sauve, on cause de noblesse. Et chacun se rue au spectacle, et parie qui perd et qui gagne. On dirait vraiment le hasard, puisqu'on joue. Alors qu'il n'y a que nécessité enchaînée. Le déclin du sport aujourd'hui vers les oppositions arrangées d'avance, montre, s'il en était besoin, où est l'attracteur principal et de quoi il s'agit en réalité. Tout va toujours vers la guerre sans risque, vers le crime et le vol, main basse sur les

hommes et sur les choses. L'usage dérive toujours de
l'abus, il y revient, de soi, quand la dérive, quand la
dérivation s'efface et ne fait plus changer sans cesse
de rival.

Toute théorie de la dérivation consiste à orienter
l'attention vers la rivalité, le mot même l'avoue.

Le furet, le ballon sont des jetons de jeu, qu'on se
passe, il est probable que ce sont des jokers. La
construction du collectif se fait avec des jokers, et
c'est un bricolage formidable. On fabrique
n'importe quoi avec n'importe quoi. Cette logique
est follement indéterminée, c'est la plus difficile à
noter.

Considérons un autre joker, si indéterminé qu'il
est, comme on le sait, un équivalent général. Il circule comme un ballon, l'argent, quasi-objet. Il
marque le sujet, il le marque efficacement : dans nos
sociétés, les méditations cartésiennes sont bientôt
écrites, je suis riche donc je suis. L'argent est intégralement mon être même. Le vrai doute est la pauvreté. Le doute radical, hyperbolique, est la misère.
Descartes a triché, il aurait dû sortir, nouveau Fran-
çois d'Assise, et se dépouiller de ses biens. Descartes
a triché, il n'a pas jeté ses ducats au ruisseau. Il n'a
jamais perdu le monde, puisqu'il a gardé son argent.
Le vrai cartésien, radical, est le cynique. Descartes
n'a jamais risqué de perdre le je, puisqu'il n'a jamais
risqué son argent. Il n'a jamais joué contre le malin
génie sa veste et sa fortune. Il n'est jamais descendu
au tonneau, dans la boue, sous la pluie, à demander

au roi qui passe de s'écarter de son soleil. J'ai toujours douté de ce doute qui ne va pas au zéro de la possession. Un sot riche est un riche, un sot pauvre est un sot. Un je riche est un riche, un je pauvre est un je. On verrait alors qui est ce monsieur.

La construction du collectif vient de se faire avec n'importe qui au moyen de n'importe quoi. Le furet, ce n'est rien, une bague, un anneau, une chose quelconque, la balle est une peau ou une bulle d'air, je les passe ou les lance à qui de rencontre, qui ne reçoit rien ou quasi, cela n'a pas trop d'importance.

La question demeure toujours : quelles choses sont entre qui ? N'importe qui, toi, moi, celui-ci, l'autre. Et entre eux, ces quasi-objets, peut-être des jokers. Les stations sont des *on*, la circulation se fait par des *ça*, et nous n'avons écrit qu'une certaine logique.

De même, l'argent n'est pas grand-chose, parce qu'il est tout, on l'échange avec le premier venu, et tel le vole à tous, et tel l'enterre pour personne.

Ces quasi-objets sont blancs et ces sujets sont transparents.

Mais l'intérêt, toujours, croît avec le noir et l'opaque.

La position du parasite est de se trouver entre. Ce pourquoi c'est une question de le dire être ou relation. Or l'attribut du parasite, jusqu'à maintenant passé sous silence, est sa spécificité.

N'importe quoi ne trouble pas un message qui passe. N'importe qui n'est pas invité à la table de n'importe qui. Telle larve ne se développe que dans tel organisme ou n'est transportée que par tel vecteur.

Il faut bien qu'Orgon soit dévot pour être parasité par Laurent et Tartuffe. Dévot et quelque chose en plus pour que l'adaptation soit parfaite. Il faut bien que le brouillage épouse le canal, se glisse dans la longueur d'onde, et se superpose souplement à l'émission. Jean-François, neveu de Rameau, n'aurait pas eu de chance chez le fils de Mme Pernelle, je peux faire tout le vacarme que je veux, je n'empêcherai pas mon voisin de voir se lever le soleil. Les poux meurent sur les cailloux.

Comment se fait-il que je t'aime, toi justement parmi cent mille, moi justement, ça tombe si bien! Est-ce une illusion, le chiffrage à la dom Juan est-il une loi plus sage?

Nous sommes conduits aux limites. La reproduction des mammifères est un cycle endoparasitaire, elle en a tous les traits. Nous nous parasitons les uns les autres pour parler, pour manger, pour organiser l'injustice et les exactions légitimes, pour ces projets, tout le monde est bon. Nous nous parasitons les uns les autres pour nous reproduire et nous multiplier, mais il faut, pour cela, que ces autres soient mêmes et autres, et ils se virent nus. N'importe qui, n'importe quoi ne suffit pas dans cette affaire. Une moitié de semence, introduite dans une boîte qui lui est étrangère mais adaptée, pullule en elle et s'en nourrit, la spécificité commence. Le foetus est un parasite, protélien, il le reste un peu après la naissance. Combien de temps? Les évaluations varient. Aux limites, mieux vaut dire toujours. Le sevrage n'est que local. Le petit d'homme, d'autre part, ne se nourrit pas seulement de pain, de lait, d'air et de chaleur, il lui faut encore de la parole, l'information et la culture qui sont un environnement, un milieu sans quoi il mourrait. Ce milieu est humain, proprement humain, produit par le groupe restreint, couple parental, famille, tribu, clan, je ne sais. Si le parasitisme en général suppose que l'hôte est milieu, ou que les productions de l'hôte constituent l'environnement, la niche nécessaire à la survie de qui s'y fixe ou s'y déplace, nous sommes tous des parasites de nos langues. Je comprends seulement aujourd'hui ma langue maternelle, pourquoi ma langue est ma mère logicielle. Il arrive que ceux qui ont manqué de mère se jettent, éperdus, dans la langue. Peut-être faut-il peindre l'événement de Pentecôte comme un groupe de nouveau-nés pendus aux langues de feu et les tétant goulûment. Ma parole est branchée sur ma langue. Je parais maintenant émettre et donner alentour, je reçois mon verbe de cette niche, parler, c'est se nourrir. Parler, c'est sucer le sein de la maternité logicielle commune. Le verbe naît de cette mère, virginale toujours, puisque toujours quelque part intacte, la langue excède ma parole. Ici le parasite-bruit est identique à celui qui dîne à table d'hôte. Je me nourris sans fin au buffet de ma langue, je ne pourrai jamais lui rendre ce qu'elle m'a donné. Je suis le bruit de son harmonie compliquée, ou le vagissement de sa rumeur. Je mourrais de ne pas écrire, je mourrais de ne pas prendre mon repas de paroles avec quelques amis, de qui, en quelque manière, je la tiens. Je ne serai jamais sevré de langue.

Non pas de langue en général, mais de la mienne. Spécifiquement de la mienne, qui me donne le jour dans le vacarme noir des langues étrangères. J'aime son côté musique de chambre, la pudeur presque sourde, muette, de ses accents toniques, sa distinction un peu nobiliaire, son hellénicité secrète, et ses terres rares. Elles redevient vierge, ma mère, au moment de mourir, nul n'use plus de ses mots locaux, elle est rabattue sur mille emplois courants, ils s'en servent tous comme d'une carpette, comme d'une putain. Ils tentent de violer leur mère, tandis qu'elle agonise. Je la voudrais belle et vivante comme aux temps de Bougainville. Comme aux temps où qui, sur la terre, voulait de la beauté parlait ma mère, et se nourrissait de sa modestie. Elle réussissait ce miracle d'être chaste, universellement.

Entre l'Égypte et le pays de Canaan, aux jours de famine et de vaches maigres, circule du blé sur les ânes des caravanes et, dans les sacs de blé, l'argent que Joseph a reçu de ses frères, que Joseph a rendu, qui circule dans les deux sens, qui n'a donc pas de sens, et circule la coupe dans le sac de Benjamin, la coupe de Joseph qui marque Benjamin, la coupe du plus jeune frère qui marque le plus jeune frère. Joseph a été victime et Benjamin, par le fait de Joseph, peut être à nouveau la victime. Il est marqué du signe de la coupe. La tunique à manches longues fut tachée par le sang du bouc et la coupe était vide, en ce temps-là, de vin. Marqués tous deux par l'absence de leur sang et par l'absence de leur vin.

Je ne parviendrai pas à me nourrir jamais d'une langue d'argent, langue plate et sans goût comme un billet de banque gras. Sans odeur, sans saveur, luisant, visqueux, on en trouve des tonnes dans les grandes surfaces. Lorsque la langue converge vers l'argent, elle monotonise son flux, elle tend vers le quasi-objet le plus blanc, le plus plat. Elle étend son empire en même temps que la monnaie. Elle construit des collectivités temporaires et molles. Dont la puissance est parallèle à la viscosité.

Des paroles de langue, on n'en mange pas seulement, on y goûte. Ceux qui s'alimentent, vite fait bien fait, comme on se mouche, comme on se couche et se touche, trouvent ça un peu dégoûtant, répugnant. Il y a les gourmands. On parle comme on mange, style et cuisine sont, ensemble, de conséquence, vulgaires de conserve ou raffinés en chœur. On échange des mots comme on passe les plats, ou à la va-vite, courons à autre chose de plus important, le travail, par exemple, ou dans une atmosphère attentive d'extase. Cela dépend de nous que certains des quasi-objets deviennent des sujets. Ou plutôt : il n'y a de nous que si cette transformation s'opère.

Les mots, le pain, le vin sont entre nous, êtres ou relations. Nous les paraissons échanger entre nous alors que nous sommes connectés sur la même table ou la même langue. Ils tètent la même mère. L'échange parasite, croisé entre le logiciel et le matériel, trouve ici son explication. A la Pentecôte, les apôtres nouveau-nés tètent les langues de feu, divisées à partir d'un socle unitaire, à la Cène, tous parasites à la table du maître, boivent le vin, mangent le pain, le partagent, le passent. Le mystère de transsubstantiation est là, clair, lumineux, transparent. Mangeons-nous jamais autre chose, quand nous sommes ensemble, que la chair du verbe ?

Nos quasi-objets sont de spécificité croissante. Nous mangeons le pain de nos mœurs, nous buvons le vin de notre culture, nous parlons seulement les mots de notre langue, je parle bien sûr des inaptes de mon genre. Et l'amour, vous dis-je, et l'amour unique ? Voici venue la spécificité.

Nous ne sommes pas des individus. Nous avons déjà été divisés, nous sommes toujours menacés de l'être, à nouveau. Zeus, mécontent de nos insolences, nous a coupés en deux, cela se voit bien au nombril, où la peau se rassemble comme par le cordon d'une bourse. Nous étions jadis quadrupèdes et quadrumanes, le cou rond, deux visages, quatre yeux, forts et rapides, et lorsque nous courions, nous tournions sur nous-mêmes en faisant la roue sur nos huit membres, à une prodigieuse vitesse. Zeus nous a schizés, il peut le faire encore, nous en serions réduits à cloche-pied. L'individu réel a-t-il un pied, deux pieds, ou quatre ? A l'inverse d'Œdipe, je ne sais pas les pieds de l'homme. Or donc nous étions de trois sortes, mâles, femelles, androgynes, selon nos équipements : deux organes semblables ou deux organes différents. Dès que la punition de Zeus fut accomplie, les moitiés, sevrées, douloureuses, se précipitèrent les unes sur les autres pour s'enlacer, s'unir et retrouver leur plénitude. L'amour est une chimère, les retrouvailles des parties schizées. Ainsi parlait Aristophane, le comique, à la table de la tragédie.

Ainsi parlait la comédie, parasite de la tragédie. Tout le monde aujourd'hui est invité par Agathon, le Bien, vainqueur couronné au concours tragique, tout le monde, y compris la philosophie. Chacun boit le vin de la tragédie. Chacun est l'hôte du Bien, nous sommes tous dans l'hospitalité tragique, ou dans l'hostilité de cette morale. Nous parlons tous d'amour pour payer notre écot du banquet. L'amour est le discours de ce remboursement. Le vin et le pain se transsubstantient en ce verbe, dû intégralement à la tragédie. Je parle d'amour pour acquitter au tragique les aliments que je lui dois. S'il existe, quelque part, une balance, l'amour est dans un plateau, il tare le tragique, il cherche à l'équilibrer.

Qui sommes-nous, aux dires de la comédie ? Nous sommes des tessères, des tessères d'hospitalité. Quasi-objet ou, plutôt, demi-quasi-objet. Tablette, cube ou osselet que des camarades, pour le lit, que des copains, pour la table et le couvert, que l'hôte, en bref, et son parasite partagent en les cassant. Ils rompent la tessère et font ainsi une mémoire. Cela est mémorable, dit Plaute, vous ferez ceci en mémoire de moi. La fracture de la tessère n'est pas

franche, elle est quasi fractale, compliquée en tout
cas, si hasardeuse qu'elle en est individuée, si dentelée qu'elle en est unique. La tessère est individu, elle
est hasard, elle est complexe, elle est mémoire. Qui
suis-je, assurément? Unique, bourré d'information
jusqu'à la gueule, compliqué, inattendu, jeté dans le
ressac de l'aléatoire, mon corps, de part en part, est
mémoire. Les hôtes se sont quittés, ils conservent la
tessère, à chacun sa moitié frangée. Ils voyagent, ils
meurent, ils aiment, peut-être ne se verront-ils jamais
plus. Ils donnent la tessère à leurs enfants, à leurs
amis, à leurs petits neveux, à ceux qu'ils veulent, à
ceux qu'ils aiment. Passé le temps ou ailleurs dans
l'espace, qui l'aura dans la main reconnaîtra son
autre exact, par ce signe, par ce rapprochement, par
cet emboîtement adapté, spécifique. Nulle autre clef
possible pour une telle serrure, par la stéréospécificité.

Nous sommes tessères, serrures. Des êtres de
reconnaissance, comme des sémaphores. Des jetons,
faux ou vrais. Le faux s'adapte à tout le monde,
putain comme une vieille pantoufle. Mon corps est
tout entier la mémoire de toi. Si je t'aime, je te rappelle.

Ἕκαστος οὖν ἡμῶν ἐστιν ἀνθρώπου σύμβολον...
Le mot tessère est un terme latin qui n'est jamais
vraiment resté dans la mémoire de ma langue, le
mot grec est le mien, chacun de nous est un symbole
d'homme. Qui suis-je, à nouveau? Un symbole, mais
surtout le symbole de l'autre.

Le symbolique est là, il court depuis le furet, se
partage et ne se partage pas. Qu'est-ce que le symbole? Une stéréospécificité?

Il est quasi-objet aussi. Le quasi-objet, lui-même, est sujet. Le sujet peut être un quasi-objet.

Le nous, parfois, est passation du je.

Sur la route de Compiègne, lamentables mendiants, trois aveugles crient aux passants. Le clerc du fabliau donne un besant, il ne leur donne pas ce besant. Ils l'ont, aveugles, ils ne l'ont pas. Ils festinent toute la nuit, mangent et boivent, chantent. Le quasi-objet tend vers zéro, tend vers l'absence, dans un collectif noir. Ce qui passe entre les trois aveugles peut être, simplement, un mot sans référent. Par réciproque : sans référent, nous ne sommes que des aveugles. Nous ne vivons que des rapports.

Fou, quasi fou, passant pour fou, l'hôte est assez payé par un exorcisme.

La table vide

De l'amour

Ils festinent autour d'Agathon le jour de sa victoire en tragédie. Ce n'est pas tous les jours que gagne le Bien : événement, miracle. Encore n'a-t-il triomphé que sur les planches et derrière les masques. Ce n'était donc pas pour de vrai. Ce n'est encore pas, hélas, pour aujourd'hui. Dans la maison du Bien, à sa table, ils festinent, ils boivent le bon vin du Bon Dieu. Qui sont-ils ? Sont-ils des dieux, inextinguibles ?

On rapporte ici un récit dont quelqu'un d'autre se souvient de l'avoir entendu relaté par un tiers, qui... Médiations, reports, retenues, on peut faire semblant de se perdre dans cette cascade fractale. Un branchement quelconque est aussitôt libre ou repris ailleurs (on dit pour un nœud, courant et dormant), les bifurcations se succèdent, le rapporteur est supplanté toujours. Évaluons les pertes de la balle à ce jeu de passes. La comparaison entre ce qui est restitué du message par Xénophon et par Platon donne tout aussitôt la victoire, non à l'hôte qui la fête, mais aux parasites. Non, ce n'était pas la tragédie, c'était la course de chevaux des grandes panathénées, la maison n'était pas celle du vainqueur, mais celle de son père, non, ce n'était pas Agathon, c'était Autolycos, non, Pausanias n'y était pas, mais il y avait Critobule... Tout a changé, rien n'est constant, la chaîne a mutilé jusqu'à méconnaissance le visage du message. La victoire est aux mains des puissances du bruit. Nous ne sommes plus en mathématiques, nous sommes en philosophie de l'histoire, ou du moins non loin de là. On en vient à douter de l'existence et de l'unicité de l'événement, dont on dit qu'il est le référent des textes. Le seul invariant est Socrate, mais tellement défiguré que le seul invariant est son nom. Un Socrate a-t-il bu avec quelques amis ? Victoire aux parasites, ceux qui mangent et boivent, et qui se sont si bien cachés qu'on ne sait plus leur nom, ni leur nombre ni leur présence, des ombres, victoire aux parasites de la chaîne qui effacent la chaîne même à son passage, victoire aux parasites qui effacent en passant la trace même de leurs pas, victoire aux parasites disparus, nommés, apparaissant pour se substituer les uns aux autres, buvant et bus, dévorant, dévorés, happant le pain et happés par l'histoire.

L'histoire (en général) telle qu'on l'écrit ou la rapporte est un réseau de bifurcations où transitent des parasites. Ils interdisent, de leur bruit, qu'on entende le bruit des parasites qui mangent, qu'on entende le bruit de l'histoire qu'ils font.

Des parasites font l'histoire, festin, banquet, bruit de mâchoires, des parasites la font oublier.

Ce bruit ne vient pas toujours du fond du monde. Mais il en vient parfois.

Le bruit entendu à la porte arrête temporairement les rats de ronger les reliefs d'ortolans. Pourquoi toujours le point de vue des rats? Pourquoi ne pas penser ce qui arrive à l'hôte? Il ne voit jamais qu'il y a des rats. La porte s'ouvre, plus personne. La table est immobile et l'obscurité calme. Il ne s'est rien passé. L'hôte ferme la porte et revient se coucher, le bruit reprend, celui des mâchoires, l'histoire. Il se relève, inquiet. Ouvre l'huis, brusquement. Il n'y aura jamais de rats.

L'observateur fait fuir l'observé en traînant avec lui ses sonnailles, la langue. Les sandales font crisser le bois de l'escalier. Il a dit à sa femme qu'il allait y voir.

On parle toujours de cette lumière indispensable au regard et à l'observation. Il en faut même au démon de Maxwell.

On ne parle presque jamais du bruit attaché comme un fil à la langue, indispensable à la parole, on ne parle presque jamais du signal attaché au

signe. Bruit de bouche, de lèvres, de dents, si proche
du bruit répugnant de qui mange.

L'histoire qu'on rapporte fait un bruit de langue.
La science, la logique font des bruits de logos. On ne
peut les tenir pour nuls.

Qui ces bruits font-ils fuir?

Quasi aveugle, en haillons, lamentable, perdant
ses membres par moignons et sa peau par plaques, le
lépreux s'avance, la crécelle à la main. Fuyez, bonnes
gens, la maladie arrive. Le signal, devant le lépreux,
fait le désert. Personne. Parfois, en charité, l'écuelle
et le pain, le banquet. Il laisse derrière lui d'infectes
pellicules.

On entend, çà et là, des langues, qui, de leur bruissement, font fuir les choses dont elles parlent. Cla-
rines, clochettes, sonnailles. Le signal de leur signi-
fiant fait s'échapper leur référent.

Elles laissent derrière elles des fragments. Des
morceaux de textes, des références. Demain, il n'y
aura plus que des citations. Après Platon et Xénophon, les *Déipnosophistai* d'Athénée de Naucratis
pourraient être signés Bouvard et Pécuchet : copier,
copier, copier, comme autrefois. Attacher des fragments détachés, lépreux.

Ceci. Voici ceci. *Ecce homo.* J'en fais l'histoire, j'en
parle, comme on dit. Cela fait tant de bruit qu'il
efface tout ce qu'il dit.

L'intuition écrit silencieux ou parle doux assez pour ne jamais effaroucher les choses, pour les apprivoiser un peu. Huiler la porte et assourdir ses pas pour surprendre les rats, un peu avant la débandade. Peut-être les filmer au milieu des os et des rogatons. Mais seuls les parasites ont ce génie, d'être invisibles, justement. Je définis le poste de Gygès, c'est-à-dire de Jupiter en Amphitryon, etc., et l'histoire, hélas, recommence.

L'histoire la plus objective est la parasite. Elle supplante toutes les autres.

Couvrir les bruits par des bruits ou passer sous silence?

Qui attache la clochette à qui? Au chat? Les rats, s'ils peuvent. A la vache? Les éleveurs. Et c'est le parasite-bruit du parasite qui mange.

La science fait un bruit assourdissant, depuis le jour d'Hiroshima et de Nagasaki. Elle laisse aussi de monstrueux fragments derrière elle. Qui fuit à l'écoute de ces explosions? Le monde? Les hommes?

L'observateur est peut-être l'inobservable. Il faut au moins qu'il soit dernier sur la chaîne des observables. S'il est supplanté, il devient observé. Donc il est en position de parasite. Pas seulement parce qu'il prend l'observation qu'il ne rend pas, mais aussi parce qu'il joue la position ultime de la suite. Dans la

gamme du visible, du regard et de l'évidence, ou il
est invisible, comme Gygès ou comme un sujet parmi
les objets, ou il est le moins visible possible. Ne te fais
pas remarquer, tiens-toi sous le vent, pour la gamme
des fragrances. Ainsi le parasite est-il le plus silencieux d'entre les êtres, et c'est là le paradoxe puisque son nom veut aussi dire bruit. Petit, protozoaire,
insecte, il est invisible, on ne le sent pas, il mime
pour disparaître, il met une blouse blanche sans
tache, il se tait, il écoute. Il observe. Non. Non, puisque les rats dans le grenier font le bruit que vous
savez à la table du fermier. En fait, ils en font moins
que la porte qui grince, et les pas de celui qui
s'apprête à l'ouvrir. En fait l'observateur n'a pas vu
les rats parce qu'il n'a pas évalué son propre bruit
par rapport au leur. L'observateur toujours fait
moins de bruit que l'observé. Il est donc inobservable par l'observé. Et c'est pourquoi il trouble et
n'est jamais troublé, c'est pourquoi il est opérateur
asymétrique. Il supplante par essence et par fonction.

Il est dans la position du sujet.

Le sujet, en dessous jeté, comme son nom
l'indique, est le dernier dans la série. S'il n'est pas le
dernier, il n'est plus le sujet. Ce n'est pas celui qui
ne fait pas de bruit, c'est celui qui en fait le moins.

La connaissance joue à la main chaude.

On relate, on raconte, on remonte. Au bout du
bout de ce bout sans bout, on joue avec l'illusion
d'assister au festin d'immortalité lui-même. Sont-ils

des dieux, ceux qui mangent et boivent là, puisqu'on sait maintenant qu'ils ne sont pas des hommes?

La suite des récits ou des relations mime-t-elle ces pistes semi-effacées où se lancent les chercheurs de mythes d'origine? Séries pures de lumière et d'ombre, où l'essentiel n'est jamais que la loi de série et jamais ce vers quoi elle conduit.

Sont-ils des dieux, alors? Non pas, certes. A la rigueur, des allégories, des prosopopées, des figures de style. Peut-être sont-ils des Idées : la comédie, Aristophane; la philosophie, Socrate; la médecine, etc. Les genres boivent, les Idées font la fête, elles parlent d'amour sur les lits du Bien. Un palais d'abstractions.

Supposons, puisque nous y sommes, qu'une Idée platonicienne soit là, devant nous, assise ou couchée, peu importe. On sait qu'elle joue le rôle d'attribut commun aux choses sensibles qui lui ressemblent, qui participent d'elle et en reçoivent leur nomination. Tous les lits de ce monde tirent leur apparence de ce lit commun, idéal, tous les hommes du monde sensible de cet homme idéal, assis ou couché sur ce lit, peu importe. Si le concept se réalise, si on fait de l'Idée, homme ou lit, une entité donnée, existante, même hors du sensible, il est clair qu'elle se juxtapose, quoique dans un autre espace, aux choses dont elle est l'Idée. Il faut alors, dans un troisième espace, un troisième homme, assis ou couché, peu importe, sur un troisième lit, pour rendre compte à la fois des choses et de leur Idée, qui se mettraient alors à participer de ces mêmes troisièmes, en recevraient leur apparence et leur nomination. Le troisième homme est l'attribut commun à l'ensemble formé par l'ensemble des hommes sensibles plus l'homme idéal, couché ou assis, peu importe. Et l'opération recommence, elle est, on s'en était douté, interminable. Les philosophes ne détestent pas ces infinis peu coûteux. Il faut dire que cet universel fait difficulté : si je me représente l'homme en général, ou bien la comédie en général, assise ou couchée sur le lit en général, ce lit qui posséderait tous les caractères communs à tous les lits, et ceux-là seulement, serait individualisé aussitôt par cette exclusion même. Il devient dès lors singularité, non, il devient singulier. Alors Aristophane le comique est tout bêtement sur son lit, assis ou couché, peu importe. Il faut recommencer. On appelle cette figure l'argument du troisième homme. L'Idée devient une image, elle fuit dans le palais de glace des images, série de pure lumière et d'ombre, où l'essentiel reste la loi de la série, où jamais on ne trouve cela même vers quoi elle conduit.

Nous ne serons jamais au pied du lit des dieux. Le récit pousse devant lui ce qu'il raconte. Apollodore le tient d'Aristodème, je ne sais plus, quelqu'un d'autre le tient de Phénix, cela ne m'étonne guère. Ce genre de relations et de passes continuées renaît sans cesse de ses cendres. Jouez avec l'idée que Phénix est le fils de Philippe, le Philippe bouffon et parasite du *Banquet* de Xénophon, qui fait rire en imitant les danseurs, grotesquement. Le récit renvoie sans arrêt à un autre récit. Nous ne connaissons pas l'argument du troisième, il n'apparaît qu'au *Parménide* (132a), mais il est là, déjà, vivant, je veux dire parlé. Je crois bien qu'il est toujours là, dans les philosophies qui ont horreur du monde. Elles disposent toutes d'une petite mécanique stratégique pour rejeter le référent, indéfiniment devant.

Ou dans l'histoire, ou dans le philosophème; ou dans le récit raconté, ou dans le raisonnement recommencé.

Soit un petit système simple, par exemple une relation, unique, entre deux points ou instances quelconques. Supposons un moment que cette relation fonctionne mal, qu'il se trouve du bruit dans le canal, du grésillement, bref, des parasites. Cela peut arriver, cela peut arriver par hasard, et c'est justement peut-être cela, le hasard.

Il faut intervenir pour rétablir la relation. Malebranche disait de Descartes que son Dieu devait à tout instant régler l'horloge du monde, toujours en train de se déglinguer. Leibniz avait préféré une boîte à musique préétablie pour la suite des temps, Dieu étant au repos. D'où le mal minimal et la communication harmonique. Intervenons pour rétablir ce qui n'est pas ici préétabli. Nous le faisons pour faciliter la relation, l'optimiser, la simplifier. Du coup, l'intervention complique le système, elle multiplie les branches de son graphe. Elle entre en bifurcation dessus, elle fait une greffe. Le système, plus complexe, reçoit probablement plus de bruit, s'expose à plus de parasites. Cette croissance est fatale. Il faut encore intervenir, on construit un troisième système. Les branchements nouveaux sont parasites. Cela ne cesse pas, c'est cela le système, c'est cela son histoire. La panne qui arrive à celui qui

court réparer la panne. Le mal court, dit-on. Il envahit l'espace.

S'il y a quelque part quelque difficulté, créez donc
une commission. Elle se réunit en séance plénière
pour inventer des solutions. Je les entends déjà se
disputer, moi qui ne suis jamais qu'à la porte. Qui
sera président, qui représente qui, etc. Il faut passer
au contentieux. Cela n'a pas de fin.

L'argument du troisième se nourrit de lui-même.
Platon, c'est remarquable, rapporte des récits de
banquets où l'on raconte, mais de banquets tout de
même. L'argument du troisième se nourrit à la table,
il est parasitaire. Le parasite est tiers, il est même
indéfiniment tiers.

Or donc le jour de la naissance d'Aphrodite, les
dieux donnent un festin. Non, ce n'est pas Socrate
qui parle, c'est Diotime, non c'est Apollodore, enfin
c'est Diotime, l'étrangère de Mantinée, qui venait de
loin, moins d'un lieu, je crois, que d'un chiffre, où
vous lisez à livre ouvert la prophétesse ou la divina-
tion. Le dépliement ne cesse pas, double fond, triple
fond, la boîte dans la boîte. Noire.

Enfin, nous y sommes, nous sommes enfin à la
porte du festin des dieux. Nous sommes arrivés au
lieu stable, au référent final. Nous allons enfin voir
et savoir. Le banquet du banquet du banquet, la fin
de la série, le point d'accumulation.

Non, nous restons à la porte. Elle s'entrouvre un
peu et laisse le passage à Poros. A Poros, petit dieu,
complètement soûl de nectar, de nectar puisqu'en

ces temps-là les hommes n'avaient pas inventé le vin.
Mais qui est Poros, qui sort de la boîte noire? Hélas!
il est le passage lui-même, la voie. Poros est le nom
du passage.

L'initiation est malhonnête. Nous sommes floués,
complètement floués. Nous courons depuis le début
de discours en discours, transcrits ou relatés, nous
allons de boîte en boîte, chacune est vide et contient
la suivante, l'explication ou la lecture va d'implication en implication, nous sommes hors d'haleine,
attentifs, suspendus. Enfin, la boîte noire est là, enfin
la vraie, le vrai banquet, celui des dieux, non plus
celui des idées ou des genres, non plus celui des allégories, des figures de style, des paroles vaines, mais le
banquet, enfin, où l'on boit pour de vrai la boisson
d'immortalité, où le bien gagne en réalité, où
l'amour est enfin l'amour et non pas une punition,
où le vin n'est pas bu pour des illusions et la gueule
de bois, mais où l'ambroisie donne, enfin, la
constance de ce qui est. Nous y sommes. La porte
s'ouvre. Nous n'entrons pas. Quelqu'un sort par la
porte. Qui est-ce? La porte même. On s'est moqué
de nous. La seule information qui sort de la boîte
noire est qu'il y a un canal par où passe l'information. Le seul message sorti de la voie est qu'il y a une
voie par où passe le message. De la boîte sort un fil.
Par le canal ne passe que le nom du canal.

Moi lecteur, essoufflé, n'ayant encore rien lu après
avoir tant lu, et tant couru, suis dans la position de
Pénia, la misère. Affamée, collée à la porte. Mendiante. J'attends du pain, j'attends du vin, je
demande qu'on me nourrisse. Pénia ne demande
pas autre chose qu'un bout de quelque chose à se

mettre sous la dent. Je requiers enfin un peu de
référent. Rien. Pénia se fait engrosser. On ne lui
donne rien que ce qui ne coûte rien. On dit, bien
entendu, qu'elle a eu cette idée toute seule. Elles le
veulent bien! Si vous rencontrez une femme affamée, faites-lui donc un enfant, cela risque de la
nourrir. Tricheur, voleur, écornifleur. Ils gardent
tout et ils ne donnent rien. Voici déjà longtemps que
je suis la misère, la misère du pauvre monde, ce n'est
pas ici que j'ai chance de prendre une miette. Ces
dieux-là ne laissent jamais un morceau tomber.

Agathon est ici, le tragique. Il est le Bien et il n'est
pas le Bien. S'il est l'idée du Bien, je crois bien qu'il
faut un troisième bien pour que nous puissions
concevoir Agathon et le Bien ensemble. Ainsi du
dieu Eros : à supposer qu'il aime, il faut bien un troisième Eros pour que nous puissions concevoir à quoi
participe Eros quand il aime. Il faut une troisième
comédie à laquelle participeraient Aristophane et sa
comédie. Et ainsi autant qu'on le veut. C'est l'argument du troisième homme. Ensuite du quatrième
homme. L'argument ne s'arrête pas, comme
l'argent. C'est l'argument du troisième banquet. Du
quatrième, du cinquième, cela n'a pas de fin. Il faut
toujours une troisième idée à laquelle participerait
le couple formé par l'objet d'ici-bas et l'idée de
l'objet. Série de banquets, donc série de discours ou
plutôt série de récits, et la chaîne d'Apollodore, Aristodème, etc., trouvera forcément un Phénix au
milieu pour qu'elle renaisse indéfiniment de ses

cendres. Le récit ne parle pas du banquet, mais d'un autre récit qui parle, non pas encore du banquet, mais d'un autre récit qui, de nouveau... C'est l'argument, non, ici, la pratique du troisième récit. On parle bien, de fait, de ce dont il s'agit : de bifurcations, de branchements. C'est-à-dire des parasites. Le récit chasse indéfiniment devant lui ce dont il parle. Et j'ai faim.

Pénia est engrossée, elle accouche d'Amour. Peut-être va-t-on savoir, enfin, par ce biais. Amour va sortir, lui aussi, d'une boîte noire, comme Poros. La boîte conjuguée de la faim et de la plénitude, de la ressource et de la pauvreté. Mauvais fœtus ou enfant viable, naissance ou avortement, qu'en dis-tu, vieil accoucheur ? Qui est Amour ? Regardez-le bien. Il est relation, il est l'intermédiaire, μεταξύ, il est le passage encore, il est la passe, il est ce qui passe, quasi-objet, quasi-sujet, comme je le disais tantôt. Il est la loi de la série que nous suivons depuis le commencement. Qui est Amour ? Il est le tiers. Il est le troisième homme, fils de manque et de passage, passe et manque. Nous revenons encore en arrière, floués, trompés, volés, mystifiés. Ce qui sort de la boîte est cette loi opératoire qui impose la suite des boîtes.

L'amour est le tiers lui-même, il est le troisième, entre deux. Il est exactement le tiers inclus. Toujours milieu, entre la science et l'ignorance, ni dans l'indigence ni dans l'opulence, ni dans la mort ni dans l'immortalité, il se pose sans précision et rigoureusement dans les lois de la logique du flou, il

habite le flou du seuil, sans domicile et près des
portes. Il est le tiers, le troisième homme, exclu et
inclus, il est la loi du platonisme et la loi de ce livre
même, il est, il n'est que la loi du récit, de la succession, de la série ou de la suite des récits. Le vieil
argument du troisième, c'était bien le tiers indéfiniment exclu, indéfiniment inclus, double frénésie.

Miséreux, je cherchais à manger, on me fait voir la
porte. Affamé d'amour, j'ai trouvé l'amour, ce
n'était que la logique. Du discours, toujours du discours. Devant l'océan même de la beauté, je
n'accoucherai que de beaux discours. Point de
référent, de pain, de vin ni de tendresse, dans cette
galerie d'ombres et de lumière. Pas un morceau, pas
une miette, le désert de la chose même.

Attention! Alcibiade rentre, complètement soûl, à
son tour. Mais qui est-il donc? Je crois le
reconnaître. Poros était sorti, en titubant, il revient,
ma parole!

Toute la scène se renverse.

Une minute, je vous prie, avant de revenir à
l'entrée d'Alcibiade.

Trois façons de guérir le hoquet : interrompre sa
respiration, se gargariser longuement à l'eau, se cha-
touiller le nez jusqu'à éternuement.

Le couvert est mis, on parle d'amour, chacun à
son tour. C'est le moment d'Aristophane. Or, le

hoquet l'empêche de parler. Bruit parasite qui interrompt la suite des discours. Il faut l'éliminer, il faut donc interrompre la suite des spasmes sonores. Il faut, pour cela, interrompre la suite des inspirations. Cela ne réussit pas? Faites du bruit, dit Eryximaque, le médecin. Soit le bruit continu de la gargouille ou chute d'eau, bruit de fond canonique, en cascade, soit le bruit éclatant et catastrophique du signal qui absorbe toutes les fonctions de notre âme. Et cela réussit enfin.

Platon dit aussi bien qu'Horace et La Fontaine avec deux rats. Les parasites d'Agathon paient en discours le repas que le tragédien paie à sa victoire. On fait tourner l'oraison à l'amour plutôt que le pot de vin. Le repas est interrompu. Par le discours. Qui est interrompu. Par le hoquet. Qui est interrompu. Par un éternuement. Des bruits.

Il n'en est pas ainsi exactement. Ou plutôt, cela est vrai dans le global. Localement, les choses sont plus fines. Aristophane, le comique, le grand, cède son tour au médecin Eryximaque, dont le nom contient, comme on le sait, le rot. L'éructation du reître. Tout ce qui peut se faire avec la bouche est ici dénombré, le rot et le hoquet, le gargouillis, l'éternuement, la respiration, le discours (sur l'amour : le baiser), le boire et le manger. Ils s'interrompent l'un l'autre, ils se paralysent l'un l'autre, petit modèle, à l'entour du lieu de la bouche, de la représentation grande nommée banquet.

Le médecin rotant et militaire vient de guérir le comique hoquetant. Et celui-ci de s'étonner : comment se fait-il que l'ordre, le bon ordre du corps, ait eu besoin de ce vacarme? Doit-on chasser un désordre par un autre désordre? L'éternuement (ou respectivement le gargarisme) chasse le hoquet, rétablit la parole, ce qu'on appelle l'ordre du discours. Un bruit ramène l'ordre. Est-ce déjà l'idée de l'ordre par le bruit? Aristophane savait les nuages et le chaos, c'était un physicien profond.

C'était un médecin profond. Relisez le discours de la lutte roteuse. L'amour est l'harmonie. La médecine fait la concorde entre les éléments, ainsi font la musique et l'astronomie. L'amour et la concorde. Qu'est-ce que la santé? Le silence entre les organes ou le silence des organes. Pas de bruit parasite, c'est l'harmonie.

Et pourtant j'éternue, et voilà que je suis guéri.

Nous ne saurons jamais à quoi un bruit peut être utile. A quoi un parasite sert. Quel bruit, pour le coup, fait le silence des organes?

La bouche est l'organe du parasite. Sa polyvalence est admirable : on y mange, on y parle, on y crie, on y chante, on y rote, on y hoquette, on y gargouille. Tout est bien là en place, et rien n'est oublié.

Observons tout d'abord en silence la séquence croissante des bruits. Les premiers petits bruits de bouche parasitent la parole, un peu supérieurs en intensité au discours, ils chassent le discours : hoquet. Le rot, l'éternuement, le gargarisme, un peu supérieurs à ce hoquet, le chassent. Ils rétablissent le discours. Un bruit efface un ordre et en reconstitue un autre. Le bruit détruit, le bruit peut produire.

Ici, voix avinée, la flûte, Alcibiade bouscule brutalement ce que dit l'hôtesse de Mantinée : la porte extérieure de la cour résonna, comme sous les coups redoublés d'un cortège. Observons tout d'abord, dans un coin, la séquence de seuils et de portes : Socrate en extase dans le vestibule de la maison voisine ; Poros, la voie, sortant par la porte de la boîte aux dieux ; Amour découche, près des portes et dans les rues ; Alcibiade et la Musique font résonner la porte de la cour, heurts et vacarme. Toutes les apparitions, toutes les manifestations n'ont lieu que dans le flou du seuil. De la philosophie, des dieux, de l'amour, ou de tout autre chose. Ici apparaît... la musique, le bruit, le tintamarre et la musique. Le bruit détruit un ordre, celui du discours, il annonce aussi un autre ordre. Le désordre est la fin de l'ordre, et parfois son commencement. Le bruit se retourne, comme une porte. Début, fin d'un système, pour lui ; entrée ou sortie, pour elle. Exclusion, inclusion.

La logique du parasite, du côté du bruit, reste cohérente à la logique de la porte, par où entrent les parasites qui vont boire ou qui viennent de boire.

Poros sort de la boîte où nous ne sommes pas admis, celle des dieux, nous restons à la porte, dans la position de Pénia. Le lecteur, vous ou moi, sommes dans la misère, la misère même. Or Alcibiade rentre, je dis bien rentre. Il entre en Tragédie accompagné de la Musique, l'allégorie est trop facile. Ivre, il a perdu son principe d'individualisation. Il entre comme Poros, ivre, non de nectar, et il

entre peut-être d'où Poros est sorti. Le fait est
qu'enfin nous y sommes. La porte s'est retournée au
nouveau régime du bruit, nous accédons enfin à la
boîte noire. En musique.

L'observateur est enfin tout au milieu des observables. Et Alcibiade parle. Il parle de Socrate. Il
continue simplement la série. Simple éternuement,
son entrée ; elle rétablit la suite. Alcibiade fait l'éloge
de Socrate, c'est-à-dire de l'amour. Qui est l'amour ?
C'est Socrate. Et il est là. Joie ! enfin le référent.
Quelque chose ou quelqu'un à se mettre sous la
dent.

Déception. Chez Xénophon, Socrate ou la philosophie étaient déjà intermédiaires, courtiers
d'amour ou proxénètes. Μεταξύ ici, tout à l'heure,
et μαστροπεία, maintenant. Déception, c'est encore
pire. Socrate ressemble aux silènes. Ceux-ci font du
bruit par leur syrinx et leurs flûtes, mais surtout ils
sont des boîtes qu'il faut ouvrir. Le cauchemar de la
série interminable reprend, je n'ai pas cessé d'être la
misère.

Mais Alcibiade, qui m'a fait entrer au festin, ouvre
pour moi la boîte. Et j'y suis avec lui.

C'est la nuit. Le piège a bien fonctionné. Socrate
est venu dîner. Enfin le vrai festin. Nouveau piège, il
reste coucher. La nuit est tombée, la lampe est
éteinte, boîte noire de boîte noire. Les esclaves sont
partis, et la porte est fermée, boîte close. Tout dort,
ténèbres. Nous tenons l'amour en chair et en os.

Enfin.

Que se passe-t-il ?

Rien.

Dédain, dérision, insulte. Il ne fait pas l'amour. Et

c'est cela, dit-on, sa gloire, sa valeur, la statue merveilleuse. Ils n'ont jamais fait que parler, parler, parler de parler, parler pour dire qu'ils vont parler, philosophie parlière. Pas de référent, pas de chose, pas
de pain pour Pénia, pas de chère pour les invités, pas
d'amour pour les amoureux. Des mots pour vous
endormir, du vin pour vous endormir, des mots et
du vin pour endormir le tragique et le comique de
l'existence. Pas de pain pour les pauvres, pas
d'amour pour les hommes, pas de vin pour les fêtes,
rien, toujours rien, du vent, rien que du vent.
Ceux-ci ne vous donnent rien, ils gardent tout pour
eux, ils ne donneront rien, pas une miette, pas un
verre, pas une seule chose, des mots rien que des
mots.

Il n'y avait dans ce banquet rien à se mettre sous la
dent. Vieille philosophie, nouvelle cuisine.

Debout, réveillé, lucide enfin, je boute ce discours
par la fenêtre ouverte.

Pour une fois, l'explication a réussi. Un pli, deux
plis, trois plis, les plis de pli, la loi des plis, la théorie
des plis, quand tout est déplié, il n'y a rien dedans, le
vide et le blanc. La succession des boîtes noires vides
n'était que les plis d'une feuille blanche.

Ce n'était que prestidigitation, illusionnisme. Que
de temps, que de vie perdus!

Je m'y connais, je suis bien préparé à faire ce récit.
Je montais de Phalère à la ville quand un homme de
ma connaissance me reconnut et me héla, de loin.
Hé! Attends-moi!

Holà! Attends-moi! Non, il n'a pas attendu. Nous avons tous couru derrière lui, monté la côte, époumonés, depuis plus de deux millénaires. Il n'a pas attendu. Et il n'a rien laissé. Quand il a, enfin, endormi tout le monde, tranquille, vainqueur, il est parti s'occuper de lui-même, au gymnase. Comme à son habitude.

Il court, il court le furet, le furet du bois, mesdames.

Le dialogue est une galère vide où jouent des ombres et de la lumière, où règnent des bruits de paroles, un petit enfer compliqué d'illusions et de vanité.

Explication. Je fus marin, je sais donc faire des nœuds compliqués, follement beaux, utiles. On en fait même théorie, belle aussi, en topologie de salon et dans la même science, sérieuse. Si vous les placez dans ce sens, et les forces de cette manière, ils font une merveilleuse tenue. Si vous tirez sur chaque brin, ils se défont quasi tout seuls, reste le bout, plat et lisse. Le nœud s'explique, il se défait, il se dénoue, il n'était rien, rien que plis, ganses et boucles. Expliqué, le banquet laisse voir aux affamés sa table vide et nulle.

Le Diable
De l'amour

Alcibiade, complètement soûl, couronné de violettes et de bandelettes, entre au banquet avec fracas. Brouhaha, vacarme, à la porte de la salle, voix avinées, joueuse de flûte, la jeunesse riche et dorée fait la vie. Alcibiade vient boire à la table des invités, il interrompt les éloges d'Amour, il est donc deux fois parasite, par le bruit et la soif. Il l'est par sa position dans la société athénienne.

Amour vient d'être défini comme un intermédiaire, μεταξύ. Il n'est ni dieu ni mortel, ni opulent ni pauvre, il tient de même le milieu entre savoir et ignorance. On peut penser l'Amour parmi les sous-ensembles flous. Il est le tiers inclus. Il est entre. Il dort près des portes, ni dedans, ni dehors, ni exclu, ni inclus, dans le flou du seuil. Dans l'entrebâillement de la porte ouverte et fermée. Pauvre, dur et sec, sans souliers, ses petits pieds nus dans la neige, astucieux, chasseur et rusé, on dirait Jean-François, Jean-François Rameau lui-même, parasite misérable et follement intelligent, jamais dehors, jamais dedans, liminaire, subliminal. Ce qu'il gagne, il le perd. Il le liquide, flou.

Alcibiade, trébuchant, vient s'asseoir, se coucher à côté d'Agathon. Il court, bien entendu, directement à l'hôte. Il est amoureux et jaloux de lui. Attention. Agathon est l'hôte, il est le bien-aimé, il est le Bien. Pensons en même temps trois choses, qu'Alcibiade court vers le Bien, en allégorie, vers son amour, pour exemple au discours, et vers qui donne à boire pour le parasiter. Une idée en trois personnes ou trois idées en un nom propre. On peut y réfléchir. Platon a tout dit, mais il a tu le parasite.

Les bandelettes se défont, comme les nœuds de tout à l'heure, et le viveur en est un peu aveuglé. Agathon commande qu'il s'attable en tiers : ôtez-lui ses chaussures ! Alcibiade, un moment dessoûlé : qui est le troisième homme ? Suis-je tiers, qui est tiers ? L'argument est là, le principe aussi, dans les nuées du vin de Thasos, et sur le lit du Bien.

Voici la Trinité, le terne : la philosophie, son objet, je veux dire Socrate et le Bien en personne, plus ce jeune homme soûl, entre les deux. Et s'il est entre, il est l'Amour. Pieds nus, on vient justement de le déchausser, venant du seuil et de la porte, entre deux vins, la tête floue, ignorant et savant, démagogue et honteux, ni exclu ni inclus, invité par force et jetant le trouble et la confusion, mais poursuivant pourtant, au-delà du bruit, par le bruit, l'ordre du discours. Il est entre, il est parasite, il veut obtenir de Socrate son rapport au Bien.

Il aime Agathon, il veut être aimé de Socrate, et il ne veut pas que Socrate aime Agathon. Il veut détourner son rapport au Bien. Il est bien parasite. Il entre dans la chaîne des discours, il fait l'éloge de Socrate et donc, selon la règle du _Banquet_, il a fait l'éloge d'Amour et Socrate est l'Amour. Du coup, il faut que Socrate se place entre Alcibiade et Agathon. Il intercepte leur amour, il est entre, il est parasite. Mais Alcibiade, qui aime Agathon, demande qu'Agathon se place entre lui et Socrate, pour que chacun le voie et le touche, mais le philosophe refuse pour une raison touchant à l'ordre du discours, comme à l'accoutumée. Il ne peut supporter que le Bien soit dans la situation de l'Amour. Les combinaisons possibles sont toutes épuisées. Chacun des trois est tiers entre les deux autres.

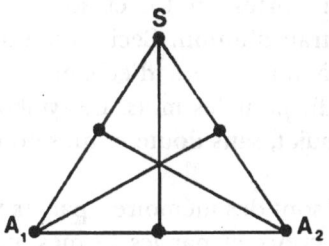

Ce tiers peut être invité sur le lit, à manger, à boire, à chanter, ou à prononcer des éloges. Il est inclus. Il peut jeter la brouille entre les deux autres, et, situé au beau milieu, les empêcher de se voir, de s'entendre : il intercepte toutes leurs relations. Il faut passer par lui pour se passer la coupe, ou quelque chose en général, il faut passer par lui pour se faire la passe. Pour que cesse la brouille, il faut qu'il soit exclu. Le dialogue sauvé, réussi, est ce tiers exclu. Nous y sommes.

La question n'est plus de l'amour. Elle est plus générale. Du tiers : ce qu'il est, ce qu'il fait. J'étais autrefois chez un hôte, ou mon père, ou mon frère,

ou quelqu'un que j'aimais. J'en ai reçu jadis une tessère. Si complexe, si dentelée, fractale, qu'elle est
une mémoire. Elle est reconnaissance, deux fois. Du
côté du savoir : il s'agit de tel au milieu des autres, la
tessère est reconnaissance par spécificité. Seul dans
le monde ce volume s'emboîte au mien, parfaitement. Stéréospécificité, dont nous savons depuis
qu'elle mime des choses cachées au fond de notre
corps par leur petitesse, mais aussi des choses moins
cachées, cependant secrètes. Du côté du sentiment,
elle est remerciement. Je porte sur moi et en moi le
symbole. Tu portes en toi et sur toi le symbole.
Comme un trait d'union. Ceci est à moi, sur moi, il
est en toi, à toi, tessère d'échange, trait d'union
comme on dit pour les mots. Le symbole est quasi-
objet, quasi-sujet, sans doute es-tu, sans doute suis-je
symbole.

Nos corps sont des mémoires, par les rides, par les
plis, par les creux et par les formes, une sculpture
individuée du temps, ce qui reste de son style.
Complexité si dentelée, singulière, qu'elle est une
tessère. Ce symbole nous rapproche, mortaises multiples et multiples tenons, nous réunit, nous jette
ensemble. Ce tiers disparaît quand deux ne font plus
qu'un. Passées les retrouvailles, on jette le jeton. Le
dialogue réussi est encore ce tiers exclu. Si deux
égalent un, alors trois égalent zéro. Curieuse arith-
métique de l'amour. Le symbole s'efface devant sa
fonction, nous le savions.

Il n'y a plus d'asymétrie dans ce nouvel espace.
L'échange est assuré, il est équilibré. Faut-il parler
d'échange symbolique? On peut, en effet. Mais

est-ce nécessaire ? Pas vraiment, puisque symbole est ce rapprochement qui est condition de l'échange.

La valeur primitive est la valeur d'abus, la relation primaire est asymétrique. Il faut un symbole, un rapprochement, pour que l'échange ait lieu ou soit possible.

Rudyard Kipling fait quelque part s'aimer deux êtres séparés par deux océans et trois mers, qui, depuis leur petite enfance, voyagent par le même espace de songes et y avancent par les mêmes étapes, dans un archaïsme, une préhistoire figés. Leur spécificité commune est la carte de leur Utopie. Elle est spatiale, c'est une stéréospécificité. Elle est complexe, dentelée, fractale, c'est une quasi-mappemonde. La géographie est pleine de tessères, les départements à bords compliqués s'emboîtent les uns dans les autres, le Finistère plonge dans l'Iroise, mais, de plus, à grande distance, l'Afrique, séparée des Amériques, depuis des temps profonds comme les plaques sous-marines, se souvient par sa forme de son ancien emboîtement. Le monde tel quel est un puzzle, et pas seulement par les bords des hommes arbitraires. Tout se passe comme si notre histoire — folie, meurtres et hasards — ne faisait, au bout de tout compte, que reproduire l'immobile mouvement des tectoniques les plus enfouies.

Les deux êtres de Kipling se déplacent dans un espace. Le tracé complexe de leur voyage est le symbole de leur union. La mappemonde baroque du Tendre est, peut-être, l'universelle psyché. Voici plus

de trois siècles, cela se passait par figures et mouvements, avant Descartes même. On se déplaçait de
lieu en lieu, de singularités locales en singularités
locales de l'espace. A-t-on jamais pensé autrement
que *l'Astrée*? Par déplacements et condensations,
c'est-à-dire par mouvements et par figures. Est-il
nécessaire de surcharger la chose d'énergétique et
de topologie, d'une théorie transcendante de la
nomination? Peut-être, mais il faut avouer que cela
n'en dit pas plus long que Rudyard Kipling, c'est-à-
dire que ces chartes précartésiennes, c'est-à-dire que
la tessère. L'âme symbolique est une étendue où des
singularités se déplacent, voyagent. Et le symbole est
une carte.

Passé l'éloge qu'Alcibiade vient de faire de lui,
Socrate ironise et joue sur un mot. Ce jeu est un
nœud, une singularité, de nouveau. Tu as tourné,
dit-il, autour du pot avec tes circonlocutions, Alcibiade : περιβαλλόμενος. Ton discours élogieux
déplace l'attention, tu as un autre but que le but
évident, tu le caches. En fait, tu veux nous brouiller,
Agathon et moi : διαβάλλειν. Tu tournes autour de
nous pour nous séparer, jaloux, tu es jaloux de lui et
de moi, tu tournes là pour nous brouiller, pour
t'asseoir ou pour te coucher entre nous deux :
διαλάβη. Pour te situer entre. Ces deux derniers
font jeu d'allitération, un petit bruit d'appel. Une
fascination joue de ce côté-là, en faisceau, en nœud
sonore. Les deux premiers font jeu de sens, ils
attirent vers le mot répété, leur verbe commun. Or,

tout à coup, voici qu'ils font jeu ensemble avec le συμβάλλειν du symbole. Attention. Tu tournes, Alcibiade (περί), tu cherches la place entre nous, tu vises notre brouille (διά), tu ne veux pas que nous soyons unis (σύν). Συμβάλλειν, réunir; διαβάλλειν, séparer. *Le Banquet* finit mal, nous sommes loin des tessères merveilleuses d'Aristophane. Celui qui est entre sépare, semble-t-il, plus qu'il ne réunit.

Voici le jeu du tiers, il est simple comme bonjour, et ce n'est plus un jeu de mot, cela peut être un jeu de mort. Il tourne, il rôde, il attend. Il guette, il épie. Il se place entre, il intercepte, il interdit. Σύν ou διά. Il réunit ou il sépare. L'un et l'autre, l'un ou l'autre. Il travaille lui aussi, lui encore, à l'exclusion et à l'inclusion, de même qu'il était l'objet, le passif, la victime parfois, des deux opérations. Il en est maintenant, le sujet.

S'il inclut, il est le symbole. S'il exclut, il est le diabole.

Apparition du Diable, en personne.

En blanc, silencieux et absent.

Platon ne le dit pas, il ne peut pas le dire, il n'en a pas formé le concept. Dans le carré du jeu, dans le carré logique ou dialogique du dialogue, la place du Diable reste blanche et vacante.

Bruit, brouhaha, rumeur. Un vacarme global, désordre général, recouvre cette découverte, comme une cataracte. Au moment où ils se levaient pour changer de place, à qui sera le Diable, à qui obligera qui à être le Diable, au moment où Socrate avait

gagné à ce jeu-là, le salaud. L'inondation de bruit
efface le crime.

Cela, bien entendu, se passe auprès de la porte.
Non plus un fêtard aviné, Poros ou Alcibiade, mais
toute une bande, une foule. Ils entrent, dit le texte,
parce que quelqu'un sortait. *L'input* et *l'output*, bien
distingués quand le dieu Ressource sortait ou que le
jeune homme entrait avec sa flûte et ses violettes,
sont maintenant brouillés, mélangés. Le flou du
seuil devient le flou de sa fonction. Ce n'est plus une
soupape, ce n'est plus une semi-conduction, les deux
sens fonctionnent ensemble. On ne sait plus qui
entre, on ne sait plus qui sort, tout entre et tout sort,
non plus un parasite, mais une séquence, une
bande, Alcibiade ou Poros au pluriel; quand un système admet un parasite, celui-ci se multiplie tout
aussitôt, se reproduit, fait chaîne, foule, nombre,
inondation. Au bout de quelques heures un seul
microbe en a produit plusieurs millions. L'épidémie.
La bande joyeuse fonce droit sur les lits, vers la table.
Elle occupe l'espace, elle suce les pots.

Un vacarme global emplit à ce moment la salle,
rien n'alla plus en ordre désormais οὐκέτι ἐν κόσμῳ
οὐδενί. Le bruit a détruit le système. Il s'en allait
temps. Ou plutôt, ce bruit-là est peut-être la figure
même de ce qui ne fut pas dit, ou de celui qu'on ne
reconnut pas, couché là sur le lit, monstrueux. Victoire aux puissances du bruit, victoire aux parasites,
à tous les parasites. A ceux qui désormais vont boire
du vin sans mesure (πίνειν πάμπολυν οἶνον) ou y
seront obligés, premier sens; à ceux qui vont produire un tohu-bohu indescriptible, deuxième sens; à
ceux qui détruisent le système dont ils se nour-

rissent, en s'y multipliant, troisième sens. Et le désordre règne enfin, par l'infection, la mise à plat des stocks et la rumeur.

Le Diable a gagné la partie. Au début des discours, on disait que l'Amour était le dieu d'entre les dieux, c'était le Diable. Tout le monde l'avait cru symbolique, il était diabolique.

Le dialogue ne disait rien. Il s'effondre dans le bruit. Dévoré par les parasites. Le blanc même est couvert de caviars.

Le symbolique et le diabolique boivent en se regardant jusqu'à ce que l'un des deux, vaincu, s'endorme. Ils se passent la coupe tierce. Ils sont trois. Ils sont deux. Ils sont un. Selon.

Il faut recommencer, une dernière fois, par-delà l'ivresse et la nuit. Les parasites sont désormais neutralisés. Quelques invités ont quitté la salle où les bruits se sont apaisés, les autres, soûls d'avoir bu toute la nuit, ronflent affalés sur les lits. Longue est l'obscurité, voici l'aube, le coq chante au dieu Soleil.

Nouveau bruit, au-dehors, l'ordre du Bien revient, qui va régner sur les pseudo-cadavres de la caverne ivre. L'observateur endormi ouvre l'œil. Le terne est encore debout. Aristophane, auteur du symbole, y a remplacé Alcibiade, fauteur du Diable. Les trois boivent à en perdre le souffle, ils parlent, ils parlent toujours. Ils se passent la coupe en rond, dextrogyre.

Hoc memorabile est; ego tu sum, tu es ego; uni animi sumus. A la passe du quasi-objet, nous sommes les mêmes, symbole. Y sommes-nous, enfin?

Non, non, encore non. La philosophie au cœur glacé, à la stratégie militaire, gloire à Socrate courageux au combat, la philosophie, aux boîtes noires, au livre blanc, ne veut pas de cela, elle veut distinguer, elle veut séparer, elle veut se séparer, se distinguer, être maîtresse et rare. Oui, Agathon, oui, Aristophane, vous êtes mêmes entre vous, buvez ensemble et passez-vous la coupe, la tragédie, c'est la comédie, la comédie, c'est la tragédie, tiers inclus, ceci est autre chose, principe d'individuation aboli. Ces deux font un, et ils s'endorment. Allons, il est bien vrai que le théâtre est le théâtre, un opium quelconque pour ensommeiller. Du coup, j'ai dit que la comédie d'Aristophane est le Bien soi-même! Nous le savons tous, et depuis longtemps.

Socrate tire son épingle du jeu, comme on dit. Sa belle individuation différente et méchante. Laide et méchante. Il court s'occuper d'elle au gymnase. L'assouplir, la nettoyer, la rendre efficace.

Le Diable s'occupe-t-il d'autre chose que du Diable? Connais-toi donc toi-même, et jamais un autre.

La définition la pire

Ulysse a gagné le concours : faire passer une flèche simple, la relation, irréversible, sans retour, par des emmanchures alignées de haches, le fer qui sépare.

Fin de *l'Odyssée*, au milieu des cadavres.

Le parasite ne s'arrête pas. Il ne s'arrête pas de manger ni de boire, de crier, d'éructer, de faire mille bruits, de remplir l'espace de son pullulement et de son brouhaha. Le parasite est expansion, il court, et croît. Il envahit et il occupe. Il déborde, soudain, de ces pages. Inondation, crue.

De rumeurs, de tohu-bohu, fureur, tumulte et incompréhension.

D'asymétrie, de violence, meurtre et carnage, flèche et hache.

De misère, de faim : la pauvreté, mendiante aux portes ; ceux qui mangent trop, soûls, ceux qui n'ont jamais rien à se mettre aux dents que du vent.

De maladies, d'épidémies, de peste.

De métamorphoses bestiales : microbes, insectes, rats, loups, lions et renards ; animaux dévorés par le politique, fleurs du bouquet d'amour mangées par un lièvre venu, amants séparés par le Diable.

Inondation d'enfer, crue d'histoire. Voici le Diable, donc; non, non, je ne l'attendais pas. Lui venu, ce livre s'achève, comme brûlé. Je ne savais pas qu'il était, irrémédiablement, un livre du Mal. Un livre d'histoire, un livre du Mal. Mal de bruit, de ramage d'enfer, tonitruant. Mal de faim, maladie, douleur. Mal habillé en bêtes et maintenant déshabillé en homme, nu. Du Mal méchant, tout simplement. Repas, banquet, festin du Diable.

Il se sépare enfin de moi. Ainsi l'horrible insecte était sorti lentement de ma chambre, par la porte, en crissant, un matin de mai, à Venise.

Quelque chose avait commencé.

Tranquille, serein, sans angoisse. La haute mer.

Décembre 1975-août 1979.

Histoires, animaux

MOLIÈRE   *Le Tartuffe* ou *l'Imposteur*
               Amphitryon

ROUSSEAU   *Les Confessions*
               Rousseau, juge de Jean-Jacques

Table des matières